7.00

CHILD PSYCHOLOGY

A CONTEMPORARY VIEWPOINT

McGRAW-HILL SERIES IN PSYCHOLOGY

CONSULTING EDITORS

Norman Garmezy

Lyle V. Jones

Adams   Human Memory
Berkowitz   Aggression: A Social Psychological Analysis
Berlyne   Conflict, Arousal, and Curiosity
Blum   Psychoanalytic Theories of Personality
Bock   Multivariate Statistical Methods in Behavioral Research
Brown   The Motivation of Behavior
Brown and Ghiselli   Scientific Method in Psychology
Butcher   MMPI: Research Developments and Clinical Applications
Campbell, Dunnette, Lawler, and Weick   Managerial Behavior, Performance, and Effectiveness
Cofer   Verbal Learning and Verbal Behavior
Crafts, Schneirla, Robinson, and Gilbert   Recent Experiments in Psychology
Crites   Vocational Psychology
D'Amato   Experimental Psychology: Methodology, Psychophysics, and Learning
Dollard and Miller   Personality and Psychotherapy
Edgington   Statistical Inference: The Distribution-free Approach
Ellis   Handbook of Mental Deficiency
Ferguson   Statistical Analysis in Psychology and Education
Fodor, Bever, and Garrett   The Psychology of Language: An Introduction to Psycholinguistics and Generative Grammar
Forgus   Perception: The Basic Process in Cognitive Development
Franks   Behavior Therapy: Appraisal and Status
Ghiselli   Theory of Psychological Measurement
Ghiselli and Brown   Personnel and Industrial Psychology
Gilmer   Industrial and Organizational Psychology
Gray   Psychology Applied to Human Affairs
Guilford   Psychometric Methods
Guilford   The Nature of Human Intelligence
Guilford and Fruchter   Fundamental Statistics in Psychology and Education
Guilford and Hoepfner   The Analysis of Intelligence
Guion   Personnel Testing
Haire   Psychology in Management
Hetherington and Parke   Child Psychology: A Contemporary Viewpoint
Hirsch   Behavior-Genetic Analysis
Hirsh   The Measurement of Hearing
Hjelle and Ziegler   Personality Theories: Basic Assumptions, Research, and Applications
Horowitz   Elements of Statistics for Psychology and Education
Hulse, Deese, and Egeth   The Psychology of Learning
Hurlock   Adolescent Development
Hurlock   Child Development

E. MAVIS HETHERINGTON
University of Virginia

ROSS D. PARKE
The Fels Research Institute

CHILD PSYCHOLOGY

A CONTEMPORARY VIEWPOINT

McGraw-Hill Book Company

New York   St. Louis   San Francisco   Auckland   Düsseldorf
Johannesburg   Kuala Lumpur   London   Mexico   Montreal   New Delhi
Panama   Paris   São Paulo   Singapore   Sydney   Tokyo   Toronto

CHILD
PSYCHOLOGY

A CONTEMPORARY VIEWPOINT

34567890 DODO 79876

This book was set in Vega Light by Rocappi, Inc.
The editors were Richard R. Wright and David Dunham;
the designer was Anne Canevari Green;
the production supervisor was Dennis J. Conroy.
The chapter-opening illustration was done by Cathy Hull;
the drawings were done by Eric G. Hieber Associates Inc.

Library of Congress Cataloging in Publication Data

Hetherington, Eileen Mavis, date
   Child psychology: a contemporary viewpoint.

   Includes bibliographies and index.
   1. Child study. I. Parke, Ross D., joint author.
II. Title. [DNLM: 1. Child psychology. WS105
H589c]
BF721.H418   155.4   74-26810
ISBN 0-07-028430-X

CONTENTS

PREFACE

The aim of this book is to provide an overview of the current state of the field of child psychology. We used a number of distinctive features in developing this book. First of all, it is topic-oriented rather than chronologically organized. It is organized by topics such as cognition, intelligence, language, early experience, genetics, social development, sex typing, and moral development. Within each specific topic area, the significant developmental changes that occur are discussed. This topical organization permits a more adequate and sophisticated presentation of the theories that guide research in each area and recognizes that there are few universal theories of child behavior, but rather smaller theories to guide research in specific topic areas. A second feature of this book is an emphasis on the processes of development. In each topic area the processes that are responsible for the changes in the child's development are stressed. As a result, the student not only knows the content of development, but understands the processes underlying development. This process focus is the distinguishing feature of child psychology in the last fifteen years. A third feature, in line with our emphasis on child psychology as a scientific discipline, is the illustration and discussion of the research methods used by workers in the field in order to ensure that the student gains an understanding of the methodological approaches that are unique to child psychology. To reflect recent methodological advances in the field, naturalistic field studies as well as laboratory studies are emphasized. A fourth feature is the attempt to show the implications of scientifically derived information for applied and socially relevant problems such as the effects of TV, sex typing, and women's liberation, and early education efforts such as day care centers and Head Start programs. The continuity between scientific data and social problems is repeatedly illustrated.

Finally, our aim is to present the best of contemporary ideas and issues in child psychology in a way that students at all levels can understand and appreciate.

A special note of recognition and acknowledgment to Diana Arezzo Slaby who contributed Chapter 8 on language development. We are very grateful for her contribution.

A number of individuals—Michael Maratsos, Aletha H. Stein, and Sandra Scarr-Salapatek—reviewed various sections of the manuscript for us and offered a number of constructive criticisms. Terry Faw provided us a very helpful full-scale review of the entire manuscript.

Special thanks to Frances Hall and Kay Chabot for their professional assistance in preparing the manuscript.

E. Mavis Hetherington
Ross D. Parke

CHILD
PSYCHOLOGY

A CONTEMPORARY VIEWPOINT

1

INTRODUCTION

The field of psychology has expanded at an accelerating pace in the past ten years. As a result of this rapid growth, it is increasingly difficult to offer a comprehensive definition of child psychology. We have chosen instead to present a series of examples from the wide range of research activities that are subsumed under the child psychology label. From these examples you should gain a good idea of the content as well as the methods of child psychology today.

There are two central issues that concern the child psychologist: how do children change as they develop, and what are the determinants of these developmental changes? There are a variety of approaches that one can employ in investigating these issues, but there are certain characteristics that are common to all approaches to modern child psychology.

Unlike earlier approaches, contemporary child psychology is no longer only a description of age-related changes; rather, it is concerned with the processes that produce and account for these changes. It is this emphasis on the processes of development that best characterizes the current field. This volume is organized around these processes of development. In the later sections of the book we have tried to illustrate how these processes may account for specific aspects of the child's development. Within each of the topics developmental and age-related changes are recognized, but the focus is on the manner in which change takes place. This organization around specific topics and processes reflects the way that scientific information about children is generated. The field is highly specialized with various viewpoints predominating in each topic area. Some theories are more appropriate for explaining language, while other theories provide a better framework for understanding socialization. Our central assumption is that child psychology is a science; therefore, in this volume, the emphasis is on our current understanding of the child as derived from scientific theory and investigation. As you will see shortly, there are a variety of methodologies and research strategies employed to understand children, ranging from the laboratory experiment to observational studies of children in natural settings. In this chapter we will examine some of the primary approaches used to generate the building blocks of this volume, empirical data about children. Our emphasis on a scientific approach to child psychology does not mean that the information does not have applied implications and relevance to real-life events and problems. Throughout this book we will try to illustrate the implications and applications that child psychology can have for applied problems and real-life events.

In the next section, we present a sampling of the topics, trends, and methods that characterize the field of child psychology. Then we will discuss in detail some of the methods used in this field.

A SAMPLE OF RECENT RESEARCH IN CHILD PSYCHOLOGY

Now we turn to contemporary child psychology and a sample of recent research in the field. These examples will not only introduce you to the wide diversity of issues, topics, and questions studied by developmental psychologists, but also provide some examples of different methodological approaches employed in child psychology. After this sampling of investigations we will turn our attention to a detailed examination of the methods of this field.

Is the capacity for language present at birth?

A central issue that has baffled child psychologists concerns the origins of language. Is language learned because the child is encouraged and rewarded for speaking or imitating the speech of his parents, or is the capacity for language innate? Although the answer is by no means clear, there have been some advances in recent years to indicate that linguistic capacities may be present very early in life.

Can the five-month-old infant discriminate between consonants, such as "bah" and "gah"? Until very recently it was virtually impossible to find out if infants could make such a discrimination, but advances in techniques for measuring infants' heart rates have given investigators access to the infants' perceptual and linguistic capacities. Babies' heart rates show a habituation, or response decrement, with repeated testing. In short, an infant quits reacting to the same old sight or sound; however, upon presentation of a novel, or new, stimulus, the infant's heart rate may show renewed responsivity.

The change associated with the new input tells the investigator that the baby knows the difference between the old and new stimuli. This was precisely the paradigm that Moffitt (1971) adopted to determine whether his five-month-old infants could distinguish consonants, just as adults can. One group of babies hears sixty "bah" syllables and then ten "gah" trials; babies in a second group heard "gah" sixty times, followed by ten presentations of "bah"; a final group heard only "bah" throughout the series. Heart rate was monitored throughout to determine if the infants' reactions changed with the presentation of the new consonant. The answer was positive: babies listening to repeated "bah" showed only limited cardiac reaction, but showed a marked recovery when the other consonant ("gah") was presented. A similar effect emerged for the "gah-bah" sequence; the control babies exhibited the same level of reaction throughout the series; after all, nothing changed. Very young infants, then, are able to perceive and discriminate speech sounds, in spite of no experience in producing these sounds, relatively limited exposure to speech, and certainly with little if any differential reinforcement for this form of behavior. "It would appear that infants enter the world with some knowledge of the phonological structure of language already available to them [Moffitt, 1971, p. 729]." At least some of language is probably innate; how much is yet to be determined.

The child as shaper of adult socializing agents

Socialization research has undergone an important theoretical shift in recent years. Instead of assuming that only parents influence children—a unidirectional viewpoint— we have finally recognized that children also influence adults. The influence process, in short, is bidirectional with both adults and children exerting control over each other. Anyone who has heard an infant at 3:00 A.M. clearly knows that even infants exert an enormous impact on parents!

Interest in this general approach has led to the emergence of new research strategies designed to illustrate children's control over adult behavior. A recent study by Osofsky and O'Connell (1972) is an excellent example. Mothers, fathers, and daughters participated in this study in which the amount of dependent and independent behavior exhibited by the daughter was varied. To increase dependent responses, such as seeking advice and help, the girls were given a very difficult puzzle that they were required to complete. On the other hand, independent behavior was established by providing the child with an easy puzzle. The laboratory tasks were successful in establishing the desired dependent and independent behaviors in the children. Independent child behaviors occurred twice as often in the easy task as opposed to the difficult task condition; dependent child behaviors occurred three times as frequently in the difficult task as in the easy task. Do parents react differently to a dependent versus an independent daughter? Both parents interacted more with the child, both physically and verbally, and exhibited more controlling behavior when she acted in a dependent manner. However, there were differences between mothers and fathers; fathers tended to be less involved with their daughters than were the mothers. The type of involvement differed as well, with fathers being more action-oriented, as demonstrated by their physically helping their child or by their totally withdrawing under other circumstances. Mothers, on the other hand, were more supportive and encouraging of their daughters' efforts and were less likely to either help them immediately or withdraw totally, leaving them on their own. Moreover, the children interacted in quite different ways with mothers and fathers: the

A dependent child eliciting comforting responses from an adult. (Suzanne Szasz)

girls spent more time working on the task with their fathers, while they spent more time talking and seeking attention and support with their mothers.

This study not only illustrates the effects of child behavior on adults, but underlines the importance of considering *both* mother and father in studies of childhood socialization. Methodologically, it illustrates an interesting combination of observational and experimental approaches.

Noise and children's auditory and verbal skills

One of the most common sources of irrelevant information in the lives of many children is roadway traffic noise. Although it is usually assumed that it is annoying and undesirable, until recently little was known about the detrimental impact that noise may have on children's cognitive development. Cohen, Glass, and Singer (1973) studied children who lived in thirty-two-floor apartment buildings located close to a heavily traveled expressway to determine if there was any relationship between the noise level in their apartment and the children's auditory discrimination skills and their reading ability.

Since noise level decreased in higher floors of the building, these investigators asked if the cognitive skills of children in the lower floors were more impaired than those of their neighbors in the higher parts of the building. The children (second through fifth graders) were given an auditory discrimination test which involved listening to pairs of words, some of which differed from each other in either initial or final sound (for example, gear-beer or cope-coke); children were simply asked to determine which pairs were different. In addition, standardized reading test scores were available from school records.

For the children living in these apartments for four years or more, the lower the floor level of the apartment, the poorer was their auditory discrimination. A similar relationship between floor level and reading test scores was obtained, that is, those children who lived on lower floors showed more reading defects. Moreover, these investigators demonstrated that auditory discrimination skills and reading are related, which suggests that impairments in auditory skills may, in part, be mediating the poorer reading scores.

Of course, there could be numerous alternative explanations, besides noise, for these effects. Perhaps, poorer children who obtained less adequate physical care and whose parents were less educated lived on lower floors. However, the socioeconomic range was very restricted and the prices of apartments varied minimally across floors. More importantly, the correlations between floor level and auditory discrimination were still present even when parental educational level is controlled.

What is the explanation? The authors suggest that the children who live under prolonged exposure to unwanted noise learn to "tune out" auditory cues. This problem results from overcompensating, that is, children fail to attend between relevant parts of their auditory world, such as speech, and the irrelevant aspects, such as the traffic sounds. They appear to ignore all auditory cues in their efforts to cope with the annoying and undesirable parts of their auditory environment. As a result, the ability to distinguish speech sounds is not learned as well in this type of home, as the auditory test results clearly show. As a result of this problem, learning to read becomes more difficult. In summary, children who live in a noisy environment tend to show auditory-discrimination defects. Adapting to urban noise may be a reasonable way of coping, but there seems to be a price in cognitive skills. As this investigation clearly illustrates, research in child psychology can have clear implications for social issues and, in this case, for environmental design and planning.

When all else fails: Shock as a therapeutic technique for modifying children's behavior

Some investigators in recent years have been concerned with the elimination of harmful and undesirable behaviors in children; on occasion the tactics used are often dramatic, but justified.

Consider the report by Lang and Melamed (1969) of a case where electricity was used to suppress the chronic and life-endangering vomiting behavior of a nine-month-old infant. When these investigators first encountered their patient, he was in critical condition. From a six-month weight of 17 pounds the infant had dropped to a skinny 12 pounds, and even though he was being fed through a naso-gastric pump, he was continuing to deteriorate. The reason was obvious: he reliably regurgitated most of his food intake within ten minutes of each feeding and continued to bring up small amounts throughout the day. Before initiating treatment, Lang and Melamed did a careful evaluation of the pattern of the vomiting behavior. They reasoned that if they could detect some early signs that the child was beginning to regurgitate, they could arrange for a maximally effective presentation of the aversive event, electric shock. One of the principles derived from punishment research is that the earlier the punishment is administered, the more effective is the suppression of the undesired behavior. By the use of electromyographic recordings which detect changes in the muscle activity, they were able to determine when the child was about to vomit. At the first sign that the child was about to vomit, he received a one-second electric shock on the calf of his leg. The unpleasant shock continued at one-second intervals until vomiting was terminated. The treatment was relatively short and very effective; each session lasted less than one hour, and after two sessions shock was rarely required. By the sixth session the infant no longer vomited during the testing procedures. The number of shocks actually used was, in fact, quite low. After eight sessions, or three periods in which there was no evidence of the undesirable behavior, therapy was discontinued. A few days later there was a brief setback, but three additional sessions eliminated any further vomiting.

On the day of discharge from the hospital, the child had gained weight and was, in general, a healthy smiling contrast to the anemic child who had entered the hospital thirteen days before (see Figure 1-1). After one year the infant continued to develop

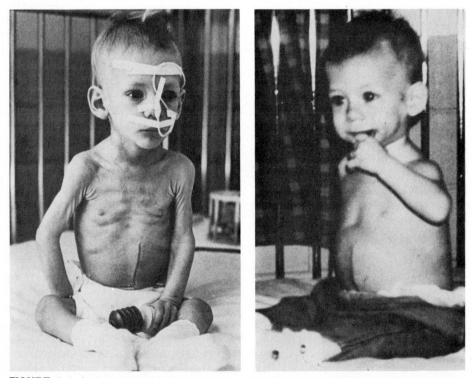

FIGURE 1-1 A nine-month-old infant before and after electric shock treatment. (From Lang & Melamed, 1969; courtesy of Peter Lang)

normally and no additional treatment was required. The remarkable success of this well-timed punishment procedure is highlighted further by the failure of all other therapeutic approaches to correct this illness. Clearly, the outcome justified the "brutality" of the shock procedures. Moreover, this study clearly indicates that principles derived from laboratory studies can have important and practical application.

THE METHODS OF CHILD PSYCHOLOGY

In this section we will examine some of the designs and methods that are used to understand the developing child. There are two principal designs or approaches to the investigation of children's development: a cross-sectional method and a longitudinal method. In the cross-sectional approach, different children at different ages are selected and studied, while in the case of the longitudinal approach, the investigator studies the same children at a variety of ages as they develop. These approaches represent plans or designs for gathering information about children of different developmental levels. In addition, the investigator has to decide on the type of *method* that he will employ. Two methodological approaches will be considered: correlational and experimental strategies. Now we turn to a detailed look at an example of each approach.

The cross-sectional approach

The main feature of this approach is the selection of different groups of children at a variety of age levels for investigation. If you wish to determine how four-, six- and eight-year-olds differ, you find separate groups of children at each of these age levels and study them. Here is an example: Children not only learn to love their mothers, but as they develop, they are increasingly willing and even eager to separate from their mothers and explore the environment. Only recently have psychologists realized how early this process of detachment from the mother occurs. Rheingold and Eckerman (1970) at the University of North Carolina set out to track the developmental course of this phenomenon. Since this was a cross-sectional study, the investigators recruited children at nine different ages: there were three boys and three girls at each half year of age between twelve and sixty months and, of course, their mothers. For their study, the semi-naturalistic setting, a large unfenced lawn, was chosen. Mother and child were placed at one end of the lawn with the mother sitting in a chair and the child free to leave. Observers were stationed in nearby windows to track the path of the child's excursions. A clear relationship between age and distance traveled emerged. The average farthest distance for one-year-olds was 6.9 meters, while by two years of age children ventured 15.1 meters; three-year-olds went 17.3 meters, while the four-year-olds ventured 20.6 meters. Stating the relationship differently, there was a linear increase in the distance traveled with increasing age. For each month of age the children went about a third of a meter farther. However, even infants less than a year old leave their mother. Ten-month-old infants participated in a laboratory study of this same phenomenon. In this case the setting consisted of two rooms, a small room and a larger room. Again, mother and child were left, and the amount of time spent with the mother was recorded. To determine some of the factors that may affect detachment, Rheingold and Eckerman left a toy in the larger room for half of the children, while the room was empty for the remaining children. The presence of the toy clearly had an effect: children in the toy group spent at least half the time playing with the toy. Of additonal interest is the fact that both groups of infants often explored in the larger room, returning to check on mother and then taking off again. One infant went out of the starting room thirteen times in ten minutes. The mother is a "secure base" from which excursions can be made into the environment. Even at this young age, the infants moved freely without any indications of distress or fear. What are the psychological advantages of this early tendency to leave the mother's side? "An increase in a store of perceptions; new opportunities to learn what can be done with an object, and what results from manipulating it; and, an increase in new techniques for controlling external events [Rheingold & Eckerman, 1970, p. 79]." These studies clearly show both the importance and prevalence of departure, a process that begins much earlier than we thought. But these examples from infancy and early childhood are precursors to an ongoing and lengthy series of departures. As the authors so aptly conclude, "If we look beyond the period of infancy, the full significance of the child's separating himself from his mother comes into view. Leaving her side is but the first step in the continuous process of achieving psychological independence [Rheingold & Eckerman, 1970, p. 83]."

The important feature of this design is that Rheingold and Eckerman were able to determine the relationship between how independence develops over age by comparing the behavior of groups of different children at different ages in the same situation. One unique feature of this approach is that data can be collected across a wide age range in a very short time; one does not have to wait until the twelve-month-old infant becomes a four-year-old toddler to evaluate developmental advances. This advantage, of course, becomes very clear when the comparisons involve even longer age periods. However, the distinctive characteristic of this approach, namely, the examination of different children at each age level, has disadvantages. This approach yields no information about the possible historical or past determinants of the age-related changes that are observed because it is impossible to know what these children were like at earlier ages. Nor is there any information about the ways in which individual children develop. How stable is independence? Is the independent child at one year likely to be more independent at five years than a peer who exhibited little independence until two years of age? A cross-sectional approach cannot answer this question, but the longitudinal method is designed to tackle this kind of issue. In the next section, this alternative methodological strategy will be explored.

The longitudinal approach: The Fels Research Institute Study

In 1929, a most ambitious project began: The Fels Longitudinal Study. By describing this undertaking, we can illustrate one of the strategies employed by child psychologists in their efforts to unravel some of the mysteries of development. When a parent enrolled his child in the study, there was a catch: the parent had to agree to have the child weighed, measured, observed, and tested for the next eighteen years. Such is the nature of longitudinal research; the subject is assessed repeatedly in order to determine the stability of the patterns of behavior of a particular individual over time. This method differs from a cross-sectional approach where age changes are determined by selecting groups of *different* individuals at each age point. For the longitudinal approach, patience is a key since one has to wait until the infants mature in order to understand adolescence. However, a question of interest to child psychologists concerns the effects of early experience on later behavior; although there are a variety of ways to answer this question, the longitudinal method offers a particularly powerful technique. By tracking children over time, the impact of early events on later behavior can be determined.

Let us take a famous illustration, the Kagan and Moss Birth to Maturity Study. In the late 1950s, Kagan and Moss brought back seventy-one of the Fels longitudinal subjects, who were then between twenty and twenty-nine years old. A number of interviews and test procedures were employed in order to assess how aggressive, dependent, and achievement-oriented these Fels subjects were as adults. Of course, these same individuals had been observed, measured, and tested throughout the first twenty years, and Kagan and Moss were able to use these early records as predictors of the adult behaviors. Typically, a Fels child and his mother are seen at six-month intervals by a trained observer in the home from birth through six years; until 1957, these semiannual home visits continued through age twelve. Detailed narrative summaries of these observations are written after each visit, and the mother's behavior is also rated on the Fels Parent Behavior Rating Scales. Dimensions of parent behavior, such as affection-rejection, autonomy-control, protectiveness and nurturance, and type of discipline, are rated. In addition, each child is observed from age three to five at the Fels Institute nursery school, which he attends twice yearly for three-week sessions. Finally, observations of peer interaction are made in a day camp setting through age twelve. Ratings are made on aggression, achievement, dependency, imitation, sex-role play, conformity, sociability, and language. It was this vast array of child and parental behavior that Kagan and Moss utilized in their search for the patterns of behavior stability and change over time.

Kagan and Moss divided the childhood data into four age periods: birth through three years; three through six years; six through ten years; and ten through fourteen years. For each age period the child's own behavior as well as his mother's behavior was rated. By relating these findings to the special adulthood assessments, these investigators sought to determine how early behavior patterns become established and the nature of the parental behaviors associated with later adult patterns. First, is behavior stable, or does it merely fluctuate randomly over time? While the first three years bear little clear relationship to adult behaviors, by the preschool years, some behaviors began to stabilize. By six through ten years most of the dependency, aggression, and achievement behaviors were quite similar to the amount of those behaviors the individual displays in young adulthood. However, the degree of stability across age between childhood and adulthood varies with the sex of the child. Boys show greater stability of aggression across time than do females; on the other hand, girls show greater stability of passive-dependent behaviors. Kagan and Moss argue that the sex-role appropriateness of the behavior determined the extent of stability; boys are expected and encouraged to behave in an aggressive, assertive fashion, while passivity is more common for girls—at least while these children were growing up in the 1930s and 1940s!

What are the advantages and disadvantages of this approach? Some of these strengths are clear: the impact of earlier events on later behavior can be determined. Differences in behavior at different points in development can also be determined, just as in the case of a cross-sectional approach. The clear advantage over the cross-sectional approach, however, is that the same children are observed at each age point and so the stability of a behavior for an individual can be noted.

But there are disadvantages to the longitudinal approach, aside from the cost and expense. There is a problem of subject loss; individuals move, become ill, or simply lose interest in being tested. The result is a shrinking sample, which not only reduces the reliability of the results, but may bias the results. Can we assume that the sample dropouts are similar to those who continue in the study? If not, the conclusions may be restricted to individuals who possess certain traits, such as immobility, scientific interest, patience.

There is another problem which plagues the longitudinal approach: cross-generational change. Is the four-year-old today similar to the four-year-old of the 1930s? Times have changed: the family structure has shifted, more women work, and more children attend nursery school and day care centers. As a result, the experiences of the four-year-old of forty years ago and the typical experience of a modern four-year-old will be quite different. Therefore, it is difficult to conclude that the long-term effects of the experiences of our 1930s four-year-old on later behavior can apply to our present four-year-old. These changes in culture, therefore, always date and limit the conclusions of longitudinal studies, particularly those which set out with a large sample and track them over time. In the Fels study, which we discussed, this problem is less serious, since a small sample of new children are enrolled each year. Therefore, it is possible to directly check on the differences between a 1930 four-year-old and a 1970 four-year-old to determine if, in fact, cultural shifts have produced changes in child behavior.

A final problem is inflexibility. It requires a rare wisdom and foresight to choose the measures that are likely to be important over a twenty-year period. Unlike a cross-sectional study where you can test your hunches and hypotheses until you find an appropriate measure to work with, in the longitudinal project you choose and hope. If you choose incorrectly, few interesting relationships may emerge. Moreover, the theory and research that is the source of hypotheses is constantly shifting, but in longitudinal research it is often not possible to take advantage of new insights and new methods. For example, in a longitudinal study of IQ, if a new test is discovered ten years after you have begun, what can the longitudinal investigator do? Several options are available: he can start over with a new sample and the new test, or alternatively, he can begin to give the test to his ten-year-olds. But then you lose the possibility of comparing the earlier results with the later findings since the test instruments are not comparable.

The short-term longitudinal project   As an alternative to extended longitudinal projects, more recently investigators have chosen a new strategy: the short-term longitudinal project. This strategy involves the tracking of a group of individuals for a short time span of one to five years. Unlike older approaches, the focus is usually more limited and restricted to a few key issues and questions which are more theoretically tied. For example, Roger Brown and his colleagues at Harvard University tracked the language development of three children over a two to five year period. This project has yielded a wealth of detailed information concerning the natural development of language and grammar, and we will be discussing some of these findings in a later chapter. What are the advantages of this approach?

> The shorter the elapsed time of data collection the less will be the attrition of the sample, and the greater the ease of maintaining the same staff and measuring instruments and procedures. Annual increments can still be studied, and the effects of different life experiences can be cancelled out or measured and statistically controlled [Bayley, 1965, p. 189].

Another advantage of this short-term approach is that the insights gained from this first project can now be utilized in designing another project. The interaction between knowledge gained from data and design can be more closely interwoven.

The cross-sectional/short-term longitudinal design This type of design combines features of the longitudinal and cross-sectional approaches. To illustrate, recent investigators (Coates, Anderson, & Hartup, 1972) were interested in changes in parent-infant interaction that occur between ten, fourteen, and eighteen months of age. According to the traditional cross-sectional approach, observations of *different* groups of children at ten, fourteen, and eighteen months would be made; alternatively the longitudinal approach would involve repeated testing of the *same* children at the three age periods. A compromise approach is possible whereby one group was tested at ten and again at fourteen months, while a second sample was tested first at fourteen months and again at eighteen months. There are distinct advantages to this method. Information concerning the patterns of interaction at the three age points can be determined just as in a usual cross-sectional study. In addition, data concerning the developmental changes that occur for individual children between ten and fourteen and between fourteen and eighteen months can also be determined. By testing both groups of children at age fourteen, one group for the second time and another group for the first time, the effects of repeated testing can be determined. Does testing the child at ten months affect his response at fourteen months? By testing another group for the first time at fourteen months, it is possible to determine this effect. A final advantage of this approach is time: approximately half the time would be required to execute this design in comparison with the complete longitudinal study.

It is clear that both cross-sectional and longitudinal studies are useful and the choice of design will depend on the type of issue under investigation. For a summary of the three main types of design see Table 1-1.

Whether a longitudinal or cross-sectional design is used, there is a choice of different research strategies. In the next section we will discuss two approaches: correlational and experimental strategies.

Table 1-1 COMPARISON OF THREE DEVELOPMENTAL DESIGNS

	Longitudinal	Cross-sectional	Cross-sectional/longitudinal
Main feature	Same group of children tested (Group A) at several age points Age Group 4 A 8 A 12 A	Different groups of children tested (Groups A, B, C) at each age point Age Group 4 A 8 B 12 C	Different groups of children (A, B) each tested at two points Age Group 4 A 8 A B 12 B
Approximate time for data collection	8 years	Time required to test each child once (typically less than 1 year)	4 years

Correlational verses experimental approaches

To illustrate these two strategies, consider how we could answer a question of considerable current concern: Does viewing TV violence affect children's behavior? Over the past ten years this question has been frequently posed, and child psychologists have used a variety of techniques to try to settle this issue. By using this issue as an example, we can illustrate the differences between correlational and experimental approaches to answer questions about children.

There are a variety of ways of investigating this issue. To illustrate one approach, consider the study of TV viewing habits and aggression reported by Eron (1963). Parents were asked about the TV habits of their sons and daughters. Specifically, the length of time that children watched TV and the extent to which violence characterized favorite programs was obtained from these parental interviews. To determine whether variations in TV viewing were related to aggression, their classmates rated these third-grade children in terms of aggressive behaviors. The results were interesting: boys who were rated as aggressive by their peers preferred violent TV programs. In other words, as the amount of violence in favorite programs increased, the rate of peer aggression increased. However, as total amount of time watched increases, aggression scores decrease. Clearly, the type of program rather than simply viewing time is a critical factor. For girls, on the other hand, there were no differences. Can we conclude that watching violent TV causes increases in aggressive behavior? Absolutely not! The results of this study merely tell us that there is a relationship between preference for violent fare and aggressive behavior. The direction of the relationship is not clear. An equally plausible explanation could be that children who prefer violent programs are already aggressive and their TV viewing may have had little effect on their level of aggressiveness. Correlational findings cannot establish causal relationships! Similarly, consider the finding that boys who watch TV are not as aggressive as boys who watch it less. "Is it because they are by temperament less active; is it because they discharge their aggressive impulses in this fantasylike way, and, thus, do not have to act them out in real life; or is it because their time is taken up in watching TV and they have less opportunity to act out aggression? [Eron, 1963, p. 195–196]." There are other problems with correlational research as well. In this study the characteristics of the TV shows are often difficult to define in a clear and unambiguous fashion. Although programs may be defined as aggressive, there are a variety of other behaviors displayed as well. Even Batman and Superman or Elliott Ness in "The Untouchables" show helpfulness and cooperation between their bouts of violence. Similarly, the usual TV films provide few female aggressive models, which may account for the failure of the Eron study to find any relationships between TV viewing and aggression for girls. It is due to the ambiguities in interpretation that this type of correlational study is only one step in the course of establishing a full understanding of the causal factors in the TV violence–aggressive behavior puzzle. To clarify the causal links, we need to turn to another approach, namely, the *experiment*.

A recent investigation by Liebert and Baron (1972) illustrates this method. One-hundred thirty-six boys and girls participated in this study; half of the children were five to six years old, and the remaining children were eight to nine years of age. Let us follow the course of events experienced by the child. In this study, the parent and child came to a laboratory where the experiment was being conducted. The parents were informed about the details of the study and a written consent for the child's participation was obtained. A common practice is to test children during school hours, and in this case, parents are informed about projects by letter; according to current ethical standards, only if the parent grants written consent can a child participate in a psychological study. The next step in the Liebert-Baron study was to randomly assign children to various experimental treatment conditions. In other words, some children were designated the experimental subjects, while others were assigned to the control condition—on a purely chance basis. By this procedure, children in the two conditions should not differ in any systematic fashion; therefore, the results should be due to effects of the experimental conditions, not to initial differences in the children. Next the experimenter, a twenty-eight-year-old female, escorted each child individually to a room containing children's furniture and a television video tape monitor. The experimenter turned on the TV and suggested that the children watch TV for a few minutes until they were ready to begin. All children watched two brief commercials selected for their humor and attention-getting value. Then the critical part of the procedure began. Half of the children, the experimental group, observed three and a half minutes of a program from the TV series, "The Untouchables." The sequence contained a chase, two fist-fighting scenes, two shootings, and a knifing. The children in the control group watched a highly active three and a half-minute video-taped sports sequence in which athletes competed in hurdle races and high jumps. Then all children watched another sixty seconds of a tire commercial. Two aspects of the procedure so far merit comment. First, the *single* difference in treatment between the children in the experimental and control conditions involved the particular type of program that they were exposed to. In all other ways their experience was similar. By carefully equating the treatments, one is reasonably certain that any subsequent differences in behavior are, in fact, *caused* by the type of TV program that the children watched. There is another important aspect of the procedure: the TV viewing was presented as part of the waiting period prior to the onset of the "real" part of the experiment. In this way, the subject's suspicions about the purpose of the experiment were reduced, and it is unlikely that the effects are attributable to the subject's prior knowledge of the experimenter's true purpose.

In the next phase, the impact of this viewing experience was assessed. The subject was seated before a panel arrayed with two buttons labeled "hurt" and "help," which was connected to another child's panel in the adjoining room. The second child was playing a game which required turning a handle. The subject was informed that if he wanted to make the handle turning easier for the other boy, he could depress the "help" button. On the other hand, by pushing the "hurt" button, the handle in the other room will feel hot and hurt the child. The amount of time that children in the two viewing conditions depressed the "hurt" button was employed as the main index of aggression. The results were clear: Children who viewed "The Untouchables" program showed reliably greater willingness to engage in interpersonal aggression than those who had observed the neutral program.

Exposure to TV violence does, in fact, *cause* increased interpersonal aggression. However, there are limitations to the study which make it difficult to generalize from this situation to the naturalistic environment. The test setting and the aggression index were artificially contrived and the TV program was edited; while it permits experimental control over the relevant variables, the legitimacy of generalization from this type of laboratory study to the field is highly questionable. There is, of course, another approach, *the field experiment*. An excellent example of a field experimental approach is the recent study by Friedrich and Stein (1973), who were interested in the impact of viewing violent TV on children's aggressive behavior. A field experiment differs from a laboratory experiment in a variety of ways. Unlike the lab studies, where the child enters into a specially created world of the experimenter, the hallmark of the field experiment is the fact that the experimenter enters the child's world. In this case, the investigators moved into the nursery school and controlled the types of TV programs that the children watched. The observations of the impact of TV viewing were made during the daily play sessions at the nursery school; adult observers recorded the frequency of aggressive and prosocial behavior. The study was conducted during a nine-week summer nursery school session. For the first three weeks, the investigators observed the children in order to achieve a baseline measure of their interaction patterns. For the next four weeks, the children watched a half-hour TV program each day. Some children always saw aggressive programs, such as Batman and Superman cartoons; other children watched a prosocial program, "Mister Rogers' Neighborhood," while the remaining children were put on a neutral TV fare of farm films, nature shows, and circus movies. In the last two weeks the long-term effects of the TV diets were assessed. To minimize bias, the adults did not know the type of programs that different children had been watching. The impact of the programs was determined by comparing the children's behavior during the first three weeks, or the baseline period, with their behavior during the period of TV viewing. Exposure to aggressive cartoons did affect the children's behavior, but the amount of aggression exhibited in the pre-TV sessions was an important factor. Children who were initially high in aggression were more aggressive following exposure to the aggressive cartoons in comparison to subjects exposed to neutral or prosocial programs. However, the behavior of children who were less aggressive during this initial period did not differ across the TV diets. Exposure to TV violence does affect interpersonal aggressive behavior if a child is already likely to behave aggressively!

One advantage of the field experimental approach over the laboratory experiment is that the results can be generalized more readily to natural environments. The TV programs were unedited and typical of the kind of fare that children are exposed to in their home environment. Moreover, the children's behavior was measured in a naturalistic setting. Any conclusion drawn from this type of study can be much more readily applied to children's daily behavior than studies conducted under more artificial circumstances. The study still retained the important feature of an *experiment*. The independent variable, namely, the type of TV program, was under the control of the experimenter. Hence, it is still possible to make causal statements; the TV diet, it appears, was the *cause* of the changes in aggressive behavior. If the children themselves had chosen the type of TV diet, we would never be sure that any changes were merely due to the possible fact that aggressive children seek out aggressive programs! That may be the case, but through experimental control, this possibility was eliminated.

Both the correlational approach and the experimental approach have a place in understanding children's behavior. Often a correlational approach is employed to suggest the factors that may be important; experiments then follow to more clearly isolate the importance of the variables indicated by the correlational approach.

AN OVERVIEW OF THE BOOK

There are two central and recurring questions that we will try to answer in this volume: How do children change as they develop, and what are the determinants of these developmental changes? Our assumption is that the development of the child can best be understood as a result of a wide number of causes. Few behaviors are singly determined; rather behavior is usually multiply determined. Throughout this volume we will emphasize the variety of causes that interact to account for different aspects of the child's development.

Consistent with our view that development has multiple causes, the first part of this volume is devoted to an overview of the biological and hereditary factors that may influence development and then to a discussion of some of the principles by which learning from the environment may affect behavior. The emphasis is not only on whether hereditary or environmental influences predominate, but on how each of these sets of influence interact to affect the developing child. In Chapter 2, some of the principles of genetic transmission are discussed. Next, the prenatal environment is examined; some of the problems and pitfalls of pregnancy are reviewed. Does smoking affect the unborn baby? What about drugs or X rays or diseases? Are there long-term results of these variations in the intrauterine environments? In Chapter 4, we take a closer look at a remarkable organism, the newborn. What are the infant's capacities? How soon and how well can he see, hear, smell, and taste? What are the reflexes of the newborn and what purpose do they serve? And how do the infant's capacities change over the weeks and months after birth? As we will discover, the newborn is much better organized and better developed than previously imagined.

Is the early environment important for later development? Do modifications in the early experience of the child, such as deprivation of normal sensory, perceptual, and social stimulation, have a lasting impact? Can these effects be modified by later experience? These are some of the issues that we will examine in Chapter 5.

In Chapter 6, the principles of learning will be presented. An understanding of the child's capacity for learning will be important, for in the remainder of the book we will encounter numerous ways in which these principles apply to specific aspects of the child's development. Different types of learning paradigms will be presented, such as classical and operant conditioning and observational learning. How do children learn to remember? How do they discriminate among features of their world and how do they notice similarities? Behaviors are suppressed as well as acquired, and principles of extinction and punishment will be reviewed. In all cases we will ask how early in life these principles operate and how their effectiveness changes with age.

In Chapter 7, we discuss motivation and emotion. What motivates us to pursue some goals and ignore others? What accounts for our emotions? Are they learned or innate or both? How do they change with age, and how do we learn to recognize and label our emotional states?

In the next three chapters, we apply some of the principles discussed in these earlier sections to the child's language and intellectual development. Chapter 8, is devoted to language development in children. How do children acquire language and how does language proficiency change with development? Are the biologically oriented theorists correct in assuming that language is an inherited set of skills? Or are the learning theorists correct in their explanation of language as environmentally determined? Finally, are there class-related differences in language development, and what implications do differences have for the child's cognitive development?

Next we turn to the child's intellectual development and examine in detail some alternative approaches with particular emphasis on Piaget's fascinating account of cognitive and intellectual development. What are the stages of cognitive development that children pass through from infancy to maturity? What are the environmental determinants of cognitive and intellectual development? Finally, how do children differ in their cognitive style? Are there different problem-solving approaches? If so, how do these develop?

Complementing this chapter is a discussion of intellectual measurement. How is intelligence measured, and what do standardized IQ tests mean? Are IQ tests culturally fair, or do they discriminate against some social classes and ethnic groups? Are there sex differences in intelligence, and what role do genetic and environmental factors play? Can intervention programs improve intellectual performance?

In the next section of the book we shift from a cognitive focus to a social viewpoint. How is the child's social behavior acquired, shaped, and modified? In Chapter 11, we examine the primary socialization agency, the family. The important role of early infant-parent attachment will be explored. Next, what are the effects of different patterns of childrearing? How do parents of different social classes treat their children? Structural factors such as family size, sex, and number of siblings and birth order will be examined. Finally, are there alternatives to the nuclear family? The impact of communes on children will be the final topic of this chapter.

In the next two chapters, sex typing and moral development are examined. Few topics have caused as much modern interest and debate as sex typing, or the ways in which the child learns the behaviors appropriate to his sex role. How important are biological factors? Or are learning principles adequate to explain sex-role acquisition? What influence does the family have on sex typing? How important is the father in sex typing?

Moral development is the next topic. How do children learn to inhibit morally unacceptable behavior? Who cheats when and why? How do children's attitudes toward moral dilemmas change? How do they justify their moral attitudes? And again, what is the development course and what determines this course? Finally, how do children learn to help and share and behave altruistically?

In the closing chapters, two other important socializing agencies are examined: the peer group and the school. Peers become increasingly influential as the child develops, and we examine some of the factors that affect peer-peer influence. What determines conformity and friendships? Are peers important in all cultures?

In conclusion, the school is considered, not just as a context for learning, but as a socialization setting as well. Does the size of the school make a difference? How does classroom organization affect children? Are boys and girls affected differently by female teachers? Do texts socialize as well as convey academic information? Finally, how do children of different social classes fare in school? Are minority groups and lower-class children at a disadvantage?

SUMMARY

In this chapter, we have introduced the field of child psychology and provided an overview of the volume. Two principal questions concern the child psychologist: How do children change as they develop, and what are the determinants of these developmental changes? The emphasis of modern child psychology is on the processes that produce and account for these changes. A number of methodological tactics were discussed, including the cross-sectional and longitudinal approaches. The cross-sectional approach involves studying different children at various age levels in order to assess developmental differences. The longitudinal approach involves the examination of the same children at different age levels. Each approach has advantages and limitations. The cross-sectional approach is more economical and less time-consuming than the longitudinal design. On the other hand, the longitudinal approach permits an examination of changes in the development of individual children and is better suited to answering questions concerning stability of behavior over time.

Two research strategies were discussed: correlational and experimental. The correlational approach involves the examination of the relationship between two events; for example, peer ratings of a child's aggressiveness were related to the child's preferences for violent TV programs, and as the preference for TV violence increased, the peer ratings of this behavior increased. However, it is impossible to determine if there is a cause-effect relationship. An alternative approach which permits the establishment of causal links is the experiment; in this approach children receive a particular treatment or experience and then their behavior is assessed. For example, by exposing children to aggressive and nonaggressive TV and then measuring their reactions, the causal link between TV watching and viewer behavior can be established. Finally, the field experiment was described; this approach involves execution of an experimental manipulation and measurement of the outcomes in a naturalistic setting. The advantage of the field experiment over the laboratory study is the greater degree to which the results can be generalized to real-life settings. In the last part of the chapter, the topics to be covered in this volume were outlined.

REFERENCES

Bayley, N. Research in child development: a longitudinal perspective. *Merrill-Palmer Quarterly*, 1965, **11,** 184-190.

Coates, B., Anderson, E. P., & Hartup, W. W. The stability of attachment behaviors in the human infant. *Developmental Psychology*, 1972, **6,** 231-237.

Cohen, S., Glass, D. C., & Singer, J. E. Apartment noise, auditory discrimination and reading ability in children. *Journal of Experimental Social Psychology*, 1973, **9,** 407-422.

Eron, L. P. Relationship of T.V. viewing habits and aggressive behavior in children. *Journal of Abnormal and Social Psychology*, 1963, **67,** 193-196.

Friedrich, L. K., & Stein, A. H. Aggressive and prosocial television programs and the natural behavior of preschool children. *Monographs of the Society for Research in Child Development*, 1973, **38** (Serial No. 151).

Kagan, J., & Moss, H. *Birth to maturity*. New York: Wiley, 1962.

Lang, P. J., & Melamed, B. B. Case report: avoidance conditioning therapy of an infant with chronic ruminative vomiting. *Journal of Abnormal Psychology*, 1969, **74,** 1-8.

Liebert, R. M., & Baron, R. A. Some immediate

effects of televised violence on children's behavior. *Developmental Psychology,* 1972, **6,** 469-475.

Moffitt, A. R. Consonant cue perception by twenty-to-twenty-four week-old infants. *Child Development,* 1971, **42,** 717-732.

Osofsky, J. D., & O'Connell, E. J. Parent-child interaction: daughters' effects upon mothers' and fathers' behaviors. *Developmental Psychology,* 1972, **7,** 157-168.

Rheingold, H., & Eckerman, C. The infant separates himself from his mother. *Science,* 1970, **168,** 78-83.

2

THE BIOLOGICAL BASES OF DEVELOPMENT

Human development can be conceived of as the interaction of genetic factors with environmental factors. It is the process by which the genotype comes to be expressed as a phenotype (Scarr-Salapatek, 1974). An individual's *genotype* is the material inherited from his ancestors which makes him genetically unique. With the exception of identical twins, no two individuals have the same genotype. An individual's *phenotype* is the way his genotype is expressed in observable or measurable characteristics. A child's genotype for high intelligence may be expressed as a phenotype in high scores on intelligence tests or good grades in school.

Some genotypes such as eye color or curly hair may be directly expressed in phenotypes. However, most of the phenotypical intellectual, social, emotional, and personality characteristics in which psychologists are interested are the result of extremely complex transactions between genetic and environmental factors during the course of development. In this chapter some of the principles and processes which guide these transactions will be reviewed. The effects of transactions among genes and between genetic and environmental factors, and the importance of the timing of such transactions, on the development of the child will be explored. In addition, a discussion of the biochemical bases of heredity will be presented. Finally, two approaches to the study of the role of genetic and environmental factors in development will be examined. The first approach involves the study of individuals having different degrees of biological relatedness. These are called consanguinity studies. In such studies a comparison is made of the similarity on a characteristic such as intelligence test performance of unrelated strangers versus that of distantly related relatives such as a child to his grandparents, cousins, aunts, and uncles, or of members of the immediate family such as parents, children, and siblings. If the score on an intelligence test is strongly influenced by inheritance it would be expected that there would be an increase in resemblance among individuals going from strangers to distant relatives to immediate relatives. However, it could also be argued that immediate relatives are more likely to be exposed to the same environment and that it will be impossible to separate the effects of heredity and environment in these studies. The study of twins, which will be discussed later in the chapter, is a special type of consanguinity study which attempts to separate these effects. The second approach to the study of the contributions of environmental and inherited factors to development involves an examination of the stability of individual attributes over time. If the squalling, irritable infant evolves into an irrascible, bad-tempered, petulant adult, one possible explanation would be that the individual has an inherited predisposition to be irritable which is manifested throughout his life span.

PHENOTYPES AND CANALIZATION

The expression of the genotype is modified by a variety of experiences. Whether or not a child's genotype for high intellectual ability is manifested in school performance will depend in part upon whether or not his parents stimulate and encourage him in intellectual pursuits. A child reared in a deprived slum environment may manifest a genotype for high intelligence by being a school dropout and becoming the most devious, skillful con artist in the neighborhood. Similarly, although a child may appear to have his grandfather's temper, any genetic predisposition for impulsive and uncontrolled behavior will be considerably modified by how "cute" his parents think his rages are and whether he eventually gets his own way and finds it rewarding to have tantrums.

The extent to which an individual's genotype is expressed in his phenotype depends on the timing, kind, and amount of environmental pressures, or pushes, to which he is exposed. Different experiences at different points in the course of development have different effects on the developing child. If a pregnant woman contracts German measles in the first three months of pregnancy, the child she is carrying, who may be genotypically predisposed to be of normal intelligence, may be born severely mentally retarded. However, if the mother contracts the disease later in pregnancy, it will have had no effect on modifying the expression of the child's intellectual genotype.

Some kinds of phenotypes are more difficult to deflect from their genetically programmed path of growth than others. These seem to have fewer possible alternative paths from genotype to phenotype, and it takes greater environmental pushes to deflect them. The term *canalization* is used to describe the limiting of phenotypes to one or few developmental outcomes (Waddington, 1962; 1966). A characteristic which is strongly canalized is relatively difficult to modify by a wide variety of environmental factors. For example, infant babbling is strongly canalized since babbling occurs even in infants who are born deaf and have never heard their own voices or the speech of others (Lenneberg, 1967).

At one time scientists were preoccupied with the question of the relative amounts contributed by genetic or environmental factors to different characteristics such as intelligence, motor skills, and personality. This resulted in what was called the nature-nurture controversy, with many psychologists assuming extreme positions on the issue. Those who were more biologically oriented emphasized the exclusive role of heredity and maturational factors in shaping development, while those who were more environmentally oriented often took an equally extreme and invalid position by denying any contribution of innate predispositions or capacities and emphasizing the exclusive role of learning and experience. Today the questions being asked are not only "How much?" but "How?" and "When?" do genetic and environmental factors and transactions affect development. The ciritical issue is to identify the processes that initiate, influence, and shape development as well as the timing of these processes. That is, "How much of an effect do specified environmental factors have on the development of X at times A, B, and C?"

CONCEPTION AND THE BEGINNINGS OF LIFE

At the time of conception, a *sperm* cell from the father penetrates and unites with the *ovum* (the egg cell) from the mother to form the *zygote*, or fertilized ovum. The cells of the zygote multiply rapidly by cell division and develop into the future child. The sperm

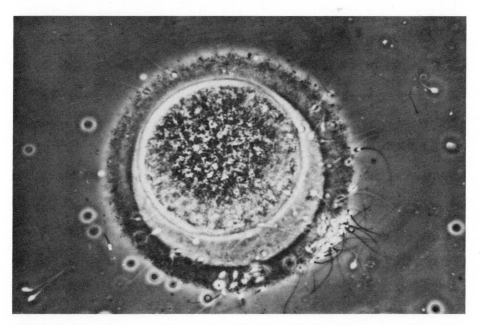

A fertilized ovum at the moment of conception. (Courtesy of the American Museum of Natural History.)

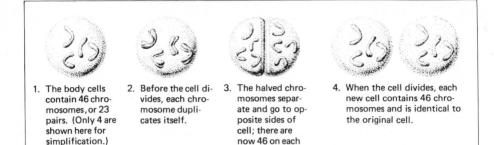

1. The body cells contain 46 chromosomes, or 23 pairs. (Only 4 are shown here for simplification.)

2. Before the cell divides, each chromosome duplicates itself.

3. The halved chromosomes separate and go to opposite sides of cell; there are now 46 on each side.

4. When the cell divides, each new cell contains 46 chromosomes and is identical to the original cell.

FIGURE 2-1 Mitosis: a process of cell replication in the zygote and body cells in which both pairs of each chromosome are reproduced. After cell division each new cell contains the identical set of 46 chromosomes (that is, 23 pairs). (Adapted from B. Sutton-Smith, *Child Psychology,* Appleton-Century-Crofts, New York, 1973, p. 60.)

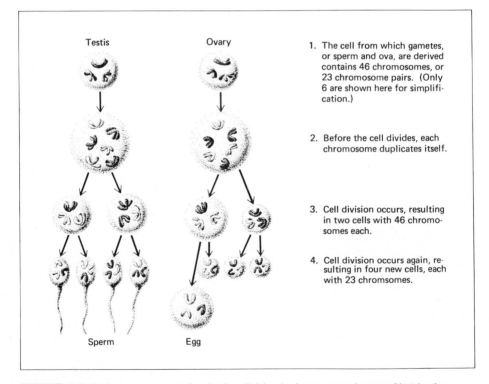

1. The cell from which gametes, or sperm and ova, are derived contains 46 chromosomes, or 23 chromosome pairs. (Only 6 are shown here for simplification.)

2. Before the cell divides, each chromosome duplicates itself.

3. Cell division occurs, resulting in two cells with 46 chromosomes each.

4. Cell division occurs again, resulting in four new cells, each with 23 chromsomes.

FIGURE 2-2 Meiosis: a process of reduction division in the ovum and sperm (that is, the gametes). Following cell division only one member of each pair of chromosomes, twenty-three chromosomes rather than twenty-three pairs of chromosomes, is present in each daughter cell. (Adapted from B. Sutton-Smith, *Child Psychology,* Appleton-Century-Crofts, 1973, p. 61.)

cell and ovum (sometimes called the *male* and *female gametes*) contain all the hereditary material of the child. Although the ovum is much larger than the sperm, both cells contribute almost equally to the inheritance of the offspring. Within each cell nucleus are threadlike entities known as *chromosomes*. Beaded along the length of the chromosomes are the *genes*, which contain the genetic code that will participate in directing an individual's development. The processes involved in the transmission of this genetic code are described in more detail in the next section.

The human body is composed of two structurally and functionally different types of cells: *reproductive cells*, or *gametes* (sometimes called germ cells), and *body cells,* which compose the bones, muscles, organs, and digestive, respiratory, and nervous systems. Each type of cell contains a different number of chromosomes and divides in a different manner. Each reproductive cell (the sperm or ovum) contains 23 chromosomes. But each body cell of most normal men and women and the nucleus of the fertilized ovum (the zygote) contains 46 chromosomes (two sets of 23 chromosomes, one chromosome in each pair coming from the mother and one from the father).

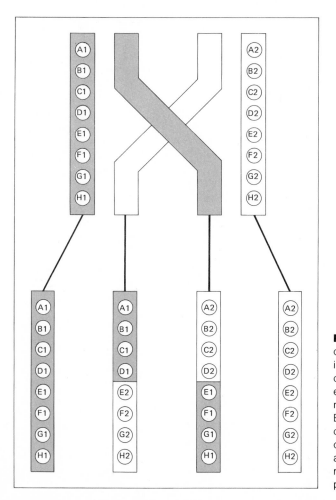

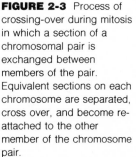

FIGURE 2-3 Process of crossing-over during mitosis in which a section of a chromosomal pair is exchanged between members of the pair. Equivalent sections on each chromosome are separated, cross over, and become re-attached to the other member of the chromosome pair.

Cell division in body cells occurs by mitosis, a process in which each of the 46 chromosomes in the nucleus of the parent cell duplicates itself. The resulting identical two sets of 46 chromosomes move to opposite sides of the parent cell. The parent cell then separates between the two clusters of 46 identical chromosomes and becomes two new cells or daughter cells. These daughter cells and all the body cells formed by mitosis in the course of human development contain 46 chromosomes which are identical to those in the zygote. The process of mitosis is shown in Figure 2-1.

Reproductive, or germ, cells divide by a different process called *meiosis*, which is essentially a process of reduction division. In the testes and ovaries a cell with 23 pairs of chromosomes divides in such a way that the daughter cells include only one member of each pair of chromosomes. This process is presented in Figure 2-2. Thus, mature sperm and egg cells contain only 23 single chromosomes rather than 23 chromosome pairs. When the sperm and egg cells with their 23 chromosomes unite, the zygote contains the 46 chromosomes, half contributed by each parent.

The great number of possible combinations of chromosomes coming from the mother and father contribute to the wide genetic variability found in offspring from generation to generation. Also contributing to genetic variability is a phenomenon called *crossing-over*, which occurs during meiosis. In this process genetic material is exchanged between pairs of chromosomes. At the beginning of meiosis two chromosomes form pairs with their lengths stretched like parallel threads, and then equivalent sections of each chromosome break away and attach themselves to the adjacent chromosome. Thus the chromosomes are actually altered because genes are exchanged between pairs of chromosomes and the genetic characteristics associated with those genes are now carried on different chromosomes. This process of crossing-over increases the already broad genetic array of possible combinations of characteristics that take place in reproduction (see Figure 2-3).

CHROMOSOMES AND GENES

Arranged along the length of a chromosome and occupying a specific location on it are segments called *genes*, which are the basic units of hereditary transmission and which specify the protein and enzyme reactions to be activated during development. A single chromosome will carry about 20,000 genes. Genes of several types direct structural development and regulate cellular, chemical, and metabolic processes.

The gene is composed of *deoxyribonucleic acid*, or DNA, which contains the genetic code that directs the functioning of *ribonucleic acid*, or RNA. RNA serves as a messenger in carrying the DNA-originated directions from the nucleus of a cell to its *cytoplasm*, which comprises the rest of the cell, where the instructions are carried out. These directions lead to the synthesis of proteins from the amino acids in the cytoplasm. Since the body is composed of protein, instructions are being relayed as to how the newly formed organism is to develop. The DNA in each gene contains instructions for a specific type of protein chain. Some of these protein chains control body processes, some are structural and form new tissues, and some regulate the functioning and turning off and on of structural genes. When even one of these genes is defective, marked developmental deviations may occur in the organism.

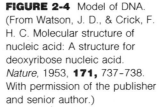

A: Adenine
T: Thymine
C: Cytosine
G: Guanine

FIGURE 2-4 Model of DNA. (From Watson, J. D., & Crick, F. H. C. Molecular structure of nucleic acid: A structure for deoxyribose nucleic acid. *Nature,* 1953, **171,** 737-738. With permission of the publisher and senior author.)

The double helix

James Watson and Francis Crick (1953) have proposed a now famous double-helix model of the structure and function of DNA, which helps to explain how genes replicate themselves during cell division. They suggest that a molecule of DNA is like a spiral staircase, or a double helix or coil, with the side strips being composed of molecules of phosphate and sugar and the steps being composed of pairs of four chemical bases. Genetic information is coded by the ordering or arrangement of these chemicals at different locations on the chromosome. Only bases that are compatible with each other form pairs; thus cytosine and guanine are paired, and thymine and adenine appear together. Watson and Crick speculate that during cell division this DNA ladder duplicates itself by separating, or unzipping, down the middle of the structure. The bases separate from their mates, cytosine from guanine, and thymine from adenine. Then each half of the DNA molecule serves as the framework to evolve a copy of the missing half from the materials of the surrounding cell and constructs a compatible half identical to the one from which it just separated. Thus, as a result of this unzipping and reconstruction of genes, every cell in the body carries the same genetic code or pattern as the original one.

Homozygotes and heterozygotes

Much of the original work which served as the basis for modern genetics was done at the end of the nineteenth century by Gregor Mendel, who worked with rather simple hereditary characteristics such as blossom color in hybridized plants. Many of the attributes he studied were ones in which a single pair of genes seemed largely responsible for the phenotypical appearance of the characteristic of the plant. Although contemporary geneticists take a more complex approach in studying the transactions among a number of genetic factors and an array of environmental effects, some of Mendel's principles dealing with *dominant* and *recessive* genes are still accepted.

At each gene *locus*, or position on the chromosome, there may be two or more alternative forms of the gene, called *alleles*. Recall that a child has two alleles of every gene in his body, one from his mother and one from his father. If the alleles from both parents are the same, a child is said to be *homozygous* at that locus; if they differ, he is said to be *heterozygous*. For example, if a child has alleles to be brown-eyed from both parents, he is homozygous; but if he has a brown-eyed allele from one parent and a blue-eyed allele from the other, he is heterozygous. Using the code ''A'' to represent one allele and ''a'' another, and considering that each of a child's two genes may exist in either allelic state, it can be seen that three types of allelic combinations may result: AA, aa, or Aa (aA), depending on the parents' alleles. In our example of eye color, if A represents brown eyes and a blue eyes, the child with an AA combination will be brown-eyed and the child with aa alleles will be blue-eyed. But what happens with the heterozygous Aa child with different alleles from each parent? If a trait is determined by a single allelic pair, there are three main ways in which a heterozygous combination of alleles can be expressed in the phenotype. In the first case, the characteristic associated with only one of the alleles may be expressed. One allele will be *dominant* over the other; that is, it would be more likely to be expressed phenotypically than the less powerful *recessive* gene. In the example of eye color, an allele for brown eyes is dominant over one for blue eyes. A second possible form in which the heterozygous combination of alleles may be expressed is in a phenotype intermediate between those carried by the individual alleles. A third means of expressing the heterozygosity is by showing codominant or combined attributes carried by the two alleles. Examples will be given to clarify these three possibilities.

Dominant and recessive genes   If the phenotype Aa is the same as the phenotype AA, the allele A is said to be dominant and the allele a is said to be recessive. An example of the interaction of dominant and recessive alleles which is perhaps more interesting than that of eye color is found in the inheritance of *phenylketonuria* (PKU). Phenylketonuria is a disorder caused by a recessive gene which leads to the absence of an enzyme necessary to metabolize certain types of proteins, some of which are unfortunately found in milk, the basic diet for infants. Thus, an infant with two recessive genes for phenylketonuria is unable to convert the protein phenylalanine into tyrosine, which results in an accumulation of phenylpyruvic acid in the body. This has damaging effects on the developing nervous system of the child, and usually results in mental retardation. The infant appears normal at birth, but with the gradual buildup of phenylpyruvic acid, increasing signs of mental retardation are shown. In addition to mental deficits, phenylketonuric children frequently have other characteristics, such as fair hair, irritability, poor coordination and awkwardness, hyperactivity, and convulsions.

The genetic transmission patterns for PKU are presented in Figure 2-5. Approximately one out of every twenty persons carries the recessive allele for phenylketonuria (p). If a heterozygote (Pp) marries an individual who carries two dominant alleles (PP)

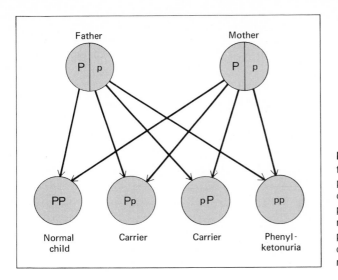

Father   Mother

P | p   P | p

PP   Pp   pP   pp

Normal   Carrier   Carrier   Phenyl-
child   ketonuria

FIGURE 2-5 The genetic transmission of phenylketonuria in the children of two heterozygous parents carrying the recessive allele for phenylketonuria (P is the dominant gene, p is the recessive gene).

for normal metabolizing of phenylalanine, their children will be normal. However, if two of these heterozygotes (Pp) marry, they will have one chance in four of producing a phenylketonuric child (pp).

A method has been developed for testing potential parents for heterozygosity for PKU (Hsia et al., 1956). The subject swallows a dose of L-phenylalanine, and subsequent tests may reveal an abnormally high level of phenylpyruvic acid in the blood. When parents have such information, they are aware of their potential risks in reproduction and can prepare for the immediate testing of their child for PKU in order to plan for dietary therapy at birth. Many hospitals also routinely test infants for PKU in the first

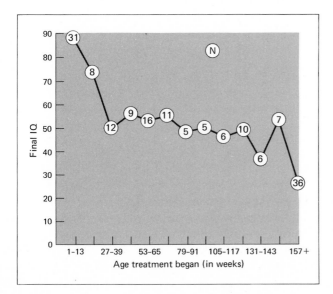

Final IQ

Age treatment began (in weeks)

FIGURE 2-6 The relationship between age of starting dietary control and intelligence in phenylketonuria. (From Baumeister, A. A. The effects of dietary control on intelligence in phenylketonuria. *American Journal of Mental Deficiency*, 1967, **71**, 840-847.)

week of life by assessing the level of phenylpyruvic acid in the blood after the infant has eaten protein. This test is sometimes inaccurate since phenylpyruvic acid has not yet had time to accumulate; therefore, in many states a urine test is required about six weeks after birth.

The progress of PKU can be inhibited if infants are fed an early diet of milk substitutes, which limits their intake of phenylalanine. Children can be kept on this diet until about middle childhood, when the brain has developed to the point where it cannot be injured by the accumulation of phenylpyruvic acid. The importance of early dietary therapy is demonstrated graphically in Figure 2-6, which shows the relation between the start of treatment and eventual IQ of PKU patients. It can be seen that the effects of starting treatment decrease rapidly after the first few months of life, and that starting dietary remedies as early as seven months can do little to reverse the destructive course of the disorder.

Homozygotic phenylketonurics seldom reproduce, but when they do, the results are disastrous. Male phenylketonurics pass on only one recessive gene for the disorder to their offspring, which may be counteracted by a normal gene in the women they marry. However, female phenylketonurics seem to present their children with a damaging prenatal intrauterine environment as well as a defective gene. Howell and Stevenson (1971) reported that of 121 babies born to 33 PKU women, only 16 were normal; the others died young, had PKU, or were mentally retarded, often with microencephaly (a disorder characterized by an extremely small skull and brain). The most common attribute of these infants was retarded prenatal growth, often manifested in deviant development of the nervous system and accompanying mental retardation. These investigators suggest that although pregnant phenylketonuric women are put on diets to limit their intake of phenylalanine, the harm to the fetus may have occurred in the first month of pregnancy before pregnancy and PKU have been diagnosed and treatment begun.

Many other genetic anomalies are associated with deleterious recessive chromosomes. Since the same chromosomal pattern is carried in each of the parents' cells, a new procedure in which cells from the prospective parents are examined for chromosomal abnormalities has been effective in detecting the carriers of some genetic disorders. In addition, some chromosomal abnormalities can be detected in the fetus in utero through a procedure called *amniocentesis*. A sample is drawn of the amniotic fluid in which the infant floats in utero. The cells in the amniotic fluid are the same as those in the infant and can be checked for some chromosomal abnormalities.

Intermediate expression of heterozygosity　In some cases a heterozygous child may exhibit a phenotype which appears to lie somewhere between the characteristics carried on the two differing alleles. For example, a single pair of alleles controls the six basic types of singing voices for males and females. The bass voice in males and soprano in females are associated with the same homozygous alleles (AA), as are tenors and altos (aa); however, heterozygosity (Aa) results in a baritone voice in male offspring and a mezzosoprano for females. Hence, if a Leontyne Price (soprano) married an Enrico Caruso (tenor), their offspring would have a voice like Rise Stevens (mezzosoprano) or Leonard Warren (baritone). A similar intermediate phenotype is often found in characteristics such as height or skin color, where tall and short parents may produce a child of average height or where a very light- and a very dark-skinned parent may have a child with only a moderately dark complexion.

Codominance   Finally some heterozygotes show *codominant* or combined charac-teristics where the effects of both alleles are represented in the phenotype. In relation to some alleles which control chemical substances in the blood, the heterozygotic child will contain both the blood substances which are contained singly in the blood of each parent. Neither dominance nor the intermediate expression of the parents' alleles are found in such a case. In a parallel manner, although the inheritance of eye color is often cited as an example of the effects of simple dominance of a brown allele over a reces-sive blue allele, it has recently been noted that two apparently blue-eyed parents can produce brown-eyed children. On closer examination it is found that these apparently blue-eyed parents have minute, often barely discernable, flecks of brown pigment in their irises. This mixed pigment might be considered a codominant representation of the discrepant alleles. It is clear that it cannot be attributed to a simple manifestation of dominance.

Gene interactions

At one time a rather simple genetic model of one gene determining one characteristic was widely accepted. However, it is now recognized that the phenotypic expression of an allele is often determined partly by interactions with *modifier genes* at other locations on the chromosome, and that a single gene may have effects on the inheritance of more than one characteristic. The latter phenomenon is called *pleiotropism.*

Modifier genes   A *modifier gene* is a gene that modifies or influences the action or phenotypical expression of another gene. The action of a modifier gene is clearly dem-onstrated in the inheritance of early cataracts. The occurrence of cataracts is deter-mined by a dominant gene; however, the type of opacity and location on the lens of the cataract seems to be determined by modifier genes.

Similarly, children with phenylketonuria have differing phenylalanine levels. In spite of the fact that they have identical genes at the critical locus for phenylketonuria, modifier genes at other loci determine the variation in phenylalanine levels and in intelligence levels in untreated cases.

Pleiotropism   The effects of some genes are not limited to influencing a single char-acteristic. In PKU children the finding that most phenylketonuric Caucasian children are blond and blue-eyed is an example of such multiple gene actions, or *pleiotropism.* The gene for PKU apparently is also associated with hair and eye color.

The multiple effects of a gene are not always present in the same individual, but may appear across generations. In an inherited disorder known as *Marfan's syndrome*, heart defects, long fingers, and a misplaced eye lens are frequently but not consistently found together. These traits are so unusual that their conjoint appearance cannot be attributed to chance. That these effects are controlled by a single gene with partly expressed multiple effects is supported by studying patterns of emergence of these characteristics over generations. A long-fingered parent without a misplaced lens will have children with heart defects and a misplaced lens as frequently as a parent who possesses both defects.

Penetrance and expressivity　*Penetrance* refers to whether or not phenotypical expression of a gene occurs regardless of the intensity or form of expression, whereas *expressivity* is defined by the extent, variability, or form the characteristic assumes. If an individual has a genotype for allergies, penetrance would refer to the occurrence of any allergic response. Expressivity would include whether the allergic genotype appears as hay fever, asthma, or skin rashes, how severe the attacks are, and the substances which cause the allergic reaction. A mother may express her allergic genotype in having asthmatic responses to cats; her son may express it in developing hay fever when exposed to spring pollens.

In summary, it can be seen that simple relationships between genotypes and phenotypes are rare. One genotype can become many different phenotypes, and the same phenotype may have many different underlying genotypes. The complex network of the effects of transactions among genes, with one gene modifying the action or expression of another, and transactions between genetic and environmental factors at different points in development all contribute to the uniqueness and variability among individuals.

Sex chromosomes and sex-linked characteristics

Of the 23 pairs of chromosomes, 22 pairs are *autosomes*; that is, they are possessed equally by males and females. In contrast, the twenty-third pair, the *sex chromosomes*, differ in males and females. The female has two X chromosomes (XX), and the male has an X and a Y (XY) chromosome. The X chromosome is about five times as long as the Y chromosome and carries more genes on it. Since the mother is XX, her ovum always contains an X chromosome. However, sperms may carry either an X or a Y chromosome. If a sperm with an X chromosome fertilizes the egg, the offspring will be female (XX); if the sperm carries a Y chromosome, the offspring will be male (XY). The sex of the child is thus determined by the father.

Since the chromosomal composition of the sex genes is different for males and females, the inheritance of characteristics determined by genes of these chromosomes is not equivalent for the two sexes. In other words, the fact that some genes on the X chromosome have no equivalent genes on the Y chromosome results in the appearance of sex-linked, recessive characteristics in males. Since a male has only one X chromosome, if the recessive allele for a defect is present on the X chromosome, the disorder will be manifested since there is no equivalent allele on the Y chromosome to counteract its effect. In women the phenotypical expression of a recessive allele for a defect will be determined by its interaction with the matching allele on the other X chromosome. If the matching allele is a dominant one for normal development, it will overrule the effects of a damaging recessive allele. For example, color blindness is a sex-linked recessive trait carried on the X chromosome. Since it is recessive, if a female receives the deleterious recessive gene from one parent, unless the matching gene from the other is also for color blindness, she will have normal color vision. In contrast, if a male receives the color-blindness gene from the mother on the X chromosome, there can be no counteracting gene from the father and the son will be color-blind.

There are many X-linked characteristics in addition to color blindness. These include hemophilia (a disease in which the blood does not clot), certain types of night blindness, one form of muscular dystrophy, diabetes, atrophy of the optic nerve, and a disorder resulting in an inability to produce antibodies to cope with certain bacterial infections. Also, the high rate of miscarriage, infant mortality, and childhood deaths in males is partly attributable to their greater vulnerability to sex-linked disorders. Even resistance to certain childhood diseases appears to be sex-linked. Thus, although a ratio of 106 males to 100 females are born, this numerical imbalance is rapidly eliminated in the early years of development. Even before birth, it has been estimated that 50

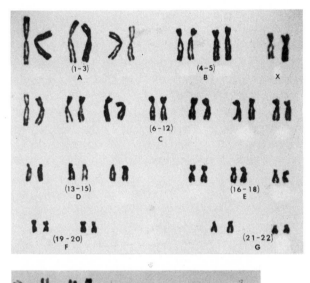

Pictures of the chromosome pairs in a male and female. The twenty-third pair in males shows the difference in size in the large X chromosome and the smaller Y chromosome. (Omikron)

percent more male than female fetuses die or are miscarried. This higher mortality rate of males continues throughout development. In the first month of life, deaths of male infants exceed female deaths by 40 percent; in the first year, by 33 percent; between five and nine, by 44 percent; between ten and fourteen, by 70 percent; and between fifteen and nineteen, by 145 percent (Montague, 1959). The high rate of mortality for males in later years may not be entirely due to their greater genetic vulnerability. Partially it may be attributable to the more adventurous risk-taking activities of males and to such things as their participation in war. In any event, the presence of only a single X chromosome is a genetic liability for males.

Chromosome abnormalities

Developmental disorders sometimes appear because of defects or variations in chromosomes, or chromosome matching. Some of these deviations occur in the autosomes; others occur in the sex chromosomes.

Down's syndrome A disorder known as *trisomy 21*, or *Down's syndrome*, was for some time regarded as a nongenetic disorder attributable to the effects of physiological and biological factors in aging of the mother on the infant in utero. As can be seen from Table 2-1 the incidence of Down's syndrome does increase dramatically with maternal age.

The disorder is characterized by physical and mental retardation and a rather typical appearance which is illustrated in Figure 2-7. Children with Down's syndrome have almond eyes with eyelid folds that many early observers found to be similar to those of the Mongoloid race, round heads often flattened on the back, short necks, protruding tongues, and small noses. In addition, they frequently have other unusual characteristics such as webbed fingers or toes, a rare long simian crease which extends across the hand, dental anomalies, and an awkward flat-footed walk. Their greater susceptibility to leukemia, heart disorders, and particularly to respiratory infections normally resulted in extremely early deaths. At one time it was unusual to see these individuals as adolescents or postadolescents; however, since advances have been made in the treatment of these disorders (such as the use of antibiotics for pneumonia), their lifespan has greatly increased. Children with Down's syndrome have affectionate, placid, cheerful temperaments and are therefore more likely to be kept in the home for a longer period of time

Table 2-1 RISK OF DOWN'S SYNDROME BY MATERNAL AGE

Age of mother	Risk of Down's syndrome in child	
	At any pregnancy	After the birth of a mongoloid
-29	1 in 3,000	1 in 1,000
30-34	1 in 600	1 in 200
35-39	1 in 280	1 in 100
40-44	1 in 70	1 in 25
45-49	1 in 40	1 in 15
All mothers	1 in 665	1 in 200

Source: Reprinted from C. O. Carter and D. MacCarthy, Incidence of mongolism and its diagnosis in the newborn, *British Journal of Social Medicine*, 1951, **5,** 83-90.

than are children with other forms of mental retardation associated with hyperactive, wild, uncontrollable behavior. In spite of this fact, over 10 percent of institutionalized retardates are persons with Down's syndrome.

Recently, it has been demonstrated that Down's syndrome is related to a deviation in the twenty-first set of autosomes, where individuals with the syndrome have three chromosomes or a part of a third chromosome instead of the usual pair. This deviation is the result of an abnormal chromosome complement from one parent with the customary single chromosome from the other. Although it might be possible that either parent could carry the deviant chromosome, the correlation between maternal age and Down's syndrome suggests that it is most often attributable to the egg rather than the sperm. It is now believed that as women grow older abnormal effects occur in the reproductive system which lead to alterations in the chromosomes in the eggs.

The role of genetic factors in this disorder is supported by comparative studies of identical, or *monozygotic* (MZ), twins and fraternal, or *dizygotic* (DZ), twins. Monozy-

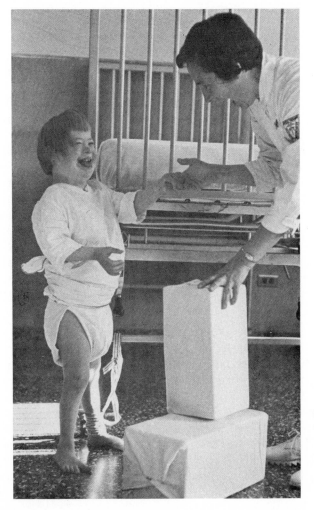

FIGURE 2-7 A young Down's syndrome child. (From Robinson, H. B. & Robinson, N. M. *The Mentally Retarded Child.* New York: McGraw-Hill, 1965. P. 100. By permission of the publisher.)

gotic twins are created by the separation of the zygote following fertilization of a single egg by a single sperm. Following the separation of the zygote, two fetuses develop instead of one. In contrast, dizygotic twins develop from two eggs that have been fertilized by two different sperms, also producing two fetuses. It can be seen that the genetic endowment, or genotypes, of the monozygotic twins are identical, whereas the genotypes of the fraternal twins are no more alike than those of separately born siblings. If a characteristic is genetically determined, the *concordance rate*, or agreement between presence or absence of a trait, is higher in identical than in fraternal twins. In all pairs of identical twins, if one infant has Down's syndrome, so does the other; whereas the occurrence of the disorder in both fraternal twins is relatively rare.

Down's syndrome is one of the genetic disorders which can be detected in the fetus through amniocentesis (an analysis of the chromosomal pattern of cells in the amniotic fluid). However, unlike phenylketonuria, there is no way of treating this disorder.

Sex chromosome abnormalities In addition to abnormalities in the autosomes, problems in sexual differentiation sometimes occur based on deviations in the number of sex chromosomes. Diagnosis of such individuals can be made on the basis of chromosome counts from cells drawn from samples of skin or mouth tissue and prenatally through amniocentesis.

Turner's syndrome. One type of sex chromosome abnormality is *Turner's syndrome.* Females having Turner's syndrome, instead of having the customary XX combination of sex chromosomes, are missing the second X chromosome and are XO. They have only 45 chromosomes. These girls remain small in stature, are usually of normal intelligence, and often have short fingers and webbed necks and unusually shaped mouths and ears. In personality they tend to be relaxed, docile, pleasant, and not easily upset. At puberty they remain infantile in the development of the mammary glands and other secondary sex characteristics because of the lack of female hormones. However, successful treatment is possible through the administration of estrogens (female hormones), which at puberty will lead to normal sexual development although the girls will remain sterile. Girls with Turner's syndrome show feminine personality characteristics and interests even without hormone treatment, and it has been concluded that the normal female XX genetic pattern is not essential for the development of a feminine identity and behaviors.

Klinefelter's syndrome. In contrast with Turner's syndrome, Klinefelter's syndrome in males involves an additional X chromosome (XXY) rather than a lack of a chromosome. These males have testes although they do not produce sperms; they have many female characteristics such as breast development and a rounded, broad-hipped female figure. Although they are sometimes mentally retarded and often show a great reduction in sexual activity, they are frequently not diagnosed correctly until puberty when normal sexual development fails to occur. Females with Turner's syndrome have a low incidence of abnormal psychological characteristics and personality problems; however, there seems to be a greater amount of antisocial, aggressive, and delinquent behavior among boys with Klinefelter's syndrome. Klinefelter's syndrome patients are overrepresented in groups of mentally retarded males with antisocial behavior problems (Forssman & Hambert, 1966).

There has recently been considerable interest and controversy about the effects of an extra Y chromosome in males. These XYY males have been reported to be found more often in populations of retardates, prisoners, and men charged with violent crimes (Hook, 1973).

Intersexuality. The precise relation of deviations in the sex chromosomes to the development of *intersexuality*, or *hermaphroditism*, that is, the presence of some of the sexual characteristics or reproductive systems of both males and females, is open to question. Although some intersexual individuals may be developmental accidents, or mutations, it is also believed that rare recessive or sex-linked genes may also cause these conditions. There are great variations in intersexuality. Some individuals have both ovaries and testes; others possess the internal reproductive system of one sex and the external genitalia of the other. However, intersexes never have both a complete male and female sexual system, and in most cases they are sterile.

Mutation and selection

Genetic variability results not only from the vast number of genetic combinations possible from the chromosomes in the gametes and the exchange of genetic material in the process of crossing-over during meiosis, but also from the development of *mutations*. Mutations are changes in the genes which may produce new phenotypes. In some cases a mutation occurs because of transformations in the gene; in other cases it may be the result of alternations in the arrangement of genes or the quantity of chromosomal material. Down's syndrome, which was discussed earlier, is one of the most frequently cited examples of a mutation developing from the addition of chromosomal material to the twenty-first pair of chromosomes.

The survival of a mutation depends upon a variety of factors; primarily its survival depends upon its adaptability in relation to the environment in which it must develop. The vast majority of mutations are deleterious, or lethal, and do not survive. Theories of evolution are based on the notion of the interaction between mutations with physical and environmental factors in the selective survival of individuals having certain characteristics. Some characteristics such as sickle-cell anemia, which will be discussed later, may be advantageous in one environment but detrimental in another.

Causes of mutation

The reasons for spontaneous mutations in genes are not well understood and are of great concern to contemporary geneticists. Some mutations are controlled by special genes called *mutator genes*, which increase the rate of mutations in individuals who carry them. Other mutations occur because of external agents, or factors, the best known of which are *high temperatures* and *radiation*.

High temperatures   High temperatures can contribute to increased rates of mutation in animals. Michael Lerner (1968) offers the following provocative speculation about the transactions between clothing, temperature, and mutations in human beings.

Most mammals have a temperature-regulating device that keeps the body warmer than the scrotum. Swedish investigators found that wearing tight trousers can raise scrotal temperatures from 30.7°C to 34°C. This, on the basis of crude estimates of known mutation rates and the temperature effect, could increase the incidence of mutation by 85 percent, that is, nearly double it. It is an amusing possibility that perhaps half of what is considered to be spontaneous mutation originating in males is in reality contributed by current sexual taboos, and that the Scottish kilt may have more merits than its wearers suspect [Lerner, 1969, p. 204].

Radiation Radiation is the most extensively studied and controversial external source of mutations. In some cases radiation occurs naturally through variations in the amount of radioactive material in the soil in different parts of the world or through eating radioactive foods. Studies of the relationship between levels of naturally occurring radiation and abnormal development show that in areas where there is a high level of radiation more developmental deviations are found in infants (Gentry et al., 1959). However, this cannot be regarded as a clear demonstration that natural radiation actually leads to genetic mutations; it may be that the radiation interferes with the development of the infants in utero and that no transmissible genetic effects are present. In other cases, developmental deviations occur through man-made radiation, such as x-rays or radiation from atomic fallout.

Since the advent of nuclear weapons, considerable attention has been focused on the effects of radiation on the possible occurrence of mutations. However, although a continued accumulation of atomic fallout effects through nuclear testing or in the event of atomic warfare would have disastrous results, at the present time these effects are minimal when compared with those resulting from the use of x-rays (Lerner, 1968).

In lower organisms it has been demonstrated that radiation of sperm increases the rate of production of mutations. The relative severity of the effects of a single exposure to high amounts of radiation or several exposures to smaller amounts distributed over a longer period of time seems to vary with the species being studied. Although radiation of pregnant mothers has detrimental effects on offspring and excessive radiation may have harmful or lethal effects on adults, the genetic transmission of radiation effects has not been demonstrated conclusively in humans. Careful studies of children of radiologists (Crow, 1955) and of Japanese populations exposed to radiation from atomic attacks (Neel & Schull, 1956; Schull & Neel, 1958) found no differences from those in nonexposed populations in the incidence of abnormal characteristics in their offspring if the parents were not pregnant with the child at the time of exposure. However, if women were pregnant during exposure, they were more likely to miscarry or have a stillborn child than were nonexposed mothers. Even their children who survived had an unusually high incidence of mental retardation, microcephaly (small heads), decrements in height and weight, and leukemia (cancer of the blood). Massive doses of radiation are clearly disastrous to a great many developing fetuses.

In addition, excessive exposure to high levels of radiation may lead to sterility, leukemia, cancer, and tumors in the exposed individual. Higher than normal death rates, especially from leukemia, have been found in the 100,000 survivors who were closest to the centers of the atomic blasts at Nagasaki and Hiroshima. These victims and a group of Marshall Islanders who were inadvertently exposed to radiation during nuclear tests in

Bikini also were found to show many chromosomal abnormalities. However, as yet there is no evidence that these radiation-induced chromosomal abnormalities are transmitted to their children in the form of genetic aberrations.

We may conclude that individuals (including infants in utero) who are exposed to massive doses of radiation show an array of detrimental effects. One of these effects is chromosomal abnormalities such as the shifting of the location of genes or breaking of genes. In spite of the facts that these chromosomal aberrations may occur in radiated humans and that in lower organisms radiation of gametes has been shown to increase mutations, firm evidence does not exist as to relationships between radiation in parents and the development of abnormalities in children who are conceived after radiation.

Hemophilia: An example of a recessive sex-linked mutation

The genetic history of families is not usually available in sufficient detail to identify when a new characteristic has emerged which can be attributed to mutation. This is particularly the case when the pattern of transmission of the mutation is that of a recessive rather than a dominant gene. With a recessive gene, the characteristic may have been carried in a heterozygous state for several generations, masked by the effect of the dominant gene. Family members are unlikely to recall that four generations ago an ancestor had had that same trait.

Fortunately for geneticists, the diseases and disorders of European royal families have been recorded in considerable detail. This has made it possible to trace the occurrence of hemophilia (a disease of the blood in which there is difficulty in clotting) in the royal family to a mutation which occurred in the chromosomes of one of Queen Victoria's parents or to her own prenatal development. At one of these points Queen Victoria became the carrier for the recessive sex-linked disorder hemophilia. Since it is a recessive sex-linked disorder, its transmission pattern is the one previously described for such traits. That is, it emerges in females only when both X alleles carry the recessive gene, and thus females are seldom affected. However, in males it acts like a dominant gene since there is no equivalent allele on the Y gene to counteract or dominate the hemophilic recessive X gene. Because of the intermarriage among members of European royal families, this hemophilic mutation which first appeared in Queen Victoria was to affect not only the British Royal family but many other royal dynasties in Europe. The pattern of transmission of this disorder through Queen Victoria's descendants is presented in Box 2-1.

Sickle-cell anemia: An example of selective survival of a mutation

One of the most dramatic examples of the interaction of genetic factors and environment in selective survival is found in the history of a blood disease called sickle-cell anemia. A mutation appearing in the red blood cells proved adaptive in one environment and destructive in another. The history of the investigation of this disorder reads like a contemporary genetic detective story.

A blood test of a random sample of American blacks would reveal that under conditions of low oxygen the erythrocytes (red blood cells) of about 8 percent of these subjects assume unusual crescent, sickle, or holly-leaf shapes. In most of these individuals the tendency of the blood to sickle is not associated with any deleterious symptoms, and these individuals are said to have the *sickle-cell trait*, or *sicklemia*. However, one in forty of these persons will be afflicted with a severe, chronic, often fatal form of anemia called *sickle-cell anemia*.

Two questions puzzled geneticists: What was the underlying genetic basis for the

---

BOX 2-1 HEMOPHILIA

Blood clotting is a rather complex process. It requires thirteen different identified substances, starting with fibrinogen, a soluble protein in the blood plasma (plasma is blood from which blood cells have been removed; serum is plasma without fibrinogen) which is converted into fibrin, the substance that forms a clot. Deficiency of any one of the thirteen substances will result in failure of clotting and consequently in continuous bleeding. All of them are probably under genetic control. Nine genes have been definitely identified as controlling one or another of these substances, and at least six more are suspected to have such a function. The best known of these genes is a sex-linked recessive responsible for the deficiency of factor VIII, the antihemophilic globulin that causes the disease spoken of as classical hemophilia.

The disease has been known since ancient times and, even though its genetic basis could not be properly explained until the discovery of sex linkage, some knowledge of the pattern of transmission from mother to son was evident in the early years of our era. Thus, in Talmudic law, boys whose two older brothers bled to death from circumcision were excused from the rite, on the basis of what is essentially a sib test. The exemption also extended to sororal nephews of mothers of such children, i.e., to sons of her sister—but not to the fathers' sons by other women. To the contemporaries of those who made them, these provisions were no doubt thought of only as typical examples of the intricacies of Talmudic law; but the provisions indicate some degree of understanding of the basis of inheritance of hemophilia.

The best known pedigree in which the disease appears is that of the descendants of Queen Victoria of Great Britain (1819–1901), an ancestor of many members of European royalty and nobility.

As the pedigree shows, the British royal descendants escaped the disease, because King Edward VII, and consequently all his progeny, did not inherit the defective gene. Similarly, no evidence of the disease is found in other royal families descended from Victoria, except for two. In Russia, the only son of the last Tsar was a hemophiliac. Lacking an understanding of the nature of the disease, his mystically inclined mother, Tsarine Alexandra, became increasingly reliant on a series of faith healers to control her son's affliction. The most notorious of them was the illiterate and dissolute Gregory Rasputin, whose baleful influence at court, financial manipulations, and personal debauchery contributed a great deal to the events leading to the Tsar's abdication and to the subsequent murder of his whole immediate family. Rasputin himself was assassinated on the eve of the Russian revolution by a group of conspirators that included a Grand Duke, another relative of the Tsar by marriage, and a member of the Russian parliament.

Two sons of the last king of Spain, Alfonso XIII, were also hemophiliacs. Although there is no dramatic connection between the disease and the Spanish revolution that sent Alfonso into exile, the gene inherited from Queen Victoria certainly added little joy to the family life of the Bourbons.

Source: From Lerner, I. M. *Heredity, evolution and society.* San Francisco: W. H. Freeman and Company, 1968, p. 200.

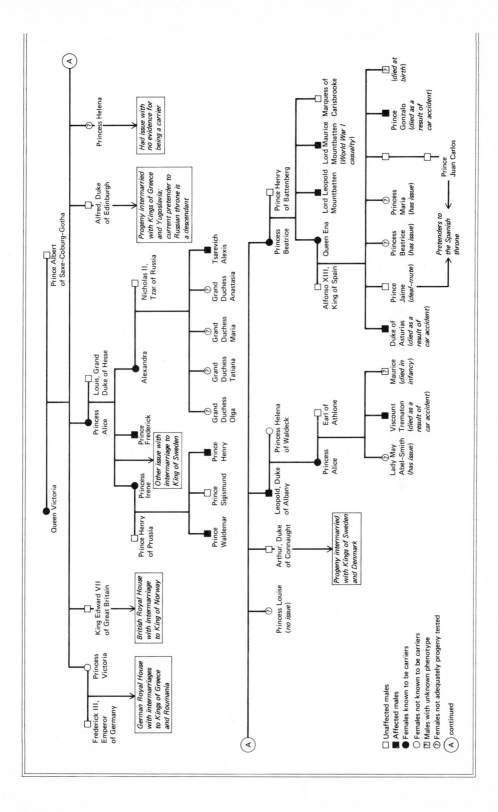

Queen Victoria
Prince Albert of Saxe-Coburg-Gotha

Frederick III, Emperor of Germany — Princess Victoria

German Royal House with intermarriages to Kings of Greece and Roumania

King Edward VII of Great Britain

British Royal House with intermarriage to King of Norway

Princess Alice — Louis, Grand Duke of Hesse

Alfred, Duke of Edinburgh

Progeny intermarried with Kings of Greece and Yugoslavia; current pretender to Russian throne is a descendant

Princess Helena

Had issue with no evidence for being a carrier

Prince Henry of Prussia — Princess Irene

Other issue with intermarriage to King of Sweden

Prince Frederick

Alexandra — Nicholas II, Tzar of Russia

Prince Waldemar
Prince Sigismund
Prince Henry

Grand Duchess Olga
Grand Duchess Tatiana
Grand Duchess Maria
Grand Duchess Anastasia
Tsarevich Alexis

Arthur, Duke of Connaught

Progeny intermarried with Kings of Sweden and Denmark

Leopold, Duke of Albany — Princess Helena of Waldeck

Princess Louise (no issue)

Princess Alice — Earl of Athlone

Lady May Abel-Smith (has issue)
Viscount Trematon (died as a result of car accident)
Maurice (died in infancy)

Prince Henry of Battenberg — Princess Beatrice

Lord Leopold Mountbatten
Lord Maurice Mountbatten (World War I casualty)
Marquess of Carisbrooke

Alfonso XIII, King of Spain — Queen Ena

Duke of Asturias (died as a result of car accident)
Prince Jaime (deaf-mute)
Princess Beatrice (has issue)
Princess Maria (has issue)
Prince Gonzalo (died as a result of car accident)
(died at birth)

Prince Juan Carlos

Pretenders to the Spanish throne

□ Unaffected males
■ Affected males
● Females known to be carriers
○ Females not known to be carriers
? Males with unknown phenotype
? Females not adequately progeny tested
Ⓐ continued

sickle-cell trait and for sickle-cell anemia? Why was the incidence of sickling relatively prevalent in blacks but rare in Caucasians? It was found (Neel, 1949) that a recessive sickling gene exists which results in the sickle-cell trait in a heterozygous state and leads to sickle-cell anemia in a homozygous state. Thus both parents of a child having sickle-cell anemia will themselves have the sickle-cell trait. In its homozygous state in the child this sickling gene causes chemical changes in the hemoglobin molecule, but only rarely do overt adverse symptoms appear in the heterozygotic parents.

The high incidence of the sickle-cell trait in blacks and particularly in some African tribes, such as the Baamba where 39 percent of the population have this trait, was baffling to geneticists. Since sickle-cell anemia sufferers die early and only a small percentage have children, how could this high rate of transmission of a recessive characteristic be explained? It was noted that the unusually high rates of the sickle-cell trait often occurred in areas with a high incidence of malaria. Investigators found a much lower rate of presence of the malarial parasite in sicklers than in nonsicklers, particularly if the subjects were children who had not yet had the opportunity to acquire immunity to malaria (Allison, 1954). The incidence of malarial parasites in 290 Ganda children, aged five months to five years, are presented in Table 2-2. The sickle-cell trait was found to be associated with a resistance to malarial infection. Thus, in malarial regions the heterozygous presence of the sickling gene actually has a selective advantage in survival. Heterozygotes, having a higher rate of survival, reproduce and maintain the frequency of the gene in the population. This is not the case in nonmalarial areas where there is no positive adaptive function served by the sickle-cell gene. In the United States it is likely that through death associated with sickle-cell anemia this disorder will decrease.

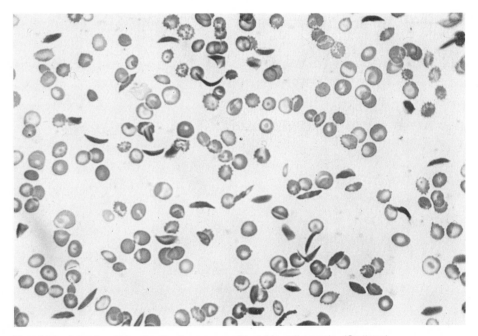

The sickle-shaped red blood cells of a person with sickle-cell anemia. (Omikron)

Table 2-2 INCIDENCE OF MALARIAL PARASITES IN GANDA CHILDREN

	With parasitaemia	Without parasitaemia	Total
Sicklers	12 (22.9%)	31 (72.1%)	43
Nonsicklers	113 (45.7%)	134 (53.3%)	247

Source: From A. C. Allison, Protection afforded by sickle-cell trait against subtertian malarial infection. *British Medical Journal*, 1954, **1**, 290–94.

Although sickle-cell carriers have few adverse symptoms, under certain environmental circumstances they, too, can suffer from their genetic endowment. The Air Force Academy at Colorado Springs recently announced that it would not admit any heterozygotic sickle-cell trait carriers because a combination of exercise and the high altitude at the mountain school had resulted in three deaths of sickle-cell carriers in the last few years. At high altitudes, severe oxygen deprivation resulting from extreme physical exertion can cause a sickle-cell crisis in heterozygotes. Under oxygen deprivation these heterozygotes have 30 to 40 percent sickled cells, which clog blood vessels and can cause not only severe pain and tissue damage but death by blocking critical vessels in the brains and lungs.

The effects of the sickle-cell gene thus vary from an adaptive effect in high malarial areas, which increases the selective survival of the mutation, to a destructive effect in nonmalarial areas, particularly those areas with high altitudes, which leads to increased mortality rates.

STUDIES OF GENETIC INFLUENCES ON HUMAN DEVELOPMENT

The study of similarities in characteristics of family members is one of the most frequently used procedures in investigating the transactions between heredity and environment in the production of phenotypical traits. Because of the unique genetic patterns in twins, many of these studies involve comparing the similarities in certain attributes of identical, or monozygotic (MZ), twins and of fraternal, or dizygotic (DZ), twins. In these studies the assumption is made that monozygotic twins are more similar than dizygotic twins in genetic endowment, since they developed from a single zygote, and the implicit assumption is also made that environmental influences are similar for both types of twins. If identical twins are much more similar with respect to a particular trait than are fraternal twins, who have different genotypes, it is assumed that the appearance of the trait is strongly influenced by genetic factors. If sets of identical and fraternal twins who have shared the same home resemble each other almost equally on a characteristic, it is assumed that this characteristic is more strongly influenced by environmental than genetic factors.

The assumption of similar environmental influences for both types of twins has been questioned by some investigators, for it seems possible that because identical twins are more similar in appearance and other attributes they elicit more similar social responses, especially in treatment by parents. Some evidence for this is found in studies in which the parents have incorrectly classified the zygosity of their twins. These misclassifications are surprisingly high, ranging from 12 percent in some monozygotic (identical) pairs to 35 percent in dizygotic (fraternal) pairs (Smith, 1965). The similarity of parental treatment seems to be determined by genetic rather than believed similarity. That is, mothers of monozygotic twins, whom they wrongly believe to be dizygotic, treat them more like correctly identified monozygotic twins; and mothers of dizygotic twins, whom they wrongly believe to be monozygotic, treat them more like correctly classified dizygotic pairs. Despite the mothers' erroneous beliefs the twins are recognized as having similarities and differences appropriate to their degree of genetic relatedness (Scarr, 1968).

Other investigators have argued that prenatal as well as postnatal factors must be considered in evaluating experiential similarities of twins (Allen, 1965; Corney & Aherne, 1965; Price, 1950; Strong & Corney, 1967). Infants in utero are carried in a sac called the chorion. About 30 percent of monozygotic twins share the same chorion in utero; the remaining 70 percent are in separate chorions, as are dizygotic twins. When monozygotic twins share the same chorion, there is a high probability that fetal crowding will occur and that one twin will obtain a significantly larger share of the maternal blood supply and nourishment than the other. This leads to functional and physical differences in monozygotic twins, and they may often show greater differences in birth weights than do dizygotic twins. Thus, in some cases twins who are genotypically identical may be less overtly similar at birth than fraternal twins but will become increasingly similar with age.

Physical and physiological characteristics

Monozygotic twins are more similar than dizygotic twins in a variety of traits associated with physical measures and measures of biological functioning. In height, weight, shoulder width, hand length, and hand width, identical twins are more alike than fraternal twins (Huntley, 1966; Mittler, 1969; Newman et al., 1937). They are also more similar in facial and dental characteristics and in body build.

Studies of twins indicate that heredity is an important factor in rate of physical maturing as measured by such things as age of first menstruation, ossification of the bones in the hand (which is used as a measure of maturity), and longevity. Even in old age, after exposure to a wide range of environmental influences, identical twins are more similar than fraternal twins in pattern and timing of the formation of wrinkles, loss of teeth, and graying and thinning of hair (Kallman & Sander, 1949).

Of interest to psychologists is the similarity in identical twins in functioning of the brain and of the *autonomic nervous system*, that system that is so closely related to emotional arousal and responsiveness. Variations in responses in the autonomic nervous system have been related to the way individuals adapt to stress and anxiety-arousing situations, control their impulses, and deal with emotional conflicts. In recordings of electrical brain-wave patterns, it has been found that young adult monozygotic twins have recordings as similar as two recordings from the same person on two different occasions. Thus, it is possible to predict the pattern of electrical impulses in the brain of one identical twin from the recordings of the brain of the other as accurately as it is to predict the patterns of impulses of the same individual from one recording to another. In contrast, there is only a modest relationship between the brain-wave recordings of fraternal twins.

Jost and Sontag (1944) found great similarity in monozygotic twins on a composite measure of autonomic functioning, the *index of autonomic stability*, which included blood pressure, respiration rate, galvanic skin response (electrical conductance rates on the skin), salivation, and heart rate. In a more recent study Lader and Wing (1966) compared changes in electrical skin-conductance rates of identical and fraternal twins during the presentation of twenty tones. When the size of the initial galvanic skin response was controlled for, the *habituation*, or change, in the response over the series of tones was much more similar for identical twins than for fraternal twins. The frequency of spontaneous fluctuations, or *lability*, in galvanic skin responses (that is, changes that are not induced by external stimuli but seem to be internally generated) was also highly correlated in identical twins but not significantly related in fraternal twins. In addition to resemblance on these measures of skin conductance, near the end of the series of tones heart rates were highly correlated for identical but not fraternal twins.

In earlier studies the same experimenters found that similar measures of autonomic habituation and lability differ in patients having severe anxiety and in normal subjects with no known emotional disorders. Other investigators have found that lability in autonomic measures, even in infants, is associated with later behavioral impulsivity (that is, a tendency to respond quickly, make errors, and have a short span of attention). Therefore it may be possible that impulsivity is partially genetically based and associated with inherited differences in the functioning of the nervous system. Since the autonomic nervous system plays a key role in anxiety reactions and in psychomatic disorders in which emotional conflicts result in physical symptoms such as ulcers, high blood pressure, and asthma, it also may be that there is a strong hereditary component in predisposition to these disorders.

Intellectual characteristics

The results of studies on similarities in intelligence test scores (IQ) of twins have been remarkably consistent. Performance on intelligence tests is heavily weighted by genetic factors. The closer the genetic kinship bonds, the more similar the IQ.

The results of an ambitious summary of fifty-two different investigations from four continents and eight countries are presented in Table 2-3. In interpreting the correlations it should be remembered that a *correlation coefficient* is an estimate of how two measures vary together. Correlations can range from + 1.00, which indicates that as one measure increases the other shows a fixed, predictable increase, to 0, which shows only a chance relationship between the two variables, to − 1.00, which shows that as one measure increases the other shows a fixed predictable decrease. Thus, the plus or minus sign shows the direction of the relationship and the size of the correlation shows the extent to which two variables are related. If no plus or minus sign is present, we assume the relationship is positive (+).

As might be expected, the correlations of IQs for unrelated persons are extremely small; we cannot predict the IQ of one unrelated person from another effectively even if they are reared together. However, as genetic similarity increases, so does similarity in intelligence test scores. It can be seen that a marked drop in the correlation of intelligence test scores occurs as kinship bonds become further removed. Also, the correlation is lower in dizygotic twins than in monozygotic twins. Even monozygotic twins reared apart, and thus exposed to different home environments, have intelligence test scores more similar than those of dizygotic twins raised in the same home. This pattern of differences in the correlations of identical and fraternal twins is more marked for tests

Table 2-3 CORRELATION COEFFICIENTS FOR INTELLIGENCE TEST SCORES FROM FIFTY-TWO STUDIES INVOLVING FAMILY RELATIONSHIPS WITH DIFFERENT AMOUNTS OF GENETIC SIMILARITY

Relationship		Median correlation	Approximate range of correlations	Number of groups
Unrelated persons	Reared apart	-0.01	-0.03-0.03	4
	Reared together	0.23	0.15-0.32	5
Fosterparent-child		0.20	0.18-0.38	3
Parent-child		0.50	0.23-0.80	12
Siblings	Reared apart	0.40	0.35-0.46	2
	Reared together	0.49	0.32-0.78	35
Twins				
Dizygotic (DZ)	Opposite sex	0.53	0.40-0.65	9
	Like sex	0.53	0.45-0.88	11
Monozygotic (MZ)	Reared apart	0.75	0.63-0.85	4
	Reared together	0.87	0.76-0.95	14

Source: From L. Erlenmeyer-Kimling & L. F. Jarvik, Genetics and intelligence. *Science*, 1963, **142,** 1477-1479.

of intellectual performance that attempt to be relatively culture free, such as intelligence tests, than it is for tests that are heavily culturally and educationally weighted such as achievement tests (Newman et al., 1937). Environmental factors play a greater role in performance on achievement tests than on intelligence tests (Burt, 1966) although they influence both. Other studies have suggested that the genetic contribution is higher in nonverbal tests, such as those involving visual-motor skills, than it is in verbal or linguistic measures.

Another type of study which is frequently used to investigate the contribution of genetic factors to intelligence involves comparisons of the intellectual performances of foster and adopted children with those of their biological or adoptive parents (Burks, 1928; Leahy, 1935). Even if placement has been in the first year of life, the intellectual performance of school-age children correlate with those of their natural parents more closely than those of their adoptive parents.

The results of these studies of foster and adopted children cannot be assumed to indicate that the adoptive parents do not influence their children's IQs (Scarr-Salapatek, 1971). In the only study which included natural mothers' IQ scores rather than intellectual estimates made on the basis of education, it was found that adopted children often averaged twenty or more IQ points higher than their natural mothers. This may be due to the more stimulating environment provided by the brighter adoptive parents. The children's average IQs and the distribution of their IQs more closely resemble their adoptive (average IQ above 100) than natural parents (average IQ 85). However the rank ordering of the children's IQs more closely resembles the rank ordering of their natural parents' IQs, which is what a correlation coefficient measures.

Personality

The contribution of genetic factors to personality characteristics appears to be less than it is to intellectual characteristics. However, this may be attributable partially to the problems that exist in defining and measuring personality traits. Most investigators do not agree on precisely what attributes define assertiveness, sociability, dependency, nurturance, anxiety, and so on. The scales used to measure these characteristics vary more than do intelligence measures, and therefore personality measures tend to be less reliable than measures of intelligence.

In spite of these problems, one dimension of personality which seems to have a hereditary component is a trait which has been variously called *sociability* or *introversion-extraversion*. Sociability ranges from inhibited, apprehensive, and withdrawn behavior to outgoing, self-confident, and gregarious behavior. Monozygotic twins reared either together or apart are more similar than dizygotic twins in sociability (Gottesman, 1963, Scarr, 1969; Shields, 1962). In studies in which the behavior of sets of identical and fraternal twins were rated once a month for the first year of life sociability, smiling, and fear of strangers were very similar for identical twins but not for fraternal twins (Freedman & Keller, 1963). It is interesting that sociability is also a remarkably stable characteristic over time, according to findings from longitudinal studies of children (Kagan & Moss, 1962; Schaeffer & Bayley, 1963). This stability is more marked for boys than girls. Sociability and interpersonal apprehension in adolescence can be predicted for girls from the early school years, but in boys these behaviors are consistent from the first year of life.

A second personality characteristic which may be influenced by genetic factors and in which wide individual differences occur is a preference for different types and amounts of *stimulation*. Some individuals seem to enjoy an environment full of excitement and changing sights and sounds; others seem to prefer a quieter and less changing or turbulent milieu. It has been proposed that some people are *stimulus-reducers* and others are *stimulus-augmenters* (Petrie, 1967). On receiving the same actual amounts of stimulus input, stimulus-reducers subjectively experience the stimulus as less stimulating while stimulus-augmenters experience it as more stimulating. Thus, if an electric shock were administered, the reducers would phenomenally experience it as being less painful than the augmenters. A turbulent environment would seem no more stimulating to a stimulus-reducer than a relatively unchanging setting would to a stimulus-augmenter.

These two groups of individuals show divergent preferences for optimal levels of stimulation. A reducer prefers greater amounts and more complex stimulation than an augmenter. Reducers have been demonstrated to drink alcohol and coffee, to smoke, to have more friends and be more active and attentive to others in social situations than are augmenters. They actually are more likely to seek out novel and complex social situations (Sales, 1972; Sales et al., 1974). Reducers are clearly more extraverted or sociable than augmenters. It has been argued that individual differences in the responsiveness of the nervous system to stimulation may underlie variations in both introversion-extraversion (sociability) and augmenting and reducing (Sales, 1972; Sales et al., 1974).

It has been suggested that so-called psychopaths (individuals who repeatedly get into difficulty, are thrill seekers, do not seem to learn from experience, and show few signs of guilt or remorse) are reducers and neurotics (inhibited individuals who often show excessive anxiety and guilt) are augmenters. This leads to stimulus seeking in psychopaths and avoidance of large amounts of stimulation in neurotics. What would happen to psychopaths and neurotics if we bombarded them with massive amounts of stimulation or isolated and restrained them and greatly reduced stimulation? Sykrzypek (1969) studied the effects of stimulus deprivation and exposure to large amounts of stimulation on responses to novelty and complexity and on anxiety scores of neurotic and psychopathic delinquents. Neurotic delinquents became more anxious and decreased in their preference for complex stimuli following exposure to large amounts of stimulation. In contrast, psychopathic delinquents showed no effects following exposure to large amounts of stimulation but showed a marked increase in their preference for complex stimuli after being subjected to a period of stimulus deprivation. Apparently large amounts of stimulation were disruptive for neurotics but readily adapted to by psychopathic delinquents; also, the effects of stimulus deprivation led to active stimulus seeking in psychopathic delinquents. On the basis of such findings, it might be speculated that solitary confinement would be more distressing for psychopathic delinquents than for neurotic delinquents.

Although most of the research on augmenters and reducers has been done on adolescents and adults, variations in response to stimulation by infants have also been studied. Brazelton (1962) has commented on the apparent ability of some infants to shut out unwanted stimulation by erecting a *stimulus barrier* comprised of a group of responses similar to those found in deep sleep, such as changed patterns of electrical brain waves, decreased motor activity, and slow breathing. When the stimulation is too much, the infant turns it off.

Activity is a personality characteristic that might be conceived of as another form of stimulus-seeking. Reducers are more physically active and enjoy the stimulation of contact sports more than augmenters. Under boring or stimulus-depriving conditions they are more likely to stimulate themselves by moving about the room, shifting position, wiggling their feet and tapping their fingers, and talking to themselves. There is evidence that activity is influenced by hereditary factors. There is greater similarity in activity measures of monozygotic than dizygotic twins (Scarr, 1966; Willerman, 1973). As was true in sociability, activity tends to be a relatively stable characteristic. Fetuses that are most active in the last month before birth become the most active neonates and develop certain motor skills earlier. However, these active neonates are often more irritable and show more difficulties in early adjustment than less active neonates. These neonatal differences in activity tend to be stable into adolescence (Kagan & Moss, 1962; Neilon, 1948) and persist in a twenty-year period from adolescence into maturity (Tuddenham, 1959).

In addition to individual variations in preferences for different amounts of stimulation, variations occur in the types of stimulation preferred. In infants, differences in irritability, in responsiveness to different types of stimulation, and in the relative effectiveness of different types of stimulation in soothing also have been noted. Some infants are *cuddlers* and are soothed by physical contact, holding and restraint; others, the *noncuddlers*, intensify their protests when such techniques are used and are more readily soothed by auditory and visual stimulation or by being walked (Schaffer & Emerson, 1964). Noncuddlers are generally more restless, physically active, and advanced in motor development than cuddlers.

Although genetically based temperamental predispositions in personality exist, the results of longitudinal studies indicate that the role of environmental factors in their expression cannot be ignored. The responsiveness of parents to the temperamental variations in their infants and to their stimulus preferences plays an important role in modifying the phenotypical expression of these traits. Depending on the responses of parents, the same temperamental genotype may be manifested in very different personality characteristics in children. The study presented in Box 2-2 illustrates the interaction

---

BOX 2-2 STABILITY OF TEMPERAMENTAL CHARACTERISTICS IN DIFFICULT CHILDREN

In this study the relationship between early, presumably inherited, temperamental characteristics and later personality development was investigated. A total of 136 children from birth to ages six to twelve in 85 families were studied. A variety of methods were used to obtain information on the children over the course of the study, including frequent parent interviews, home and school observations, teacher interviews, and psychological tests. Measures of child behavior and temperament were obtained by parent interviews at three-month intervals during the first eighteen months of age, at six-month intervals until five years, and at yearly intervals thereafter. Considerable consistency over the first two years of life was found in intensity of responses, rhythmicity (the regularity of cycles of such things as sleeping, eating, elimination, and irritability), adaptability, and threshold of responsiveness.

Before the age of two a group of fourteen *difficult children* with a set of specific temperamental characteristics were defined. These characteristics included biological irregularities in sleep, feeding, and elimination; avoidance, withdrawal, or distress in response to new stimuli or experiences; slow adaptability to new situations; and a prevalence of a negative mood including extremes of fussiness and crying. Of these children, 70 percent developed later behavior disorders, a much higher percentage than in the rest of the sample.

When these difficult children were infants, their parents did not seem to treat them markedly differently from other children, and therefore it is not possible to say their temperamental differences were caused by systematic differences in the way they were reared. However, as these children grew older, their parents started to cope with their behavior in a variety of ways—sometimes with guilt and self-blame, sometimes with anger, resentment, and punishment, and sometimes with flexibility and sensitivity to the needs of the child. The particular form of later behavior disorders to a large extent seemed to be determined by these parental responses, together with later social learning experiences. Some parents were able to moderate the behavior of these temperamentally difficult children; the responses of other parents led to intensification of their children's difficult behavior.

Thus although temperamental differences may have hereditary bases, their specific manifestations are shaped through social interactions, particularly early interactions within the family.

Source: Adapted from Thomas, A., Chess, S., Birch, H., Hertzig, M., & Korn, S., *Behavioral individuality in early childhood*. New York: New York University Press, 1963, and Chess, S., Thomas, A., & Birch, H. G., Behavioral problems revisited, in S. Chess, & H. Birch (Eds.), *Annual Progress in Child Psychiatry and Child Development*. New York: Brunner Mazel, 1968, pp. 335–44.

between possible genetically produced traits and social learning experiences (Thomas et al., 1963; Chess et al., 1968).

Deviant behavior

Although in the study of twins many forms of pathology have been the focus of research, schizophrenia has received the greatest attention. Schizophrenia is a severe mental disorder in which emotional and cognitive disorders occur often, resulting in bizarre behavior and beliefs. In studies of specific disorders such as schizophrenia, rather than using a correlation as is done in studies of IQ, the *concordance rates* of monozygotic and dizygotic twins are compared. A concordance rate is a measure of the percent of time in which the disorder is present in both members of the twin pair. For example, a 100 percent concordance rate would indicate that when one twin had schizophrenia the other twin also always had schizophrenia. One of the problems in using concordance rates in the study of mental disorders such as schizophrenia is that if one twin has the disorder at the time of the study and the other does not, the nondeviant twin may still develop it at a later time. This difficulty in controlling for age of occurrence has not yet been coped with adequately. Differences in specific populations studied, the ages of the subjects, and the criteria for labeling a person schizophrenic, all contribute to variations in concordance rates. Table 2-4 presents a summary of concordance rates for a wide range of studies in a variety of countries. It can be seen that in all these studies monozygotic twins show significantly higher concordance rates than dizygotic twins. Many other disorders such as manic depressive psychoses, alcoholism, homosexuality, and juvenile delinquency and adult crime also show greater concordance rates in monozygotic twins than in fraternal twins.

A study by Heston (1966) lends further support to the theory that there may be a partial genetic basis for schizophrenia. A group of children of schizophrenic mothers, separated from their mothers at birth, were compared to offspring of nonschizophrenic mothers. About half of each group were placed in adoptive homes and half remained in institutions. Both groups were compared on a variety of disorders at about age thirty-five. The higher rates of deviant behavior in the children of schizophrenics, presented in Table 2-5, suggests that the genetic mechanism involved may be manifested in a range of psychological anomalies, including schizophrenia, depending on the effects of life experiences.

As mentioned previously, studies of male criminal populations have found a disproportionately high incidence of XYY and XXY chromosomal patterns compared to those found in a normal population (Bartlett et al., 1968; Telfer et al., 1968). It may be that chronically antisocial behavior is just one possible manifestation of such chromosomal anomalies and that as genetic research progresses they may be found to be correlated with other intellectual or personality deviations.

The fact that there are correlations between chromosomal anomalies and deviant behavior, or the pattern of concordance rates in pathological populations should in no way lead to the conclusion that genetic factors cause the specific form of pathology. Genetic factors may predispose an individual toward mental disorders, but experiential and cultural factors such as social class, family interactions, and the unique frustrations of his life will determine the occurrence, timing, intensity, and form of the disorder.

Table 2-4 CONCORDANCE RATES OF TWIN STUDIES OF SCHIZOPHRENIA

Investigator	Date	Monozygotic pairs			Dizygotic pairs		
		Number of twin pairs	Concordant twin pairs	Percent	Number of twin pairs	Concordant twin pairs	Percent
Luxenberger	1928	19	11	58	13	0	0
Rosanoff et al.	1934	41	25	61	53	7	13
Essen Moller	1941	11	7	64	27	4	15
Kallmann	1946	174	120	69	296	34	11
Slater	1953	37	24	65	58	8	14
Inouye	1961	55	33	60	11	2	18
Kringlen	1967	69	31	45	96	14	15
Fischer et al.	1969	25	14	56	45	12	26
Tienari	1971	20	7	35	23	3	13
Allen et al.	1972	121	52	43	131	12	9
Gottesman & Shields	1972	26	15	58	34	4	12

Source: Adapted from I. I. Gottesmann, & J. Shields. Genetic theorizing and schizophrenia. *British Journal of Psychiatry*, 1973, **122,** 17–18.

Table 2-5 COMPARISON OF SEPARATED OFFSPRING OF SCHIZOPHRENIC AND NORMAL MOTHERS

	Offspring of normal mothers ($N = 50$)	Offspring of schizophrenic mothers ($N = 47$)
Age, mean	36.3	35.8
Adopted	19	22
Mental health ratings	80.1	65.2
Schizophrenia	0	5
Mental deficiency	0	4
Sociopathic	2	9
Neurotic disorder	7	13
More than one year in penal or psychiatric institution	2	11
Total years institution	15	112
Felons	2	7
Number serving in armed forces	17	21
Discharged from armed forces	1	8
Mean IQ	103.7	94.0
Years in school	12.4	11.6
Divorces	7	6

Source: From L. Heston & D. Denny. Interactions between early life experiences and biological factors in schizophrenia. *Journal of Psychiatric Research*, 1968, **6,** 363–76.

SUMMARY

One of the basic interests of geneticists and developmental psychologists is the study of how genetic and environmental factors transact throughout the course of development in shaping the phenotypical characteristics of the child. At certain times in development the child is more vulnerable to certain kinds of environmental factors than at other times.

Genetic factors play an important role in the emergence of many physical, intellectual, and behavioral characteristics. A simple one gene to one characteristic approach to the appearance of individual differences has been modified in accord with current genetic understanding of the chemical processes and multiple gene interactions involved in genetic transmission and the modification of these genotypes through environmental factors. One genotype may lead to many different phenotypes, and a variety of genotypes may underlie the same phenotype.

The appearance, transmission, and survival of genetically based characteristics depend on a variety of factors. Some of these are related to whether the characteristic is transmitted on a dominant or recessive gene or whether it is a sex-linked trait which is transmitted by the X chromosome and occurs more frequently in males. The phenotypical expression of genes may also be modified by interactions with other genes and by the expressivity or penetrance of the genetic characteristic. In addition, biological factors—such as the age of the mother, intrauterine environment, postnatal experiences, and the adaptability of a trait to the environment in which the individual must survive—influence the frequency and phenotypical expression of genetically based characteristics.

Two approaches to the study of the role of genetic factors in development are the use of comparative concordance rates in monozygotic and dizygotic twins and the investigation of the stability of behavior over time in longitudinal studies. Results of such studies suggest that genetic factors play a role in many physical characteristics: in the functioning of the brain and the autonomic nervous system; in intelligence, sociability, and emotional responsiveness; in the preference for certain types and levels of stimulation; and in some psychotic and character disorders. However, the occurrence of these disorders and the phenotypical manifestations of these genetic predispositions are also influenced by environmental and experiential factors.

REFERENCES

Allen, G. Twin research: problems and prospects. In A. G. Steinberg & A. G. Bearn (Eds.), *Progress in medical genetics*. New York: Grune & Stratton, 1965. Pp. 242-69.

Allison, A. C. Protection afforded by sickle-cell trait against subtertian malarial infections. *British Medical Journal*, 1954, **1,** 290-294.

Bartlett, H. W., Hurley, W., Brand, C., & Poole, E. Chromosomes of male patients in a security prison. *Nature,* 1968, **219,** 351-354.

Baumeister, A. A. The effects of dietary control on intelligence in phenylketonuria. *American Journal of Mental Deficiency*, 1967, **71,** 840-847.

Brazelton, T. B. Observations of the neonate. *Journal of American Academy of Child Psychiatry*, 1962, **1,** 38-58.

Burks, B. S. The relative influence of nature and nurture upon mental development: a comparative study of foster parent-foster child resemblance and true parent-true child resemblance. *27th Yearbook of the National Society for the Study of Education* Chicago: The University of Chicago Press, 1928. Part 1, 219-316.

Burt, C. The genetic determination of differences in intelligence: a study of monozygotic twins reared together and apart. *British Journal of Psychology,* 1966, **57,** 137-153.

Carter, C. O., & MacCarthy, D. Incidence of mongolism and its diagnosis in the newborn. *British Journal of Social Medicine*, 1951, **5,** 83-90.

Chess, S., Thomas, A., & Birch, H. G. Behavioral problems revisited. In S. Chess & H. Birch (Eds.), *Annual progress in child psychiatry and child development*. New York: Brunner Mazel, 1968. Pp. 335-344.

Corney, G., & Aherne, W. The placental transfusion syndrome in twins. *Archives of Disease in Childhood*, 1965, **40,** 264-270.

Crow, J. F. A comparison of fetal and infant death rates in the progeny of radiologists and pathologists. *American Journal of Roentgenology, Radium Therapy and Nuclear Medicine*, 1955, **73,** 467-476.

Erlenmeyer-Kimling, L., & Jarvik, L. F. Genetics and intelligence. *Science*, 1963, **142,** 1477-1479.

Forssman, H., & Hambert, C. Incidence of Klinefelter's syndrome among mental patients. *The Lancet,* 1963, **1,** (7284), 1327-1328.

Freedman, D. An ethological approach to the genetical study of human behavior. In S. G. Vandenberg (Ed.), *Methods and goals in human behavior genetics*. New York: Academic, 1965. Pp. 141-161.

Freedman, D. G., & Keller, B. Inheritance of behavior in infants. *Science*, 1963, **140,** 196-198.

Gentry, J. T., Parkhurst, E., & Bulin, G. V., Jr. An epidemiological study of congenital malformations in New York State. *American Journal of Public Health*, 1959, **49,** 1-22.

Goodnight, C. J., Goodnight, M. C., & Gray, P. *General zoology*. New York: Reinhold, 1964.

Gottesman, I. I. Heritability of personality: a demonstration. *Psychological Monographs*, 1963, **77** (Whole No. 572).

Heston, L. Psychiatric disorders in foster-home reared children of schizophrenic mothers. *British Journal of Psychiatry*, 1966, **112,** 819-825.

Heston, L., & Denny, D. Interactions between early life experiences and biological factors in schizophrenia. *Journal of Psychiatric Research*, 1968, **6,** 363-376.

Hook, E. B. Behavioral implications of the human XYY genotype. *Science*, 1973, **179,** 131-150.

Howell, R. R., & Stevenson, R. E. The offspring of phenylketonuric women. *Social Biology Supplement*, 1971, **18,** 519-529.

Hsia, D. Y., Driscoll, K. W., Troll, W., & Knox, W. E. Detection by phenylalanine tolerance tests of heterozygous carriers of phenylketonuria. *Nature*, 1956, **178,** 1239-1240.

Huntley, R. M. C. A study of 320 twin pairs and their families showing resemblances in respect of a number of physical and psychological measurements. Unpublished Ph.D. thesis, University of London, 1966.

Jost, H., & Sontag, L. The genetic factor in autonomic nervous system function. *Psychsomatic Medicine*, 1944, **6,** 308-310.

Kagan, J., & Moss, H. A. *Birth to maturity*. New York: Wiley, 1962.

Kallman, F. J., & Sander, G. Twin studies in senescence. *American Journal of Psychiatry*, 1949, **106,** 2-26.

Lader, M., & Wing, L. Physiological measures, sedative drugs and morbid anxiety. *Maudsley Monographs*, No. 14. London: Oxford University Press, 1966.

Leahy, A. M. Nature-nurture and intelligence. *Genetic Psychology Monographs*, 1935, **17,** 235-308.

Lenneberg, E. H. *Biological foundations of language*. New York: Wiley, 1967.

Lerner, I. M. *Heredity, evolution and society*. San Francisco: Freeman, 1968.

Mittler, P. Psycholinguistic skills in four-year-old twins and singletons. Ph.D. thesis, University of London, 1969.

Mittler, P. *The study of twins*. Baltimore: Penguin, 1971.

Money, J., & Mittenthal, S. Lack of personality pathology in Turner's syndrome: relation to cytogenetics, hormones and physique. *Behavior Genetics*, 1970, **1,** 43-56.

Montague, A. *Human Heredity*. New York: Harcourt, Brace & World, 1959.

Neel, J. V. The inheritance of sickle cell anemia. *Science*, 1949, **110,** 64-66.

Neel, J. V., & Schull, W. J. Studies on the potential genetic effects of the atomic bombs. *Acta Genetics*, 1956, **6,** 183-189.

Neilon, P. Shirleys' babies after fifteen years: a personality study. *Journal of Genetic Psychology*, 1948, **73,** 175-186.

Newman, H. I., Freeman, F. N., & Holzinger, K. J. *Twins: a study of heredity and environment*. Chicago: The University of Chicago Press, 1937.

Petrie, A. *Individuality in pain and suffering*. Chicago: The University of Chicago Press, 1967.

Price, B. Primary biases in twin studies: a review of prenatal and natal differences producing factors in monozygotic pairs. *American Journal of Human Genetics*, 1950, **2,** 293-352.

Robinson, H. B., & Robinson, N. M. *The mentally retarded child*. New York: McGraw-Hill, 1965.

Scarr, S. Genetic factors in activity motivation. *Child Development*, 1966, **37,** 663-673.

Scarr, S. Environmental bias in twin studies. *Eugenics Quarterly*, 1968, **15,** 34-40.

Scarr, S. Social introversion-extraversion as a heritable response. *Child Development*, 1969, **40,** 823-832.

Scarr-Salapatek, S. Unknowns in the IQ equation. *Science*, 1971, **174,** 1223-1228.

Scarr-Salapatek, S. Genetics and the development of intelligence. In F. Horowitz (Ed.), *Review of child development research*. Vol. 4. Chicago: The University of Chicago Press, in press.

Schaeffer, W. S., & Bayley, N. Maternal behavior, child behavior and their intercorrelations from infancy through adolescence. *Monographs of the Society for Research in Child Development*, 1963, **28** (Serial No. 87), 1-127.

Schaffer, H., & Emerson, P. Patterns of response to physical contact in early human development. *Journal of Child Psychology and Psychiatry*, 1964, **5,** 1-13.

Schull, W. J., & Neel, J. V. Radiation and the sex ratio in man. *Science*, 1958, **128,** 343-348.

Shields, J. *Monozygotic twins brought up together and apart*. London: Oxford University Press, 1962.

Shields, J., Gottesman, I., & Slater, E. Kallman's 1946 schizophrenia twin study in the light of new information. *Acta Psychiatrica Scandinavica*, 1967, **43,** 485-496.

Smith, R. T. A comparison of socioenvironmental factors in monozygotic and dizygotic twins; testing an assumption. In S. Vandenberg (Ed.), *Methods and goals in human behavior genetics*. New York: Academic, 1965. Pp. 45-61.

Strong, S. J., & Corney, G. *The placenta in twin pregnancy*. New York: Pergamon Press, 1967.

Sykrzypek, G. J. Effects of perceptual isolation and arousal on anxiety, complexity preference and novelty preference in psychopathic delinquents. *Journal of Abnormal Psychology*, 1969, **74,** 321-329.

Telfer, M., Baker, D., Clark, G., & Richardson, C. Incidence of gross chromosomal errors among tall criminal American males. *Science*, 1968, **157,** 1249-1250.

Thomas, A., Chess, S., Birch, H., Hertzig, M., & Korn, S. *Behavioral individuality in early childhood*. New York: New York University Press, 1963.

Tuddenham, R. D. The constancy of personality ratings over two decades. *Genetic Psychology Monographs*, 1959, **60,** 3-29.

Waddington, C. H. *New Patterns in Genetics and Development*. New York: Columbia, 1962.

Waddington, C. H. *Principles of development and differentiation*. New York: Macmillan, 1966.

Watson, J. D., & Crick, F. H. C. Molecular structure of nucleic acid: a structure for deoxyribose nucleic acid. *Nature*, 1953, **171,** 737-738.

3
PRENATAL DEVELOPMENT AND BIRTH

At one time it was thought that prenatal development occurred within a benign and protected intrauterine environment. It is now recognized that the prenatal organism is vulnerable to a variety of factors that can influence the course of its development. Some of these factors are genetic mechanisms, and some are variations in prenatal environment due to the physical and possibly the emotional condition of the mother. A variety of adverse agents such as maternal disease, X rays, drugs, and dietary deficiencies can contribute to deviations in development. Surprisingly, some of these agents previously regarded as harmless, such as commonly prescribed drugs which may have no deleterious effects on the pregnant mother, can lead to abnormalities in her unborn child.

In this chapter the effects of these genetic and environmental factors on prenatal development will be discussed. First, what are the most important factors? Second, how does the timing of variations in the prenatal environment modify their impact on the developing fetus? Third, what are the effects of conditions of birth and the status of the child at birth on later development? Finally, what postnatal environmental factors sustain or modify the effects of prenatal and perinatal factors?

STAGES OF PRENATAL DEVELOPMENT

The ten lunar months (usually about 280 days) of prenatal development include three periods: the period of the *ovum*, the period of the *embryo*, and the period of the *fetus*. These periods should be thought of as continuous phases of development, for from the moment the sperm penetrates the ovum the development of the organism involves a systematic series of sequential changes by which the organism becomes increasingly complex and differentiated.

The period of the ovum

The period of the ovum includes approximately the first two weeks of life, extending from fertilization until the fertilized ovum, or zygote, proceeds down the fallopian tube and becomes implanted on the wall of the uterus. Tendrils from the zygote penetrate the blood vessels in the wall of the uterus, and the zygote forms the physiologically dependent relationship with the mother which will continue throughout the course of prenatal development. The establishment of this relationship marks the beginning of the second period, the period of the embryo, a state of rapid growth which lasts until the end of the eighth week.

The period of the embryo

Differentiation of the most important organs and physiological systems occur at this time, and by the end of this period, the embryo is recognizable as a partially functioning tiny human being. From the time of fertilization until the end of this period the infant increases 2 million percent in size. Because rapidly developing and differentiating organisms are most vulnerable to adverse environmental effects, the period of the embryo is the phase in which environmental intrusions caused by such things as maternal disease, faulty nutrition, and drugs may result in devastating, irreversible deviations in development.

In the period of the embryo the inner mass of the zygote differentiates into three layers: the *ectoderm*, the *mesoderm*, and the *endoderm*. From the ectoderm develop the hair, nails, and part of the teeth; the outer layer of the skin and skin glands; and the sensory cells and the nervous system. From the mesoderm evolve the muscles, skeleton, excretory and circulatory systems, and inner skin layer; and from the endoderm come the gastrointestinal tract, trachia, bronchia, eustachian tubes, glands, and vital organs such as the lungs, pancreas, and liver.

In addition, in this period, three other important auxiliary structures develop: the *amniotic sac*, the *placenta*, and the *umbilical cord*. The amniotic sac contains *amniotic fluid*, a watery liquid in which the developing embryo floats and which serves as a protective buffer against physical shocks and temperature changes. The tendrils which attach the embryo to the uterine wall increase in size and complexity to form a fleshy disc called the *placenta*. The embryo is joined at the abdomen to the placenta by the third accessory apparatus, the *umbilical cord*, which attains a final length slightly greater than that of the fetus and permits considerable fetal mobility. Although the umbilical cord is composed of blood vessels carrying blood to and from the infant and placenta, there is no direct connection between the bloodstream of the mother and child. The bloodstreams of the mother and child are separated in the placenta by semipermeable membranes, which permit transmission of chemicals with fine molecular structure, such as those found in nutrients and waste products. In this way the placenta carries nourishment to the child and removes its waste products. Early in gestation the nutrients in the mother's bloodstream exceed the needs of the embryo and are stored by the placenta for later use. Certain drugs, hormones, viruses, and antibodies from the mother, which may have destructive effects on the embryo, are also transferred through the placental

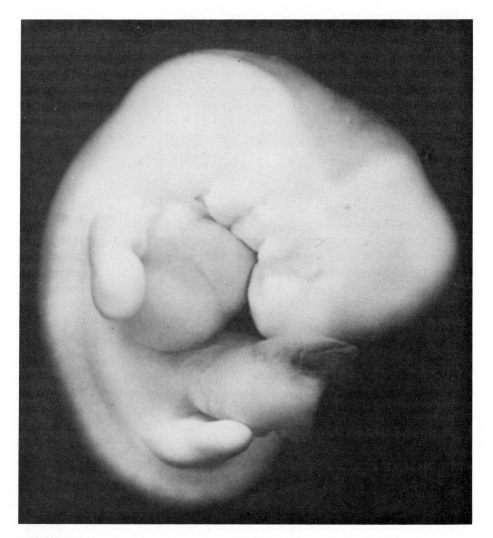

FIGURE 3-1 A human embryo at thirty-eight days. (From Rugh, R., and Shettles, L., *Conception to Birth: The Drama of Life's Beginnings,* with permission.)

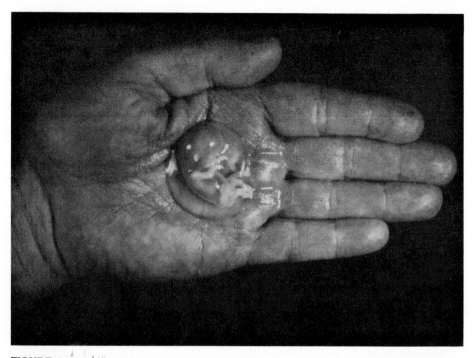

FIGURE 3-2 A human embryo at two months of age. (From Rugh, R., and Shettles, L., *Conception to Birth: The Drama of Life's Beginnings,* with permission.)

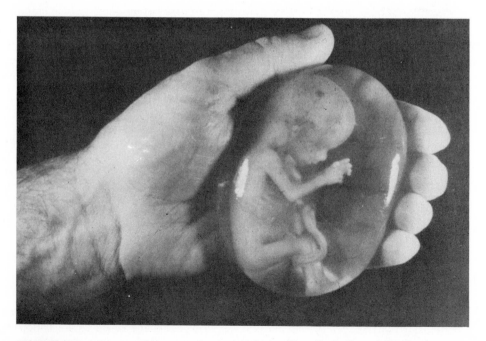

FIGURE 3-3 A human embryo at twelve weeks of age. (From Rugh, R., and Shettles, L., *Conception to Birth: The Drama of Life's Beginnings,* with permission.)

membranes. The rapid emergence and development of new organs and systems in this period make the embryo particularly vulnerable to environmental assault, and thus it is the period when most congenital anomalies occur.

> The neural folds appear about day 19 and began to close 2 days later; if they fail to close, spina bifida results. The future lens of the eye is recognizable at 28 days. The limb buds appear in the 5th week; the hand is defined at the 30th day, the fingers and toes about the 35th. The lateral elements of the future lips and palate are fusing in the 5th and 6th weeks. In these same weeks, the heart and the great vessels are shifting toward their ultimate pattern [Corner, 1961, p. 14].

By the end of the period of the embryo, the face and its features are delineated, and fingers, toes, and external genitalia are present. At six weeks the embryo can be recognized as a human being, although a rather strangely proportioned one in that the head is almost as large as the rest of the body. Primitive functioning of the heart and liver, as well as the peristaltic movement of ingestion, have been reported late in this period.

Most miscarriages or spontaneous abortions occur during this period; the embryo becomes detached from the wall of the uterus and is expelled. It has been estimated that the rate of spontaneous abortion is as high as one in four pregnancies but that many remain undetected because they occur in the first few weeks of pregnancy. This high rate of abortion may be advantageous to the species since the great majority of aborted embryos have gross chromosomal and genetic disorders. The most severely affected embryos are spontaneously eliminated.

The period of the fetus

The final stage of prenatal development, the period of the fetus extends from the beginning of the third month until birth. During this time, muscular development is rapid and the gradual maturing and differentiation of the nervous system leads to the emergence of more refined and circumscribed reflexes and responses. By the end of the fourth month, mothers usually report movement of the fetus. By the age of five months reflexes such as sucking, swallowing, and hiccoughing usually appear. In addition, a Babinski reflex of a fanning of the toes in response to stroking of the foot occurs. After the fifth month, the fetus develops nails and sweat glands, a coarser, more adultlike skin, and a soft hair which covers the body. Most fetuses shed this hair in utero, but some continue to shed it after birth. By six months the eyes have developed and opening and closing of the eyes occurs. If an infant is born prematurely at six months his regulatory processes and nervous and respiratory systems still are usually not mature enough for survival. The age of twenty-eight weeks, sometimes referred to as the *age of viability*, is an important point in fetal development since at this time the physical systems of the fetus are sufficiently advanced so that if birth occurs, the child may survive.

PRENATAL INFLUENCES ON DEVELOPMENT

During the course of prenatal development many agents may raise the incidence of deviations or produce malformations in the fetus. These agents are called *teratogenes* and include maternal diseases and blood disorders, diet, irradiation, drugs, temperature, and oxygen level. In addition, maternal characteristics such as age, emotional state, and the number of children she has borne influence prenatal development. Certain general principles describe the effects of teratogenes on prenatal development (for recent reviews on the topic see Beck & Lloyd, 1965; Clegg, 1971; and Wilson, 1961).

1. The effects of a teratogene vary with the developmental stage of the embryo. Teratogenes acting on newly differentiated cells may damage developing but yet unformed organ systems. Since the various organ systems begin and end their prenatal development at different times, their sensitivity to agents varies over time. The vulnerable period for the nervous system is from fifteen to twenty-five days, for the eye from twenty-four to forty days, for the heart from twenty to forty days, and for the legs from twenty-four to thirty-six days (Tuchmann-Duplessis, 1965). Before implantation and after the beginning of the fetal stage the organism is less vulnerable than during the embryonic period. During the fetal stage, teratogene-induced abnormalities tend to occur only in locations or systems which are still maturing such as the cerebellum, palate, and some cardiovascular and urogenital structures (Clegg, 1971).

2. Since individual teratogenes influence specific developmental processes, they produce specific patterns of developmental deviations. Rubella (German measles) affects mainly the heart, eyes, and brain; and the drug thalidomide results primarily in malformations of the limbs. This finding, in conjunction with the information on the critical vulnerable periods for these developing systems reported in the first principle,

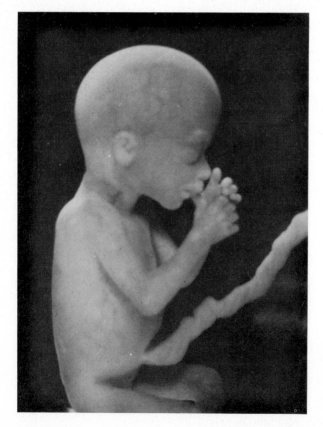

FIGURE 3-4 A human fetus at seventeen weeks. (From Rugh, R., and Shettles, L., *Conception to Birth: The Drama of Life's Beginnings,* with permission.)

suggests that although the form of the deviations resulting from rubella and thalidomide vary, the organism's period of greatest vulnerability to them is in approximately the same timespan during the embryonic period, that is, between the fourth and sixth weeks.

3. Both maternal and fetal genotypes can affect the developing organism's response to teratogenic agents and may play an important role in the appearance of abnormalities in offspring. Not all pregnant women who use the drug thalidomide or have German measles or poor diets produce defective infants. Those who do may themselves be genetically predisposed to being more vulnerable to those particular teratogenes or may have fetuses who are so predisposed.

Genetic differences in the vulnerability to biochemical changes associated with maternal emotional arousal is demonstrated in a study by Thompson and Olian (1961). Exposure of a pregnant organism to stressful situations is though to affect the offspring through increases in production of adrenal hormones. Injections of adrenalin were given to groups of pregnant mice of three different inbred strains in their second trimester of pregnancy. When the activity of the offspring was subsequently tested in an open-field situation under normal and stressful conditions, it was found that prenatal adrenal condition led to no changes in one strain, increased activity in the second strain under both normal and stressful conditions, and decreased activity in the third strain under the

FIGURE 3-5 A human fetus at eight months. (From Rugh, R., and Shettles, L., *Conception to Birth: The Drama of Life's Beginnings*, with permission.)

stressful testing condition only. This experiment demonstrates the interaction of genetic factors, teratogenes, and eliciting situational factors in affecting the behavior of off-spring.

4. Levels of teratogenic agents which will produce malformations in the offspring may show no or mild detrimental effects on the mother. With a variety of drugs, diseases, X-irradiation, and dietary deficiencies the mother may show no abnormalities but gross deviations may appear in the child.

5. One teratogene may result in a variety of deviations, and several different terato-genes may produce the same deviation. Rubella may lead to deafness, cataracts, mental retardation, or heart disorders in the early months of pregnancy depending on the time at which the disease was contracted. However, deafness in infants can be caused not only by maternal rubella but but also by the mother taking drugs such as quinine or streptomycin.

Maternal diseases and disorders

A wide range of maternal diseases and disorders can affect prenatal development, and, in accord with the principles noted previously, the effects are correlated with the stage of fetal development. Even mild attacks of rubella may produce cardiac disorders, cataracts, deafness, and mental retardation in the infant. It has been argued that the primary effects of rubella are the physical and sensory deficits such as blindness and deafness which limit the information available to the child and interfere with his development. The suggestion is that the appearance of retardation in these children is one not directly produced by the rubella virus but is a result of these other physical and sensory liabilities which interfere with his intellectual growth (Dodrill et al., 1974). The occurrence of deviations decreases from 50 percent if the mother contracts rubella in the first month, to 17 percent if she contracts it in the third month; and there is almost no probability of abnormalities occurring if the mother contracts rubella after that time (Rhodes, 1961). Another maternal disease, mumps, also results in a higher incidence of malformations if contracted in the first trimester rather than later in pregnancy.

Chronic infections like venereal diseases (gonorrhea and syphilis), which invade the developing embryo and remain active, have their worst effects at later stages of development. The deleterious effects of the syphilis spirochete on the fetus do not occur before eighteen weeks of age, and therefore early treatment of a syphilitic mother may avert abnormalities in the child. If the mother is untreated, invasion of the fetus by the syphilis spirochetes from the mother may result in abortion or miscarriage, mental retardation, blindness, or other physical abnormalities. In some cases the deleterious effects of syphilis are not apparent at birth but gradually emerge during the early years of development in the form of juvenile paresis, involving deterioration in thought processes, judgment, and speech, and in a decline in motor and mental abilities and eventual death.

Other maternal conditions such as *high blood pressure, diabetes,* and *blood incompatibilities* between mother and fetus may affect fetal development. The increase in miscarriage and infant and maternal mortality rates are directly correlated with the degree of high blood pressure in pregnant women suffering from hypertension. Infants of diabetic mothers have a relatively high proportion of infant mortality and abnormalites, particularly of the circulatory and respiratory systems (Gellis & Hsai, 1959). It is difficult to determine whether this relatively high incidence of malformations is attributable to the influence on the fetus of the mother's high blood sugar or to the effects of insulin, which the mother takes as medication for diabetes (Corner, 1961).

In addition, an incompatibility can occur between the blood types of mother and child. Although many forms of blood incompatibilities occur, Rh blood incompatibility is the most frequent and destructive. The incompatibility between an Rh-positive baby and an Rh-negative mother can cause miscarriage or infant death through *erythroblastosis*, a destruction of the red blood corpuscles resulting in an inadequate supply of oxygen to the fetus. Antigens are produced in the blood of the Rh-positive fetus and transmitted through the placenta to the blood of the Rh-negative mother; toxic antibodies are produced in the mother's blood and are returned to the infant, resulting in erythroblastosis. Maternal sensitivity to the Rh-positive antigens increases with successive pregnancies, and although the first pregnancy may be normal, later ones are less likely to be so.

Several advances have been made in treating this condition. One is to give the infant in utero blood transfusions to purge it of the destructive antibodies. A second and more promising method is to inoculate and immunize Rh-negative mothers prior to their first pregnancy before they have the opportunity of becoming sensitized to Rh-positive antigens. Finally, some very recent and promising work is being done in which maternal antibody level is controlled through drugs.

Drugs

Thalidomide   The *thalidomide* disaster in the late 1950s and early 1960s brought into public awareness the often unknown and potentially horrendous effects of the use of drugs by pregnant women. At this time an increase began to occur in the birth of children with an unusual group of abnormalities. The cluster of abnormalities included such things as eye defects, cleft palate, depressed bridge of the nose, small external ears, facial palsy, fusing of fingers and toes, dislocated hips, and malformations of the digestive and genitourinary tract and heart. However, the most unusual and characteristic deformity was *phocomelia*, an anomaly where limbs are missing and the feet and hands are attached directly to the torso like flippers (Karnofsky, 1965). It was partly the rarity of this anomaly that called attention to the fact that the mothers of these malformed infants had been prescribed thalidomide as a sedative or antinausea drug in the early months of pregnancy.

The problems in establishing the consequences of maternal intake of a drug during pregnancy on offspring is illustrated clearly in the case of thalidomide. The pregnant women showed no adverse effects of the thalidomide. (Even in instances where adults have ingested massive quantities of thalidomide in suicide attempts, it has resulted in nothing more serious than deep sleep, headaches, and nausea.) Only a small percentage of pregnant women who used thalidomide produced deviant children and in some of the animal species studied no effects of thalidomide on offspring were obtained.

Although there is some controversy about the intelligence of thalidomide babies, the evidence suggests that among noninstitutionalized infants who are reared in a normal home situation and who do not suffer from gross sensory deficits (such as blindness, deafness, or paralysis, which might be expected to seriously handicap the development of a child), the intelligence quotients of thalidomide babies differ little from those of normal children. However, in the study by Decarie (1969) of twenty-two thalidomide children under four years of age, suffering from malformations involving either or both the hands and arms or legs and feet, a typical profile of developmental abilities in thalidomide infants was found, which was rather unexpected. This study used both institutionalized and family-raised limb-deficient thalidomide children, and although the latter had a higher average intelligence quotient on the Griffith Developmental Scale, the configuration of the developmental profile was similar for both groups. The profile for the total sample is presented in Figure 3-7.

Surprisingly, the area of ability most adversely affected was language, as measured by the hearing and speech subscale; the area least affected was eye-hand coordination. In order to make the test appropriate for these limb-deficient children, the administration of the Eye-Hand Scale was made more flexible than in the standard test administration; thus, items such as "Can hold pencil as if to mark paper" were given credit when the pencil was held successfully with the toes, mouth, or hands. The pattern of findings on the subscales were attributed to two factors:

(1) interruption in the normal developmental sequence due to the limb deficiencies which especially interfere with locomotor development thereby resulting in the impetus in fine mo-

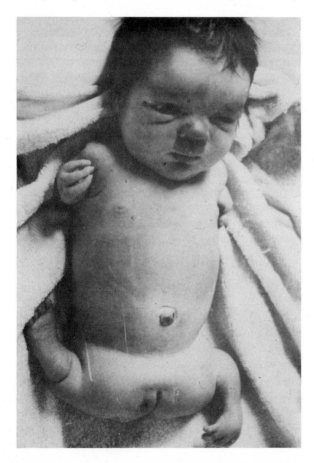

FIGURE 3-6 A baby whose mother had taken thalidomide during pregnancy. (Omikron)

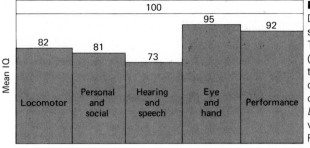

FIGURE 3-7 The Griffith Developmental Profile of a sample of thalidomide children. The overall mean IQ is 85. (From Dacarie, T. G. A study of the mental and emotional development of the thalidomide child. In B. M. Foss (Ed.), *Determinants of infant behavior,* vol. 4. London: Metheun, 1969. Pp. 167–187.)

tor development, and (2) lack of sufficient stimulation from the human milieu so that the child is forced to search for his satisfactions from the only other source available, the inanimate world of objects, with the only other instrument available, his deficient arms and hands [O'Neill, 1965, p. 136].

Inadequate amounts of stimulation in institutional settings have been demonstrated frequently, and even in the home, handicapped children are not given sufficient stimulation from caretakers to compensate for their lack of initiative. There is less interaction between handicapped children and adult caretakers than between normal children and adults (Spock & Lerrigo, 1965). It may be that this lack of stimulation and interaction is partly responsible for the retardation in language development in thalidomide children. An active, talking, responsive adult is essential for the development of speech in the infant.

Although the deleterious effects of thalidomide are the most widely known, other drugs ingested by the mother also may affect the fetus. For example, the use of quinine for the treatment of malaria in pregnant women can result in congenital deafness in the child. In addition, it has recently been found that drugs which are commonly administered to pregnant women for therapeutic reasons may have deleterious effects. Maternal ingestion of reserpine, a tranquilizer, may lead to infant respiratory problems. Some of the drugs (such as the tetracyclins) used to combat maternal infections may depress infant skeletal growth. The intake of certain anticonvulsant drugs has been related to cleft lip and palate and problems in blood coagulation in the neonate. Even the common aspirin, if taken in high doses by pregnant women, may produce blood disorders in offspring (Eriksson et al., 1973).

Labor and delivery medication Recently concern has been focused on the administration of drugs to ease pain and sedate women during labor. Early studies demonstrated short-term effects of such anesthetics on the newborn child. Offspring of mothers who received certain drugs during labor showed a decrease in cortical activity for several days after birth (Hughes et al., 1948), disruptions in feeding responses (Brazelton, 1961; Kron et al., 1966), and general neonatal depression (Shnider & Moya, 1964). Attentional behavior (such as looking at pictures exposed at one-minute intervals) in two- to four-day-old infants has also been impaired by maternal intake of a depressant during labor (Stechler, 1964).

The timing of the administration of a drug during labor seems particularly important. Moya and Thorndike (1962) surveyed the results of a large group of studies on the use of a variety of narcotics during labor and found that if the infant is born less than one hour or more than six hours following a mother's intake of a drug, there is a decrease in its effects.

A recent study (Conway & Brackbill, 1970) presented in Box 3-1 suggests that the effects of medication administered during delivery may be more long-lasting than was previously realized. In addition, parent-infant interaction is changed as a result of medication. Mothers who receive a large amount of medication during labor touch and rock their infants more than mothers who receive little medication (Parke, O'Leary & West, 1972). During feeding, others who have had high doses of medication give more stimulation to their infants to suck and attend (Richards & Bernal, 1971). These mothers seem to be adapting to their children's depression, problems in attending, and disruptions in feeding.

BOX 3-1 EFFECTS OF OBSTETRICAL MEDICATION ON INFANT
DEVELOPMENT

Does the obstetrical medication that a mother may receive during labor and delivery affect the infant? To answer this question Conway and Brackbill investigated the relation between the potency of maternal medication and the developmental status of the child at ages two days, five days, and one month. They employed a group of motor, mental, sensory, and physiological measures of development, including a measure of habituation, or gradually ceasing to respond to repeated stimuli. The measure of habituation used in this study was the number of exposures to bursts of a noise before the infant ceased making a startle response to the noise. This measure has previously been demonstrated to be a significant index of cortical functioning.

The findings showed that obstetrical medication influences the sensorimotor functioning of the infant and that some of these effects are still present at one month of age. These effects were not restricted to one sensory modality but were found in muscular, visual, and neurological development. At all three ages the ability to habituate to the noise was impaired. Even at one month of age, infants whose mothers had received no anesthetics during delivery habituated, or adapted to the noise, two and one-half times more rapidly than infants whose mothers had received general anesthetic. In addition, infants of anesthetized mothers performed poorly at two and five days on a scale designed to assess behavioral deficit in neonates, the Graham Scale (Graham, 1956). Finally at one month, potency of medication was related to impairment on the Bayley Motor scales (Bayley, 1965a), which measure such things as muscular strength and coordination, head movements, postural adjustments, visual following and eye coordination, and response to sounds.

It can be seen that obstetrical medication during labor results in short-term deficiencies and in impairment of attentional and motor abilities that is still present at one month of age.

Source: Adapted from Conway, E., & Brackbill, Y. Delivery medication and infant outcome: An empirical study in the effects of obstetrical medication on fetus and infant, by Bowes, W. A., Jr., Brackbill, Y., Conway, E., & Steinschneider, A. *Monographs of the Society for Research in Child Development*, 1970, **35,** 24-34.

Heroin, Methadone, and LSD   In addition to drugs used for therapeutic reasons, in this "turned-on" age, the prenatal effects of drugs such as heroin, morphine, methadone, and LSD (lysergic acid diethylamide) are of increasing concern. Mothers who are heroin or morphine addicts have offspring who are also addicted and are observed to go through withdrawal symptoms such as hyperirritability, vomiting, trembling, shrill crying, rapid respiration, and hyperactivity which may result in death in the first few days of life (Brazelton, 1970). Female addicts seem to have reduced fertility; however, when they do conceive, their infants are often premature and of low birthweight, which makes them even less prepared to cope with the trauma of withdrawal symptoms (Eriksson, Catz & Yaffe, 1973). The severity of the neonate's symptoms are related to how sustained and intense the mother's addition has been (Burnham, 1972). If the mother stops taking drugs in the months preceding birth, the infant usually is not affected in this way.

There has been a great controversy in the past ten years over the use of methadone as a less deleterious substitute for heroin. However, it has been found that the use of methadone by pregnant women leads to withdrawal symptoms in their infants that are believed by some experts to be even more severe than those resulting from heroin.

The evidence for the effects of LSD during pregnancy are less conclusive than those for heroin. Chromosomal breakages have been found in both humans and animals exposed to high and sustained doses of LSD. In animal studies some developmental anomalies have been associated with LSD, but in human studies no firm conclusions can be drawn about the relation between defects in children and maternal use of LSD (Eriksson, Catz & Yaffe, 1973). In studies of maternal use of LSD, as in those of other illegally used drugs, it is difficult to isolate the specific effects of the drugs. Frequently these mothers have been multiple-drug users, are malnourished, and may have poor prenatal and delivery care, all of which could contribute to producing anomalies in their infants.

Smoking   Maternal smoking, which also can be regarded as drug use, influences the cardiovascular system of the fetus by frequently, but not invariably, increasing the fetal heart rate (Sontag & Wallace, 1935). In addition, women who are chronic smokers have premature infants almost twice as often as nonsmokers (Frazier et al., 1961; Simpson, 1957); also, the rate of prematurity is directly related to the amount of maternal smoking. Even with full-term babies, infants of nonsmokers are heavier than those of smokers. In observing such findings Bernard (1962, p. 43) has commented that "the choice between a dessicated weed and a well cultivated seed seems often to be a quite difficult one."

In summary, the effects of maternal drug intake on fetal development are difficult to predict. Many of the drugs which produce unfortunate effects had been tested on animals and nonpregnant adults and found to be harmless. We cannot make valid generalizations from tests performed on animals and human adults to the rapidly developing fetus since teratogenes may affect different species at different stages of development in diverse ways. Although it is apparent that great caution should be used in the administration of drugs to women during pregnancy and labor, physicians prescribe an amazingly high number of drugs to pregnant women. Peckham and King (1963) found that pregnant women were prescribed an average of 3.6 drugs. Four percent of the women had been prescribed ten or more drugs while they were pregnant.

Maternal diet

It is difficult to separate the effects of maternal malnourishment from those of a variety of other deleterious factors. The mother who is malnourished often exists in an environment of poverty and disadvantage characterized by poor education, inferior sanitation and shelter, and inadequate medical care (Birch & Gussow, 1970). In this country a high maternal and infant mortality factor is associated not only with socioeconomic factors but also with ethnicity.

People who are both nonwhite and poor are exposed to more of these harmful environmental factors and experience more of their destructive effects. Figure 3-8 presents a table of infant mortality rates related to sex and race. It can be seen that males, particularly black and Indian males, are more likely to die in infancy. In addition, infant and maternal mortality rates are higher in low income families. The increase in infant mortality rates for Puerto Ricans and blacks with low-income levels in New York City can be seen in Figure 3-9. In the United States, nonwhites tend to be less affluent, begin childbearing early and end it later, and have poorer diets, more illegitimate births, and poorer prenatal and delivery care. Adverse prenatal conditions are followed by the environment of poverty which sustains and compounds their effects.

A study which gave equivalent prenatal medical care to low-income black and white women found that although maternal mortality rates decreased in both groups, the decrease was greatest for the white women, who had a lower death rate initially (Whit-

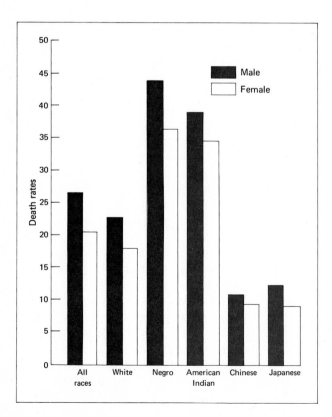

FIGURE 3-8 Infant mortality rates by sex, race, or national origin: United States, 1966. (Death rates under one year per 1,000 live births.) (From White House Conference on Children, *Profiles of Children*. Washington: Government Printing Office, 1970. P. 49.)

ridge & Davens, 1952). On the basis of such findings Birch and Gussow conclude: "It seems clear that it is not simply differences in the age or marital status of the non-white population that explains its relatively high risk of death. Rather, the different death rates in the white and non-white groups are the consequence of a constellation of factors in which the depressed population differs from the majority [Birch & Gussow, 1970, p. 44]."

Studies on a variety of populations have shown that gross dietary deficiencies, especially in some vitamins and in protein, in the diets of pregnant women are related to increased rates of abortions, prematurity, stillbirths, infant mortality, and physical and neural defects in infants (Bayley, 1965*b*; Burke et al., 1943; Knoblack & Pasamanick, 1966; Pasamanick & Knoblock, 1966; Tompkins, 1951; Wortis, 1963). Even when gestation period and prematurity are controlled for, offspring of malnourished mothers are smaller in length and weight. Middle-class mothers are more likely to have an adequate intake of protein, vitamins, and minerals than lower-class mothers although there are no class differences in the consumption of fats, carbohydrates, and calories (McCance, Widdowson & Verdon Roe, 1938).

Studies of severely malnourished animals and infants suggest that early malnutrition may interfere with the development of the nervous system, and, again, we find that the specific form the damage takes depends on the age at which malnutrition occurs. Early gross malnutrition disrupts myelination, the development of an insulating fatty sheath around nerves, which facilitates the speed of transmission of neural impulses. If malnu-

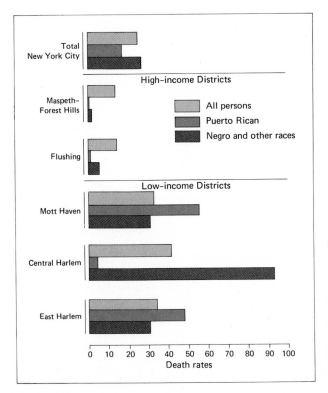

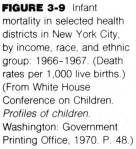

FIGURE 3-9 Infant mortality in selected health districts in New York City, by income, race, and ethnic group: 1966–1967. (Death rates per 1,000 live births.) (From White House Conference on Children. *Profiles of children.* Washington: Government Printing Office, 1970. P. 48.)

trition occurs during the period of myelination of the brain, defective myelination may be associated with mental retardation (Davison & Dobbing, 1966).

In the prenatal period and in the first six months of life the brain grows mainly by cell division; after that time it grows through the intake of fats and proteins, not by the formation of additional cells (Winick, 1968; 1970). Autopsies on malnourished animals and children suggest that early malnutrition leads to a decreased number of cells in the brain that later dietary deficiencies result in decreases in the size of the brain cells. Autopsy studies of malnourished children in Uganda (Brown, 1966) and India (Parekh et al., 1970) show brain-weight deficits up to 36 percent. Similar findings were obtained in a study of 252 American urban children who were stillborn or died within forty-eight hours after birth, and whom it is assumed were not as grossly malnourished as children in economically deprived countries. Autopsies on these American children showed that the brains of the lower-class infants weighed 15 percent less than those of children from more affluent families (Naeye et al., 1969).

The reports of the deleterious effects of maternal malnutrition on prenatal development have led to many studies in which the diets of malnourished pregnant women are supplemented. Although the study reported in Box 3-2 is one of the first on the effects of dietary supplementation on development, it remains one of the best since it determined, rather than assumed, that the pregnant women really had dietary deficiencies before their diets were supplemented. In addition, the study points out that even when mothers do not show marked adverse effects of malnutrition, their infants may be harmed.

BOX 3-2 THE EFFECTS OF PRENATAL DIET ON MOTHER AND CHILD

In this study the effects of variations in diet on pregnant women and their infants were studied. From a group of 210 women who attended a University of Toronto clinic and who were determined to have inadequate diets, 90 were given dietary supplements which resulted in an adequate diet during the last portion of pregnancy; the remaining 120 continued on inadequate diets. The women were studied throughout pregnancy and the infants in the first few months of life.

Although few direct signs of malnutrition were manifested in either of the groups of mothers, the offspring of the mothers on inadequate diets showed greater neonatal risk, developmental deviations, and poorer health than those of mothers who had been given dietary supplements. During the first six months of life, the infants of poorly nourished mothers had a higher incidence of such disorders and diseases as rickets, anemia, tetany, pneumonia, colds, and bronchitis. Also, mothers on inadequate diets had more physical difficulties during pregnancy, including miscarriages, premature and stillbirths, bleeding anemia, and toxemia. In addition, the period of labor averaged about five hours longer for these mothers. This study clearly demonstrates the importance of a well-balanced diet to pregnant women and their offspring.

Source: Adapted from Ebbs, H. H., Brown, A., Tisdall, F. F., Moyle, W. J., & Bell, M. The influence of improven prenatal nutrition upon the infant. *Canadian Medical Association Journal,* 1942, **46,** 6-8, and Ebbs, H. H., Tisdall, F. F., & Scott, W. A. The influence of prenatal diet on mother and child. *Millbank Memorial Fund Quarterly,* 1942, **20,** 35-36.

The results of such studies should not lead to the conclusion that a massive national program of dietary supplementation for malnourished pregnant women could be undertaken easily or casually. The very poor women, who suffer most from the effects of malnutrition, frequently do not seek medical care during pregnancy and hence would be unlikely to be identified in time to benefit from dietary supplementation. Also, it has been found that under some conditions selective supplementation may have detrimental effects, depending on the previous nutritional status of a woman. Tompkins and Wiehl (1951) found that although administering vitamin and mineral supplements reduced prematurity in young mothers who had few previous children, the same supplementation in women over thirty who had more than two children led to a rate of prematurity even higher than that of a poorly nourished control group. It seems that in some cases of severe nutritional deprivation the body may be unable to adapt to, or compensate for, selected supplement-induced nutritional imbalances. These factors suggest that to be effective, continuing programs for dietary supplementation should be concerned with the population as a whole.

Maternal emotional state

The causal factors in the frequently cited finding that emotionally disturbed women produce disturbed children are difficult to isolate. It might be attributable to genetic transmission of emotional characteristics or the fact that emotionality in a pregnant woman induces metabolic or biochemical changes, such as alterations in adrenalin level, which affect the fetus. It also seems probable that the woman who is emotionally disturbed during pregnancy is also more likely to be an emotionally unstable and inadequate caretaker following pregnancy when she will be the main social influence on the infant. Emotional stress in women may therefore be a contributing factor to both problems in pregnancy and delivery and later intellectual and emotional deviations in offspring. Genetic or prenatal factors or early infant learning and experiences could all play a role in the findings of the following studies.

Maternal emotional disturbance has been related to complications both during pregnancy and delivery. High maternal anxiety has been associated with nausea during pregnancy, prematurity, abortion, prolonged labor, and delivery complications (Ferreira, 1969; Joffe, 1969; McDonald, 1968). It might be expected that greater emotional stress would be found in women having psychiatrically diagnosed emotional disorders. Sameroff and Zax (1973) compared the difficulties during pregnancy and delivery of schizophrenic, neurotic depressive, personality-disorders, and normal women. Normal women had fewer difficulties during pregnancy and delivery than the women with severe emotional problems. However, there were no differences in the frequency of perinatal complications among the disturbed groups. The occurrence of obstetrical problems was related to the severity of disturbance rather than the psychiatric classification. Those who had had the most prolonged history of emotional disturbance with the most frequent contacts with psychiatrists and hospitalization, regardless of diagnostic classification, had the most perinatal difficulties.

Women who are anxious and emotionally disturbed during pregnancy have infants who are physically more active in utero. These infants also are hyperactive, irritable, and have feeding and sleep problems after birth (Montagu, 1950; Sontag, 1941; 1944). It has even been argued that stress in the first trimester of pregnancy may lead to bio-chemical changes that inhibit the normal spontaneous abortion of malformed fetuses (Stott, 1971). More frequent reports of intense emotional stress during pregnancy are made by women who subsequently bear children with Down's syndrome or nonfamilial (thus unanticipated) cleft lip and palate (Drillien & Wilkinson, 1964; Drillien, Ingram & Wilkinson, 1966).

The disturbance and apprehension of women during pregnancy may just be selected symptoms in a broader continuing pattern of maladjustment, and this pattern of distur-bance may be continued later in the handling of their infants. Women who have positive attitudes toward pregnancy have had happy childhoods and close family relationships and regard themselves as currently having satisfying marital, sexual, and social relation-ships; the reverse is true of women who have negative attitudes toward pregnancy

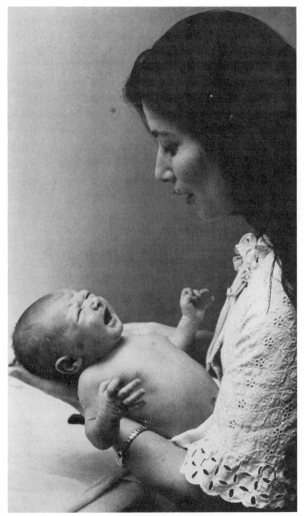

A mother soothing a crying, irritable baby. (Suzanne Szasz)

(Despres, 1937). Mothers of excessively crying or colicky infants are highly anxious and tense during pregnancy and discontinue work and sexual intercourse early during pregnancy. Also they feel less secure and accepting in their roles as women and mothers and are more pessimistic and depressed following birth (Lakin, 1957; Stewart et al., 1954). The depression is not unexpected. In one of these studies the criterion used in determining excessive crying was episodic crying over a period of seven weeks in the first month of life, occurring at least once a day and lasting a minimum of ninety minutes, not related to apparent physical discomfort. Such excessive crying could result in a lack of sleep and increased tension leading to depression in almost any mother. The timing of the occurrence of the crying suggests that it is at least partially a result of learning based on tension in early mother-child relations. Differences between groups of infants with high and low rates of crying did not appear until after two weeks of age. By six weeks the low criers stopped crying when approached by an adult, which suggests the development of trust in early social relationships; in contrast, the excessively crying infants intensified their crying at the approach of an adult which could be a result of the association of discomfort with caretaking by anxious mothers.

In summary, emotional stress in the mother may contribute to complications during pregnancy and birth and to a harmful emotional climate following birth that will lead to developmental disturbances in the child.

Maternal age and parity

The development of offspring is related both to the age of the mother and to maternal parity, or the number of children she has borne, and these two factors interact. Women who have their first child when they are over thirty-five are likely to experience more problems during pregnancy and difficulties and complications during delivery than younger women. Mothers under age thirty-five tend to have lower rates of maternal and infant mortality and infant anomalies than older mothers. The incidence of two-egg twinning, mental retardation, hydrocephaly (mental retardation resulting from the accumulation of fluid in the brain), microcephaly (mental retardation associated with a small skull and brain), Down's syndrome, low birth weight, and a variety of other congenital deviations increases in mothers over thirty-five, particularly when the mother is bearing her first child.

THE EFFECTS OF BIRTH FACTORS ON DEVELOPMENT

Although labor and birth are normal processes in human development and in the majority of cases occur with no lasting adverse influences, they sometimes do deleteriously affect the infant. In prolonged labor or in difficult births (such as a breech birth where the buttocks appear first and the head last) the chance of neurological damage through pressure or hemorrhage in the brain or through anoxia (lack of oxygen in the brain) is greatly increased. This can result in various types of physical and mental disabilities, such as mental retardation, cerebral palsy, paralysis, lack of motor coordination, sensory defects (particularly in vision and audition), and even in death.

Other important birth factors that are related to developmental deviations and infant mortality are prematurity and low birth weight. In early studies an infant weighing less than 5½ pounds was classed as premature; however, the sole use of weight as an indicator of prematurity has been criticized, and some investigators are now considering criteria such as weight relative to stature of the parent, gestational age, nutritional condition of the mother, and a variety of skeletal, neurological, and biochemical indexes of maturity (Drillien, 1964; Mitchell & Farr, 1965).

Such conditions as toxemia or bleeding and certain diseases during pregnancy, premature separation of the placenta, the development of the placenta in the lower portion of the uterus so that it blocks the uterine opening, or prolapse of the umbilical cord so that it precedes the baby through the cervix are all associated with greater intellectual and physical deficits in infants (Bishop et al., 1965; Pasamanick & Lilienfeld, 1955).

More males than females are born with anomalies. This has been attributed in part to the role of the sex chromosomes (discussed in the previous chapter) and in part to the larger size of, and hence greater pressure on, a male's head during birth. The majority of infants do not suffer serious impairment at birth, however. Less than 10 percent have any type of abnormality, and many of these disappear during the subsequent course of development.

Anoxia

All infants undergo some oxygen deprivation and retention of carbon dioxide during the birth process; however, abnormalities in the mother and conditions during labor and delivery can lead to severe anoxia, which results in brain damage, functional defects, or even death of the infant.

Infants born with no complications during birth and with an average duration of labor of six to ten hours show fewest detrimental effects. It may seem surprising that extremely short as well as excessively long periods of labor are associated with severe anoxia. Infants delivered after a period of labor of less than two hours or those delivered by caesarean section suffer less brain injury from pressure or the use of instruments during birth but are often exposed to oxygen too suddenly, have difficulty beginning to breathe, and hence may be damaged by anoxia (Schwartz, 1956).

One of the most extensive investigations of the effects of anoxia is the longitudinal study presented in Box 3-3. This study is important, not only because of the multiple measures used, but also because it demonstrates the importance of evaluating the

---

BOX 3-3 EFFECTS OF PERINATAL ANOXIA ON DEVELOPMENT: A LONGITUDINAL STUDY

The aim of this study was to determine the long-term effects of perinatal anoxia on the development of the infant. Graham and her colleagues studied 713 newborns, and on the basis of clinical signs of prenatal or intrauterine anoxia and of respiratory delay, classified them as anoxic or nonanoxic infants. An index composed of these signs of anoxia plus measures of central-nervous-system damage was used as a measure of severity of anoxia. These infants were studied as newborns (Graham et al., 1956), three year olds (Graham et al., 1962), and seven year olds (Corah et al., 1965).

In the initial testing the anoxic neonates were found to have disrupted functioning in maturity of sensorimotor functioning, irritability, muscle tension, and responsiveness to pain and visual stimuli. Infants with the most severe anoxia manifested the most impairment. At three years of age, 191 of the nonanoxic and 132 of the anoxics were selected from the original sample and assessed on a series of neurological, cognitive, perceptual-motor and personality measures, including a parent questionnaire and psychologists' ratings of the children's behavior. The most marked and consistent differences between groups at this age were found in cognitive functioning. On the Stanford-Binet Intelligence Scale, a vocabulary test, and a concept-formation test the anoxic children performed less adequately than the nonanoxics. The deficit was relatively greater in the concept-formation test than in vocabulary, which parallels findings with organically impaired adults where abstract reasoning and concept formation often are markedly impaired. The neurological examination also showed more deviations for the anoxic children than for nonanoxics. No differences were found on perceptual-motor tests; and although in a composite measure of personality characteristics the anoxic group was rated less favorably than the nonanoxic group by both parents and psychologists, the only individual trait on which they differed significantly was distractibility.

At age seven, about 85 percent of the sample were examined again by Corah and co-workers. The earlier differences between anoxics and nonanoxics in general intelligence and neurological impairment had disappeared although anoxics still performed more poorly in tests of verbal abstract abilities and were less able to copy designs. Only on these two tests out of twenty-one cognitive and perceptual measures did the anoxic children still show deficits. Parents' ratings of the children's behavior on the Vineland Social Maturity Scale indicated that the anoxic children were less well socialized and were more socially immature and lacking self-sufficiency in such things as feeding and dressing and instigating goal-directed activity than nonanoxic children. Parents of anoxic children also regarded their children as being more maladjusted. Psychological examiners rated the anoxic children as being more impulsive and distractible; and on the basis of play sessions with the children and the information on the parents' questionnaires, psychiatrists rated the anoxic children as exhibiting more signs of organicity, more emotionally explosive, lacking in social sensitivity, unable to maintain adaptive behavior, and using words and gestures excessively and inappropriately, resulting in a lack of communication.

These results suggest that behavioral manifestations of deficits due to perinatal anoxia vary with age. Some deficits are developmentally stable, and some increase and others decrease with age. Distractibility and deficits in attentional factors and abstract cognitive abilities were stable over the age range studied; general intellectual and neurological impairment decreased, and personality problems and lack of social adaptability increased. It is interesting to speculate about what may lead to the later problems in social adjustment and personality. It may be that parents respond to the early distractibility and motor and cognitive deficits with overprotection or rejection that results in the later adjustment problems.

The experimenters also conclude that although there is a modest association between the composite newborn measure of severity of anoxia and later impairment, it would be difficult to make accurate predictions about future deficits in any given infant except in extreme cases or in those with multiple complications.

Source: Adapted from Graham, F. K., Ernhart, C. B., Thurston, D., & Craft, M. Development, three years after perinatal anoxia and other potentially damaging newborn experiences. *Psychological Monographs,* 1962, **76,** no. 3, and Corah, N. L., Anthony, E. J., Painter, P., Stern, J. A., & Thurston, D. Effects of perinatal anoxia after seven years. *Psychological Monographs,* 1965, **79,** no. 3.

changing effects of perinatal anoxia over time; different deficits appear and diminish at different ages. Other studies have corroborated the diminishing effects of anoxia on intellectual development with age, and some investigators find that the deficits disappear in the preschool years (Apgar et al., 1955; Keith et al., 1953; Ucko, 1965).

Prematurity and low birth weight

Both extremely low and extremely high birth weights are associated with intellectual impairment. Examination of the findings on low-birth-weight children show that significant impairment in IQ occurs only among children with extremely low birth weights, that is, under 4 pounds (Caputo & Mandel, 1970). More low-birth-weight children than normal-weight children are found among both institutionalized and noninstitutionalized mental retardates and high school dropouts. In a review of eighteen studies of prematurity, only one investigator reported no impairment of intelligence in prematurely born infants (Weiner, 1962); and in contrast with anoxia, deficits associated with very low birth weights tend to be more enduring. Retardation in other cognitive skills such as reading, language, arithmetic, and spelling are also associated with prematurity and low birth weight. Deviant behavior of a disorganized, hyperactive type and disorders such as autism and accident-proneness are more frequently found in prematures than in maturely born infants.

Since deviations in neurological functioning and motor and physical development are also characteristic of prematures and infants with extremely low birth weights, particularly in the early months of life, many of these children have often been considered to be suffering from *minimal brain disfunction* (Knoblock & Pasamanick, 1966). Investigators who use this label are saying that the behavior exhibited by these children is similar to those of children with known organic brain damage and therefore they may be suffering from organic abnormalities which our neurological tests cannot detect. It is believed that in the syndrome of minimal brain damage many of the early neurological abnormalities often show gradual improvement over time. However, although neurological indicators of abnormality may disappear, a suggestion of an undetectable disfunction remains in the lack of integrative and attentional abilities seen in the behavior and learning disorders of these children. Many psychologists have objected to the "I can't see it and I can't measure it, but it must be there" implications in the use of the concept of minimal brain dysfunction.

Another provocative consideration in the development of extremely low birth weight and premature infants is that most of these children spend their early weeks of life in the monotonous, unstimulating environment of an incubator or isolette where there is minimal sensory, tactual, and emotional stimulation. Sensory deprivation has been demonstrated to have disruptive effects on the behavior of adults, and it seems probable that these effects may be even more severe on the rapidly developing neonate.

The findings of several recent studies suggest that additional sensory stimulation can counteract some of the effects of low birth weight, and that the early sensory deprivation experienced by such children in the isolettes may contribute to some of their deficits. It has been found that rocking the isolettes (Freedman, 1969) or human stimulation such as handling, cuddling, talking and rocking, and singing (Powell, 1974; Scarr-Salapatek & William, 1973; Siqueland, 1970; Solkoff et al., 1969) have positive effects on the intellectual and social development of premature infants.

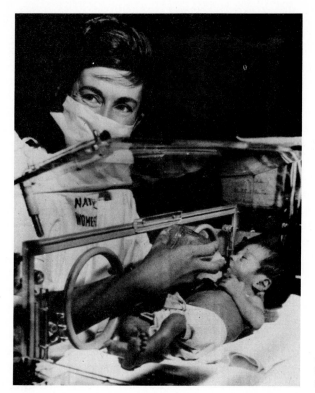

A premature infant in the sterile, sensory-depriving environment of an isolette. (Omikron)

It has been pointed out that behavior associated with prematurity may also be the outcome of a number of related factors, such as delivery complications, low birth weight, the early period of isolation in an incubator, neonatal anomalies other than prematurity, and the treatment by parents in response to the infants' apparent frailty and small size (Braine et al., 1966; Parmalee & Haber, 1973).

Two continuums: reproductive casualty and caretaking casualty

It has been proposed that there is a *continuum of reproductive casualty* (Pasamanick & Knoblock, 1966); that is, there are variations in the degree of reproductive complications which result in abnormalities in the child, ranging from relatively minor perceptual, attentional, intellectual, motor, and behavioral disabilities to extremely gross anomalies. However, more recently it has been suggested that in order to make predictions about the developmental course of such disorders, the transactions between the continuum of reproductive casualty and the *continuum of caretaking casualty* must be considered (Sameroff & Chandler, in press). The continuum of caretaking casualty ranges from an environmental and family situation in which there are few adverse factors to one in which there are multiple, severe deleterious factors.

Although 10 percent of all children are born with some kind of handicap or anomaly (Niswander & Gordon, 1972), many of these defects decrease or disappear with age. How do these children overcome their deficits? What factors contribute to the retention and increase of these handicaps or the gradual overcoming of these liabilities?

> Self-righting influences are powerful forces toward normal human development, so that protracted developmental disorders are typically found only in the presence of equally protracted, distorting influences. . . .Even if one continues to believe that a continuum of reproductive casualty exists, its importance pales in comparison to the massive influences of socio-economic factors on both prenatal and postnatal development [Sameroff & Chandler, in press].

In order to predict later development from neonatal condition the transactions between multiple measures of infant state and the environmental conditions in which the child will develop are necessary. This is vividly demonstrated in an outstanding longitudinal study of the effects of birth complications on the development of the entire population of 670 children born on the island of Kauai in the Hawaiian Islands in 1955 (Werner et al., 1971). At the time of birth 3 percent of the neonates showed severe complications, 13 percent showed moderate complications, 31 percent showed mild complications, and 56 percent showed no complications. Since all the mothers participated in a prepaid health plan and had good prenatal care, correlation between birth difficulties and socioeconomic status was not obtained.

When the children were reexamined at twenty months of age, 12 percent were rated as deficient in social development, 16 percent were deficient in intellectual functioning, and 14 percent were deficient in health. The more severe the complications of birth and the poorer the neonatal performance of the infants had been, the less adequate was the developmental level of children in these areas. Of more interest was the relationship between perinatal difficulties and environmental factors, notably those associated with socioeconomic status. Infants living in unstable, lower socioeconomic family situations with mothers of low intelligence showed a 19- to 37-point difference in average IQ scores between the group with severe perinatal complications and the groups with mild or no complications. In contrast, infants in stable, high socioeconomic family environments with mothers of high intelligence showed only a 5- to 7-point difference between the group with severe and the group with no perinatal complications.

By age ten the effects of environmental variables had almost obliterated those of perinatal damage. No relationship was found between perinatal measures and a child's IQ at this age; instead the correlation between a child's intellectual performance and his parents' IQs and socioeconomic status increased with age, with lower-class children showing marked deficits on cognitive measures. The main effects of deviations caused by reproductive casualty occurred early in a child's development, and after that development was increasingly influenced by environment, or the continuum of caretaking casualty. The investigators note that at the conclusion of their study "ten times more children had problems related to the effects of poor early environment than to the effects of perinatal stress [Werner et al., 1971]."

SUMMARY

The infant in utero goes through a sequence of three developmental stages: the periods of the ovum, the embryo, and the fetus. The infant is most vulnerable to the effects of teratogenes (deviation- or malformation-producing agents) in the period of the embryo. A variety of factors such as maternal diseases and disorders, drugs, diet, radiation, blood incompatibilities, emotional state, age, and parity can all result in developmental deviations in the child.

The effects of teratogenes are influenced by such things as the stage of development of the fetus, the organ systems that are developing at the time of exposure, and the genotypes of mother and child. An agent which may damage the infant may have no effects on the mother. This is dramatically exemplified in the results of the intake of thalidomide during pregnancy.

Anoxia and extremely low birth weight have also been found to be associated with a variety of physical, neurological, cognitive, and emotional deficits. The effects of low birth weight are more long lasting than those of anoxia, which tend to disappear with age.

It has been proposed that there are two interacting continuums which effect the appearance and maintenance of abnormalities in the child: the continuum of reproductive casualty and the continuum of caretaking casualty. Although in extreme instances of reproductive casualty (such as massive brain damage) the effects of environment cannot overcome the effects of perinatal complications, environmental conditions, in general, play a major role in sustaining or eliminating early deficits.

REFERENCES

Apgar, V., Girdany, B. R., McIntosh, R., & Taylor, H. C. Neonatal anoxia—a study of the relation of oxygenation at birth to intellectual development. *Pediatrics*, 1955, **15,** 653-662.

Bayley, N. Bayley infant scales of motor and mental development. University of California and National Institutes of Health. Unpublished Research Form, 1965. (a)

Bayley, N. Comparisons of mental and motor test scores for ages 1-15 months by sex, birth order, race, geographic location and education of parents. *Child Development*, 1965, **36,** 379-411. (b)

Beck, F., & Lloyd, J. B. Embryological principles of teratogenesis. In J. M. Robson, F. M. Sullivan, & R. L. Smith (Eds.), *Symposium of embryopathic activity of drugs*. Boston: Little, Brown, 1965. Pp. 1-17.

Bernard, H. W. *Human development in western culture*. Boston: Allyn and Bacon, 1962.

Birch, H. G., & Gussow, J. D. *Disadvantaged children. Health, nutrition and school failure*. New York: Grune & Stratton, 1970.

Bishop, E. H., Israel, S. L., & Briscoe, C. C. Obstetric influences on premature infant's first year of development: a report from the collaborative study of cerebral palsy. *Obstetrics and Gynecology*, 1965, **26,** 628-635.

Braine, M. D. S., Heimer, C. B., Wortis, H., & Freedman, A. M. Factors associated with impairment of the early development of prematures. *Monographs of the Society for Research in Child Development*, 1966, **31** (106), 1-92.

Brazelton, T. B. Effects of maternal medication on the neonate and his behavior. *Journal of Pediatrics*, 1961, **58,** 513-518.

Brazelton, T. B. Effects of prenatal drugs on the behavior of the neonate. *American Journal of Psychiatry*, 1970, **126,** 1261-1266.

Brown, R. E. Organ weight in malnutrition with special reference to brain weight. *Developmental Medicine and Child Neurology*, 1966, **8,** 512-522.

Burke, B. S., Beal, V. A., Kirkwood, S. B., & Stuart, H. C. The influence of nutrition during pregnancy upon the conditions of the infant at birth. *Journal of Nutrition*, 1943, **26,** 569-583.

Burnhan, S. The heroin babies are going cold turkey. *New York Times Magazine*, Jan. 9, 1972.

Caputo, D. V., & Mandell, W. Consequences of low birth weight. *Developmental Psychology*, 1970, **3,** 363-383.

Clegg, D. J. Teratology. *Annual Review of Pharmacology*, 1971, **11,** 409-423.

Conway, E., & Brackbill, Y. Delivery medication and infant outcome: an empirical study. *Monographs of the Society for Research in Child Development*, 1970, **35** (137), 24-34.

Corah, N. L., Anthony, E. J., Painter, P., Stern,

J. A., & Thurston, D. Effects of perinatal anoxia after seven years. *Psychological Monographs*, 1965, **79,** 3.

Corner, G. W. Congenital malformations: the problem and the task. In *Congenital malformations: papers and discussions presented at the First International Conference on Congenital Malformations*. Philadelphia: Lippincott, 1961. Pp. 7-17.

Davison, A. N., & Dobbling, J. Myelination as a vulnerable period in brain development. *British Medical Bulletin*, 1966, **22,** 40-44.

Decarie, T. C. A study of the mental and emotional development of the thalidomide child. In B. M. Foss (Ed.), *Determinants of infant behavior.* Vol. 4. London: 1969.

Despres, M. A. Favorable and unfavorable attitudes toward pregnancy in primiparas. *Journal of Genetic Psychology*, 1937, **51,** 241-254.

Drillien, C. M. *The growth and development of the prematurely born infant.* Baltimore: Williams & Wilkins, 1964.

Drillien, C. M., Ingram, T. T. S., & Wilkinson, F. M. *The causes and natural history of cleft lip and palate.* Edinburgh: Churchill Livingstone, 1966.

Drillien, C. M., & Wilkinson, E. M. Emotional stress and mongoloid birth. *Developmental Medicine and Child Neurology*, 1964, **6,** 140-143.

Ebbs, H. H., Brown, A., Tisdall, F. F., Moyle, W. J., & Bell, M. The influence of improven prenatal nutrition upon the infant. *Canadian Medical Association Journal*, 1942, **46,** 6-8.

Ebbs, H. H., Tisdal, F. F., & Scott, W. A. The influence of prenatal diet on mother and child. *Millbank Memorial Fund Quarterly*, 1942, **20,** 35-36.

Eriksson, M., Catz, C. S., & Yaffe, S. J. Drugs and pregnancy. In H. Osofsky (Ed.), *Clinical obstetrics and gynecology: high risk pregnancy with emphases upon maternal and fetal well being.* Vol. 16. New York: Harper & Row, 1973. Pp. 192-224.

Ferreira, A. *Prenatal environment.* Springfield, Ill.: Charles C Thomas, 1969.

Frazier, T. M., Davis, G. H., Goldstein, H., & Goldberg, I. D. Cigarette smoking and prematurity: a prospective study. *American Journal of Obstetrics and Gynecology*, 1961, **81,** 988-996.

Freedman, D. G. Remarks. In J. A. Ambrose (Ed.), *Stimulation in early infancy.* New York: Academic, 1969.

Gellis, S. S., & Hsai, D. Y. The infant of the diabetic mother. *American Journal of Diseases of Children*, 1959, **97,** 1.

Graham, F. K. Behavior differences between normal and traumatized newborns. I. The test procedures. *Psychological Monographs*, 1956, 70, No. 20.

Graham, F. K., Ernhart, C. B., Thurston, D., & Craft, M. Development three years after perinatal anoxia and other potentially damaging newborn experiences. *Psychological Monographs*, 1962, **76** (3, Whole No. 522).

Graham, F. K., Matarazzo, R. G., & Caldwell, B. M. Behavioral differences between normal and traumatized newborns. II. Standardization, reliability and validity. *Psychological Monographs*, 1956, **70** (21, Whole No. 428).

Hughes, J. G., Ehemann, B., & Brown, U. A. Electroencephalography of the newborn. *American Journal of Diseases of Children*, 1948, **76,** 626-633.

Joffe, J. M. *Prenatal determinants of behavior.* Oxford: Pergamon, 1969.

Karnofsky, D. A. Drugs as teratogenes in animals and man. *Annual Review of Pharmacology*, 1965, **5,** 477-482.

Keith, H. M., Norval, M. A., & Hunt, A. B. Neurologic lesions in relation to the sequelae of birth injury. *Neurology*, 1953, **3,** 139-147.

Knoblock, H., & Pasamanick, B. Prospective studies on the epidemiology of reproductive casuality: methods, findings and some implications. *Merrill-Palmer Quarterly of Behavior and Development*, 1966, **12,** 27-43.

Kron, R. E., Stein, M., & Goddard, K. E. Newborn sucking behavior affected by obstetric sedation. *Pediatrics*, 1966, **37,** 1012-1016.

Lakin, M. Personality factors in mothers of excessively crying (colicky) infants. *Monographs of the Society for Research in Child Development*, 1957, **22,** (64).

McCance, R. A., Widdowson, E. M., & Verdon Roe, C. M. A study of English diets by the individual method. III. Pregnant women at different economic levels. *Journal of Hygiene*, 1938, **38,** 596.

McDonald, R. L. The role of emotional factors in obstetric complications: a review. *Psychosomatic Medicine*, 1968, **30,** 222-237.

Mitchell, R. G., and Farr, V. The meaning of maturity and the assessment of maturity at birth. In M. Dawkins and W. G. MacGregor (Eds.), *Gestational age, size and maturity.* London: Spastics Society Medical Education and Information Unit, 1965. Pp. 83-99.

Montagu, M. F. A. Constitutional and prenatal factors in infant and child health. In M. J. E. Senn (Ed.), *Symposium on the healthy personality.* New York: Josiah Macy, Jr., Foundation, 1950. Pp. 148-75.

Moya, F., & Thorndike, V. Passage of drugs across the placenta. *American Journal of*

Obstetrics and Gynecology, 1962, **84,** 1778-98.

Naeye, R. L., Diener, M. M., & Dellinger, W. S. Urban poverty: effects of prenatal nutrition. *Science*, 1969, **166,** 1206.

National Center for Health Statistics: Infant Fetal and Maternal Public Health Service Publication No. 1000, Series 20, No. 3. Washington, 1966.

Niswander, K. R., & Gordon, M. (Eds.), *The collaborative perinatal study of the National Institute of Neurological Diseases and Stroke: the women and their pregnancies.* Philadelphia: Saunders, 1972.

O'Neill, M. Preliminary evaluation of the intellectual development of children with congenital limb malformations associated with thalidomide. These de licence inedite, Universite de Montreal, 1965.

Parekh, V. C., Pherwani, A., Udani, P. M., & Mukherjie, S. Brain weight and head circumference in fetus, infant and children of different nutritional and socio-economic groups. *Indian Pediatrics*, 1970, **7,** 347-358.

Parke, R., O'Leary, S. E., & West, S. Mother-father-newborn interaction: effect of maternal medication, labor and sex of infant. *Proceedings of the American Psychological Association*, 1972, **7,** 85-86.

Parmalee, A. H., & Haber, A. Who is the "risk infant?" In H. J. Osofsky (Ed.), *Clinical obstetrics and gynecology: high risk pregnancy with emphases upon maternal and fetal well being.* Vol. 16. New York: Harper & Row, 1973. Pp. 376-387.

Pasamanick, B., & Knoblock, H. Retrospective studies on the epidemiology of reproductive casualty: old and new. *Merrill-Palmer Quarterly of Behavior and Development*, 1966, **12,** 7-26.

Pasamanick, B., & Lilienfeld, A. Association of maternal and fetal factors with the development of mental deficiency. I. Abnormalities in the prenatal and perinatal periods. *Journal of the American Medical Association*, 1955, **159,** 155-160.

Rhodes, A. J. Virus infections and congenital malformations. *Papers and discussions presented at the First International Conference on Congenital Malformations.* Philadelphia: Lippincott, 1961. Pp. 106-116.

Richards, M. P., & Bernal, J. F. Social interactions in the first days of life. In H. R. Schaffer (Ed.), *The origins of human relations.* New York: Academic, 1971. Pp. 3-13.

Sameroff, A. J., & Chandler, M. J. Reproductive risk and the continuum of caretaking casualty. In F. Horowitz (Ed.), *Review of child development research.* Vol. 4. Chi-

cago: The University of Chicago Press, in press.

Sameroff, A. J., & Zax, M. Perinatal characteristics of the offspring of schizophrenic women. *Journal of Nervous and Mental Diseases*, 1973, in press.

Schwartz, P. Birth injuries of the newborn. *Pediatric Archives*, 1956, **73,** 429-450.

Simpson, W. J. A preliminary report on cigarette smoking and the incidence of prematurity. *American Journal of Obstetrics and Gynecology*, 1957, **73,** 808-815.

Siqueland, R. R. Biological and experimental determinants of exploration in infancy. Paper presented at the First National Biological Conference, 1970.

Shnider, S. M., & Moya, F. Effects of meperidine on the newborn infant. *American Journal of Obstetrics and Gynecology*, 1964, **89,** 1009-1015.

Solkoff, N., Yaffe, S., Weintraub, D., & Blase, B. Effects of handling on the subsequent developments of premature infants. *Developmental Psychology*, 1969, **1,** 765-768.

Sontag, L. W. The significance of fetal environmental differences. *American Journal of Obstetrics and Gynecology*, 1941, **42,** 996-1003.

Sontag, L. W. War and fetal maternal relationship. *Marriage and Family Living*, 1944, **6,** 1-5.

Sontag, L. W., & Wallace, R. F. The effect of cigarette smoking during pregnancy upon the fetal heart rate. *American Journal of Obstetrics and Gynecology*, 1935, **29,** 3-8.

Spock, B., & Lerrigo, M. *Caring for Your Disabled Child,* New York: Macmillan, 1965.

Stechler, G. A longitudinal follow-up of neonatalapned. *Child Development*, 1964, **35,** 333-348. (a)

Stechler, G. New born attention as affected by medication during labor. *Science*, 1964, **144,** 315-317. (b)

Stewart, A. H., Weiland, I. H., Leider, A. R., Mangham, C. A., Holmes, T. H., & Ripley, H. S. Excessive infant crying (colic) in relation to parent behavior. *American Journal of Psychiatry*, 1954, **110,** 687-694.

Stott, D. H. The child's hazards in utero. In J. G. Howells (Ed.), *Modern perspectives in international child psychiatry.* New York: Brunner Mazel, 1971.

Thompson, W. R., & Olian, S. Some effects on offspring behavior of maternal adrenalin injection during pregnancy in three inbred mouse strains. *Psychological Reports*, 1961, **8,** 87-90.

Tompkins, W. T. The clinical significance of nutritional deficiencies in pregnancy. *Bulletin of the New York Academy of Medicine,* 1948, **24,** 376-88.

Tompkins, W. T., & Wiehl, D. G. Nutritional deficiencies as a casual factor in toxemia and premature labor. *American Journal of Obstetrics and Gynecology,* 1951, **62,** 898-919.

Tuchmann-Duplessis, H. Design and interpretation of teratogenic tests. In J. N. Robson, J. M. Sullivan, & R. L. Smith (Eds.), *Symposium of embryopathic activity of drugs.* Boston: Little, Brown, 1965. Pp. 56-87.

Ucko, L. E. A comparative study of asphyxiated and nonasphyxiated boys from birth to five years. *Developmental Medicine and Child Neurology,* 1965, **7,** 643-657.

Werner, E., Bierman, J. M., & French, F. F. *The children of Kauai.* Honolulu: University of Hawaii, 1971.

White House Conference on Children. *Profiles of children.* Washington: Government Printing Office, 1970.

Whitridge, J. & Davens, E. Are public health maternity programs effective and necessary? *American Journal of Public Health,* 1952, **42,** 508-515.

Wiener, G. Psychologic correlates of premature birth: a review. *Journal of Nervous and Mental Diseases,* 1962, **134,** 129-144.

Wilson, J. G. General principles in experimental teratology in congenital malformations. *Papers and Discussions Presented at the First International Conference on Congenital Malformations.* Philadelphia: Lippincott, 1961. Pp. 187-194.

Winick, M. Nutrition and cell growth. *Nutrition Reviews,* 1969, **26,** 195-197.

Winick, M. Nutrition and nerve cell growth. *Federation Proceedings,* 1970, **29,** 1510-1515.

Wortis, H. Social class and premature birth. *Social Casework,* 1963, **45,** 541-543.

4

INFANCY AND GROWTH

In the previous chapters genetic and prenatal determinants of behavior were presented. In this chapter, we shall take a closer look at the outcome, the newborn child. How alert is the newborn and how do his states of alertness change? What is in the newborn's repertoire of reflexes? What are the sensory and perceptual capacities of the neonate and how do these capacities improve as the infant develops? It has been stated that the newborn's world is a "blooming, buzzing confusion." However, research findings indicate that the very young infant has a wide range of available reflexes and capacities, and even his primitive abilities permit him to respond selectively and organize the stimulation he is receiving. Recent methodological advances, particularly those in psychophysiology, have permitted developmental psychologists to gain a clearer understanding of the capabilities and response systems of the infant.

What are the motor achievements of the developing infant? When does he reach, crawl, and walk? Finally, what is the pattern of growth? Have growth patterns changed over past generations? Are we growing taller and, if so, why? These are the questions we shall explore in this chapter.

THE NEWBORN CHILD

Unlike the beautiful creatures in the advertisements for diapers, cribs, and safety pins, the newborn, or neonate, is generally a homely organism. As one writer put it, "even a fond mother may experience a sense of shock at the first sight of the tiny wizened, red creature that is her offspring [Watson, 1962, p. 140]." At birth the average child weighs approximately 7½ pounds and is about 20 inches long; from birth on boys are slightly larger and heavier than girls. Part of the neonate's unusual appearance is derived from his odd bodily proportions, odd at least in comparison with adults (see Figure 4-1). For example, he seems to be "all head," and, in fact, the head represents ¼ of his body length (the head is only 1/20 of the full-grown adult).

What is this odd-looking creature capable of doing? An understanding of how well equipped, behaviorally speaking, the new arrival is on entering the world is crucial for understanding the relative importance of genetic and experiential variables. Is he the passive, nonreacting organism that scientists for many years assumed he was? Hardly! In fact, as we shall see, he is a highly competent organism with a surprisingly well-developed set of reflexes and sensory responses, even at birth. Nor are his responses random and disorganized; rather he shows a capacity to respond in an organized, meaningful way from a much earlier time than was originally assumed. John B. Watson exaggerated: The newborn baby's world is something more than a "blooming, buzzing confusion."

INFANT STATES AND SOOTHABILITY

One of the fascinating and at times troublesome aspects of the newborn infant is his *state*, which refers to a continuum of consciousness or alertness ranging from vigorous activity to regular sleep. The importance of the concept of state in understanding the newborn is that the impact of environmental stimulation will vary considerably depending on the baby's state. The presence, direction, and amount of the response will depend on the baby's state at the onset of stimulation. Even reflexes may not appear to be present in some states. Many investigators have been frustrated when after attaching a wide array of electrodes, wires, and recording equipment to an infant subject, the infant has burped and happily drifted off to sleep before the experimental procedures could be

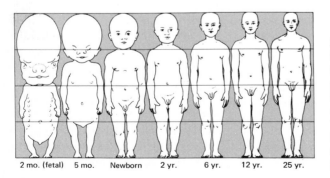

2 mo. (fetal)   5 mo.   Newborn   2 yr.   6 yr.   12 yr.   25 yr.

FIGURE 4-1 Changes in body form and proportion during prenatal and postnatal growth. (From C. M. Jackson (ed.), *Human Anatomy*, 9th ed. Copyright 1933 by Blakiston Division, McGraw-Hill Book Company, and published with permission.)

executed. In addition, at times some infants seem to sleep with their eyes open; although visually they appear to be awake, recordings of their physiological functioning suggest that they are really in a sleeplike state. In such cases failure to attend or respond on the part of the infant may be due to his state rather than his capacities.

In light of the central role of state in determining infant responsiveness, many researchers view state, not only as an obstacle to be controlled for, but also as a phenomenon to be understood in its own right. It is clear that before the infant's reflex repertoire is examined and his sensory and perceptual capacities are probed, a look at the many states of the infant is necessary.

Classification of infant states

How can infant states be classified? Wolff (1966) has offered the following criteria for infant states:

Regular sleep: His eyes are closed and he is completely still; respirations are slow and regular; his face is relaxed—no grimace—and his eyelids are still.

Irregular sleep: His eyes are closed; engages in variable gentle limb movements, writhing and stirring; grimaces and other facial expressions are frequent; respirations are irregular and faster than in regular sleep; interspersed and recurrent rapid eye movements.

Drowsiness: He is relatively inactive; his eyes open and close intermittently; respirations are regular, though faster than in regular sleep; when eyes are open, they have a dull or glazed quality.

Alert inactivity: His eyes are open and have a bright and shining quality; he can pursue moving objects and make conjugate eye movements in the horizontal and vertical plane. He is relatively inactive; his face is relaxed and he does not grimace.

Waking activity: He frequently engages in diffuse motor activity involving his whole body. His eyes are open, but not alert, and his respirations are grossly irregular.

Crying: He has crying vocalizations associated with vigorous diffuse motor activity.

Developmental changes in states

To illustrate the state changes that occur as the infant develops, two extreme states are examined—sleep and crying.

Sleep   The proportion of time that an infant spends in these various states not only differs for individual infants, but also varies for each infant as he develops. As he becomes older, a larger proportion of the infant's time is spent in awake states, which provide increased opportunities to interact with the environment; in turn, the proportion of time spent sleeping is reduced. The newborn sleeps about 30 percent of the time, and, of course, not continuously; rather, sleep time is distributed across the day in a series of short and long naps. By four weeks of age, fewer but longer periods of sleep are typical, and by the end of the first year, the infant sleeps through the night.

However, not only the amount and temporal pattern of sleep change with age, but the kind of sleep changes as well. By recording brain activity of infants and adults at different ages, investigators have distinguished different phases of sleep. The most important distinction is between REM (rapid-eye-movement) and non-REM sleep. Often termed *dream sleep*, REM sleep is a period characterized by rapid eye movements as well as fluctuations in heart rate and blood pressure. In adults, dreaming occurs in this period, and one might expect increased motor activity: but the body is wisely organized so that there is no physical acting-out of dreams during REM sleep. Apparently dreaming is not simply a pleasant nighttime entertainment. We need a certain amount of REM sleep, and if we are deprived, we spend more of our later sleep in REM activity (Dement, 1960). There is some evidence that if people are wakened as soon as REM sleep begins, obtaining very little REM sleep, their subsequent waking behavior is irritable and disorganized.

Of particular interest is the change that takes place in the percentage of REM and non-REM sleep as the infant develops. In the newborn, 50 percent of sleep is REM sleep, and as the infant develops, the percentage drops dramatically (see Figure 4-2). As yet there is no way of determining if infants dream, and if this high amount of REM sleep is associated with dream activity. The organization and sequence of different phases of sleep also changes from infancy to adulthood. For example, normal adults usually have an hour of non-REM sleep before drifting into REM sleep. In contrast, newborns enter REM sleep from almost any waking or sleeping state; only 25 percent of newborn REM sleep is preceded by non-REM sleep, and usually the babies go into REM sleep from a drowsy, crying, or waking state (Korner, 1968, 1972).

An *autostimulation* theory has been proposed to account for the high level of REM sleep in newborns: The REM mechanism provides stimulation to higher brain centers, and the high degree of REM activity in infancy may therefore stimulate the development of the central nervous system of the young infant (Roffwarg et al., 1966). As the infant develops and becomes increasingly alert and capable of processing external stimula-

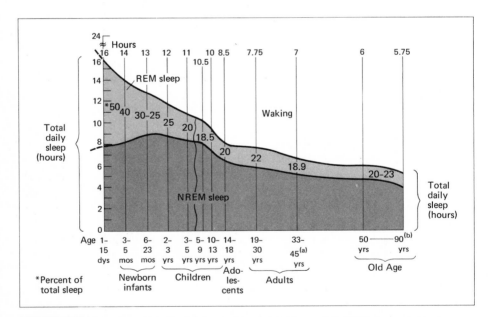

FIGURE 4-2 Age changes in the total amounts of daily sleep, daily REM sleep, and in percentage of REM sleep. (From Roffwarg, Muzio, and Dement, 1966; revised since publication in *Science* by Dr. Roffwarg. By permission of the senior author.)

tion, this type of built-in stimulation becomes less necessary. Although it is speculative, this theory makes good sense.

Crying   At the other extreme of the continuum of infant states is crying, which, like sleep, is not a simple homogeneous state. Crying is considered important as one of the infant's means of communicating his needs to his caretakers. In light of this communicative role, it is not surprising that different types of crying patterns can be distinguished. Three distinct patterns of crying have been identified:

1. A basic pattern, linked amongst other factors to hunger which starts arhythmically and at low intensity, but gradually becomes louder and more rhythmical.
2. The "mad" or angry cry, characterized by the same temporal sequence as the basic pattern (namely cry-rest-inspiration-rest) but distinguished from it by differences in the length of the various phase components.
3. The pain cry, which is sudden in onset, is loud from the start and is made up of a long cry, followed by a long silence (during which there is breath holding) and then by a series of short gasping inhalation. [Schaffer, 1971, p. 61]

Most mothers maintain that they are able to easily distinguish among these different types of crying, and research has demonstrated that this is true. For example, when mothers who were alone in a room heard a tape recording of a baby's pain cry from an adjacent room, they reacted with distress; but when they heard a tape in which the time sequences of the crying were changed by shortening the long silent pause, the mothers showed less concern (Wolff, 1969). The unique temporal characteristics of each cry pattern therefore have an important social signaling function.

Experience with infants helps in recognition of different types of crying patterns. In an extensive Swedish study, midwives, children's nurses, and mothers were superior to women who had less experience with children in identifying different crying patterns (Wasz-Hockert et al., 1968). However, even the least experienced women were able to identify the various crying patterns well above a level of accuracy that can be attributed to chance. Since comparative data on men are not available, we do not know whether women are superior to men in their sensitivity to crying because of their usual greater caretaking responsibility.

As every parent knows, crying is a very effective technique for eliciting adult attention. Moss and Robson (1968), in fact, found that 77 percent of the 2,461 crying episodes they studied were followed by maternal intervention but only 6 percent were preceded by contact with the mother. At first, crying is initiated by internal organic stimuli, but as a result of the consistent experience of having mother appear, crying becomes a deliberate means for the infant to gain contact with his caretakers. However, as the infant develops other means of signaling his caretakers, the reliance on crying subsides. In fact, the changes in state that occur as the child develops can be viewed as part of a changing set of means of successfully interacting with the environment. Just as REM sleep decreases as the child's external input increases, so does the child's reliance on crying as a social signaling system decrease as his motor and language capacities increase.

Soothing Techniques

Although general developmental changes from sleep to wakefulness and from agitation and crying to quieter states appear to follow a regular and preprogrammed course, there has been considerable interest in identifying specific techniques that are effective in shifting the infant's state. Of particular interest are soothing techniques, which can reduce agitation and distress in the baby.

Soothing techniques are obviously of practical importance for salvaging the nerves of the harried new mother. In addition, the state of the infant determines how much he will respond to his external environment, and therefore soothing techniques are important because they tend to shift the baby into a state that is more optimal for responding to the external world. The interesting sights and sounds in the outside environment are lost on the agitated crying baby; more optimal for the baby's development is a state of *alert inactivity*. As Korner (1972) recently noted, "the visual exploratory behavior which often attends this state may be one of the main avenues at the neonate's disposal for getting acquainted with his environment and for early learning [Korner, 1972, p. 88]." Infants who spontaneously spend a great deal of time in alert inactivity also tend to be most capable of fixating and following a visual stimulus [Korner, 1970]. In short, the state of alert inactivity is optimal for early learning, and so there has been interest in determining whether certain types of stimulation that a mother or caretaker might provide an infant are effective in shifting the baby into this state.

The caretaker as soother   Korner and Thoman (1970) assessed the effectiveness of six different soothing techniques, or kinds of stimulation, in shifting newborn infants from either a crying or sleeping state into a state of alert inactivity.

1. The infant was lifted from the examining table and put to the shoulder, head supported.
2. The infant was lifted horizontally and cradled in arms in the nursing position.
3. Bending over the supine infant, the assistant held the infant close, simulating another nursing position. Care was taken not to move the infant in any way.
4. The infant who had previously been placed in an infant seat was raised to the upright position.
5. The infant in the infant seat was moved horizontally, as if in a perambulator.
6. The infant was talked to in a high pitched voice, simulating "mother talk." The voice was used as a marker to avoid bias in picking a time during which to observe alerting in the absence of any intervention. This was decided after a preliminary study showed that the voice elicited no more attention than occurred spontaneously without any intervention. [Korner and Thoman, 1970]

Figure 4-3 indicates the results; by far the most effective technique for eliciting visual alertness was putting the infant to the shoulder; this position evoked bright-eyed scanning in 77.5 percent of the infants. Korner (1972) noted several implications of her findings:

> Mothers, in soothing their crying infants by picking them up will inadvertently provide them with a great many visual experiences. . . . If the earliest forms of learning occur mostly through visual exploration, vestibular stimulation which evokes a great deal of visual alertness in the neonate may be the more important form of stimulation during this stage of

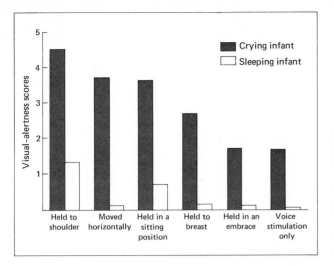

FIGURE 4-3 Effects of stimulation on visual alerting. (From A. Korner and E. Thoman, Visual alertness in neonates as evoked by maternal care. *Journal of Experimental Child Psychology*, 1970, **10,** 68-78. By permission of the senior author and publisher.)

development than . . . body contact. . . . It makes good sense for the vestibular system to be an excellent mediator for early stimulation. It appears that this system is one of the earliest to develop and is fully mature at birth [Korner, 1972, p. 91].

Figure 4-3 also clearly illustrates that the same type of stimulation will have either a strong or minimal effect, depending on the infant's state at the time of intervention. For example, the same stimulation had a much greater impact on the infant who was crying than on the sleeping infant.

Of course, a variety of other techniques are effective in soothing infants, including rocking (Pederson & Ter Vrugt, 1973) and swaddling (Lipton, Steinscheider, & Richmond, 1965). Neither of these appear to be dependent on learning or experience, but are effective shortly after birth. Centuries of mothers can testify on behalf of the effectiveness of these techniques.

The infant as a self-soother   To some extent, an infant is a self-sufficient pacifier and can shift from one state to another independently of outside stimulation. One way that an infant can often reduce his own distress is by *sucking*, a highly organized response pattern that is ready to operate at birth.

Sucking as the principal means of feeding is important for infant survival, and for many years it was assumed that the pacifying effects of sucking were due to the association of sucking and feeding. However, sucking on a pacifier—without any accompanying food—is an effective means of reducing distress. In fact, sucking on a pacifier functions as a stress reducer immediately after birth—even before the first postnatal feeding (Kessen et al., 1965). In short, sucking tends to reduce activity and movement in the newborn and may be viewed as a congenital stress reducer.

Soothability and individual differences   There are wide and reliable individual differences in babies, not only in their rhythms, states, and activity levels, but also in their ability to be soothed (Birns et al., 1966). There are sex differences: Moss (1967) found that boys are more difficult to pacify than girls. And there are race differences: Freedman and Freedman (1969), in assessing Chinese-American and European-American newborns, found marked differences in temperament and soothability. The European-American babies shifted between states of contentment and disturbance more frequently than the Chinese-American babies, and the Chinese-American babies tended to calm themselves more readily when upset (a self-quieting ability) and were more easily consoled by adult caretakers.

THE NEWBORN'S REPERTOIRE OF REFLEXES

It is against this temperamental backdrop that the neurological assessment of newborn reflexes and the examination of the sensory and perceptual capacities must be executed. Next we take a brief look at the infant's initial equipment—his reflexes; then we discuss the sensory and perceptual capacities of the infant. In attempting to unravel the mysteries of infancy, it is becoming increasingly obvious how adaptively organized the young human organism really is. The confusion that psychologists traditionally have attributed to the newborn might better be attributed to the psychologists themselves. However, now that we are letting the organism speak for himself, even psychologists are becoming less confused.

First consider the newborn's repertoire of *reflexes*, which are involuntary responses to external stimuli. These may be elicited at birth as a test for the soundness of the infant's central nervous system. Moreover, a neurological examination of the newborn has predictive value; signs of abnormality which may be evident in the first days or weeks may disappear during a "silent period" and not reappear as abnormal functions until months or even years later (Precht & Bientema, 1964). In Table 4-1, some of the reflexes of the newborn are described. Note that some reflexes are permanent while others may disappear after a few months.

SENSORY AND PERCEPTUAL CAPACITIES OF THE INFANT

Problems of investigation

Neonates and young infants are not easy organisms to understand; in fact, they guard the secrets about their abilities extremely well. Part of the difficulty is that many of the methods used to investigate the sensory and perceptual capacities of older children and adults cannot be used with infants. Infants' motor repertoires are limited: They cannot reach or point with any degree of accuracy, nor can they crawl. In addition, they cannot be asked whether one tone is louder than another or whether they prefer red to green. So many well-refined adult techniques of investigation which depend on motor and verbal responses are useless in studying infants. There are other problems as well. How can you be sure that the standards defined by the adults (for example, as to what constitutes a sweet, pleasant taste) apply to infants? Perhaps subjective judgments change with age.

Techniques of investigation have been developed to capitalize on the responses that the infant can make. The autonomic nervous system, which controls such things as

Table 4-1 NEWBORN REFLEXES

Name	Testing method	Response	Developmental course	Significance
Blink	Light flash	Closing of both eyelids	Permanent	Protection of eyes to strong stimuli
Biceps reflex	Tap on the tendon of the biceps muscle	Short contraction of the biceps muscle	In the first few days it is brisker than in later days	Absent in depressed infants or in cases of congenital muscular disease
Knee jerk or patellar tendon reflex	Tap on the tendon below the patella or knee cap	Quick extension or kick of the knee	More pronounced in the first two days than later	Absent or difficult to obtain in depressed infants or infants with muscular disease; exaggerated in hyperexcitable infants
Babinski	Gentle stroking of the side of the infant's foot from heel to toes	Dorsal flexion of the big toe; extension of the other toes	Usually disappears near the end of the first year; replaced by plantar flexion of great toe as in the normal adult	Absent in defects of the lower spine
Withdrawal reflex	Pin prick is applied to the sole of the infant's foot	Leg flexion	Constantly present during the first ten days; present but less intense later	Absent with sciatic nerve damage
Plantar or toe grasp	Pressure is applied with finger against the balls of the infant's feet	Plantar flexion of all toes	Disappears between eight and twelve months	Absent in defects of the lower spinal cord
Palmar or automatic hand grasp	A rod or finger is pressed against the infant's palm	Infant grasps the object	Disappears at three to four months; increases during the first month and then gradually declines; replaced by voluntary grasp between four and five months	Response is weak or absent in depressed babies; sucking movements facilitate grasping

Moro reflex	(1) Sudden loud sound or jarring (for example, bang on the examination table); or (2) head drop—head is dropped a few inches; or (3) baby drop—baby is suspended horizontally, and the examiner lowers his hands rapidly about 6 in. and stops abruptly	Arms are thrown out in extension, and then brought toward each other in a convulsive manner; hands are fanned out at first and then clinched tightly; spine and lower extremities extend	Disappears in six to seven months	Absent or constantly weak moro indicates serious disturbance of the central nervous system
Stepping	Baby is supported in upright position; examiner moves the infant forward and tilts him slightly to one side	Rhythmic stepping movements	Disappears in three to four months	Absent in depressed infants
Rooting response	Cheek of infant is stimulated by light pressure of the finger	Baby turns head towards finger, opens mouth, and tries to suck finger. Disappears at approximately three to four months	Absent in depressed infants; appears in adults only in severe cerebral palsy diseases	
Sucking response	Index finger is inserted about 3 to 4 centimeters into the mouth	Rhythmical sucking	Sucking is often less intensive and less regular during the first three to four days	Poor sucking (weak, slow, and short periods) is found in apathetic babies; maternal medication during childbirth may depress sucking
Babkin or Palmarmental reflex	Pressure is applied on both of baby's palms when lying on his back	Mouth opens, eyes close, and head returns to midline	Disappears in three to four months	General depression of central nervous system inhibits this response

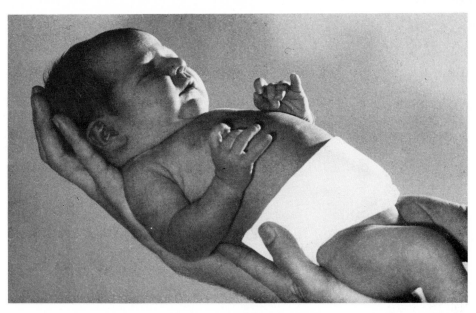

(a)

(b)

FIGURE 4-4 Some examples of newborn reflexes. The moro reflex (above): (a) initial position before the infant's head is dropped and (b) the moro response to the sudden loss of support. The rooting reflex (next page): (c) stimulation of cheek, (d) infant moves toward stimulation source, (e) infant grasps the finger. (All reflex photos from H. Prechtl and D. Beintema, The neurological examination of the fullterm newborn infant, *Little Club Clinics in Developmental Medicine,* 1964, number 12, 41. London: Spastics Society Medical Information Unit and William Heinemann Medical Books, Ltd. By permission.)

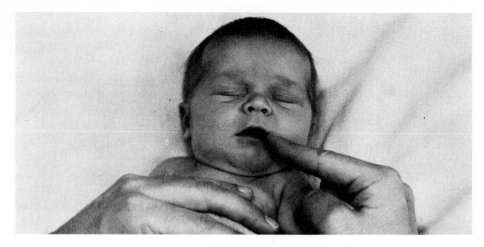

(c)

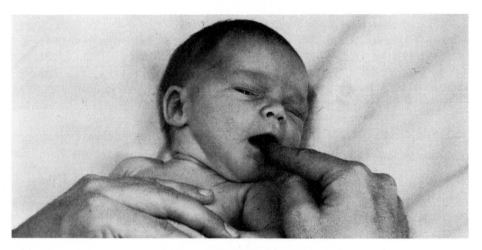

(d)

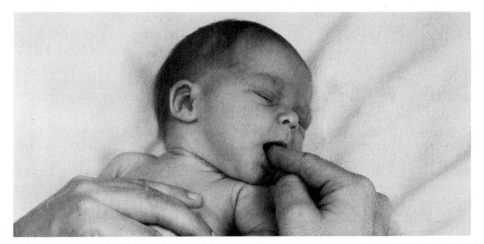

(e)

heart rate, muscle reactions, and respiration, has been receiving much attention in recent years partly because the child psychologist can use psychophysiological functions to probe the infant's sensory capacities. A change in respiration contingent upon a change in the pitch of a sound suggests that the infant is sensitive to changes in this auditory dimension. The neonate's motor responses, although limited, can give a clue to his sensory systems as well. In fact, one of the earliest means of detecting sensory capacities was the stabilimeter, an apparatus that monitors changes in an infant's movement. Recently, researchers have capitalized on the infant's well-developed sucking pattern as an index of the effect of the sensory input.

Hearing

Although the neonate's hearing has not been as extensively investigated as vision, there have been some exciting discoveries about the newborn's auditory capacities in the last decade. Just how soon after birth the neonate begins to hear is still a controversial issue since fluid in the inner ear may prevent proper assessment of infant's hearing capacities until a few hours after birth. It is clear, however, that as soon as a fair (for example, unobstructed) test can be made, the infant's hearing is remarkably well developed.

The newborn can discriminate among sounds of different *duration*: however, their behavioral effects are still unclear. Early studies suggested that short sounds (two to three seconds) were alerting and arousing while longer sounds (fifteen seconds or longer) were soothing and tended to decrease activity (Pratt, 1954). More recently, Brackbill (1970) has demonstrated that continuous sound does, in fact, have a soothing impact on the infant.

The newborn can also discriminate among sounds of different *loudness*. It has been shown that a neonate's heart rate increases as the loudness of a tone increases (Bartoshuk, 1964).

Not only can the newborn discriminate among sounds of different duration and loudness, but they can discriminate among sounds of different *pitches* as well. It has been found that infants with a mean age of fifty-eight hours can discriminate among tones of 200 and 1,000 cycles per second, as measured by bodily and leg movements and breathing patterns (Leventhal and Lipsitt, 1958). Sounds of a low pitch (ranging from 500 to 900 cycles per second) elicit more reliable and consistent responses than do high-pitched sounds (4,000 to 4,500 cycles per second) such as that of a whistle (Eisenberg et al., 1964). Moreover, the response patterns to different pitches are markedly varied: High-pitched sounds produce more marked startle responses than low-pitched sound.

Since experience can play only a minor role in accounting for these different response patterns, these findings suggest that human neonates are prepared at birth to respond differently to specific auditory characteristics, including duration, loudness, and pitch the first time they encounter them. Even more provocative evidence of the existence of a genetically based auditory mechanism comes from recent investigations of newborn responses to the human voice. Freedman (1971) found that newborns responded to the sound of a female voice more often and more vigorously than to the sound of a bell. Another group of investigators who have noted this selective responsivity to potentially important social stimuli have commented:

"The structure of the human auditory apparatus at birth ensures . . . that the voice at normal intensities is nonaversive and pre-potent. The survival value of the differential responsivity may be in the part it plays in the development of the affectional bond between parent and child [Hutt et al., 1968]."

Nor is this kind of selective responsivity to adult vocalizations limited to humans. Similar results have been found using young rhesus monkeys (Sackett & Tripp, 1968). After monkeys were reared for the first thirty days of life without hearing the vocalizations of adult monkeys, their responsivity to six levels of pitch was assessed. The monkeys were watched on closed-circuit TV, and a behavior change within two seconds of the onset of a tone was the criterion of responsivity. Sackett and Tripp found that response to pitch was selective: Maximal response occurred at the low and high pitches, with significantly less response occurring at the three middle-frequency pitches. Of significance is the fact that the vocalizations of adult female monkeys have pitches with frequency ranges that are similar to the frequencies that the newborn monkeys responded to. Moreover, the vocalizations of younger monkeys do not have these frequency ranges, which suggests that the adult female vocalizations are unique. The implication is that "at birth or soon after rhesus monkeys possess a tuned auditory mechanism that produces maximal responsiveness to the vocalization of adult females. Thus, the neonate does not have to learn to respond to the mother's vocalization—the auditory system is prewired for these sounds [Sackett, 1970, p. 12]."

In humans, there is accumulating evidence that infants are not only born with a general sensitivity to sounds in the normal range of human speech, but they also have a capacity to be "tuned in" to fine-grained aspects of adult speech. Consider this recent observation: While infants listen to adult speech, they synchronize their body movements precisely to the sound patterns of the speech. Amazingly, this synchronization occurs as early as the first day of life. Condon and Sander (1974) used very sophisticated techniques to film and minutely analyze these infant movement patterns. Infants ranging in age from twelve hours to two weeks (most were two days old or younger) were filmed while listening to a variety of sounds, including natural speech (English or Chinese), disconnected vowel sounds, and tapping sounds. Analysis revealed that if the infants were already moving when the speech stimulus began, they quickly synchronized the movements of their heads, hands, elbows, hips, legs, and even toes to the exact acoustic structure of the speech. Coordinated segments of the infants' movements were found to start, stop, or change form in precise correspondence to the speech segments (for example, phonemes, syllables, or words). For instance, a movement pattern involving several of an infant's body parts might start exactly when a word (or syllable) began and stop exactly when the word (or syllable) ended. The time segments involved were only fractions of a second, and the precise synchrony was sustained by two-day-old infants over sequences as long as 125 words.

Synchrony of movement to sound was equally precise for both English and Chinese speech. But this high degree of synchrony patterns to sound patterns was not observed in infants' responses to either the disconnected vowel sounds or to the tapping sounds; nor was synchrony observed in a control condition in which the movement patterns of an infant filmed during silence were compared with those in response to speech samples used with the other infants. These results suggest that the phenomenon of movement synchronization may be specific to natural human speech. This research provides the earliest and perhaps the most dramatic evidence to date that from the beginning of life the human organism is genetically prepared to selectively attend and respond to human speech in very special ways.

In addition to these remarkable observations, there is other evidence of the early responsivity of the human infant to language sounds. [Recall our discussion in Chapter 1 of the twenty-week-old infant's ability to distinguish consonants (Moffitt, 1971.] It is becoming increasingly clear that at a very early age the infant is capable of auditory discriminations that have functional significance for later social and language development.

Vision

Some animals, such as kittens, cannot see at all for many days after birth, but at birth the eye of the human newborn "is physiologically and anatomically prepared to respond differentially to most aspects of its visual field [Reese & Lipsitt, 1970, p. 36]." In spite of this ability to respond to the visual environment, until recently little was known about how much the infant could actually see.

Visual sensitivity in infants   Let us begin with some of the simplest dimensions. First, is the newborn sensitive to changes in *brightness*? Using the pupillary reflex (closing of the eyelid in response to bright light) as their index of responsivity, a number of researchers have found that the infant is sensitive to brightness changes immediately after birth (for example, Sherman, Sherman & Flory, 1936). More recently it has been demonstrated that brightness sensitivity undergoes rapid development in the first two months of life. The intensity of brightness required to elicit a response decreases as the infant matures. Similarly, other studies indicate that in response to brightness changes both the speed and amount of pupillary constriction increase with age.

Can the infant detect *movement* in his visual field? Haith (1966) exposed infants ranging in age from twenty-four to ninety-six hours to intermittent moving lights. To assess the infants' reactions to the light movement, they simultaneously monitored the newborns' sucking on a pacifier. It was found that infants engaged in measurably less sucking activity during the experimental trials with moving lights than during control trials employing nonmoving lights.

Moreover, it has been found that newborns have the capacity to follow a visual stimulus. Greenman (1963) presented a 4-inch red ring above infants' heads and moved it in a horizontal arc from one side to the other and then vertically. Immediately after birth 26 percent of the infants were able to follow the ring with their eyes, and in twelve to forty-eight hours 76 percent of the infants were able to do so. Also, it was found that following a horizontal stimulus is easier for the newborn than following than a vertical stimulus. In relation to our earlier discussion of infant states, it is interesting to note that when cradled in the examiner's arms in the feeding position, many infants followed the stimulus who had not done so previously.

Pattern perception in infancy   Is the visual world of the infant organized into patterns, images, and forms? The answer to this difficult question has important implications for theoretical formulations as to how perceptual development proceeds. Two positions can be distinguished: One view, the *naturalist* position, suggests that the infant comes into the world capable of perceiving forms and patterns; the *empiricists*, on the other hand, argue that only through experience can the infant develop the ability to construct "forms" out of the chaos of visual input. Probably the person who has been most responsible for reviving interest in this long-standing controversy is Robert Fantz. In Box 4-1, Fantz's work on pattern discrimination in infants is presented. The studies of Fantz suggest that the newborn can discriminate among patterns at a very early age; moreover, faces may have a particular appeal even to two-day-old infants.

BOX 4-1 PATTERN PERCEPTION IN INFANCY

Can the infant discriminate among patterns? To find out, Fantz (1961) developed a procedure in which he measured the amount of time that an infant would look at a visual target. Figure 4-5 illustrates the apparatus. An observer located above the baby recorded the amount of time that the infant directed his gaze at each target. If the infant looked longer at one form than another form, it was assumed that the infant preferred that form. In Figure 4-6 the results of one study are presented. These data support the *naturalist* position: Young infants can discriminate among visual patterns. The subjects looked longer at a face, newsprint, and bull's-eye pattern than at nonpatterned stimuli. However, the youngest infants in this study were two months of age at the commencement of testing; since opportunities for learning had been available, perhaps experiential factors did, in fact, contribute to the infants' ability to discriminate among patterns.

Fortunately, data on even younger infants are available. Fantz (1963), in a related study, found that babies under forty-eight hours of age looked longer at patterned targets, such as faces, and concentric circles, than at targets of color, such as circles of red, white, or yellow. These results suggest that pattern perception in human organisms may be innate or at least acquired after very little environmental experience.

Source: Adapted from Fantz, R. L. The origin of form perception. *Scientific American*, 1961, **204,** 66-72, and Fantz, R. L. Pattern vision in newborn infants. *Science,* 1963, **140,** 296-97.

In support of Fantz, other investigators (Freedman & Jirari, 1971) using a different approach—a head-turning response—found that newborn infants do, indeed, prefer facelike figures over figures in which the pattern features are scrambled (see Figure 4-7). As shown in Figure 4-8, the newborn moved his head to follow a facelike figure to the greatest degree. Perhaps the newborn is preprogrammed to be responsive to the human face, which is clearly adaptive for later socialization. However, as we shall see soon, there are still many skeptics and the case for innately determined recognition of human faces remains open to debate and further investigation.

A wide array of subsequent studies have been addressed to this issue of visual pattern discrimination in infancy. Perhaps the most integrative study was done by Brennan and coworkers (1966), who tested infants at ages three, eight, and fourteen weeks using checkerboards of varying levels of complexity. They found that three-week-old infants fixated simple patterns more than complex ones, but that this trend began to reverse itself at eight weeks and by fourteen weeks the most complex patterns received the most attention. Preferences for degree of complexity in patterns, then, may be age-dependent. Moreover, as we shall see in subsequent chapters, the attention of infants is affected by novelty of and familiarity with the stimulus pattern as well as its complexity.

Perhaps the most important methodological advance in the study of pattern perception in infants is the work of Salapatek and Kessen (1966) at Yale University, who substituted an infrared camera for the human observer. By this technique it was possible to determine not only that an infant was looking at an object, but precisely on what parts of the object his eyes were focused. When Salapatek and Kessen photographed the exact position of infants' eye movements on a triangle target, they found that the infants' attention was concentrated on the angles and was *not* distributed over the whole form.

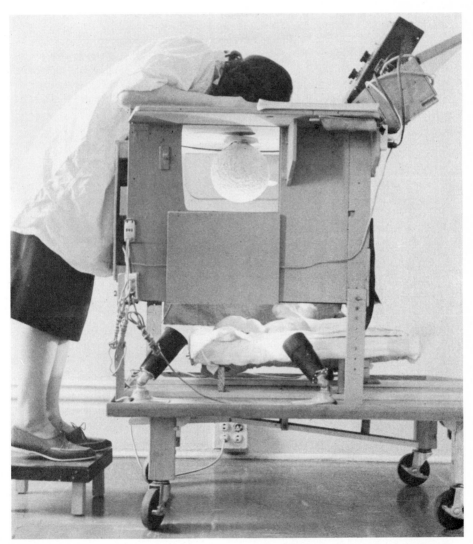

FIGURE 4-5 The Fantz Looking Chamber was used to test the visual interests of chimpanzee and human infants. Here a human infant lies on a crib in the chamber, looking at objects hung from the ceiling. The observer, watching through a peephole, records the attention given each object. (By permission of R. Fantz and through the courtesy of D. Linton, photographer.)

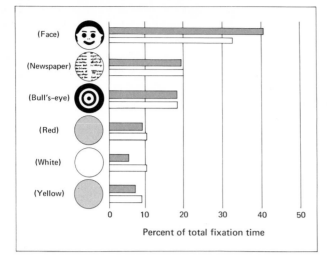

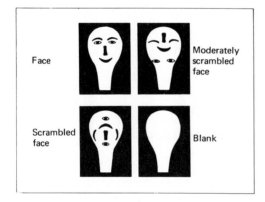

FIGURE 4-7 Facelike figures used in assessment of newborn visual preferences. (From Freedman and Jirari, 1971. By permission of the author and publisher.)

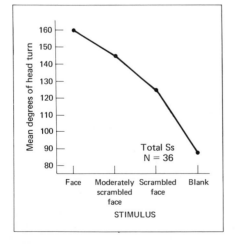

FIGURE 4-8 Head turning in newborns to stimuli varying in degree of "faceness." (Maximal score is 90° to each side or 180°.) (From Freedman & Jirari, 1971. By permission of the author and publisher.)

This suggests that certain elements of complex patterns may elicit infant attention, but it is not fair to conclude that young infants perceive a pattern. Instead, they appear to be attracted to specific elements of a pattern, particularly a vertex or boundary. Later research (Salapatek, 1969) found that the four- to six-week-old infants continue to show the fixation of the newborn on angles and edges but by two months of age, there is visual tracing of both the edge of the pattern as well as the center or internal areas. As Brennan and coworkers noted, "it seems possible that part of the age-related changes in response to complexity may be attributable to changes in patterns of scanning [Brennan et al., 1966, p. 356]."

Some later visual landmarks: Depth perception and size constancy   Our survey of the infant's visual capacities would not be complete without a discussion of two other aspects of visual behavior: *depth perception* and *size constancy.*

Depth perception. As adults we possess the ability to distinguish depth; the adaptive value of this capacity is obvious—it prevents us from routinely walking off cliffs and the edges of tall buildings. But how soon does the infant show depth perception? To investigate this issue, Gibson and Walk (1960) developed an apparatus that they termed the *visual cliff* (see Figure 4-9). As you can see, it consists of an elevated glass platform divided into two sections: One section has a surface that is textured with a checkerboard pattern, while the other has a clear glass surface with a checkerboard pattern several feet below it. The investigators hypothesized that if an infant can, in fact, perceive depth, he should remain on the "shallow" side of the platform and avoid the "cliff" side since it has the appearance of a chasm. In the natural world, of course, it is possible to misjudge the perception of depth; for example, the reflections from the surfaces of water may mislead a person to think that the water is not deep. However, in this visual-cliff apparatus, the glass surfaces are lighted in such a way as to eliminate any reflections. Thirty-six infants ranging in age from six to fourteen months were tested. All infants eagerly approached their mothers when the mothers were on the "shallow" side of the platform but refused to cross the "deep" side in spite of the mothers' encouragements.

This study is important for it suggests not only that human infants can discriminate depth as soon as they can crawl, but that the ability to avoid a visual brink may not be as dependent on experience as was once assumed. However, six months may be sufficiently long to acquire this ability through experience, and therefore tests with younger human infants are necessary before it can be concluded that depth perception is an innate ability.

More recently, Campos and coworkers (1970) overcame the problem of testing the premotor infant for depth perception and provided a test using very young infants. Instead of indexing whether or not infants would crawl over the deep side of the visual cliff they placed forty-four- to one-hundred-fifteen-day-old infants on both the deep and shallow sides of the visual cliff and measured changes in their heart rates. It was hypothesized that if the infant is capable of depth perception, his heart rate should increase when he is placed on the deep side. The infants' heart rates did increase, which clearly supports the hypothesis that infants as young as one and a half months perceive depth. This finding is consistent with experiments involving animals with independent

FIGURE 4-9 The visual cliff. (From Gibson and Walk, 1960. Photo by William Vandivert. Used with permission.)

locomotion shortly after birth, which show that chicks, kids, and lambs avoid the deep side of the visual cliff when they are one day old. Together these studies support an interpretation that the ability to perceive depth is innate.

Size constancy. Next, we turn to the genesis and development of size constancy. As adults we are able to judge the size of an object, regardless of its distance from us; for example, even though a truck looks toylike at a great distance, we still recognize it as a "truck" with real-life proportions. This ability is called *size constancy* and is defined as the tendency of an object to retain its size in our perception regardless of changes in viewing distance, even though the size of the retinal image changes (Bower, 1966, p. 80). (See Figure 4-10.) Again, the question arises: How early does the infant show size constancy? This question is, of course, important: If the ability does not depend on experience, very young infants should possess it; on the other hand, failure to demonstrate this ability in early infancy would support the empiricist view, namely, that size constancy is a capacity acquired through direct experience with real objects at varying distances. Progress in resolving this controversy has been hampered by inadequate

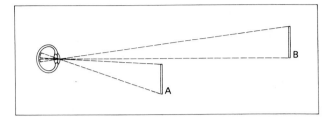

FIGURE 4-10 Size constancy. Two objects of the same physical size may produce very different retinal image sizes and yet be seen as the same size. (From T. G. R. Bower, "The Visual World of Infants." Reprinted with permission. Copyright © 1966, by Scientific American, Inc. All rights reserved.)

research techniques for assessing this ability in young infants. As the study in Box 4-2 indicates, Bower (1966) has removed the methodological roadblock and demonstrated that infants do possess this capacity very early in life.

BOX 4-2 SIZE CONSTANCY IN INFANCY

How early do infants show size constancy? To find out, Bower (1966) rewarded a group of six- to eight-week-old babies for a simple head-turning response with a "peek-a-boo!" Once the head turning was well established, he reinforced an infant for its head turning only when a 12-inch cube was present 3 feet in front of the infant. Now to determine whether the infant possessed *size constancy,* the experimenter systematically varied the size and distance of the cube. An empiricist would predict that an infant should maintain a high rate of head-turning response even if the original stimulus object, the cube, were changed as long as the new stimulus object continued to project onto the retina an image identical to that of the original stimulus.

To produce this condition, Bower displayed a 36-inch cube at a distance of 9 feet from the infant; the retinal image produced by this arrangement is the same as the retinal image produced by the original 12-inch cube presented at 1 foot (see Figure 4-11). If the infant does not yet have size constancy, and is responding on the basis of retinal image, he should respond equally in these two conditions. However, as a nativist would argue, if the infant does have size constancy and can respond to the actual size of the original stimulus (12-inch cube) and not simply to the retinal image produced by the cube, he should maintain a high rate of head turning to the 12-inch cube—regardless of its distance from him.

To evaluate the adequacy of these viewpoints, infants were tested with either 12- or 36-inch cubes placed 9 feet away from them. The infants turned to the 12-inch cube regardless of distance, while they did not turn their heads when only the retinal image was the same as the original. In summary, the infants demonstrated size constancy: they did not use the retinal image as their guide for responding, but the true size of the object. The change in distance did not affect the infant's recognition of the original stimulus— even though a retinal image from a distance of 9 feet would be, of course, much smaller than its image at a distance of 3 feet. The results support the nativist viewpoint: size constancy may be an innately determined ability.

Source: Adapted from Bower, T. G. R. The visual world of infants. *Scientific American,* 1966, **215(6),** 80–92.

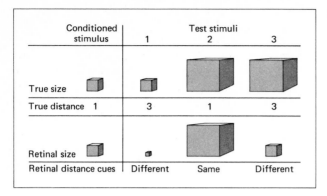

FIGURE 4-11 Size constancy was investigaged with cubes of different sizes placed at different distances from the infants. The conditioned stimulus was 30 centimeters on a side and 1 meter away, test stimuli 30 or 90 centimeters on a side and 1 or 3 meters away. The chart shows how test stimuli were related to the conditioned stimulus in various respects. (From T. G. R. Bower, "The Visual World of Infants." Reprinted with permission. Copyright © 1966, by Scientific American, Inc. All rights reserved.)

Smell and taste

Although the olfactory and gustatory response systems probably play a less significant role in the human infant's development than vision and hearing, in order to illustrate the extent of the infant's sensory competence, a brief summary of these more primitive capacities will be presented.

Smell   Until recently there was little clear-cut evidence concerning the newborn infant's capacity to smell. Most of the early studies (Pratt, 1954) were marred by methodological deficiencies or failed to be replicated by other investigators. As in most areas of infant research, the success of more recent efforts can be attributed largely to the development of more sophisticated methodologies and measurement techniques, which have eliminated the need for subjective judgments and allowed infant responses to be automatically and objectively recorded under well-controlled conditions.

A study by Engen and colleagues (1963) demonstrates that the young human can, indeed, respond differentially to various odors. Twenty infants, ranging in age from thirty-two to sixty-eight hours old, were presented with either a dry Q-tip (control) or a Q-tip soaked in an odorous liquid. Dry and odor trials were alternated, with each infant receiving ten presentations of each odor. To determine whether an infant could smell the difference between the dry and odorous stimuli, leg withdrawal, bodily activity, and respiration were continuously monitored. If the changes in these responses were greater on the odor trial than on the control trial, it was assumed that the infant could discriminate the particular odor.

Although the data clearly indicated that the neonate could discriminate the four different odors employed, it is not clear whether pleasantness or intensity of the odors was the basis for the different degrees of infant response. Finally, as a later study shows, the intensity of an odor necessary for detection by an infant decreases as the infant develops. Although infants can detect odors in the first few days of life, sensitivity to odor does improve with age (Lipsitt et al., 1963).

Taste Although controversy still exists concerning the exact taste preferences of the human newborn, there is little doubt that the neonate is selectively responsive to different gustatory stimuli. Over forty years ago, Jensen (1932) utilized changes in sucking as an index of taste and found that infants' sucking responses to water and glucose and various concentrations of salt solutions differed from their responses to milk; moreover, their sucking responses varied for different concentrations of salt solutions. Recent advances in measurement techniques should aid in more clearly specifying the taste sensitivity of the newborn.

In summary, the infant's sensory and perceptual apparatus is well developed very early in life, which suggests that he is well prepared to profit from interactions with both his social and physical environment. Next, we turn to a brief examination of the infant's motor development and then finally to a discussion of growth.

MOTOR DEVELOPMENT

What course does the infant's motor development follow? How soon can an infant crawl and walk? The remarkable achievement of the development of posture and locomotion in infants was plotted by Shirley (1933), and her results are shown in Figure 4-12. One of the important implications of these motor achievements is the increasing degree of independence that the child gains. He can explore his environment more fully and initiate social contact with peers and caretakers. However, there are variations in the age at which walking begins. In Figure 4-13, the results of a comparison of five European cities are presented. Not only are the differences in the cities noteworthy, but even more striking are the wide range of differences in individual children. Although neither sex nor social class can account for these differences, it is possible that nutritional and environmental factors may contribute to these patterns.

It has been a long accepted doctrine that motor skills such as walking develop relatively independently of opportunities for practice of these emerging skills. Consider the classic work of Dennis and Dennis (1940) on the development of walking in humans

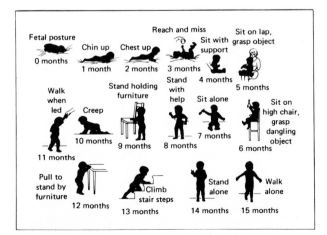

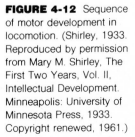

FIGURE 4-12 Sequence of motor development in locomotion. (Shirley, 1933. Reproduced by permission from Mary M. Shirley, The First Two Years, Vol. II, Intellectual Development. Minneapolis: University of Minnesota Press, 1933. Copyright renewed, 1961.)

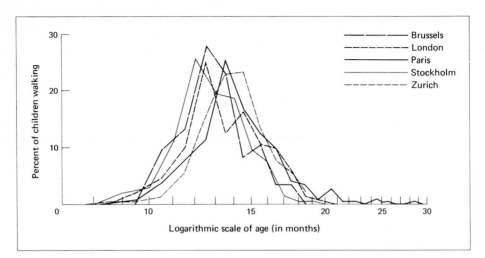

FIGURE 4-13 Differences in age of first walking in five European longitudinal samples. (From Hindley, C.; Filliozat, A.; Klackenberg, G.; Nicolet-Meister, D.; and Sand, E., 1966. Differences in age of walking in five European longitudinal samples, *Human Body,* 1966, **38,** 364-379. By permission of the senior author and Wayne State University Press.)

reared under conditions of restricted practice. Hopi Indians were the subjects in this early study and for a very good reason: In some villages of this tribe it was the custom to keep infants on a cradle board for the first year of life. Comparisons between these restricted infants and Hopi infants from other villages who were not cradled indicated almost no differences in beginning ages of walking: Cradle-board babies began to walk at an average of 14.98 months, while the noncradle-board babies reached this developmental milestone in 15.07 months—nearly identical time. A similar practice, swaddling of infants, which is common in the Balkans, Russia, and Poland, apparently has little effect on the age of walking.

However, more recent studies by Dennis and Najarian (1957) have indicated that very severe restriction of opportunities for practice of motor skills (such as found in some orphanages) may, in fact, retard motor development. Under extreme conditions, therefore, the onset of walking may be delayed. As we will discuss in Chapter 5, development is typically determined by both genetic and environmental factors

GROWTH

One of the most heavily investigated areas of child development is physical growth. For many years psychologists have tracked and plotted the manner in which the young infant grows. A brief description of the general growth trends is in order before we discuss some of the determinants of growth.

As a culture, we are very concerned about how tall and heavy we are. Parents hope that their boys won't be too short or their girls too tall. Consider these interesting observations of our concern about height that appeared in a Sunday newspaper supplement:

The Metropolitan Life Insurance Company reports that average life insurance coverage is twice as much for six-footers; bishops average 5'10-½", rural preachers 5'8-¾", presidents of major universities are 1" taller than those of smaller colleges and of high school principals; sales managers hit 5'10", their salesmen average 1" shorter, railroad presidents are 5'11", station agents 5'9-½"; in the depression of the 1930s shorter men were first to be laid off; in fifteen presidential elections victory went to the taller candidate (Lincoln was the tallest at 6'4", L.B.J. next at 6'3") [summarized by Krogman, 1972, pp. 28–29].

Although taller isn't necessarily better, it seems to help. It is not just height that we are concerned about. The monthly appearance of another new diet book or the announcement of a recently formed Weight Watchers club also testifies to our concern about weight.

Age and sex differences in height and weight

How does a child's height and weight change with age? Are the patterns of growth similar for boys and girls? Are there national, ethnic, and socioeconomic differences in height and weight? Figures 4-14 and 4-15 summarize curves for height and weight for boys and girls in the United States. Of interest are the sex differences: In height the girls' curve crosses the boys' curve at about 9½ years of age, and until 13½ the girls are taller than boys on the average. Similarly, notice the weight curves: Girls are lighter than boys until nearly nine years of age and then are heavier than boys until about age fourteen. However, these curves do not tell the complete story; it is of interest not only to determine the average height and weight at various age points, but to isolate periods of accelerated growth. The periods of peak growth occur at different ages for boys and girls. Between seven and ten and a half for both boys and girls the differences between successive age groups are relatively consistent. For boys the greatest mean change occurs at thirteen and a quarter years, while for girls the peak is earlier at eleven and three quarter years. Not only does their growth spurt occur earlier, but girls reach their mature height earlier than boys. A similar pattern is evident for weight: Boys start their spurt in weight gain at twelve and a quarter years, while girls start their weight spurt about 1½ years earlier when they are ten and three-quarter years old. Table 4-2 summarizes these growth spurt data for boys and girls.

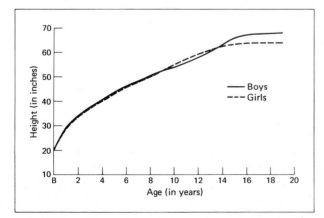

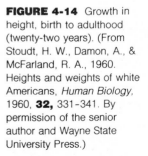

FIGURE 4-14 Growth in height, birth to adulthood (twenty-two years). (From Stoudt, H. W., Damon, A., & McFarland, R. A., 1960. Heights and weights of white Americans, *Human Biology*, 1960, **32,** 331–341. By permission of the senior author and Wayne State University Press.)

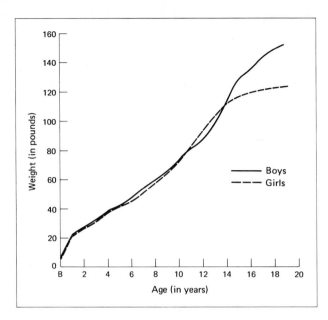

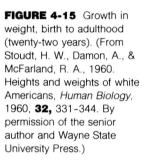

FIGURE 4-15 Growth in weight, birth to adulthood (twenty-two years). (From Stoudt, H. W., Damon, A., & McFarland, R. A., 1960. Heights and weights of white Americans, *Human Biology,* 1960, **32,** 331–344. By permission of the senior author and Wayne State University Press.)

These differences have important implications for the social and emotional adjustment of boys and girls, and these issues will be discussed in later chapters.

National differences in height and weight

There are ethnic and national differences as well as age and sex differences. For example, there are variations within Europe. Northwestern and western Europeans, especially Scandinavians, are taller than southern Europeans, such as Italians. And, of course, there are even more extreme examples in Africa where the Niloties grow 7 feet tall, while Pygmies are approximately 4 feet tall. Figure 4-16 illustrates the wide variation in height around the globe.

Are we growing taller?

Height is on the rise. Estimates of the average Englishman between the eleventh and fourteenth centuries have been made by careful measurements of bones exhumed from

Table 4-2 PERIODS OF SPURT GROWTH FOR BOYS AND GIRLS

	Height			
	Start	Peak	End	Duration
Boys.	11¾	13¼	14½	2¾
Girls	10¼	11¾	12½	2¼
		Weight		
Boys.	12¼	13¾	15	2¾
Girls	10¾	12¼	13¼	2½

Source: From Hamil, P., Johnston, F., & Lemeshow, S. *Vital Statistics,* Series 11, No. 124; 1973. The National Center for Health Statistics, Health Resources Administration, Department of Health, Education, and Welfare. By permission.

British cemeteries and he was approximately 5 feet, 6 inches tall. In contrast, in 1972, the average male is 3 inches taller at 5 feet, 9 inches. Serious measurement of these group trends in size has indicated that we need to be constantly updating our norms of height and weight. Figure 4-17 documents these shifts between 1880 and 1960, and in most parts of the culture we are still growing bigger. However, there are social class differences in height and weight; as the 1972 government survey revealed, children in

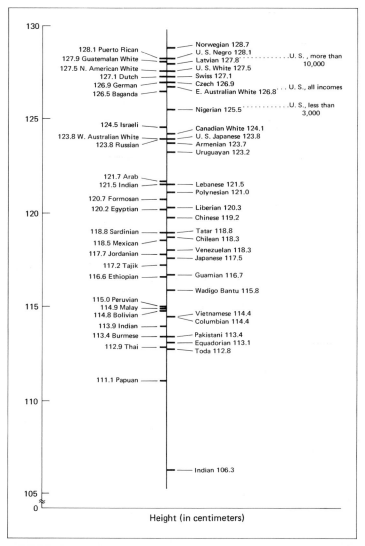

FIGURE 4-16 Relation of heights of three United States income groupings of eight-year-old boys to those of the rest of the world. (From Meredith, H. V., Changes in the stature and body weight of North American boys during the last 80 years. In L. P. Lipsitt and C. C. Spiker (Eds.), *Advances in child development and behavior,* 1963, vol. 1. New York: Academic Press, 1963. By permission of author and publisher.)

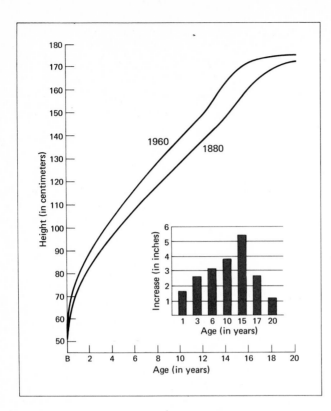

FIGURE 4-17 Schematic curves of mean stature of North American white boys for 1880 and 1960. Inset shows differences between the curves at selected ages. (From Meredith, H. V., Changes in the stature and body weight of North American boys during the last 80 years. In L. P. Lipsitt and C. C. Spiker (Eds.), *Advances in child development and behavior*, 1963, vol. 1. New York: Academic Press, 1963. By permission of author and publisher.)

families of over $10,000 annual income were both taller and heavier than children of families with less than $3,000 in yearly income. Moreover, the changes were more marked for the upper income groups. However, recent indications are that in the upper classes of the United States the increases have stopped; individuals in the higher socio-economic classes have apparently reached the upper level of their growth potential. Increases in the remaining segments of the society continue.

There are several possible reasons for the trends that Americans are growing taller and heavier (Krogman, 1972):

1. Health and nutrition have both improved; specifically there has been a decline in growth-retarding illness, particularly in the first five years. There has been an improvement in the amount and balance of nutritional intake. Medical care and personal health practices have improved.

2. Socioeconomic conditions have improved; child labor is less frequent and living conditions have improved.

   In the 19th century child labor in coal mines and the big mills extracted a repressive toll upon the health and stamina of the growing child. . . . Additionally, the crowding within and around industrial centers made for wretched living conditions. Child labor in England and Scotland, as in the USA, has been greatly reduced so that children are freed to grow up under far less repressive circumstances [Krogman, 1972, p. 40].

3. Genetic factors, including interbreeding which produces increases in height and weight in the offspring. An additional factor may be selective mating of tall individuals.

Finally, we are not only growing taller, but our feet are growing longer due to the fact that we are growing taller. Your grandfather probably wore a size 7 A or B, while now the average American male wears a size 9 to 10 B. This represents about a ⅓-inch gain in length each generation. Krogman (1972) has spelled out the economic implications of this change: "About 650 million pairs of shoes are sold annually; add ⅓ inch of leather needed per generation and you get about 6,800 miles of additional shoe leather—diagonally from Maine to California [Krogman, 1972, p. 42]." If this demand continues, we may have a leather crisis in addition to an energy crisis. Finally, it is worth noting that sexual maturity is being achieved at an earlier age as well.

Nutrition and growth

Growth is determined not only by genetic factors which set limits to normal adult stature, but also by the environmental context. In a favorable environment, there is a great deal of similarity in the growth curves; when nutrition is inadequate, however, growth rates are seriously depressed. Evidence of the controlling role of nutrition in physical growth comes from studies comparing growth before and during wartime periods in which nutritional intake was reduced. During World Wars I and II, there was a general growth retardation while there was a general secular increase during 1920 to 1940, the be-tween-war period. However, weight was affected more than height and boys more than girls. Age of puberty is affected by nutritional factors as well. During World War II, girls in occupied France did not achieve menarche until an average age of sixteen years, approximately three years later than the prewar norm (Howe & Schiller, 1952).

A variety of other environmental factors affect growth as well, including illness, disease, climate, and psychological disturbance (Tanner, 1970). In addition, there is a season of the year effect: Growth in height is fastest in the spring and growth in weight fastest in the fall.

Overcoming environmental deficiencies: catchup growth   As we have seen earlier in our discussions of the effects of prenatal deficiencies on later development, there is a strong corrective tendency to regain the normal course of development after an early setback. A similar corrective principle operates in the case of physical growth following environmental injury or deprivation. As Tanner notes:

> Children, no less than rockets, have their trajectories governed by control systems of their genetical constitution and powered by energy absorbed from the natural environment. Deflect the child from its growth trajectory by acute malnutrition or illness, and a restoring force develops so that as soon as the missing food is supplied or the illness terminated the child catches up toward its original curve. When it gets there, it slows down again to adjust its path onto the old trajectory once more [Tanner, 1970, p. 125].

A child who had reduced food intake during two periods of psychological disturbance showed a compensatory increase in growth rate after each period of reduced growth. However, the degree of "catchup" will depend on a variety of factors: duration, severity of timing of the deprivation and the nature of the subsequent treatment or therapy. The effects of intervention following severe malnutrition will illustrate (Graham, 1966). When infants with varying degrees of malnutrition were treated, those with a 5 percent deficit in body length caught up; those with a 15 percent deficit benefited only somewhat, but remained significantly shorter. In general, the earlier and more prolonged the stress, the more difficult it is for regulation to be fully effective in achieving the normal level of growth.

SUMMARY

The newborn infant is not a "blooming, buzzing confusion." Rather, the newborn has a well-organized set of reflexes and sensory capacities. Since assessment of the newborn's capacities are affected by his state of alertness, developmental changes in sleep and crying patterns were examined. A state of alert inactivity is optimal for responding to external stimulation. Soothing techniques such as holding the baby on the shoulder, rocking, swaddling, and sucking were discussed. There are wide differences among individuals, sexes, and races in soothability.

The newborn's repertoire of reflexes—involuntary responses to an external stimulus—were examined; these assessments are employed as a test of the soundness of the infant's central nervous system. Next the sensory capacities of the newborn were examined. At birth the infant can discriminate sounds of different intensity, duration, and pitch. Some evidence suggests that the newborn may be particularly responsive to human voices and is capable of discriminating certain aspects of language.

Visual capacities are also well developed in the infant. The newborn is sensitive to changes in brightness, movement, and can track a moving object. Pattern preferences are evident early, with indication that infants prefer facelike stimuli. Other evidence suggests that very young infants respond to only small segments of a visual stimulus such as angles and lines and only later does true pattern perception develop. Infants possess depth perception and size constancy in the first months of life.

Changes in the infant's locomotion skills from creeping to walking were discussed next. Although these kinds of motor skills are to a large degree maturationally determined, extreme variations in the early environment can retard the developmental sequence of motor skills.

Finally, growth patterns in height and weight from infancy on were discussed. Sex differences were noted, with girls showing faster rates of maturation than boys. Cross-generation comparisons indicate that we are growing taller and heavier; however, the upper classes appear to have reached their growth potential but the remaining segments of the population continue to show this increasing trend. Growth is a self-regulating process which compensates for temporary interference by illness or dietary deficiency by a period of accelerated growth.

REFERENCES

Bartoshuk, A. K. Human neonatal cardiac responses to sound: a power function. *Psychonomic Science*, 1964, **1**, 151-152.

Birns, B., Blank, M., & Bridger, W. H. The effectiveness of various soothing techniques on human neonates. *Psychosomatic Medicine*, 1966, **28**, 316-322.

Bower, T. G. R. The visual world of infants. *Scientific American*, 1966, **215**(6), 80-92.

Brackbill, Y. Continuous stimulation and arousal level in infants: additive effects. *Proceedings, 78th Annual Convention, American Psychological Association*, 1970, **5**, 271-272.

Brennan, W. M., Ames, E. W., & Moore, R. W. Age differences in infants' attention to patterns of different complexities. *Science*, 1966, **151**, 354-356.

Campos, J. J., Langer, A., & Krowitz, A. Cardiac responses on the visual cliff in prelocomotor human infants. *Science*, 1970, **170,** 196-197.

Condon, W. S., & Sander, L. W. Neonate movement is synchronized with adult speech: interactional participation and language acquisition. *Science*, 1974, **183,** 99-101.

Dement, W. C. The effect of dream deprivation. *Science*, 1960, **131,** 1705-1707.

Dennis, W., & Dennis, M. G. The effect of cradling practice upon the onset of walking in Hopi children. *Journal of Genetic Psychology*, 1940, **56,** 77-86.

Dennis, W., and Najarian P. Infant development under environmental handicap. *Psychological Monographs*, 1957, **71** (Whole No. 436).

Eisenberg, R. B., Coursin, D. B., Griffin, E. J., & Hunter, M. A. Auditory behavior in the human neonate: a preliminary report. *Journal of Speech and Hearing Research*, 1964, **7,** 245-269.

Engen, T., Lipsitt, L. P., & Kaye, H. Olfactory responses and adaptation in the human neonate. *Journal of Comparative and Physiological Psychology*, 1963, **56,** 73-77.

Fantz, R. L. The origin of form perception. *Scientific American*, 1961, **204,** 66-72.

Fantz, R. L. Pattern vision in newborn infants. *Science*, 1963, **140,** 296-297.

Freedman, D. G. Behavioral assessment in infancy. In G. B. A. Stoelinga & J. J. Van Der Werff Ten Bosch (Eds.), *Normal and abnormal development of brain and behavior,*. Leiden: Leiden University Press, 1971. Pp. 92-103.

Freedman, D. G., & Freedman, N. C. Behavioral differences between Chinese-American and European-American newborns. *Nature*, 1969, **224,** 1227.

Gesell, A., & Amatruda, C. S. *The embryology of behavior.* New York: Harper, 1945.

Gibson, E. J., & Walk, R. R. The "visual cliff." *Scientific American*, 1960, **202,** 2-9.

Graham, G. G. Growth during recovery from infantile malnutrition. *Journal of American Medical Women's Association*, 1966, **21,** 737-742.

Greenman, G. W. Visual behavior of newborn infants. In A. J. Solnit & S. A. Provence (Eds.), *Modern perspectives in child development,* New York: Hallmark, 1963.

Haith, M. M. The response of the human newborn to visual movement. *Journal of Experimental Child Psychology*, 1966, **3,** 235-243.

Hamill, P. V. V., Johnston, F. E., & Lemeshow, S. Height and weight of youths 12-17 years. *Vital and Health Statistics*, 1973, Series 11, No. 124.

Hindley, C. B., Filliozat, A. M., Klackenberg, G., Nicolet-Meister, D., & Sand, E. A., Differences in age of walking for five European longitudinal samples. *Human Biology*, 1966, **38,** 364-379.

Howe, P. E., & Schiller, M. Growth responses of the school child to changes in diet and environmental factors. *Journal of Applied Physiology*, 1952, **5,** 51-61.

Hutt, S. J., Hutt, C., Lenard, H. G., Bernuth, H. V., & Muntjewerff, W. J. Auditory responsivity in the human neonate. *Nature*, 1968, **318,** 888-890.

Jackson, C. M. (Ed.). *Human anatomy* (9th ed.). New York: McGraw Hill, 1933.

Jensen, K. Differential reactions to taste and temperature stimuli in newborn infants. *Genetic Psychology Monographs*, 1932, **12,** 363-479.

Kessen, W., Leutzendoff, A. M., & Stoutsenberger, K. Age, food deprivation, non-nutritive sucking and movement in the human newborn. *Journal of Comparative and Physiological Psychology*, 1967, **63,** 82-86.

Korner, A. F. REM organization in neonates: theoretical implications for development and the biological function of REM. *Archives of General Psychiatry*, 1968, **19,** 330-340.

Korner, A. F. Visual alertness in neonates: individual differences and their correlates. *Perceptual and Motor Skills*, 1970, **31,** 499-509.

Korner, A. F. State as variable, as obstacle and as mediator of stimulation in infant research. *Merrill-Palmer Quarterly*, 1972, **18,** 77-94.

Korner, A. F., & Thoman, E. Visual alertness in neonates as evoked by maternal care. *Journal of Experimental Child Psychology*, 1970, **10,** 67-78.

Krogman, W. M. *Child Growth.* Ann Arbor: The University of Michigan Press, 1972.

Leventhal, A. S., & Lipsitt, L. P. Adaptation, pitch discrimination, and sound localization in the neonate. *Child Development*, 1964, **35,** 759-767.

Lipsitt, L. P., Engen, T., & Kaye, H. Developmental changes in the olfactory threshold of the neonate. *Child Development*, 1963, **34,** 371-376.

Meredith, H. V. Changes in the stature and body weight of North American boys during the last 80 years. In L. P. Lipsitt & C. C. Spiker (Eds.), *Advances in child development and behavior.* Vol. 1. New York: Academic, 1963. Pp. 69-114.

Lipton, E. L., Steinschneider, A., & Richmond, J. B. Swaddling, a child care practice: historical, cultural, and experimental. *Pediatrics*, 1965, **35,** 521-567.

Moffitt, A. R. Consonant cue perception by twenty- to twenty-four-week old infants. *Child Development*, 1971, **42,** 717-732.

Moss, H. A. Sex, age and state as determinants of mother-infant interaction. *Merrill-Palmer Quarterly*, 1967, **13,** 19-36.

Moss, H. A., & Robson, K. S. The role of protest behavior in the development of mother-infant attachment. Paper presented at the American Psychological Association, San Francisco, 1968.

Pederson, D. R., & Tervrugt, D. The influence of amplitude and frequency of vestibular stimulation on the activity of two-month-old infants. *Child Development*, 1973, **44,** 122-128.

Prader, A., Tanner, J. M., & Von Harnack, G. A. Catch-up growth following illness or starvation. *Journal of Pediatrics*, 1963, **62,** 646-659.

Pratt, K. C. The neonate. In L. Carmichael (Ed.), *Manual of Child Psychology* (2d edition). New York: Wiley, 1954, Pp. 215-291.

Prechtl, H. F. R., & Beintema, D. J. *The neurological examination of the full term newborn infant*. Little Club Clinics in Developmental Medicine, No. 12. London: Spastics Society Medical Information Unit and William Heinemann Medical Books, 1964.

Reese, H. W., & Lipsitt, L. P. (Eds.), *Experimental child psychology*. New York: Academic, 1970.

Roffwarg, H. P., Muzio, J. N. & Dement, W. C. Ontogenetic development of the human sleep-dream cycle. *Science*, 1966, **152,** 604-619.

Sackett, G. P. Innate mechanisms, rearing conditions and a theory of early experience effects. In M. R. Jones (Ed.), *Miami symposium on the prediction of behavior: early experience*. Coral Gables: University of Miami Press, 1970.

Sackett, G. P., & Tripp, R. Innate mechanisms in primate behavior: identification and causal significance. Paper presented at US-Japan Seminar on Regulatory Mechanisms, Emory University, Atlanta, July 1968.

Salapatek, P. The visual investigation of geometric pattern by the one- and two-month-old infant. Paper presented at the meeting of the American Association for the Advancement of Science, Boston, December 1969.

Salapatek, P., & Kessen, W. Visual scanning of triangles by the human newborn. *Journal of Experimental Child Psychology*, 1966, **3,** 155-167.

Schaffer, H. R. *The growth of sociability*. London: Penguin, 1971.

Sherman, M., Sherman, I. C., & Flory, C. D. Infant behavior. *Comparative Psychology Monographs*, 1936, **12,** No. 4.

Shirley, M. M. *The first two years*. Minneapolis: The University of Minnesota Press, 1933.

Stoudt, H. W., Damon, A., & McFarland, R. A. Heights and weights of white Americans. *Human Biology*, 1960, **32,** 331-341.

Tanner, J. M. *Growth at adolescence* (2d ed.). Oxford: Blackwell Scientific Publications, 1962.

Tanner, J. M. Physical growth. In P. H. Mussen (Ed.), *Carmichael's manual of child psychology*. Vol. 1. New York: Wiley, 1970. Pp. 77-155.

Watson, R. I. *Psychology of the child*. New York: Wiley, 1962.

Wasz-Hockert, O., Lind, J., Vuorenkoski, V., Partanen, T. and Valanné, E. *The infant cry: a spectrographic and auditory analysis*. Suffolk: Lavenham Press, 1968.

Wolff, P. H. The causes, controls and organization of behavior in the neonate. *Psychological Issues*, 1966, **5** (1, Whole No. 17).

Wolff, P. H. The natural history of crying and other vocalizations in early infancy. In B. Foss (Ed.), *Determinants of infant behavior*. Vol. 4. London: Methuen, 1969.

5
EARLY
EXPERIENCE

In the previous chapters we examined the role of biological factors in development, prenatal determinants of behavior, and the early capacities of the young organism. In this chapter the focus will be on the importance of the early environment for the child's normal development. Since the late 1940s under the influence of Donald Hebb's classic work, *The Organization of Behavior,* in which he elegantly argued that a certain minimal amount of environmental stimulation of the sense organs was necessary for the proper development of the central nervous system, there has been a flurry of activity aimed at determining the effects of variations in the early environment on later development. A number of questions can be asked. Do normal patterns of behavior—motoric, intellectual, and social—emerge in a predetermined fashion regardless of the nature of the early experiences of the child? Or, are there some minimal conditions that are necessary for proper development? Another issue concerns the timing of experience. Are early experiences more important than later ones? Are some periods of development more critical for proper development than others? Finally, can patterns of behavior that are established early be modified by later experience? How much plasticity is there in human development?

In order to answer these questions, psychologists have employed two closely related approaches, both of which involve a systematic tampering with the environmental rearing conditions of the organism. On the one hand, the effects of reductions in the normal level of sensory, perceptual, and social stimulation have been examined in order to isolate the necessary conditions for normal development. In contrast to this deprivation approach, another technique has been to provide the organism with "extra experience" in which the environment is enriched beyond the typical amount of sensory and perceptual stimulation typically found in the normal rearing environment.

To illustrate these two approaches to understanding the effects of early experience, a series of experimental and naturalistic studies employing a wide range of species will be presented. First, a series of experimental studies of the impact of environmental deprivation and enrichment on the development of the underlying physiological structures of the central nervous system will be examined. Second, the effects of social and sensory deprivation on the development of social and intellectual competence in monkeys will be discussed. Third, naturalistic studies of human deprivation found in orphanages and institutions will be presented. In all sets of studies the prime interest will be the modifiability of the effects of early environmental deprivation on later behavior. Finally, the importance of early opportunities for social interaction with other members of the species for normal social and intellectual development will be emphasized.

EARLY EXPERIENCE AND THE MODIFICATION OF THE CENTRAL NERVOUS SYSTEM'S EARLY DEVELOPMENT

The importance of the early environment for the proper development of the central nervous system was demonstrated many years ago. In fact, at the turn of the century A. J. Carlson (1902) demonstrated that the physiological structures of the visual system of birds could be altered by variations in stimulation. However, Carlson was much ahead of his time and his demonstration had little impact on psychological views of development. Rather, the maturationalists were to have their heyday before a similar kind of demonstration over forty years later would point the way to serious consideration of the effects of early experience. In 1947, Austin Reisen reported his classic experiments on the effects of reduced sensory stimulation on the development of the visual system of the chimpanzee. He found that the retinal structures of a chimp that had spent the first sixteen months of life in the dark failed to develop properly. Specifically, there was a loss of ganglion cells in the retina, those neurons whose axons form the optic nerve, which connects the retina with the rest of the nervous system. Moreover, even when the animals were returned to lighted conditions, their retinas failed to develop properly and they became permanently blind. Other studies (Reisen, 1950) have confirmed these original results. It is clear that even the anatomical structures of the central nervous system, the foundation blocks of maturation, require a certain amount of early environmental stimulation for proper development.

More recent research has indicated that the physiological effects of variations in early experience are not restricted to the peripheral aspects of the visual system but may actually modify the size of the brain itself. (Rosenzweig, 1966; Krech, Rosenzweig, & Bennett, 1962). In order to test the modifiability of the brain, these investigators, in Rosenzweig's words:

> . . . decided to set up two markedly different experimental situations, to put the rats in one or the other at an early age when their brains might be most plastic and to maintain the animals in these situations for a prolonged period. Animals were therefore assigned at weaning (about 25 days of age) and kept for 80 days in either an enriched environment—environmental complexity and training (ECT)—or in an impoverished condition (IC). . . . In the enriched situation the animals are housed in groups of 10 to 12 in a large cage that is provided with "toys" such as ladders, wheels, boxes, platforms, etc. . . . The toys are selected each day from a larger group. To enrich the rats further, we gave them a daily half-hour exploratory session in groups of 5 or 6 . . . in a 3 × 3 food field with a pattern of barriers that is changed daily. . . . After about 30 days some formal training is given in a series of mazes. In contrast the animals in the impoverished condition live in individual cages with solid side walls, so that an animal cannot see or touch another. These cages are placed in a separate, quiet, dimly lighted room, while the ECT (enriched) cages are in a large, brightly lighted room with considerable incidental activity [Rosenzweig, 1966, pp. 321–322].

What impact do these different rearing conditions have on brain weight and on brain chemistry? In the early stages of their research program, these investigators disregarded brain anatomy, since they, like most psychologists and physiologists, had accepted the dogma of absolute stability of brain weight. Records of brain weights were routinely recorded, however, and after two years it became apparent that their environmental manipulations *were* affecting the *actual weight of the animal's brain*—in spite of historical beliefs to the contrary. As Figure 5-1 indicates, separate analyses were performed for the cerebral cortex and the rest of the brain; this was fortunate, since not all areas, it turned out, were equally affected. The variations in early environment had their greatest impact on the cortex region, with the enriched animal's cortex weighing about 4 percent more than the cortex of his restricted littermates. Not only does the cerebral cortex differ from the rest of the brain in its response to the differential rearing experiences, but all regions of the cortex are not equally altered. The occipital region, for example, shows

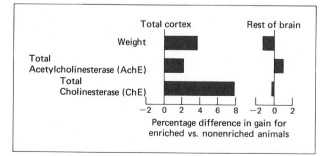

FIGURE 5-1 The effects of enriched rearing environment on brain chemistry and brain weight in rats. (Note that the enriched animals made the larger gains.) (From Rosenzweig, 1966, with permission of the author and the American Psychological Association.)

the largest changes in weight, 6 percent, whereas the somesthetic area showed only 2 percent increase in weight. Other experiments indicate that there may be systematic relationships between the nature of the enrichment program and the particular region of the cortex that is affected. Rearing rats in darkness results in a shrinkage of the visual cortex. There is some suggestion of parallel effects at the human level. Donaldson in 1892 (cited by Rosenzweig, 1966) carried out a postmortem examination of the brain of a human blind deaf-mute and found deficient development of the cortical areas controlling speech and visual and auditory functions. The skin senses region of the cortex, on the other hand, was apparently normally developed. Careful investigation may show that there is an anatomical as well as a behavioral basis for the overcompensation phenomenon wherein loss of one sense results in heightened sensitivity in the other sense organs.

What about the biochemical effects? To assess these effects the activity of two enzymes, acetylcholinesterase (AchE) and cholinesterase (ChE), was measured. These enzymes play an important role in synaptic transmission of nerve impulses between neurons. Specifically, they act on acetylcholine, the chemical transmitter that conveys messages from one neuron to the next. Examination of Figure 5-1 reveals that the total activity of both enzymes increases significantly as a result of the enriched rearing experience. As in the case of the weight changes, the cortex is again the area most responsive to the rearing conditions. The rats used in the original studies were young and for good reason: it was assumed that their brains would show their greatest plasticity prior to maturity. However, later studies showed that the weight and biochemical effects are *not* restricted to the immature brain. Rats exposed to the deprived or enriched experience after spending their early days under normal laboratory rearing conditions showed similar weight and biochemical effects. "The cortex of the adult brain is as capable of adaptive growth as is the cortex of the young animal [Rosenzweig, 1966, p. 327]."

A final question explored by the Rosenzweig group concerned the relationship between cerebral changes and learning ability. In other words, do bigger brains mean brighter rats? At this time, it is not clear. Some early evidence indicated that the two groups of rats differed in their learning abilities, at least on difficult discrimination tasks. They did not differ in their performance on simple tasks (Krech et al., 1962). Giving rats enrichment for twenty-four hours a day produced both bigger brains and smarter rats, while a two-hour-a-day enrichment produced the brain changes but not the improvements in learning. The extra twenty-two hours added to the animal's learning capacity, even if it didn't further alter the organism's brain weight. This finding suggests that while some changes in learning ability may be reflected as anatomical changes, such as brain weight, many may be more subtle than present techniques permit us to adequately measure. Brain changes and the changes in problem-solving capacities may simply run in parallel.

Moreover, it is not clear yet to what extent these findings are species specific. The main efforts to test for species generality have been to subject other species of rodents to differential environments. La Torre (1968) found weight and enzyme effects for mice, and more recently Rosenzweig and Bennett (1970) found similar effects for Mongolian gerbils. Although it can safely be concluded that these results are not restricted to rats, we are still a long way down the phylogenetic ladder from human beings. The implications for human development are still only suggestive.

EFFECTS OF EARLY EXPERIENCE ON SOCIAL, EMOTIONAL, AND INTELLECTUAL DEVELOPMENT

The effects of early experience are not limited to emerging motor behaviors. Variations in the early environment may exert profound effects on the individual's emotional, social, and possibly his intellectual development. The child's capacity for responding flexibly and adaptively to changing stimulus conditions, a necessity for proper development, may be impaired if his early experience is impoverished. A wide range of species have participated in these studies, including dogs, monkeys, fish, birds, and even humans. Although the details of the particular kinds of effects have varied considerably across species, the broad picture that emerges is clear: an animal reared in an environment that is low in sensory and perceptual stimulation and does not allow opportunities for interaction with other members of his species during some period of his early life will be socially, emotionally, and perhaps intellectually inadequate. To document this proposition two sets of studies will be examined in detail: Harlow's studies of the effects of sensory and social deprivation on the development of the rhesus monkey, and studies of children reared in impoverished institutional environments.

There are a number of reasons for examining the monkey data. In the first place, although cross-species generalization is always risky, the recent monkey research has implications for human development, since monkeys undergo "a relatively long period of development analogous to that of the human child [Harlow & Harlow, 1962, p. 138]." Second, because these are carefully controlled experimental studies, they permit quite refined statements about cause and effect relationships. By comparing these experimental findings with the nonexperimental data yielded by the studies of institutionalized children, firmer conclusions about the impact of variations in early experience on human development may be possible.

Effects of social and sensory isolation on monkeys

One of the most thorough and systematic attempts to investigate the effects of early environmental deprivation on later development has been the work of Harry Harlow and his colleagues at the University of Wisconsin. To study the impact of depriving young rhesus monkeys of sensory and social stimulation, Harlow has devised a number of experimental rearing procedures.

In some cases the animals were reared in total social isolation which the Harlows have described as follows:

> At birth the monkey is enclosed in a stainless steel chamber where light is diffused, temperature controlled, air flow regulated and environmental sounds filtered. Food and water are provided and the cage is cleaned by remote control. During its isolation the animal sees no living creature, not even a human hand [Harlow & Harlow, 1972, p. 276].

In another condition, partial isolation, animals are reared alone in wire cages; but in contrast to the totally isolated monkeys, they can see and hear other young monkeys. Although they do have some sensory and perceptual input and some social stimulation, no physical interaction with other monkeys is allowed.

These drastic modifications in the natural early environment of young monkeys are appreciated more fully in contrast to the rearing conditions of control of normal monkeys. The animals with the most "normal" backgrounds are, of course, feral monkeys who are born in the jungles of Southeast Asia and are brought to the laboratory for study at various ages. Close approximations of "normality" in the laboratory are achieved in two ways: the mother-peer rearing condition, in which animals are raised by a real mother in a large cage where the infants have daily access to age-mates in an adjacent play area; and the nuclear family environment (Harlow, 1971), in which the infants have continual access to their mothers, fathers, and siblings. Characterizing all three of these conditions is a healthy dose of sensory and perceptual stimulation and plenty of opportunity to interact with other monkeys.

In some cases, observations of the animal's behavior were made in his own cage, while more extensive tests of the social and emotional competence of the monkeys took place in a playroom, where two isolation-reared animals were paired with two other cage-reared monkeys. Trained observers recorded the "monkey business' from behind a one-way-vision screen; the frequency of behaviors such as exploration, play, and fear were systematically noted. Since duration of the deprivation experience may be important, animals were isolated for varying periods of time. Some were deprived for the first three months of life and others were sentenced to a six-months stay, while a third group spent a full year in isolation prior to being tested.

What are the effects of isolation on the development of young rhesus monkeys? First, let us examine the *partial isolates*, who were totally deprived of mothering, fathering, and the opportunities for physical interaction with their peers (Cross & Harlow, 1965). Compared to monkeys raised by real monkey mothers and permitted extensive peer play, these isolates showed a number of abnormal behavior patterns, such as self-biting and self-clasping, fear grimacing, rocking, huddling, and a variety of stereotyped movements. When presented with a fear stimulus (a black-gloved hand), the mother-peer-

The total withdrawal of an isolated monkey. (Wisconsin Primate Laboratory.)

raised monkeys responded appropriately—they directed their threats toward either the fear object or the experimenter. In contrast, the isolates engaged in episodes of self-biting and ignored the external fear elicitor. In summary, depriving the animal of opportunities for physical contact with other monkeys resulted in abnormal motor patterns, agitation and disturbance, and an inability to direct hostility toward appropriate targets.

To examine the effects of even further environmental deprivation, we turn to the *total isolation* studies. Confining the animal for only the first three months in this highly impoverished situation does not appear to produce serious or long-lasting effects. In fact, when tested in the playroom, they did not differ from wire cage-reared age-mates, the partial isolates. They experienced a post-isolation depression for a few weeks, but after recovery they showed no behavioral deficits (Griffin & Harlow, 1966). Total isolation, then, if it lasts for three months, is no more damaging than the partial isolation treatment. But if the confinement period is six months, the effects are more dramatic. As Figure 5-2 shows, these animals exhibited a much higher level of general emotional disturbance, a composite of fear, withdrawal, rocking, and huddling behaviors. Their social inadequacy was not permanent, and although they were never as socially competent as their control group partners, they did improve with age. To produce a full-fledged social incompetent, a full year of isolation was necessary. Unlike normal monkeys, these social misfits played and explored very little; were generally inactive, fearful, and withdrawn; and were frequently the victims of aggressive attacks by their test partners (see Figure 5-3). "Whereas 6-month isolates are social misfits, monkeys isolated for the first

Self-biting of an adult male monkey raised in isolation for the first six months of life. (Wisconsin Primate Laboratory.)

year of life seem to be little more than semi-animated vegetables [Suomi & Harlow, 1971, pp. 506-507]."

However, the length of deprivation is not the only important temporal variable; the timing of the *onset* of the deprivation experience is critical as well. To investigate this issue, another group of animals were reared in wire cages in an enclosed cage with a cloth surrogate mother for the first six months of life. The second half of the first year was spent in total isolation. Does the partial isolation experience of the first six months serve to reduce the impact of the total isolation experience? Not completely. These animals were both hyperactive and hyperaggressive in contrast to the withdrawn animals isolated for the *first* six months of life. However, these late isolates displayed higher levels of play and exploration than the monkeys in their comparison group, which suggests that these monkeys were still capable of engaging in some positive social behaviors. In spite of their abnormal behavior patterns, they were clearly superior to their peers who experienced a similar duration of deprivation but who experienced the isola-

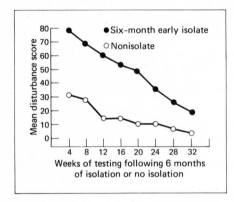

FIGURE 5-2 Amount of disturbed behavior (fear, withdrawal, rocking, and huddling) after isolation for the first six months for rhesus monkeys. (From Rowland, 1964.)

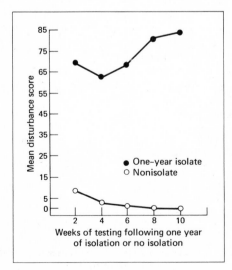

FIGURE 5-3 Amount of disturbed behavior (fear withdrawal, rocking, and huddling) after one year of isolation for rhesus monkeys. (From Rowland, 1964)

tion from birth. Both *duration* and *timing* are important determinants of the impact of early deprivation. As Sackett (1968) pointed out in a summary of these studies:

> there was a critical age for exposure to social stimulation at which later qualitative changes in the characteristics of social behavior can be produced. . . . This critical age seems to be between 3 to 6 months for quantitative deficits and 6 to 8 months for producing complete destruction of social ability [1968, p. 7].

Later effects of isolation

Do the social deficiencies of these isolated monkeys persist or are they merely transitory? To find out, Sackett (1967) tracked the social development of the early isolates and found clear evidence that as adolescents and adults these monkeys were still *social misfits.* At three and one-half and four and one-half years of age, the social behavior of totally or partially isolated animals was compared with animals reared with both mother and peer experience. Reactions displayed in the presence of a strange monkey constituted the test for social adequacy. As Table 5-1 shows, social initiative and motor activity were both depressed in the total isolates, whereas fearfulness was high, especially in the case of the animals isolated for a full year. Other research confirms this general picture of social inadequacy (Mitchell, Raymond, Ruppenthal, & Harlow, 1966). When tested in a playroom with a range of partners—age-mates, younger juveniles, and older adults—the total isolates were more fearful and less playful than mother-peer-raised monkeys. Their main social behavior was a high level of misdirected hostility; unlike normal animals, they aggressed against infant monkeys. "Or the isolates make a single, sacrificial, suicidal sortee against a large adult, an act never attempted by socially experienced adolescents [Harlow & Novak, 1973, p. 468]." The total isolates are sexual incompetents, even though they are endocrinologically adequate sexually by two or three years of age.

> Their gymnastic qualifications are only quaint and cursory as compared with sexual achievement customary at these ages. Isolates may grasp other monkeys of either sex by the head and throat aimlessly, a semierotic exercise without amorous achievements. . . . This exercise leaves the totally isolated monkey working at cross purposes with reality [Harlow & Novak, 1973, p. 468].

The above describes the six-month total isolate; twelve-month isolates did not even bother to engage in these misguided sexual overtures. These sexual failings may be a

Table 5-1 PERSISTENT EFFECTS OF EARLY SOCIAL DEPRIVATION

Measure	1-year isolate	6-month early isolate	Wire-cage partial isolate	Mother-peer condition
Contact initiation	3.1*	3.4	8.5	16.6
Motor activity	86	121	117	229
Aggression	6.8	4.2	5.6	10.2
Fear-withdrawal	97	25	34	12

*Number of seconds in a ten-minute social interaction test.
Source: Adapted from Sackett, G. P. Some persistent effects of differential rearing conditions on pre-adult social behavior of monkeys. *Journal of Comparative and Physiological Psychology,* 1967, **64,** 364.

virtue in disguise since those isolate females that have become pregnant (artificially or accidentally) are generally inadequate mothers that often reject or brutally mismanage their young offspring.

One interesting and provocative sidelight: males seem to be more devastated by isolation than females. Pratt (1967) found that male monkeys isolated for the first nine months of life showed more fear and disturbance and a lower incidence of nonsocial play and exploratory behavior than did their deprived female peers. Similar sex differences were found for partially isolated subjects that were raised in wire cages. Are the social behaviors characteristic of normal males more complex and demanding and thus susceptible to disruption by this early deprivation? It is an intriguing difference, but the basis for it is still unclear. In any case, these findings leave little doubt that early deprivation does exert a lasting impact on later social and emotional adjustment.

Early deprivation and intellectual development

The isolated animals are clearly socially inadequate, but are they intellectually deficient as well? It seemed likely that early deprivation would have a marked impact on the animal's learning abilities. In fact, a number of experiments with animals farther down the phylogenetic scale indicated that learning deficits often resulted from a deprived childhood. It was somewhat surprising, therefore, to find absolutely no evidence of retarded learning in the isolated monkeys. The total isolate did as well as the wire cage controls (Rowland, 1964; Griffin & Harlow, 1966). Part of the reason for the immunity of intellectual abilities to the typically debilitating impact of deprivation is revealed in a more recent study (Harlow, Harlow & Schiltz, 1968). In addition to confirming the original findings of no learning ability deficits, these investigators found clear-cut differences in the degree of emotionality displayed by the isolated and nonisolated subjects in the test situations used for assessing learning abilities. The totally isolated animals took much longer to adapt to the learning environment than did the partially isolated subjects. In other words, even total isolates possess the ability, but may fail to show it as a result of their heightened emotionality in the test situation. Adaptation to the test environment was an absolute necessity for isolated monkeys, because these monkeys avoid novel and complex stimuli and display competing emotional responses. By carefully familiarizing the isolated animal with the testing apparatus, a fair test of learning ability was possible; these monkeys revealed no intellectual arrest as a result of the deprivation.

The critical features of deprivation: sensory or social

It is, of course, impossible to decide which aspects of the deprivation experience were responsible for the social and emotional damage. Reductions in sensory and perceptual stimulation are accompanied by alterations in the social environment of the monkeys as well. However, other rearing conditions suggest that the loss of opportunities for physical interaction with peers is particularly critical. Harlow and Harlow (1962) report that animals who have been reared in the company of peers, even though they lack contact with a mother, exhibit normal social and emotional behavior. More recent research by Pratt (1967) further underscores the importance of ''social'' rather than merely sensory or perceptual deprivation for producing abnormal monkeys. This investigator tried to overcome the effects of isolation by providing extra visual stimulation, in the form of color slides of other monkeys, people, and nature scenes, to monkeys during the isolation confinement period. Compared to their nonstimulated controls, they were just as socially retarded. Stimulation per se apparently is not sufficient for normal monkey development, and as Box 5-1 indicates, for overcoming the effects of abnormal rearing. However, more recent studies from the Harlow laboratories reveal that a nuclear family rearing environment may produce even more socially sophisticated monkeys than rearing with mothers and peers (Ruppenthal, Harlow, Eisele, Harlow, & Suomi, 1974; Suomi, 1974).

BOX 5-1 THE REVERSIBILITY OF EARLY DEPRIVATION: THE MONKEY
THERAPISTS

Can the effects of total isolation be reversed? Suomi, Harlow, and McKinney (1972) have demonstrated that the devastating impact of six months of isolation can be overcome. Since most efforts to rehabilitate isolates by exposing them to normal age-mates have failed, these investigators tried a new approach. Normal animals overwhelm the socially inexperienced and incompetent isolate; therefore instead of normal age-mates, they paired the isolates with three-month-old animals. Unlike older animals, monkeys of this age would initiate social contact without displaying social aggression and would exhibit simple social responses which gradually became more sophisticated. Four male monkeys that had served six months in total isolation were the "patients"; after their isolation ordeal they showed little exploration or locomotive behavior but high levels of rocking, huddling, and self-clasping. Four three-month females that had been reared with peers and were socially normal served as "therapists." Individual therapy sessions involving one isolate and one therapist were held two hours a day, three days a week, while group therapy periods (two isolates and two therapists) were held on two other days each week. After six months of therapy, the isolates were virtually indistinguishable from the therapists in terms of their social behaviors (see Figure 5-4). After this six-month period,

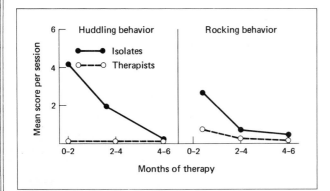

FIGURE 5-4 The effects of peer therapy on rhesus monkeys after isolation rearing. The figure shows the amount of huddling and rocking behavior during the therapy period. (From Suomi, Harlow, & McKinney, 1972, with permission of the authors and the American Psychiatric Association.)

the isolates and therapists were placed in a large group living pen. At two years of age, the isolates showed complete recovery—even sexual behavior was normal. More recently, Harlow and Novak (1973) have reported considerable success in treating twelve-month isolates by the use of four-month-old therapists.

These findings bring into question critical period notions that suggest the importance of particular time periods for adequate social development, and they clearly stress the modifiability of early established patterns by later experience.

Source: Suomi, S. J., Harlow, H. F., & McKinney, W. T. Monkey psychiatrists. *American Journal of Psychiatry*, 1972, **128,** 41–46.

INSTITUTIONALIZATION: STUDIES OF EARLY DEPRIVATION IN HUMANS

At the human level, the environment that most closely resembles the isolation rearing conditions of Harlow's rhesus monkeys is the old-fashioned orphanage or institution. In fact, institutional rearing environments are an unfortunate but naturally occurring deprivation which permits us to determine the impact of depriving the young child of a single caretaker and the effect of considerable reduction in sensory and perceptual stimulation as well. Here is the description of one institution studied in the 1940s by Goldfarb, one of the pioneering investigators of the effects of this kind of environment:

> The children had been reared in institutions outstanding for their standards of physical hygiene. To prevent epidemic infection babies below nine months of age were kept singly in separate cubicles. They had brief, hurried contacts with adults when they were cleaned and fed by the nurse. During the first year of life, therefore, each child lived in almost *complete isolation* [Goldfarb, 1955, p. 108]. [italics added].

Nor is this institution very different from other institutions studied in the 1930s and 1940s, as the following description by Spitz indicates:

> The infants lay in cots with bed sheets hung over the railings so that the child was effectively screened from the world. . . . Probably owing to the lack of stimulation, the babies lay supine in their cots for many months and a hollow is worn into their mattresses . . . this hollow confines their activity to such a degree that they are effectively prevented from turning in any direction [Spitz, 1945, p. 63].

Add to these descriptions the following characteristics: a typical caretaker-child ratio of 1:8, little individualized attention, propped bottles, few if any toys, and minimal opportunities for peer-peer interaction. The result is a fairly accurate picture of these child rearing environments.

Compared to the infant reared in a normal home environment, the institutionalized child is markedly deprived both in terms of the amount and variation of sensory stimulation and in terms of the degree of social attention. It is, of course, always hazardous to describe a "typical" institution, and fortunately most modern orphanages and other child-care centers do not conform to this dismal picture. However, institutions of the kind described did exist in the 1930s and 1940s and even in the 1950s, and it is the impact of these deprived rearing environments that is our concern. As a result of increased awareness of the debilitating effects of these situations that we are about to describe, few current institutions can be legitimately labeled *deprivation laboratories* in the same way that these older institutions could be.

The effects of institutionalization

What are the effects of this kind of impoverished early environment on the child's social, emotional, and intellectual development? (For detailed reviews, see Yarrow, 1961, 1964; Casler, 1961, 1967.) As in the case of the Harlow monkeys, social development is markedly affected, with the major disturbances centering around interpersonal relationships. Children tended to show two predominant patterns. On the one hand, some were socially indifferent, with little motivation or capacity to form meaningful social attachments with their caretakers or later with their peers. Social discrimination was also retarded; institutionalized infants often show similar reactions to both familiar caretakers and total strangers. In contrast to this picture of social apathy, some children show a second pattern characterized by an *affect hunger,* to borrow Spitz's term, which is characterized by a seemingly insatiable desire for individual social attention and affection. Nor are these personality and social abnormalities limited to the young child. Goldfarb (1943, 1949), for example, has reported that even as adolescents, many institutionalized children continue to show social deficiencies in the form of heightened aggression, impulsivity, and antisocial behavior. In contrast to the monkey studies, intellectual behavior is affected by institutionalization. Many studies have reported severe retardation with the severity of the IQ deficit typically increasing with the length of the institutional stay. Language development, in particular, is often markedly affected, and a number of researchers have reported evidence of deficiencies in abstract thinking and conceptual abilities as well. The one area that is least affected is motor development, although some studies do find evidence or retarded emergence of motor skills, such as walking (Dennis, 1960). More often investigators have noted extremes in activity level. These variations, either hyperactivity or marked passivity and withdrawal, present an interesting parallel in the motor sphere to the social apathy and heightened attention-seeking characterizing the social behavior of institutionalized children. In addition, bizarre motor patterns similar to Harlow's "rocking and huddling" monkeys have been reported. Table 5-2 provides a useful summary of the impact of institutional rearing on the infant's motor, social, and cognitive development. These observations are based on an extensive study of seventy-five institutionalized infants by Provence and Lipton (1962). Although this institution was not as physically impoverished as some of the earlier ones, it was similar in the lack of individualized social interaction between infants and caretakers.

This summary of the effects of institutionalization underlines emphatically the importance of the child's early environment for his later social and intellectual development. But are these effects reversible? Is it true, as some theorists have argued, that an early deprivation experience produces irreversible damage, or is it possible for children to recover from these early experiences?

In Box 5-2, we examine a study by Harold Skeels that attempted to answer this question. Mentally retarded women served as substitute mothers for a group of institutionalized infants, and their social and intellectual development markedly improved. It seems that stimulation from an interested responsive caretaker, even if that caretaker is mentally retarded, is preferable to a depriving institutional environment.

Table 5-2 EFFECTS OF INSTITUTIONAL REARING ON MOTOR, LANGUAGE, AND SOCIAL
DEVELOPMENT

Age, months	No retardation	Retardation	Unusual or deviant behavior
		Motor behavior	
0 ↑	Reflex responses	Kicking activity	Failure to adapt to holding
	Arm activation	Support of weight on lower extremities	
	Hand engagement Rolling: prone to supine		
		Head control: pull to sit	Rocking (excessive)
	Emergence of hand-to-mouth maneuver	Rolling: supine to prone	Disappearance of thumb sucking
	Maturation of grasping patterns	Foot play (hand-foot; foot-mouth)	Absence of self-touching
	Lifting legs high in extension (supine)	Sitting erect	Decreasing skill in coordination of movements
	Head control in prone	Changing position: sitting to prone and back; pivoting Reaching out to people, toys Creeping (mild retardation) Pulling to stand	Unusual motility patterns: hand waving, hand posturing, "athetoid" movements Inhibition of movement Poor modulation of movement (poor modulation of motor
12 ↓		Walking	impulse discharge)

Age, months	No retardation	Retardation	Unusual or deviant behavior
		Language behavior	
0 ↑ ↓ 12	Early ah, eh, uh sounds	Cooing	
	Emergence of vowel sounds	Spontaneous vocalization to toys, self, to adult	Quietness
	Emergence of consonants Changes in tonal range of voice (high pitch, low pitch, etc.)	Vocal social responses Chuckling and laughing	
		Use of voice to initiate social contact	
		Differentiation of vocal signs (pleasure, eagerness, recognition, displeasure, anxiety, etc.) Use of language for communication Specificity of mama, dada words Understanding verbalizations of others	Discrepancy between maturation and function
		Responses to people	
0 ↑	Visual attentiveness	See also Motor and Language Behavior	Intensity of visual regard of adult
	Responsive smile Spontaneous smile	Recognition of nurse Discrimination of face vs. mask	Failure to establish a personal attachment: tenuousness of emotional ties
		Reflection of facial mimic Anxiety to the stranger Participation in social games (peek-a-boo, pat-a-cake, etc.)	Failure to seek out the adult either for pleasure or when in distress
↓ 12		Initiation of social games Reaching out to adult to touch, caress, explore or act aggressively	

Table 5-2 EFFECTS OF INSTITUTIONAL REARING ON MOTOR, LANGUAGE, AND SOCIAL
DEVELOPMENT (*continued*)

Age, months	No retardation	Retardation	Unusual or deviant behavior
		Responses to toys (inanimate objects)	
0 ↑	Visual and acoustic attention Early grasping efforts		
		Memory for hidden toy	Decreasing interest in toys Rarity of spontaneous play with toys
		Investigatory behavior	Rarity of mouthing of toys and other objects
		Combining of toys Simultaneous attention to two or more toys Preference for one toy over another Recovering toy when obstacle is introduced	
12 ↓			Absence of transitional object

Source: Provence, S., & Lipton, R. C. Infants in institutions. New York: International Universities Press, 1962.

BOX 5-2 THE REVERSIBILITY OF EARLY EXPERIENCE DEFICITS: THE
SKEELS STUDY

In the late 1930s, Skeels set out to determine whether the debilitating impact of early institutionalization could be overcome by exposure to a more enriched environment. Two groups of children were involved in this investigation: Due to crowding, one group of children was transferred from the orphanage to a mental retardation institution; children in the comparison group remained in the orphanage.

The two environments were in marked contrast. The orphanage was a typical 1930s institution: few staff; little social attention; sheet-covered cribs, which limited opportunities for visual exploration; and few toys. The institution for the mentally retarded to which the "subjects" of this study were transferred could easily be described as "enriched" in comparison to the orphanage. It was not simply a more varied and stimulating environment, but one that provided abundant opportunities for social and emotional development as well.

In the case of almost every child, some one adult (older girl or attendant) became particularly attached to him and figuratively "adopted him." As a consequence, an intense one-to-one adult-child relationship developed which was supplemented by the less intense but frequent interactions with the other adults in the environment. Each child had some one person with whom he was identified and who was particularly interested in him and his achievements. This highly stimulating emotional impact was observed to be the unique characteristic and one of the main contributions of the experiment setting [Skeels, 1966, p. 17].

The thirteen children who were sent to this setting at an average age of nineteen months of age were considered mentally retarded, with an average IQ of 64.3. The twelve children in the control group who stayed in the orphanage were close to normal in terms of intelligence, with a mean IQ of 86.7. To assess the impact of living under these contrasting conditions, the children's intellectual status was reassessed about one and one-half years after the transfer had taken place. The experimental subjects showed a marked increase in mental growth, with the average gain being a dramatic 28.5 IQ points. These "mental retardates" now had an average IQ of 91.8. The losses of the children who stayed in the orphanage were just as spectacular: the average loss was 26.2 IQ points, resulting in a mean IQ of 60.5 for the control group. The two groups had reversed positions over the two-year period. Skeels was interested in determining whether the gains achieved by the experimental subjects would last. His first follow-up study was conducted two and one-half years after the termination of the initial study. Of the original group of thirteen children, eleven were adopted while two remained institutionalized until adulthood. The adopted children maintained their intellectual status: the mean IQ for these children was 101.4, but the reinstitutionalized children dropped in IQ. The unfortunates in the control group, of course, remained wards of the state and in spite of slight gains were still classified as mentally retarded; the mean IQ for this group was 66.1. However impressive these results appear to be, some skeptics will argue that the effects of early deprivation may be reflected in maladjustments in adulthood. To more convincingly illustrate the reversibility of the effects of early environmental deprivation, Skeels (1966) assessed the adult status of the two groups and found no evidence of any late-emerging defects in the experimental subjects. Twenty-one years elapsed between the first follow-up study and this final assessment; by this time the "children" were between twenty-five and thirty-five years of age. Did the groups maintain their divergent patterns of competence into adulthood? Clearly they did. All of the subjects in the experimental group were self-supporting, including the nonadopted children. Of the twelve children in the control group, one died in adolescence after continued institutionalization, while another four children were still under state care. The educational and occupational achievements of the two groups were markedly different as well; for example, half of the experimental group completed the twelfth grade; in contrast half of the control subjects had not completed the third grade. In fact, in terms of education, occupation, and income, the eleven adopted children were indiscriminable from the rest of the "normal" population, as assessed by the 1960 United States census figures. According to Skeels, "Their adult status was equivalent to what might have been expected of children living with natural parents in homes of comparable sociocultural levels [Skeels, 1966, p. 55]." Although no IQ data were available, it seems safe to conclude that the eleven adopted children were functioning as normal adults. Also, children of the experimental subjects were in no way retarded. Of their twenty-eight offspring, the mean IQ was 104 and school progress was normal.

Finally, a political-economic footnote is in order. Many times intervention programs are not initiated because of the presumed cost to the taxpayer. However, in the case of the subjects in the Skeels' study, nonintervention meant that the subjects in the control group cost the state five times as much as the experimental group. Clearly nonintervention in this case had little economic justification.

The implication of this study is clear: the deleterious effects of early environmental restriction can be effectively reversed. Similarly, these findings suggest that continued deprivation has obviously harmful effects. In general, prediction of the adult's status is affected by all periods of development up to that point, not just by the first one and one-half years. Long-range relationships between early periods of life and later age points in childhood, adolescence, or adulthood can *only* be understood by a close examination of the intervening environmental factors that are present at any developmental period. In short, it is not just "early" experience but experience at all age points that needs to be continuously considered in attempting to understand the child's development.

Source: Skeels, H. Adult status of children with contrasting early life experiences. *Monographs of the Society for Research in Child Development,* 1966, **31,** No. 3.

Alternate explanations of institutionalization effects

Although these studies of institutionalization have been severely criticized on methodological grounds, there is general agreement that this kind of early environment does have devastating emotional, social, and intellectual effects on the developing child. The issue is no longer *what* happens, but *why* it happens. In this section we shall examine alternative explanations for the effects of institutionalization.

The perceptual-deprivation position Some investigators have argued that it is the lack or deficit of perceptual and sensory stimulation that is responsible for the low level of intellectual and social functioning of the institutionalized child. This approach is, of course, consistent with the theme that has been developed in this chapter: sensory stimulation is necessary for proper development. The chief spokesman for this viewpoint is Lawrence Casler (1961, 1967) who specifically suggests that "the physical, intellectual and emotional defects often observed in individuals deprived of 'mothering' during early infancy can best be explained in terms of perceptual deprivation [1961, p. 42]."

The perceptual-deprivation position is a compelling one, and it has the attraction of pointing the way to readily specifiable stimulus dimensions that are amenable to experimental manipulation, such as the amount, kind, and schedule of tactual, visual, auditory, and kinesthetic input typically received by the institutionalized child. In addition to being a useful framework for conceptualizing the institutional environment, it has prompted research concerning the effects of additional perceptual stimulation on the development of the institutionalized child. To evaluate the adequacy of the perceptual-deprivation hypothesis, we turn to a sample of these studies.

Casler (1965) systematically provided a group of institutionalized infants with extra tactile stimulation to determine if this additional sensory imput would arrest the decline of the intellectual and social development typically observed in these infants. The experimental subjects were significantly superior to the nonstimulated babies although both groups showed a general decline in their social and cognitive development. Although important, Casler's data suggest that tactile stimulation alone is not sufficient to ensure proper social and intellectual development.

Further support for the importance of stimulation comes from studies of individual differences in reaction to environmental deprivation. As noted earlier in this chapter, there are clear constitutionally based individual differences among children in activity level. Would hyperactive and quiet, passive infants be affected by the reduced stimulation associated with institutionalization to the same degree? Probably not. A highly active infant is likely to shift position more, thus providing himself with more proprioceptive and kinesthetic stimulation than his less active peer. The postural changes are likely to increase the infant's chances of encountering new sights and sounds as well. Finally, heightened activity level has been found to be associated with greater alertness to the external environment. So the highly active baby is not only more likely to have greater opportunities for visual and auditory stimulation, but is also more likely to notice changes in his external environment. The prediction is clear: The self-stimulating infant would be less adversely affected by the reduction in environmental input than less active infants. Schaffer (1966) has presented evidence that is consistent with this expectation. The developmental quotients of highly active infants were significantly less altered by a short-term institutional stay than were the scores of less active subjects. Further support for this position comes from White's study (Box 5-3) which suggests that the development of visually directed reaching can be enhanced by extra sensory and perceptual stimulation.

BOX 5-3 EXPERIMENTAL MODIFICATION OF VISUALLY DIRECTED REACHING

Evidence of the plasticity of the human organism comes from a series of experimental studies of the modification of visual-motor behavior. During the first half year of life, normal infants in average environments proceed through a rather remarkable set of landmarks that culminate in visually directed reaching for objects at about five and one-half months of age. Before this time, the hand and eye are simply not well coordinated. At first, the infant may attend to an object placed in his visual field, but only in the second month can any swiping action be seen. Gradually the young infant learns to use his eye and hand together, so that he not only swings at the target but eventually can accurately and consistently contact the object with his hand. Burton White and his colleagues (White, Castle, & Held, 1964; White & Held, 1966; White, 1967) have shown, however, that the speed of development of visual-motor coordination can be rather drastically altered by enriching the visual world of infants whose environments were deficient in opportunities and rewards for visually directed reaching. The subjects were institutionalized infants, whose visual-motor development generally lags behind the pace of normal home-reared infants due to the rather monotonous visual environment of the institution. In order to enrich the infants' surroundings, these investigators suspended a colorful stabile over the cribs, substituted printed multicolored sheets for the standard white ones, and adorned the side of the baby beds with brightly colored bumpers. (See Figure 5-5.) In addition, the infants were given extra handling by their caretakers and placed in a prone position for a short time each day to further enrich their visual input. These "treated" infants exhibited visually guided reaching by ninety-eight days, an advance of forty-five days over the control babies, who were given only routine institutional care. In another related experiment, visually enriched subjects reached this developmental milestone even earlier, at day 89. Stating these findings somewhat differently, the experimental infants developed visually directed reaching in approximately 60% of the time required by the control group children.

However, it is not clear how much advance can be achieved for normal, home-reared infants by this type of environmental supplement. These kinds of infants already receive a great deal of handling and visual stimulation, and the boundaries of plasticity for children reared in normal environments is not yet determined. However, the White study leaves little question that severely deprived environments can have delaying effects which, in turn, can be overcome by extra sensory and perceptual stimulation.

However, the White data illustrate another point in addition to clearly demonstrating the plasticity of visual-motor development. Timing of the enrichment experiment is important

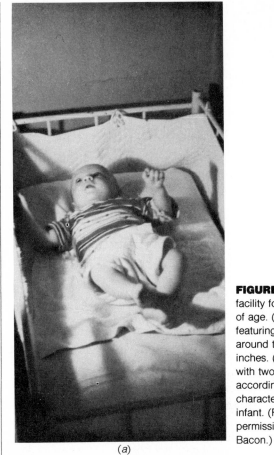

(*a*)

FIGURE 5-5 (*a*) The typical nursery ward facility for control infants one to four months of age. (*b*) Massive enrichment condition featuring many brightly colored objects around the infant at distances of 5 to 36 inches. (*c*) Modified enrichment condition with two highlighted pacifiers placed according to postural and visual characteristics of the four- to eight-week-old infant. (From White & Held, 1966, with permission of the authors and Allyn and Bacon.)

as the early studies of the effects of practice on the emergence of maturational skills clearly indicated (for example, Gesell & Thompson, 1929; Hilgard, 1932). White's infants who were given a massive dose of visual stimulation tended to show less rather than more looking behavior during the first five weeks of the procedure. Once the infants began to engage in prehensory contacts with the stabile over their beds and the figured bumpers along the sides of their cribs, visual attention increased sharply. However, in the initial period they not only ignored the novel objects but showed much more crying than did the control subjects. Enrichment, then, came too early and in too large a dose to be maximally effective. Probably the most effective enrichment provides a proper match of impact to internally developing structures. Maturation, then, clearly limits the effect of externally imposed stimulation; the problem of producing maximal acceleration involves providing the child with new experiences that are paced just ahead of his emerging capacities, but not so far ahead of him that with effort he cannot incorporate these inputs into his emerging response repertoire. We will discuss this issue again in our consideration of Piaget's theory of cognitive development.

Source: White, B. L., & Held, R. Plasticity of sensorimotor development in the human infant. In J. Rosenblith & W. Allinsmith (Eds.), *The cause of behavior: readings in child development and educational psychology.* Boston: Allyn and Bacon, 1966, pp. 60–70.

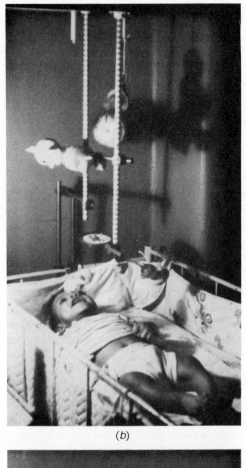

(b)

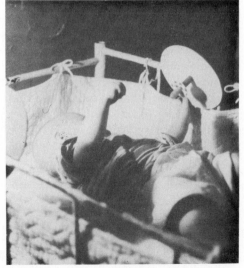

(c)

While the evidence points clearly to the importance of sensory and perceptual stimulation for adequate development, is Casler correct in his suggestion that "perhaps any source—an impersonal caretaker, or even a machine would be satisfactory, so long as the dosage of stimulation were approximately correct [Casler, 1965, p. 141]"? Or, are more than simple doses of stimulation necessary for proper social and intellectual development?

Some of the monkey data is worthwhile reexamining in this regard. We have already seen that monkeys reared in cages that permitted a good deal of auditory, visual, and olfactory stimulation, but no opportunities for physical interaction with other animals, were still impaired in their later social development. Similarly, Pratt's (1967) attempt to overcome the effects of isolation by providing extra visual stimulation to isolated monkeys in the form of color slides was essentially a failure. In spite of extra perceptual variation, they were still socially inept. Stimulation, at least of the kind and dosage provided, was not sufficient to ensure the proper development of these animals raised without mothers; however, those provided with an opportunity to interact with age-mates did develop adequate social behavior repertoires.

The importance of a responsive social environment   These data suggest that we need to reformulate the issue and ask not whether stimulation per se is important, but in what forms, in what amounts, and in what ways and by whom should stimulation be provided to ensure adequate development. More specifically, the monkey research points to the necessity of sustained interaction with other members of the species as a necessary condition for adequate social development. Are there any human data to support this viewpoint?

A reexamination of the contrasting environments of the Skeels study that we discussed earlier provides an important clue. Although it is impossible to isolate with precision the critical variables distinguishing the two rearing conditions, Skeel's own analysis pointed to the "intense one-to-one adult-child relationship which was supplemented by . . . frequent interactions with other adults in the environment" as "the unique characteristic and one of the main contributions of the experimental setting [Skeels, 1966, p. 17]."

However, the original institution was an extremely deprived environment, and the intervention increased the quantity as well as the quality of the stimulation. Recently, a more adequate test of the impact of opportunities for sustained social interaction of the development of institutionalized children has been executed. As the report of this study in Box 5-4 clearly demonstrates, it is the quality of stimulation, not merely the quantity, that is important for proper intellectual development. Moreover, as Rheingold (1956) has shown, personalized contact clearly increases social responsiveness as well.

BOX 5-4 THE EFFECTS OF PART-TIME MOTHERING ON
INSTITUTIONALIZED CHILDREN

The aim of this study was to determine the impact of extra individualized attention on the development of institutionalized children. Two institutions which were similar in staff, organization, and degree of physical and intellectual stimulation were studied. The children ranged in age from sixteen months to six years. In contrast to the 1940s institutions, these were "model" institutions. The two institutions differed in one respect: A foster-grandparent program was introduced in one of the institutions. Foster grandparents were impoverished elderly persons who were employed part time to provide personal relationships for the children. The typical routine was as follows:

Foster-grandparents worked 5 days a week, 4 hours per day. Each was assigned two children as his "own." Their specific activities naturally varied according to the age of the children. For example, in the nursery, the foster-grandparents rocked, fed, walked, talked to, and played with "their" babies. For an older child, in any one day a foster-grandparent might read stories or play a special game, take the child for a walk on the grounds (including visits to other cottage units where the child might have a sibling), encourage him to practice skills, talk with him and listen to his complaints or tales of accomplishments, or simply sit on the side-lines and watch him play, being available as required to tie his shoe-lace or offer comfort after a bump. Generally, regardless of the specific activity, there was a pronounced affective quality to the interactions between each foster-grandparent and his or her "own" children [Saltz, 1973, p. 167].

Does this personalized care make any difference to the child's intellectual development? Yes; the children in the foster-grandparent program scored significantly higher on a standard IQ test than did children in a similar institution without the extra personal interaction. Moreover, the effects were most marked after a long period of institutionalization (35 months), which suggests that the foster-grandparent program aided in maintaining an average rate of intellectual development. What aspects of the program were responsible for the effects? It is unlikely that the effects were simply due to an increase in the quantity of stimulation, since both institutions offered the children extensive physical and sensory stimulation. Rather "the primary contribution of the foster-grandparents was to improve the quality of stimulation [Saltz, 1973, p. 169]." This type of program benefited not only the infants and children; the opportunity to perform a useful function enhanced the self-esteem and self-worth of the foster grandparents as well.

Source: Saltz, R. Aging persons as child-care workers in a foster-grandparent program: psychosocial effects and work performance. *Aging and Human Development*, 1971, **3,** 314–340; and Saltz, R. Effects of part time "mothering" on IQ and SQ of young institutionalized children. *Child Development,* 1973, **9,** 166–170.

It is clear that the old-time institutions did not provide these opportunities. Under the typical orphanage regime the child had less frequent contact with his caretakers; responsiblity for the child's care was distributed among a large group of individuals; and most importantly, the child was treated in a highly mechanical and routinized fashion. It is simply easier and less time-consuming to care for the child according to a fixed schedule. Demands on the caretaking staff allowed little opportunity to adjust routines to accommodate the idiosyncracies and special demands of individual children. They were picked up when it was feeding time, and were changed when it was diaper-changing time; but their bids for attention at other times generally passed unnoticed. The child was assigned a passive role in the infant-caretaker interaction schedule. This analysis of the caretaking routines of an orphanage suggests that the amount of stimulation per se is not the only dimension along which an institutional environment may differ from the home situation. Rather the schedule and tempo of the caretaker-infant interaction differs as well. Specifically, in this impoverished situation, input is less likely to be contingent on (that is, closely follow) the infant's behavior; rather it is more likely to be on a schedule that is to a large degree independent of the behavior of the child.

Effects of a nonresponsive environment What are the implications of growing up in an environment that allows the infant so little opportunity to shape and alter his environmental inputs and provides him with little direct encouragement in the form of consistent and contingent feedback for his emerging social and language skills such as smiling, crying, and vocalizing? There are at least two important implications. First, some degree of contingent feedback from the environment attendant upon the performance of certain social responses may be necessary for the adequate development of these responses. An environment that is responsive to emerging behaviors and skills is necessary for adequate development.

Learning to control the environment There is a second and possibly more important limitation of the kinds of caretaking regimes found in these orphanages and institutions. There are a few opportunities for the kind of social interaction in which a child gains experience in successfully modifying the behavior of other individuals. In fact, this type of experience may be necessary for the development of a generalized expectancy or belief in his own ability to control his social environment (Lewis & Goldberg, 1969). Moreover, this lesson is probably learned independently of the acquisition of specific social behaviors of the kind discussed above. The institutionalized environment, however, promotes the development of a precisely opposite expectation, namely, that little if anything that one does will make any difference in what happens to one. The world proceeds on schedule, regardless of individual needs and demands. In light of this, it is not at all surprising that such descriptive adjectives as apathetic, passive, and withdrawn are frequently applied to institutionalized infants. In an environment one is helpless to alter, one simply gives up and stops trying to have any effects on others. It is interesting to note that this pattern of passive withdrawal is not seen initially in infants who have had six months or more home-rearing experience prior to being institutionalized. (As we will see in a later chapter, the first half year of life is a particularly important period for the infant to learn the lesson that he can control his caretaker's behavior.) Rather than being passive, these infants often vigorously attempt to elicit responses from their institution handlers, as they were able to do in the more personalized home environment. Of course, these early attempts to elicit the attention of their new caretakers typically fail, and a new and familiar phase in the life of the institutionalized child ensues—passivity and withdrawal. The child learns that it is useless to try, so he simply does not try any longer. In the language of the learning theorist (and the next chapter) the child's efforts are extinguished.

Helplessness in children Some recent experimental work by Watson and Ramey (1969, 1972) illustrated how "helplessness" can develop. To compare the effects of exposure to visual stimulation that was either contingent on the infant's behavior or independent of his activities, these investigators designed a special remotely controlled "mobile." In one case, by means of a pressure-sensitive pillow, the mobile made a one-second turn each time the infant moved his head. In this condition, the infant had control; the movement of the mobile was contingent on the infant's behavior. During the fourteen days of exposure, the infants in the other two groups were powerless to control the activity of their mobiles. In one case, during the ten-minute daily exposure period, the mobile remained stationary. In the other condition, the mobile periodically turned by itself. The movement was independent of the infant's behavior in the same way that environmental changes are often on a noncontingent basis in an institutional environment. Of central interest is the impact of experiencing this dose of noncontingent input on later behavior. Specifically, what will happen when the infants have the opportunity to control external events at some later time? Will they remain passive as a result of their earlier failure to exercise control over their environment? To find out, Watson and Ramey exposed the infants to the mobiles again, but on this occasion all the infants could control the movement of their mobiles. Both the infants who had viewed the noncontingently turning mobile were unsuccessful in controlling their mobiles. Even after six weeks without further exposure to the mobiles, the results were the same: the infants who had experienced the uncontrollable mobile failed to exercise control even when they had the opportunity to do so. Like the institutionalized child, these infants apparently learned that they were unable to control their environment and so gave up trying to exercise any control.

A similar phenomenon has been demonstrated by Maier, Seligman, and Solomon (1970), using aversive noncontingent stimulation. In these investigations dogs were exposed to a series of inescapable and painful electric shocks. Regardless of the animal's behavior, he was always shocked. Following this initial session, where the animal had been restrained by a harness, the animal was placed in a different situation where it was possible to escape the painful shock by jumping over a barrier to the other side of the test chamber. Dogs typically learn to escape from the shock in this type of situation very rapidly. However, when this test was preceded by the session of unavoidable shock, 67 percent of the animals failed to learn to escape from the punishment. What makes this finding impressive is that, unlike the Watson and Ramey study where the original exposure and test contexts were similar, the training and test situations were very different. The dogs had *generalized* their experience concerning the futility of escape from the training situation to the very different environment of the test situation. To use Solomon's term, the animals learned a generalized "helplessness."

This research nicely illustrates how the kind of apathy observed in institutionalized children may develop. Finally, before closing this section, it is worthwhile examining Russian institutions which indicate quite clearly that "competent" infants can develop in an institutional setting if attention is paid to social and cognitive as well as physical development (see Box 5-5).

BOX 5-5 A MODEL INSTITUTION

Not all institutions are as unstimulating and devastating to the child's development as the institutions that we have described. In fact, some of the Russian institutions for infants and preschoolers are highly effective environments for childrearing. Bronfenbrenner, in an exerpt from his *Two Worlds of Childhood: US and USSR*, describes these settings:

From the very beginning, considerable emphasis is given to the development of self-reli-

ance, so that by 18 months of age the children are expected to have completed bowel and bladder training and are already learning more complex skills such as dressing themselves. Physical activity outdoors is encouraged and it is usually followed by rest, with the windows wide open and the smallest children swaddled in thick quilts.

During the first year of life, especial attention is focused on language training. The following passage from the official manual on the pre-school programme provides an accurate summary of our own observations:

The upbringer exploits every moment spent with the child for the development of speech. In order that the infant learns to discriminate and understand specific words, the upbringer speaks to him in short phrases, emphasizes by her intonation the main words in a given sentence, pauses after speaking to the child, and waits for him to do what was asked. It is important that the words coincide with the moment when the child engages in the action, looks at the object which the adult has named, or is watching a movement or activity being performed by the adult. The speech of the upbringer should be emotional and expressive, and should reflect her loving, tender relation to the child.

In activities with children of this age, the upbringer develops the understanding of speech and enriches the children's impressions. Toward this end she carries the baby to different objects and shows him large colorful sound-making and wind-up toys; with children eight to nine months of age, she encourages them to pick out from a collection of many toys the one which she names; in order to acquaint the child with names of adults and other children, she conducts games of hide and seek.

In order that the child can learn the words associated with certain actions (''Clap your hands,'' ''Goodbye,'' ''Give me your hand,'' ''So-o big,'' and so on), she teaches these actions, accompanying them with the appropriate words. The upbringer encourages the child to duplicate sounds which he already knows how to pronounce, as well as new ones, and structures his babbling and imitation of simple syllables.

The development of speech becomes the vehicle for developing social behaviour. Thus, in speaking of the nine to twelve months age level, the manual states:

It is important to cultivate in the baby a positive attitude toward adults and children. At this age the child's need to relate to the adults around him increases. Interest develops in what others are doing. Sometimes children of this age play together: they throw balls into the same basket, roll downhill one after the other, smile at each other, call to one another. If the upbringer is not sufficiently attentive to the children, negative relations may arise among them; for example, the result of the attempt by one child to take a toy held by another. From the very beginning, stress is placed on teaching children to share and to engage in joint activity. Frequent reference is made to common ownership: ''Moe eto nashe; nashe moe'' (mine is ours, ours is mine). Collective play is emphasized. Not only group games, but special complex toys are designed which require the cooperation of two or three children to make them work. Music becomes an exercise in social as well as sensory-motor articulation. As soon as children are able to express themselves, they are given training in evaluation and criticizing each other's behavior from the point of view of the group. Gradually, the adult begins to withdraw from the role of leader or coordinator in order to forge a ''self-reliant collective,'' in which the children cooperate and discipline themselves—at meal times and in play activities, too.

Play itself often takes the form of role playing in real-life social situations, which gradually increase in complexity (taking care of baby, shopping, in the doctor's office, at school). Beginning in the second year of nursery and continuing through kindergarten children are expected to take on ever-increasing communal responsibilities, such as helping others, serving at table, cleaning up, gardening, caring for animals, and shoveling snow. The effects

> *of these socializing experiences are reflected in the youngsters behaviour, with many chil-*
> *dren giving an impression of self-confidence, competence and camaraderie.*
>
> Source: Bronfenbrenner, U. *Two Worlds of Childhood: U.S. & U.S.S.R.* New York: Russell Sage
> Foundation, 1971, pp. 17-23.

In summary, early experience is important, but the detrimental impact of drastic modifications in the child's early rearing environment can be altered. Of particular importance for the proper development of behavior—motoric, social, and intellectual—is not only sensory and perceptual stimulation, but a responsive environment that permits the acquisition of a critical belief, the belief that he can modify his social and nonsocial world.

SUMMARY

The impact of early experience on the later development was the focus of this chapter. Two approaches to understanding this problem were employed: a deprivation approach involving modification of the normal environment by a reduction in sensory, perceptual, and social stimulation; and an enrichment approach involving an increase in the level of normal stimulation.

First, a series of experimental studies of the modifiability of the central nervous system by rearing rats in an enriched environment were discussed. Significant increases in the size and weight of the cortex were obtained as a result of being reared in an enriched situation.

Next, investigations of the effects of severe sensory, perceptual, and social deprivation on the social and intellectual development of monkeys were presented. A number of factors, such as the length, the completeness, and the timing of the deprivation experience, were important determinants of both the short-range and long-range effects of deprivation. Total isolation involving reduced sensory and perceptual stimulation as well as no contact with other animals was more debilitating than partial isolation wherein the monkey could see and hear but not physically interact with other monkeys. The impairment in social behavior increased as the length of the deprivation increased, with one year of total isolation producing a total social misfit. Deprivation immediately after birth was more damaging than deprivation after a period of social experience. Intellectual capacity was not affected by the deprivation experiences if the monkeys were adapted to the testing environment before intellectual assessments began. Finally, the impact of early deprivation is reversible. A technique involving the use of younger age-mates as therapists was found to be particularly effective.

Institutionalization in which there was a reduction in sensory and perceptual stimulation as well as limited opportunities for social interaction had a debilitating effect on the child's social, intellectual, and motor development. However, as in the case of the monkeys, these effects of early deprivation are reversible. Evidence was presented which indicated that perceptual and sensory stimulation was important, but the critical factor for adequate development was a responsive social environment. Institutional effects often occur because of the development of a state of helplessness in the infants and young children.

REFERENCES

Bronfenbrenner, U. *Two Worlds of Childhood: U.S. and U.S.S.R.* New York: Russell Sage Foundation, 1970.

Carlson, A. J. Changes in Nissl's substance of the ganglion and the bipolar cells of the retina of the brandt cormorant phalacrocorax pencillatus during prolonged normal stimulation. *American Journal of Anatomy,* 1902/3, **2,** 341–347.

Casler, L. Maternal deprivation: a critical review of the literature. *Monographs of the Society for Research in Child Development,* 1961, **26,** No. 2.

Casler, L. The effects of extra tactile stimulation on a group of institutionalized infants. *Genetic Psychology Monographs,* 1965, **71,** 137–175.

Casler, L. Perceptual deprivation in institutional settings. In G. Newton & S. Levine (Eds.), *Early experience and behavior.* New York: Springer, 1967.

Cross, H. A., & Harlow, H. F. Prolonged and progressive effects of partial isolation on the behavior macaque monkeys. *Journal of Experimental Research in Personality,* 1965, **1,** 39–49.

Dennis, W. Causes of retardation among institutional children: Iran. *Journal of Genetic Psychology,* 1960, **96,** 47–59.

Gessell, A., & Thompson, H. Learning and growth in identical twin infants. *Genetic Psychology Monographs,* 1929, **6,** 1–124.

Goldfarb, W. Effects of early institutional care on adolescent personality. *Child Development,* 1943, **14,** 213–223.

Goldfarb, W. Rorschach test differences between family reared, institution-reared, and schizophrenic children. *American Journal of Orthopsychiatry,* 1949, **19,** 625–633.

Goldfarb, W. Emotional and intellectual consequences of psychological deprivation in infancy: a revaluation. In P. H. Hoch and J. Zubin (Eds.), *Psychopathology of childhood.* New York: Grune & Stratton, 1955.

Griffin, G. A., & Harlow, H. F. Effects of three months of total social deprivation on social adjustment and learning in the rhesus monkey. *Child Development,* 1966, **37,** 533–547.

Harlow, M. K. Nuclear family apparatus. *Behavioral Research Method and Instrumentation,* 1971, , 301–304.

Harlow, H. F., & Harlow, M. K. Social deprivation in monkeys. *Scientific American,* 1962, **207,** 137–146.

Harlow, H. F., & Harlow, M. K. The young monkeys. *Readings in psychology today.* Delmar Publishers, CRM Books, 1972.

Harlow, H. F., & Novak, M. A. Psychopathological perspectives. *Perspectives in Biology and Medicine,* 1973, **16,** 461–478.

Harlow, H. F., & Schiltz, K. A., & Harlow, M. K. Effects on social isolation on the learning performance of rhesus monkeys. *Proceedings of the Second International Congress of Primatology,* 1970.

Hebb, D. O. *The organization of behavior.* New York: Wiley, 1949.

Hilgard, J. R. Learning and maturation in preschool children. *Journal of Genetic Psychology,* 1932, **41,** 36–56.

Krech, D., Rosenzweig, M., & Bennett, E. L. Relations between brain chemistry and problem-solving among rats raised in enriched and impoverished environments. *Journal of Comparative and Physiological Psychology,* 1962, **55,** 801–807.

La Torre, J. C. Effect of differential environment enrichment on brain weight and on acetylcholinesterase and cholinesterase activities in mice. *Experimental Neurology,* 1968, **22,** 493–503.

Lewis, M. Infant attention: response decrement as a measure of cognitive processes, or what's new, Baby Jane? Paper presented at the meeting of the Society for Research in Child Development, New York, March, 1967.

Lewis, M., & Goldberg, S. Perceptual-cognitive development in infancy: A generalized expectancy model as a function of mother-infant interaction. *Merrill-Palmer Quarterly,* 1969, **15,** 81–100.

Maier, S., Seligman, M. E., & Solomon, R. L. Fear conditioning and learned helplessness. In R. Church & B. Campbell (Eds.), *Punishment and aversive behavior.* New York: Appleton-Century-Crofts, 1970.

Mitchell, G. D., Raymond, E.J., Ruppenthal, G. C., & Harlow, H. F. Long-term effects of total social isolation upon behavior of rhesus monkeys. *Psychological Reports,* 1966, **18,** 567–580.

Pratt, C. L. Social behavior of rhesus monkeys reared with varying degrees of early peer experience. Unpublished M. A. thesis, University of Wisconsin, 1967.

Provence, S., & Lipton, R.C. *Infants in institutions.* New York: International Universities Press, 1962.

Reisen, A. H. Arrested vision. *Scientific American,* 1950, **183,** 16-19.

Rheingold, H. L. The modification of social responsiveness in institutional babies. *Monographs of the Society for Research in Child Development,* 1956, **21,** No. 63.

Rosenzweig, M. R. Environmental complexity, cerebral change and behavior. *American Psychologist,* 1966, **21,** 321-332.

Rosenzweig, M. R., & Bennett, E. L. Effects of differential environments on brain weights and enzyme activities in gerbils, rats and mice. *Developmental Psychobiology,* 1970, **2,** 87-95.

Rowland, G. L. The effects of total social isolation upon learning and social behavior in rhesus monkeys. Unpublished doctoral dissertation, University of Wisconsin, 1964.

Ruppenthal, G. C., Harlow, M. K., Eisele, C. D., Harlow, H. F., & Suomi, S. J. Development of peer interactions of monkeys reared in a nuclear family environment. *Child Development,* 1974, **45,** 670-682.

Sackett, G. P. Some persistent effects of differential rearing conditions on pre-adult social behavior of monkeys. *Journal of Comparative and Physiological Psychology,* 1967, **64,** 363-365.

Sackett, G. P. The persistence of abnormal behavior in monkeys following isolation rearing. In R. Porter (Ed.), *The role of learning in psychotherapy.* London: J & A Churchill, Ltd., 1968.

Saltz, R. Aging persons as child-care workers in a foster-grandparent program: psychosocial effects and work performance. *Aging and Human Development,* 1971, **3,** 314-340.

Saltz, R. Effects of part time "mothering" on IQ and SQ of young institutionalized children. *Child Development,* 1973, **9,** 166-170.

Schaffer, H. R. Acitivity level as a constitutional determinant of infantile reaction to deprivation. *Child Development,* 1966, **37,** 595-602.

Skeels, H. Adult status of children with contrasting early life experiences. *Monographs of the Society for Research in Child Development,* 1966, **31,** No. 3.

Spitz, R. A. Hospitalism: an inquiry into the genesis of psychiatric conditions in early childhood. *Psychoanalytic Study of the Child,* 1945, **1,** 53-74.

Suomi, S. J. Social interactions of monkeys reared in a nuclear family environment versus monkeys reared with mothers and peers. *Primates,* 1974, in press.

Suomi, S. J., & Harlow H. S. Abnormal social behavior in young monkeys in J. Helmuth (Ed.), *Exceptional Infant: Studies in Abnormalities.* Vol. 2. New York: Brunner Mazel, 1971, pp. 483-529.

Suomi, S. J. & Harlow, H. F. Social rehabilitation of isolate-reared monkeys. *Developmental Psychology,* 1972, **6,** 487-496.

Suomi, S. J., Harlow, H. F., & McKinney, W. T. Monkey psychiatrists. *American Journal of Psychiatry,* 1972, **128,** 41-46.

Watson, J. S., & Ramey, C. T. Reactions to responsive contingent stimulation in early infancy. Paper presented at the biennial meeting of the Society for Research in Child Development, Santa Monica, Calif., March, 1969.

Watson, J. S., & Ramey, C. T. Reactions to responsive contingent stimulation in early infancy. *Merrill-Palmer Quarterly,* 1972, **18,** 219-227.

White, B. L. An experimental approach to the effects of environment on early human behavior. In J. P. Hill (ed.), *Minnesota Symposium on Child Psychology.* vol. I. Minneapolis: University of Minnesota Press, 1967.

White, B. L., & Held, R. Plasticity of sensorimotor development in human infant. In J. Rosenblith & W. Allinsmith (Eds.), *The causes of behavior: readings in child development and educational psychology.* Boston: Allyn and Bacon, 1966.

White, B. L., Castle, P., & Held, R. M. Observations on the development of visually directed reaching. *Child Development,* 1964, **35,** 349-364.

Yarrow, L. Maternal deprivation: toward an empirical and conceptual re-evaluation. *Psychological Bulletin,* 1961, **58,** 459-490.

Yarrow, L. J. Separation from parents during early childhood. In M. L. Hoffman & L. W. Hoffman (Eds.), *Review of child development research.* Vol. I. New York: Russell Sage Foundation, 1964, 89-136.

6
LEARNING

The purpose of this chapter is to detail those principles and processes which determine to a large degree the extent to which genetically determined capacities will reach their full potential and the direction that genetically controlled behaviors will follow in their developmental course. These principles do not deny or in any way invalidate the previous chapters on the roles of genetic, hereditary, and maturational factors in behavioral development.

First, two traditional approaches to learning will be examined: classical and operant conditioning. What factors determine the effectiveness of these two forms of learning in children? How early can infants be classically or operantly conditioned, and what is the developmental course of these types of conditioning? Next, observational learning will be examined. What are the processes involved in this type of learning, and how long do the effects last? How important is observational learning from TV for cognitive and social development? In the next section, the development of memory is explored. How do children's memory capacities and their strategies change with age? How do children learn to discriminate between relevant and irrelevant information in their environ-ment? Alternatively, how do children learn to generalize and transfer their behaviors to new situations? Does this ability to generalize shift with age? Next, techniques for pro-ducing inhibition, including extinction and punishment, are explored. Again, the factors that modify the effectiveness of these alternative tactics are examined. What are the negative side effects associated with the use of punishment? Finally, we will consider whether learning is a unitary phenomenon or a multifaceted set of different abilities.

CLASSICAL AND OPERANT CONDITIONING

Classical conditioning

The first and most famous demonstration of the kind of learning termed *classical condi-tioning* was carried out by Ivan Pavlov over sixty years ago. A harnessed dog heard a bell ring just as food was placed in his mouth. The dog, of course, salivated. What was significant was the fact that after a series of occasions in which the bell and food were presented together, the dog began to salivate whenever he heard the bell. The presen-tation of the food was unnecessary; the bell had become an effective elicitor of the salivary reaction.

With this example in mind, let us examine the characteristic features of this type of learning. The food in our example is termed the *unconditioned stimulus, or US:* it is a reliable elicitor of a particular response. The presentation of food always evokes saliva-tion, which is termed the *unconditioned response, or UCR.* The stimulus that is paired with the US (that is, the bell) is labeled the *conditioned stimulus, or CS.* The main characteristic property of this stimulus, the bell, is its inability to evoke salivation reac-tions prior to being systematically paired with the unconditioned stimulus. To complete this procedure we have a *conditioned response, or CR,* the response (salivary re-sponse) that closely resembles but is not identical with the unconditioned response originally produced by the unconditioned stimulus, but which is now evoked by the conditioned stimulus alone. The CR may differ from the UR, for example, in terms of strength of response.

This type of conditioning can be found frequently in everyday life. Consider the child who cries when he sees a physician who gave him a painful injection on a previous visit. On the first visit, he did not cry when he saw the physician. It was only as a result of the pairing of the painful needle (unconditioned stimulus) with the physician (conditioned stimulus) that the sight of the doctor alone elicited crying.

Operant conditioning

Unlike classical conditioning, operant conditioning requires that the organism first make a response and then experience some consequence for his behavior. The strength of the response that is followed by a reinforcing outcome is increased (that is, condi-tioned).

Consider two examples—one is famous; the other is relevant. First, the famous dem-onstration of instrumental conditioning will be discussed. A lowly white rat is wandering about his cage and accidentally presses a bar extending out of one wall of his cage.

rat + bar

Immediately after the press, a click is heard and a food pellet drops into a cup near the bar. The rat presses the bar again, and again food is delivered. Soon the rat has given up his tour of the cage and is seen avidly pressing the bar and eating food pellets. He has been conditioned to press the bar. Or, as one rather precocious white rat once commented, "I've sure got him (that is, the experimenter) conditioned; everytime I press the bar he gives me another food pellet."

Now, let us consider an example with children, for this type of learning is extremely important in understanding the development of infant and child behavior. Rheingold, Gewirtz, and Ross (1959), for example, demonstrated that vocalizing in three-month-old infants could be modified by the use of operant conditioning. First, an adult leaned over the baby's crib and recorded the frequency of the infant's vocalizations. However, during this early session, the adult gave no reaction to the vocalization. To determine whether positive feedback would increase vocalizing, the adult began to smile, say "tsk," and touch the infant immediately after a vocalization. The results were striking: the adult's response increased the frequency of infant vocalization. In short, through operant conditioning the infant's vocalizations had been modified.

Unlike classical conditioning where the response to be conditioned is readily and reliably elicited by the unconditioned stimulus, the operant conditioning method can be used to increase the frequency of behaviors that are often not emitted by the child. The process is termed *shaping*, and the following example of a child who seldom attended to his teacher's actions will illustrate this process. This pupil spent most of his day either looking at classmates, gazing out the window, or staring blankly at his desk. The school year might have been over before the child ever looked at the teacher, so it would have been highly inefficient to wait for the desired response to spontaneously occur. The solution is to reinforce or reward (by approval, candy, etc.) the child for approximations of the final response that is desired. For example, whenever the child looked to the front of the class, the "experimenter" dispensed a candy, even though the child didn't look directly at the teacher. By gradually reinforcing the child for closer and closer approximations of the final response, the child eventually begins to look at his teacher.

The complexity and variety of behavior patterns that can be learned through operant shaping procedures are virtually unlimited; the only restrictions are the ingenuity and patience of the experimenter. Skinner (1953), for example, received considerable recognition for demonstrating that pigeons could even be taught to play Ping-Pong through shaping tactics. In fact, numerous animal trainers have used these techniques for teaching seals, lions, and other assorted circus performers to do complex and amusing stunts.

Factors affecting operant conditioning   A variety of variables affect the success of operant conditioning. Time parameters are important. In general, the sooner the reinforcement occurs after the response, the more successful will be the learning. Reinforcement that is delivered immediately upon the execution of the response is more effective than a delayed reinforcement.

However, the age of the child makes a difference; for young infants, even brief delays may severely disrupt learning. In a recent study of operant conditioning of vocalization rate in three-month-old infants, Ramey and Ourth (1971) found that delaying the presentation of the reward by a mere three seconds prevented the occurrence of operant conditioning. This is not simply due to an inability to learn. As we saw in the study of infant vocalization, three-month-old infants can be operantly conditioned if the positive reinforcement is delivered immediately after the response. Probably the increase in memory capacity that occurs with age contributes to the greater ability of the older child to learn under conditions of longer reinforcement delays. The child is able to remember the response that he has made until the time that the reinforcer is delivered.

Another important factor is the schedule of reinforcement, or the pattern with which reinforcement is delivered. There are a variety of schedules of reinforcement. Under ratio schedules, the reinforcement is delivered only after the child has made a certain number of responses. For example, the reinforcer is delivered every third or every fifth response, not every response. Under interval schedules, reinforcement is delivered only after a certain time interval since the last reinforcement has elapsed. Both ratio and interval schedules can be either fixed or variable; a fixed schedule is one where every fifth or tenth response is reinforced or reinforcement comes a set interval (for example, thirty seconds) after the last reinforcement. In everyday life, meal times, the presence of father, or opportunities for interaction among school-age siblings usually occur on a fixed-interval schedule. That is, they occur with predictable regularity at the same times of the day. Fixed-ratio schedules are less common in naturalistic settings. Perhaps the most usual reinforcement patterns are variable ratio and interval schedules. In the case of variable-ratio schedules, the reinforcement comes after differing numbers of responses (3, 5, 2, 6), but the average is one reinforcement for every so many responses (for example, 4). Similarly, according to a variable-interval schedule, reinforcement comes on an average of every thirty seconds, but the actual intervals between reinforcement may vary (for example, sixty, twenty, or ten seconds). In most everyday situations, most reinforcement is intermittent; that is, a combination of schedules are employed whereby both the ratio of responses to reinforcement and the interval between reinforcements vary. Mothers don't praise their children on a regular schedule; on some days praise may be frequent, but on other occasions when mother is tired and irritable, even the most loving mother may reward infrequently.

How early can children be conditioned?

For the past forty years, there has been considerable controversy over the issue of how early children can be conditioned. Some investigators (for example, Spelt, 1948) have attempted to demonstrate classical conditioning in the unborn fetus; however, the results were inconclusive due to methodological inadequacies. But, can the newborn infant be classically conditioned? Probably not. Recently Sameroff (1971, 1972) reviewed the evidence and concluded that there was no convincing proof for classical conditioning in newborn infants.

Although classical conditioning has not been successfully achieved with newborns, the infant's behavior can be modified by operant conditioning. Sameroff (1968) has demonstrated that the sucking response of the newborn can be modified by the presentation or withholding of milk. Specifically, sucking can be divided into two distinct components: an *expression* response involving the squeezing of the nipple between the tongue and palate, and a *suction* component in which the floor of the mouth is lowered and creates a partial vacuum in the oral cavity during the suction. Sameroff provided milk for the baby as a direct consequence of suction applied to the nipple or in response to direct sucking or squeezing the nipple. The infants were able to adjust their style of sucking depending on the component that was followed by nutrient. If the milk was contingent upon the suction component, suction sucking increased; pressure sucking increased if nutrient delivery was contingent on this type of sucking action. This study clearly indicates that operant conditioning involving very subtle and complex discriminations is possible in the first few days of life.

However, this study and other successful demonstrations of operant conditioning in the newborn have involved existing organized patterns of behavior which are of considerable biological importance to the infant's survival. While Sameroff employed sucking, in another successful demonstration of operant conditioning in the newborn, head turning, an already existing organized component of the rooting-sucking-feeding complex was used (Siqueland, 1968). Clearly some responses are more easily modified than other responses. Newborn infants, like members of any species, have certain response systems that are biologically prepared to operate efficiently very early in life. For the human newborn infant, these *prepared responses,* to use Seligman's (1970) term, are associated with feeding and through evolution have been selected as a result of their importance for survival. In short, the infant is best organized in early life to perform behaviors that are functionally adaptive (Sameroff, 1972).

In the same sense, it appears that the newborn infant is biologically prepared for instrumental conditioning, but not for classical conditioning. The demands of classical conditioning are simply too great for the newborn. In classical conditioning, unlike operant conditioning, the infant must coordinate or associate a new stimulus with the established response (that is, the tone with sucking behavior). This complex ability to form associations between a new stimulus and a familiar response does not appear to be possible in the newborn period. Only later in infancy is classical conditioning possible (Sameroff, 1972).

It is of interest to determine not only how early conditioning can occur; psychologists have traced age changes in conditionability as well. In Box 6-1, a study of Papousek demonstrates these changes over the first three months of infancy.

BOX 6-1 DEVELOPMENTAL TRENDS IN INFANT CONDITIONING

In addition to knowing how early learning can occur, child psychologists have been interested in determining whether the child's capacity to learn in this way improves with age. Papousek (1967), a Czechoslovakian investigator, has provided the most systematic data on this issue. Using a combination of operant and classical conditioning techniques, he studied the development of conditioning in infants at three age levels: newborn, three months, and five months. Head turning, the unconditioned response employed in these studies, was elicited by a tactile stimulus to the side of the mouth. A bell, paired with the tactile unconditioned stimulus, served as the conditioned stimulus. Up to now, this paradigm is an example of classical conditioning. However, when the infant turned his head to the US, he received a milk reinforcer. The addition of the milk brings this procedure close to an instrumental conditioning paradigm. It is a mixed classical-instrumental conditioning paradigm. To review, on a typical trial, a bell sounded followed by presentation of milk whenever the infant turned his head to one side. The bell continued to sound until the baby began sucking the milk. Gradually the sound of the bell alone was sufficient to elicit the head-turning response. However, the number of trials necessary to reach a criterion of five consecutive head-turning responses in the ten trials of a daily session clearly depended on the age of the child. For newborns, an average of 177 trials were required to reach this criterion, while 42 trials were sufficient for the three-month old infants; by five months, still more rapid conditioning occurred: only 28 trials were necessary. In short, conditionability does improve with age. These findings are consistent with the notion that the opportunity for experience with auditory stimuli in the natural environment is a prerequisite for conditioning. Although additional opportunities to interact with the environment are probably important, maturation of the central nervous system may be important as well. There is evidence that the dramatic improvement over the first three months found by Papousek may, in fact, be due to changes that take place in the organization of the central nervous system around the third month of life. First, it is at this age that Ellingson (1967) has reported that the infant electroencephalographic, or EEG, activity patterns first approximate adult patterns. A second indication of the increasing maturity of the central nervous system is the disappearance of a number of primitive reflexes at this age. Finally, autopsy analyses of a group of South American children who died in the first six months of life of respiratory ailments found that the deoxyribonucleic acid (DNA) content in the brain showed a rapid increase during the first few months and reached a peak at the three- to four-month age period (Winick, unpublished; cited by Lewis, Goldberg, & Campbell, 1969, p. 25).

Source: Papousek, H. Conditioning during early postnatal development. In Y. Brackbill & G. G. Thompson (Eds.), *Behavior in infancy and early childhood.* New York: Free Press, 1967. Pp. 259-274.

LEARNING THROUGH OBSERVATION

Although a great deal of learning takes place through direct contact with the environment, as we have seen in the cases of operant and classical conditioning, learning can occur vicariously as well. Merely observing the behavior of peers, parents, and teachers can significantly expand the behavioral repertoire of the observer. Research has clearly demonstrated that new responses can be acquired and old responses elicited and modified through imitation. Indeed, it would be extremely unfortunate if a child were forced to acquire all of his responses through either operant or classical conditioning. For example, consider how uneconomical it would be to learn to drive a car through operant conditioning alone. Bandura (1962) offers the following rather humorous analysis of such a predicament:

As a first step our trainer, who has been carefully programmed to produce head nods, resonant hm-hms, and other verbal reinforcers, loads up with an ample supply of candy, chewing gum and filter-tip cigarettes. A semi-willing subject who has never observed a person drive an automobile, and a parked car complete the picture. Our trainer might have to wait a long time before the subject emits an orienting response toward the vehicle. At the moment the subject does look even in the general direction of the car, this response is immediately reinforced and gradually he begins to gaze longingly at the stationary automobile. Similarly, approach responses in the desired direction are promptly reinforced in order to bring the subject in proximity to the car. Eventually, through the skillful use of differential reinforcement, the trainer will teach the subject to open and to close the car door. With perseverance he will move the subject from the back seat or any other inappropriate location chosen in this trial-and-error ramble until at length the subject is shaped up behind the steering wheel. It is unnecessary to depict the remainder of the training procedure beyond noting that it will likely prove an exceedingly tedious, not to mention an expensive and hazardous enterprise [Bandura, 1962, pp. 212–213].

Another form of conditioning?

Are we justified in treating this apparently common-sense phenomenon as another form of learning, a form governed by a set of principles that are separate and discrete from either operant or classical conditioning? Many theorists have tried to reduce imitation to a special case of either instrumental or classical conditioning. Skinner (1953) has argued that it is the frequent rewarding of a child for imitating that increases the frequency of modeling. Imitation, according to this viewpoint, is simply a set of response tendencies that are developed and maintained according to well-established operant conditioning principles. The most serious challenge to this position comes from Bandura and his colleagues at Stanford University. They argue that imitation is, in fact, a separate and distinct form of learning, and a separate set of principles is required for its understanding.

An illustrative experiment   To illustrate, let us consider an early but classic experiment. In this study, Bandura, Ross, and Ross (1963) brought nursery-school-age children into a room to sit and watch an adult pummel, hit, and kick a large inflated Bobo doll. Some of the model's verbal and motor responses are both bizarre and novel, unlike anything the typical nursery schooler has likely ever seen before, much less ever performed previously. The adult model is neither praised nor punished for his antics; similarly no consequences in the form of either rewards or punishment accrue to the child as he watches the model. So neither observer nor model are reinforced. To determine whether any learning has taken place under these seemingly impoverished conditions, the child is left alone with the same Bobo doll that had previously been the object of the model's aggression. And for comparison purposes, other children who had not observed the model were left alone with the Bobo toy. Hidden assistants recorded the frequency with which the child's behavior matched the behavior of the model. The children who had been exposed to the model were much more likely to exhibit matching responses than the children in the no-model condition. Moreover, many of the bizarre and novel responses exhibited by the adult were accurately reproduced by the child observers. Learning, in the absence of any reinforcers delivered to either the model or the viewer, clearly had taken place; imitation, then, is another means by which novel responses can be acquired. In addition, the experimenters noted the frequency of forms of aggressive behavior that were different from the model's aggressive responses. Again, the children who observed the model scored higher. Watching a model apparently serves another function, namely, eliciting previously acquired responses that belong to the same class of behaviors as those of the model. In the case of the present example, other forms of aggressive expression that already existed in the observer's behavior repertoire, such as poking and name calling, were more likely to be displayed after watching the model act aggressively.

In summary, new responses can be acquired and previously acquired responses can be elicited by observing the behavior of another individual. Moreover, reinforcement is not necessary for these acquisition and eliciting processes to operate.

The acquisition-performance distinction   Although responses can be acquired in the absence of reinforcement, this does not imply that the reinforcement contingencies associated with the model's behavior are unimportant. Consider a related study by Bandura (1965). In one condition, the young children saw the adult lavishly rewarded with candy and juice for performing the aggressive acts, while in a second condition, other children saw the model punished. The kind of consequences that the model experienced was important; in the subsequent test for imitation, children who saw the model rewarded displayed more aggressive responses, both imitative and nonimitative, than the children who viewed the punished model. Is our earlier conclusion that reinforcement is unnecessary for acquisition by observation incorrect? To answer this question, it is necessary to examine the second part of Bandura's experiment. In this phase, which followed immediately after the test for imitation, the children in all of the experimental conditions were offered candy incentives to reproduce as many of the model's responses as possible. In spite of the earlier differences between the model-rewarded and model-punished groups, both sets of child observers reproduced almost exactly the same number of model responses. The question is answered: The children who viewed different outcomes to the model differed in their performance of the observed acts, but as the follow-up phase indicates, both groups had "learned," or acquired, the same amount of information during the viewing period. Response consequences, in other words, affect the child's likelihood of performing the model's behavior; these consequences have little effect on the acquisition of responses through imitation.

Long-term effects   Moreover, the effects of exposure to models may have long-lasting effects. Hicks (1965) exposed preschool boys and girls to filmed aggressive models. In addition to assessing the immediate effects of exposure, Hicks brought his subjects back to the experimental setting after a six-month period and assessed the amount of imitative aggressive behavior they displayed in a free play session. Although the amount of imitative aggressive behavior markedly decreased over time, in comparison to control subjects who had never viewed a model, there was still evidence that exposure to an aggressive model had an effect even up to six months after the initial viewing. More recently Eron and his colleagues (1972, 1975) reported that TV viewing may affect aggressive behavior even after a ten-year period.

Representation processes in observational learning

In order to account for the occurrence of imitative learning in the absence of reinforcement, Bandura has offered an information processing theory of observational learning. He has summarized the theory as follows: "While the observer views the model's behavior, the observer codes the modeled actions in the form of verbal or symbolic images that can later be retrieved when the observer performs the model's actions [Bandura, 1971, p. 17]."According to this theory, the observer's symbolic or representational responses in the form of images and verbal associates of the model's behavior are clearly central in accounting for imitation learning. The role that symbolic representation plays in observational learning is illustrated in an experiment by Bandura, Grusec, and Menlove (1966). On the assumption that the observer's verbalizations would affect the representational process, a group of six- to eight-year-old boys and girls were instructed to verbalize the actions of a film model who was exhibiting some novel play behaviors. This verbalization procedure was intended to facilitate the development of symbolic representations of the models' responses. While other children passively observed, a third group was instructed to count, an activity that was assumed to interfere with and retard the acquisition of imaginal correlates of the model's behavior. In support of the theory, subjects in the facilitating symbolization condition were clearly superior in reproducing the model's responses. (See Figure 6-1). Later research by Coates and Hartup (1969), however, suggests that the importance of verbalization for acquisition and retention of imitative responses is dependent on the age of the child. In a study of four- and seven-year-old children, they compared passive observation with two types of verbalization: *induced verbalization,* in which the subject was told how to describe the model's actions during exposure; and *free verbalization,* in which the subject was asked to describe the model's actions in his own words during exposure. A number of interesting findings emerged from this experiment. Since children tend to verbalize spontaneously to a greater extent as they grow older, it was not surprising to find that the verbalization procedures benefited the younger children more than their older peers. While both induced and free verbalization increased the younger children's reproduction of the model's responses, the induced verbalization procedure was superior. Probably this is due to young children's limited practice in verbalization production which, in turn, resulted in the children in the free verbalization condition emitting fewer accurate verbalizations during the exposure period than subjects in the induced verbalization group.

In order to understand the role of symbolic mediators on imitative learning, both age and the type of coding activity clearly need to be considered. However, these experiments indicate that the nature of the observer's activity during the viewing period can markedly influence observational learning. More specifically, this research suggests that symbolization clearly enhances the acquisition of and retention of imitative responses.

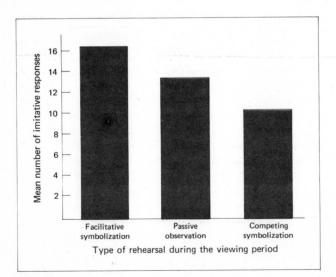

FIGURE 6-1 The effects of different types of viewer rehearsal on observational learning. (Plotted from Bandura, Grusec, & Menlove, 1966.)

Finally, these experiments question the adequacy of theories which stress the necessity of reinforcement for the occurrence of imitative learning.

Finally, it should be noted that learning by imitation is not restricted to mere mimicry, whereby the observer is limited to merely the exact reproduction of the model's responses. Zimmerman and Rosenthal (1974), in a comprehensive review, have clearly shown that children are able to abstract conceptual rules from instances of modeled behavior that permit a wide degree of transfer to new tasks and new situations. Observational learning, for example, has been found to be effective in teaching children generalized linguistic rules, concepts, and problem-solving and question-asking strategies. Children have learned rules for using prepositions, passive tenses, and other particulars of English grammar through imitation. For an applied example of the effects of observational learning on children's cognitive development, turn to Box 6-2 where "Sesame Street" is discussed. In summary, observational learning is an important avenue for the acquisition of new behaviors and the modification of old response patterns, and most importantly, it is a technique for the acquisition of not only specific, but highly generalizable and flexible response patterns. Throughout the remaining chapters, numerous instances of observational learning will be presented.

BOX 6-2 OBSERVATIONAL LEARNING AND TELEVISION: "SESAME STREET"

An important and innovative application of recent advances in observational learning was the introduction of the educational program "Sesame Street." The show aimed toward improving the cognitive skills of preschoolers so that they would be better prepared for elementary school education. By using TV as a medium, the Children's Television Workshop hoped to bring the educational message to a large portion of children who normally have no preschool education. Only 1 in every 5 three- and four-year-olds attend preschool programs. So, the Cookie Monster, Bert, Ernie, and their zany companions made their debut in 1969. However, it was not merely cartoon characters and a host of clever attention-holding tactics, but a well-defined set of cognitive goals that made "Sesame Street" so successful. And it has worked, as demonstrated in evaluations conducted by Ball and Bogatz (1972). Children were tested on a variety of items such as body parts, letters, numbers, geometric forms, sorting, and classification before and after a six-month viewing period.

Although there was an initial concern that enough children would watch to permit an evaluation, nearly everyone watched occasionally. Therefore, children were divided into four groups based on their frequency of watching the program: Group 1 watched "Sesame Street" rarely, group 2 watched two or three times a week, children in group 3 viewed four or five times a week, and group 4 viewers saw the program more than five times a week. Children who watched "Sesame Street" showed a marked improvement in a variety of cognitive skills; more importantly, as Figure 6-2 clearly shows, as viewing became heavier the amount of improvement increased. The more one watched, the more one learned. Nor was the viewing context important; children who watched at home and those who watched the program in a preschool setting both gained. Finally, the results were not restricted to middle-class children; disadvantaged children who watched showed marked improvements as well. Perhaps one of the most interesting outcomes is that reading skill improved, even though this was not specifically taught on "Sesame

Observational learning, such as that on "Sesame Street," has been found to be effective in teaching children. (Children's Television Workshop.)

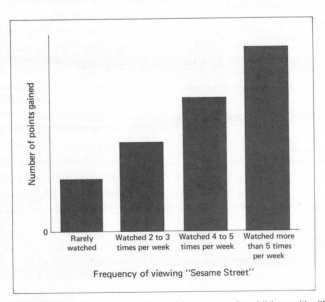

FIGURE 6-2 Improvement in total test scores for children with different amounts of viewing experience. (Based on Ball & Bogatz, 1972.)

Street.'' These results leave little doubt that children learn by observation and that television can be a potent educational tool.

Source: Ball, S., & Bogartz, J. Summative research of Sesame Street: Implications for the study of preschool children. In Anne D. Pick (Ed.), *Minnesota symposia on child psychology, Volume 6.* Minneapolis: University of Minnesota Press, 1972. Pp. 3–17.

MEMORY AND HOW CHILDREN LEARN TO REMEMBER

Up to now we have focused on children's acquisition of new behaviors; but that is only one aspect of learning. Children remember people, places, and events that are no longer present. There are two types of memory: short-term and long-term. Short-term memory refers to the capacity to remember over a brief period of time (for example, thirty seconds); long-term memory, on the other hand, refers to material that is stored for later retrieval (for example, two days).

First, it is clear that short-term memory improves with the age of the child, but the more interesting question is "Why?" What are the older children doing that results in their improved memory capacity?

A number of processes have been suggested to account for differences in memory in children. Opportunities for rehearsal, as we have already seen in the case of observational learning, are important. First, teaching children to name the objects that they have to remember increases children's recall of the objects more than merely looking at them (Hagen & Kingsley, 1968). In addition to rehearsal of the material at the time of exposure by verbal labeling, rehearsal (for example, repeating the words) during the interval between exposure to the words or objects improves memory as well. For example, in one study, six- to seven-year-old children who spontaneously rehearsed showed greater recall than nonrehearsers. However, when the nonrehearsers were trained to rehearse and then were instructed to rehearse before a recall task, they recalled as much as spontaneous rehearsers (Keeney, Cannizzo, & Flavell, 1967). It is clear that rehearsal is an effective means of increasing recall, but the *spontaneous* use of rehearsal strategy increases with age. Since younger children do not spontaneously rehearse in trying to retain material, it has been found that training and rehearsal benefit young children more than their older peers.

One of the most interesting recent advances in our understanding of memory is the role of organization of material. When faced with the task of remembering a set of pictures or words, children tend to group or cluster the material into different conceptual categories. Moreover, there is a relationship between increasing recall and clustering with age. However, it is not so much that conceptual clustering per se is an age-specific phenomenon; rather the organizational bases for recall appear to change with age. Rossi and Wittrock (1971) found marked differences in the organizational bases for free recall among children with mental age ranges from two to five years. They used a list of words (for example, sun, hand, men, peach, hat, bark, apple, dogs, fat) that could be organized in a number of different ways during recall. At the youngest age (mental age two) rhyming (for example, sun-fun; fat-hat) was the predominant mode of organizing the words. At the next age level (mental age three) syntactical organization (for example, dogs-bark; men-work) was the most evident strategy. Clustering (for example, peach-apple; leg-hand) was higher than the other techniques at age four, while the children at the oldest mental age level (five) used serial ordering (for example, the order in which they heard the words) most often. As we will see in more detail in a later chapter, these results are consistent with Piaget's theory of a development from concrete to abstract functioning and from perceptual to conceptual responding.

Probably it is the ability to employ appropriate organizing strategies that develops with age. Just as spontaneous rehearsal and spontaneous labeling increase with age, it has been observed that the spontaneous clustering of items increases with age and that this clustering is related to the number of items subsequently recalled (Moely, Olsen, Hawles, & Flavell, 1969).

Another way that children remember is by forming mental images of the objects. A recent study by Wolff and Levin (1972), which demonstrates the usefulness of imagery for improving memory, is presented in Box 6-3. In summary, children use a number of strategies in remembering, and the application of these strategies seem to vary with the age of the child.

BOX 6-3 IMAGES: AIDS FOR REMEMBERING

Does forming mental images improve your memory? That was the question that Wolff and Levin (1972) investigated. Children in kindergarten and third grade were presented with pairs of toys (for example, giraffe, truck, watch, airplane). Later, only one toy was presented and the child was asked to recall the other toy in the pair. Children received one of four different kinds of training. Children in the control condition were shown the pairs and told to remember which toys went together. In the imagery group, they were instructed to form a mental image of the toys in each pair "playing together." Children in another condition were instructed to manipulate the toys in a manner described by the

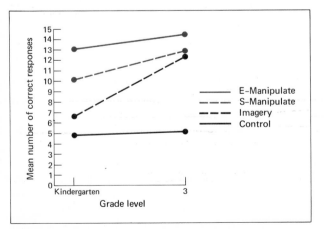

FIGURE 6-3 The effects of different ways of presenting information on children's ability to remember. Mean number of correct responses by kindergarten and third-grade children in each of four presentation conditions. (From Wolff & Levin, 1972, with permissions of the authors and the Society for Research in Child Development.)

experimenter (for example, the bear jumped into the truck). Subjects in the final condition were asked to devise their own ways of having the toys in each pair play together by actually manipulating the toys. As Figure 6-3 illustrates, active manipulation of the toys resulted in improved memory regardless of whether the experimenter or the child himself initiated the manipulation sequence. However, the mental imagery instructions were effective only for the third graders; the kindergarten children did not benefit from these instructions. Motor manipulation appears to be a helpful aid for the five-year-old, while more abstract techniques like imagery are effective only at older ages.

Source: Wolff, P., & Levin, J. R. The role of overt activity in children's imagery production. *Child Development,* 1972, **43,** 537–548.

ATTENTION AND DISCRIMINATION LEARNING

One of the requirements for successful learning is the ability to attend to relevant and ignore irrelevant information in the environment. Obviously everything is not equally important, and selectively attending is one of the most important abilities that the child acquires as he develops. In learning situations very young children are easily distracted by irrelevant features and therefore learn the critical aspects of the task at a slower rate. As children mature, they pay less attention to irrelevant information and learn to concentrate on the central and critical aspects of a task. It is apparent that in situations in which there is no specific learning task involved, attention to a wide array of stimuli in the environment may be interesting and beneficial.

There are a variety of ways to study the development of attention in children. One technique for studying attention is to photograph the children's visual scanning patterns by means of an eye camera, which takes a picture of the object that the child is attending as well as exactly where he is focused. Vurpillot (1968) asked children between the ages of six and nine to examine pairs of pictures and decide whether they were the same or different. Of course to correctly make this kind of judgment, children ought to scan both pictures in detail before deciding. But, in fact, the younger children were not very systematic in their scanning strategies; rather they looked at only parts of the pictures and as a result made more errors than the older children who more systematically scanned the features of the pictures. This is, of course, reminiscent of the behavior of infants who spend a large amount of time investigating the angles of a triangle, but rarely scan the full outline of the figure (Salapatek & Kessen, 1966). With increasing age, children improve in their capacity to attend selectively with their eyes to those portions of visual stimuli which contain the most information.

However, it is not just the lack of systematic scanning, but the young child's failure to distinguish irrelevant from relevant information that often accounts for poor learning. A study by Hagen (1967) will illustrate this process. Children at grades one, three, five, and seven saw cards containing two pictures: an animal and a household object. Half the children were instructed to remember the locations of the animals, while the remaining children were asked to remember the household objects. However, after completing the learning task, the children were asked to recall not only the locations of the animals or household objects, but were unexpectedly asked to pair each animal with the household object with which it had appeared; in other words, children had to locate the card with the picture of the animal even though they had originally been asked to remember only the household objects. There were two measures: the *central memory score,* consisting of the number of correct responses for materials that adults asked the child to remember; and the *incidental memory score,* consisting of the number of correct responses for incidental materials (for example, the materials the child presumably was to ignore). Central memory performance improved with increasing age level, while incidental performance declined at the oldest age level. Moreover, younger children who were able to do well on the central task did well on the incidental task; but for the oldest children, those who did best on central memory were able to ignore the incidental information. In a later study, Druker and Hagen (1969) reported that older subjects usually only scanned and covertly labeled relevant pictures, while younger children reported more scanning and labeling of both pictures.

Children engage in a similar selective process of ignoring irrelevant features as they get older when more naturalistic materials, such as films, are used. Hale, Miller, and Stevenson (1968) showed elementary grade children an interesting film and then quizzed the children for their recall of both central plot and irrelevant aspects of the film (for example, "What was the color of the lady's dress?"). Memory for central features improved with age, while recall of irrelevant features showed a gradual increase up to the seventh grade when there was a decline. In early adolescence, attention to irrelevant material appears to wane. Together these findings suggest that "with increasing age, the ability to maintain task performance by excluding certain kinds of information develops [Hagen, 1972, p. 299]."

However, a question remains. Can young children be trained to selectively attend to relevant features of their environment? According to recent studies by Tighe and Tighe (1969), the answer is clearly "yes." By giving children training in distinguishing critical features of an object (for example, height versus brightness) *before* a discrimination test, the children's discrimination performance was markedly superior to their non-pretrained peers. In fact, some recent theorists such as Gibson (1969) have argued that the principal process underlying successful learning is the discovery of distinctive features that separate objects in the environment. Attention to and isolation of the critical and distinguishing characteristics are the important tasks; according to this view, reinforcement is unnecessary for learning, just as reinforcement is unnecessary for observational learning. Reinforcement may serve to increase motivation and maintain persistence and interest, but the basic learning process is essentially a perceptual differentiation process. The Tighe and Tighe training study is certainly compatible with this viewpoint. This kind of selectivity is not limited to visual learning tasks, as Maccoby's research on auditory attention clearly illustrates (Box 6-4). Next we turn to generalization of responses to new situations.

BOX 6-4 AUDITORY ATTENTION: OR LEARNING TO LISTEN SELECTIVELY

Children learn to attend selectively to information coming from their auditory environment as well as from their visual world. Often two people are talking, but we are able to tune out one conversation while we attend to the other. Similarly, we ignore street noise and barking dogs and "hear" a TV program or a call for dinner. An experimental analogue of this type of double auditory message is the dichotic listening situation. Two different messages are presented to the two ears simultaneously: one is a man's voice and one is a woman's voice. The child was instructed to attend to the messages (simple English words) and to repeat them after the voices stopped. The child's ability to listen selectively improves between ages five and fourteen, according to research by Maccoby (1967, 1969). Some of her research illustrates an important variable in selective attention, namely the expectation to respond. Children were told either before or after the presentation of the message which voice they would have to remember. As Figure 6-4 illustrates, hearing the instruction set *before* the two messages were received greatly improved the child's ability to selectively report a particular message. The expectation or set to respond is an important determinant of success in a dichotic listening task.

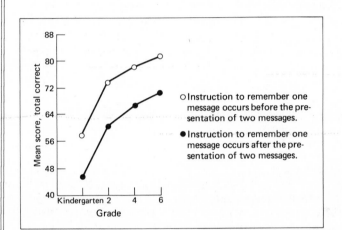

FIGURE 6-4 The effects of the age of a child and the timing of an instruction to listen to a particular message on selective auditory attention. (From Maccoby, 1967, with permission of the author and Academic Press.)

Source: Maccoby, E. E. Selective auditory attention in children. In L. P. Lipsitt & C. C. Spiker (Eds.), *Advances in child development and behavior.* Vol. 3. New York: Academic, 1967. Pp. 99–125; and Maccoby, E. E. The development of stimulus selection. In John P. Hill (Ed.), *Minnesota symposia on child psychology.* Vol. 3. Minneapolis: University of Minnesota Press, 1969. Pp. 68–96.

GENERALIZATION AND TRANSFER

Stimulus generalization

Not only must the child develop the ability to detect differences among stimuli that he encounters, but he has to determine how closely these new inputs match previously encountered events. In other words, a child need not learn to respond to every situation as a unique and novel experience; he can draw upon his past history to help him decide how to react by noticing the similarities between the present context and past situations. This process of transferring previously acquired responses or habits from one stimulus situation to a new context is known as *stimulus generalization*. Its importance stems from the time and energy that it saves the child; generalization makes daily living a much more economical and effortless business, and therefore this capacity has clear adaptive significance. But, generalization can have unfortunate and detrimental consequences as well. The following example will serve two functions: to illustrate the principle of stimulus generalization, and to indicate some of the negative, maladaptive consequences of overgeneralization.

The following letter was taken from an advice column of a metropolitan newspaper:

> Dear Abby:
> My girlfriend fixed me up with a blind date and I should have known the minute he showed up in a bow tie that he couldn't be trusted. I fell for him like a rock. He got me to love him on purpose and then lied to me and cheated on me. Every time I go with a man who wears a bow tie, the same thing happens. I think girls should be warned about men who wear them.
> AGAINST BOW TIES
>
> Dear Against:
> Don't condemn all men who wear bow ties because of your experience. I know many a man behind a bow tie who can be trusted.
> [Cited by Bandura & Walters, 1963]

As the amusing exchange indicates, overzealous generalization can lead to unfortunate consequences; discrimination is necessary as well. Bandura and Walters point out the lesson of these letters as follows:

> A generalized response is inappropriate when it occurs to a stimulus element that is not regularly correlated with the other elements of the stimulus complex in which the response was originally learned. The letter-writer had generalized a whole pattern of behavior to the bow tie, an object which one would not expect to be regularly associated with the response characteristics of the wearer [Bandura & Walters, 1963, p. 9].

A number of variables affect the degree of stimulus generalization. The physical similarity of the two stimulus situations is one important determinant. A five-year-old boy who is chased by a large Afghan hound is more likely to react with fear and flight at the sight of a German shepherd than a miniature poodle; the physical similarity between the Afghan and the German shepherd is likely to suggest that their reactions to small boys might be similar as well.

This observation can be summarized by the following principle: The greater the similarity that exists between the original and the generalization situations, the greater the probability that the same behavior will be exhibited in the two situations. This principle is termed a *gradient of generalization*.

Other types of stimulus generalization occur as well; these depend not so much on the physical similarity that exists between two situations, but rather on the perceived similarity as a result of the two situations sharing the same meaning or the same conceptual label or belonging to the same class or linguistic grouping.

Semantic generalization Here is an example of semantic generalization whereby a response conditioned to one word generalizes to other words on the basis of their semantic relations. Russian researchers Luria and Vinogradova (1959) reported that subjects who were shocked upon hearing the word violin gave a similar emotional reaction to related words such as violinist, bow, string, and mandolin but little emotional response to neutral words.

Words are related in a wide variety of semantic relationships, such as synonyms (right-correct), antonyms (right-wrong), and homophones (right-write). A number of years ago, Reiss (1946) found that generalization is most readily obtained by different semantic relationships at different ages. First, children heard a word (for example, male) at the same time that a buzzer sounded. Through classical conditioning procedure the word alone came to elicit an emotional reaction. To test for semantic generalization, a series of words with different semantic relationships to the conditioned word "male" were presented. For example, some words were synonyms (for example, man), while others were antonyms (for example, female) and others were homophones (for example, mail). Generalization was indicated by the similarity of the emotional reaction to the original word (male) and the new word. For seven- to nine-year-olds, generalization was best to homophones, while ten- to twelve-year-olds responded more to synonyms. The fourteen- and eighteen-year-old subjects showed maximum generalization to the synonyms. Semantic relationships, therefore, do provide the basis for generalization, but the nature of the semantic dimension shifts with age. As the Reiss study shows, young children respond to words of similar sounds rather than those of similar meaning. Only as language becomes more highly developed does the child shift to meaning as a basis for generalization. Interestingly, feeble-minded individuals and adults under conditions of fatigue or under the influence of drugs which suppress activity of higher cortical centers respond on the basis of word sounds (Slobin, 1971). It is clear that "the phenomenon of semantic generalization reflects a relatively mature and highly developed level of cortical functioning [Slobin, 1971, p. 84]."

Age changes in stimulus generalization The degree of stimulus generalization may vary with the age of the child. In a study that tested boys ranging in age from seven to twelve years, subjects were exposed to a horizontal row of eleven lamps and were required to push a button whenever the center lamp was lit. Intermittently, the peripheral rather than the center lamp would be lit in order to test the degree to which the children generalized their button pushing. Stimulus generalization was greater in the younger children, indicating that stimulus generalization lessens as the child matures. (Mednick & Lehtinen, 1957). However, it is not just chronological age that is important in stimulus generalization. Mental age or the child's intellectual age may be important. Mental age represents the age level of the child's performance on an intelligence test. For example, a mental age of six means that the average children of this age perform at that level. Six-year-olds, therefore, may have differing mental ages; some may have a mental age of four, while others have a mental age of six or even eight. It has shown that stimulus generalization is greater among children of lower mental age than among children of higher mental age (Tempore, 1965). The child's level of intellectual development, as well as his age, are important determinants of stimulus generalization.

Response generalization

Children generalize not only along stimulus dimensions, but along response dimensions as well; they learn to substitute different but related responses to the same stimulus. Let us turn again to our dog-fearing child to illustrate this type of generalization. One reaction to the sight of a dog might be to cry. However, the emotion of fear can be expressed in a variety of ways, and crying is only one manifestation of fear. The child could have hidden his face in his hands, screamed for help, or run away from the frightening animal. The same fear stimulus evoked a slightly different response, illustrating the principle of response generalization.

Or consider some examples of response generalization of aggression. Children who are encouraged to punch tend to kick and scratch often as well, even though these behaviors were never involved in the original training. These other responses generalized from the original training in punching behavior. Response generalization can often occur between verbal and physical behaviors as well; for example, a child who attacks with angry, hostile words may on a later occasion generalize his aggressiveness and punch his or her target rather than simply call him a nasty name. Recent research has shown that young children or adolescents who were rewarded for speaking aggressive words were more likely to act in a physically aggressive fashion toward one of their peers (Parke, Ewall, & Slaby, 1972; Slaby, 1975). These findings illustrate the process of response generalization.

INHIBITION OF BEHAVIOR

Not only are procedures that increase the occurrence of a behavior important, but tactics to weaken or eliminate undesirable behaviors are also of both practical and theoretical interest. Indeed, during childhood socialization the child must learn acceptable, prosocial behavior, but in addition, he or she must learn to inhibit or suppress undesirable and unacceptable behaviors. Moreover, maladaptive responses, such as excessive fears, often require weakening in order to permit adequate development. Procedures that inhibit behavior, therefore, play an important role in both naturalistic socialization and in therapeutic situations as well. In this section two methods for weakening or inhibiting children's responses will be discussed: extinction and punishment.

Extinction

In the case of operant conditioning, the presentation of the reinforcement maintains behavior; similarly, withholding the reinforcement following the response will weaken and eventually eliminate the behavior. In the case of classical conditioning, continue to present the conditioned stimulus (CS) without pairing it with the unconditioned stimulus (US) and eventually the CS will lose its power to elicit the conditioned response. These procedures are termed experimental extinction.

The effectiveness of an extinction procedure is nicely illustrated by a case study of excessive crying reported by Williams (1959). The subject was a twenty-one-month-old child who regularly protested being separated from his parents at bedtime by insistently screaming and crying until someone attended to him. The attention that his tantrum behavior produced, however, served only to increase the strength of this undesirable behavior. The parents tried a new approach; they ignored his crying behavior after bedtime routines had been completed. As Figure 6-5 illustrates, the results were dramatic. There was a marked decrease in the duration of the tantrum episode, and within

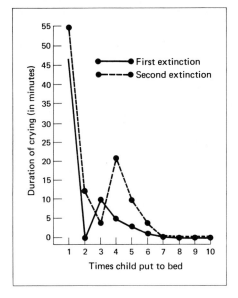

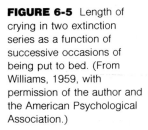

FIGURE 6-5 Length of crying in two extinction series as a function of successive occasions of being put to bed. (From Williams, 1959, with permission of the author and the American Psychological Association.)

a week the troublesome behavior had virtually disappeared. It was necessary to repeat the extinction procedure a short time later due to the intervention of a "helpful" grandmother who insisted on responding to the infant's crying. However, extinction was again successful, and no adverse side effects were apparent after a two-year follow-up.

One factor that affects the rate of extinction is the previous reinforcement history of the individual. Extinction is slower following intermittent reward than after continuous reinforcement. A study by Brackbill (1958) on infant smiling provides an illustration of this principle. Using eight infants between three and one-half and four and one-half months of age as subjects, she first secured baseline levels of smiling to a motionless and expressionless face. Following this period, Brackbill placed four infants on a continuous reinforcement schedule and the remaining four infants first on a continuous, then on an intermittent, schedule. Reinforcement consisted of the experimenter smiling, speaking softly to the infant, picking it up, patting it, and talking to it. When reinforcements were discontinued, the experimenter stood motionless and expressionless. During the extinction period there was a decline in the mean number of responses given by both groups of infants. However, as Figure 6-6 indicates, the intermittently reinforced infants smiled at a higher rate during extinction than did the continuously reinforced subjects. These data illustrate another feature of the early stages of extinction, namely a heightened rate and intensity of responding. That is, the infant appears to be protesting the cessation of the reinforcement and therefore exerts a greater effort in order to reinstate his vanished rewards. Often emotional responses different from the behavior previously reinforced can be detected as well. In the Brackbill experiment this can be seen quite clearly; the incidence of crying and fussing increased in the early stages of extinction.

Intermittently reinforced children have greater difficulty determining when reinforcement has occurred for the last time, whereas continuously rewarded subjects should

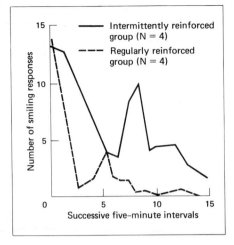

FIGURE 6-6 Mean rates of smiling response during extinction period as a function of regular or intermittent reinforcement. (From Brackbill, 1958, with permission of the authors and the Society for Research in Child Development.)

experience an abrupt and easily recognized shift when extinction begins. Research with children (Kass & Wilson, 1966), in fact, has supported this explanation of the persistence of intermittently reinforced behaviors.

But extinction may be too slow a technique to employ for behaviors which may be unusually bothersome, injurious, or undesirable. An alternative technique for suppressing unwanted behaviors is punishment.

Punishment

In punishment, a noxious stimulus is associated with a particular response and thereby makes this response less likely to occur. The anxiety or fear that is generated by the unpleasant event (for example, a swat on the bottom, a verbal rebuke, or an electric shock) comes to be associated via classical conditioning with the originally pleasant and rewarding response. The result is suppression of the punished behavior. Punishment has been used for many years by parents, although the "experts" in psychology assumed that punishment was an extremely ineffective means of controlling human behavior. Possibly the harried and harrassed parents who have used punishment as a way of disciplining their charges have been wiser than the experts, for recent research has shown that punishment can be an effective control technique (Parke, 1972).

Factors affecting the operation of punishment Recent laboratory studies of the effects of punishment on children's behavior have revealed that its effectiveness is dependent on a variety of factors, just as we saw in the case of positive reinforcement. The factors that seem to be most important in punishment are the timing, the severity, the consistency, and the relationship between agent and recipient of punishment.

As in the case of positive reinforcement, temporal factors are critical. A number of years ago at Harvard's Laboratory of Human Development, Black, Solomon, and Whiting (1960) undertook a study of the timing of punishment for producing "resistance to temptation" in a group of young puppies. Two training conditions were used. In one case, the dogs were swatted with a rolled-up newspaper just *before* they touched a bowl of forbidden horsemeat. The remaining pups were punished only *after* eating a small amount of the taboo food. On subsequent tests, even though deprived of food, the animals punished as they approached the food showed greater avoidance of the prohibited meat than did animals punished after committing the taboo act. This study is the prototype of a number of studies carried out with children, and it illustrates the importance of the *timing* of the punishment for producing effective control over children's behavior.

In these studies of the effects of timing of punishment on children's behavior, the rolled-up newspaper has been replaced by a verbal rebuke or a loud noise, and an attractive toy stands in place of the horsemeat. For example, Walters, Parke, and Cane (1965) presented subjects with pairs of toys, one attractive and one unattractive, on a series of nine trials. The six- to eight-year-old boys were punished by a verbal rebuke, "No, that's for the other boy," when they chose the attractive toy. As in the dog study, one group of children was punished as they approached the attractive toy, but before they actually touched it. For the remaining boys, punishment was delivered only after they had picked up the critical toy and held it for two seconds. Following the punishment training session, the subjects were seated before a display of three rows of toys similar to those used in the training period and were reminded not to touch the toys. The resistance-to-deviation test consisted of a fifteen-minute period during which each boy was left alone with an unattractive German-English dictionary and, of course, the prohibited toys. The extent to which the subject touched the toys in the absence of the external agent was recorded by an observer located behind a one-way screen. The

Punishment—Does It Help or Hurt? *depends what kind.*

There is still some controversy regarding how beneficial punishment really is. (*Science World,* vol. 22, no. 4, March 1, 1971.)

children's data paralleled the puppy results: the early punished children touched the taboo toys less than did the boys punished late in the response sequence. Extensions of this experimental model indicate that this finding is merely one aspect of a general relation: The longer the delay between the initiation of the act and the onset of punishment, the less effective the punishment for producing response inhibition (Aronfreed, 1968).

The delay periods used in all of these studies were relatively short. In everyday life, detection of a deviant act is often delayed many hours, or the punishment may be postponed, for example, until the father returns home. The father's delayed discipline may be effective if he describes the deviant act just before he punishes the child. In fact, one experiment demonstrated that this approach successfully increased the effectiveness of a punishment delivered four hours after the commission of a deviant act (Walters & Andres, 1967). An equally effective, if less practical procedure used by these investigators involved exposing the children to a video tape recording of themselves committing the deviant act just prior to the long-delayed punishment. A partially analogous situation involves parental demonstration of the deviant behavior just before delivering the punishing blow. In any case, symbolic reinstatement of the deviant act seems to be a potent way of increasing the effectiveness of delayed punishment.

If a parent is going to punish a child, a forceful rebuke will probably be more effective than a gentle one. Intensity of the punishment, in other words, is important; the effectiveness of punishment increases as the intensity of the punishment increases. However, the aim is to achieve a level that "hurts" so that the child will be motivated to cease the deviant activity; often a gentle tap is treated as "play" and amusement, which, of course, leads to an increase rather than a decrease in the deviant behavior. Ethical and practical limitations are clearly necessary, however; it is unlikely that a severe child beating is very effective in achieving much other than a demoralized and battered child. Obviously parental control is a prerequisite to the effective utilization of punishment as a method of child control.

The nature of the relationship between the agent and recipient of punishment is a third determinant. Punishment delivered by a parent who has previously established a warm and nurturant relationship with a child is much more likely to be effective than the same kind of punishment delivered by a cool and aloof parent. Sears, Maccoby, and Levin (1957) studied a group of mothers, who were rated as warm and affectionate and who made relatively frequent use of physical punishment; these mothers reported that they found spanking to be an effective means of discipline. In contrast, cold, hostile mothers who made frequent use of physical punishment indicated that spanking was ineffective. Moreover, according to the mothers' reports, spanking was more effective when it was administered by the warmer of the two parents. Subsequent studies (Parke, 1969; Parke & Walters, 1967) have confirmed these childrearing findings in a controlled laboratory situation.

To complete our list, consistency deserves mention. Although it is often difficult to punish the child on a consistent, regular basis, research has shown that erratic administration of punishment is likely to lead to little inhibition (Parke & Deur, 1972). Inconsistency can take a variety of forms. Sometimes one parent punishes the child, while the other either ignores or encourages the child for a similar type of misbehavior. This is known as *interagent inconsistency*. When the same person treats the same response differently from one time to another, we have an example of *intraagent inconsistency*. As illustrated in the Deur and Parke (1970) study, detailed in Box 6-5, the use of inconsistency may reduce the effectiveness of continuous punishment for controlling undesirable behavior.

BOX 6-5 INCONSISTENT PUNISHMENT AND AGGRESSION

The aim of this study was to examine the impact of inconsistent punishment on the persistence of aggression under conditions of extinction or continuous punishment. Does inconsistent punishment increase the persistence of the behavior? In this study an automated Bobo doll was used to measure aggression (see Figure 6-7).

The child punches a large padded stomach of the clown-shaped doll and the frequency of hitting is automatically recorded. To familiarize themselves with the doll, the six- to nine-year-old boys used in this study punched freely for two minutes. Following this

FIGURE 6-7 The automated Bobo doll used to measure aggression in this study.

warm-up or baseline session, the subjects underwent one of three training conditions. In one case the boys were rewarded with marbles each time they punched the Bobo doll for eighteen trials. Subjects in the second training condition received marbles on nine trials, while on the other nine trials punching was neither rewarded nor punished. The final group of boys was rewarded on half of the trials, but heard a noxious buzzer in the other nine trials of the training session. The children were informed that the buzzer indicated that they were playing the game "badly." In these last two training groups the order of the outcome (for example, rewards, punishments) over the 18 trials was randomly determined. In the next part of the study, half the children in each of the three groups were neither rewarded nor punished for hitting the Bobo doll. In the learning theory terms, these subjects were on an *extinction* schedule. The remaining subjects heard the noxious buzzer each time they punched; in other words, they were exposed to a *continuous punishment* schedule. The purpose of the study was to determine how persistent the boys would be in the face of either extinction or continuous punishment after being exposed to different training schedules. The main measure of persistence was the number of hitting responses that the child gave before he voluntarily ended the game. To overcome any reluctance in quitting, the experimenter informed the boys at the outset of the training session that they could terminate the punching game whenever they wished. The results are shown in Figure 6-8. As expected, the punished subjects made fewer hitting responses than did subjects in the extinction group; these results suggest that the punishment was effective in inhibiting the aggressive behavior. The training schedules produced particularly interesting results. The inconsistently punished subjects showed the greatest resistance to extinction. Moreover, these previously punished children tended to persist longer in the face of consistent punishment than did the boys in the other training groups. The implication is clear: The socializing agent using inconsistent punishment builds up resistance to future attempts to either extinguish it or suppress it by consistently admin-

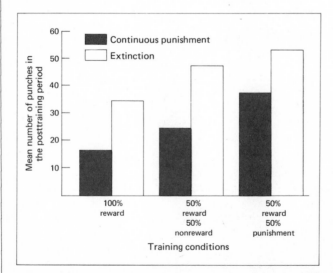

FIGURE 6-8 The effects of different types of reward and punishment training on persistence during extinction and continuous punishment for six- to nine-year-old boys. (After Deur & Parke, 1970, with permission of the American Psychological Association.)

istered punishment. It is possible that parents who inconsistently punish their children may build up strongly established patterns of aggressive and deviant behavior which are highly resistant to the use of punitive control.

Source: Deur, J. L., & Parke, R. D. The effects of inconsistent punishment on aggression in children. *Developmental Psychology,* 1970, **2,** 403–411.

Applications of punishment   In recent years, punishment has been increasingly employed by child clinical psychologists as a therapeutic procedure. A recent highly dramatic study of this type will illustrate not only the effectiveness of punishment, but its application as a treatment technique as well.

To illustrate that severe punishment in the form of electric shock can have therapeutic value, consider the work of Ivor Lovaas, who has applied punishment techniques to the treatment of retarded and mentally disturbed children. Here is one case:

John was a seven-year old boy, diagnosed as retarded (IQ 25), with psychotic-like behaviors. He had been self-injurious since he was two years of age, a behavior which necessitated his hospitalization one year prior to his being studied at UCLA. During that year he had to be kept in complete restraints (legs, waist, and with a camisole to restrain his arms) on a 24-hour a day basis. When removed from restraint he would immediately hit his head against the crib, beat his head with his fists, and scream. He looked extremely frightened when removed from restraints. He was so unmanageable that he had to be fed in full restraints; he would not take food otherwise. His head was covered with scar tissue, and his ears were swollen and bleeding [Bucher & Lovaas, 1968, p. 86].

Only after other techniques had failed did Lovaas resort to electric shock. Consider the results for a simple extinction procedure, for example. On the assumption that attention in the form of sympathetic comments by ward personnel often increased rather than decreased self-destructive behavior, the child was left alone without restraints with no attention given to his self-destructive actions. Although after eight days the child's self-destructive behavior was nearly extinguished, he still hit himself nearly 10,000 times in the process.

Punishment, an electric shock, produced dramatic results. The self-destructive behavior was virtually eliminated by the administration of a total of twelve shocks over fifteen sessions. In addition, the child cried less and avoided attending adults less following the treatment. In this case, at least, the punishment was not only an effective therapeutic procedure, but even resulted in some positive side effects. However, this is probably not always true and only in the most unusual circumstances would the use of such severe punishment be ethically and morally justified. In the present case, there is little question; punishment was a humane treatment.

Side effects of punishment   Punishment can have undesirable side effects, which may limit its usefulness. Parents who use physical punishment may be inadvertently providing an aggressive model. Bandura (1967) has summarized this viewpoint:

When a parent punishes his child physically for having aggressed toward peers for example, the intended outcome of this training is that the child should refrain from hitting others.

The child, however, is also learning from parental demonstration how to aggress physically. And, the imitative learning may provide the direction for the child's behavior when he is similarly frustrated in subsequent social interactions [Bandura, 1967, p. 43].

Support for this possibility comes from childrearing field studies (Becker, 1964; Eron, Walter, Huesmann, & Lefkowitz, 1974) as well as from laboratory studies (Parke, 1972; Gelfand, Hartmann, Lamb, Smith, Mahan, & Paul, 1974). Another negative side effect is the avoidance of the punishing agent. This is illustrated in a recent study by Redd, Morris and Martin (1975) in which five-year-old children interacted with three different adults who employed various control strategies. One adult behaved in a positive manner and smiled and made positive comments ("Good," "Nice boy," "Tremendous") while the child performed a color-sorting task. A second adult dispensed mild verbal reprimands whenever the child deviated from the sorting task (for example, "Stop throwing the tokens around," "Don't play with the chair"). A third adult was present but didn't comment on the child's behavior. While the results indicated that the punitive adult was most effective in keeping the child working on the task, the children tended to prefer the positive and neutral agents more than the punitive adult. When asked to indicate which adult they wished to work with a little longer, the children always chose the positive adult. Similarly, the children always avoided the punitive adult as their partner on other tasks or as a playmate. The implication is clear: punishment may be an effective modification technique, but the use of punishment by adults may lead the child to avoid that socializing agent and therefore undermine the adult's effectiveness as a future influence on the child's behavior.

This review leaves little doubt that punishment can be an effective means of controlling children's behavior. The operation of punishment, however, is a complex process and its effects are quite varied and highly dependent on such parameters as timing, intensity, consistency, and the affectional relationship between the agent and recipient of punishment.

It is unlikely that a socialization program based solely on punishment would be very effective; the child needs to be taught new appropriate responses in addition to learning to suppress unacceptable forms of behavior.

In fact, in real-life situations the suppressive effect of punishment is usually only of value if alternative pro-social responses are elicited and strengthened while the undesirable behavior is held in check. The primary practical value of studies of parameters that influence the efficacy of punishment is . . . to determine the conditions under which suppression will most likely occur [Walters & Parke, 1967, p. 217].

From this viewpoint, punishment is only one technique which can be used in concert with other training techniques, such as positive reinforcement, to shape, direct, and control the behavior of the developing child.

Is learning a unitary phenomenon?

Common observation suggests that children learns some types of material at different rates than other types of material. Recently psychologists have begun to systematically ask this question: Is learning a unitary phenomenon, or is there a general learning ability? One way to answer this issue is to examine the consistency of children's learning scores across a variety of different learning tasks. Stevenson and his colleagues (Stevenson, Hale, Klein, & Miller, 1968) presented to over 600 children in grades three through seven a dozen different types of tasks ranging from memory and discrimination learning to more complex problem-solving tasks, such as concepts of probability and anagram puzzles. The results were clear: there was only a very modest degree of consistency among the tasks with the median correlation being around + .30. However, it could be argued that learning is more integrated for younger children, and as the child develops, more specific learning abilities emerge. To find out, Friedrichs and his co-workers (1971) tested four- and five-year-olds on eight different tasks and the results were similar to the earlier findings. There was as little relationship at age four, as there was at age twelve, across different types of learning tasks. The implication of these studies is clear: it is sheer folly to assume that learning is a unitary, undifferentiated ability; rather, children learn different learning problems differently, a lesson that educators and parents would do well to remember.

SUMMARY

A variety of different aspects of learning were presented in this chapter. First, classical and operant conditioning were distinguished. Classical conditioning involves the pairing of two events, such as a noise and food, with the result that *both* noise and the food elicit reactions (salivating) that were previously only linked with the food. This type of learning is not evident in newborn infants but is evident after the first few months of life. Operant conditioning, unlike classical conditioning, requires that the child first make a response and then experience some consequence for his behavior. According to this type of learning, conditioning occurs when a response is followed by a reinforcing event. Even newborn infants can learn in this way, but only if the delay interval between response and reward is brief. The schedule of reinforcement is an important determinant of the effectiveness of operant learning. Intermittent schedules tend to increase the persistence of the response.

Imitation learning by observation of others is another effective learning technique. Children acquire new responses and modify existing behaviors as a result of exposure to peer and adult models. A variety of factors affect this type of learning, particularly the consequences (reward or punishment) experienced by the model. Age changes in observational learning occur, as do shifts in the effectiveness of different types of strategies for coding and remembering the model's behavior.

Children's memory was the next topic. As children develop, their memory capacities improve; a number of factors that help children remember were discussed. Rehearsal, verbalization, and organization of material were noted as being important memory aids. Symbolic aids, such as mental imagery, appear to be particularly effective as the child develops, while motor manipulation strategies are effective at younger ages.

Learning to attend selectively to critical features of the environment and to ignore irrelevant aspects is an important developmental phenomenon. In early adolescence, children show marked improvement in their ability to ignore the incidental and tangential parts of tasks; by doing so, learning often improves. Other studies dealing with selective listening indicated the importance of preparatory sets in learning. Knowing what to expect helps to attend to the relevant dimension.

Children not only develop the ability to detect differences among stimuli but they learn to notice similarities. The process of transferring previously acquired responses to a new situation is known as stimulus generalization. Age changes were noted, with older children showing less stimulus generalization than younger ones. Response generalization involves the substitution of a different but related response to a similar stimulus. Children cry on one occasion but may run at the sight of the same fear stimulus on another occasion.

Procedures that weaken or eliminate behaviors were considered. Extinction, a procedure involving the removal of the conditions that maintain a behavior, was discussed. The decrease in the occurrence of a response after removal of reinforcement illustrates extinction. Punishment, another technique for producing inhibition, was discussed. It was suggested that punishment can be effective, but a variety of controlling factors such as timing, intensity, and consistency need to be considered.

In a final section, the relationships among different types of learning were considered. Learning is not a unitary phenomenon; rather children learn different learning tasks at different rates and in different ways.

REFERENCES

Aronfreed, J. *Conduct and conscience.* New York: Academic, 1968.

Ball, S., & Bogatz, J. Summative research of Sesame Street: implications for the study of preschool children. In Anne D. Pick (Ed.), *Minnesota symposia on child psychology, Volume 6.* Minneapolis: University of Minnesota Press, 1972. Pp. 3–17.

Bandura, A. Social learning through imitation. In M. R. Jones (Ed.), *Nebraska symposium on motivation: 1962.* Lincoln: University of Nebraska Press, 1962. Pp. 211–269.

Bandura, A. Influence of model's reinforcement contingencies on the acquisition of imitative responses. *Journal of Personality and Social Psychology,* 1965, **1,** 589–595.

Bandura, A. The role of modeling processes in personality development. In W. W. Hartup & N. L. Smothergill (Eds.), *The young child.* Vol. I. Washington: National Association for the Education of Young Children, 1967. Pp. 42–58.

Bandura, A. (Ed.), *Psychological Modeling.* Chicago: Atherton, 1971.

Bandura, A., Grusec, J., & Menlove, F. L. Observational learning as a function of symbolization and incentive set. *Child Development,* 1966, **37,** 499–506.

Bandura, A., Ross, D., & Ross, S. A. Imitation of film-mediated aggressive models. *Journal of Abnormal and Social Psychology,* 1963, **66,** 3–11.

Bandura, A., & Walters, R. H. *Social learning and personality development.* New York: Holt, 1963.

Becker, W. C. Consequences of different kinds of parental discipline. In M. L. Hoffman & L. W. Hoffman (Eds.), *Review of child development research,* Vol. 1. New York: Russell Sage Foundation, 1964.

Black, A. H., Solomon, R. L., & Whiting, J. W. M. Resistance to temptation in dogs. Cited by Mowrer, O. H., *Learning theory and the symbolic processes.* New York: Wiley, 1960.

Brackbill, Y. Extinction of the smiling response in infants as a function of reinforcement schedules. *Child Development,* 1958, **29,** 115–124.

Bucher, B., & Lovaas, I. Use of aversive stimulation in behavior modification. In M. R. Jones (Ed.), *Miami symposium on the prediction of behavior 1967: Aversive stimulation.* Miami: University of Miami Press, 1968.

Coates, B., & Hartup, W. W. Age and verbalization in observational learning. *Developmental Psychology,* 1969, **1,** 556–562.

Deur, J. L., & Parke, R. D. The effects of inconsistent punishment on aggression in children. *Developmental Psychology,* 1970, **2,** 403-411.

Druker, J. F., & Hagen, J. W. Developmental trends in the processing of task-relevant and task-irrelevant information. *Child Development,* 1969, **40,** 371-382.

Ellingson, R. J. The study of brain electrical activity in infants. In L. P. Lipsitt & C. C. Spiker (Eds.), *Advances in child development and behavior.* Vol. 3. New York: Academic, 1967.

Eron, L. D., Lefkowitz, M. M., Huesmann, L. R., & Walder, L. O. Does television violence cause aggression? *American Psychologist,* 1972, **27,** 253-263.

Eron, L. D., Walder, L. O., Huesmann, L. R., & Lefkowitz, M. M. The convergence of laboratory and field studies of the development of aggression. In J. de Wit and W. W. Hartup (Eds.), *Determinants and origins of aggressive behavior.* The Hague: Mouton, 1975.

Friedrichs, A. G., Hertz, T. W., Moynahan, E., Simpson, W. E., Arnold, M. R., Christy, M. D., Cooper, C. R., & Stevenson, H. W. Interrelationships among learning and performance tasks at the preschool level. *Developmental Psychology,* 1971, **4,** 164-172.

Gelfand, D. M., Hartmann, D. P., Lamb, A. K., Smith, C. L., Mahan, M. A., & Paul, S. C. The effects of adult models and described alternatives on children's choice of behavior management techniques. *Child Development,* 1974, **45,** 585-593.

Gibson, E. *Principles of perceptual learning and development.* New York: Appleton-Century-Crofts, 1969.

Hagen, J. W. The effect of distraction on selective attention. *Child Development,* 1967, **38,** 685-694.

Hagen, J. W. Strategies for remembering. In S. Farnham-Diggery (Ed.), *Information processing in children.* New York: Academic, 1972.

Hagen, J. W., & Kingsley, P. R. Labeling effects in short-term memory. *Child Development,* 1968, **39,** 113-121.

Hale, G. A., Miller, L. K. & Stevenson, H. W. Incidental learning in film content: a developmental study. *Child Development,* 1968, **39,** 69-77.

Hicks, J. Imitation and retention of film-mediated aggressive peer and adult models. *Journal of Personality and Social Psychology,* 1965, **2,** 97-100.

Kass, N., & Wilson, H. Resistance to extinction as a function of percentage of reinforcement, number of trials, and conditioned reinforcement. *Journal of Experimental Psychology,* 1966, **71,** 355-357.

Keeney, T. J., Cannizzo, S. R., & Flavell, J. H. Spontaneous and induced verbal rehearsal in a recall task. *Child Development,* 1967, **38,** 953-966.

Lewis, M., Goldberg, S., & Campbell, H. A developmental study of information processing within the first three years of life: response decrement to a redundant signal. *Monographs of the Society for Research in Child Development,* 1969, **34,** Serial No. 133.

Luria, A. R., & Vinogradova, O. S. An objective investigation of the dynamics of semantic systems. *British Journal of Psychology,* 1959, **50,** 89-105.

Maccoby, E. E. Selective auditory attention in children. In L. P. Lipsitt & C. C. Spiker (Eds.), *Advances in child development and behavior.* Vol. 3. New York: Academic, 1967. Pp. 99-125.

Maccoby, E. E. The development of stimulus selection. In J. P. Hill (Ed.), *Minnesota symposium on child psychology.* Vol. 3. Minneapolis: University of Minnesota Press, 1969. Pp. 68-96.

Mednick, S. A., & Lehtinen, L. E. Stimulus generalization as a function of age in children. *Journal of Experimental Psychology,* 1957, **53,** 180-183.

Moely, B. E., Olsen, F. A., Hawles, T. G., & Flavell, J. H. Production deficiency in young children's clustered recall. *Developmental Psychology,* 1969, **1,** 26-34.

Papousek, H. Conditioning during early postnatal development. In Y. Brackbill & G. G. Thompson (Eds.), *Behavior in infancy and early childhood.* New York: Free Press, 1967. Pp. 259-274.

Parke, R. D. Effectiveness of punishment as an interaction of intensity, timing, agent nurturance and cognitive-structuring. *Child Development,* 1969, **40,** 213-235.

Parke, R. D. Some effects of punishment on children's behavior. In W. W. Hartup (Ed.), *The young child.* Vol. 2. Washington: National Association for the Education of Young Children, 1972. Pp. 264-283.

Parke, R. D., & Deur, J. L. Punishment and inhibition of aggression in children. *Developmental Psychology,* 1972, **7,** 266-269.

Parke, R. D., Ewall, W., & Slaby, R. G. Hostile and helpful verbalizations as regulators of non-verbal aggression. *Journal of Personality and Social Psychology,* 1972, **23,** 243-248.

Parke, R. D., & Walters, R. H. Some factors determining the efficacy of punishment for inducing response inhibition. *Monographs of the Society for Research in Child Development,* 1967, **32,** Serial No. 109.

Ramey, C. T., and Ourth, L. L. Delayed reinforcement and vocalization rates of infants. *Child Development,* 1971, **42,** 291–297.

Redd, W. H., Morris, E. K., & Martin, J. A. Effects of positive and negative adult-child interactions on children's social preferences. *Journal of Experimental Child Psychology,* 1975, in press.

Reiss, B. F. Genetic changes in semantic conditioning. *Journal of Experimental Psychology,* 1946, **36,** 143–152.

Rheingold, H., Gewirtz, J. L., & Ross, H. W. Social conditioning of vocalizations in the infant. *Journal of Comparative and Physiological Psychology,* 1959, **52,** 68–73.

Rossi, S., and Wittrock, M. C. Developmental shifts in verbal recall between mental ages two and five. *Child Development,* 1971, **42,** 333–338.

Salapatek, P., & Kessen, W. Visual scanning of triangles of the human newborn. *Journal of Experimental Child Psychology,* 1966, **3,** 155–167.

Sameroff, A. J. The components of sucking in the human newborn. *Journal of Experimental Child Psychology,* 1968, **6,** 607–623.

Sameroff, A. J. Can conditioned responses be established in the newborn infant: 1971? *Developmental Psychology,* 1971, **5,** 1–12.

Sameroff, A. J. Learning and adaptation in infancy: a comparison of models. In H. W. Reese (Ed.), *Advances in child development and behavior.* Vol. 7. New York: Academic, 1972. Pp. 169–214.

Sears, R. R., Maccoby, E., & Levin, H. *Patterns of Child Rearing.* Evanston, Ill.: Row, Paterson, 1957.

Seligman, M. E. P. On the generality of the laws of learning. *Psychological Review,* 1970, **77,** 406–418.

Siqueland, E. R. Reinforcement patterns and extinction in human newborns. *Journal of Experimental Child Psychology,* 1968, **6,** 431–442.

Skinner, B. F. *Science and human behavior.* New York: Macmillan, 1953.

Slaby, R. G. The effects of aggressive and altruistic verbalizations on aggressive and altruistic behaviors. In J. de Wit & W. W. Hartup (Eds.), *Origins and determinants of aggression.* The Hague: Mouton Publishers, 1975.

Slobin, D. I. *Psycholinguistics.* Glenview, Ill.: Scott, Foresman, 1971.

Spelt, D. K. The conditioning of the human fetus in utero. *Journal of Experimental Psychology,* 1948, **38,** 375–376.

Stevenson, H. W., Hale, G. W., Klein, R. E., & Miller, L. K. Interrelations and correlates in children's learning and problem solving. *Monographs of the Society for Research in Child Development,* 1968, **33,** Serial No. 123.

Tempore, V. J. Stimulus generalization as a function of mental age. *Child Development,* 1965, **36,** 229–235.

Tighe, L. S., & Tighe, T. J. Facilitation of transportation and reversal learning in children by prior perceptual training. *Journal of Experimental Child Psychology,* 1969, **8,** 366–374.

Vurpillot, E. The development of scanning strategies and their relation to visual differentiation. *Journal of Experimental Child Psychology,* 1968, **6,** 632–650.

Walters, R. H., & Andres, D. Punishment procedures and self-control. Paper presented at the Annual Meeting of the American Psychological Association, Washington, D.C., 1967.

Walters, R. H., & Parke, R. D. The influence of punishment and related disciplinary techniques on the social behavior or children: theory and empirical findings. In B. A. Maher (Ed.), *Progress in experimental personality research.* Vol. 4. New York: Academic, 1967. Pp. 179–228.

Walters, R. H., Parke, R. D. & Cane, V. A. Timing of punishment and the observation of consequences to others as determinants of response inhibition. *Journal of Experimental Child Psychology,* 1965, **2,** 10–30.

Williams, C. D. The elimination of tantrum behavior by extinction procedures. *Journal of Abnormal and Social Psychology,* 1959, **59,** 269.

Wolff, P., & Levin, J. R. The role of overt activity in children's imagery production. *Child Development,* 1972, **43,** 537–548.

Zimmerman, B. J., & Rosenthal, T. L. Observational learning of rule governed behavior by children. *Psychological Bulletin,* 1974, **81,** 29–42.

7
MOTIVATION AND EMOTION

What motivates children to pursue some goals and not others? In this chapter, traditional as well as more recent approaches to understanding motivation will be presented. Are primary drives, such as hunger and thirst, the main sources of motivation? Or are there other sources of motivation in infants and children?

A second and closely related theme of this chapter will be the development of emotion in children. Using two expressions of emotion, fear and smiling, a number of questions will be asked. What is the basis of emotion? How do genetic and environmental factors contribute to the development of emotion? Are emotions genetically determined, or are they learned through principles of operant, classical, or observational learning? Alternatively, are emotions determined by perceptual and cognitive discrepancies in the environment? In addition to examining the origins and development of emotions, the ways in which emotions can be altered or modified will be discussed. Next, how does the expression of emotions change as a child develops? A final set of questions concerns the ways in which children learn to recognize and label their own emotions and the emotional expressions in other people. What are the consequences of mislabeling emotional states?

MOTIVATION

A traditional view of motivation: primary drives

Motivation is the term that describes the external conditions or internal states that force the organism to act or react to his environment. Early theories of motivation stressed the role of primary drives, such as hunger and thirst. For many years psychologists thought that *all* behavior was controlled by these basic drives. There is no doubt that primary drives can control behavior; numerous animal studies document the impact of food and water deprivation on animal motivation. Similarly, most of us who have missed lunch have experienced an increased desire for dinner. However, it is equally clear that many of our activities are not directly related to primary drives. We seek acceptance from peers, we relish the thrill of a roller coaster ride, and we line up for hours for a concert. There is no doubt that we are motivated, but it is very difficult to reduce these activities to primary drives. When all behaviors could not be directly related to the basic drives, the concept of acquired drives was invented to account for the power of other motivations. It was assumed, for example, that affection developed as a result of the infant's early satisfaction of his hunger drive through the intervention of his mother. As a result of the mother's link with hunger reduction, a drive to maintain contact with her developed. Recently, however, serious questions have been raised about the necessity of primary needs as the basis for the child's motivation. Just as the original documentation of primary drive theory developed out of animal research, so did the research that was to seriously undermine the validity of this original position.

A famous challenge: the Harlow surrogate mother study

Perhaps the most famous challenge to this traditional view of motivation came from Harlow and Zimmerman (1959). Using infant rhesus monkeys as subjects, they showed that feeding is of much less importance than *contact comfort* as an antecedent of attachment formation. The monkeys were raised on two surrogate mothers, one of wire construction and one of terry cloth. (See Figure 7-1.) Although both mothers were always available to the infants, half of the monkeys were fed on the wire mother and the remainder on the cloth monkey. If the drive-reduction view is correct, the infants should spend the majority of their time on the mother that fed them. However, the infants fed on the lactating wire mother spent a decreasing amount of time in contact with her and an increasing amount of time with the nonlactating cloth mother. (See Figure 7-2.) "This is a finding completely contrary to any interpretation of derived-drive in terms of which the mother-form becomes conditioned to hunger-thirst reduction [Harlow, 1958, p. 676]." Moreover, the infant monkeys favored the cloth mother as a safe base from which to explore the environment, and they tended to seek the proximity of the cloth mother rather than that of the wire mother when in the presence of a fear stimulus. Harlow was so impressed by the infant's preference for the cloth mother that he attributed this attraction to a need for contact comfort. Margaret Ribble (1944) has argued that tactile stimulation is important for the development of the human infant as well; however, visual and auditory stimulation probably plays an even more important role in human development (Walters & Parke, 1965).

The evidence against the assumption that oral gratification is necessarily the principal antecedent of social responsiveness does not imply that the feeding situation itself is not of considerable importance as a context for social and cognitive development. As

FIGURE 7-1 Wire and cloth surrogate mothers. (From Harlow & Zimmerman, 1959 with permission of the authors and the American Association for the Advancement of Science.)

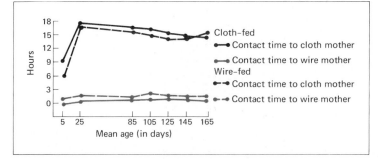

FIGURE 7-2 Contact time to cloth and wire surrogate mothers for young rhesus monkeys. (From Harlow & Zimmerman, 1959, with permission of the authors and the American Association for the Advancement of Science.)

noted in the last chapter, stimulation is extremely important for development and mothers often provide their infants with auditory and visual and physical stimulation during feeding. Moreover, Igel and Calvin (1960) have shown that need-reduction variables may play a role in social development and attachment formation. In a study that paralleled Harlow's original experiment with mother surrogates, these investigators found that infant puppies preferred a lactating cloth surrogate to a nonlactating cloth mother. "Similarly, one would expect a human infant to form a stronger attachment to a caretaker who feeds him and provides contact comfort and visual and auditory stimulation than to one who supplies a similar amount of distance receptor stimulation but little contact comfort or participates minimally in the feeding situation [Walters & Parke, 1965, pp. 64–65]."

Nor do these findings alter the fact that under conditions of severe food deprivation, hunger can be a strong motivating force. What is brought into question is the doctrine that all behavior is motivated by primary drives either directly or through association with these primary drives. They are not the only source of motivation.

Other challenges to a primary-drive-reduction viewpoint

There were other serious challenges to traditional drive-reduction theory. For example, Butler (1953) demonstrated that monkeys would "work" by pressing a lever for the mere opportunity of peering out of their cages. In other studies, animals have been found to exert great effort in order to examine a simple lock-and-chain "puzzle."

Similar examples abound at the human level as well. How would a hunger-thirst-reduction position explain why a young child will take a piece of cloth and "make it go to sleep [Gilmore, 1966, p. 355]." Or, how can the play behavior of a freshly fed and diapered infant be explained? Infants will stare at their mobiles, shake their rattles, clap their hands, and wave their arms, and then laugh and smile. They will repeat the sequence and laugh again. These are not just anecdotal observations of how an infant might fill his spare moments; a number of investigators have experimentally confirmed these speculations: infants will work when their only "payoff" is some interesting sight or sound (Rheingold, Stanley, & Cooley, 1962; Leuba & Friedlander, 1968).

An alternative approach to motivation: effectance

How do you explain these activities that are unrelated to basic drives? Drive-reduction theory is clearly not sufficient. Various answers have been offered, but a consistently recurring theme throughout many different approaches has been the important role of the child's need to master and understand his environment. R. W. White (1959) introduced the term *effectance motivation* to aid our understanding of this early and pervasive tendency of children to gain mastery and control over their environment. This theory suggests that children's constant attempts to understand their world may be the basis for the curiosity, exploration, and play that they exhibit from a very early age. The importance of curiosity and exploratory behavior is clear: the child is oriented to new and different aspects of his or her environment and increases the variety and range of stimuli with which to interact. Not only do children learn to recognize and become familiar with new aspects of their world; new opportunities for learning emerge as well.

Novelty, curiosity, and surprise as motivators

Even curiosity, or preference for unfamiliar and novel experiences, changes with age; one might expect the young infant to prefer the familiar, but as he grows and develops he shifts his preferences toward more novel events. Recently, Weizmann, Cohen, and Pratt (1971) tested the hypothesis suggested by Hunt (1963) that the interest in novelty follows a two-stage process:

> The infant begins to recognize recurrent patterns of stimulation by comparing them to their internal representations. . . . When infants first develop this ability to recognize objects, they show manifest pleasure at and become attracted to objects they can recognize. Once this recognition process has become commonplace, however, it no longer serves as a basis for attraction. The infant's interest in familiar stimuli now becomes replaced by the increased attention to the novel [Weizmann, Cohen, & Pratt, 1971, p. 149].

In a study aimed at documenting this developmental trend, Weizmann and his co-workers exposed thirty-two four-week-old infants to a stabile above their cribs for thirty minutes a day over a period of one month. At six weeks and again at eight weeks the infants were tested for their preference, a novel stabile or the familiar one that they had previously seen each day. Table 7-1 presents the results: at six weeks the infants preferred to watch the familiar stabile; by eight weeks the novel stimulus was preferred. Clearly, the preference for novelty develops out of the infant's ability to store prior experience in memory and suggests that attraction to novelty may proceed from an interest in familiar events.

As Charlesworth (1964) has shown with preschoolers and first- and third-graders, *surprise* as well as novelty may be an important motivator for children. As the author notes:

> Surprise was produced by violating, by means of a trick, the law governing conservation of substance. The expectancy that physical substances—marbles in the present case—are not changed in color or number by merely shaking them in a container is known to be already present in the preschool child. It was assumed that if such a violation was observed to occur, the subject would be surprised since such an event would contradict his expectations. The surprise reaction would then instigate him to demand to see the event again [Charlesworth, 1964, p. 1170].

As a subject in the surprise condition of this experiment your experience would be something like this: After being seated in front of a machine, you place five bright-red

Table 7-1 MEAN FIXATION TIME (IN SECONDS) FOR NOVEL AND FAMILIAR STABILES

Age, wk	Stabile familiarity	
	Novel	Familiar
six	62.5	93.1
eight	90.9	72.25

Source: Weizmann, F., Cohen, L. B., & Pratt, R. J. Novelty, familiarity, and the development of infant attention. *Developmental Psychology*, 1971, **4,** 149–154.

marbles in a slot at one side of the apparatus; the machine shakes the marbles and then eight yellow marbles roll out into a cup on the other side of the apparatus. The appearance of the eight yellow marbles is, of course, contrary to your expectation that the five red marbles would come out of the machine. In short, you are surprised. Your experience would be less dramatic if you were a subject in the nonsurprise condition: You insert your five bright-red marbles, and the machine shakes them around and then five red marbles reappear. All is according to your expectations, and hence no surprise. To measure the motivating properties of surprise, Charlesworth told the children that they could play the game as long as they wanted and then measured the number of times that the children played the marble game under these different conditions. As predicted, children in the surprise condition persisted at the marble game longer than children who were not surprised. Moreover, in comparison with children in a novelty condition who had the color, number, or order of marbles varied from trial to trial, children in the surprise condition persisted longer. Not only does violation of an expectation serve to maintain responding, but it may even be a better motivator than novelty. In this case, nonconformation led to approach rather than avoidance behaviors. Surprise also motivated more questioning than did nonsurprise conditions.

Another index of children's curiosity, namely, questioning, has received extensive study by Berlyne and Frommer (1966). In their study, pictures and stories representing different degrees of novelty, surprisingness, and incongruity were presented to children ranging in age from kindergarten to grade six. Novelty was manipulated by changing the characters in a familiar story; for example, Aesop's famous fable "The Fox and the Raven" was presented in the usual way and in a second version with two unfamiliar animals—a tayra and an auk—replacing the principal characters. For surprise, Berlyne and Frommer presented a story of a little boy who wouldn't eat and was finally blown away with a kite; the story ended with the boy starting to eat again. An example of an incongruity item was a picture of an animal with an elephant's head, a horse's forelegs, a lion's body, and a dog's tail, while the corresponding but nonincongruous pictures were normal elephants and birds. Questioning frequency increased with age, while novelty and surprisingness and incongruity all increased the incidence of questions at all age levels.

These examples and findings all tell a similar story: from infancy onward the child is an active, stimulus-seeking, and highly curious organism. Viewing motivation as governed by biological deficits alone is simply no longer tenable.

EMOTIONS

Children show a wide range of emotional reactions. But why are they sometimes elated and happy, at other times depressed and sullen, and on other occasions angry? And what are the determinants of our emotions? How do emotional responses originally develop? How do they change with age? What are the circumstances that lead to one emotion rather than another? There are, of course, a number of possible theories of emotion, but three viewpoints predominate. According to one position, emotions such as fear, sadness, and joy are largely constitutionally determined. A second position regards emotions as reactions learned and acquired through interaction with the environment. A final position, the perceptual-discrepancy hypothesis, focuses on reactions to violations of familiar or expected events as a way of explaining emotional development.

To illustrate these approaches, we will first examine the development of fear; then we will apply these same viewpoints to the development of positive affective states.

Fear

The early developmental course of fear Much attention has been devoted to documenting the variety of stimuli that elicit fear responses during infancy. Jersild (1946) reported the following frequencies of various fear situations for infants in the first two years: noise and agents of noise (27 percent); pain (18 percent); falling, loss of support, and high places (13 percent); animals (7 percent); sudden unexpected movement plus lights, flashes, and shadows (6 percent). Other more recent investigations and reviews (Scarr & Salapatek, 1970) have confirmed that infants show fear reactions to loud, sudden, unexpected events; to depth, as indexed by the visual cliff (see Chapter 4); and to pain and rapid or abrupt displacement in space.

Of particular interest have been social fears, such as the fear of unfamiliar people that occurs for some infants in the latter part of the first year (eight to nine months). However, the onset of *fear of strangers* is not abrupt or sudden, but is usually preceded by a period characterized by less smiling and unresponsiveness to unfamiliar adults. One investigator, Rene Spitz (1950), was so impressed with the regularity of the time course followed by this fear reaction that he termed it *eight-month anxiety,* in recognition of the fact that this kind of fear peaked in the seven- to nine-month period.

Although fear of strangers has become enshrined in the psychological literature as a developmental milestone, it is far from a universal and inevitable reaction. In fact, Rheingold and Eckerman (1973) have recently criticized the continued treatment of stranger fear as a typical reaction, and suggest that greeting and smiling may be a frequent reaction to strangers for some infants.

In spite of this controversy, there is little doubt that many infants do show fear or at least wariness in reaction to unfamiliar people, but the timing of onset, the frequency of occurrence, and the intensity of the reaction are modified by a variety of factors. In Box 7-1, Morgan and Ricciuti present data which present a serious challenge to Spitz's eight-month-anxiety position. These investigators present evidence that the fear reaction is greater at twelve months, rather than eight months, as observed by Spitz. Moreover, the context in which the assessment was conducted was important. Infants who sat in their mothers' laps while the stranger approached did *not* show any fear reaction; only when placed in infant seats a few feet away from their mothers was there any negative emotional response. Just as the presence of a familiar caretaker may affect the child's reaction to strangers, the familiarity of the context is important as well. Sroufe, Waters, and Matas (1974) reported little fear reaction when ten-month-old infants were tested at home for their reaction to a stranger, but nearly fifty percent of the infants showed fear when tested in an unfamiliar laboratory.

BOX 7-1

Morgan and Ricciuti recently investigated the developmental course followed by the fear of strangers reaction; their findings seriously challenge Spitz's view that the stranger anxiety reaction reaches a peak at eight months.

Eighty infants participated, with eight boys and eight girls at each of five age points: four and one-half, six and one-half, eight and one-half, ten and one-half, and twelve and one-half months. In the critical test, a strange adult, smiling and talking, gradually approached and finally touched the infant under two conditions: with the baby on the mother's lap or in a feeding table about 4 feet from the mother. An observer recorded the infant's facial expressions, vocalizations, and gross visual and motor activity in reaction to the stranger and the masks. From these data, a score indicating the degree of positive and negative responses was calculated for the infants at each of the five age levels. The age trends are plotted in Figure 7-3. The younger infants were generally positive, but with increasing

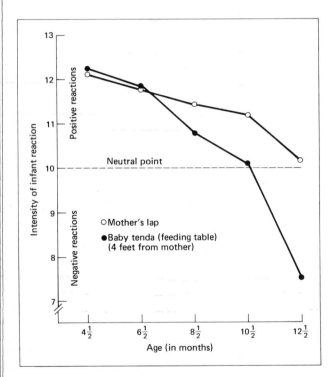

FIGURE 7-3 Infants' response to strangers as a function of age and distance from mother. (From Morgan & Ricciuti, 1969, with permission of the authors, the publisher, and the Tavistock Institute of Human Relations.)

age, negative reactions became more prevalent. By the twelve and one-half-month age point, more negative than positive reactions to the stranger were found. No sex differences were present.

Even after the end of the first year, the infants showed an increasing reaction to the stranger. Another important finding concerns the effect of the closeness of the mother on the amount of stranger fear. As the graph clearly shows, the reaction was less when the baby was in the mother's lap than when in a tenda (table) a short distance from the mother.

Source: Morgan, G. A., & Ricciuti, H. N. Infants' responses to strangers during the first year. In B. M. Foss (Ed.), *Determinants of infant behavior.* Vol. 4. London: Methuen, 1969, 253–272.

Do infants show fear reactions to all unfamiliar people—children as well as adults? To find out, Lewis and Brooks-Gunn (1972) examined the reactions of infants between seven and nineteen months of age to strange male and female adults, a strange child (four-year-old girl), their mothers, and the self (as reflected in a mirror). The infants' responses were measured at four distances: 15 feet away; 8 feet away; 3 feet away; and touching the infants. Reactions were measured on a five-point scale: a score of 3 indicates a neutral response, with 1 being the most negative and 5 being the most positive responses. The facial expression scale varied from a broad smile to a puckering cry-like expression, while the motor scale varied from reaching toward the person to twisting away and reaching to mother. Figure 7-4 shows the results. First, it is not the mere *presence* of a stranger that elicits negative emotional reactions; the child's affective reaction depends on the distance of the stimulus person from the infant. As the individuals came closer, both positive and negative reactions were greater; the negative reaction to the strange adults became clear, while the positive reactions to the mother and mirror image of the self were more marked. Of principal interest is the child's reaction to the unfamiliar child; in contrast to their reaction to the adult, the infants showed a mild positive reaction. The stimulus characteristics of the stranger are an important determinant of whether or not a stranger will elicit fear. It is clear that infants do not show fear

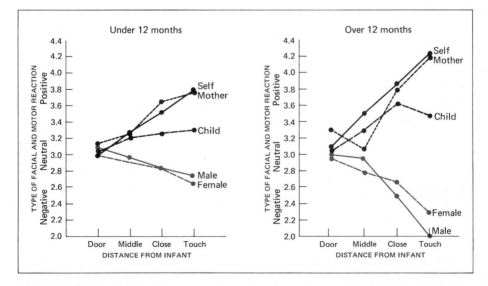

FIGURE 7-4 The amount of positive and negative facial and motor responses of human infants in reaction to self and to familiar and unfamiliar individuals. (From Lewis & Brooks-Gunn, 1972.)

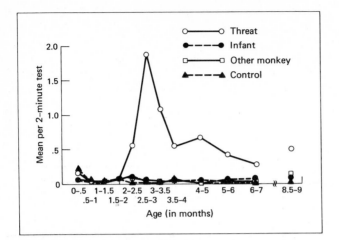

FIGURE 7-5 The amount of disturbance behavior of infant rhesus monkeys in response to different types of pictures viewed during nine months of isolation. (From Sackett, 1966, with permission of the author and the American Association for the Advancement of Science.)

of all kinds of strangers. Next we examine some alternative viewpoints that may account for the development of fear.

Fear as a genetically determined phenomenon   According to this viewpoint, fear has a constitutional basis and is not dependent on specific learning experiences. Freedman (1965) has offered some evidence that the age of onset of fear of strangers is influenced by genetic factors. Specifically, he found greater concordance of onset age between identical than between fraternal twins. Although it is possible that the experiences, such as frequency of exposure to strangers, may be more similar for identical than for fraternal twins, this is a rather weak and unlikely possibility.

Another kind of evidence in favor of a constitutional argument comes from cross-cultural studies of the development of fear of strangers. In spite of childrearing practices that differ greatly from Western customs, both infants raised in Uganda (Ainsworth, 1963) and babies reared on a Hopi Indian reservation (Dennis, 1940) show the stranger-anxiety reaction at approximately eight months, the same time as Western infants. Probably the most convincing evidence of the genetic basis of fear comes from a study of fear emergence in rhesus monkeys by Sackett (1966). In this experiment a group of eight monkeys were raised from birth to nine months in isolation. Their only input was a series of colored slides depicting monkeys of various ages engaged in a range of typical monkey activities, such as threatening, exploring, and playing. In addition, a set of control slides of nonmonkey scenes were included. Two methods of slide presentation were employed: In one case, the slides were projected for a two-minute period in a daily exposure session, but the monkey had no direct control over the onset or duration of the picture. Under the second procedure the animal could expose itself to the pictures by touching a lever which turned on the picture for a fifteen-second period. Behavioral reactions to the slides, such as vocalization, disturbance, playing, and exploration, were recorded by an observer hidden behind a one-way-vision screen. Of particular interest was the disturbance reaction, which includes rocking, huddling, self-clasping, fear, and withdrawal. Figure 7-5 shows that the isolated monkeys were highly selective in their fear reaction in terms of both the object and the timing. Only one slide evoked much disturbance, the threatening monkey picture. Throughout the nine-month period the other slides provoked little fear response. Even more striking is the fact that the fear reaction began abruptly at two to two and one-half months and peaked at about three months. By three and one-half months, there was a decline in fear of the picture. When the monkey had control over the things that he looked at, a similar pattern emerged.

> Since the isolation rearing conditions precluded opportunities for learning the significance of the visual threat of another monkey, the data suggest that this threat pattern may be an *innate releasing stimulus* for fearful behavior in rhesus monkeys. Although the initial onset may be maturationally governed, it is unlikely that the decline observed in this experiment would be found under normal rearing conditions where the threat is often backed up with actual physical attacks. These data suggest that while certain aspects of communication may lie in acquisition through social learning processes during interactions with other animals, the initial evocation of such complex responses may have an inherited species-specific structure [Sackett, 1966, p. 1472].

Fear as a learned phenomenon According to other theorists, fear is not innate or constitutionally determined; rather, children *learn* to fear certain aspects of their environment. Sometimes this can be accomplished in a very direct manner through either instrumental conditioning or classical conditioning, learning paradigms that were discussed in Chapter 6. A familiar example of instrumental fear conditioning is the young child who touches a hot stove; the *consequence* of touching the stove is pain, and as a result of this unpleasant outcome the child learns to fear the hot stove and avoids it on later occasions.

Another approach is the classical conditioning position, which stresses not the outcomes but rather the events that are temporally associated with a particular response. According to this viewpoint, the young child learns to fear objects and even people in his environment by their association with an unlearned fearful stimulus. For example, as we noted in an earlier chapter, children who are punished by an adult may avoid this parent or socializing agent. In classical conditioning terms, the loud noise would be the unconditioned stimulus, or UCS; any object that was temporally linked with this UCS would be termed the conditioned stimulus or CS. The theory assumes that as a result of the frequent pairing of the previously neutral or nonfearful stimulus with the anxiety-arousing event, this neutral event would serve as a fear elicitor as well.

The case of "little Albert" illustrates this approach to fear development. Watson and Raynor (1920) found that the loud noise produced by striking a steel bar evoked fear reactions in this eleven-month-old boy; few other things caused him any anxiety or fear. A white rat, to which the child showed no fear, was chosen as the object to be conditioned. Over a series of trials, Watson and Raynor presented the white rat but, at the same time, clanged the steel bar. Although the child had not previously feared the white rat, presentation of the animal—without the noise—was sufficient to produce marked fear reactions. Little Albert had been classically conditioned to fear the rat. Moreover, the child showed evidence of generalized fear of similar objects: furry and wooly objects in his environment, such as a white rabbit, a dog, a fur coat, cotton, and wool. In fact, he even showed a fear reaction to a Santa Claus mask! To determine whether the generalization effect was merely transitory, Watson and Raynor retested Albert after one month. Although the emotional reactions were reduced, there was still evidence of generalized conditioned fear. Later studies with both children (Jones, 1931) and animals (Miller, 1948) have confirmed this classical conditioning theory of fear acquisition.

However, direct experience with the critical object is not the only way in which fears are learned. Observation of the emotional reactions of other people to environmental events will often shape the onlookers' reactions to these events. In a recent experiment Venn and Short (1973) exposed nursery-school-age children to a film showing a five-year-old male model scream and withdraw when the mother presented a plastic figure of Mickey Mouse; in response to another previously neutral stimulus, a plastic figure of Donald Duck, the film model gave only a neutral reaction. A later test revealed that the children avoided Mickey Mouse, the fearful stimulus, more than Donald Duck, the neutral stimulus. In this study, classical conditioning had been achieved, but merely through observation. In other naturalistic situations, a similar phenomenon may occur. Parents,

A fearful child. (Suzanne Szasz.)

for example, may be inadvertently teaching their children to fear certain objects by showing marked fear themselves in the presence of the object. Children who witness a parent jumping back and screaming at the sight of a snake may show a similar fear reaction when they themselves directly encounter a snake on some future occasion. In this case the child's fear of snakes develops through observing the parent's emotional reactions.

Perceptual-recognition hypothesis   In 1946 Hebb reported a classic experiment involving the development of fear in the chimpanzee. There were two critical conditions in this study. In the first condition, the chimps were given normal visual experience, including the experience of seeing other chimpanzees. In the second condition, the animal was reared with a blindfold which prevented him from seeing the other chimps. Both groups were then exposed to the critical stimulus, a plaster replica of the head of a chimpanzee. The results were striking: for the animals who had been reared under normal conditions and allowed to interact with age-mates, the sight of the "chimpanzee head" caused extreme fear and flight; for the animals lacking this opportunity for visual learning, the sculpture caused either little reaction or a mild curiosity. The main thing is that these animals showed no fear reaction. Why the difference? Hebb (1946; 1949) proposed that the normally reared chimps had learned a particular perceptual pattern which defined the concept of "chimpanzee." This familiar pattern included not only a head, but, of course, a body, legs, and arms as well. It was the sight of the head alone, partially familiar but incomplete, that caused the animals' upset. Their expectation based on past experience with the familiar object, the chimpanzee was violated by this incomplete duplication of the familiar pattern. It was, according to Hebb, this violation of the expectation that evoked fear. It is now easy to see why the blindfolded animals failed to show any fear. They were deprived of the opportunity to build a standard of familiarity. Until the pattern has been learned or centrally coded, incongruous or violating stimulation is precluded.

At the human level, the phenomenon that most closely resembles the reactions of Hebb's chimpanzees is a fear of strangers anxiety reaction, such as crying, whimpering, and withdrawal, whenever a strange adult is present. Part of the reason for this reaction may be due to the apparent discrepancy the infant notices between his familiar care-taker and the stranger. They share some similarities, just as the plaster head shared some similarities with the chimp's familiar experiences, but there were some discrepancies as well. It may be that the discrepancy between the familiar and the partially familiar causes the anxiety. If this position has any merit, certain predictions would follow. Since the central proposition involves the learning of a unique pattern—the characteristics of the mother, for example—then the extent of the anxiety reaction should vary with the exclusiveness of the mother-infant relationship. The infant who sees only his mother is more likely to notice or detect the difference between the well-established pattern of mother and a strange female. On the other hand, a child who sees babysitters, grand-mothers, day care center aids, and next door neighbors, as well as the mother, will have a more diffuse concept of "mother" and will, therefore, be less likely to show a fear of strange adults. Evidence in support of this prediction comes from a study by Schaffer (1966). Using human infants, he found that fear of strangers was evidenced earlier in families with a small number of children and when the number of strangers typically seen by the child was small. These data, then, are clearly consistent with the perceptual-discrepancy approach to fear development.

Which explanation is correct?   It should be obvious to the reader by now that no single viewpoint is "correct"; all views have some evidence in their favor. It is not unreasonable to assume that different types of fear may, in fact, develop according to different sets of principles. Moreover, it is possible, as Bronson (1968) has proposed, that the contribution and importance of these viewpoints may vary with the developmental stage of the organism. For example, in the first few months of life, the constitutional and classical conditioning positions are probably much more useful in explaining "fear" than is the perceptual-recognition hypothesis. This latter viewpoint will be relevant only "when the child is cognitively mature enough to distinguish between familiar and unfamiliar and to recognize discrepancies in the appearance of a familiar stimulus [Bronson, 1968, p. 424]." These cognitive attainments are related to Piaget's concepts of schema and object permanence, which will be discussed in Chapter 8. The task, then, is not to decide which explanation is correct, but to determine how each set of principles contributes to our understanding of the development of this complex emotional response pattern. With the present paucity of empirical data, to choose among these alternatives is premature.

Longitudinal development of fear   Interesting as the infant data may be, one would like to know if this information is predictive of later behavior. Is knowledge of fearfulness in infancy helpful in determining the probable degree of fear observed at later stages of development? In other words, is there continuity in emotional behavior between infancy and later childhood?

Bronson (1970) has provided a partial answer in his analysis of the development of fear over the first eight and one-half years of life. The boys and girls who participated were part of the Berkeley Growth Study, a longitudinal investigation of physical and mental development. Bronson took advantage of the opportunities provided by the repeated testing of the same children at different ages to track changes in fearfulness. From the records of the child's reactions to the examiner and the examination situation, two main indexes of fear were chosen: age of onset of fearfulness, and "shyness ratings," which measured diverse signs of wariness including crying. Although there were wide discrepancies in the age of onset fearfulness, stable individual differences in the degree of fear were evident by the end of the first year. Therefore, the average shyness ratings during ten and fifteen months were used to index fearfulness in infancy. To test for continuity between this early stage and later childhood, three age periods were selected: two and-one-half to three and one-half years, four to six years, and six and one-half to eight and one-half years. The correlations between individual ratings of shyness during infancy with ratings made at later ages were presented in Table 7-2. The most striking feature of these results is the difference between boys and girls. For boys, the level of fearfulness remains relatively stable over the first eight and one-half years of life. Girls, on the other hand, show little consistency in their fear reactions from infancy to early childhood. Similarly, relative precocity of fear onset was a reliable predictor of

Table 7-2 CORRELATIONS BETWEEN RATINGS OF SHYNESS IN THE
PERIOD 10-15 MONTHS AND SHYNESS RATED AT LATER
PERIODS

	Age period (yr)		
Group	2-3½	4-6	6½-8½
Boys	0.56*	0.46†	0.41‡
	($N = 26$)	($N = 26$)	($N = 24$)
Girls	0.21	0.18	0.28
	($N = 24$)	($N = 24$)	($N = 21$)

* $P = 0.01$.
† $P = 0.02$.
‡ $P = 0.05$.
Source: Bronson, G. W. Fear of visual novelty, *Developmental Psychology*, 1970, **2**, pp. 33–40.
By permission of the author and the American Psychological Association.

later fearfulness for boys. Those boys who showed early fear of novelty tended to remain more fearful than their peers who exhibited their first fear reaction at a later stage of infancy. Again, in the case of girls, there was little stability between age of onset of fear and later shyness ratings. Males and females, however, did *not* differ in the average degree of fearfulness at any age; this finding suggests that boys and girls, as groups, were not subject to differential treatment. "In males, but not in females, a relatively enduring predisposition towards a particular level of fearfulness was set by factors that were operative at or before the age of onset of fear [Bronson, 1970, p. 13]."

Developmental changes in specific fears Even though the general level of fearfulness may show some individual stability over time, it is likely that the specific objects and situations that evoke fear change as children develop. In fact, tracking the development of specific fears has been a favorite task of psychologists since the 1930s.

For an up-to-date look at the nature of children's fears, we turn to a recent study by Barnett (1969). A group of 228 seven- to twelve-year-old girls participated in this project. She found that overall fear did not differ at various age levels, but several specific categories of fear changed with age. Figure 7-6 illustrates age changes in particular fears. Notice that as the child grows older, fears concerning imaginery creatures and personal safety show a decline; probably this trend is due to the child's more sophisticated understanding of the laws governing physical reality. As adolescence approaches there is another marked change: school and social concerns show a rapid rise. Other data support these general age trends. Scherer and Nakamura (1968), for example, report that nine- to eleven-year-old boys and girls include the following as their most common fears: being hit by a car or truck, failing a test, getting poor grades, being sent to the principal's office, and bombing attacks. Again school anxieties are clearly in evidence. Similarly, Angelino and his coworkers (1956) found in their study of fear development that fears relating to personal safety and animals declined with age, while fear of school and social situations showed increases between nine and seventeen years of age. These developmental changes move the child closer to the adult fear profile, which is characterized by a high degree of social fear and little concern of imaginery fears.

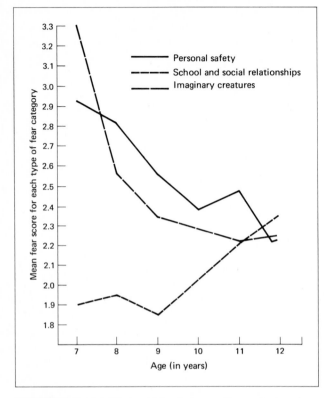

FIGURE 7-6 Variation in children's fears with age for imaginary creatures, school and social relationships, and personal safety. (From Barnett, 1969.)

Fear measurement: the integration of various indexes of fearfulness Although many studies of children's fear have relied on verbal reports of what children (or
their parents) *say* they fear, until recently little attention has been directed to the interrelationships between verbal reports and actual fear behavior. In other words, do children
who say they are afraid *act* afraid? Similarly, do emotional measures of fear relate to
verbal and behavioral indexes? The importance of these questions is underlined by
recent studies of fear in adults. Lang (1968), for example, found little relationship among
verbal responses and overt responses, both in the form of avoidance of the feared
object and physiological measures of fear among college students. Saying one is not
afraid is a poor predictor of how one will act or how one's heart will react when confronted by the actual fear object. Whether or not the three systems of fear are integrated
to a greater extent during childhood is one of the questions that Barnett (1969) tried to
answer. Two groups of girls participated: 10 nine- to eleven-year-olds drawn from local
Brownie and Girl Scout organizations and 20 nine- to eleven-year-olds from a local
Catholic school. Children came individually to the university laboratory, where a variety
of measures of fear were collected. First, the girls watched a series of slides depicting
either neutral pictures of nonfrightening animals, such as deer, raccoons, and rabbits,

and then a series of three critical slides of three different snakes. To measure the children's physiological reaction, heart rate was continuously monitored during the slide show. To index the children's verbal expressions of fear, the subjects rated their fear of the snake pictures. As a further measure of the children's reactions to snakes generally, the snake questionnaire for children was administered. This instrument is composed of eleven items describing scenes with harmless snakes; the children merely indicate how fearful they would be if they were in each scene. Confrontation with a live snake followed. In this behavioral assessment phase of the study, each girl was asked to execute a series of increasingly intimate acts, first with a small kitten and then with the test animal, a 4-foot boa constrictor. Here is a list of the eleven acts that the children were asked to perform:

1. Walk up to a white line 2 feet from the cage.
2. Walk directly up to the cage.
3. Look directly at the animal in the cage.
4. Put hand in the glass of the cage.
5. Remove the cover from the cage.
6. Place hand in the cage.
7. Touch the animal for the count of one.
8. Stroke the animal for the count of three.
9. Stroke the animal for the count of five.
10. Lift the animal an inch off the ground.
11. Lift the animal out of the cage.

The child's behavior fear score was the number of tasks actually completed, with the higher scores representing less fear. Finally, the child was asked to rate her own fear during the snake test. Now let us examine the results. Barnett confirmed the fact that most children, or girls at least, are not afraid of kittens. Twenty-five out of twenty-seven girls completed all tasks with the live kitten. In contrast, only seven children completed the eleven tasks with the live boa constrictor. Of particular interest is the relationship of the girls' behavior with other fear measures, the self-report and heart rate. The children's self-ratings during the slide presentation and their evaluations of their own fearfulness in the presence of the snake both predicted accurately the actual behavioral performance. Children who said earlier that they feared snakes hovered around the back of the room and would not touch the snake. Those who said they were not afraid touched, picked up, and even held the snake close to their bodies. Similarly, the high correlation between the snake questionnaire results and children's performance suggests that this is a valid instrument for fear assessment in children. Apparently children do as they say. However, the self-reported overall fear level, measured by the children's Fear Survey Schedule which measured fear of a wide range of objects, did *not* relate to the children's behavior in the snake test. The close link between word and deed is present only in the case of specific fears. Knowing that a child regards herself as highly fearful in *general* may be a poor predictor of how she will actually behave in *particular* fear situations.

The relationships between emotional reactions indexed by heart rate and the self-report and behavioral measures of fear were also impressive. With the snake questionnaire scores as a basis, the children were divided into high-and low-fear groups and then the heart rate responses in reaction to the snake slides of these two samples was examined. Heart rate acceleration was higher for the high-fear girls than for their peers who reported being less afraid of snakes. Similarly, heart rate acceleration was greater for the girls who rated their fear of the snake as greater. Finally, the verbal rating of fear during performance with the live snake followed the same pattern of relationship of heart rate measure. In summary, somatic and self-report indexes among these girls showed a consistent and positive relationship. Again evidence of a high degree of interrelation between these two fear indexes was found: the high-fear subjects as indexed by the completion of few tasks with the snake showed greater heart rate acceleration than the low-fear girls.

Unlike adults, in children the three fear systems—self-report, behavioral, and psychophysiological—show a well-integrated pattern. Girls who say they are afraid tend to react that way both behaviorally and physiologically. As Barnett suggested, "it may be the case that while in adults separate variables control the various systems of fear response, the extent of this differential learning has not taken place with children 7 to 12 years of age [Barnett, 1969, p. 33]." Clearly, data on older children would be of interest in tracking the emergence of the highly differentiated control of fear responsivity that is observed in adults. Moreover, in light of Bronson's (1970) data concerning the sex differences in stability of fear reactions over time, one wonders whether the same degree of integration would be present for boys. Cultural norms dictating less fearfulness for boys may contribute to weaker links between self-report measures and other indexes of fear.

Ways of overcoming children's fears   One advantage of a learning theory approach to fear development is that it points directly to therapeutic techniques for reducing children's fears. Just as conditioning could be used to account for fear acquisition, these same principles can aid in fear reduction.

Counterconditioning. For counterconditioning, the fearful stimuli that typically evoke emotional reactions are presented in conjunction with pleasant activities. In a classic application of this technique, Mary Cover Jones (1924) used food as the pleasant stimulus. The subject, Peter, a boy of thirty-four months, showed many of the same reactions as "little Albert," the infant in the Watson and Raynor study. Both children showed strong fear reactions to furry objects, such as fur coats, feathers, cotton, wool, and animals, especially rabbits. To reduce his fear of the rabbit, Jones placed the caged animal in the room with the child at the same time that he was eating. She was careful not to put the cage too close so that Peter's eating was disrupted. Each day the cage was moved a little closer, and finally the animal was released from his cage. At the end of the treatment period, the child showed no fear, even when the rabbit was placed on the eating table. In fact, the child spontaneously expressed his fondness for the animal; by pairing the animal with the highly pleasant activity of eating, the positive affect associated with eating generalized to the rabbit and counterconditioned Peter's fear of the rabbit. Generalization tests, moreover, indicated that his previous fears of furry objects had been successfully eliminated as well.

Desensitization. A more recent approach to overcoming children's fear is *desensitization.* According to this approach, the therapist trains the child in physical relaxation techniques, constructs a graduated list of fearful stimuli, and then asks the child to imagine events in increasing order of fearfulness. Each time that a fearful stimulus is visualized, the child is required to relax. By inducing a state of calm in the presence of the fearful stimulus, the associated anxiety is extinguished or counterconditioned. Relaxation, then, instead of food is used in this procedure. As the child overcomes his fear of weaker events, the therapist gradually moves up the fear scale so that eventually the most fearful event becomes completely neutralized and elicits no anxiety. Instead of visualizing fear items, more concrete techniques of stimulus presentation, such as slides and pictures of the fear stimuli, have been employed with children.

To illustrate the procedure, here is an example for a snake-fearing child. The child and therapist first construct a list of snake-related objects that the child fears. There may be as many as twenty steps between the least and most feared items. The least feared item might be seeing a snake skin belt on a department store counter, while a middle-level item might be seeing a snake 20 feet ahead on a path in the forest. The highest item might be picking up and handling a nonpoisonous snake. After a few sessions of relaxation training, the child in the first desensitization session is asked to imagine seeing the belt and to relax. He has repeated visualization of this first item with relaxation instructions until he no longer reports fear and anxiety upon visualizing the belt on the store counter. Then he moves on to the next item in his hierarchy and goes through repeated exposure to this item while he engages in the incompatible muscle relaxation procedure. Gradually, the child works up to the point where he can even pick up and handle the previously feared snake without anxiety.

This technique has been applied to a wide range of fears in both children and adults, including fear of spiders, snakes, airplanes, hospitals, and schools. Children with severe examination anxiety have had their performance on tests improved through desensitization (Mann & Rosenthal, 1969). Reading achievement scores of desensitized children improved and their anxiety test scores dropped significantly in contrast to a group of nontreated control children. Moreover, observers of the treatment procedure benefited to the same extent as the direct participants; this suggests a further manner in which fears can be reduced: modeling. In the next section we will examine the impact of modeling techniques for promoting fear reduction.

Exposure to a fearless model.   Just as many fears can be acquired merely by observing the actions of other individuals, many fearful responses can be eliminated in this same manner. A study by Bandura, Grusec, and Menlove (1967) illustrates that a fear of dogs can be overcome by exposure to a fearless peer model. Qualifications for participation in this project were few: one merely had to be a nursery schooler who exhibited a strong fear of dogs. Then, each child was assigned to one of four treatment conditions designed to help him overcome his dog phobia. Children in one group watched a four-year-old model perform increasingly "brave" and intimate interactions with a dog over a series of eight brief sessions. For example, in the first session the child merely stayed close to the dog, who was enclosed in a wooden pen. In later sessions the child climbed into the pen and fearlessly played with the animal. All of the sessions took place in the context of a "jovial party" to determine whether a positive viewing atmosphere would further reduce and counteract the young children's anxieties. A child assigned to the second condition would see the same graduated series of model-dog interactions, but in a neutral rather than a party context. Since repeated exposure to the feared animal alone might be therapeutic, some of the children merely watched the dog, and although the party atmosphere was retained, no peer model ever appeared. Finally, for the last group, the only experience offered would be the jovial party; neither dog nor model was ever present. Following treatment, the children's fear behavior in reaction to two different dogs was assessed twice: once immediately after the final session and again a month later.

According to Bandura:

> The avoidance test consisted of a graded sequence of interactions with the dog. The children were asked, for example, to approach and pet the dog, to release it from the playpen, remove it from its leash, feed it with dog biscuits and spend a fixed period of time alone in the room with the animal. The final and most difficult set of tasks required the children to climb into the playpen with the dog and after having locked the gate, to pet it and remain alone with it under these confining fear-arousing conditions [Bandura, 1968, p. 203].

As Figure 7-7 indicates, the modeling treatment was successful in producing stable *and* generalized reduction in the children's avoidance of dogs. In comparison to the other two groups, children exposed to the fearless peer model displayed significantly greater approach behavior, not only toward the experimental dog, but to an unfamiliar dog as well. A generalized reduction in fear had been produced by these modeling procedures. Modeling alone apparently accounted for these changes since the party atmosphere contributed little to the fear reduction. Stating their results differently, an impressive 67 percent of the children in the modeling treatment conditions were eventually able to remain alone in the room and confined with the dog in the playpen; only a few children in the control conditions could manage this terminal task.

In recent studies, Liebert (1973) has successfully applied these techniques to children's fear of the dentist. A child overcame his fear of the dentist by observing a film of another child who overcame his initial fear and successfully completed a dental visit. At

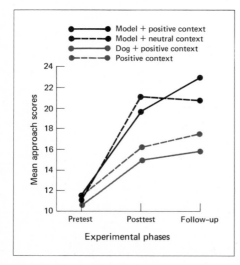

FIGURE 7-7 Mean approach scores achieved by children in each of the treatment conditions on the three different periods of assessment. (From Bandura, Grusec, and Menlove, 1967, with permission of the authors and the American Psychological Association.)

Photographs of children, who were apprehensive about dogs, engaging in fearless interactions with dogs after exposure to a series of therapeutic films. (From Bandura & Menlove, 1968.)

the end of his brave performance, the film model was rewarded with a large red tooth-brush. It is clear that exposure to film models is an effective technique for reducing childrens' fears.

In the next section we turn to a discussion of the development of positive emotions and examine smiling, laughter, and humor.

Smiling, laughter, and humor

Just as negative emotions can be viewed from a variety of angles, the development of the child's positive expressions of emotion and affect can be examined from a diverse series of viewpoints. Take the smiling response of the infant as an example. This response has received a great deal of attention because it is one of the first expressions of social responsivity observable in the human infant. Again, we ask a series of questions concerning the determinants of its development. Is its developmental course constitutionally determined? Or, is it simply a conditioned response? Alternatively, how well does the perceptual-recognition hypothesis account for the development of smiling? Let us examine the data.

The developmental course of smiling   Much of the research on smiling has been concerned with the types of stimulus conditions effective in eliciting and maintaining smiling at various developmental stages. The earliest phase of smiling in the human infant has been termed *spontaneous* or *reflex smiling* (Gewirtz, 1965). Watson's (1924) elicitation of an infant smile by stroking the lips or cheeks is an example of the reflex smile; spontaneous smiles appear to be dependent mainly on the infant's internal state. Early smiles have been attributed to "gas," although recent research suggests that gas per se has little to do with it. In their first three or four weeks, infants are likely to smile when they are comfortable and in REM (rapid-eye-movement) periods of sleep or drowsiness (Ende and Koenig, 1969). The exact nature of the intraorganic stimulus remains a mystery. Recent findings suggest that girls engage in more spontaneous smiling than boys in the newborn period (Korner, 1969; Freedman, 1971). Possibly "girls are genetically more prone to affiliative modes of behavior [Freedman, 1971, p. 95]." Moreover, other evidence indicates that frequent smilers in the newborn period tend to have lower thresholds for later social smiling (Freedman, 1964). This period of spontaneous smiling is relatively brief and between the third and eighth week social smiling begins as the infant smiles in response to a wide variety of external, and often social, stimuli. Influenced by ethological conceptions of an innate releasing stimulus, it was originally proposed that the smiling face of an adult is the best elicitor of infant smiles. However, recent research has shown that a wide variety of stimuli are effective, including auditory and tactual as well as visual stimuli. Although the earliest elicitor of the smile appears to be a high-pitched human voice (Wolff, 1963), in general, a combination of voice and face, particularly a moving face, is the most reliable elicitor of smiling over the first six months of life (L'Allier, 1961; Laroche & Tcheng, 1963).

Recent studies of the development of smiling in blind infants provide further support for the view that visual stimuli are not *necessary* elicitors of smiling. Freedman (1965) and Dunn (1962) both reported that congenitally blind children could smile in response to social stimulation; the timing of the occurrence of smiling was between one and one-half and four months, approximately the same time as their sighted siblings. Even deaf and blind children reportedly are able to smile (Thompson, 1941). However, Freedman has observed that the nature of the smiling may differ.

> In each of the four (blind) subjects these first elicited smiles were extremely fleeting, i.e., they quickly formed and disappeared as in normal eyes-closed smiling in the first weeks of life. By six months there are indications that these fleeting smiles gradually change to normal prolonged smiling. Possibly, in these early months prolonged social smiling required visual regard as a maintaining stimulus [Freedman, 1965, p. 10].

However, the critical aspects of the human face that are effective elicitors of smiling in normal infants change as the infant matures (Ahrens, 1954). Figure 7-8 illustrates this developmental sequence; at first the configuration of the eyes are important, followed by the mouth, and finally the details of the face's features and expressive characteristics take on importance. As Box 7-2 shows, however, the child-rearing environment may affect the rate of the development of smiling.

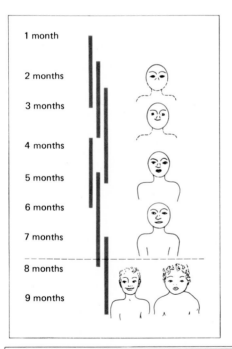

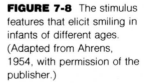

FIGURE 7-8 The stimulus features that elicit smiling in infants of different ages. (Adapted from Ahrens, 1954, with permission of the publisher.)

BOX 7-2 THE DEVELOPMENT OF SMILING IN DIFFERENT CHILDREARING SETTINGS

The development of smiling was examined in three different childrearing settings: the kibbutz, the normal family, and a residential institution. In both the kibbutz and the normal family the infant had plenty of opportunities to interact with adults. Recall that on the kibbutz, although the responsibility for childrearing was shared by the mother and metapelet, the infant was in no sense deprived of human social contact. On the other hand, in the residential institution the frequency of interaction between the infant and his caretakers is much less frequent. Smiling should develop at a slower rate in the institutional environment. Examination of Figure 7-9 indicates that this is the case. The family and kibbutz curves peak at four months, while the institution curve reaches its peak about one month later, at five months. The development of smiling varies with the type of childrearing environment.

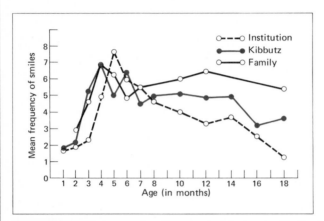

FIGURE 7-9 Frequency of smiling among infants raised in three different environments. (From Gewirtz, 1965, with permission of the author, the publisher, and the Tavistock Institute of Human Relations.)

Source: Gewirtz, J. L. The cause of infant smiling in four child-rearing environments in Israel. In B. M. Foss (Ed.), *Determinants of infant behavior. Vol. 3.* London: Methuen, 1965. Pp. 205–248.

The origins of smiling A source of considerable controversy and disagreement has been the genesis of smiling. Some have regarded smiling as innately determined (for example, Spitz, 1946), while others have emphasized the role of instrumental or classical conditioning (for example, Gewirtz, 1965). Finally, some theorists (for example, Kagan, 1967) have championed a perceptual-recognition hypothesis to explain smiling.

The genetic viewpoint. Some support for the heredity side of the debate about the origins of smiling comes from Freedman (1964), who has found that identical twins exhibit greater concordance than fraternal twins in the time of onset and in the amount of social smiling. Such studies indicate only that genetic factors may play a role; they tell nothing about the nature of this role. For example, is smiling determined in a direct fashion by hereditary influences, or are more fundamental processes, such as activity level, genetically determined? There may be links between activity level, amount of adult attention elicited by the infant, and speed of onset of smiling; since this is so, similarity in activity level, a stable and genetically determined individual difference, may mediate the observed concordance between identical twins.

The learning viewpoint. In support of a learning position is the study by Brackbill (also discussed in Chapter 6) which demonstrated instrumental conditioning of the smiling response in infants between the ages of three and one-half and four and one-half months (Brackbill, 1958). More recently, Etzel and Gewirtz (1967) have found that smiling behavior can be instrumentally conditioned in infants even as young as six weeks of age. Moreover, they were able to demonstrate the incompatibility of smiling and crying. By systematically ignoring crying and reinforcing smiling, they were able to both increase the frequency of smiling and inhibit excessive crying. Finally, as we shall see later in our discussion of the family, not all social agents are equally effective reinforcers; mothers are more effective conditioning agents than are strange females (Wahler, 1967). The major significance of these studies is their demonstration that the smiling response may be strengthened or weakened according to well-established learning principles. It should be noted, however, that these studies do *not* argue against genetic components in the development of smiling; the infant was already smiling at the onset of these conditioning procedures. It was the rate of smiling that was altered; conditioning may not be necessary for the initial occurrence of smiling. In short, the capacity to smile may be genetically determined, but the rate of occurrence of smiling behavior may be modified by conditioning.

The perceptual-recognition viewpoint. The perceptual-recognition view of smiling has been championed by Kagan (1967). According to Kagan, the infant can be viewed as an information processing organism who is attempting to impose structure or meaning on incoming stimulation. One way in which the infant makes sense of the external world is by forming representations of external events; these internal pictures are called *schemas.* Achieving a match between the schema and an incoming stimulus is the infants' means of understanding, and Kagan argues that this achievement or creation of a schema for an event is a source of pleasure which is indexed by a smile.

Data collected by Kagan and coworkers (Kagan, Henker, Hen-Tov, Levine & Lewis, 1966) illustrate interesting relationships between the nature of facial configuration, age of the infant, and smiling behavior. When four-month-old infants were shown either a photograph of a regular face or a three-dimensional sculptured face, they smiled much more often than they smiled to either a schematic version of a face or a distorted, disordered version of a face. Kagan offered a number of explanations for this finding. He argued that the mother's face has become a secondary reward; the regular face stands for pleasure because it has been associated with care and affection from the mother; as a result, it elicits more smiles. An alternative interpretation is that the smile response has become conditioned to the human face via reciprocal contact between mother and infant. A third interpretation, not necessarily exclusive to these, is that the smile can be elicited when the infant matches stimulus to schema—when he has an "aha" reaction, that is, when he makes a cognitive discovery. The four-month-old infant is cognitively close to establishing a relatively firm schema of a human face. When a regular representation of a face is presented to him, there is a short period during which the stimulus is assimilated to the schema and then after several seconds a smile may occur. The smile is released following the perceptual recognition of the face and reflects the assimilation of the stimulus of the infant's schema, a small but significant act of creation. This hypothesis is supported by the fact that the typical latency between the onset of looking at the regular face (in the four-month-old) and the onset of smiling is about three to five seconds. The smile usually does not occur immediately, but only after the infant has studied the stimulus. If one sees this phenomenon in real life, it is difficult to avoid the conclusion that the smile is released following an act of perceptual recognition.

Other studies offer more definitive support for this analysis. Shultz and Zigler (1970) studied smiling in infants eight to eighteen weeks of age. These investigators argued that recognition of a novel clown figure would occur more quickly if it were presented in a stationary position, while it would take longer for the infant to familiarize himself with the object if it were presented in motion. On the assumption that smiling will occur only after the infant has mastered the details and learned to recognize the object, they predicted earlier smiling to the stationary versus the moving clown. Their results confirmed their expectation: the infants smiled to the stationary clown after 1.70 minutes, while only after 7.21 minutes to the moving stimulus. Vocalizing followed a parallel pattern. Kagan (1971) and Zelazo and Komer (1971) have offered similar demonstrations. These data suggest an interesting explanation of Ahren's observations of the developmental changes in the facial stimuli necessary for smiling behavior. As the Gewirtz study (Box 7-2) indicates, the extent to which the infant has opportunities to learn the characteristics of social stimuli, such as faces, will determine the speed with which he reaches each of these developmental points.

Returning to the controversy over the contribution of genetic and learned factors in the development of smiling, it is clear that the present data permit no firm conclusion.

> Smiling occurs so soon after birth that there can be little doubt about smiling as a physiological response is innately determined. However, the question remains whether there is an unconditioned stimulus or releaser that evokes a social smile. While recent evidence suggests that certain auditory or visual stimuli may be "releasers" of this kind, no definite conclusion can be reached on this point. There is no doubt, however, that social smiles are to a large extent elicited, maintained, and modified through the presentation of visual and auditory stimuli [Walters & Parke, 1965, p. 69].

Laughter and humor   Infants not only smile, but at approximately four months of age they begin to laugh. Laughter, like smiling, may play an important role in caretaker-infant interaction; specifically, the infant's laughter may serve to maintain the proximity of the mother or other caretaker and hence is a very adaptive response pattern. Until recently, little was known about the early development of laughter.

Recently, Sroufe and Wunsch (1972) have helped fill this gap in our knowledge by their investigation of laughter in the first years of life. Using mothers as their experimental assistants, these investigators examined the amount of laughter elicited by a wide array of visual (human mask, disappearing object), tactile (bouncing on knee, blowing in hair), auditory (lip popping, whispering, a whinnying horse sound), and social (peek-a-boo, covering baby's face, and sticking out tongue) stimuli. Infants from four to twelve months participated and Figure 7-10 shows their results. After the onset of laughter at the age of four months, there is a clear increase with age in the number of situations eliciting laughter; the increase is most apparent between the second and third trimesters of life. Moreover, the nature of the stimuli that elicit laughter change as the child develops. Tactile stimuli that are effective in younger infants become less potent in the eight- to twelve-month period; on the other hand, most visual items and some social items

Laughter plays an important role in parent-infant interactions. This infant's laughter is being elicited by tactile and social means. (Suzanne Szasz.)

become increasingly successful across the age range studied. These shifts parallel the argument of Walters and Parke (1965) which is that distance receptors play an increasingly important role in social development as the child matures. Although there are a variety of explanations, these data are consistent with the perceptual-recognition hypothesis. As Sroufe and Wunsch note, "such a formulation can be fitted readily to the general pattern of our findings, including the relationship between age of laughter and independently rated 'cognitive sophistication' of items [Sroufe & Wunsch, 1972, p. 1,339]."

Just as the infant tends to smile and laugh at stimuli that may require effort to comprehend, there is some indication that a similar set of processes may account for children's appreciation of humor at later ages. In one study of this problem, children indicated not only whether a series of cartoons were funny, but also whether they had comprehended the message, or "got the joke" (Zigler, Levine & Gould, 1966). Children from second to fifth grade participated, and while there was little relationship between funniness ratings and comprehension among the children in the lower grades, at the fifth-grade level there was a positive relationship between the difficulty of the cartoon and the "funniness" score. At the younger age levels, even the easy cartoons require effort to understand, but as the child's cognitive abilities expand, these "easy" cartoons

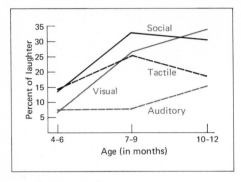

FIGURE 7-10 Laughter of infants in the first year of life in response to four different classes of stimuli. (From Sroufe & Wunsch, 1972, with permission of the authors and the Society for Research in Child Development.)

simply fail to stretch the subjects' capacities. It is, then, the most difficult cartoons that challenge the children; it is precisely these cartoons that the fifth-graders found most humorous.

More convincing support for this hypothesis would come from a demonstration that moderately difficult cartoons are appreciated most, regardless of the child's age level. This is exactly the relationship that was uncovered in a later study (Zigler, Levine, & Gould, 1967). Instead of showing all the children the same cartoons, a special series containing easy, moderate, and difficult cartoons was constructed for each age level. Children rated the moderately difficult cartoons as funnier than cartoons that were very easy or very difficult to understand. However the case is not yet closed as indicated by a recent critical review by McGhee (1974).

The perceptual-recognition hypothesis clearly has far-ranging implications: It can account for smiling and laughter in the infant and humor appreciation in older children with equal facility.

RECOGNITION AND LABELING OF EMOTIONS

A final problem deserves attention: How and when do children learn to recognize their own emotions and the emotional states of other individuals?

Labeling of emotions

As children mature, they learn an increasingly differentiated vocabulary for describing their emotional states. This ability to categorize accurately one's emotions facilitates communication between individuals since they can then share a common emotional labeling system. When one person says to another, "I'm angry" or "I love you," it is important that both share the same meaning for the word "angry" or "love." In a recent study in which changes in children's descriptions of emotions were investigated, children in the second, fourth, sixth, and eighth grades were asked to describe their experiences of happiness, sadness, love, anger, and fear (Farmer, 1967). The older the children, the more detailed and differentiated descriptions they gave, probably due to their greater verbal facility. More importantly, the study showed that the more mature the children were, the more their descriptions approximated those of adults; in fact, the more a particular aspect is stressed in an adult's description of an emotional state, the earlier it appears in the children's verbal reports of emotions. (For example, in describing ''sadness,'' adults as well as children mention ''discomfort'' in their descriptions.) The subtler and less emphasized aspects of adult descriptions of emotional states, in turn, tend to appear at later age points among the children in this study. Both the range and richness of emotional experiences shift with age, and accompanying these changes in an increasing ability to accurately label and describe one's emotions.

Recognition of facial expressions

Vocabulary increases are not the only index of the child's understanding of different emotional states—facial expressions provide another important clue. ''To the developing child, facial expressions are an important source of information and communication, the expressions of others serve to communicate significant information to the child about the people and things around him while his own productions of expression function to communicate attitudes and needs to others [Odom & Lemond, 1972, p. 359].''

To find out how successfully children of different age levels can discriminate and reproduce facial expressions was the aim of a recent study conducted by Odom and Lemond (1972). To assess the ability to discriminate expression, five- and ten-year-old children were required to match up pictures of similar facial expressions, while in another task the subjects matched pictures and descriptions of situations. For example, ''being chased by a dog'' and ''gotten a bowl of ice cream'' were to be matched with facial expressions of joy, sadness, distress, disgust, etc. For the production phase, children were asked to ''see how well you can make faces when I ask you to.'' In other cases, they were requested to imitate different facial expressions. The findings were clear: children at both ages were better able to discriminate than produce facial expressions, and secondly, the older children made more correct discriminations and productions than the younger children. This developmental increase in the child's capacity to distinguish and produce facial expressions probably contributes to the more frequent and successful peer group participation and increasingly more sustained and sophisticated social interactions. The apparent universality of these types of emotional expressions is illustrated in Box 7-3.

BOX 7-3 THE UNIVERSALITY OF FACIAL EXPRESSIONS OF EMOTION

Are facial expressions of emotion universal, or does each culture develop its own unique ways of expressing emotions such as happiness, sadness, and disgust? This is the question that Paul Ekman and his colleagues have tried to answer in their research program. Observers from five cultures (Argentina, Chile, Brazil, Japan, and the United States) were shown a series of photographs of human faces depicting different emotions. Subjects categorized each photo into one of the following emotion categories: surprise, fear, disgust, sadness, anger, and happiness. If each culture has a unique set of facial expressions for conveying different emotions, little agreement would be expected; however, if there is some universality in our expressions of emotion, cross-cultural agreement would be predicted. In twenty-eight out of thirty pictures a facial expression was judged as showing the same emotion regardless of the culture. But, do individuals from different cultures show similarity in their facial expression of emotion? To find out, Japanese and

American students watched a stressful movie and recordings were made of their facial expressions. Marked similarities were noted in the facial expressions of the Japanese and American viewers. However, the judgment data do not necessarily prove the existence of universal facial expressions of emotion. Possibly, in cultures that share the same mass media outlets, such as TV films, and magazines, people can and do learn their facial expressions from the same media models and will therefore have learned the same facial expressions. To eliminate this argument, Ekman studied two isolated preliterate cultures in New Guinea; these cultures had little or no exposure to the mass media, to Caucasians, or to each other. Children in one tribe heard a story designed to connote a particular emotion and were then asked to choose the photograph that best depicted the emotion. By comparing how often the observers in these preliterate cultures chose the same facial expression for a particular emotion as had people in literate cultures, these investigators were able to determine the universality of facial expression of emotions. With some minor exceptions, there was striking agreement between the ratings of the Fore and Dori tribes of New Guinea and ratings from literate groups. In addition, other members of these tribes were asked to "show how his face would appear if he was the person described in one of the emotion stories [Ekman, 1971, p. 273]." The videotapes were then rated by American students, who were able to accurately judge four of the six emotions: happiness, disgust, anger, and sadness. Fear and surprise were not as accurately judged. Together these findings provide strong support for the view that both the recognition *and* the expression of facial emotion are universal. Learning, of course, does play a role. The elicitors, the particular events which activate different affective expressions, are socially learned during childhood and are culturally determined. Moreover, many of the consequences of an aroused emotion are culturally bound; in some cultures attack is often associated with anger, while in other cultures withdrawal is the typical response to anger. Again, learning plays a part. But the facial muscular movement which occurs for a particular emotion appears to be universal.

Source: Ekman, P. Universals and cultural differences in facial expressions of emotion. In J. K. Cole (Ed.), *Nebraska symposium on motivation*. Lincoln: University of Nebraska Press, 1971. Pp. 207-283.

Sometimes emotional messages may be contradictory. For example, criticism may be delivered in a pleasant voice or may be accompanied by a smile. The father who smiles benignly at his son as he says blandly, "Don't swear at your mother," is communicating a very different message than the father who makes the same communication in a stern voice accompanied by a scowl. It has been found that in interacting with their children, mothers are more likely to make this type of inconsistent communication than fathers. When a father smiles while talking to his child, he is likely to be making a more positive approving statement than when he is not smiling. In contrast it has been found that mothers are likely to smile when criticizing their children as well as when praising them. (Bugental, Love, & Gianetto, 1971).

It is interesting that children are aware that the female smile is an unreliable indicator of true emotion. In a paper aptly entitled "Perfidious Feminine Faces" it was reported that when children view mothers making joking messages such as criticism with a smile, they are more likely to regard this as hostile than when the same inconsistent message is delivered by a father. If mother smiles and says, "You're a complete idiot," the child accepts her words. Father's smile means the communication is a teasing, more positive, even affectionate message.

Children differ from adults in their ratings of how positively or negatively they view such communications. Children in the presence of conflicting information, particularly from women, are more likely than adults to resolve the incongruity by assuming the worst. Adults tend to place less credence in a critical statement if the speaker smiles (Bugental, Love, & Gianetto, 1971).

Learning to recognize our own emotions

These studies tell us when capacities for labeling and recognition of emotions may occur. But what is the nature of the process by which we decide when we are happy rather than sad, angry, or disgusted? Attempts to define emotions by identifying stimuli that elicit different emotions have not been successful. In fact, the *same* stimulus can produce laughter at one time and fear on another occasion. Let us take an example: Scarr and Salapatek (1970), in their study of fear, found that a mask worn by a stranger produced withdrawal and fear in their infants, while Sroufe and Wunsch (1972) reported that a similar mask worn by the infant's mother elicited laughter. Rothbart (1973) offers a parallel illustration of the paradox:

> If a man suddenly appears to a child and says, "I'm going to get you," and the man is a stranger, the child is likely to run away. If, however, the man saying "I'm going to get you" is the child's father, the child may laugh and beg the father to repeat the threat. In the former case, the child is aroused in a situation subsequently labeled dangerous; in the latter case he is aroused in a "safe" situation [Rothbart, 1973, p. 251].

It is clear that the *same* stimulus, whether it is a loud sound, a mock attack, or a masked face, is capable of eliciting either fear *or* laughter.

Perhaps there are different physiological correlates of emotions such as fear, anger, and embarrassment. But emotions appear to be more than physiological states, and those early attempts to discover different physiological bases of emotions were largely unsuccessful. Rather, it appears that the physiological reactions determine only the *intensity* of our emotional reactions; they do not provide information concerning the *identity* of the emotion that is being experienced. In fact, the physiological states appear to be surprisingly similar for all emotions. We learn to label or catalog these similar states of arousal by reference either to clues in the present environment or to our past experience in related situations. For example, the infant knows that his father is playing when he says, "I'm going to get you," and so the baby laughs; when hearing these words from a stranger, the baby interprets them as threatening and so exhibits fear. In short, we have to learn to interpret the events that produce our physiological states; only then do we have *emotions*. This two-factor approach to understanding emotions—a state of undifferentiated physiological arousal and a set of external cues whereby an interpretation is attached to this state—can be illustrated by an experiment by Schachter and Singer (1962).

In this study, late adolescents (college students) were aroused by an injection of adrenaline; other subjects, those in the control condition, were given a placebo injection. In addition, some students were given an accurate account of the drug's effects; they were told that "your hand will start to shake, your heart will start to pound, and your face may get warm and flushed . . . these are side effects lasting about 15 or 20 minutes [Schachter, 1971, p. 6]." Other groups of individuals were either not informed or deliberately misinformed; they were told that "your feet will feel numb, you will have an itching sensation over parts of your body, and you may get a slight headache [Schachter, 1971, p. 6]." According to the theory, in a "state of physiological arousal for which the individual has no adequate explanation, cognitive factors can lead the individual to describe his feelings with any of a variety of emotional labels [Schachter, 1964, p. 56]." The same physiological state, in other words, could be labeled happiness, anger, sadness, or disgust. It depends on the situational cues which help the person define his state of physiological arousal. To test how labile the emotional labeling process might in fact be, Schachter exposed some of his "drugged" subjects to an experimental confederate who was trained to act in a euphoric manner, while the remaining subjects were exposed to an angry, aggressive stooge.

For subjects who had a completely satisfactory explanation of their bodily feelings, the presence of the angry or euphoric confederates had little effect on the emotional labeling process of the subjects. Subjects who were ignorant of the drug's effects took their cue from the social situation and rated themselves as angry or euphoric, depending on how others were acting. However, the state of arousal is necessary; subjects in the placebo condition were not influenced by the social cues available. Emotional labels are dually determined; both physiological arousal and social-cognitive cues are involved in defining an emotion. A similar set of processes are useful for understanding why the *same* stimulus can produce both laughter and fear on different occasions and in different contexts.

How might children acquire labels for these emotional states? Consider a young child who strikes out or screams and is told on these occasions, "Don't be angry," and thus learns to identify emotional-arousal states that are accompanied by certain classes of potentially pain- or distress-producing responses as instances of the manifestation of anger. Parents, then, play an important role in helping the child to identify and label his behavior in terms of commonly accepted cultural judgments. Later, a highly aroused child who contemplates, imagines, or anticipates aggressive actions that he may carry out will identify his emotion as anger, even though aggressive behavior does not actually occur.

The problem of mislabeling our emotions

In more recent work, Schachter and his colleagues have pointed out the implications of incorrectly labeling one's bodily states and responses. For example, some mothers may answer a young baby's cry with food, regardless of the bodily state that motivated the distress signal. The mother may feel that by offering food she is showing her affection. The child may eventually come to associate eating with love, and in times when he or she is feeling rejected or unloved the child may satisfy these needs through overeating. If the mother persists in feeding her child and fails to discriminate among his or her different internal cues, the child may overgeneralize the one label that he has learned well, hunger, to cover a wide variety of internal rumblings and discomforts. Any state of arousal may incorrectly be labeled "hunger" with the result that overeating may become a regular pattern. The outcome, of course, may be obesity. Another possibility is that some individuals never learn to discriminate any internal cues, but rather become dependent on the stimuli impinging on them from their external environment. In fact, this seems to be the case for obese individuals; it isn't that they overgeneralize and mislabel the internal state—they ignore it. To demonstrate this, Schachter, Goldman, and Gordon (1968) decided to directly manipulate the state of hunger: One group was fed roast-beef sandwiches, while another group missed a meal and was deprived of the sandwiches as well. In a test which followed, the subjects, some obese and some normal, were required to taste as many crackers as they wished in order to make taste judgments. For fifteen minutes the subjects tasted and rated crackers, and Schachter and his coworkers simply kept count of the number of crackers that each person ate. If the theory is correct, the obese subjects should eat just as many on a full stomach as on an empty stomach. Normal individuals, on the other hand, should regulate their cracker consumption according to how full they are already. Hunger and the state of the stomach should show some correspondence in normals. Normal subjects ate approximately fifteen crackers when their stomachs were full of roast-beef sandwiches, but they ate twenty-two crackers when their stomachs were empty. The obese people were different and, apparently, indifferent, at least to the state of their own stomachs. They ate the same amount (eighteen crackers) when they were full as when they were deprived of food and operating on an empty stomach. Obese people, it seems, fail to use the information available from their internal systems to define their emotional state or to regulate their behavior. The disastrous outcome associated with overeating underlines the importance of learning to read the body's internal cues in childhood.

SUMMARY

Traditional theory in motivation stressed the role of primary drives, such as hunger and thirst, and many psychologists assumed that all behavior was under the control of these biological drives. Moreover, secondary drives, such as affection and dependency, were assumed to develop as a result of their association with the satisfaction of these more basic innate forces. Few accept this view of motivation any longer. Demonstrations that infants, children, and even animals are motivated to behave in various other ways in the absence of any primary drives dealt a serious blow to the doctrine. The opportunity to explore and examine without any extrinsic payoff is often sufficient.

Three approaches to the development of fear were considered: a genetic hypothesis, a learning-theory position, and the perceptual-discrepancy viewpoint. According to the genetic position, fear has a constitutional basis and is not dependent on specific learning experiences. Evidence indicates greater concordance of onset age in identical than in fraternal twins; there is also evidence of some agreement across different cultures in terms of the age of appearance of fear. Further support for a genetic position comes from animal research which found fear reactions to specific threatening pictures, even in the absence of any prior experience with this type of fear stimulus.

An alternative viewpoint stresses the importance of learning in the development of fear. Both operant conditioning and classical conditioning may play a role in the emergence and shaping of fear responses. However, fears may also be acquired vicariously by watching another individual express fear in the presence of a previously nonfeared object.

A third position, the perceptual-discrepancy hypothesis, suggests that the sight of an incongruous or slightly unfamiliar event may evoke fear reactions. In addition to animal data, studies of human infants fear of strangers were cited in support of this position. When few strangers are typically viewed, fear of strangers tends to be found at an earlier age.

How stable is fear from infancy to later childhood? For boys, the level of fearfulness over the first nine years remains relatively stable, but girls show little stability. Evidence indicates that the nature of children's fear changes with age; as the child grows, fears concerning imaginery creatures and personal safety decline, while school and social anxieties begin to predominate.

Measurement of fear was briefly examined. Children, unlike adults, tend to react to fearful stimuli in an integrated fashion: there is a high degree of correspondence between their verbal reports of what they say they are afraid of and their actual behavior in fear situations.

Two approaches to overcoming children's fears were considered: counterconditioning and modeling. In the first approach, the fear stimulus is associated with a pleasant activity (for example, eating) and the child's fear is gradually reduced. Another technique to lessen children's fears involves exposing a fearful child to a nonfearful model. Children who feared dogs were eventually able to interact without fear or flight after watching a peer play with the originally feared animal.

The development of a positive emotional reaction, smiling, was considered from three viewpoints as well. Again, genetic, learning, and perceptual-discrepancy positions were presented. As in the case of fear, age of onset was closer for identical than for fraternal twins, which suggests that genetic factors may play a role. Operant conditioning has been shown to play an important part in the modification of the smiling response; possibly, this type of learning may contribute to the development of this type of emotional reaction. Data in support of the perceptual-discrepancy account of smiling was presented as well. Finally, there is evidence that humor in older children can be handled by this same hypothesis. Cartoons that were moderately difficult to comprehend were rated as funnier than very easy or very difficult cartoons. These data are consistent with the hypothesis that cartoons that required some effort to understand were most appreciated.

Finally, how do children learn to recognize and label their emotions? A two-level approach to understanding the problem of how children categorize specific emotional states was presented. Since the physiological state characterizing different emotions is generally similar, children learn to describe or label specific emotions in terms of external events. For example, being aroused and at the same time seeing food might lead one to label his emotion as hunger, while the sight of a burglar might lead to a label of fear. One of the consequences of mislabeling emotional states, obesity resulting from identifying all states as hunger, was briefly discussed.

REFERENCES

Ahrens, R. Beitrag zur entwicklun des physionomie und mimikerkennens. *Z. F. Exp. U. Angew. Psychol.*, 1954, **2**, 599-633.

Ainsworth, M. D. The development of infant-mother interaction among the Ganda. In B. M. Foss (Ed.), *Determinants of infant be-*

havior. Vol. 2. New York: Wiley, 1963. Pp. 67-104.

Angelino, H., Dollins, J., & Mech, E. V. Trends in the "fears and worries" of school children. *Journal of Genetic Psychology,* 1956, **89,** 263-267.

Bandura, A. Modeling approaches to the modification of phobic disorders. In R. Porter (Ed.), *The role of learning in psychotherapy.* London: Churchill, 1968. Pp. 201-217.

Bandura, A., Grusec, J. E., & Menlove, F. L. Vicarious extinction of avoidance behavior. *Journal of Personality and Social Psychology,* 1967, **5,** 16-23.

Bandura, A., & Menlove, F. L. Factors determining vicarious extinction of avoidance behavior through symbolic modeling. *Journal of Personality and Social Psychology,* 1968, **8,** 99-108.

Barnett, J. T. Development of children's fears: the relationship between three systems of fear measurement. Unpublished M.A. thesis, University of Wisconsin, 1969.

Berlyne, D. E., & Frommer, F. D. Some determinants of the incidence and content of children's questions. *Child Development,* 1966, **37,** 177-189.

Brackbill, Y. Extinction of the smiling response in infants as a function of reinforcement schedule. *Child Development,* 1958, **29,** 115-124.

Bronson, G. W. The development of fear in man and other animals. *Child Development,* 1968, **39,** 409-431.

Bronson, G. W. Fear of visual novelty. *Developmental Psychology,* 1970, **2,** 33-40.

Bugental, D. E., Love, L. R., & Gianetto, R. M. Perfidious feminine faces. *Journal of Personality and Social Psychology,* 1971, **17,** 314-318.

Butler, R. A. Discrimination learning by rhesus monkeys to visual exploration motivation. *Journal of Comparative and Physiological Psychology,* 1953, **46,** 95-98.

Charlesworth, W. R. Instigation and maintenance of curiosity behavior as a function of surprise versus novel and familiar stimuli. *Child Development,* 1964, **35,** 1169-1186.

Dennis, W. Does culture appreciably affect patterns of infant behavior? *Journal of Social Psychology,* 1940, **12,** 305-317.

Dunn, M. R. Interpersonal relations in blind infants. Unpublished manuscript, 1962. In D. G. Freedman's Smiling in blind infants and the issue of innate *vs.* acquired. *Journal of Child Psychology and Psychiatry,* 1964, **5,** 171-184.

Ekman, P. Universals and cultural differences in facial expression of emotion. In J. K. Cole (Ed.), *Nebraska symposium on motivation.* Lincoln: University of Nebraska Press, 1971. Pp. 207-283.

Ende, R. N., & Koenig, K. L. Neonatal smiling and rapid eye movement states. *Journal of the American Academy of Child Psychiatry,* 1969, **8,** 57-67.

Etzel, B. C., & Gewirtz, J. L. Experimental modification of caretaker-maintained high rate operant crying in a 6- and a 20-week-old infant: extinction of crying with reinforcement of eye contact and smiling. *Journal of Experimental Child Psychology,* 1967, **5,** 303-317.

Farmer, C. Words and feelings: a developmental study of the language of emotion in children. Unpublished doctoral dissertation, Columbia University, 1967.

Freedman, D. G. Smiling in blind infants and the issue of innate vs. acquired. *Journal of Child Psychology and Psychiatry,* 1964, **5,** 171-184.

Freedman, D. G. Hereditary control of early social behavior. In B. M. Foss (Ed.), *Determinants of infant behavior.* Vol. 3. London: Methuen, 1965. Pp. 149-156.

Freedman, D. G. An evolutionary approach to research on the life cycle. *Human Development,* 1971, **14,** 87-99.

Gewirtz, J. L. The course of infant smiling in four child-rearing environments in Israel. In B. M. Foss (Ed.), *Determinants of infant behavior.* Vol. 3. London: Methuen, 1965. Pp. 205-248.

Gilmore, J. B. Play: a special behavior. In R. N. Haber (Ed.), *Current research in motivation.* New York: Holt, 1966. Pp. 343-355.

Harlow, H. F. The nature of love. *American Psychologist,* 1958, **13,** 673-685.

Harlow, H. F., & Zimmermann, R. R. Affectional responses in the infant monkey. *Science,* 1959, **130,** 421-432.

Hebb, D. O. On the nature of fear. *Psychological Review,* 1946, **53,** 250-275.

Hebb, D. O. *The organization of behavior.* New York: Wiley, 1949.

Hunt, J. McV. Piaget's system as a source of hypotheses concerning motivation. *Merrill-Palmer Quarterly,* 1963, **9,** 263-276.

Igel, G. J., & Calvin, A. D. The development of affectional responses in infant dogs. *Journal of Comparative and Physiological Psychology,* 1960, **53,** 302-305.

Jersild, A. T. Emotional development. In L. Carmichael (Ed.), *Manual of child psychology.* New York: Wiley, 1946. Pp. 752-790.

Jones, H. E. The conditioning of overt emotional responses. *Journal of Educational Psychology,* 1931, **22,** 127-130.

Jones, M. C. The elimination of children's fears. *Journal of Experimental Psychology,* 1924, **7,** 383-390.

Kagan, J. On the need for relativism. *American Psychologist*, 1967, **22**, 131-147.

Kagan, J. *Change and continuity in infancy.* New York: Wiley, 1971.

Kagan, J., Henker, B., Hen-Tov, A., Levine, J., & Lewis, M. Infants' differential reactions to familiar and distorted faces. *Child Development*, 1966, **37**, 519-532.

Korner, A. Neonatal startles, smiles, erections and reflex sucks as related to state, sex and individuality. *Child Development*, 1969, **40**, 1039-1053.

L'Allier, L. Smiling as a result of aural stimuli. Ph.D. thesis, University of Montreal, Canada, 1961.

Lang, P. J. The mechanics of desensitization and the laboratory study of human fear. In C. M. Franks (Ed.), *Assessment and status of the behavior therapies.* New York: McGraw-Hill, 1968.

Laroche, J. L., & Tcheng, P. *Le Souivre et Nourisson.* Louvain: University of Louvain, 1963.

Leuba, C., & Friedlander, B. Z. Effects of controlled audio-visual reinforcement on infants' manipulative play in the home. *Journal of Experimental Child Psychology*, 1968, **6**, 87-99.

Lewis, M., & Brooks-Gunn, J. Self, other and fear: the reaction of infants to people. Paper presented at the meeting of the Eastern Psychological Association, Boston, April 1972.

Liebert, R. Observational learning: Some applied implications. In P. Elich (Ed.), *Social Learning.* Bellingham: Western Washington State Press, 1973. Pp. 59-79.

Mann, J., & Rosenthal, T. L. Vicarious and direct counterconditioning of test anxiety through individual and group desensitization. Unpublished manuscript, University of Arizona, 1969.

McGhee, P. E. Cognitive mastery in children's humor. *Psychological Bulletin*, 1974, **81**, 721-730.

Miller, N. E. Studies of fear as an acquirable drive. I. Fear as motivation and fear reduction reinforcement in the learning of new responses. *Journal of Experimental Psychology*, 1948, **38**, 89-101.

Morgan, G. A., & Ricciuti, H. Infants' responses to strangers during the first year. In B. M. Foss (Ed.), *Determinants of infant behavior.* Vol. 4. London: Methuen, 1969. Pp. 253-272.

Odom, R. D. & Lemond, C. M. Developmental differences in the perception and production of facial expressions. *Child Development*, 1972, **43**, 359-370.

Rheingold, H. L., & Eckerman, C. O. The fear of strangers hypothesis: a critical review. In

H. Reese (Ed.), *Advances in child development and behavior.* Vol. 8. New York: Academic, 1973. Pp. 185-222.

Rheingold, H. L., Stanley, W. C. & Cooley, J. A. Method for studying exploratory behavior in infants. *Science*, 1962, **136**, 1054-1055.

Ribble, Margaret A. Infantile experiences in relation to personality development. In J. McV. Hunt (Ed.), *Personality and the behavior disorders, II.* New York: Ronald Press, 1944. Pp. 621-651.

Rothbart, M. K. Laughter in young children. *Psychological Bulletin*, 1973, **80**, 247-256.

Sackett, G. P. Monkeys reared in isolation with pictures as visual input: evidence for an innate releasing mechanism. *Science*, 1966, **154**, 1468-1473.

Scarr, S., & Salapatek, P. Patterns of fear development during infancy. *Merrill-Palmer Quarterly*, 1970, **16**, 53-90.

Schachter, S. The interaction of cognitive and physiological determinants of emotional state. In L. Berkowitz (Ed.), *Advances in experimental social psychology.* Vol. 1. New York: Academic, 1964. Pp. 49-80.

Schachter, S. *Emotion, obesity and crime.* New York: Academic, 1971.

Schachter, S., Goldman, R., & Gordon, A. The effects of fear, food deprivation and obesity on eating. *Journal of Personality and Social Psychology*, 1968, **10**, 91-97.

Schachter, S., & Singer, J. E. Cognitive, social and physiological determinants of emotional state. *Psychological Review*, 1962, **69**, 379-399.

Schaffer, H. R. The onset of fear of strangers and the incongruity hypothesis. *Journal of Child Psychology and Psychiatry*, 1966, **7**, 95-106.

Scherer, M. W., & Nakamura, C. Y. A fear-survey schedule for children: a factor analytic comparison with manifest anxiety. *Behavior Research and Therapy*, 1968, **6**, 173-182.

Shultz, T. R., & Zigler, E. Emotional concomitants of visual mastery in infants: the effects of stimulus movement on smiling and vocalizing. *Journal of Experimental Child Psychology*, 1970, **10**, 390-402.

Spitz, R. A. The smiling response: a contribution to the ontogenesis of social relations. *Genetic Psychology Monographs*, 1946, **34**, 67-125.

Spitz, R. A. Anxiety in infancy: a study of its manifestations in the first year of life. *International Journal of Psycho-Analysis*, 1950, **31**, 138-143.

Sroufe, L. A., Waters, E., & Matas, L. Contextual determinants of infant affectional response. In M. Lewis and L. Rosenblum (Eds.), *Origins of fear.* New York: Wiley, 1974.

Sroufe, A. L., & Wunsch, J. P. The development of laughter in the first year of life. *Child Development,* 1972, **43,** 1326-1344.

Thompson, J. Development of facial expression of emotion in blind and seeing children. *Archives of Psychology,* 1941, **37,** No. 264, 1-47.

Venn, J. R., & Short, J. G. Vicarious classical conditioning of emotional responses in nursery school children. *Journal of Personality and Social Psychology,* 1973, **28,** 249-255.

Wahler, R. G. Infant social attachments: a reinforcement theory interpretation and investigation. *Child Development,* 1967, **38,** 1079-1088.

Walters, R. H., & Parke, R. D. The role of the distance receptors in the development of social responsiveness. In L. P. Lipsitt & C. Spiker (Eds.), *Advances in child development and behavior.* Vol. 2. New York: Academic, 1965. Pp. 59-96.

Watson, J. B. *Psychology from the standpoint of a Behaviorist.* Philadelphia: Lippincott, 1924.

Watson, J. B., & Raynor, R. Conditioned emotional responses. *Journal of Experimental Psychology,* 1920, **3,** 1-14.

Weizmann, F., Cohen, L. B., & Pratt, R. J. Novelty, familiarity and the development of infant attention. *Developmental Psychology,* 1971, **4,** 149-154.

White, R. W. Motivation reconsidered: the concept of competence. *Psychological Review,* 1959, **66,** 297-333.

Wolff, P. H. Observations on the early development of smiling. In B. M. Foss (Ed.), *Determinants of infant behavior.* Vol. 2. London: Methuen, 1963. Pp. 113-134.

Zelazo, P. P., & Komer, M. J. Infant smiling to nonsocial stimuli and the recognition hypothesis. *Child Development,* 1971, **42,** 1327-1339.

Zigler, E., Levine, J., & Gould, L. Cognitive processes in the development of children's appreciation of humor. *Child Development,* 1966, **37,** 507-518.

Zigler, E., Levine, J., & Gould, L. Cognitive challenge as a factor in children's humor appreciation. *Journal of Personality and Social Psychology,* 1967, **6,** 332-336.

8
LANGUAGE
DEVELOPMENT

New developments in linguistics have dramatically demonstrated that language is probably the most complex system of rules a person ever learns. Yet, the task of learning the bulk of these rules is accomplished readily by all normal children around the world in an astonishingly short period of time, approximately between the first and fourth birthdays. Despite the fact that during acquisition each child hears a different set of language utterances, the same basic rules for understanding and speaking are acquired by all children exposed to a given language or dialect. Furthermore, some of the language a child hears from adults does not conform perfectly to the rules he or she must learn, since adult utterances often include false starts, idiosyncrasies, or errors. In addition, the language a child hears from other children is not always consistent with adult grammar. The more we study language acquisition, the more remarkable an accomplishment it seems.

The field of *psycholinguistics* was formally created at two interdisciplinary conferences in the early 1950s which brought together linguists and psychologists. This new field represents a resurgence of interest in the acquisition and use of structured language. Developmental psycholinguistics, which will be the main concern of this chapter, specifically deals with children's acquisition of a structured language system. This has been a dynamic area of study and one that has seen some of the liveliest controversies in psychology. The present chapter will emphasize changing issues and trends in the study of language development. This interdisciplinary area provides an interesting example of the workings of science, that is, the interplay of theory and research, and the discrepancies that can arise as a result of different theoretical and methodological approaches being applied to the same phenomenon.

Despite great initial optimism, the satisfactory combination of two very different fields has proven to be surprisingly difficult. Developments in the field have forced many psychologists to seriously rethink fundamental questions about learning theory, possible biological bases for behavior, and even the appropriateness of experimental techniques for studying certain areas of language and thinking. Although psycholinguists have shattered traditional notions of how language is acquired, they have not yet provided satisfactory new explanations of acquisition. Nevertheless, there has been a vast increase in our knowledge of the systematic nature of children's language, including developmental changes in the language system as it approaches the adult model.

Developmental psycholinguistics has been greatly influenced by a recent revolution in the field of linguistics. We will, therefore, begin with a brief discussion of new thinking on the nature of the language system itself.

LINGUISTICS: OLD AND NEW

Linguists have emphasized that knowing a language primarily means knowing a structured system of rules which allows one to speak or understand an unlimited number of sentences. Using the language system is thus a creative act. The vast majority of sentences one hears, speaks, reads, or writes are novel sentences never encountered before. You are able to understand the sentence you are now reading, despite the fact that you have probably never seen or heard it before. And you are able to create a novel sentence (one that you have never before encountered) to effectively communicate an experience, a thought, or a plan. In fact, language users do both of these things all the time. Linguists describe this aspect of language as *infinite generativity,* in that a finite number of rules are used by the speaker-hearer to generate a potentially *infinite* set of meaningful sentences.

Structural versus transformational grammar

A linguist formulates a *grammar* in an attempt to describe the rules used (without awareness) by all native speakers of a given language. Traditional (or structural) linguists divide language into types of sentences, divide sentences into types of phrases or words, and describe how these parts are put together by language users. The big change came when Noam Chomsky (1957) pointed out that this way of dividing up sentences did not adequately account for all the knowledge and intuitions that a native speaker possesses about his language.

For example, a native speaker knows that the sentence "Visiting relatives can be a nuisance," is an ambiguous sentence having two distinct meanings. It may refer either to "going to visit relatives" or to "relatives that are visiting." Traditional linguistic analysis cannot account for the fact that a speaker-hearer knows there are two meanings. Furthermore, some sentences have the very same structure according to the traditional approach, but there is a clear difference in the relationship between the words, for example:

> John is easy to please.
> John is eager to please.

In the first sentence, John himself is pleased. In the second, John pleases someone else.

Also consider the fact that language users recognize that certain sentences mean the same thing, even though their structure is very different, for example:

> Mary threw the ball.
> The ball was thrown by Mary.
> Mary did throw the ball.

Other sentences with different structures are also related in meaning to the above three, for example:

> Did Mary throw the ball?
> Mary did not throw the ball.
> Mary is throwing the ball.
> Mary will throw the ball.
> etc.

Traditional linguists treat each of these sentences as a different structural type. Thus, they do not account for the fact that the language user understands that these sentences are related to each other in particular ways. One sentence asks in a question form about the same meaning stated in another sentence; one sentence negates the meaning of another; three of the sentences have the same content except that the action takes place in the past, in the present, or in the future; etc.

From these few examples we have seen that language users are able to determine the meaning of sentences and the relationships between sentences somewhat independently of the sentence structures alone (that is, the way the words are ordered and grouped). In order to account for these facts, Chomsky proposed two levels of linguistic structure for each sentence. The *deep structure* is an abstract construct which indicates the meaning; it is not actually spoken. The *surface structure* is the actual order of the words in the spoken sentence. The deep structure is changed into the surface structure by a set of rules called *transformational rules*. Hence, Chomsky's system is known as *transformational grammar.*

According to this system, "Mary threw the ball," and "The ball was thrown by Mary" would have the same deep structure (the same meaning); different transformational rules are applied to produce the two different surface structures. "Visiting relatives can be a nuisance" would have two *different* deep structures (two different meanings); transformational rules happen to produce the same surface structure from the two different deep structures. Thus, transformational grammar is better able to account for what language users know about the meaning of sentences. Also, from a technical point of view, transformational grammar has been demonstrated to be a far more efficient system than traditional grammar. That is, fewer rules are required to describe a given aspect of language, and these rules apply more broadly.

It is important to understand before we proceed that both deep structure and transformational rules were developed (and are being reformulated) by linguists in an attempt to efficiently describe the language system itself. They form a kind of linguistic theory, but were never meant to directly describe psychological structures or processes. As formulated, transformational rules can change deep structure to surface structure on paper, but these transformations do not *necessarily* occur in the mind of the child or adult.

Competence and performance

A very important distinction to make, and one that is critical in some of the controversies to be discussed, is the linguistic distinction between language competence and language performance. *Language competence* is all of the knowledge a language user has about his language, knowledge which he relies on just as much in understanding as in speaking. It includes such things as his intuitions, his judgments about which sentences are grammatical and which sentences are related to each other, and his recognition of ambiguity in sentences. Transformational linguists consider competence to be the ability to infer the deep structure from the surface structure. They generally consider grammar to be a formalized account of language competence, the ideal knowledge of an ideal speaker-listener.

Language performance, on the other hand, is what language users actually do when they speak or listen. It is not a perfect reflection of language competence. Language performance includes many ungrammatical utterances and misunderstandings since it is subject to psychological factors such as memory, fatigue, anxiety, expectations, and so on. Not surprisingly language performance, actual observable behavior, is the aspect of language with which American psychologists have primarily been concerned. This has brought criticism from linguists who maintain that the essential aspect of language is competence, which is not directly observable.

In summary, then, linguists have been compiling a grammar, an abstract system to describe ideal knowledge (competence) about the language system itself, theoretically apart from psychological factors that affect performance. Psychologists, impressed by new insights into the nature of language, have tried to apply and test aspects of linguistic theory, but they have dealt primarily with actual language performance as their source of data.

The issue of competence and performance has been a special problem in *developmental* psycholinguistics. One cannot directly assess the language competence of young children by asking them about their linguistic intuitions, as is often done with adults. When one researcher tried asking a two-year-old, "Adam, which is right, 'two shoes' or 'two shoe'?", the child replied, "Pop goes the weasel" (Brown & Bellugi, 1964). Thus, researchers in developmental psycholinguistics are particularly dependent on studying language performance and must use performance to infer underlying linguistic competence.

Phonology, semantics, and syntax

The study of language has usually been divided into three areas: phonology, semantics, and syntax. *Phonology* describes the system of sounds for a language, that is, how the basic sound units (phonemes) are put together to form words and how the intonation patterns of phrases and sentences are determined. A *phoneme* can be defined as the shortest speech unit in which a change produces a change in meaning, for example, the difference in meaning between "*bat*" and "*cat*" is accounted for by the different initial phoneme; "b*a*t" and "b*i*t" differ in their middle phoneme.

Although we will not emphasize phonology in this chapter, it is important to realize that phonological rules, like rules at other linguistic levels, are generative. That is, speaker-hearers know the proper stress and intonation patterns for novel sentences they have never heard before, as well as knowing the sound relationships allowable in novel words. For example, a native speaker knows that the nonsense word "kib" is a possible sound pattern in the English phonological system, but that the nonsense word "bnik" is not possible. Thus, even the rules of phonology form a system, and they are "general rules" in the sense that they are applicable beyond the cases from which they are derived.

Semantics is the study of the meaning of words and of sentences. Because language is meaningful, communication is possible. There is a connection, though an imperfect one, between language and those things to which it refers. According to the best known theory of semantics (Katz & Fodor, 1963), every word has a set of *semantic features*, each of which specifies part of the word's meaning. For example, the words "man" and "boy" share in common the semantic features male and human, but differ with regard to age. In addition, there are semantic restrictions on how individual words may be combined to form meaningful sentences. Thus, "The man hurt herself" is semantically ill-formed. The relationships between word meanings and sentence meanings, as well as the relationships among individual word meanings, are complex and not clearly defined. At the present time, semantics is the least well-understood aspect of language.

Not surprisingly, the development of semantic competence is also poorly understood. Knowledge of the many aspects of meaning requires not only experience with words themselves, but also an understanding of features and relationships in the world. Thus, semantic knowledge continues to increase substantially throughout the school years as the child matures intellectually. A preschool child may use the words "animal" and "dog" appropriately in many contexts. However, his incomplete understanding of the meanings of these words might be demonstrated when he calls a pony a dog, or when he makes statements such as "Lassie is not an animal, she's a dog."

Syntax describes the structure of a language, the underlying rules which specify the order, and the function of words in a sentence. Application of syntactic rules provides the greatest opportunity for linguistic creativity. Each language has specific syntactic rules for expressing grammatical relations, such as negation, interrogation, possession, and juxtaposition of subject and object. Because we share the same syntactic knowledge of sentence structure, when I say either "Bill hit John" or "Bill was hit by John," you know who did the hitting and who got hit. We can agree that the sentence "You didn't go, did you?" is an acceptable (grammatical) sentence, whereas "You didn't go, didn't you?" is unacceptable and ambiguous.

One category of syntactic rules consists of those which specify how to vary or form words to express grammatical relations. Syntactic word variations are called *inflections*. The following are examples of inflections: go-going, mouse-mice, Mary-Mary's, be-is-was-am, and he-him.[1] The syntax of some languages, such as Latin and Russian, depends much more heavily on inflections than does English. In English the order of words is relatively important for expressing syntactic relations. Linguists have demonstrated the vast complexity of the underlying syntactic system. Yet, in contrast to semantic development, acquisition of the basics of syntactic competence is nearly complete by four or five years of age. This chapter will concentrate on the development of syntax.

Developmental psycholinguists, following the transformational grammarians, initially focused almost exclusively on the syntax of children's earliest sentences. Little emphasis was placed on semantics per se. However, syntax and semantics are not fully separable. The structure of a sentence and its meaning are intrinsically related, as Chomsky and others have pointed out. There has recently been an increased effort to combine the study of syntax and semantics and to specify the relationship between structure and meaning. This trend is evident both in the field of theoretical linguistics (for example, Schlesinger, 1971) and in research on language development (for example, Bloom, 1970, 1975; Nelson, 1973).

RESEARCH TRENDS AND THEORIES

The count studies

Several diary studies of individual children, often relatives of the investigators, were done in the first half of this century. As a result of the strong behavioral trend in American psychology in the 1930s and 1940s, the diary studies were largely rejected as unscientific. They were replaced by studies which dealt with aspects of language that could be easily recorded, counted, and statistically processed, such as number and kinds of words used and length of utterance. These studies compared large numbers of children of different ages, sexes, and backgrounds; made statements about language development in general; and specified developmental milestones in language development (for example, the average age of the first babbling sound, the first word, the first two-word combination, etc.). Because of their methodology, they have come to be called *count studies* (Bloom, 1975). A typical finding of this kind of research is that vocabulary size increases spectacularly in the preschool years. (See Figure 8-1.)

Although the count studies provided some useful information about early language, we can see from the modern linguistic perspective that they failed to treat language as a system of rules. One cannot directly study how a child uses rules if one looks only at such countable things as vocabulary, number of verbs used, and length of sentence. Even more importantly, these studies were normative-descriptive accounts which were not concerned with developmental processes. They were not concerned with how the individual child's use of the language system changes over time, which has become the main concern today.

---

[1] Rules of inflectional word variation are usually considered one aspect of syntax, as in this chapter. However, in some cases, the term "syntax" has been reserved for the system of combining whole words into sentences (Gleason, 1961); according to this categorization, inflectional rules would not be considered part of syntax.

Behavioral theories

The behaviorally oriented count studies, as well as a great deal of laboratory research on learning, served as the bases for behavioral explanations of language development. These behavioral theories, which are also referred to as learning theories or S-R (stimulus-response) theories, have taken many forms. They are concerned primarily with speech (one aspect of language performance), and not with language competence. Furthermore, behaviorists have treated speech as an overt behavior acquired according to the same learning principles that presumably explain all other behaviors. These learning principles have largely been derived from laboratory studies of simple behaviors in animals and humans. They include classical and operant conditioning, discrimination learning, shaping through successive approximations, associative learning, and stimulus and response generalization.

As an extreme example, let us look at Skinner's early theory of language acquisition, proposed in a book which is appropriately called *Verbal Behavior* (1957). According to Skinner, the parent first selectively reinforces those parts of the child's spontaneous babbling sounds which are most like adult speech, thereby increasing the frequency of vocalization of these sounds by the baby. Parental reinforcement serves to gradually shape the child's verbal behavior through "successive approximations," until it becomes more and more like the adult's speech. Thus, "wahwah" becomes "wahda" and "wahda" becomes "watah," etc., as the adult reinforces only closer and closer approximations to "water." Similarly, reinforcement is also used to gradually shape sentences. At the same time, the child becomes capable of *self-reinforcement* whenever his utterances match those of the caretaker. Others who advocate very similar theories also propose that the child learns to imitate through *secondary reinforcement*, since the

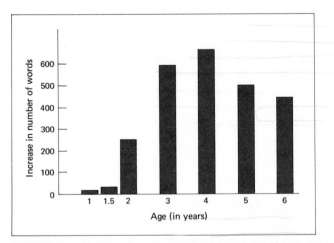

FIGURE 8-1 Number of spoken words added to vocabulary each year from ages one to six. (Smart, M. S., & Smart, R. C. *Children: development and relationships.* New York: Macmillan, 1972. P. 260. Adapted from Smith, M. E. An investigation of the development of the sentence and the extent of vocabulary in young children. *University of Iowa Studies in Child Welfare,* 1926, 3,5.)

caretaker's vocalizations are associated with the primary reinforcement of being fed (Staats & Staats, 1963).

Skinner suggests that the child learns specific *sentence frames* into which he can substitute words through generalization. For instance, a child may learn "I want more cookies" as a sentence that is reinforced, and from this he can substitute words to produce such sentences as "I want more pennies," "I want more toys," etc. Words and eventually sentences are elicited by appropriate environmental cues, which may be generalized across similar situations. Thus, the child will learn to say "water," and later will learn to say "I want water" when he is thirsty.

A slightly modified learning theory position gives more weight to imitation in its own right, rejecting as unnecessary the concepts of secondary reinforcement and gradual response shaping. According to this view, the child picks up words, phrases, and sentences directly by imitating, and then through reinforcement and generalization he learns when it is appropriate to use and combine these responses.

Some behavioral theories have postulated more sophisticated learning mechanisms, such as higher-order conditioning and S-R mediational processes. However, all the behavioral theories basically portray the child as passively or mechanically responding to environmental stimuli. Specific responses are learned, and environmental stimuli in the form of reinforcers, models, and cues determine not only the acquisition process but also the conditions for elicitation of speech responses.

As is characteristic of behaviorism in general, these theories tend to portray language learning as a *quantitative* increase in learned responses. Indeed, the count studies can be called upon to demonstrate that such things as vocabulary and average length of a sentence increase quantitatively over time. These theories are not concerned with qualitative changes in the child's use of the language system, nor do they deal at all

This child is learning word sounds through the behavioral theory of imitation. (Suzanne Szasz.)

satisfactorily with the child's use of abstract rules. Thus, it is not hard to see why linguists and those influenced by linguists would take issue with the behavioral approach to language.

Linguists challenge behavioral theories

Chomsky's (1959) all-encompassing attack on Skinner's theory of language acquisition, which is actually an attack on the entire S-R approach, is a classic example of a clash between two entirely different scientific approaches to an area. Theoretically, the linguists have argued that the ability to infer the deep structure of language is the critical aspect of language acquisition. Since the deep structure itself is never directly available (that is, is never spoken or heard), it cannot possibly be imitated or reinforced. A related argument states that the rules of language form an abstract system on the phonological, semantic, and syntactic levels. These rules are never explicitly stated, and therefore cannot be learned through imitation or reinforcement. It has been argued that S-R mechanisms, *in principle*, are unable to explain how a finite set of rules can generate an infinite system (McNeill, 1968).

Aside from the more theoretical arguments, linguists have pointed out that the number of specific S-R connections that would be necessary to even begin to explain language is so enormous that there would not be enough time to acquire these connections in a whole lifetime, not to mention a few short years. Furthermore, the vast majority of language utterances can in no way be directly predicted from specific "environmental eliciting cues." Utterances which are closely tied to environmental cues, such as "Hello," "Watch out!" or "You're welcome," are rare. For most sets of circumstances, language affords an enormous degree of creative latitude, which linguists argue is not accounted for by S-R theories.

Learning theorists respond by arguing that linguists have interpreted learning theory principles too narrowly, and that traditional concepts (such as reinforcement, imitation, and generalization) may in fact be important in explaining language development. This conclusion is based in part on experimental demonstrations that certain aspects of verbal behavior can be modified. For instance, the types of questions produced by an adult model have been shown to affect the types of questions subsequently produced by sixth-grade children; this finding indicates the influence of imitation (Rosenthal, Zimmerman, & Durning, 1970). Learning principles obviously play some part in language learning and in shaping subsequent language behavior as well.

Here is an example (Liebert, Odom, Hill, & Huff, 1969). An adult modeled (or gave examples of) ungrammatical sentences which ended with a preposition, for example, "The boy went *the house to*," or "The goat was *the door at*." These sentences were considered to embody a "new rule." Children in three different age groups were required to make up sentences and were told to pay close attention to those sentences the experimenter would indicate were especially good. When the adult model said a "new rule sentence," the experimenter praised him (for example, "I like that sentence"); then the experimenter asked the child to repeat the sentence. When the child said a new rule sentence of his own, he was also praised and, in addition, was given a token reward.

Children in the oldest group (averaging fourteen years of age) showed a dramatic increase in their use of the new ungrammatical rule. Children in the middle group (averaging eight years of age) showed some increase in their use of the new rule, though a much less substantial increase than the fourteen-year-olds. However, children in the youngest group (averaging about five and a half years of age) showed no tendency to learn the new rule. The authors concluded that "the results of this experiment lend additional support to the general hypothesis that children's adoption of language rules may be influenced by a combination of modeling and reward procedures . . . [Liebert, Odom, Hill, & Huff, 1969, p. 185]."

However, a qualification is necessary since psycholinguists have shown that the vast majority of actual language rules are "adopted" by children even *younger* than the youngest group used in the study. This experiment, therefore, though perhaps relevant to the rule-learning behavior of older children, provides no evidence that modeling and rewards influence *initial* language acquisition.

Another behavioral theorist attempted to take linguistic developments into account in proposing a simple type of rule learning through generalization (Braine, 1963a). According to this theory, children learn the position of words within two-word phrases (that is, first or second) and later the position of phrases within sentences. Braine used an artificial "language," consisting of a small set of meaningless nonsense words, to experimentally demonstrate that preschoolers are, in fact, capable of this type of learning. Position learning may well play an important part in early language acquisition. Braine's experiments are especially convincing in this regard since his subjects were young enough to be in the primary language acquisition years.

Nevertheless, linguists have convincingly argued that even this behavioral theory is ultimately unsatisfactory since word order is only a superficial aspect of real languages (as discussed briefly in the first section of this chapter). The grammatical function of a word cannot be predicted by position alone. For example, the first word (or phrase) in a sentence may be the subject *or* the object of the sentence, or neither. A child learning a natural language learns much more than the relative position of words and phrases.

Finally, it should be noted that a demonstration that modeling or reinforcement can shape language in an older child is not evidence that the child actually learns language initially through these strategies. In fact, psychologists have thus far not been able to demonstrate that traditional learning principles play a *critical* role in the normal acquisition of language rules by the young child. However, as we will note later in this chapter, learning principles may play a very important and useful role in modifying language usage and in overcoming language deficits in some individuals. Lovaas (1967), for example, has made remarkable demonstrations of the usefulness of imitation and reinforcement principles in overcoming speech deficits in autistic children.

Nativist and biological theories

The nativist position (or innate theory) of language development was first proposed largely on the basis of linguistic arguments. The abstractness and complexity of language, the remarkable rapidity and consistency of its acquisition by the child, and the proposed inaccessibility of the deep structure led to the assertion that some aspects of language must be innate. The nativist position became increasingly popular in the 1960s largely because of growing research evidence against the learning theory explanations.

Nativist theory, like learning theory, takes many forms. A representative example is Chomsky's proposal that the human nervous system contains a mental structure which includes an innate concept of human language (Chomsky, 1968). Some nativists maintain that specific aspects of language are innate. For example, they may claim that certain "universal features," common to all human languages, are innate; or that a set of innate "language hypotheses" are used by the child in deriving rules from the language "data" he hears; or even that aspects of the deep structure are in some sense innate.

These more extreme or literal statements of the nativist position are highly controversial. It has been argued, for instance, that the theories are not testable and that the "innateness" label is simply being used to explain away behavior we do not yet understand. Nativist speculation involving deep structure (for example, McNeill, 1966) is especially questionable because the linguistic concept of deep structure itself is controversial and very much in flux.

Most nativists have not spelled out exactly what they consider to be innate. They do agree, however, that at the very least, every normal human child is in some way biologically "ready" or "predisposed" to learn any human language with ease. They uniformly view language as an abstract system of rules which is not learned by way of traditional learning principles. These more general aspects of the nativist position have become fairly widely accepted and have been influential even among empirical psychologists.

By far the most thorough and precise case for biological determinants of language has been presented, with considerable supporting data, by Eric Lenneberg (1967). Lenneberg's position is that the uniquely human ability to generate and understand language is an inherited species-specific characteristic of man. He argues that language is based on highly specialized biological mechanisms which not only predispose but actually shape the development of language in the child. These biological determinants include, among other things, the articulatory apparatus, specific brain centers for language, and a specialized auditory system which processes speech sounds in a qualitatively different way than other sounds. For example, we can process phonemes at a much faster rate than we can process nonspeech sounds. We can process up to thirty phonemes per second of speech, but we cannot discriminate thirty nonspeech sounds in the same one-second interval (Liberman, 1967). Furthermore, the perception and categorization of phonemes (even when not in the context of speech) is radically different than the perception of nonspeech sounds.[2]

Infant speech perception Some of the most convincing arguments for language-specific neurological structures come from growing evidence that very young infants, as

---

[2] This unique aspect of speech perception is called *categorical perception*. Speech sounds are always perceived as belonging to discrete categories (phoneme categories), even though the acoustic characteristics of the sounds vary continuously. For example, "b" and "p" are produced in the same way except that the vocal cords begin to vibrate later for "p" than for "b". Liberman (1967) demonstrated categorical perception by artificially synthesizing a series of sounds that varies *continuously* along an acoustic dimension corresponding to the timing of vocal cord vibration. As the stimulus is varied, subjects perceive a "b" sound over a wide range of variation and then suddenly perceive a "p" sound over another wide range of variation. Within the "b" or the "p" ranges, variations in the stimulus cannot be discriminated. In contrast to the categorical perception of speech sounds, nonspeech sounds are discriminated on a continuous basis.

well as adults, have specialized linguistic capacities. Specifically, there is evidence of mechanisms which selectively direct the infant's attention to speech and to particular features of speech. From the end of the first month, infants can distinguish between the human voice and other sounds, and the voice is much more effective in stopping crying (Wolff, 1966). Differential smiling to the voice of the mother and the voice of an unfamiliar female has been reported for infants as young as four months of age (Laroche & Tcheng, 1963). Infants under one year of age are sensitive to the intonation patterns of both individual syllables and sentences. They modify their own babbling according to the intonation and pitch qualities of the adult speech they hear. For instance, compared to the babbling of American babies, the babbling of six-month-old Chinese babies shows much more pitch variation, reflecting the Chinese language they hear (Weir, 1966). Also, a ten-month-old and a thirteen-month-old infant were each found to babble in a higher pitch when the mother was present than when the father was present (Lieberman, 1967).

Consistent with a biological view of language is the finding that newborns synchronize their body movement in coordination with the sound patterns of adult speech, (Condon & Sander, 1974). This intriguing study was discussed earlier in Chapter 4.

Another interesting aspect of the infant's receptive language abilities involves phoneme perception. A heart rate habituation measure was used to demonstrate that five-month-old infants can discriminate between the phonemes ''b'' and ''g'' in ''bah'' and ''gah'' (Moffitt, 1971, described in Chapter 1). Similarly, a sucking response was used to demonstrate that infants as young as one month old can discriminate between ''p'' and ''b'' (Eimas, Siqueland, Jusczyk, & Vigorito, 1971). In this second experiment, the loudness of a continuous recording of either ''pa'' or ''ba'' was electronically maintained by the infant's sucking on a pacifier. When the infant's sucking rate began to decrease, the recording switched to the alternate syllable. The infants in the study then quickly began sucking more frequently to keep the new syllable audible, indicating that they had discriminated the change. In the control condition, the initial syllable was continued and the infants' sucking continued to decrease (see Figure 8-2). An important aspect of the study was that the infants showed the same specialized perception of phonemes characteristic of adult speech perception.

Thus, even in early infancy, humans demonstrate specialized language abilities, including selective attention, voice discrimination, imitation of aspects of speech, movement synchronized to speech patterns, and specialized phoneme perception. All of this evidence supports the hypothesis of an innate capacity and readiness in the human infant to learn language.

Further evidence of the biological position   Lenneberg points out that the unfolding ''milestones'' of language acquisition occur in a regular and fixed order in all normal children around the world, and that they occur at very much the same rate despite cultural or environmental variation. For example, children all over the world begin babbling at about six months, say their first word near the end of the first year, begin using two-word combinations near the end of the second year, and master the basic syntax of their language by the time they are four or five years old. Lenneberg considers this regular unfolding process to be tied to biological maturation, in much the same manner as the stages involved in learning how to walk are maturationally determined. In fact, he has demonstrated the correspondence in time between milestones in motor development and milestones in language (see Table 8-1). Lenneberg suggests that the only requirement for this preprogrammed ''unfolding'' of language milestones is exposure to a minimal number and variety of normal language examples. In cases in which maturation is abnormally slow, such as in Downs' syndrome, the language milestones develop in the same order as in normal children, but correspond to the slower overall maturation of the child.

Lenneberg proposed that because of the functional importance of language to man, the biological language system has evolved with very strong built-in resistance to disruption. Deaf children can acquire standard language, at least in written form. The sign language of the deaf is also a true linguistic system. Normal language occurs in blind children, who manage to acquire words for many objects which have no tactile referents (such as ''mountain,'' ''cloud,'' etc.). Children suffering neglect, or even certain kinds of severe retardation, nevertheless develop language.

genetic evidence

When congenital language deficits are observed, they are often related to specific chromosomal abnormality and are not necessarily related to intelligence. Several other

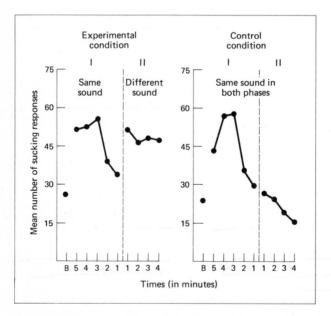

FIGURE 8-2 Discrimination of ''pah'' and ''bah'' by four-month-old infants. The figure shows the mean number of sucking responses to presentation of the same sound across both phases of the experiment and to presentation of a different sound in the second phase of the experiment. The dashed line indicates the occurrence of the stimulus shift to a new sound, or in the case of the control group the time at which the shift would have occurred. The letter *B* stands for the base line rate. Time is measured with reference to the moment of stimulus shift and indicates the five minutes prior to and the four minutes after shift. (Adopted from Eimas, P., Siqueland, E. R., Jusczyk, P., and Vigorito, J., Speech perception in infants. *Science*, 1971, **171,** 303–306; with permission of senior author and American Association for the Advancement of Science.)

sources of evidence, including studies of the language development of identical twins, suggest that language ability is genetically based.

Another source of support for specific biological involvement is evidence that humans learn language far more easily and quickly during a certain period of biological development, that is, from infancy to puberty. Before puberty, a child can achieve the fluency of a native speaker in any language (or even in two or more languages simultaneously) without special training. After puberty, language learning is more difficult and usually requires study, and the speaker rarely approaches the fluency of a native

Table 8-1 DEVELOPMENTAL MILESTONES IN MOTOR AND LANGUAGE DEVELOPMENT

At the completion of:	Motor development	Vocalization and language
12 weeks	Supports head when in prone position; weight is on elbows; hands mostly open; no grasp reflex	Markedly less crying than at 8 weeks; when talked to and nodded at, smiles, followed by squealing-gurgling sounds usually called *cooing,* which is vowel-like in character and pitch-modulated; sustains cooing for 15-20 seconds
16 weeks	Plays with a rattle placed in his hands (by shaking it and staring at it), head self-supported; tonic neck reflex subsiding	Responds to human sounds more definitely; turns head; eyes seem to search for speaker; occasionally some chuckling sounds
20 weeks	Sits with props	The vowel-like cooing sounds begin to be interspersed with more consonantal sounds; acoustically, all vocalizations are very different from the sounds of the mature language of the environment
6 months	Sitting: bends forward and uses hands for support; can bear weight when put into standing position, but cannot yet stand with holding on; reaching: unilateral; grasp: no thumb apposition yet; releases cube when given another	Cooing changing into babbling resembling one-syllable utterances; neither vowels nor consonants have very fixed recurrences; most common utterances sound somewhat like ma, mu, da, or di
8 months	Stands holding on; grasps with thumb apposition: picks up pellet with thumb and finger tips	Reduplication (or more continuous repetitions) becomes frequent; intonation patterns become distinct; utterances can signal emphasis and emotions
10 months	Creeps efficiently; takes side-steps, holding on; pulls to standing position	Vocalizations are mixed with sound-play such as gurgling or bubble-blowing; appears to wish to imitate sounds, but the imitations are never quite successful; beginning to differentiate between words heard by making differential adjustment

Source: Lenneberg, E. *Biological foundations of language.* New York: Wiley, 1967. Pp. 128-130. With permission of author and publisher.

Table 8-1 DEVELOPMENTAL MILESTONES IN MOTOR AND LANGUAGE DEVELOPMENT (*cont'd*)

At the completion of:	Motor development	Vocalization and language
12 months	Walks when held by one hand; walks on feet and hands, knees in air; mouthing of objects almost stopped; seats self on floor	Identical sound sequences are replicated with higher relative frequency of occurrence and words (mamma or dadda) are emerging; definite signs of understanding some words and simple commands (show me your eyes)
18 months	Grasp, prehension, and release fully developed; gait stiff, propulsive, and precipitated; sits on child's chair with only fair aim; creeps downstairs backward; has difficulty building tower of three cubes	Has a definite repertoire of words— more than three, but less than fifty; still much babbling but now of several syllables with intricate intonation pattern; no attempt at communicating information and no frustration for not being understood; words may include items such as thank you or come here, but there is little ability to join any of the lexical items into spontaneous two-item phrases; understanding is progressing rapidly
24 months	Runs, but falls in sudden turns; can quickly alternate between sitting and stance; walks stairs up or down, one foot forward only	Vocabulary of more than 50 items (some children seem to be able to name everything in environment); begins spontaneously to join vocabulary items into two-word phrases; all phrases appear to be own creations; definite increase in communicative behavior and interest in language
30 months	Jumps up into air with both feet; stands on one foot for about two seconds; takes few steps on tip-toe; jumps from chair; good hand and finger coordination; can move digits independently; manipulation of objects much improved; builds tower of six cubes	Fastest increase in vocabulary with many new additions every day; no babbling at all; utterances have communicative intent; frustrated if not understood by adults; utterances consist of at least two words, many have three or even five words; sentences and phrases have characteristic child grammar, that is, they are rarely verbatim repetitions of an adult utterance; intelligibility is not very good yet, though there is great variation among children; seems to understand everything that is said to him
3 years	Tiptoes three yards; runs smoothly with acceleration and deceleration; negotiates sharp and fast curves without difficulty; walks stairs by alternating feet; jumps 12 inches; can operate tricycle	Vocabulary of some 1000 words; about 80% of utterances are intelligible even to strangers; grammatical complexity of utterances is roughly that of colloquial adult language, although mistakes still occur
4 years	Jumps over rope; hops on right foot; catches ball in arms; walks line	Language is well-established; deviations from the adult norm tend to be more in style than in grammar

This pictograph, in which pictures are used as symbols for words, is a true linguistic system. (Omikron.)

speaker. When a family moves to a foreign country, the parents sometimes must depend on their young children, who pick up the language quickly, to serve as translators. Furthermore, in cases of speech disruption due to brain damage, young children often recover their language capacity rapidly and completely; if the brain damage occurs after puberty, the prognosis for the recovery of language is poor (Lenneberg, 1967).

If language ability is an inherited species-specific characteristic, all languages of the species must share common basic characteristics, or universal features. In examining features such as the sounds used in speaking, the way words are organized, and how meaning is determined in various languages, investigators have concluded that a set of common principles underlie all human languages (Greenberg, 1966). For instance,

Common properties of languages

speakers of all languages create a vast number of spoken words by combining a small set of meaningless sounds of a particular type. All languages use only a limited sample of vocal sounds, of all the possible sounds humans can make; for example, no language makes use of snorting or clapping sounds. Words are always combined into structured sequences we call sentences. All languages have grammars, and linguists claim that these grammars share certain formal properties as well.

Although Lenneberg's formal theory is still speculative in certain respects and may be somewhat overstated, he has brought together from many sources a great deal of evidence which suggests that humans, and humans alone, are biologically destined in some sense to acquire a language system possessing specific characteristics. This evidence, of course, has added substantial support to some of the earlier theoretical arguments of the nativists.

Evidence that children use general language rules The previously presented arguments in support of a biological approach to language acquisition gain strength from evidence that children do learn and apply general language rules in their own unique yet systematic way.

One of the best examples of such evidence is the fact that children all over the world show *overregularization* of rules they acquire. They apply a rule to form regularities in cases where the adult form is irregular and does not follow the rule. For instance, a young child may use the words "went" and "came" correctly. But after learning that "-ed" forms the past tense for many verbs, the child will use this ending on *all* verbs and will switch to saying "goed" and "comed" (Ervin, 1964). Similarly, a child often uses the word "feet" until the regular plural ending "-s" is learned; at that time he or she switches to "foots" (or sometimes "feets"). In some cases it has been reported that after learning that some plurals are formed by adding "-es" (such as "boxes"), the child may then say "footses" for a time. According to reinforcement theory, the child would have been reinforced initally when he or she did say the correct words (for example, "went" and "feet"). Neither reinforcement nor imitation theory can explain why the child would ever replace these presumably reinforced imitations with deviant forms like "comed" and "feets" which he or she had probably never heard and had never been reinforced for saying.

not just imitation of adults

Children also sometimes "create" regularized singular words from an irregular plural. For example, a child the authors knew used the word "clothes" and insisted on calling one piece of clothing "a clo." A different type of overregularization was demonstrated by a child who said, "I'm magic, amn't I?" It has been observed that young children in the Soviet Union and other countries also broadly apply the rules they learn to form novel "regularized" words and phrases that do not occur in adult speech (Slobin, 1966).

Overregularization is only one example of the fact that children's speech is unique and qualitatively different from adult speech in many ways and thus not *directly* a product of imitation. For instance, such utterances as "Allgone hot," "Allgone window," "More page," or "More up" are not simplified imitations of any adult sentence, but rather are truly creative combinations. The same is true of more complex sentences such as "Cowboy did fighting me" and "No I see truck," which are not likely to be imitations (Brown & Bellugi, 1964).

creative not imitative?

Use of the auxiliary verb "will" provides a striking example of how children's speech often differs from the adult model in characteristic ways. It was found that mothers in three separate families nearly always contracted the word "will" in such sentences as "I'll fix it later," "You'll ruin it," and "It'll be a little one." But their three children went through a period in which they used only the full word "will" in such sentences as "I will read you book," "You will gone away," and "They will get dry?" The children's consistent use of "will" was therefore not a direct copying. When the mother said, "I'll get it," the child said, "I will get it." Similarly, adults may say, "Put on the dress," or "Put the dress on"; but when using the pronoun "it," they always say, "Put it on." Despite the consistent adult modeling of the sentence "Put it on," children will often apply their own rule, treat "put on" as a unit, and creatively say, "Put on it."

Ask a young child to repeat "Why can't the dog go?" and he will be likely to rephrase it to match the form of his current spontaneous questions, perhaps, "Why the dog can't go?" The power of an internalized syntactic rule system is illustrated by the fact that children are extremely persistent in applying their own rules even when they are under direct pressure to change. Witness the following dialogue:

> Child: Nobody don't like me.
> Mother: No, say, "Nobody likes me."
> Child: Nobody don't like me.
> (8 repetitions of above)
> Mother: Now listen carefully, say, "Nobody likes me."
> Child: Oh! Nobody don't likes me [McNeill, 1970, pp. 106–107].

With regard to the reinforcement explanation of language acquisition, there is little evidence for selective reinforcement of "correct" speech. Adults are likely to respond to all types of babbling sounds, and not only to those that resemble words. More importantly, it has been demonstrated that parents' approval or disapproval is determined primarily by the truth value of the child's speech, and hardly at all by the correctness of the syntax (Brown, Cazden, & Bellugi, 1969). That is, parents frequently "reinforce" *un*grammatical statements that are true (or in some other way pleasing to the parent), whereas they correct grammatical but untrue statements. In one actual example, a child said, "Mama isn't boy, he a girl." The adult replied, "That's right," presumably reinforcing an ungrammatical sentence. Similarly, the ungrammatical sentence, "Her curl my hair," was approved because the mother was, in fact, curling Eve's hair. On the other hand, the *grammatical* sentence, "There's the animal farmhouse," was disapproved because the building was a lighthouse. If a child were to say "The sky is green" or "I'm asleep"—both perfectly grammatical—the adult would be likely to disagree and perhaps show disapproval. This observation is in direct contradiction to the reinforcement explanation of syntactic development.

Thus we have seen that imitation and reinforcement theories, which emphasize the direct effect of environmental stimuli on the child, are contradicted by research evidence about language development, as well as by theoretical arguments. These traditional explanations fail not only to treat language itself as a system of rules, but also to account for the active and creative part the child takes in forming and re-forming linguistic systems.

Trends in development psycholinguistic research

Beginning in the 1950s, researchers in the area of developmental psycholinguistics have tried to assess the development of language competence and the child's functional knowledge of the rules of his language system. Attempts have also been made to write syntactic grammars specifically for the speech of young children. This recent research has involved fewer children than did the count studies, but it has delved into the development of the individual child's language system in greater depth. There have been two basic research strategies which have sometimes been used in conjunction: experiments involving manipulation of linguistic or situational variables, cleverly designed to assess language competence; and detailed longitudinal sampling and analyses of children's spontaneous speech, recorded at frequent intervals during the period of early syntactic development.

Manipulative experiments One ingenious manipulative experiment clearly demonstrated that children as young as three to five years of age can infer a great deal about the functional meaning of a nonsense word simply from the way it is used in an English sentence (Brown, 1957; see Box 8-1). In another experiment, Berko (1958) studied children's productive use of word inflections. Examples of common English inflections are the plural ending "-s," the past tense ending "-ed," and variations of each. Berko presented a series of nonsense words, such as "wug" or "bix," in conjunction with drawings. For instance, she showed children drawings of strange bird-like creatures and said, "This is a wug. Now there is another one. There are two of them. There are two _____." (See Figure 8-3.) It should be noted that the sound of the required plural endings varies with the word, for example, wug(z), bix(es), and zat(s). Even four-year-olds could produce the proper plural forms of the nonsense words in a large proportion of test sentences. Similar demonstrations have used other inflections, such as the past tense endings. These results are consistent with the phenomenon of overregularization discussed in the previous section. They clearly demonstrate that children learn *general rules* for plural inflection and not just individual plural words. Since general rules can be applied to novel material, they form the core of any generative language system.

BOX 8-1 TO SIB, OR NOT TO SIB

Through clever use of nonsense words and pictures, Roger Brown (1957) was one of the first researchers to demonstrate experimentally that young children know underlying linguistic rules, which they can use in a novel situation. The children were three to five years old.

The nonsense words "niss," "sib," and "latt" were each used in sentences in three different ways. When "sib" was used as a verb, for instance, the child was asked: "Do you know what it is to sib? In this picture you can see sibbing." The picture which was shown to the child simultaneously depicted an action, a particular object, and a mass substance. For example, one of these pictures showed hands manipulating a mass of confetti-like material which was overflowing a striped container. The child was then shown three related pictures, each of which depicted one component of the first picture. In the above example, one picture showed the moving hands, one the confetti-like mass, and one the container. Presenting the three pictures, the experimenter said to the child, "Now show me another picture of sibbing."

Ten out of sixteen children responded appropriately to the verb questions by pointing to the action picture (for example, the moving hands). Similarly, when asked analogous questions about a "sib," "a latt," or "a niss," eleven out of sixteen children pointed to the picture of the particular object (for example, the container). When asked about "some sib," "some latt," or "some niss," twelve out of sixteen children pointed to the mass substance (for example, the confetti-like mass).

Several children also spontaneously indicated that they could use the nonsense words appropriately in other sentences. When asked "Can you show me another sib?" one child pointed to an odd object in the room and said, "There's a sib." When (with regard to the picture described above) the investigator said, "There is some latt in this picture," one child observed, "The latt is spilling."

Source: Brown, R. Linguistic determinism and the part of speech. *Journal of Abnormal Social Psychology*, 1957, **55,** 1–5. With permission of author and publisher.

These and other studies in the 1950s provided evidence that young children acquire a functional knowledge of certain kinds of linguistic rules (phonological and inflectional rules, for instance) which are never directly spelled out for the child or the adult. However, prior to the 1960s, very little was understood about the development of a grammatical system for combining words into larger units or sentences.

Transformational linguists focused attention on the syntax of sentences. Consequently, in the 1960s, developmental psycholinguists were most interested in children's developing syntactic systems for understanding and forming sentences. Interesting experimental studies of sentence comprehension have been carried out. In one such study, three-year-olds were presented with pairs of sentences and corresponding pictures. Then, after hearing one of the sentences repeated, they were asked to point to the appropriate picture. For example, they were asked to point to the picture of either "The boy pushes the girl" or "The girl pushes the boy." The children had little trouble understanding this type of sentence, which is called an *active* sentence. However, most of them misinterpreted the corresponding *passive* sentence. That is, when asked to show "The boy is pushed by the girl," they pointed instead to the boy pushing the girl. This systematic error suggests that three-year-olds process passive sentences as if they were active sentences, incorrectly assuming the first noun is the actor (Fraser, Bellugi, & Brown, 1963). This finding is consistent with the observation that in their own early speech, children almost always place the subject before the verb.

This is a wug.

Now there is another one. There are two of them.

There are two _____

FIGURE 8-3 One of the drawings used to test children's productive use of word inflections. (From Berko, J. The child's learning of English morphology. *Word*, 1958, **14,** 50–177.)

Another ingenious technique used to study comprehension involves having the child imitate a sentence that is too long for his immediate memory span. If the child comprehends the sentence, even though he cannot repeat it verbatim, he will be able to rephrase it in a way that retains the meaning:

Adult: The little boy is eating some pink ice cream.
Child: Little boy eating some pink ice cream [Slobin & Welsh, 1973, p. 487].

If he does not comprehend it, his reformulation will not preserve the meaning:

Adult: The boy the book hit was crying.
Child: Boy the book was crying [Slobin & Welsh, 1973, p. 494].

By the above reasoning, it may be concluded that the child in these examples comprehended the first sentence, but not the second sentence. The first sentence illustrates the child's ability to pick out the underlying meaning even of sentences too long for him to repeat. Another interesting experimental study of children's comprehension was done by Carol Chomsky (see Box 8-2). This study illustrates that although the basic syntactic system is acquired in the preschool years, specific complex aspects of syntax continue to develop into the elementary school years.

BOX 8-2 COMPREHENSION OF COMPLEX SYNTAX

In order to make sense of a number of English sentences, the child must learn to violate some of the rules he has previously acquired. These semantically complex sentences may resemble simpler forms at the surface level. For example, in the two sentences "John is eager to please" and "John is easy to please" the subject, John, takes on two very different functions. In "John is eager to please," John is doing the pleasing. But in "John is easy to please," John is the logical object, the one being pleased; this sentence is unusual in that the subject of a sentence is more often the actor than the recipient of action. Most children younger than eight or nine years old are not able to understand this type of sentence in which the subject is also the logical object.

This phenomenon was investigated by Carol Chomsky (1969). In one of her experiments she used a sentence with the same form as "John is easy to please." Her subjects were individually presented with a blindfolded doll and asked, "Is the doll easy to see or hard to see?" After responding, the child was asked, "Why is the doll easy/hard to see?" Finally, the child was asked to make the doll easy or hard to see (opposite to his previous response).

Most of the youngest children (the five-year-olds) misinterpreted the sentence. They initially said the blindfolded doll was "hard to see," and then took off the doll's blindfold in an effort to make her "easy to see." In contrast, all of the nine-year-olds said the doll was "easy to see," and then hid the doll or covered their own eyes in an effort to make her "hard to see," thus demonstrating the correct interpretation of the sentence. The six-, seven-, and eight-year-olds showed intermediate levels of correct interpretations. This is one of several recent experiments which demonstrate that children's use of specific aspects of syntax continues to develop well into the school years, although the basic syntactic system is acquired in the preschool years.

Source: Chomsky, C. *The acquisition of syntax in children from 5 to 10.* Cambridge, Mass.: M.I.T., 1969.

Longitudinal studies and child grammars   The most important research trend of the 1960s and the 1970s was extensive longitudinal sampling of children's spontaneous speech. This approach, a more rigorous version of the early diary studies, has provided a wealth of information. Its main advantage over the manipulative experimental approach is that only by studying the same child extensively over a period of time is it possible to analyze in detail how the individual child's language system changes and develops. So far, very few children have been involved, perhaps a few dozen in total, including children in non-English-speaking countries. However, the enormous quantity of language acquisition data that has been collected from these children has permitted analysis and reanalysis by the original investigators as their thinking changed. Also, other researchers have analyzed these data with different goals in mind. The best-known children were initially studied by Roger Brown and associates (Brown, 1973). In the literature they are called Adam and Sarah (each studied for over two years) and Eve (studied for nine months).

Box 8-3 presents examples taken from the records of Adam's speech, first when he was twenty-eight months old, and then (only ten months later) when he was thirty-eight months old. Notice the increase in length and complexity of his utterances which took place in this short time.

BOX 8-3 SPEECH SAMPLES, TEN MONTHS APART

These samples of speech are from the records of Brown and Bellugi (1964). The first is from a boy at 28 months of age, and the second is from the same boy at 38 months of age.

Child—28 months	Adult
What dat . . . somebody pencil	Whose pencils are they?
Floor	Floor?
Where birdie go? Birdie Birdie up dere Birdie Read dat?	
Read dat?	Will you read it to me?
What innere?	Is that a hammer, Adam?
Hammer Hit hammer, mommy No Cromer _____, mommy? Hurt	Poor Adam. Did you hurt yourself? What happened, Adam?
Screw (did) happen	Screw happened? You didn't even have a screw.

have screw
————no down there . . .
table . . . get broom

Does that one fit?

Yep, it fit
Yep, it fit

Does it fit?

No . . . fit
Put suitcase . . . for?

What did you put it in the suitcase for?

What dat?

That's tape. We'll use that one tomorrow.

All right 'morrow

Shall we use it tomorrow?

Yep
Use morrow, yep
Sure, use 'morrow

Child——38 months

Adult

I like a racing car
D'you like some?
I broke my racing car

Oh, did you used to have one?

Yes
Look at dat one
Like dis part broke

What part broke?

Dis part broke, like that
It's got a flat tire
What is dat?
It's a what?
He . . . his mouth is open
What shall we shall have?
Why he going to have some seeds?

Why it's not working?

You got some beads?

Yes

Just like me?
I got bead 'round myself
Hit my knee

Hit my knee

Hit your knee
What dat teacher will do?

Why you pull out?

Who put dust on my hair?

Dust in your hair

Can you tell Ursula what the lesson is . . .
on the blackboard?

On the black which board?
We going see another one
We can read 'bout dis
You wanto read?

What is dat?
What is dat got?
It's got a flat tire
When it's got flat tire, it's
    needs to go to the . . . to
    the station.
The station will fix it.
Tank come out through what?
Really . . . tank come out through
    . . . here
Mommy don't let my buy some
What is dis?   That's a marble bag
A marble bag for what?   For marbles. It would be good to carry tiny cars.

What is dat?
Can I keep dem?
Why I can keep dem?
Now can I keep dem?
We don' do some games
It's broked?

Source: Cited in McNeill, D. *The acquisition of language: the study of developmental psycholinguistics.* New York: Harper & Row, 1970. Pp. 16–19.

One striking fact that has emerged from the longitudinal studies is that young children often omit words or word endings that would be found in adult speech, and that these omissions are not random. Children omit the small words (such as "of," "on," "the," etc.) and word endings, both of which carry relatively little meaning. The words they do speak are the most important meaningful words, called *content words*. The resulting speech has been called *telegraphic,* and this speech includes sentences such as "There no more these." In addition to the selection of certain types of words to speak, the child usually orders these words in a systematic way. For instance, one of the first syntactic rules used by children seems to be that the subject comes before the verb; this has been found in several different countries for children learning their native language (Slobin, 1973). The words that are spoken in a telegraphic sentence are usually in the same order as in the corresponding adult sentence. Even when a young child is imitating an adult sentence (spontaneously or on request), he will usually produce a telegraphic version. No matter how long the model sentence is, the child's imitation will be only about as long as the sentences he makes up on his own at that point in his development. Thus, "I showed you the book" becomes "I show book"; "He's going out" becomes "He go out"; "No, you can't write on Mr. Cromer's shoe" becomes "Write Cromer shoe" (Brown & Bellugi, 1964).

By using language samples from the longitudinal studies, various researchers attempted to infer the grammatical structures and rules of the earliest language combinations. It was initially hoped that the linguists' evolving transformational grammar could be empirically linked in some way to the child's acquisition of language rules. In certain

telegraphic sentences [handwritten marginal note]

areas, such as the study of children's questions and negations, the transformational framework has proven to be relatively important and useful. For instance, it has been found that in the early stages of question formation, children simply place a question word, such as "where," "what," or "why" (or "why not"), at the beginning of an otherwise declarative sentence without further modifying its form. Examples of spontaneous early questions from Adam, Eve, and Sarah are

Where my mitten?
Where Daddy going?
What me think?
What the dollie have?
Why you smiling?
Why not he eat?
Why not cracker can't talk?

Similarly, the earliest negative sentences are formed by adding a negative word, usually "no" in English, to an affirmative sentence, for examples:

No fall.
No drop mitten.
No want soup.
No the sun shining.
Get car no.
[Klima & Bellugi, 1966]

Children in the Soviet Union, Japan, and France apparently form early negative sentences in the same way as American children. They choose *one* negative word and consistently add that one word to sentences. This is especially interesting because the rules of negation in the adult grammars of these languages are different: single negation is the rule in English, double negation is common in the Soviet Union, and two words are required in French (for example, "non . . . pas") (McNeill, 1968; Slobin, 1970). These early forms of children's questions and negations closely resemble the deep structure postulated by some linguists for adult questions and negations. This has led to speculation that children may somehow first speak the deep structure of questions and negations and only later learn the transformations of their particular language.

In general, however, transformational grammar has been disappointing as a direct tool for understanding language development. One reason for this is that the methods used in formulating child grammars were inconsistent with the transformational approach. Whereas transformational linguists stressed underlying meaning and competence, child language researchers initially analyzed only the form of children's utterances, that is, the distribution of words and particularly the order of words. The best known product of this strategy was the postulation of *pivot grammar,* an attempt to explain children's first two-word utterances strictly in terms of word order (Braine, 1963b).

Pivot grammars consist of two classes of words. *Pivot* words are frequently occurring words, which are usually used in combination with a variety of other words. Each pivot word occurs fairly consistently in either the first or the second position of two-word utterances (usually first position). All the other words spoken are considered to be in a complementary *open class*. The child increases his vocabulary primarily by adding words to the open class, that is, by combining new words with his existing pivot words. Thus, in sentences like "more milk," "more shoe," and "more ride," the word "more" is the pivot word, and "milk," "shoe," and "ride" (as well as any other word that might follow "more") are open-class words. Similarly, "go" is the pivot word in "baby go," "dolly go," "he go," etc.

New emphasis: semantics and cognition Pivot grammars describe a certain aspect of early language, that is, the tendency of children to experiment by combining new words with familiar words. However, several psycholinguists have recently pointed out that pivot grammars offer only a superficial description of children's utterances (Brown, 1972; Bloom, 1975). Because they account for word order alone, they cannot explain the child's growing mastery of the rules for inferring meaning from the form of a sentence, or for expressing a desired meaning by way of a sentence. In other words, pivot grammars are inadequate to deal with early *semantic* development, which is increasingly considered to be of critical importance in understanding language acquisition.

We have seen that adult utterances (such as "Visiting relatives can be a nuisance") may be ambiguous, with the meaning dependent on context. The meaning of a young child's short idiosyncratic utterance is often especially difficult to interpret. If such utterances are taken out of context, as was done in the earlier formulation of pivot grammars, it becomes almost impossible to determine meaning. For instance, twenty-one-month-old Kathryn, who was studied by Bloom (1970), was observed to say "Mommy sock" in two separate contexts: when Kathryn picked up her mother's sock, and when mother was putting Kathryn's sock on Kathryn. Pivot grammar would describe this sentence in one way, that is, according to the word order, thereby failing to account for the fact that in the first context Kathryn was probably describing the sock as belonging to Mommy, whereas in the second context she probably meant that Mommy was doing something involving a sock. Theoretically, "Mommy sock" might express many things, including "Mommy is that a sock?" "Mommy, give me the sock," or perhaps even "Mommy, go sock Daddy!" As another example, Bloom (1970) has pointed out that the observed negative sentence "No dirty soap" could be interpreted in at least four ways: There is no dirty soap; the soap isn't dirty; that isn't dirty *soap;* and I don't want the dirty soap.

Since the meaning is ambiguous from word order alone, Bloom has made the important suggestion that the child's immediate behavior and the context in which the language occurs be carefully recorded and evaluated as a clue to the meaning. She sees this as necessary in studying the child's progress in expressing meaning syntactically. One sign that other researchers agree is the increasing use of video tape recordings instead of just audio recordings of children's language in order to help specify the context.

Interest in the child's intended meaning and in specifying ongoing behaviors is, in part, a reflection of the trend toward analyzing the child's language development in relation to his changing ways of perceiving and thinking about his word. "Cognitive" theorists, and especially Piaget, have been especially influential in this regard. Attempts are being made to link cognitive processes to both the structure and the content of early language. First, with regard to structure, the Piagetian viewpoint is that a linguistic system (for example, a grammar) is just one kind of cognitive system which is not qualitatively different from other cognitive systems. Grammatical rules, including transformational rules, are considered to develop in the same way as other cognitive operations. So far, there is little specific data to support this aspect of the cognitive position.

Second, cognitive theorists maintain that the content of what children say must stem from their general cognitive functioning at any given stage in development. For example, they point out that children all over the world who are beginning to speak use similar types of relations in their early speech, such as agent-action relations, disappearance, and reappearance. This is presumably because these particular relations are significant in the children's cognitive processes at that time. The claim that there is a strong relationship between semantic and cognitive development has received some empirical support (for example, Bloom, 1970; Nelson, 1973).

A major implication of the cognitive approach to language is that the regularities observed in language development around the world may perhaps be accounted for in terms of regularities already demonstrated in the development of more general cognitive processes. As yet this is merely a hypothesis, but it does provide a potential alternative to the strict nativist interpretation that regularities in language development result from language-specific genetic factors.

Social class and ethnic differences

The influence of linguistic and nativist theories has led to a heavy research emphasis on regularities in language development, as opposed to individual or group differences in development. The recent longitudinal studies of children's language acquisition, from which generalizations about regularity have been made, have exclusively involved middle-class white toddlers. Despite the lack of detailed information about the early linguistic development of lower-class children or black children, there exists a raging controversy about differences in the rate, quality, and function of language development in "disadvantaged" children compared to middle-class children.

For years, educators, psychologists, and others have worked under the influence of the *verbal deficit* model, that is, under the assumption that the language used by poverty children is inferior or deficient, and that this language deficiency leads to cognitive deficiency. Language of a certain caliber is considered a prerequisite for adequate intellectual functioning. Under this model, teaching "correct" language is expected to improve poor performance on standardized tests and in school, and to help eliminate the vocational and social discrimination presumably related to substandard speech.

Many of the programs which have attempted to implement this strategy at the preschool level, such as Head Start, have been unsuccessful in producing lasting educational effects. However, at least one influential preschool program based on the deficit model, the Bereiter-Engelmann program of precise patterned language drill, has demonstrated relatively long-lasting effects on standardized tests and school performance (see Box 8-4). The results differed from those of other programs in that the tested children continued to make academic gains in the year following the program, rather than showing the typical pattern of losing the initial gains (Osborn, 1968). The Bereiter-Engelmann program is very intensive and has a high teacher-child ratio; these are probably important factors contributing to its success. Moreover, the total program also involves training in other areas, including arithmetic, reading, and writing. Therefore, it cannot be stated with certainty that the oral language training per se led to the children's subsequent improved performance.

BOX 8-4 A PRESCHOOL LANGUAGE TRAINING PROGRAM

Bereiter and Engelmann have designed a highly structured language training program for "disadvantaged" preschool children. In a typical twenty-minute language training session, the teacher leads a group of about five or six children in a fast pattern of alternating statements, questions, and responses. The children speak rhythmically, first in unison and then individually. The goal of the fast pace and frequent change of task is to keep the children working in a highly disciplined and energetic manner. The initial procedure is as follows:

a. Present and object and give the appropriate identity statement. "This is a ball."
b. Follow the statement with a yes-no question. "Is this a ball?"
c. Answer the question. "Yes, this is a ball."
d. Repeat the question and encourage the children to answer it.
e. Introduce what questions after children have begun to respond adequately to the yes-no *questions. ("What is this?" "This is a ball.")*
[Bereiter & Engelmann, 1966, p. 140]

Similar pattern drills are then used with more complex sentence types in a sequenced order. In the beginning language program the following sentence patterns are used:

First order Statements— *. . . This is a* _____.
The not statement: This is not a _____.
Plural statements: These are _____.
Second Order Statements— *. . . This* _____ *is* _____.
Polar: This cup is big.
      This cup is not big.
      This cup is little.
      This cup is not little.
Prepositions: This cup is on the table.
Color: This cup is white.
Pattern: This cup is striped.
Categories: This animal is a zebra . . .
Shape: This cup is round.
Made of: This cup is made of plastic.
[Osborn, 1968, p. 43]

After each sentence pattern is mastered, it is used in a variety of contexts utilizing different objects, categories, etc. The advanced language pattern involves more complex aspects of language, including verb tenses, personal pronouns, and the use of "and," "or," and "if-then." The Bereiter-Engelmann program is based heavily on imitation, repetitive drill, and immediate feedback (often in the form of verbal praise). Earlier we indicated that imitation and reinforcement are probably not key factors in normal language acquisition. Nevertheless, the success of the Bereiter-Engelmann program, in at least improving language performance, suggests that these strategies do have value in an intervention setting.

Source: Bereiter, C., & Engelmann, S. *Teaching disadvantaged children in the preschool.* Engelwood Cliffs, N.J.: Prentice-Hall, 1966.

An essential distinction which is often blurred or ignored is the distinction between social class differences on the one hand and ethnic differences on the other. The verbal deficit model received its greatest formal impetus from Bernstein's (1961) theorizing on *social class* differences in British speech. He postulated that lower-class speech, as well as lower-class mother-child verbal interactions, involves a "restricted" linguistic code characterized by simple statements made in general terms, limited expressive range, and many commands and repetitions. According to Bernstein, those using the restricted code fail to verbally specify rationales, intentions, causation, or other abstract concepts.

In contrast, middle-class speech and mother-child verbal interactions supposedly involve an "elaborated" code which is more differentiated, complex, and precise, as well as being more "grammatical" and logical. The elaborated code is said to allow expression of a wider and more abstract range of thought. A hypothetical example which has been given is a middle-class mother saying, "Would you keep quiet a minute? I want to talk on the phone," in contrast to a lower-class mother saying, "Shut up!" (Hess & Shipman, 1965). Whereas the middle-class speaker is presumably capable of using either the restricted or elaborated codes in different situations, the lower-class speaker is presumably only capable of using the restricted code. According to Bernstein, this language difference between classes has far-reaching implications, not only for cognitive and educational functioning, but also for such characteristics as attitude towards authority, self-control, social competence, and moral behavior.

The influence that Bernstein's work has had, especially in the United States, is both surprising and dismaying for several reasons. For one thing, although his claims are often cited as if they were established fact, they are actually highly speculative. The main related study of his own which Bernstein cities, in which he found that middle-class boys hesitate more in speaking than lower-class boys, can only remotely be construed as evidence for his theory (Bernstein, 1962). Another important consideration is that despite his protestations to the contrary, Bernstein makes value judgments that can be called "classist." He clearly judges the linguistic style as well as many other values and characteristics of the middle class to be more desirable than those of the lower class. Social class stereotyping is certainly involved in his very broad descriptions. As if all this is not enough, Bernstein's work is often applied in the United States to black-white language differences, which involve other issues in addition to social class, as we will see. Perhaps Bernstein's work has been so widely accepted and cited, despite its inadequacies, because it feeds into preconceived notions of the "inferiority" of lower-class speech, and especially of lower-class black speech.

The most specific support for certain aspects of Bernstein's hypothesis on class differences has been provided by Hess and Shipman (1965, 1967). They used interviews as well as direct observations in a structured setting to study mother-child interactions in lower- and middle-class black families. They concluded that social class differences in language perpetuate themselves because in the lower-class home the child's cognitive growth is constricted by parent-child communication systems which "offer predetermined solutions and few alternatives for consideration and choices [Hess & Shipman, 1965, p. 869]." Among other variables, "maternal teaching style" was assessed by observing the mothers as they attempted to teach three simple tasks to their four-year-old children. Compared to middle-class mothers, the lower-class mothers did less well in teaching these tasks, and their children did less well in learning them.

Differences in maternal teaching styles are illustrated by the following passage. The task of the mother was to teach the child to sort a number of plastic toys by color and then by function:

> The first mother outlines the task for the child, gives sufficient help and explanation to permit the child to proceed on her own. She says:
> "All right, Susan, this board is the place where we put the little toys; first of all you're supposed to learn how to place them according to color. Can you do that? The things that are all the same color you put in one section; in the second section you put another group of colors, and in the third section you put the last group of colors. Can you do that? Or would you like to see me do it first?"
> Child: "I want to do it."
> A second mother's style offers less clarity and precision. She says in introducing the same task:
> "Now, I'll take them all off the board; now you put them all back on the board. What are these?"
> Child: "A truck."
> "All right, just put them right here; put the other one right here; all right put the other one there."
> This mother must rely more on nonverbal communication in her commands; she does not define the task for the child; the child is not provided with ideas or information that she can grasp in attempting to solve the problem; neither is she told what to expect or what the task is, even in general terms [Hess & Shipman, 1965, p. 88].

Middle-class mothers in this study were more likely than lower-class mothers to use the first type of teaching approach. Children whose mothers used this more explicit and more verbal teaching approach performed better than children whose mothers used the second teaching approach. They performed better not only on the task itself, but also on unrelated cognitive tests. Maternal teaching style was even more important than the mother's IQ or social class in predicting the child's performance. These findings led the authors to conclude that maternal teaching style is very important to the child's cognitive and language development (Hess & Shipman, 1967). With regard to social class differences, several studies have produced results similar to those of the Hess and Shipman studies. However, a few others have produced contradictory results, indicating that the actual and intended communication of lower-class black mothers may have been underestimated by Hess and Shipman (Baldwin, 1969).

Cognitive psychologists in particular are fundamentally at odds with the verbal deficit model. Piaget does not view language as the key to cognitive development, but conversely maintains that intellectual processes underlie and direct language functioning. More generally, many psychologists protest that there has been much too heavy an emphasis on the "debilitating" effects of family patterns and childrearing practices on the cognitive and educational functioning of poor and minority children. They point out that we should be aware of possible cultural bias in the studies themselves. Most importantly, school or standardized test performance is not to be taken as proof of intellectual or linguistic competence. The failure of "disadvantaged" children in the middle-class white school system is largely the result of cultural and language *differences* that are not necessarily deficiencies (Ginsburg, 1972; Baratz & Baratz, 1969).

Standard English, which is important for school achievement, is only one of various dialects spoken in the United States. Sociopolitical considerations, and not intrinsic linguistic superiority, determine which dialect is considered standard. Labov (1970) has conclusively demonstrated that "black English" (as spoken by poor black adolescents in Harlem, New York) has its own complex structure with a complete and consistent set of rules (see Box 8-5). Labov wrote, "When linguists say that black English is a system we mean that it differs from other dialects in regular and rule-governed ways, so that it has equivalent ways of expressing the same logical content [Labov, 1970, p. 185]."

BOX 8-5 TWO ENGLISH DIALECTS

Standard English (STE)	Black English (BE)
1. This is John's mother.	1. This is John mother.
2. This is John's.	2. This is John's.
3. I have lived here.	3. I have live here. (or: I lived here)
4. He is going home.	4. He goin' home.
5. Didn't anybody see it?	5. Didn't nobody see it?
6. I see it.	6. I see it. (present)
7. I saw it.	7. I see it. (past)
8. I don't see it.	8. I don't see it. (present)
9. I didn't see it.	9. I ain't see it. (past)
10. He's with us.	10. He with us. (at the moment)
11. He's with us.	11. He be with us. (generally)

From a linguistic point of view, the dialect of English that is considered standard English (STE) and a dialect that has been called "black English" (BE) are not very different.* In general, the deep structures of sentences and semantic and grammatical categories are the same in STE and BE. The differences occur mostly in the transformational and phonological rules that determine the final form (the surface structure) of sentences.

The above sentences were chosen to illustrate a few of the differences and commonalities between the dialects. In sentence 1, BE does not "mark" the possessive with "'s"; the sentence is nevertheless unambiguous in referring to the mother of John. If the second noun is deleted, as in sentence 2, BE *does* require the "'s" marker; in this case "This is John" would have a different meaning than "This is John's."

In sentence 3, STE marks the present perfect verb tense in two ways: with the auxiliary verb "have" *and* with the "-ed" ending on the verb "live." BE requires only one element (either one in this case) to mark this verb tense. The same is true for a different verb tense in sentence 4—double marking in STE, single marking in BE. The converse also occurs: STE marks negation only once, but double and triple negatives are common in BE (sentence 5), just as they are in Russian.

Many common irregular verbs are not marked for the simple past tense in BE; for example, the past tense forms of "come" and "see" are "come" and "see" (sentence 7). However, the existence of the concept of the past in BE is indicated by the fact that the present and past tenses are negated differently (sentences 8 and 9).

There are some cases where BE makes a grammatical distinction that STE does not make. For instance, BE uses the verb "be" to indicate habitual or general state. "He be workin'" means he generally works, perhaps at a regular job; whereas, "He workin'" means he is working at the moment (sentences 10 and 11).

To summarize these examples:

Some grammatical features are marked twice in STE and once in BE (sentences 3 and 4), whereas other features are marked twice in BE and once in STE (sentence 5).

Some features are marked in STE but not in BE (sentences 6 and 7), whereas other features are marked in BE, but not in STE (sentences 10 and 11).

Some features are marked in one context, but not marked in another context (sentences 1 and 2; sentences 6, 7, 8, and 9).

*The following discussion of BE is based primarily on studies of lower-class black adolescents in Harlem (Labov, 1970). It of course does not represent the speech of all black Americans, which varies widely by region and social class.

Source: The above discussion and examples have been adapted from Dale, P. S. *Language development: structure and function.* Hinsdale, Ill.: The Dryden Press, 1972. Pp. 244–247.

Thus, black English is functionally equivalent to standard English. It definitely is not a collection of sloppy or random mistakes, or a simplified version of standard English, as has been assumed by many researchers and educators. The incorrect assumption that black English is inferior has undoubtedly put black children at a disadvantage on standardized tests and in school. We must realize, however, that to say that the standard and black dialects are equivalent as linguistic systems is not necessarily to say that the languages are *used* equivalently by all different subgroups. For example, lower-class black or white preschoolers may still show verbal inadequacies within their respective language systems. This is an empirical question and an important one.

There is substantial evidence that middle-class children show more advanced vocabulary development than lower-class children; this has been demonstrated for various ethnic groups and for preschool as well as elementary school children (Templin, 1957; Stodolsky, 1965; Stodolsky & Lesser, 1967). Vocabulary growth, though important, cannot be equated with the development of language as a system of rules. In contrast to the evidence for vocabulary growth, clear-cut social class differences in *syntactic* development have not been demonstrated. No differences between middle-class and lower-class white children were found in either of two experiments with assessed syntactic competence through the use of nonsense words and sentences (LaCivita, Kean, & Yamamoto, 1966; Shriver & Miner, 1968). Two separate investigators compared the spontaneous speech of lower-class black and middle-class white preschoolers. One concluded that despite equating for dialect differences, the lower-class black children had a more limited range of syntactic constructions (Osser, 1966). But the other investigator concluded that the rate of syntactic development for the two groups was similar (Cazden, 1970). Thus, the question of social class differences in syntactic development is by no means settled. At present, however, the lack of evidence of differences tends to support the nativists' position that syntactic development is relatively independent of environmental variation. Bernstein's class-difference hypothesis has so far received little support with regard to the development of syntax.

Surprisingly, as we have pointed out, there is as yet virtually no psycholinguistic data on the language acquisition process in young lower-class or black children. There are many indications from studies of older black children that the language performance

Children often display sophisticated verbal and artistic systems in their graffiti. (Omikron.)

they demonstrate in school and in testing situations probably has led to an underestimation of their linguistic competence. For example, Houston (1970) showed that poor black children about eleven years of age use two modes of communication. The "school register" is used with persons in authority and is characterized by nonfluency, shortened utterances, simplified syntax, and lack of expressiveness. However, the "non-school register," used with friends and in natural settings, is very expressive and shows all the syntactic characteristics expected of eleven-year-olds. Houston noted that the children engaged in constant language games, verbal contests, and narrative improvisations. She wrote, "To the observer able to elicit the nonschool register . . . the natural linguistic creativity and frequent giftedness of the so-called linguistically deprived child become apparent [Houston, 1970, p. 953]."

Similarly, it has been pointed out that the poor black adolescent gang members studied by Labov display an extremely sophisticated verbal system and place a very high value on verbal skill. Individual gangs often have a "verbal leader" who leads other members in the ritualized tradition of "toasts," or gang-originated epic poems partly recited from memory and partly invented, which frequently have high literary value. The linguistic skills demonstrated by the boys among themselves stands in marked contrast to the consistent failure of these same boys in the school system (Ginsburg, 1972).

Clearly, detailed studies of the language acquisition process of lower-class children and of minority children are necessary, both to answer questions about the verbal deficit model and to broaden our understanding of language development in general.

SUMMARY

The study of language can be divided into three areas: phonology, semantics, and syntax. Phonology describes the system of sounds for a language and how the basic sound units, or phonemes, are combined to form words and how the intonation patterns of phrases and sentences are determined. Semantics is the study of the meaning of words and of sentences, while syntax describes the structure of a language, the underlying rules which specify the order, and the function of words in a sentence.

The main focus of this chapter was on the development of syntax in children. A variety of approaches to syntax development and language learning in general have been proposed. Behavioral theories have been principally concerned with speech development, which is treated as an overt behavior acquired according to learning principles of reinforcement, classical and operant conditioning, and imitation. In spite of some demonstrations that modeling and reinforcement can shape language, there is considerable doubt that these are necessary strategies for language acquisition. However, learning principles are important in modifying language usage and in overcoming language deficits in children.

In contrast to the behavioral approach, modern psycholinguistics views language learning as involving the abstraction and application of rules rather than merely learning specific responses. The child's language is a complex, rule-governed system at any given point in its development. The discrepancies between a given child's language and adult language are not simply due to the child's random mistakes; rather, they represent differences in the respective rule systems. Language acquisition is viewed as a creative process. To account for the development of language, some theorists have taken a nativist position, which suggests that some aspects of language are innate. The existence of some kind of human biological predisposition to learn language has gained considerable acceptance, though the exact nature of this predisposition is quite debatable. Almost all children, including those with limited general intelligence, are born with the ability to discover the abstract rules and structure of language in their first few years. The claim that all human languages are similar in structure and share other universal features is also used as evidence of a biological basis for language. However, the severe minimization of the role of experience by some nativists seems to have been an overraction.

Critics note that languages of the world also differ greatly, as any adult studying a foreign language realizes. Even if we accept the core assumptions of the nativist position, each child must at least learn the particulars of his own language. He must learn from the actual speech that he hears. The inadequacy of previous learning explanations does not negate the fact that learning of some kind must occur. Some nativists have considered language learning to be analogous to a maturational process. It may be more appropriate to conclude that children have innate abilities which lead to language learning, but which are not necessarily *limited* to language. What these abilities may consist of, as well as *how* language is learned or discovered, are still fascinating and largely unanswered questions.

The concept of underlying linguistic competence (or knowledge) remains a crucially important one. However, it is no longer assumed that either underlying knowledge or innate abilities are best represented by the technical transformational grammars. Psycholinguists are no longer looking toward theoretical linguistics for a ready-made blueprint for language development. Interest has begun to focus instead on the relationship between language development and the child's overall cognitive development. One result of this trend is that researchers have recently been trying to determine and analyze the intended meaning of children's early speech, rather than focusing on word order.

Partly for theoretical reasons, regularities in the language development process have been stressed at the expense of individual or group differences in development. The earlier longitudinal studies sometimes grouped together the utterances of different children and concluded that there were great similarities in children's development of syntax. However, analyzing each child's development individually, investigators have recently found that children learning the same language may differ markedly in the "strategies" they use in both syntactic development and semantic development.

A final focus of this chapter was on social class and ethnic differences in language. A verbal deficit viewpoint which assumes that the language used by some groups is inferior or deficient and, in turn, leads to poorer performance on cognitive tasks was discussed. Although there is some evidence to support this position, more recent research suggests that speakers in various social classes and ethnic groups use equally complex but different means of expressing the same information. Cultural acceptance of middle-class English as standard may, in part, be responsible for the poor academic achievement of lower-class children.

Fundamental differences in the assumptions, goals, and methods of the linguists on the one hand and the psychologists on the other hand have led to heated disagreements and sometimes misunderstandings about the nature of language development. The controversies continue in this very lively interdisciplinary field, but fortunately there have been shifts in position as well. Current theories and research are moving away from the earlier nature-nurture polarities and are attempting to answer more subtle and more specific questions about the language acquisition process.

REFERENCES

Baldwin, C. P. Information exchange in mother-child interactions. Paper presented at the Biennial Meeting of the Society for Research in Child Development, Santa Monica, Calif., 1969.

Baratz, S., & Baratz, J. Early childhood intervention: the social science base of institutional racism. Paper presented at the Biennial Meeting of the Society for Research in Child Development, Santa Monica, Calif., 1969.

Bereiter, C., & Engelmann, S. *Teaching disadvantaged children in the preschool.* Englewood Cliffs, N.J.: Prentice-Hall, 1966.

Berko, J. The child's learning of English morphology. *Word*, 1958, **14,** 50-177.

Bernstein, B. Social class and linguistic development: a theory of social learning. In A. H. Hakey, J. Floud, & C. A. Anderson (Eds.), *Education, economy and society.* New York: Free Press, 1961. Pp. 288-314.

Bernstein, B. Linguistic codes, hesitation phenomena and intelligence. *Language and Speech*, 1962, **5,** 31-46.

Bloom, L. *Language development: Form and function in emerging grammars.* Cambridge, Mass.: M.I.T. Press, 1970.

Bloom, L. Language development review. In F. Horowitz (Ed.), *Review of child development research.* Vol. 4. New York: Russell Sage, 1975.

Braine, M. D. On learning the grammatical order of words. *Psychological Review*, 1963, **70,** 328-348. (a).

Braine, M. D. The ontogeny of English phrase structure: the first phase. *Language*, 1963, **39,** 1-13. (b)

Brown, R. Linguistic determinism and the part of speech. *Journal of Abnormal Social Psychology*, 1957, **55,** 1-5.

Brown, R. *Psycholinguistics: selected papers by Roger Brown.* New York: Free Press, 1970.

Brown, R. Development of the mother tongue in the human species. Paper presented at the Annual Meeting of the American Psychological Association, Honolulu, 1972.

Brown, R. *A first language.* Cambridge, Mass.: Harvard University Press, 1973.

Brown, R., & Bellugi, U. Three processes in the child's acquisition of syntax. In E. H. Lenneberg (Ed.), *New directions in the study of language.* Cambridge, Mass.: M.I.T., 1964.

Brown, R., Cazden, C., & Bellugi, U. The child's grammar from I to III. In J. P. Hill (Ed.), *1967 Minnesota symposia on child psychology,* vol. 2. Minneapolis: The University of Minnesota Press, 1969. Pp. 28-73.

Cazden, C. The acquisition of noun and verb inflections. *Child Development,* 1968, **39,** 433-448.

Cazden, C. The neglected situation in child language research and education. In F. Williams (Ed.), *Language and poverty.* Chicago: Markham Publishing Company, 1970, pp. 81-101.

Chomsky, C., *The acquisition of syntax in children from 5 to 10.* Cambridge, Mass.: M.I.T., 1969.

Chomsky, N. *Syntactic structures.* The Hague: Mouton, 1957.

Chomsky, N. Review of "Verbal Behavior," by B. F. Skinner. *Language,* 1959, **35,** 26-58.

Chomsky, N. *Language and mind.* New York: Harcourt, Brace & World, 1968.

Condon, W. S., & Sander, L. W. Neonate movement in synchronized with adult speech: interactional participation and language acquisition. *Science,* 1974, **183,** 99-101.

Dale, P. S. *Language development: structure and function.* Hinsdale, Ill.: The Dryden Press, 1972.

Deese, J. Behavior and fact. *American Psychologist,* 1969, **24,** 515-522.

Eimas, P., Siqueland, E. R., Jusczyk, P., & Vigorito, J. Speech perception in infants. *Science,* 1971, **171,** 303-306.

Ervin, S. Imitation and structural change in children's language. In E. H. Lenneberg (Ed.), *New directions in the study of language.* Cambridge, Mass.: M.I.T., 1964.

Fraser, C., Bellugi, U., & Brown, R. Control of grammar in imitation, comprehension and production. *Journal of Verbal Learning and Verbal Behavior,* 1963, **2,** 121-135.

Ginsburg, H. *The myth of the deprived child, poor children's intellect and education.* Englewood Cliffs, N.J.: Prentice-Hall, 1972.

Gleason, H. A. *An introduction to descriptive linguistics* (2d ed.) New York: Holt, 1961.

Greenberg, J. H. *Language universals.* The Hague: Mouton, 1966.

Hess, R., & Shipman, V. Early experience and the socialization of cognitive modes in children. *Child Development,* 1965, **34,** 869-886.

Hess, R., & Shipman, V. Cognitive elements in maternal behavior. *Minnesota symposium on child psychology.* Vol. 1. Minneapolis: The University of Minnesota Press, 1967.

Houston, S. H. A re-examination of some assumptions about the language of the disadvantaged child. *Child Development,* 1970, **41,** 947-963.

Katz, J. J., & Fodor, J. A. The structure of semantic theory. *Language,* 1963, **39,** 170-210.

Klima, E. S., & Bellugi, U. Syntactic regularities in the speech of children. In J. Lyons and R. Wales (Eds.), *Psycholinguistic papers.* Edinburgh: Edinburgh University Press, 1966. Pp. 183-207.

Labov, W. The logic of nonstandard English. In F. Williams (Ed.), *Language and poverty.* Chicago: Markham Publishing Company, 1970.

La Civita, A., Kean, J. M., & Yamamoto, K. Socio-economic status of children and acquisition of grammar. *Journal of Educational Research,* 1966, **60,** 71-74.

Laroche, J. L., & Tcheng, F. C. Y *Le sourire du nourrisson.* Louvain: Publications Universitaires, 1963.

Lenneberg, E. *Biological foundations of language.* New York: Wiley, 1967.

Liberman, A. M., Cooper, F. S., Shankweiler, D. P., & Studdert-Kennedy, M. Perception of the speech code. *Psychological Review,* 1967, **74,** 431-461.

Lieberman, P. *Intonation, perception, and language.* Cambridge, Mass.: M.I.T., 1967.

Liebert, R. M., Odom, R. D., Hill, J. H., & Huff, R. L. Effects of age and rule familiarity on the production of modeled language constructions. *Developmental Psychology,* 1969, **1,** 108-112.

Loban, W. D. *The language of elementary school children.* Champaign, Ill.: National Council of Teachers of English, 1963.

Lovaas, I. A behavior therapy approach to the treatment of childhood schizophrenia. In J. P. Hill (Ed.), *Minnesota Symposia on Child Development,* Vol. I. Minneapolis: University of Minnesota Press, 1967. Pp. 108-159.

McNeill, D. Developmental psycholinguistics. In F. Smith & G. Miller (Eds.), *The genesis of language.* Cambridge, Mass.: M.I.T., 1966.

McNeill, D. On theories of language acquisition. In D. Horton & T. Dixon (Eds.), *Verbal behavior and general behavior.* Englewood Cliffs, N.J.: Prentice-Hall, 1968.

McNeill, D. *The acquisition of language, the study of developmental psycholinguistics.* New York: Harper & Row, 1970.

Moffitt, A. R. Consonant cue perception by twenty to twenty-four week old infants. *Child Development,* 1971, **42,** 717-732.

Moskowitz, A. I. The two-year-old stage in the acquisition of English phonology. *Language,* 1970, **46,** 426-441.

Nelson, K. Structure and strategy in learning to talk. *Monographs of the Society for Research in Child Development,* 1973, **38** (Nos. 1 and 2).

Osborn, J. Teaching a teaching language to disadvantaged children. In M. A. Brottman (Ed.), Language remediation for the disadvantaged preschool child. *Monographs of the Society for Research in Child Development*, 1968, **33** (8), 36–48.

Osser, H. The syntactic structures of five-year-old culturally deprived children. Paper presented at Eastern Psychological Association Annual Meeting, New York, 1966.

Rosenthal, T. L., Zimmerman, B. J., & Durning, K. Observationally induced changes in children's interrogative classes. *Journal of Personality and Social Psychology*, 1970, **16**, 681–688.

Schlesinger, I. M. Production of utterances and language acquisition. In D. I. Slobin (Ed.), *The ontogenesis of grammar*. New York: Academic, 1971. Pp. 63–101.

Shriner, T. H., & Miner, L. Morphological structures in the language of disadvantaged and advantaged children. *Journal of Speech and Hearing Research*, 1968, **11**, 605–610.

Skinner, F. F. *Verbal behavior*. New York: Appleton-Century-Crofts, 1957.

Slobin, D. I. The acquisition of Russian as a native language. In F. Smith & G. Miller (Eds.), *The genesis of language*. Cambridge, Mass.: M.I.T., 1966. Pp. 129–148.

Slobin, D. I. Cognitive prerequisites for the development of grammar. In C. A. Ferguson (Ed.), *Studies of child language development*. New York: Holt, 1973.

Slobin, D. I. Universals of grammatical development in children. In G. B. Flores d'Arcais & J. M. Levelt (Eds.), *Advances in Psycholinguistics*. New York: American Elsevier, 1970. Pp. 174–184.

Slobin, D. I., & Welsh, C. A. Elicited imitation as a research tool in developmental psycholinguistics. In C. A. Ferguson & D. I. Slobin (Eds.), *Studies in child language development*. New York: Holt, Rinehart & Winston, 1973. Pp. 485–497.

Smith, M. E. An investigation of the development of the sentence and the extent of vocabulary in young children. *University of Iowa, Studies in Child Welfare*, 1926, **3,** 5.

Staats, A. W., & Staats, C. K. *Complex human behavior*. New York: Holt, 1963.

Stodolsky, S. Maternal behavior and language and concept formation in Negro preschool children: an inquiry into process. Unpublished doctoral dissertation, University of Chicago, 1965.

Stodolsky, S., & Lesser, G. Learning patterns in the disadvantaged. *Harvard Educational Review*, 1967, **37,** 546–593.

Templin, M. *Certain language skills in children*. Minneapolis: The University of Minnesota Press, 1957.

Weir, R. H. Some questions on the child's learning of phonology. In F. Smith & G. Miller (Eds.), *The genesis of language*. Cambridge, Mass.: M.I.T., 1966. Pp. 153–168.

Wolff, P. H. The natural history of crying and other vocalizations in early infancy. In B. M. Foss (Ed.), *Determinants of infant behavior*, Vol. 4. London: Methuen, 1966. Pp. 81–109.

9

INTELLECTUAL DEVELOPMENT

The next two chapters will deal with intellectual, or cognitive, development. The terms *intelligence* and *cognition* will be used interchangeably and will refer to mental activity and behavior through which knowledge of the world is attained, including learning, perception, memory, and thinking. The concept of intelligence is such a broadly integrative concept that most of the topics covered in the previous chapters of this book have relevance for intellectual development and performance. Biological factors, environmental and experimental factors, social factors, emotions, and motivation all play a role in cognitive development.

Most of this chapter will deal with theoretical issues involving the nature of intelligence. First, factor analytic theories that focus on the variety of intellectual skills and the manner in which they are organized will be discussed. Next, a description and evaluation of Piaget's theory of the development of intelligence over age will be detailed. Finally, individual differences in cognitive and problem-solving styles will be discussed.

In contrast to the theoretical focus on

the structure and development of intelligence in this chapter, in the following chapter the discussion will focus on why one individual would exhibit more or less intelligence than another, how these differences can best be measured, and what these individual differences predict about performance in other situations.

DEFINITIONS OF INTELLIGENCE

Since there are few topics in psychology which have generated a more voluminous literature than that of intelligence, it seems anomalous that there is no widely accepted definition of intelligence. It is apparent that conceptions of the nature of intelligence will influence views of the methods most appropriate for its assessment, its stability or modifiability, and its usefulness in predicting other behaviors.

Divergence in definitions and theories of intelligence have centered around three questions. First, is intelligence a unitary, generalized function, or is it composed of a group of relatively separate abilities? If it is a generalized function, an intelligent child should perform well across a variety of intellectual tasks; if it is composed of independent factors, an individual could excel on some cognitive tasks and perform poorly on others. Second, how modifiable is intelligence? Is its development determined primarily by genetic factors, or is it more dependent upon learning experiences in environments with varying degrees of stimulation or deprivation? Finally, is intelligence an underlying construct, trait, ability, or capacity which can never be directly assessed, or should it be defined only in terms of performance on specific cognitive tests? If the latter position is accepted, the most appropriate definition of a child's intelligence might be his score on a particular intelligence test under particular circumstances.

Differing positions on these issues are reflected in the frequently cited definitions of intelligence which follow: Intelligence is "innate, general cognitive ability [Burt, 1955, p. 162]." Intelligence is "the aggregate or global capacity of the individual to act purposefully, to think rationally and to deal effectively with his environment [Wechsler, 1958, p. 7]." "Manifest intelligence is nothing more than an accumulation of learned facts and skills . . . innate intellectual potential consists of tendencies to engage in activities conducive to learning, rather than inherited capacities as such [Hayes, 1962, p. 337]."

THEORIES OF INTELLIGENCE

There are a variety of theoretical approaches to understanding intelligence. Some theories are concerned with the structure or organization of intelligence and attempt to describe the variety of abilities and skills and how they are organized. Other theoretical approaches are concerned with outlining and explaining the development of intelligence across time. Factor analytic theories, such as those of Spearman and Guilford, will illustrate the first approach to intelligence, while the theory of Jean Piaget will illustrate a developmental theory of intelligence.

FACTOR-ANALYTIC THEORIES

One of the main questions factor-analytic theorists attempt to answer is whether intelligence is unitary or whether there are different kinds of intellectual abilities that might vary within the same individual. Can people accurately be described in general terms as very intelligent or below average? Or is it more accurate to describe people in terms of specific intellectual skills, for example, "He's very articulate and verbally fluent, but is a bit of a dolt at arithmetic."

Factor analysis is a statistical procedure which groups test items which are highly related to each other and relatively independent from other clusters of items. These clusters of intercorrelated items are regarded as intellectual factors. It would be expected that an individual who does well on one item within a cluster would be likely to do well on other items within the same cluster, whereas his performance on this item would be less likely to predict his performance on items in other factors. If there was a verbal reasoning cluster and someone had performed well on one of the items within the cluster, for example, explaining the meaning of a proverb (such as "A bird in the hand is worth two in the bush"), this would probably relate more closely to other verbal reasoning items, such as explaining the similarity between an eye and an ear, than it would to items involving arithmetical computations.

The earliest attempt at defining intellectual factors through factor analysis was performed by Charles Spearman (1927), who concluded that intelligence comprises a "g," or general, factor, and a number of "s," or specific, factors. He regarded "g" as general mental energy or ability which would be involved in all cognitive tasks, and "s" factors as factors unique to a particular task. Thus someone with a high "g" would be expected to do well on all intellectual tasks. Variations in his performance among tasks would be attributable to differential amounts of "s."

Later Thurstone (1938, 1947) analyzed a large number of tests and identified seven factors of primary mental abilities: perceptual speed, numerical ability, word fluency, verbal comprehension, space visualization, associative memory, and reasoning. He went on to construct seven tests, each of which would measure one of his seven independent primary mental abilities. However, after all his careful efforts in attempting to derive pure measures of his seven mental abilities, he found scores on these abilities tended to be correlated. Spearman's general mental ability factor appeared to be emerging again, in addition to the specific primary abilities.

One of the most complex contemporary factor-analytic models of intelligence is that developed by Guilford (1966) which proposes that intelligence is comprised of 120 factors classified in terms of subdivisions of three major dimensions: operations, products, and contents. The subclassifications of these three basic dimensions are presented in Figure 9-1. Intellectual activities can be classified in terms of the interaction of four types of contents or material involved in a task with five types of processes or operations performed to respond to the problem, resulting in six possible different kinds of cognitive products. For example, a frequently used item on intelligence tests is recall of a series of digits said aloud by an examiner. In Guilford's terms the task would require the operation of "memory" and the production of numbers which are "units" having "symbolic" content. Since this is such a complicated model of intelligence, the student will not be burdened with all of the details of the subcategories within the three dimensions. Guilford has been attempting to systematically build tests to tap each of the 120 cells, but this monumental task is not yet completed. At this point he has items to assess about 75 of the 120 cells. Each individual's intelligence would be composed of a unique combination of these separate intellectual abilities.

Guilford, like other factor analysts, has focused mainly on the structure of intelligence rather than on its developmental aspects or modifiability. However, he does suggest that although even the intellect of infants must be conceived of in terms of complex factors rather than general intellectual ability, the child is able to deal with different kinds of information and experiences at different ages.

Much of the initial optimism about the usefulness of factor analysis as an instrument to further the understanding of intelligence has dissipated. Not only do different psychologists disagree on the number of factors; they even disagree on the names of the factors of intelligence. The type of factor analysis used, the selection of items serving as the initial pool for analysis, the characteristics of the subjects answering the items, and the subjectivity in the interpretation and naming of the factors lead to wide variations in results. Most of the factors obtained, even in recent factor analytic studies, such as those of Guilford, tend to be dependent and show some degree of correlation with each other. This has led many psychologists (Humphreys, 1962; McNemar, 1964; Vernon, 1965) to question both the conceptual and practical utility of such a fractionated approach to the study of intelligence. After a careful analysis of the most important of such studies, McNemar states, "The structure of intellect that requires 120 factors may very well lead the British, and some of the rest of us, to regard our fractionalization and fragmentation of ability, into more and more factors of less and less importance, as indicative of scatterbrainedness [McNemar, 1964, p. 872]." He concludes that the notion of general intelligence still has a rightful and practical place in psychology.

As will be seen in Chapter 10, from an applied as well as a theoretical point of view the notion of general intelligence has never been discarded. Intelligence tests based on the concept of global intelligence which yield a single IQ score continue to be widely used by practicing psychologists in clinical, academic, and industrial settings.

Some theory of mental organization acknowledging both general intelligence and

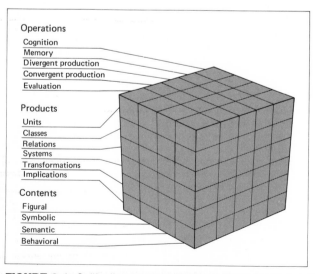

FIGURE 9-1 Guilford's structure of intellect. (From Guilford, J. P. Intelligence: 1965 model. *American Psychologist*, 1966, **21,** 20-26.)

some differentiated clusters of mental abilities would seem to most adequately fit current evidence about cognitive development. Mental abilities do tend to be correlated. Studies of exceptionally bright children (Terman, 1925) show that these children excel in a wide variety of cognitive tasks; but although their performance is above average on most tasks, they still score higher in some areas than in others.

Studies of changes in intellectual performance with age show that although general ability is marked in the preadolescent years, more specialized talents appear with increasing age (Garrett, 1946). This evolving cognitive differentiation could of course be attributed to differential training and experience.

The growth patterns of different abilities also vary with age. A factor sometimes called *fluid intelligence,* which is related to reasoning and discrimination and involves the capacity for insight into complex relations, increases until mid-adolescence and begins to decline after adolescence. Fluid intelligence is similar to the concept of "g," general intelligence. In contrast, a second factor, *crystallized intelligence,* which involves accumulated information, shows no decline with age (Horn & Cattell, 1966). Crystallized intelligence evolves through the communication of culturally relevant cognitive skills to the child. This might involve such things as language, the use of abstract concepts, or the use of written symbols. Crystallized intelligence is more dependent on environmental factors than is fluid intelligence and could be expected to be more easily depressed by deprived environments or increased by stimulating life circumstances.

PIAGET'S COGNITIVE DEVELOPMENTAL THEORY OF INTELLIGENCE

The single most important, detailed, and controversial theory of intellectual development is that of the Swiss psychologist Jean Piaget. He has been the major figure responsible for a great surge of interest in cognitive development in the past decade. If two criteria for the significance of a theory are its comprehensiveness and the amount of research it stimulates, Piaget's theory is unique in the area. Whether or not they agree with his theories, hundreds of psychologists currently are investigating Piaget's provocative formulations.

An historical overview

Piaget has been writing since 1907, when at the age of ten he published his first article on a rare albino sparrow in a natural history journal. Four years later some of his writings on mollusks led to an inquiry being made as to his possible interest in the position of curator of the mollusk collection in the Geneva Museum of Natural History. The chagrined director of the museum reneged on his offer when he discovered that the creative young biologist was a schoolboy. Piaget continued to be interested in biology and by 1920 was concerned with the relationship between biology and psychology. In the following two decades he published a remarkable series of books on the intellectual development of children. He has produced over 30 books and more than 200 articles, and his writing still continues. Since he had such a long history of prolific study and writing on cognitive development, why was it not until the early 1960s that his influence began to really shape the course of American developmental psychology? What was it about the climate of American psychology that made it inhospitable to a theorist like Piaget?

Child psychology in the 1930s and 1940s was largely a descriptive, atheoretical field. Interest in intelligence focused on mental measurement. Psychologists were more interested in the number of questions a child could answer correctly on an intelligence test, than in qualitative differences in how children of different ages arrived at these answers. When theory did impinge on child psychology in the late 1940s, it was predominantly in the form of stimulus-response theories—derived from the behaviorism of John B. Watson—which had dominated the mainstream of psychology for twenty years. Stimulus response theorists emphasized the role of learning rather than any innate predispositions, processes, or structures in intellectual development. They were not truly concerned with differences in learning over age, but tried to apply the same principles of learning across all ages. Standard laws of conditioning, reinforcement, generalization, and extinction were invoked to explain the behavior of children of all ages as well as the behavior of rats from which these principles were derived. The preferred method of behaviorists was to investigate groups of subects by using controlled manipulative experimental procedures, rather than to observe a few subjects intensively and repeatedly under naturalistic conditions. As the student reads further into the work of Piaget, it will

Jean Piaget, a Swiss psychologist, has written extensively on cognitive development and language. (Omikron.)

become clear why this behavioristic approach was incompatible with Piagetian theory and methods.

By the end of the 1950s child psychology was in a period of great growth and flux. No completely satisfying developmental theory existed. The psychoananalytic developmental theory had never been accepted by experimentally oriented academic American psychologists. The attempts to translate psychoanalytic theory into the more familiar terms of learning theory had not proved fruitful and were abating. Moreover, disenchantment with learning theory itself had set in. Some psychologists claimed it was not a real developmental theory since it did not allow for the different capacities of children at different ages. In learning theory, development was explained as a function of learning, whereas Piaget argued that learning was a function of development. Some behavioral scientists also said the child played a more active role in learning than contemporary learning theory allowed. Others, including Piaget, argued that American learning theory had little relevance or influence on educational or other practical human problems since it had evolved from work in animal laboratories. In addition to this theoretical need, the launching of Sputnik and our government's concern with competing in achievement with the Russians led to a heightened interest in understanding how intellectual abilities develop. Piaget presented an attractive alternative to the available theories of the time. His theory was a genuinely developmental theory derived from direct observations of children.

One of the major obstacles to Piaget's acceptance in this country was that he is difficult to read. His terminology was unfamiliar to American psychologists. His theory was complex and at times obscure. He did not define his constructs operationally, and he seemed to use terms with inconsistent meanings. American psychologists who had gone to Geneva to study with Piaget at the Centre of Genetic Epistemology began to return and present his work in a more readily understandable fashion. In 1963 John Flavell published *The Developmental Psychology of Jean Piaget,* a lucid, comprehensive summary and analysis of Piaget's work, and the Piaget boom was well underway.

Early in his career Piaget had worked in the Binet Laboratory in Paris with Theophile Simon, one of the developers of the first intelligence test. In contrast to the other psychologists in the laboratory, who were interested in standardizing and measuring children's ability to answer questions correctly, Piaget became interested in the similarity of the incorrect responses made by children of the same age and how they differed from errors of older or younger children. The qualitative differences in the responses made by children of different ages seemed to reveal varying developmental strategies or processes in thinking. The understanding of these developmental differences in thinking became the central goal of Piaget's investigations. For Piaget the study of *what* children know was only an avenue to understanding age changes in *how* children think.

In order to attain this goal Piaget used an unstructured method of questioning children. The child's responses and not a standardized procedure directed the questioning. Many of his conclusions are derived from detailed observation and question sessions with his own three children, Laurent, Lucienne, and Jacqueline. Later Piaget attempted to test some of his hypotheses with more controlled experiments; nevertheless the looseness of his early methodology is frequently criticized by more rigorously oriented psychologists.

Structure and function

The theory of cognitive development evolved by Piaget (1952) is one which does not focus exclusively on learning but which emphasizes the interaction of innate structures and processes with experience. Piaget uses the term *schemata* to refer to cognitive structures. Some of these schemata are inherited reaction patterns and reflexes, but the most important schemata are organized patterns of behavior or structures underlying behavior, which are based on the interaction of innate responses and experience. For example, the sucking reflex which is present in neonates is an early schema; however, in older infants this sucking schema has been elaborated through experience into a complex pattern of responses involving visual searching for the bottle, head turning, reaching, holding the bottle, and adjustment of sucking movements and pressure to the nipple.

In younger children these schemata are largely based on the interaction of sensory input and physical activity. However, in older children there is a shift from mental activities based on overt behavior to symbolically represented schemata in the form of internalized intellectual operations and systems of classification. The older child thinks in ways increasingly similar to adult thought, whereas younger children must externalize their mental operations.

In addition to schemata, the structural units of intellectual activity, there are certain unlearned and functional principles which organize behavior. The most important of these inherited principles of functioning are *organization* and *adaptation*.

Organization is the predisposition to integrate and coordinate physical or psychological structures into more complex systems. In the previously cited example of the sucking schema, the infant may initially have a sucking response, a looking response, and a grasping response which function independently. However, these separate simple behaviors are gradually organized into a higher-order system involving the coordination of all these activities.

The second functional principle, that of adaptation, involves two processes: *assimilation* and *accommodation*. When a child has a new experience, the child relates and modifies it, that is, assimilates it in accordance with his or her existing schemata. The child's current cognitive structures and level of understanding alter his or her response to the environmental event. Children reared in primitive cultures who have never seen an airplane may assimilate their first view of an airplane into a familiar conceptual framework by calling it a great white bird. A more familiar example of assimilation may be the sometimes embarrassing one of the child calling "Daddy" to a male stranger.

Accommodation is a complementary process to that of assimilation. It involves the adjustment of the organism to environmental demands. This coping with the environment results in the continuous modification of schemata. Thus the child may adapt an existing schema for babbling "BaBa" to the repeated and insistent verbalization of "Baby" by the parent, and begin identifying himself as "Baby." Piaget regards imitation, where the child matches his behavior to that of someone else, as the purest form of accommodation; he regards play, where the child's fantasy and imaginative processes are relatively independent of reality, as pure assimilation. Intelligent behavior involves an adaptive balance between assimilation and accommodation.

Cognitive development therefore is based on alterations in intellectual structures resulting from innate predispositions to organize and adapt to experience in certain ways. These functional principles or predispositions are invariant; they are found in all normal children and continue to operate throughout the life span. The child is constantly organizing and adapting, and these processes result in continuously changing schemata or cognitive structures.

Piaget's developmental stages

Piaget viewed the course of intellectual growth in terms of progressive changes in cognitive structures. All children do not go through the stages at the same age; however, all children pass through the stages in the same order. The attainments in earlier stages are essential for those in later stages and some of the earlier intellectual processes may extend into later periods of development. The stages are in no way discrete but involve gradual and continuous changes.

Piaget identifies the four main periods of intellectual development, presented in Table 9-1: the sensorimotor period, the preoperational period, the concrete operational period, and the period of formal operations.

As the child passes through these periods, he changes from an organism incapable of thought and dependent on his senses and motor activities to know the world about him, to an individual capable to great flexibility of thought and abstract reasoning. Piaget believed that every child must pass through these periods in a fixed sequence since the cognitive changes at one stage are dependent upon the intellectual attain-

Table 9-1 CHARACTERISTICS AND ACHIEVEMENTS IN STAGES OF INTELLECTUAL DEVELOPMENT ACCORDING TO PIAGET

Stage	Approximate age range, yr	Major characteristics and achievements
Sensorimotor period	0-2	Infant differentiates himself from other objects; seeks stimulation and makes interesting spectacles last; attainment of object permanence; primitive understanding of causality, time, and space; means-end relationships; beginnings of imitation of absent, complex nonhuman stimuli; imaginative play and symbolic thought
Preoperational period	2-6	Development of the symbolic function; symbolic use of language; intuitive problem solving; thinking characterized by irreversibility, centration, and egocentricity; beginnings of attainment of conservation of number and ability to think in classes and see relationships
Period of concrete operations	6 or 7 through 11 or 12	Conservation of mass, length, weight, and volume; reversibility, decentration, ability to take role of others; logical thinking involving concrete operations of the immediate world, classification (organizing objects into hierarchies of classes), and seriation (organizing objects into ordered series, such as increasing height)
Period of formal operations	11 or 12 on	Flexibility, abstraction, mental hypotheses testing, and consideration of possible alternatives in complex reasoning and problem solving

ments in the earlier periods. No child could pass from the preoperational period directly to the period of formal operations since the intervening cognitive achievements of the concrete operational period serve as the basis for the malleable, abstract hypotheses-testing approach to problem solving found in the period of formal operations.

The student will be impressed by the great richness of Piaget's theory of cognitive development in contrast to those of factor-analytic and behavioristic theories and will understand why his theory is sometimes described as the only complete theory of cognitive development.

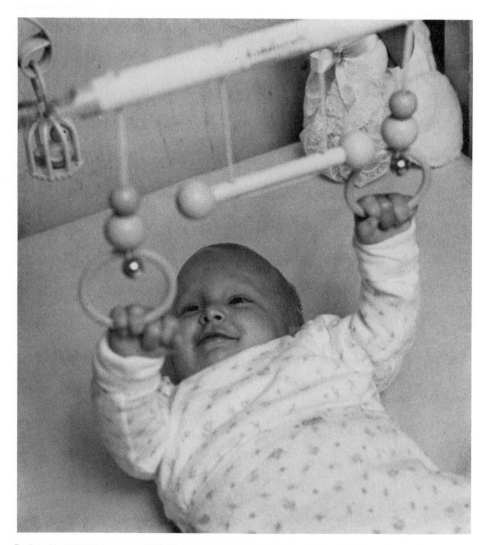

During the sensorimotor period, infants become interested in objects in their environment. (Suzanne Szasz.)

Sensoriomotor period   During the first stage, the sensorimotor period, which encompasses approximately the first two years of life, the child makes a dramatic transition from a reflexive organism to one possessing rudimentary symbolic thought.

In this period the infant shifts from an organism focused only on immediate sensory and motor experiences to one who becomes oriented toward understanding objects in the world about him. He becomes aware of spatial relationships through such motor activities as reaching and grasping. He develops concepts of the permanence of objects and of a time dimension having a before and after rather than only immediate experience. These notions are closely related to evolving concepts of causality and the appearance of intentionality and imitative behavior which also emerge in this period. Through the actions of sensing and manipulating the body and objects around him, he acquires knowledge about the properties of his environment. The infant's physical actions are essential in his evolving discovery, organization, and knowledge of reality.

Piaget speaks of the *plane of action* in the sensorimotor phase preceding and being essential for the later development of the *plane of thought.*

Piaget further divides the sensorimotor period into six substages. Again it should be emphasized that these stages involve gradual rather than abrupt transitions in behavior.

In the first month of life, the *stage of reflex activity,* infants refine their innate responses. They become more proficient in the use of reflexes, such as the sucking reflex, and in finding stimulation which will permit the functioning of these responses.

In the *period of primary circular reactions* (one to four months) the infant repeats and modifies actions which initially may have occurred by chance and which seem to be satisfying. These behaviors are primary in that they are basic reflexive or motoric functions of his or her own body; they are circular in that they are repeated. These primary circular reactions are focused on the infant's activities and body rather than on objects. The functioning of assimilation and accommodation is clearly seen in this period as schemata are altered and integrated.

Primitive anticipations begin to occur. In the neonate, sucking had occurred mainly when the infant's mouth was in contact with the nipple. Now anticipatory sucking may occur when the child is first placed in a reclining position in mother's arms. The sucking schema has come to include postural cues, in addition to sucking and the satisfaction of hunger.

In these two early periods, the infant shows no awareness of the existence of objects occurring outside of his or her immediate perception of them. Objects are not comprehended as having an existence of their own. When a toy vanishes or mother's face disappears from over his crib, the infant does not actively seek to find the lost object. For young infants it is literally the case of "out of sight, out of mind." When an object is not being perceived it does not exist.

It is not until the stage of *secondary circular reactions* (four to ten months) that the infant's attention becomes centered on the manipulation of objects rather than focused on his body, as it was in primary circular reactions. It appears that the child now repeats behavior which will reproduce stimulating events which may first have occurred by chance. The child will grasp and shake a rattle in order to hear the interesting sound it makes. The reaching, grasping, and shaking motions necessary for the movement and noise of the rattle are learned. The infant has begun to intentionally manipulate and change his or her environment.

Some increased awareness of the permanence of objects also is found. For the first time the child recognizes a partly concealed object. If a favorite toy is only partly covered by a blanket, the child will reach for it. However, if the child sees someone else placing the toy under a blanket which completely conceals it, he or she does not search for the toy under the blanket. A child who drops a toy may look around briefly for it but makes no new movements to attempt to regain the toy. If the loss of the object is associated with interruption of the child's own movements, visual searching is more likely to ensue than if it has been hidden by another person.

In the stage of *coordination of secondary schemata* (ten to twelve months) the child begins to use or combine previously acquired schemata as a means of attaining a goal. He or she intentionally utilizes schemata previously used in one situation to solve problems in a new situation. For example, a previously acquired hitting schema developed as a means of moving a mobile will be used in order to strike away a barrier in front of a toy. Two things are noticeable about this achievement: First, the schemata are generalized from one situation to another; second, a schema may be used as an intermediate step, as a means of attaining a goal.

The child in this stage starts to imitate responses initiated by other people. In the earlier stages, imitation consisted of repeating responses initiated by the infant which might be mimed by someone else. If the child was babbling and his or her mother repeated the sounds, the child would listen to her and then repeat the sounds again. This type of imitation really involved only the infant's repetition of his or her own behavior. Now if the mother initiates a new response which is similar to one the child can already perform, the child will attempt to modify the familiar response to match hers. The mother may make a new response of waving "bye-bye." This response is not too different from the child's hand-closing response in an existing grasping schema. The child will attempt to change the action of the hand closing to match the mother's finger movements. The shift here is from subject-initiated to model-initiated behavior in imitation, but the behavior involved must resemble one in an already existing schema.

In the stage of *tertiary circular reactions* (twelve to eighteen months) children actively use trial and error methods to learn more about the properties of objects. Interest is no longer focused on their own behavior and their own bodies. Their curiosity leads them to experiment with objects. Children become interested in the properties of falling objects; they experiment by dropping different toys and by varying the way the toy is dropped, the position and distance of the drop, the place from which the object is dropped, and the characteristics of the surface on which it lands. This exploration is a kind of early problem solving which leads children to accommodate to new aspects of their environment and assimilate them into their constantly changing schemata. Through experimenting they learn about characteristics of objects around them and new means of attaining goals.

The infant at this time finally is able to recognize the permanence of a visible object. A child, seeing an object being moved and hidden, will track it visually and search for it in the position where it disappeared. Piaget describes hiding his watch alternately between two cushions. His son, Laurent, consistently searched for the watch under the cushion where it had just disappeared. However, if the child saw the watch placed in a box, saw the box taken behind a cushion where it was emptied, and was then handed the empty box, he would not search for it behind the cushion. Laurent manifested object permanence only when he could observe the sequential displacement of the watch. He could not make the inferences necessary to understand invisible displacements of the watch when it had vanished into the box and then the box disappeared.

It is not until the sixth and last stage of the sensorimotor period, the *period of the invention of new means through mental combinations,* that the beginnings of thought using symbolic representations occur and true object permanence is attained. At this time the child is able to make inferences about the position of the unseen object. The child, not finding the watch in the box, will search for it behind the cushion where the box containing the watch last disappeared.

The emergence of the ability to represent an object, which is not present, through mental imagery is also manifested in the occurrence of deferred imitation. Without the presence of a model, the child now is able to imitate complex behavior exhibited by a model at a previous time. Piaget cites an occasion when Jacqueline, who did not have temper tantrums, viewed with amazement a wild tantrum in the playpen by a visiting child. The next day when Jacqueline was placed in her playpen, she exhibited the same pattern of behavior, complete with the screaming, foot stamping, and pen rattling, that she had observed in her little visitor. She must have maintained some image of the boy's tantrum in order to match his behavior so closely.

This internal representation facilitates problem solving through the invention of new means through mental combinations rather than through the overt explorations, manipulations, and behavioral experimentation which occurred in the previous stage. This primitive ability to think through problems leads to the emergence of sudden solutions to problems with little or no overt trial and error behavior. Piaget believes this type of insightful solution to problems occurs when the child discovers new relationships among familiar elements. Piaget describes Laurent's behavior on being presented with a stick at various ages. Over the course of the first year of life, although he manipulated the stick and gradually came to hit objects with the stick, he did not use it to bring attractive objects closer to him. Even at fourteen months, when he was holding the stick, he would futilely attempt to reach for distant objects by hand rather than extend the stick and pull them toward them. He was over sixteen months of age when he finally grasped the stick in the middle and attempted unsuccessfully to pull some bread toward him. He soon grasped the stick by the end and obtained the bread. After that he stopped reaching for distant objects, such as toys, with his hand and immediately used the stick. Laurent seemed suddenly to discover the usefulness of the stick with little overt trial and error. The exploration and experimentation had been interiorized.

The child's intellectual development in the first two years of life is a monumental attainment. Through rapid central nervous system development and active interaction with the environment, the child has changed from a being focused on reflex activity and sensory and motor experiences to an organism with a considerable understanding of realities in the environment, with the ability to develop new behaviors and strategies to attain goals, and the use of symbolic imagery and thought processes to help solve problems and adapt to the environment.

Although the child's cognitive achievements in this period have been marked, he or she is just beginning to use symbolic processes. It is the increasingly efficient use of these symbolic processes that leads to the rapid changes in thought which occur in the preoperational period.

Preoperational period Piaget divides the preoperational phase into two subperiods: the *preconceptual period* (two to four years) and the *intuitive period* (four to seven years).

The major characteristic of the preoperational phase is the appearance of systems of representation, such as language, which Piaget calls the *symbolic function*. In the preconceptual period the emergence of the symbolic function is shown in the rapid development of language, in imaginative play, and in the increase in deferred imitation. In the intuitive phase it is manifested in changes in thought process involving such things as new understanding of relationships, numbers, and classifications. All of these behaviors suggest that the infant is able to produce mental symbols which mediate his or her performance.

The acceleration of language development in the preconceptual period is regarded as an outcome of the development of symbolization rather than as its precursor. In accord with his belief in the achievements of one stage being built upon the attainment of earlier stages, Piaget points out the continuity between imitative responses in the sensorimotor period and language in the preconceptual period. In the second year of life Piaget reported that Lucienne, upon seeing the forward and backward motion of his bicycle, began to sway back and forth in a motion similar to that of the bicycle. He regards this imitation as a necessary sensory motor step in the attainment of a mental symbol. The imitative motion is a kind of primitive motor symbol for "bicycle." As the child gets older, there may be imperceptible tensing of muscles or motion which signifies the bicycle; this is a type of internal imitation. Gradually the mental image alone and the word "bicycle" become symbols for the same thing.

The process described thus far is predominantly one of accommodation; however, the child also assimilates the symbols to his existing schemata. The symbol is extremely personal and subjective. Most children will associate "bicycle" with a moving two-wheeled vehicle. However, a child who has been injured in a fall from a bicycle will assimilate it into an aversive schema, whereas a child who associates it with pleasant rides in the country with his father will assimilate it into a very different schema. Each child's use of the word "bicycle" will refer to personal representations based on his or her unique experiences. In spite of these differences, with most words in adult communication there is enough shared perception and understanding of what the word refers to that some consensus in the use of symbols in language is attained. Once the use of language symbols begins, it greatly broadens the child's problem-solving abilities and also permits learning from the verbalization of others.

Piaget's notion that cognitive development precedes and is the foundation for the development of language is in direct opposition to the frequently advanced position that improvement in reasoning and problem solving is a result of advances in speech. Piaget's theory is supported by studies of deaf children; the results of these studies show that children with severely restricted language development are able to reason and solve most problems as well as normally hearing children (Furth, 1971). It has been proposed that deaf children evolve their own nonlinguistic symbols as they are required for thinking and problem solving.

The symbolic process is also apparent in imaginative play. The child who has seen a train going down the track may push a series of blocks and say "toot toot"; the child has assimilated the blocks into schemata formerly involving a real train. Although Piaget's main interest was in the intellectual rather than the emotional development of the child, he does discuss the emotional importance of play in this period. Symbolic play is an attempt to cope with the demands of reality. At a time when increasing demands are being placed upon the child, he or she is able to act out conflicts with reality in a gratifying, nonstressful manner.

The term *intuitive* is applied to the child in the period from four to seven years; this term is appropriate because although certain mental "operations" (such as ways of classifying, quantifying, or relating objects) occur, the child does not seem to be aware of the principles he or she has used in the performance of these operations. Although the child can solve problems involving these operations, he or she cannot explain the reasons for solving a problem in a certain way.

Although the child's symbols are becoming increasingly complex, reasoning and thinking processes have certain characteristic limitations. Some of these limitations are reflected in the child's solution of *conservation* problems at this age. When superficial changes in an object or situation occur, the child is unable to understand that certain attributes of the object remain the same or have been conserved.

For example, a preoperational child presented with two equal-sized balls of clay and asked if they are the same size will report that they are equal in size. If the child then sees the experimenter roll one of the balls into a long sausage-like form and again is asked the same question, he or she will examine the clay objects and will report that one or the other is larger. Asked if anything was added or taken away from each clay form, the child will say "No," but will still insist they now differ in size either because of the variation in height or length of the two objects. What processes are at work that lead to this remarkable error in judgment, this lack of conservation, when the child has viewed the entire procedure?

The most important characteristic of preoperational reasoning is *irreversibility*. The child does not see that every logical operation is reversible—in this case, that if one of two balls of clay of the same size can be rolled into a sausage-shaped form, by rerolling it can be transformed back into its previous round shape again. Irreversibility is found in many different types of problems in the preoperational child.

> "A four-year-old subject is asked:
> "Do you have a brother?" He says, "Yes."
> "What's his name?" "Jim."
> "Does Jim have a brother?" "No."
> [Phillips, 1969, p. 61]

Irreversibility is associated with another type of error, the focusing on the successive states of a changing perception rather than on the process or *transformations* by which the change occurs. Piaget uses the analogy of the child viewing a motion picture as a series of successive but unrelated still pictures instead of the continuous movie which an older person would see. Likewise, in the transformation of the clay the child ignores how the experimenter changed the ball of clay by gradually reducing its height and extending its width through rolling. Flavell (1963) reports a vivid illustration of the preoperational child's difficulty in seeing transformations. The child has difficulty in arranging in order a series of drawings to reconstruct the movements of a ruler or stick which is held in a vertical position and then let fall into a horizontal position, as in Figure 9-2. He cannot identify the sequence of movements necessary for the shift of the ruler from its upright to its prone position, nor does he follow the transition stages in this process. In a similar way, in the problem with the ball of clay he does not pay attention to the gradual transition in the shape of the clay as it becomes longer and narrower as the experimenter rolls it.

Finally, our example of the lack of conservation of mass in the clay balls demonstrates *centration* in thinking. The child focuses on one dimension of the object, i.e., either on height *or* length, in giving his reasons as to why he thinks the clay is no longer equal. One child may say one ball is bigger because it is taller, another child that the other ball is bigger because it is longer. This attention to only one attribute of the objects and not to reciprocal changes between dimensions (that is, as it gets shorter some of the clay is being displaced into making it longer) contributes to the child's inability to solve the problem.

The conservation of many attributes other than mass have been studied, and the age of attainment of conservation varies for different characteristics. Some of the problems used to test conservation are illustrated in Figure 9-3. Conservation of number has usually been achieved by about age six, conservation of mass and length between six and seven, weight around nine, and finally volume sometime after eleven. Cross-cultural studies have found considerable variation in the age at which conservation is attained in different societies, but only moderate differences in the order in which different types of conservation occur. In order to illustrate this, we return to the problem of the clay balls. A child of seven who has attained the concept of conservation of mass will respond that the two different-shaped balls are the same size after seeing one rolled out. However, when the child sees the two identical round balls of clay weigh equally on a balance and then sees one ball rolled and is asked whether the sausage-shaped and round-shaped clay weigh the same, the response will be that they do not. The child will offer the same reasons that were given at a younger age for his belief that they differed in mass. Then at about age nine the child will be able to say they weigh the same but will say they differ in volume when they are rolled, although he has previously seen that they displace the same amount of water when they are placed in beakers of water in their round shape.

Piaget says the separation and sequence in achieving these three kinds of conservation are due to *horizontal decalage*. Horizontal decalage refers to the fact that even in tasks requiring similar operations there is an age separation in the chief ability to deal with the problems. He believes that mass, weight, and volume differ in degree of abstraction, with mass requiring the least abstract operations and volume the most. He also believes that the attainment of the earlier concept is essential for the development

FIGURE 9-2 Falling stick.
(From Phillips, J. *The origins of intellect: Piaget's theory.* San Francisco: Freeman, copyright © 1969.)

of the one of greater abstraction, and that increasing age is essential for progress from one concept to the next.

The Acceleration of Conservation. Because the attainment of the processes underlying conservation is regarded by Piaget as such an important intellectual achievement, many psychologists have attempted to accelerate the development of conservation through a variety of training procedures (Gelman, 1969; Goldschmid, 1968; Inhelder, 1968; Kingsley & Hall, 1967; Sigel, Roeper, & Hooper, 1966; Smith, 1968; Zimilies, 1966). These investigators question whether the operations Piaget assumes are basic in the development of conservation are the critical ones. Could children be trained to

1. Conservation of substance

A
⬤   ⬤

The experimenter presents two identical plasticene balls. The subject admits that they have equal amounts of plasticene.

B
⬤   ▬▬▬

One of the balls is deformed. The subject is asked whether they still contain equal amounts.

2. Conservation of length

A
═════

Two sticks are aligned in front of the subject. He admits their equality.

B
═════

One of the sticks is moved to the right. The subject is asked whether they are still the same length.

3. Conservation of number

A
• • • • •
• • • • •

Two rows of counters are placed in one-to-one correspondence. Subject admits their equality.

B
• • • • •
 • • • • •

One of the rows is elongated (or contracted). Subject is asked whether each row still has the same number.

4. Conservation of liquids

A

Two beakers are filled to the same level with water. The subject sees that they are equal.

B

The liquid of one container is poured into a tall tube (or a flat dish). The subject is asked whether each contains the same amount.

5. Conservation of area

A

The subject and the experimenter each have identical sheets of cardboard. Wooden blocks are placed on these in identical positions. The subject is asked whether each cardboard has the same amount of space remaining.

B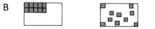

The experimenter scatters the blocks one of the cardboards. The subject is asked the same question.

FIGURE 9-3 Some simple tests for conservation. (From G. R. Lefrancois. *Of children.* Belmont, Calif.: Wadsworth, 1973. p. 305.)

conserve without attempting to alter their notions of such things as reversibility? Although children's performance on a conservation task may appear inadequate, perhaps they have the capacity to conserve under the right circumstances. The inability of children to perform on certain of Piaget's tasks may not be a result of limitations in their cognitive apparatus. Instead, it may be a limitation in certain necessary prerequisites for the use of those cognitive functions. It has been proposed that failure to conserve may occur because the child attends to irrelevant aspects of the stimulus, such as shape, length, height, color, and so on. Training procedures which modify children's attentional processes have been effective in facilitating conservation in children who were previously nonconservers. In one study children were made aware that objects possess many attributes by having them look at pairs of objects, for example, an orange and a banana, and describe how they are the same and how they are different (Sigel et al., 1966). In another study they were trained through discrimination-learning procedures to attend to the relevant dimensions of the stimuli (Gelman, 1969). Such attentional training procedures not only have improved the children's conservation on the conservation task on which they were trained; the effects have also generalized to other forms of conservation. Thus, if a child was given attentional training involving conservation of number, where the same number of pennies are grouped closely or strung out in a long row, in addition to improvement in number conservation, the attentional training would also generalize to improved conservation of mass, on which the child has had no training (Gelman, 1969). It is recognized that preoperational children have difficulty in solving conservation problems. However, the importance of these studies lies in their casting doubt on whether the acquisition of conservation is based on underlying operations, such as reversibility, as is proposed by Piaget. In addition, these results may lead to questions as to whether the sequence of attainment of cognitive skills is as invariant as Piaget suggests or whether the sequence may be modified by experience and training.

A recent innovative study by Frank Murray (1972) successfully used social interaction as a training procedure to accelerate the acquisition of conservation on a series of problems, as reported in Box 9-1. Piaget (1928) emphasized the role of interaction with peers in moral development and suggested that repeated communication conflicts between children was essential in the transition from preoperational or egocentric cognition to more advanced modes of thinking. Such conflicts lead the child to attend to other children's points of view. Murray reasons that since the ability to take another's perspective is related to other forms of operational thought, it should also play a role in the acquisition of the operations involved in conservation. His results suggest that this is true. It might also be asked if the discussions these children had with conflicting points of view about the conservation problems might not have been a kind of attentional training where children were made aware of the stimulus attributes that seem relevant to others.

BOX 9-1 ACQUISITION OF CONSERVATION THROUGH SOCIAL
INTERACTION

The aim of this study was to determine the effects of peer group interaction on the acquisition of conservation in children. Fifty-seven 6-year-old boys and girls were first given six conservation problems: two-dimensional space, number, substance, continuous quantity, weight, and discontinuous quantity. These problems constitute Form A of the Concept Assessment Kit, which contains a variety of sets of problems that differ in specific content, but are of a similar level of difficulty. On the basis of performance on these problems, subjects were divided into conservers and nonconservers; then groups were formed containing one nonconserver and two conservers.

Each group of three was then given these same problems and told they must discuss and come to some agreement as to the correct solution to each problem. Each child was asked to give an answer to the problem and explain how he arrived at this answer. Subjects were also permitted to manipulate the conservation stimuli, but no information or reinforcement was given to them for correct or incorrect responses.

One week later in a third session, subjects were tested individually on Form B, Form C, and finally the original problems (Form A) from the Concept Assessment Kit. Form B contained problems parallel to those in Form A on which the subjects had been originally tested and about which they subsequently argued and discussed in the conflict situation. Although the problems were the same, Form B used different conservation stimuli or different conservation transformations. In contrast, Form C tested the conservation of two new concepts, length and area.

Comparisons between the pre-test scores on Form A and post-test performance on Form A, Form B, and Form C indicated that the conflict situation enhanced the nonconservers performance on all tests. It is of particular interest that the effects generalized not only to new stimuli in Form B but to new concepts in Form C. Comparisons of the performance on the tests in this experiment with the standardization norms previously obtained for the Concept Assessment Kit Tests showed superior performance by the children exposed to the conflict situation. The social conflict also improved the performance of conservers on post-tests A and B, but not C.

In general it has been found easiest to obtain effects of training with nonconservers who were nearing or beginning to show some conservation. However, in this study there were no differences in amount of improvement in conservation between children who had exhibited absolutely no conservation on the pretraining measures and those who exhibited a small amount.

The author concludes:

Since there was no deliberate instruction in the present experiments, the data emphasize the effectiveness of social interaction even in the absence of any systematic instructional effort. It was the case that the children often resorted to reversibility explanations to persuade their lagging colleagues, and that in the social situations nonconservers acquiesced and generally gave conservation responses after the third problem on Form A, and generally (80%) did not give a nonconserving response after they had once given a conserving one . . . Smedslund (1966) in a review of the research on the many conditions that have been found to be inconsistently related to the acquisition of operational thought concluded that "the occurrence of communication conflicts is a necessary condition for intellectual decentration" and recommended that the key interaction needed for the growth of intelligence was not so much between the individual and the physical environment as it was between the individual and those about him. The present data support his hypothesis and emphasize, as Piaget has (Sigel, 1969), the educational role of social interaction in the transition from egocentrism to operational thought [Murray, 1972, p. 5].

Source: Adapted from Murray, F. B. Acquisition of conservation through social interaction. *Developmental Psychology*, 1972, **6,** 1–6.

Egocentrism. In addition to the limitations of thought processes underlying difficulties in the solution of conservation problems, the preoperational child's egocentrism or inability to take the view of others, also restricts cognitive performance in this period. The inability of the preoperational child to solve Piaget's famous three mountain problem demonstrates his or her difficulty in seeing things from the perspective of others. Three mountains of varying sizes are set on a square table with one chair at each side of the table. The child is seated on one chair and a doll is placed sequentially on the other chairs. The child is asked to identify what the doll is seeing from each of three positions either by selecting from a set of drawings or by using cardboard cutouts of the mountain to construct the doll's views (see Figure 9-4).

It has been argued that tasks such as the three mountains task, which are usually used to measure egocentricity, are beyond the experience and response capabilities of the young child. If the response required to demonstrate role taking was one which the young child was capable of performing he might not appear so egocentric. In addition, the particular type of role taking may influence the time at which egocentrism abates. Role-taking skills can be manifested in a variety of ways: in perceptual role taking, such as in the three mountain task; in guessing what responses and strategies another person will make in a problem-solving situation; or in awareness of the emotions other people are experiencing.

The study by Borke (1971) presented in Box 9-2 shows that very young children do have some capacity for responding empathically to the feelings of others. Borke argues that often the apparent lack of role taking in young children is because the response demanded by the experimenter is one which the child is not yet capable of making, even if he can empathize. Her study demonstrates the importance of considering the kind of response required in evaluating egocentricity. The task she used was within the capabilities of very young children since it required a behavioral response of selecting a picture rather than a verbal response. Therefore, the young child's limited language skills did not restrict him in demonstrating emotional role taking. The results of this study challenge Piaget's conception of the egocentricity of the preoperational child since children as young as three years old were found to be aware of the feelings of others and of the situations which elicit these feelings.

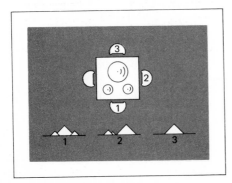

FIGURE 9-4 The three mountains problem. (From Phillips, J., *The origins of intellect: Piaget's theory.* San Francisco: Freeman, copyright © 1969.)

BOX 9-2 INTERPERSONAL AWARENESS IN CHILDREN

How young can children recognize the emotional states of other people? To find out, Borke tested 200 upper-middle-class white children ranging in age from three to eight years on a two-part measure of interpersonal awareness.

In part I the children were shown and given labels for the drawings of four faces depicting happy, sad, afraid, and angry emotional responses. The children were then told a story about another child who might be perceived as experiencing these emotions. The stories were about such things as getting lost in the woods at night, being forced to go to bed, eating a favorite snack, etc. Each story was accompanied by a picture of a child with a blank face, and the child was asked after each story to complete the picture by selecting the face that showed how the child in the story felt.

In part II the children were presented with stories in which they were described as behaving toward another child in ways that might make the child feel happy, sad, or angry, for example, sharing candy, refusing to let him play, and pushing him off a bike. This time the child was shown only happy, sad, and angry faces and was asked to point to the one which indicated how the other child felt in the situation.

The age at which children understood other people's feelings varied according to which emotion was being assessed.

Sixty percent of three to three and one-half-year-olds gave the correct response to the happy stories, and by age three and one-half to four and older almost all of the children identified happy stories correctly.

In stories in which the story character might have been expected to be fearful, three to three and one-half-year-olds were unable to respond at above a chance level; however by three and one-half to four years of age the children were responding above a chance level, and by four and one-half to five years of age twenty-two of the twenty-five children were aware that another child would be fearful in these situations.

Although three to three and one-half-year-olds were sensitive to another person's feeling sad or angry in the appropriate situation, there was not a systematic increase of sensitivity with age for these variables. In fact with the angry stories there is a drop in empathy at three and one-half to four followed by an increase from four to four and one-half years of age. However, among the oldest children only nine of twenty-five children identified the angry stories correctly in part I. Reactions to sadness or anger showed the least consistent trends with age. The findings indicate that the first differentiation children develop is between generalized pleasant and unpleasant responses.

Of special methodological interest is the fact that when shown a picture of a smiling face and asked to name the emotion, only 44 percent of the three to three and one-half-year-olds and 69 percent of the three and one-half- to four-year-olds gave the verbal response of happy spontaneously. However 60 percent and 92 percent of these children were able to select the smiling face appropriately for the happy stories. Thus the specific task used to measure awareness of emotions, in this case naming versus pointing to a picture, is a crucial factor in whether or not the child appears egocentric.

Source: Adapted from Borke, H. Interpersonal perception of young children: egocentrism or empathy? *Developmental Psychology*, 1971, **5,** 263–269.

Concrete operational period   Dramatic changes in the characteristics of thought occur in the concrete operational period, which extends from about age seven to about age eleven. In this period increased mobility of thinking due to increased understanding of reversibility and decentration and the ability to take the role of others lead to a new understanding of reality. Logic and objectivity increase. The child begins to think deductively. If all dogs are animals, then *this* dog is an animal. If 1 foot is equal to 12 inches, then 12 inches put together will equal 1 foot. The child is able to conserve quantity and number, to form concepts of space and time, and to classify or group objects *if the objects are present.* However, he is still tied to the concrete operations of the immediate world. He can solve problems only if the objects necessary for the solution of the problem are physically present. For example, if three children of varying heights are presented to the child in pairs so that in pair 1 he sees that Joan is taller than Sandra, and in pair 2 Sandra is taller than Mary, without seeing Joan and Mary together he can reason that Joan is taller than both Sandra and Mary. However, if the visual stimuli are not present and the problem is presented verbally as "Joan is taller than Sandra and Sandra is taller than Mary; who is the tallest of the three?", the concrete operational but not the formal operational child will have difficulty with its solution.

Again it has been questioned whether the solution of such problems is based on the underlying changes in mental operations proposed by Piaget. Some investigators have suggested that in tests of inference, such as the one just cited dealing with height, the deficits of the concrete operational child do not lie in being tied to the physical presence of stimuli, but in memory capacity. It is a complex series of propositions to remember. If the child could be trained to remember the rather complicated components of the problem, perhaps he or she could solve it in the absence of the stimuli, the three girls. Bryant and Trabasso (1971), in a study involving a similar problem of inferences about the length of sticks, demonstrated that when procedures are used to assure that the information is retained, even very young children can make logical inferences. The difference in memory capacity of younger and older children therefore is one of the critical factors in differences in performance on tests of logical inference.

Although memory capacity is an important factor in age differences in logical inference, it has been found that children between the ages of eight and eighteen solve problems of inference presented with concrete examples more easily than those with verbal presentations (Glick & Wapner, 1968). In the period of concrete operations the child is beginning to utilize symbolic thought and is building the foundation for logical thinking which characterizes the adolescent child.

Formal operations period   The period of formal operations begins at about age twelve. During adolescence the child's thought becomes increasingly flexible and abstract. To solve problems the child uses logical processes in which all the possibilities in a situation are considered. He or she imagines what might occur if the situation were manipulated. In contrast to the concrete operational child, who under most circumstances can solve problems of classification only in a real situation with the objects actually present, the adolescent considers a number of possible alternatives or hypotheses in a problem-solving situation and thinks of what could occur.

In addition to this system of deducing consequences from a variety of alternate hypotheses, the child can assimilate and combine information from a variety of sources.

Rather than evaluating single factors in solving a problem, as the concrete operational child does, the child at this stage is able to consider combinations of factors and simultaneous interactions of factors which will effect the solution.

It is in this flexibility, mental hypotheses testing, and appreciation of the many possibilities in a situation, as well as in the awareness of the complexity of problems that the adolescent differs from the concrete operational child.

The stage of formal operations and the flexible problem solving associated with it are not attained by all adolescents nor for that matter by all adults. This is attributable partly to cultural and educational factors and partly to general intellectual level. Subjects who score below average on standard tests of intelligence do not attain formal operational thought (Inhelder, 1966; Jackson, 1965; Stephens, McLaughlin, & Mahoney, 1971). In contrast, very bright children have been found to perform as well or better than some adults (Neimark, 1974; Neimark & Lewis, 1967).

Summary of Piaget's theory of cognitive development

The theory of cognitive development of Jean Piaget is the most influential and elaborate attempt to describe and explain the development of rational thought processes in children. The basic cognitive structures of the infant are modified and new schemata emerge through the interaction of the processes of assimilation and accommodation. Assimilation involves the modification of sensory input in accord with existing schemata. Accommodation involves a reciprocal process of adapting the mental structures or transforming the existing schemata to the characteristics of the stimuli or experiences to which the child is exposed. Through the interaction of these two processes involving reorganization of and adaptation to experience, increasingly complex cognitive structures emerge.

The child goes through an invariant sequence of cognitive growth in which the attainments of one period depend on those of the preceding period. Piaget describes the course of this development of thought in four stages which must be regarded as subdivisions of a continuous course of cognitive change.

During the first two years of life the sensorimotor period occurs. During this first period the child responds with simple motor responses to the sensory stimuli to which he is exposed. In these early years remarkable intellectual development occurs in such things as comprehending the permanence of objects; understanding means-ends relationships; using complex forms of imitation; and understanding primitive concepts of space, time, and causality. By the end of this period the child is clearly exhibiting behaviors which involve the beginnings of symbolic thought.

These symbolic thought processes become increasingly apparent in the child's use of language and elaborated symbolic play in the period of preoperational thought extending from two to six years. However, the thinking of the preoperational child in such things as the ability to solve problems dealing with numbers, concepts, relations, or classes is still limited because of certain restrictive characteristics of his or her cognitive processes. The movement away from the limitations of preoperational cognitive thought, such as egocentrism, irreversibility, and centering, is associated with the emergence of concrete operations.

During the period of concrete operations the child begins to appreciate the dynamic changing aspects of objects and to understand the relations between different attributes of objects. He or she can take the role of others and understand their perceptions, cognitions, and feelings, as well as elaborate his or her concepts of causality, time, space, and number and the operations of conservation.

Although the concrete operational child is clearly a reasoning organism capable of complex problem solving, thought processes of the child in this period differ markedly from those of the adolescent in the period of formal operations. The concrete operational child can solve problems if the stimuli are before him but has difficulty in verbal and mental manipulations.

The formal operational child is able to consider the many possible solutions to a problem and understand the relationships between many attributes or classes simultaneously. In problem solving, in this period the child uses the kind of systematic deductive reasoning that is characteristic of scientific thought, in that it involves the consideration of all possible alternative solutions and the logical elimination of those which are untenable. Everyone does not attain the level of formal operations. In contrast to the achievement of concrete operational thought, which seems to be attained to some degree in all societies, the attainment of formal operations is influenced by culture (Goodnow & Bethon, 1966). In groups which do not emphasize symbolic skills or in which educational experiences are limited, the stage of formal operations may occur late in development or may even be absent.

Commentary and evaluation of Piaget's theory

The student might ask why the theory of Jean Piaget has been discussed in such great detail. It is because of his profound impact on contemporary developmental psychology. The current concern with cognitive factors in development and the establishment of many centers for the study of cognitive psychology throughout the country are largely attributable to his influence.

Piaget presents the only well-elaborated and integrated theory of cognitive development. There are no comparable theories of intellectual growth. In spite of the frequently noted limitations and lack of objectivity of his methodology, he has asked and answered important questions in an innovative way and his provocative theory has stimulated a vast amount of research and theorizing by other behavioral scientists. It is inconceivable that our understanding of the intellectual development of children could have advanced to its present stage without the monumental work of Jean Piaget.

Recently evidence has been advanced that the sequence of intellectual growth that Piaget proposes may not be as unvarying as he suggests and that it may be modified by cultural and experiential factors, as well as by training in problem-solving strategies. In addition, there is some question that attainment of the underlying operations regarded by Piaget as necessary in solving certain problems is really essential in those tasks.

Whatever reevaluations of Piaget may occur as more investigators systematically test his theory, he will remain a giant in the history of developmental psychology. Jean Piaget must be considered one of the very few individuals whose theories, even if they are eventually rejected, have led to massive alterations in the course of developmental psychology.

COGNITIVE STYLE

Piaget was concerned with building a general theory of cognitive development which involved processes experienced by all individuals. He was looking for general principles of cognitive growth which effect the intellectual development of all persons. Guilford focused on the structure of intellect and individual variations in the abilities constituting this structure, but showed little concern with how intellect develops.

Theorists who study cognitive style are interested in individual differences rather than general principles or common structures in cognition. They are not asking, as Piaget did, what the cognitive processes and stages shared by all children are. They are saying children vary in cognitive performance. How can we best conceptualize these differences? Some children manifest relatively consistent individual differences in the way they think, perceive, remember, or use information. They show a preferred cognitive style that may be related to differences in motivation, personality, attention, or cognitive organization. Cognitive style does not refer to the level of intellectual ability as much as to the manner in which cognitive functions are executed.

The two dimensions of cognitive style which have been most extensively investigated are those of inpulsivity-reflectivity and field dependence-independence. These cognitive styles show individual differences among children and systematic changes with age and are associated with a variety of other social and cognitive measures.

Reflectivity-impulsivity

When children are asked to classify a group of objects by selecting two pictures in a set that are alike in some way, such as those presented in Figure 9-5, they may respond to the specific content or meaning of the objects. For example, are the objects women, children, flowers? Beyond this primary conceptual classification based on the specific content of the stimuli, the child may also categorize the pictures on the basis of formal qualities which are independent of content categories.

Kagan, Moss, and Sigel (1963) identified four formal conceptual categories used by children in such a classification task:

1. *Superordinate or categorical.* A categorical concept represents a shared characteristic among objects in the class. The child who groups cats and dogs because they are animals is utilizing a categorical concept.
2. *Functional-relational.* This classification is based on the relation in functions between members of the class. For example, a child who includes the matches and the pipe in the same concept because the match lights the pipe is using a functional-relational concept.
3. *Functional-locational:* The members in this class have a shared location. This basis of classification is occurring when the child says the dog and cat are alike because they both live in the pet store.
4. *Analytic.* This concept involves categorizing on the basis of similarity in a specific manifest component of each object in the class. Thus the striped shirt and zebra are alike because they have stripes.

The use of analytic categories increases with age (Sigel, 1953, 1966). Preschool children prefer functional-relational categories; older children tend to use superordinate and analytic concepts (Kagan, Rosman, Day, Albert, & Phillips, 1964). This increase in the use of analytic concepts seems to be in part based upon the older child's tendency to delay and take the time to analyze the visual stimuli carefully. Children who use analytic classifications have also been found to spend a greater amount of time in solitary tasks in the preschool years and are regarded as more emotionally controlled in kindergarten than are children who use categorical or relational concepts (Kagan et al., 1964). This suggests that children who use analytic concepts are more self-controlled and reflective in making a variety of responses.

Kagan extended this work and observed that there are relatively stable differences in the degree to which a child will wait and evaluate his response before answering. When children are asked to respond in situations where there is response uncertainty, for example, in the Matching Familiar Figures Test, some children respond slowly and with accuracy and others respond rapidly and with many errors. The former Kagan calls *reflective* children; he calls the latter *impulsives*. The Matching Familar Figures Test is a test in which the child is asked to match a standard figure, say a picture of a teddy bear sitting on a chair, with the identical stimulus in an array of six pictures of teddy bears on chairs which vary only in tiny details from the standard.

The Matching Familiar Figures Test taps two individual difference components: anxiety over errors and tempo of information processing. Impulsives and reflectives show different styles of scanning stimuli which may be related to concern about making errors. Studies have been performed in which the eye movements of children were photographed while they scanned the pictures in the Matching Familiar Figures Test (Siegelman, 1966). Reflectives carefully inspected the standard and checked between each picture in the array and the standard before making a response. Impulsives checked back and forth between the array and the standard less, and frequently did not even scan all alternatives in the array before responding.

The tempo or speed of responses dimensions may be identified as early as infancy and is predictive of conceptual tempo in the school years. Measures such as heart rate variability and activity level in play situations in the early years have been associated

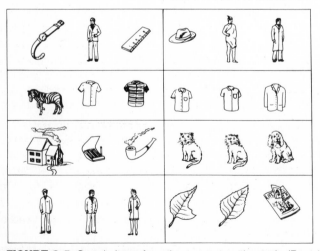

FIGURE 9-5 Sample items from the concept-sorting task. (From Kagan, J., Information processing in the child. *Psychological Monograph,* 1964, vol. 78.)

with an impulsive cognitive style. Impulsive children run around a room picking up toys, play with them for only a few minutes, and then dart off to the next plaything. In their play they are curious, exploratory, and distractible. In contrast, the reflective child considers with which toys he would prefer to play and will play with the same toy for longer periods of time.

Since much learning in the classroom requires the careful, considered, systematic behavior of the reflective, it is not surprising that impulsives have greater difficulty in the school situation. Impulsive children are less attentive and more distractible on a variety of learning tasks and more frequently show reading disabilities than do reflectives. Boys who are not promoted in the first grade are often more impulsive than their classmates who go on to second grade, although the two groups of children do not differ in scores on standard intelligence tests (Messer, 1970). In general, the relationship between IQ and reflectivity-impulsivity is small, although it is higher for girls than for boys.

Cognitive style is also related to performance on problem-solving tasks used in Piagetian studies of formal operations. Both impulsivity and field dependence, a dimension of cognitive style which will be discussed later, have been related to the use of less efficient and less advanced problem-solving strategies (Neimark, 1974; Pascual-Leone, 1973).

In addition to the relation between impulsivity and reflectivity and cognitive task performance, variations in cognitive style are related to different types of pathology (S. Wientraub, as reported in Kagan & Kogan, 1970). Preadolescent boys who showed overinhibited internalized symptoms, such as feelings of guilt and self-criticism, fears, and phobias, were much less impulsive on the Matching Familiar Figures Test than were boys who externalized their conflicts and showed hyperaggressive, antisocial, uncontrolled delinquent behavior.

Modification of reflectivity-impulsivity

The early appearance of differences in cognitive tempo, and the correlation of reflectivity-impulsivity with measures assumed to be partially genetically or constitutionally based (such as heart rate lability, activity level, and IQ) have led some investigators to conceive of cognitive style as a relatively unmodifiable attribute. However this is not the case. Shifts in cognitive style have been induced or observed in both laboratory and naturalistic settings. In general it has been found easier to modify response time than number of errors, although both can be altered. Experimenters have found a variety of techniques to be partially successful in these studies. These include giving the child verbal descriptions of other response styles and direct instructions on appropriate response tactics, and modeling a different response style where a model may demonstrate to the impulsive how to respond slowly, (Briggs, 1966; Debus, 1970; Kagan, Pearson, & Welch, 1966; Nelson, 1968). Another effective technique involves demonstrations of scanning strategies, in which the impulsive child is shown how to check back and forth between the standard and each alternative on the Matching Familiar Figure Test (Ridberg, Parke, & Hetherington, 1971), which is the strategy used by reflective children.

In the classroom even the presence of reflective or impulsive teachers can affect the cognitive style of pupils (Yando & Kagan, 1968). Children's response styles become more similar to those of their teachers, with the clearest effects occurring when impulsive boys are in a class with an experienced reflective teacher. Perhaps our impulsive, fidgety children with reading disabilities should be taught by careful, methodical, reflective teachers.

These studies demonstrate that although there may be a predisposition to respond in a reflective or impulsive manner, cognitive styles can be altered through experience and training.

Field dependence-independence

Herman Witkin and his colleagues (Witkin, Lewis, Hertzman, Machover, Meissner, & Wapner, 1954; Witkin, Dyk, Faterson, Goodenough, & Karp, 1962) for the past twenty years have studied another cognitive style dimension: field dependence-independence. Field dependence involves the tendency of some individuals to perceive the perceptual field as fused and relatively undifferentiated, and to be controlled in their perceptions by the organization of the field rather than by its parts. Field-independent persons, on the other hand, are those individuals who differentiate parts of the field as being separate from the field as a whole and are able to analyze the constituents of the field. The distinction between a field-independent and a field-dependent person can best be understood by describing their performance on the three perceptual tasks most commonly used to assess this dimension: the Embedded Figures Test, the body adjustment task, and the rod-and-frame test.

In the Embedded Figures Task the subject is asked to find a simple figure which is embedded within a larger, more complex design. A sample problem from the Embedded Figures Test is presented in Figure 9-6.

The field-dependent subject, in contrast to the field-independent subject, is so dominated by the organization of the total field that he has difficulty or may find it impossible to distinguish the simple design embedded within the more complex design.

A second task, the body adjustment task, involves a situation in which the individual must distinguish and utilize cues from his or her body rather than those from the surrounding visual field. The subject is seated on an adjustable chair which can be tilted to the left or right; the chair is located within a room which can also be tilted. Subjects are asked to adjust themselves to an upright position although the room is tilted. Field-independent subjects seem able to separate the cues from their body from those of the room and assume an upright position. Field-dependent people are pulled by the surrounding room, and if the room is tilted to the right, they may report that they are in a true upright position when their bodies are actually leaning as much as 35° to the right.

The final test commonly used to assess field dependence-independence involves being placed within a completely darkened room containing a luminous tilting picture frame and a rod which can be adjusted to the right or left. In this case the rod, rather than the person's body, is the embedded object. The subject is instructed to adjust the rod to a true vertical in spite of the organizational pull of the tilted frame.

The ability to differentiate and separate parts of the field from the whole in these three tasks is highly related. Subjects who perform in a field-independent or field-dependent way on one task tend to perform in a similar way on the others. In addition, this style of responding shows considerable stability over time, although children become more

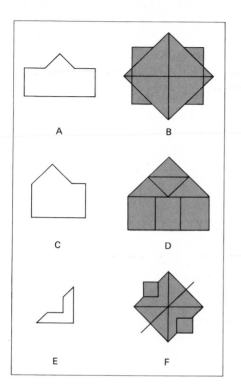

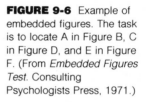

FIGURE 9-6 Example of embedded figures. The task is to locate A in Figure B, C in Figure D, and E in Figure F. (From *Embedded Figures Test*. Consulting Psychologists Press, 1971.)

field-independent with age until a leveling off occurs at about age seventeen (Witkin, Goodenough, & Karp, 1967).

Boys are more field-independent than are girls. Sex differences in field independence are usually not found in the preschool period and are most marked in the school years, particularly in high school. Greater contact with fathers and cross-sex identification, that is, closer identification with the father than the mother, are associated with greater field independence in females. In Eskimos, where daughters spend considerable time with their fathers, accompany them on extended hunting trips, and are less confined to the mother's company, there are no sex differences in field dependence.

There is some evidence that more intelligent children are more field-independent. However, even with the effects of intelligence taken into account, field-independent behavior is related to achievement behaviors (Crandall & Sinkeldam, 1964).

The relationship between field independence and social behavior is not as clear as that of field independence and achievement. In stressful social situations where an experimenter criticizes or disapproves of the child, the field-dependent child looks more at the critical experimenter and is disrupted more in his or her performance of an experimental task (Konstadt & Forman, 1965). The child seems to be more externally oriented and more affected by the responses of others than are field-independent peers. However, under ordinary nonstressful situations, such as in free play situations, this relationship is not as apparent. Thus the relation between field dependence and field independence and social behavior emerges only in certain select situations.

SUMMARY

Factor-analytic theories are among several other theories of intelligence described in this chapter. Factor-analytic theories are statistically derived and focus on the organization and structure of intelligence. Intellectual factors are derived on the basis of the clustering of scores of a long series of tests, usually paper and pencil tests. Spearman proposed that intellectual performance was influenced by the interaction of the general factor of intelligence and factors of specific ability. In contrast, Thurstone rejects the notion of general intellectual ability and identifies seven autonomous factors of primary mental ability. Finally, the most complex factor-analytic model of intelligence, that of Guilford, postulates 120 factors classified in terms of operations, products, and contents.

Piaget proposes a theory of intelligence which places more emphasis on the development of intelligence than do the factor analysts. He has evolved the most detailed and influential theory of intellectual development. Much of this theory was based on the naturalistic observation of children. It emphasizes the modification and evolution of cognitive structures through the functions of organization and adaptation. A balance between the two complementary processes involved in adaptation, those of assimilation and accommodation, result in intelligent behavior.

Piaget proposes that intellectual growth goes through an invariant sequence of stages of development. Each of the four major stages, the sensorimotor stage, the preoperational stage, the concrete operational stage, and the stage of formal operations, is characterized by different kinds of thought. The cognitive attainments in any stage are built upon and require those of the earlier stages. Over the course of development the individual shifts from being an infant focused only on immediate sensory and motor experiences to being a mature organism capable of symbolic thought and complex abstract reasoning and able to consider all possible solutions to a problem.

In addition to these general theories of intelligence, dimensions of cognitive style which focus on individual differences in the manner in which the individual copes with cognitive tasks were described. The study of reflectivity-impulsivity and field dependence-independence shows that individuals have relatively stable preferred modes or styles of cognitive behavior, and that these are associated with a variety of intellectual, social, and personality factors.

REFERENCES

Borke, H. Interpersonal perception of young children: egocentrism or empathy? *Developmental Psychology,* 1971, **5,** 263-269.

Briggs, C. H. An experimental study of reflection-impulsivity in children. Unpublished doctoral dissertation, University of Minnesota, 1966.

Bryant, P. E., & Trabasso, J. Transitive inferences and memory in young children. *Nature,* 1971, **232,** 456-458.

Burt, C. The evidence for the concept of intelligence. *British Journal of Educational Psychology,* 1955, **25,** 158-177.

Crandall, V. J., & Sinkeldam, C. Children's dependent and achievement behaviors in social situations and their perceptual field dependence. *Journal of Personality,* 1964, **32,** 1-22.

Debus, R. L. Effects of brief observation of model behavior on conceptual tempo of impulsive children. *Developmental Psychology,* 1970, **2,** 22-32.

Flavell, J. H. *The developmental psychology of Jean Piaget.* Princeton, N.J.: Van Nostrand, 1963.

Furth, H. C. Linguistic deficiency and thinking:

research with deaf subjects, 1964-1969. *Psychological Bulletin,* 1971, **76,** 58-82.

Garrett, H. E. A developmental theory of intelligence. *American Psychologist,* 1946, **1,** 372-382.

Gelman, R. Conservation acquisition: a problem of learning to attend to relevant attributes. *Journal of Experimental Child Psychology,* 1969, **7,** 167-187.

Glick, J., & Wapner, S. Development of transitivity: some findings and problems of analysis. *Child Development,* 1968, **39,** 621-638.

Goldschmid, M. L. The relation of conservation to emotional and environmental aspects of development. *Child Development,* 1968, **37,** 579-589.

Guilford, J. P. Intelligence: 1965 model. *American Psychologist,* 1966, **21,** 20-26.

Goodnow, J., & Bethon, G. Piaget's task: the effects of schooling and intelligence. *Child Development,* 1966, **37,** 573-582.

Hayes, K. J. Genes, drives and intellect. *Psychological Reports,* 1962, **10,** 299-342.

Hebb, D. O. *The organization of behavior.* New York: Wiley, 1949.

Hebb, D. O. A neuropsychological theory. In S. Koch (Ed.), *Psychology: a study of science.* Vol. 1. New York: McGraw-Hill, 1959. Pp. 622-643.

Horn, J. L., & Cattell, R. B. Refinement and test of the theory of fluid and crystallized general intelligences. *Journal of Educational Psychology,* 1966, **57,** 253-270.

Humphreys, L. G. The organization of human abilities. *American Psychologist,* 1962, **17**(7), 475-483.

Inhelder, B. Cognitive development and its contribution to the diagnosis of some phenomena of mental deficiency. *Merrill-Palmer Quarterly,* 1966, **12,** 299-319.

Inhelder, B. Recent trends in Genevan research. Paper presented at Temple University, 1968.

Jackson, S. The growth of logical thinking in normal and subnormal children. *British Journal of Educational Psychology,* 1965, **35,** 255-258.

Kagan, J., & Kogan, N. Individual variation in cognitive processes. In P. Mussen (Ed.), *Carmichael's manual of child psychology,* New York: Wiley, 1970. Pp. 1273-1365.

Kagan, J., Moss, H. A., & Sigel, I. E. Psychological significance of styles of conceptualization. In J. C. Wright & J. Kagan (Eds.), Basic cognitive processes in children. *Monographs of the Society for Research in Child Development,* 1963, **28,** 2(86), 73-112.

Kagan, J., Pearson, L., & Welch, L. Modifiability of an impulsive tempo. *Journal of Educational Psychology,* 1966, **57,** 359-365.

Kagan, J., Rosman, B. L., Day, D., Albert, J., & Phillips, W. Information processing in the child: significance of analytic and reflective attitudes. *Psychological Monographs,* 1964 (Whole No. 578).

Kingsley, R. C., & Hall, V. C. Training conservation through the use of learning sets. *Child Development,* 1967, **38,** 1111-1126.

Konstadt, N., & Forman, E. Field dependence and external directedness. *Journal of Personality and Social Psychology,* 1965, **1,** 490-494.

Krech, D., Rosenzweig, M., & Bennett, E. L. Effects of environmental training and complexity on brain chemistry. *Journal of Comparative Physiological Psychology,* 1960, **53,** 509-519.

Krech, D., Rosenzweig, M., & Bennett, E. L. Relations between brain chemistry and problem solving among rats raised in enriched and impoverished environments. *Journal of Comparative Physiological Psychology,* 1962, **55,** 801-807.

McNemar, Q. Lost our intelligence? Why? *American Psychologists,* 1964, **19**(17), 871-883.

Messer, S. Reflection-impulsivity: stability and school failure. *Journal of Educational Psychology,* 1970, **61,** 487-490.

Murray, F. B. Acquisition of conservation through social interaction. *Developmental Psychology,* 1972, **6,** 1-6.

Neimark, E. D. Intellectual development during adolescence. In F. Horowitz (Ed.), *Review of research in child development,* Vol. 5. 1974.

Neimark, E. D., & Lewis, N. The development of logical problem-solving strategies. *Child Development,* 1967, **38,** 107-117.

Nelson, T. F. The effects of training in attention deployment on observing behavior in reflective and impulsive children. Unpublished doctoral dissertation, University of Minnesota, 1968.

Pascual-Leone, J. *Cognitive development and cognitive style.* Lexington, Mass.: Heath, 1973.

Phillips, J. *The origins of intellect: Piaget's theory.* San Francisco: W. H. Freeman and Company Publishers, 1969.

Piaget, J. *The language and thought of the child.* Translated by Marjorie Worden. New York: Harcourt, Brace & World, 1928.

Piaget, J. *The origins of intelligence in children.* New York: International Universities Press, Inc., 1952.

Ridberg, E., Parke, R., & Hetherington, E. M. Modification of impulsive and reflective cognitive styles through observation of film mediated models. *Developmental Psychology,* 1971, **5,** 369-377.

Rosenzweig, M. R., Bennett, E. L., & Krech, D.

Cerebral effects of environmental complexity and training among adult rats. *Journal of Comparative Physiological Psychology,* 1964, **57,** 438-439.

Siegelman, E. Observing behavior in impulsive and reflective children. Unpublished doctoral dissertation, University of Minnesota, 1966.

Siegel, I. E. Developmental trends in abstraction ability of children. *Child Development,* 1953, **24,** 131-144.

Sigel, I. E. The attainment of concepts. In M. L. Hoffman & L. W. Hoffman (Eds.), *Review of Child Development Research.* Vol. 1. New York: Russell Sage, 1966. Pp. 209-248.

Sigel, I. E. The Piagetian system and the world of education. In D. Elkind & J. H. Flavell (Eds.), *Studies in cognitive development. Essays in honor of Jean Piaget.* New York: Oxford University Press, 1969.

Sigel, I. E., Roeper, A., & Hooper, F. H. A training procedure for acquisition of Piaget's conservation of quantity: a pilot study and its replication. *British Journal of Educational Psychology,* 1966, **36**(3), 301-311.

Smedslund, L. Les origines sociales de la centration. In F. Bresson & W. L. De Montmalin (Eds.), *Psychologie et Epistemologie Genetiques.* Paris: Dunod, 1966.

Smith, I. D. The effects of training procedures upon the acquisition of conservation of weight. *Child Development,* 1968, **39,** 515-526.

Spearman, C. *The abilities of man.* New York: Macmillan, 1927.

Stephens, B., McLaughlin, J. A., & Mahoney, E. J. Age at which Piagetian concepts are achieved. *Proceedings, APA,* 1971, 203-204.

Terman, L. M. *Genetic studies of genius.* Vol. 1. The mental and physical traits of a thousand gifted children. Stanford: Stanford, University Press, 1925.

Thurstone, L. L. *Primary mental abilities.* Chicago: The University of Chicago Press, 1938.

Thurstone, L. L. *Multiple factor analysis: a development and expansion of "the vectors of the mind."* Chicago: The University of Chicago Press, 1947.

Vernon, P. E. Ability factors and environmental influences. *American Psychologist,* 1965, **20**(9), 723-733.

Wechsler, D. *The measurement and appraisal of adult intelligence* (4th ed.). Baltimore: Williams & Wilkins, 1958.

Witkin, H. A. The perception of the upright. *Scientific American,* 1959, **200,** 50-70.

Witkin, H. A., Dyk, R. B., Faterson, H. F., Goodenough, D. R., & Karp, S. A. *Psychological differentiation.* New York: Wiley, 1962.

Witkin, H. A., Lewis, H. B., Hertzman, M., Machover, K., Meissner, P. B., & Wapner, S. *Personality through perception.* New York: Harper, 1954.

Witkin, H. A., Goodenough, D. R., & Karp, S. A. Stability of cognitive style from childhood to young adulthood. *Journal of Personality and Social Psychology,* 1967, **7,** 291-300.

Yando, R., & Kagan, J. The effect of teacher tempo on the child. *Child Development,* 1968, **39,** 27-34.

Zimilies, H. The development of conservation and differentation of number. *Monographs of the Society for Research in Child Development,* 1966, **31** (No. 6).

10
THE
MEASUREMENT
OF
INTELLIGENCE

The previous chapter was largely devoted to theories of the development and organization of intelligence and to consistencies and similarities in cognition. This chapter will deal with attempts to assess individual differences in intellectual performance.

Many of the students reading this book probably had never heard of intellectual factors, or cognitive schemata until they read Chapter 9. However, all will have heard of the *IQ,* or intelligence quotient. Many will confess their own IQ at the slightest provocation. The IQ is a term which is widely used and often misconstrued by a great many people. It is frequently regarded as some kind of innate, fixed endowment, like a baritone voice, big ears, or "your father's family's nose." It sometimes comes as a shock to find that IQs vary over age, can be modified by experience, and depend to some extent on which test is being administered under what circumstances.

In view of the many definitions and theories of intelligence, it is not surprising that there is a wide variety of intelligence tests constructed in different ways and with different goals. Most intelligence tests are a series of items of increasing difficulty which are administered in a carefully prescribed and standardized manner.

Test constructors who believe in a factor of general intellectual ability tend to select items which intercorrelate with each other. Others who believe in relatively independent factors of intellectual abilities may select items to measure these postulated abilities and would not expect these items to be interrelated.

Guilford has carefully selected items to test the types of intellectual abilities discussed in the previous chapter. He selected items to fit the cells in his theoretical model of intellectual ability. In contrast to this theoretical, multiability approach to the construction of intelligence tests, the first important test of intelligence, devised by Alfred Binet and Theophile Simon in 1905, was developed to solve an important practical problem and was based on a belief that a general ability to learn might be measured.

THE BINET-SIMON SCALE

In 1904 the administrators in the overcrowded Paris school system presented Binet and Simon with the challenging task of devising a means of distinguishing between children who were retarded and unable to learn and should be removed from traditional classes, and those who could benefit from education and had the capacity to learn.

These early psychometricians started with the premise that if children had equal opportunities to learn and equal educational experience, those children at a given age who could demonstrate more skills or information or were better able to solve problems than other children of the same age were manifesting a greater intellectual ability.

Many of the items on the original 1905 Binet-Simon scale involved skills which were taught in school, such as counting coins, naming the days of the week, and recalling details of a story after reading it. A sample of academic achievement was used to predict future achievement. It is a tribute to these testing pioneers that the modern version of the Binet-Simon intelligence test remains one of the best predictors of academic success. Binet and Simon were remarkably successful in developing a measure to serve their original goal of an academic screening device. When the items on the Binet-Simon scale were being selected, an assumption, which many contemporary psychologists would question, was being made: that *performance* in the form of such skills was assessing an underlying *capacity* to learn, and that what has been learned is a measure of what could be learned. However, what is measured on an intelligence test is performance, not capacity. Although capacity and performance may be correlated, intellectual capacity always remains only an inference on the basis of the child's responses to the test items. It cannot be directly measured. Situational, emotional, and experiential factors will influence the child's performance in any given test session.

Binet originated the concept of *mental age.* Mental age is based on the number of items the child gets correct relative to the number of items an average child of various ages gets correct. Thus, if a six-year-old child has a mental age of seven, he is performing as well as the average child whose actual chronological age is seven. Later, William Stern, a German psychologist, conceived of the intelligence quotient, which is a ratio of the child's mental age (MA) divided by his chronological age (CA) and multiplied by 100.

$$IQ = \frac{MA}{CA} \times 100$$

It can be seen that if a child had an IQ of 100, his performance would be average for a child of his age. As the IQ rises above 100, his performance is increasingly superior to other children his age; as it drops below 100, he is doing relatively less well than his peers.

Recently other ways of scoring intellectual performance have been used, notably a deviation IQ determined by the relation of a person's score to the distribution curve of scores for people his age. However, all methods of calculating IQ involve a comparative measure of the individual's performance and the performance of a group his own age. One of the important issues is what other similarities there should be between the subject and the members of the comparative group in addition to age. Should comparison groups be further broken down into factors such as education, socioeconomic class, ethnic group, and sex?

Subsequent revisions of the Binet-Simon scale and many other contemporary intelligence tests are designed to include items which are less directly influenced by academic experience. Although it is clear that items such as vocabulary items involving definitions of words or mathematical problem solving are heavily weighted by different experiences, the extent to which learning and education affect form-board tasks, building designs out of blocks, or assembling objects which have been broken up like a jigsaw puzzle is less clear. These last items are often referred to as *performance items*.

Since language and mathematics are heavily culturally and educationally influenced, much effort has been put into attempting to design tests which do not solely emphasize skills in these areas. The Wechsler Intelligence Scale for Children (Wechsler, 1952) is constructed to yield a separate verbal IQ and performance IQ. The performance IQ, which includes reasoning, memory, and concepts involving perceptual and spatial organization and pictoral representations, is assumed to be less influenced by cultural factors than is the verbal IQ.

Attempts to evolve tests entirely free of cultural influences have not been successful, and at the present time the IQ is best conceived of as a measure representing the interaction of a multitude of factors including those of innate capacity and experience.

STABILITY OF IQ

If it is assumed that intelligence tests largely measure a capacity to learn, it might be expected that the IQ would remain stable over time. Most of the information on the consistency of performance on intelligence tests over age has been obtained from longitudinal studies in which the same children were repeatedly tested over long periods of time. In some cases these multiple testings have extended from the first month of life until adulthood.

Investigators who have collected and analyzed the results of a large number of these longitudinal studies conclude that infant intelligence tests in the first year of life do not accurately predict IQ performance later in childhood although they may be useful in identifying neuromotor abnormalities or extreme intellectual deficits (McCall, Hogarty, & Hurlburt, 1972). The types of tasks used in the first year of life are largely sensorimotor tasks involving such things as reaching and grasping an object or visually following a moving object. These tasks differ considerably from the type of task used with older children which frequently tap problem-solving ability and verbal skills. After about eighteen months when items of the latter type are included on intelligence tests, the prediction of later test performance from early IQ scores improves. Table 10-1 presents items drawn from four infant tests for six-month-old and one-year-old infants. In general it has been found that the shorter the period is between repeated test sessions and the older the child is at the time of the initial testing, the more stable are the IQ scores.

Although IQ tests from the middle childhood years onward are reasonably good predictors of adult intelligence, there is still considerable variability in the IQs of individual children. An investigation of the stability of test IQs of 140 children in the longitudinal Fels Institute study was summarized as follows:

> Normal home-reared middle-class children change in IQ performance during childhood, some a substantial amount. In the present sample, the average individual's range of IQ between 2½ and 17 years of age was 28.5 IQ points, one of every three children displayed a progressive change of more than 30 points, and one in seven shifted more than 40 points. Rare individuals may alter their performance as much as 74 points. High-IQ children are likely to show greater amounts of change than low-IQ children. [McCall, Appelbaum, & Hogarty, 1973, p. 70].

Table 10-1 ITEMS DRAWN FROM FOUR INFANT TESTS FOR SIX-MONTH-OLD AND ONE-YEAR-OLD INFANTS

Gesell & Amatruda (1941)	Bayley (1933)	Cattell (1940)	Griffiths (1954)
(Key age, 28 wk)	5.8 mo. Exploitive paper play: present a piece of paper to child so he may grasp edge of it	(Key age, 6 mo)	(Key age, 6 mo)
Lifts head		Secures cube on sight: when child is sitting in upright position before table, a 1-in cube is placed within easy reach	Plays with own toes
Sits erect momentarily			Sits with slight support
Radial palmar grasp of cube	5.8 mo: Accepts second cube: when child is holding one cube, place a second in easy reach		Anticipatory movements when about to be lifted
Whole hand rakes pellet		Lifts cup: place straight-sided aluminum cup upside down within easy reach of child as he is sitting at table	Manipulates bell
Holds two cubes more than momentarily	5.9 mo: Vocalizes pleasure		Makes 4 + different sounds
Retains bell	5.9 mo: Vocalizes displeasure		Secures dangling ring
Vocalizes m-m-m and polysyllabic vowel sounds	6.0 mo: Reaches persistently: place cube just far enough away	Fingers reflection in mirror: while child is in sitting position, a framed mirror is held before him in such a	Hands explore table surface
			Holds two cubes
			(Key age, 12 months)
			Side-steps around in-

Table 10-1 ITEMS DRAWN FROM FOUR INFANT TESTS FOR SIX-MONTH-OLD AND ONE-YEAR-OLD INFANTS (*continued*)

Gesell & Amatruda (1941)	Bayley (1933)	Cattell (1940)	Griffiths (1954)
Takes solid food well	from child so he cannot reach it; credit if he reaches persistently	manner that he can see his reflection but not that of his mother or other persons	side cot or play pen holding rails
Brings feet to mouth	11.5 mo. Inhibits on command: when child puts an object in mouth or on some other pretext, say "no, no"; credit if he inhibits	Reaches unilaterally: child sits with shoulders square to front and both hands an equal distance from examiner; a 2- to 3-in door key or peg is presented in perpendicular position	Obeys simple request, "Give me cup," etc.
Pats mirror image			Plays "pat-a-cake" (claps hands)
(Key age, 52 wk)			Reacts to music vocally
Walks with one hand held			Babbles monologue when alone
Tries to build tower of cubes, fairly	11.6 mo: Repeats performance when laughed at	Reaches persistently: a 1-in cube is placed on table just out of child's reach; credit if child reaches several times	Says three clear words
Dangles ring by string	11.6 mo. Strikes doll: place small rubber whistle doll on table; hit it smartly to produce whistle, encourage child to do the same; credit if he imitates the hitting motion	Approaches second cube: child is presented with one cube; as soon as he has taken, it a second is held before him in such a position as to favor his grasping, but is not actually placed in his hand	Interested in motor car
Tries to insert pellet in bottle			Uses pencil on paper a little
Two words besides "mama" and "dada"			Manipulates box, lid, and cubes
Gives toy on request	11.7 mo. imitates words: say several words, such as mama, dada, baby, etc., and credit attempts to imitate	(Key age, 12 mo)	
Cooperates in dressing		Beats two spoons together: two spoons are taken, one in each hand, and beaten gently together while child watches; then they are presented to child, one in each hand	
Releases ball towards adult (56 wk)	12.1 mo. Spoon imitation: rattle spoon in cup with stirring motion; Credit if child succeeds in making a noise in cup by a similar motion with spoon		
	12.2 mo. Holds cup to drink. hand cup to child saying, "Take a drink"; credit if he takes it in his hands and holds it adaptively to drink	Places cube in cup: aluminum cup and 1-in cube are placed before child and he is asked to put "block" in cup; if no response, placing cube in cup is demon-	
	12.6 mo. Adjusts round block: three-hole (Gesell) form		

Table 10-1 ITEMS DRAWN FROM FOUR INFANT TESTS FOR SIX-MONTH-OLD AND ONE-YEAR-OLD INFANTS (*continued*)

Gesell & Amatruda (1941)	Bayley (1933)	Cattell (1940)	Griffiths (1954)
	board is laid on table with round hole at child's right. Give round block to him with no directions; credit if child puts block in round hole	strated and request repeated	
		Marks with pencil: piece of paper and pencil are placed before child with request, "write"; if no response, writing is demonstrated and request repeated; credit if child makes any marks on paper	
		Rattles spoon in cup: aluminum cup is placed before child and spoon is moved back and forth in it, hitting edges; then spoon is placed beside cup with handle toward child	
		Speaking vocabulary—two words ("ma-ma" and "da-da" are not credited)	
		Hits doll: rubber doll with whistle is put face up on table before child and hit gently with open hand several times; credit if child makes a definite attempt to hit doll	

Source: Kessen, W., Haith, M. M., & Salapatek, P. H. Human infancy: a bibliography and guide. In P. H. Mussen (Ed.), *Carmichael's manual of child psychology*. Vol. 1. New York: Wiley, 1970. Pp. 304–306. By permission of the publisher and the senior author.

The rate of mental growth varies among different children. Just as different children may experience a spurt or a plateau in physical growth at different ages, the ages at which sudden accelerations or leveling in cognitive development occur vary among children. These variations in rate of growth will obviously affect the reliability of IQ scores. When patterns of IQ change over age are examined, it is found that changes in IQ are most likely to occur at ages six and ten. It has been proposed that the six-year change may be associated with a shift to higher levels of abstract reasoning and conceptual process that Piaget and other investigators have discussed. There is some evidence to suggest that the intelligence of girls is more stable and predictable from infancy than that of boys, and that the developmental course of cognition varies for the two sexes. Vocalization in the first two years of life is predictive of later intellectual performance for girls but not for boys (McCall, Hogarty, & Hurlburt, 1972). With a sample of English children Moore (1967) found that an infant speech quotient was stable between six and eighteen months of age for girls but not for boys, and that the eighteen-month speech quotient predicted general IQ, vocabulary, and comprehension at age eight for girls only. In addition, an analysis of performance on the Bayley Infant Scale for the first fifteen months for children in the Berkeley Growth Study in California found that a vocalizing factor involving such items as vocalizes eagerness, displeasure, interjections, says ''da-da,'' two words, etc., again predicted verbal IQ into adulthood for girls only (Cameron, Livson, & Bayley, 1967).

In contrast, a factor of social orientation and active play in the first year of life seems to relate inversely to later childhood intellectual and verbal skills for boys but not for girls. Thus, early verbal behavior is associated with later cognitive development in girls, and low sociability and low activity in infant boys is related to subsequent intellectual development in boys.

Boys have shown larger gains in IQ with age, whereas girls more often show decreases in IQ (Sontag, Baker, & Nelsen, 1958). This is even present in young adulthood when male scores on the verbal scale of the adult Wechsler increase, in contrast to females who drop on performance scores and only remain stable on verbal scores between the ages of twenty-six and thirty-six years (Bayley, 1970).

The correlates of IQ growth for the two sexes show some similarities and a few marked differences. Children of both sexes who show marked IQ gains between ages three and twelve are described as independent, problem-solving, self-initiating, and academically competitive (Sontag, Baker, & Nelsen, 1958). IQ gains after eighteen years seem to be related to introversion and a detachment and distancing in interpersonal relations (Honzik & MacFarlane, 1970). Boys who show IQ growth tend to be better adjusted and happier than those whose IQs decrease; however, IQ gains in girls are associated with poorer social adjustment and unhappiness (Haan, 1963). It is interesting that a more masculine orientation and interests are associated with IQ growth for both boys and girls (Rees & Palmer, 1970). Perhaps independence, competitiveness, persistence, and self-confidence which are associated with IQ gains are regarded as more appropriate for males in our culture. It may be only the girl who resists social pressures to accept the stereotyped passive feminine role who develops a strong motivation toward coping with intellectual problems.

CORRELATES OF INTELLECTUAL PERFORMANCE

Genetic and constitutional factors

The role of genetic factors in intellectual development is clearly supported by the studies reported in Chapter 2 on the greater similarity of IQs of monozygotic than dizygotic twins, and in studies involving comparisons between children raised by natural or by foster parents. Even the most rabid environmentalist would not deny that heredity has some influence on cognitive development. The question is how these genetic factors are

A child identifying the parts of the body as part of a standardized intelligence test. (Suzanne Szasz.)

manifested in intellectual performance and what factors interact with and modify the effects of genetic and constitutional predispositions.

There is evidence that some intellectual abilities are more influenced by experience than are others, and that there may be individual differences in vulnerability to environmental influences. Bayley (1970) has suggested that boys and girls may be affected differently by environmental factors. She reports that intellectual development in males is more affected by early experiences and emotional conditions than it is in females. Girls' IQs may more directly reflect the underlying genotype than do boys' IQs. She reaches this conclusion from the findings that in both intact and adoptive homes the correlation of girls' IQs with their natural parents is higher than that for boys. In addition the Berkeley Growth Study found that only the boys showed persistent relationships between early maternal and child behavior and later IQs.

Bayley speculates that genetically determined nonintellective behaviors associated with temperamental or personality factors may shape the expression of inherited intellectual capacities. Thus, characteristics such as social orientation, thresholds of physiological arousal, activity, fearfulness, and attention span may retard or enhance cognitive development or performance. Support for the relationship between such temperamental characteristics, which are probably genetically based, and mental development was obtained in a recent longitudinal study in which neonatal physiological activity was compared with differences in intellectual and personality measures at age two and a half (Bell, Weller, & Waldrop, 1971). Infants who were categorized as "low intensity" neonates because they showed low respiration rates, low tactile sensitivity, and little response to interrupted sucking, were described at two and one-half years as being advanced in speech development, manipulative skills, geographic orientation, and modeling of adults. These associations were more marked for boys than for girls.

In addition to the influence of these genetically based influences on intellectual performance, physiological effects of such things as conditions of pregnancy and birth, nutrition, drugs, disease, and physical injury shape the cognitive skills of the child.

Environmental impoverishment and stimulation

It has been stated that

> Trying to predict what a person's IQ will be at 20 on the bases of his IQ at age one or two is like trying to predict how heavy a two-week-old calf will be when he is a two-year-old without knowing whether he will be reared in a dry pasture, in an irrigated pasture or in a feed lot [Hunt, 1972, p. 41].

It is apparent that the quality, amount, and patterning of stimulation received by children in different environments varies greatly. One of the problems in studying such environmental variations is that of trying to specify which attributes of the environment are the salient ones affecting cognitive performance. It is easier to identify groups of children who do not perform well on standardized tests of intelligence or achievement than it is to report what it is about their culture, homes, education, or communities which result in these deficits.

Some of the most extensively investigated groups of children who have been found to show deviations in cognitive performance are children living in isolated communities, those of low socioeconomic class, and minority group children.

Social isolation and cognitive development   Many studies have dealt with the intelligence test performance of children living in isolated conditions, which are frequently associated both with educational and economic deprivation.

Some of the earliest investigations dealt with English canal boat children and gypsies (Gordon, 1923). Both groups of children showed marked decrements in Stanford-Binet IQs. These decrements also increased with age. The mean IQ in the four- to six-year-old canal boat children was 87, but the adolescents within the same family had mean IQs of only 60. This might be attributed to the cumulative effects of an unstimulating environment since the children only went to school when the boats were docked for loading or unloading. Most of their parents were illiterate, and they had little social interaction beyond the family. However, another possible explanation is that as the children grew older, the brighter ones left the boat and sought a more exciting environment.

An increasing intellectual deficit is also found among rural children and could be attributed to the same migration effect. Several studies have been done on isolated mountain children in the United States. The IQs of children living in lonely hollows of the

Blue Ridge Mountains of Virginia were significantly lower than those of children in nearby villages, and the IQ scores of the isolated children decreased with age (Sherman & Key, 1932).

A more recent study (Kennedy, VanDeRiet, & White, 1963; Kennedy, 1969) tested 1800 black children in five Southeastern states. A subgroup of the children was retested five years later. This type of longitudinal study with repeated measures of the same child permits us to see if IQ in the same children is actually declining with age. This was the case; the older the child, the lower the IQ. Again it was found that community size was correlated with IQ. The mean IQ for the children in metropolitan areas was 83.96, in urban areas 79.37, and in rural areas 78.70. Although these residential trends were present, the most marked effect on IQ was one associated with socioeconomic level. The lower the socioeconomic level, the lower the IQ.

It may be that different environments stimulate and facilitate the development of different cognitive abilities and that standard intelligence tests do not measure a wide enough array of these abilities. One study showed that children living in remote New-foundland outpost communities had highly developed motor and perceptual abilities which might be considered adaptive in that setting, whereas their verbal and reasoning skills which might be less necessary for survival were below average (Burnett, Beach, & Sullivan, 1963).

The Pulawat islanders, who live a primitive, isolated, seafaring existence in a society with little technology or formal education, have developed an amazing navigational system. This system, which reveals an understanding of navigational rules and the relationship between winds, tides, currents, and direction, permits the islanders to navigate over long distances out of the sight of land. It seems probable that these remark-able navigators would not perform well on a standard test of intelligence or even on one of the frequently used Piagetian tasks of formal operations, although on problems which are culturally relevant they are clearly demonstrating very advanced deductive reasoning. On navigational tasks they have certainly attained the stage of formal operations. It has been argued that such observations show the importance of analyzing intellectual performance within the naturalistic, cultural context in which they occur (Gladwin, 1970). This has been advanced as an important issue not only in cross-cultural studies and studies of isolated communities but also in studies of social class, race, and ethnicity in the United States.

Social class, race, and cognitive development   Differences in performance on standardized intelligence tests among children from various ethnic and racial groups and social classes have been frequently noted (Dreger & Miller, 1960, 1968; Jensen, 1969; Kennedy, VanDeReit, & White, 1963; Kennedy, 1969; Shuey, 1966). Low-socio-economic-class children score 10 to 15 IQ points below middle-class children, and black children score on the average 15 to 20 IQ points below white children. These differences are present by first grade and the size of the difference remains the same throughout the school years (Kennedy, 1969). A similar 20 percent deficit on achievement tests such as the California Reading and Arithmetic Test appears in the early school years and increases with age in blacks (Osborne, 1960). In many studies the effects of race and social class have not been clearly separated, since in our country a disproportionate number of blacks are found in the lower classes.

Some investigators have argued that a more fruitful approach to racial and class differences is to look at differences in the patterns of cognitive skills rather than at overall elevation or depression of IQs. On what kinds of intellectual dimensions do members of different groups show the greatest relative strengths or weaknesses? Such an approach leads to construction of a profile of patterns of abilities. The carefully designed study presented in Box 10-1 investigated the relative standing on tests of verbal, reasoning, number, and spatial abilities of middle- and lower-class Chinese, Jews, Puerto Ricans, and blacks. The findings of this study are even more impressive when one realizes that it has been replicated and similar ethnic patterns of ability were found with a different sample of children.

Interpretations of cultural differences in cognitive performance   Three main types of explanations have been advanced to explain the ethnic and social class differences in intellectual performance: a position which emphasizes the inappropriateness of the tests for lower class children, a genetic position, and an environmental position.

Test bias and IQ. Advocates of the first position argue that the most widely used intelligence tests have not been standardized on minority groups, and that the items contained on these tests are not a true measure of adaptive ability or problem solving for the circumstances within which lower-class children and some ethnic groups live. The content of the usual intelligence tests draws heavily on white middle-class language, vocabulary, experience, and values. Attempts to cope with the possible bias in both tests and the testing conditions have not been very successful and some of the proposed solutions seem naïve.

BOX 10-1 ETHNIC GROUP, SOCIAL CLASS, AND MENTAL ABILITIES

This study investigated the relationship of social class and ethnic group in performance on tests of verbal ability, reasoning, number facility, and space conceptualization.

Eighty New York City children between the ages of six years and two months and seven years and five months were selected from each of four ethnic groups: Jewish, Chinese, Puerto Rican, and black. The children in each group were equally divided between lower- and middle-class children.

The investigators tried to use test materials and items that were equally familiar to all the social classes and cultural groups used in the study. The test administrators were from the same cultural background as the subjects and spoke the language of the child being tested. The test was administered in the language most familiar to the child. The items involved no writing or reading and no time limits on responding were used. Thus, a careful, systematic attempt was made to develop measures that were as culture-fair as were possible.

In order to establish rapport and reduce test anxiety, long periods of adapting to the test situation and extensive practice materials were used. The relative standing of the four

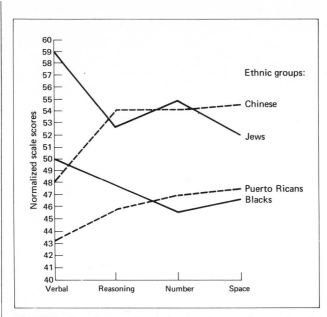

FIGURE 10-1 Pattern of verbal, reasoning, number, and spatial mental ability scores for six- and seven-year-old children of ethnic groups. (Reproduced from Lesser, G. S., Fifer, G., & Clark, D. H., 1965.)

ethnic groups is presented in Figure 10-1. It can be seen that distinctive profiles of mental ability scores emerge for the four ethnic groups: Puerto Ricans and Chinese show higher spatial abilities relative to their verbal abilities, whereas the pattern is reversed for blacks and Jews.

It was found that social class influenced the elevation but not the pattern of scores, whereas ethnicity influenced both pattern and level. When the groups were separated on the basis of socioeconomic class, the profiles of abilities for lower-class ethnic groups parallel the middle-class profiles but they are lower on all abilities. The difference between the levels for the lower- and middle-class is greatest for blacks, which suggests relatively greater socioeconomic disadvantage for lower-class blacks.

Source: Lesser, G. S., Fifer, G., & Clark, D. H. Mental abilities of children from different social class and cultural groups. *Monographs of the Society for Research in Child Development*, 1965, 30 (4, Serial No. 102), 1-115.

If the test items are experientially inappropriate, attempts to deal with such cultural bias by developing lower norms for blacks based on the performance of a large sample of blacks on a standard test such as the Stanford-Binet test or by translating these biased items into black dialect are not very sensible solutions to the problem. An example of cultural bias on the current revision of the Binet scale is cited by Williams (1970). Correct responses to the Binet item "What's the thing for you to do if another boy hits you without meaning to do it?" are such things as "'That's alright. I know it was an accident,' and walk away." Williams says that in some black communities a child must fight back as a means of survival and to walk away would mean suicide.

A little different kind of cultural bias is demonstrated in the test presented in Box 10-2. The "Dove Counterbalance General Intelligence Test" or the "Chitling Test" was facetiously developed by Adrian Dove, a black sociologist, to show that communication problems go both ways.

BOX 10-2 THE CHITLING TEST

It doesn't take a high IQ to recognize that intelligence tests have a built-in cultural bias that discriminates against black children. Tests designed to measure how logically a child can reason often use concepts foreign to the ghetto: a Harlem child who has never handled money or seen a farm animal, for example, might be asked a question that assumes knowledge of quarters and cows.

Adrian Dove, a sociologist and a Negro, for one, knows that black children have their own culture and language that "white" tests don't take into account. He saw this clearly when he worked with white civic and business leaders after the Watts riots. "I was talking Watts language by day," he says, "and then translating it so the guys in the corporations could understand it at night." Dove then designed his own exam, the Dove Counterbalance General Intelligence Test (the "Chitling Test") with 30 multiple-choice questions, "as a half-serious idea to show that we're just not talking the same language." The test has appeared in the Negro weekly Jet as well as in white newspapers, but mostly, says the 32 year-old Dove, "it has been floating around underground." Some samples (see end of story for the correct answers):

The Chitling Test
1. A "handkerchief head" is: (a) a cool cat, (b) a porter, (c) an Uncle Tom, (d) a hoddi, (e) a preacher.
2. Which word is most out of place here? (a) splib, (b) blood, (c) gray, (d) spook, (e) black.
3. A "gas head" is a person who has a: (a) fast moving car, (b) stable of "lace," (c) "process," (d) habit of stealing cars, (e) long jail record for arson.
4. "Down-home" (the South) today, for the average "soul brother" who is picking cotton from sunup until sundown, what is the average earning (take home) for one full day? (a) $.75, (b) $1.65, (c) $3.50, (d) $5, (e) $12.
5. "Bo Diddley" is a: (a) game for children, (b) down-home cheap wine, (c) down-home singer, (d) new dance, (e) Moejoe call.
6. If a pimp is up tight with a woman who gets state aid, what does he mean when he talks about "Mother's Day?" (a) second Sunday in May, (b) third Sunday in June, (c) first of every month, (d) none of these, (e) first and fifteenth of every month.
7. "Hully Gully" came from: (a) East Oakland, (b) Fillmore, (c) Watts, (d) Harlem, (e) Motor City.
8. If a man is called a "blood," then he is a (a) fighter, (b) Mexican-American, (c) Negro, (d) hungry hemophile, (e) Redman or Indian.
9. Cheap chitlings (not the kind you purchase at a frozen-food counter) will taste rubbery unless they are cooked long enough. How soon can you quit cooking them to eat and enjoy them? (a) 45 minutes, (b) two hours, (c) 24 hours, (d) one week (on a low flame), (e) one hour.

10. What are the "Dixie Hummingbirds?" (a) part of the KKK, (b) a swamp disease, (c) a modern gospel group, (d) a Mississippi Negro paramilitary group, (e) Deacons.
11. If you throw the dice and seven is showing on the top, what is facing down? (a) seven, (b) snake eyes, (c) boxcars, (d) little Joes, (e) 11.
12. "Jet" is: (a) an East Oakland motorcycle club, (b) one of the gangs in "West Side Story," (c) a news and gossip magazine, (d) a way of life for the very rich.
13. T-Bone Walker got famous for playing what? (a) trombone, (b) piano, (c) "T-flute," (d) guitar, (e) "Hambone".

Those who are not "culturally deprived" will recognize the correct answers are 1. (c), 2. (c), 3. (c), 4. (d), 5. (c), 6. (e), 7. (c), 8. (c), 9. (c), 10. (c), 11. (a), 12. (c), 13. (d).

Source: Dove, A. "The Chitling Test." In "Taking the Chitling Test," *Newsweek*, July 15, 1968. Copyright Newsweek, Inc., 1968, reprinted by permission.

Since most attempts to develop completely new culture-free tests or to modify the content of tests have not been successful in eliminating the association between social class, ethnicity, and test performance, some psychologists have attempted to develop measures which sample the child's performance on practical learning problems within his own environment. The study by Mercer presented in Box 10-3 represents an attempt to distinguish between IQ scores and adaptive ability. It demonstrates that for lower class and minority groups a standard intelligence test does not accurately distinguish individuals who cannot cope with practical problems in their environment from those who function well in the community. This is particularly important since the American Association on Mental Deficiency defines mental retardation as subaverage general intellectual functioning associated with impairment in adaptive behavior. It involves both IQ (usually an IQ score of 84 or lower or the bottom of 16 percent of the population) and adaptive ability. Many schools use only the criteria of the lowest 7 percent or a score of 75 to 79 or lower on a standard IQ test, whereas many test constructors suggest using an even more lenient criterion of only the bottom 3 percent or an IQ of 70 or lower.

The investigator, Jane Mercer, attempted to deal with three issues:

1. How is mental retardation defined and how do variations in its definition affect the labeling of minority groups?
2. Is a retarded IQ on a standard intelligence test associated with an inability to get along socially and deal with problems in the environment?
3. Is the lower average IQ scores of blacks and Chicanos related to variations in their cultural background?

The problem of labeling a child as retarded is a critical one: it influences his academic placement; it influences attitudes toward him in the classroom, in his peer group, and in the community; and it may even result in institutionalization. Once a child has been labeled retarded, the label follows him and plays a pervasive role in shaping his life experiences and the expectancies of others about him.

In addition to bias in the test content, it has been proposed that the testing conditions themselves are deleterious to the performance of low socioeconomic status and minority group children. Labov (1970) argues that the poor performance of black children on IQ tests is due to suspicion and hostility elicited by the test situation. The test is usually administered by a middle-class white psychologist, and lower-class children are less familiar with test situations and may be less likely to be motivated to perform well on tests. They also frequently bring in expectancies of failure based on past academic experience.

BOX 10-3 THE LETHAL LABELING OF LOW-IQ INDIVIDUALS

The investigator devised a test of adaptive ability involving the person's increasing ability to cope with more complex roles and practical problems as he matures. The scale consisted of a series of twenty-eight age-graded skills ranging from such things in younger children as self-care items (dressing, feeding, etc.) to more complex items in adults, such as being able to travel alone, hold a job, shop, and so on.

She compared the performance of 664 black, Mexican-American, or white persons on her adaptive behavior scale and on a standard intelligence test, usually the Stanford-Binet or the Kuhlman-Binet. It was found that if an IQ of either 84 ot 75 was used as the criterion to define retardation, many adults in this group were functioning competently in their social roles as measured by the adaptive behavior scale. Almost 100 percent could shop or travel alone, 84 percent had completed at least eight grades in school, 83 percent had held jobs, and 65 percent had semi-skilled or skilled occupations. In contrast, subjects who scored with an IQ below 70 were likely to be functioning inadequately in their environment. The investigator concludes that the cutoff level for retardation should be the lowest 3 percent (IQ below 70).

She then went on to compare quasi-retarded subjects, those who failed the IQ test but passed the test of adaptive behavior, with clinically retarded individuals, those who failed both tests at the 3 percent level.

She found that clinically retarded children had a more consistent history of learning problems, have had to repeat grades, and are likely to be in special programs. Quasi-retarded children are less likely to lag behind their age-mates or be in special classes although they too have low IQ scores.

Using the two tests to define retardation did not affect the Anglo-American children; every child who had an IQ below 70 also was in the bottom 3 percent on the test of adaptive behavior. However, 90 percent of the blacks and 60 percent of the Chicanos who had IQs below 70 passed the behavior test. Thus minority group children of low socioeconomic status are most likely to suffer from the use of an IQ score alone as a definition of retardation.

Finally, the investigator found that the more similar the black and Chicano children's homes and families were to middle-class Anglo-American homes in such things as socioeconomic status, education, family size, size of the house, home ownership, English spoken in the home, and so on, the better were their scores on IQ tests.

She concluded that the content of IQ tests is heavily biased in favor of the middle-class white cultural background, and that because of this, the dual classification system using both a standard IQ test and the test of adaptive behavior should be used in defining retardation.

Source: Mercer, J. R. IQ: the lethal label. *Psychology Today*, September 1972. P. 44; and Mercer, J. R. Sociocultural factors in labeling mental retardates. *The Peabody Journal of Education*, 1971, **48,** 188-203.

Some investigators have attempted to manipulate the race of the tester and others the motivation of the subjects. Under conditions which are not stressful, black children may actually perform better with white testers (Bucky & Banta, 1972). However, under anxiety-provoking situations where black subjects think they are not doing well or that their performance is to be compared to white norms, their performance improves with a black tester (Katz & Greenbaum, 1963; Katz, Robinson, Epps, & Waly, 1964; Katz, Roberts, & Robinson, 1965).

Attempts to elicit the best possible performance in children by familiarizing them with the test situation and test materials and by establishing rapport have been successful in improving the IQ scores of some lower-class children.

Zigler and Butterfield (1968) studied differences in IQs of lower-class nursery school children tested on the Stanford-Binet Intelligence Test under motivating and standard test conditions. Each child was tested on two different forms of the test under the two motivating conditions in the fall of one year and the spring on the following year. In the intervening period half of the subjects had nursery school experience and half did not. The motivating testing condition was one in which items were administered in such a way that easy items on which the child was likely to be successful were given early. In addition the child was not permitted to experience a sustained series of failures. Whenever he missed two items, an easy one which he could answer was interpolated. The child was gently encouraged to respond to all items. It was found that these lower-class children performed much better on intelligence tests under encouraging, supportive testing conditions than under standard conditions. In addition they showed marked improvement on IQ scores obtained under standard conditions if they had attended nursery school between the fall and spring sessions. The investigators propose that the change in IQ as a result of nursery school experience was due to a reduction in negative motivational factors in the test situation rather than an increase in intellectual competence. The children's wariness toward the adult examiner seemed to have decreased as a result of preschool experience. These results are presented in Figure 10-2.

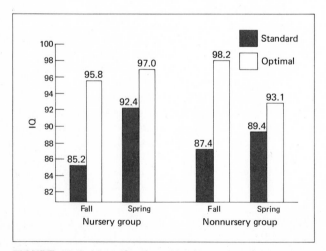

FIGURE 10-2 Mean IQs of combined nursery and nonnursery groups for standard and optimal fall and spring testings. (From Zigler, E., & Butterfield, E.C., 1968.)

Heredity and IQ. The second position that has been advanced to explain variations among social and racial groups in IQ is that these differences are based on genetic factors. One variant on this theme is that in a mobile society the brighter members of the lower class move upward and become middle class, and also that there is a tendency for people to marry within their class. This selective migration and assortative mating will tend to increase the difference between average IQ scores of the lower and middle classes over time (Burt, 1961; Herrenstein, 1971).

The most articulate exponent of the genetic position is Arthur Jensen (1969, 1973). He proposes that there are two genetically independent types of learning: *associative learning,* or level I learning, involving short-term memory, rote learning, attention, and simple associative skills; and *cognitive learning,* or level II learning, which involves abstract thinking, symbolic processes, conceptual learning, and the use of language in problem solving. The latter is clearly manifested in the ability to see relationships in such problems as:

> Which number goes in the following series?
> 2, 3, 5, 8, 12, 17, _____.
> How are an apple and a banana alike?

Most intelligence tests measure predominantly level II abilities. Some simple experimental tests, such as recalling a group of familiar objects or memory for numbers, measure level I abilities. Level I associative intelligence does not correlate with school performance. These abilities are not very important in academic learning, whereas level II intelligence as measured by IQ tests is predictive of achievement in school. Jensen suggests that level I abilities are equally distributed across social class and ethnic groups but that level II abilities are more concentrated in middle-class and Anglo-American than in lower-class or black American groups.

He further argues that on the basis of twin studies, estimates can be made that 70 to 80 percent of the contribution to intelligence is due to heredity and the remainder to environment. However, not all agree with Jensen, and next we turn to the environmental viewpoint.

Environment and IQ. Psychologists who emphasize environmental factors point to the fact that the conditions of physical and cultural deprivation imposed by poverty are adequate to explain the social class differences in cognitive performance without invoking genetic factors or systematic selection for IQ through social mobility. Poverty is associated with poor nutrition, poor health care, inadequate living conditions, and limited education. The effects of discrimination and lack of opportunity may lead to lack of motivation, low self-esteem, and feelings of helplessness, which will also influence performance on intelligence tests.

Much research in this area suggests that parental behavior may mediate some of the effects of social class. Because of this many investigators have studied differences in middle- and lower-class parent-child interactions which may influence the development of verbal and cognitive skills.

The work of Basil Berstein in England and of Robert Hess and Virginia Shipman described in the chapter on language development stressed the interaction between maternal control techniques, teaching styles, and language and the child's cognitive development. They differentiate individualistic, person-oriented control procedures ver-

Maternal communication and interaction are some of the determinants of a child's cognitive development. (Suzanne Szasz.)

sus status, role-oriented maternal approaches to control of the child. The individualistic approach used by middle-class mothers emphasizes the child's feelings, characteristics, and reasons for actions and orients the child toward attending to relevant cues in problem-solving situations in the environment. The mother makes the child aware of the complexities of his or her social and physical environment. She organizes information for her child and uses a more complex linguistic code to do so. In contrast, the lower-class mother who uses status-oriented control is less likely to individualize responses and uses a simplistic stereotyped restrictive form of language. This type of maternal communication is less likely to facilitate the kinds of discriminations and classifications necessary for later problem-solving skills in the child.

Studies of social-class differences in parent-child interactions have been criticized for some of the same reasons as have reports of race and class differences in IQ. It is frequently said that the laboratory situations in which many of the studies are conducted are more unfamiliar and anxiety-provoking for lower-class or minority group mothers than middle-class white mothers. Resentment or apprehension in the situation may cause lower-class minority group mothers to interact with their children in a manner which is not representative of their behavior in the home or more familiar situations. In addition, it is argued that the teaching situations used in many interaction studies where the mother must teach the child to solve a problem, build a house of blocks, or put together a puzzle are biased toward the experiences of middle-class mothers who already are probably doing this kind of thing at home with their children.

A study of mother-child interaction comparing mothers having high school education or less to mothers with college education or more indicates that the interaction task is important (Streissguth & Bee, 1972). When a play situation where the child was allowed to play freely with toys was used, interaction differences between the two groups of mothers were less than when a teaching situation was used. The teaching situation involved having the mother teach the child selected motor items from an infant intelligence test, such as putting blocks in a cup or completing a form board.

The patterns of evaluative comments which differed for the two groups of mothers and varied in the two situations are presented in Figure 10-3. The results are summarized by the investigators as follows:

> All mothers were much more active with their infants in the teaching situation than in the free play, apparently perceiving the teaching situation as requiring more active intervention. However, the two groups of mothers differed significantly in their teaching styles, particularly in their differential use of feedback to the infant about his performance. In free play, both groups used about the same amount of positive reinforcement (statements of approval and praise [such as "good girl"]) but the mothers with lower education used much more negative reinforcement (statements of disapproval and criticism [such as "not that way"]). These differences were intensified when the mothers were asked to teach their infants to solve a problem. Although the two groups of mothers gave their infants the same amount of overall feedback in the teaching situation, the higher education mothers used four times as much positive as negative reinforcement while the lower education mothers used almost the same amounts of negative and positive reinforcement. These same feedback patterns held for mothers of infants of each age: 9-, 12-, 15- and 18-months. It also appears that mothers with lower education used more demonstrations in teaching the task and were generally more specific in the type of help and suggestions they gave their infants, while mothers with higher

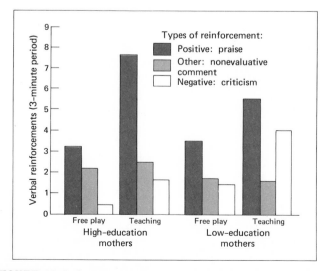

FIGURE 10-3 Average number of verbal reinforcements used by mothers with high school education or less compared with mothers with college education or more, interacting with their infants in a free-play and a teaching situation. (From Streissguth, A. P., & Bee, H., 1972.)

education used teaching strategies that were aimed at maintaining the infant's attention and focusing him on the task, but did not give as much specific instruction on how to solve the problem [Streissguth & Bee, 1972, pp. 172–73].

The finding of the more frequent use of praise for problem-solving performance by middle-class mothers has been related to the greater emphasis these mothers place on achievement and to the subsequent motivation their children may have to do well on intellectual tasks.

This focus on parent-child interaction as playing a mediating function on the association between social class and cognition has led many psychologists to include or focus on intervening in this interaction in attempting to improve the cognitive skills of children.

In addition to pointing to physical, emotional, and social factors which vary among social class and racial groups and would effect IQ, environmentalists seek evidence for their position in the late emergence of intellectual differences among such groups. In rebutting a genetic position they point out that no social class or racial differences are found on infant intelligence tests, but that these differences gradually emerge over the preschool years and therefore are attributable to cumulative effects of adverse experience. Jensen argues that infant intelligence tests use fewer items that involve level II abilities than do tests for older children such as the Stanford-Binet, and that the differential genetic salience of level II cognitive skills emerges only with age. He is arguing that it is not necessary for a genetically based trait to be present at birth in order to conclude that it is hereditary, and that the phenotypical manifestations may vary over age and may only appear in certain stages of development.

Environmentalists also argue that Jensen's estimate of a 70 to 80 percent heritability factor in IQ is not valid, and that the contribution of genetic factors to intelligence will vary with the population being studied and the environmental conditions under which they develop. Jerome Kagan (1969) uses the example of stature to illustrate this point. In the United States under conditions of reasonable nutrition and immunization against disease, height is largely genetically determined. Because the majority of Americans are well-nourished, the genes associated with height express themselves fairly directly in phenotypical or actual height. However, the differences in height between these well-nourished American children and children suffering from disease and malnutrition in another, less affluent culture is not mainly genetically determined. Extremely adverse health and nutritional factors overwhelm and minimize genetic contributions to stature. Most starving children remain small in stature. Since the contribution of heritability to height in the two cultures is not the same, it is inappropriate to use heritability indexes calculated on the basis of studies in one population and generalize these findings to different populations.

In a twin study Sandra Scarr-Salapatek investigated this problem directly by looking at the relationship between heritability and IQ in black and white lower- and middle-class children (Scarr-Salapatek, 1971). The investigator assumed that lower-class children and most blacks have limited experiences with environmental factors relevant to the development of academic skills or performance on intelligence tests. Therefore, just as the range of stature is smaller under conditions of extreme malnutrition, variability in scores on cognitive tests will be less for these groups than for white middle- or upper-class children. This was found to be the case. Genetic intellectual variations are more directly expressed in the performance on cognitive tests of white middle- or upper-class children than in lower-class or black children.

Finally, environmentalists argue that some compensatory education preschool programs aimed at improving the cognitive skills of children of poverty have been successful, and that the social class differences are reversible and thus cannot be genetically based. It is interesting to note that although the effects of some of the programs have washed out rapidly when treatment terminated or by the early school years, the ones that have been most successful have been those that were begun early and involved the parents in the training of their children. It is difficult to maintain gains if children are put in a cognitively stimulating school environment but return to the unchanged home situation which has previously shaped their cognitive performance.

Programs in which the focus is on the parent-child relation rather than only on placing the child in an educationally stimulating program are sometimes called "home start" as contrasted to "head start" programs.

Projects which have attempted to use parent education programs in neighborhood or child-care centers have not been very successful in either changing parent attitudes or affecting parental behavior (Chilman, 1973). One of the difficulties in such projects is in maintaining the involvement, interest, and attendance at meetings of the parents, especially of the fathers. Many lower-class parents see child-care workers' attempts to teach them how to be good parents as condescending and offensive. Others have reported that there are too many adverse reality factors in their lives, such as crowded or inadequate housing, lack of money, unemployment, and so on, to make concerns like improving child-care practices important.

The most successful programs seem to be those in which low-income parents are actively involved in the education of their children. In some cases the mothers are employed as teaching aids in the preschool centers; in other studies mothers are visited in their homes and instructed and supported in their educational activities with the child. The educational activities themselves vary widely in different studies; reading, demonstration of educational toys, exercises aimed at improving cognitive development, and even play have been used. The wide range of types of parent-child activities that have been successful in modifying the child's intellectual performance suggests that it may be increased positive interaction between mother and child rather than the specific content of the tasks that is leading to the changes. The description of a toy program developed by Merle B. Karnes, which is used to facilitate mother-child interaction, is presented in Box 10-4.

The effects of such programs are not restricted to the target child. In one study IQs of the mothers improved, and in a group involving active participation of both mother and child in a preschool center, one-third of the mothers subsequently enrolled in school to finish their high school work (Miller, 1967). The experience of actively participating in their child's education and of feeling responsible for instigating changes in the child may help develop a sense of competence and initiative in the mother which partially mitigates the feelings of helplessness and of being externally controlled that are frequently found in lower-class people.

The effects also extend to siblings of the child receiving the enrichment program. Younger siblings of the children involved in such activities show superior test performance to those in homes where the older child is not in an enrichment program (Klaus & Gray, 1968; Miller, 1967).

BOX 10-4 MOTHERS' TRAINING PROGRAM

In the home training sessions, the child's curiosity and growth are encouraged by the use of various simple educational materials and toys, many of which the mothers learn not only to use effectively with their babies, but also to make by themselves from inexpensive materials. Within a budget of $50 per child, the following materials are provided for each of the children in the program: (1) a table and chair set; (2) 11 educational toys; (3) crayons, scissors, play dough, slate, and chalk; (4) four inexpensive books; and (5) a plastic laundry basket for storage of materials. A lending library of 30 wooden inlay puzzles and simple object lotto games is available for all the children.

The most seemingly ordinary objects, such as the table and chair and the laundry basket, play a central role in revolutionizing the environment of mother and child. These objects help to establish an order in the home and to define the pattern of roles and behavior which is maintained in every training session. During these sessions the child always works sitting at his table, on his chair. Each day, the mother takes the training toys from the laundry basket, and at the end of each session she returns them to the basket for safe storage.

Working with the toys, the child learns finger coordination and gross motor skills, concepts of relative size, basic shapes, and verbal skills. One training session might find mother and child playing with a set of five nested cans which the mother has collected herself. Starting with two, she teaches the baby to stack them, saying "Put the *little* one *on top of* the *big* one. Put the *little* one *in* the *big* one." Later, the mother teaches him body parts, antonyms and prepositions, and visual matching. Scrapbook making and dramatic storytelling are also included in the training sessions at a later stage. Often older brothers and sisters help in making the scrapbook, which the mother and baby "read" together, and the scrapbooks become a source of pride to both mother and child. For most of the mothers it comes as a surprise that these scrapbooks and simple toys, which encourage the child to manipulate and explore, are better than expensive electrical toys which he merely watches. They learn that the best kind of toy is often one that they can make themselves.

In addition to the regular program toys, there are several "fun toys" such as pounding bench and busy box—again, these are toys that will help the baby develop new skills or concepts. They are to be played with any time, not just during training sessions; and since a number of mothers have reported that their babies do not want to stop when the training session is ended, these "fun toys" are suggested as "transfer toys." The mother simply hands the child one of these toys as a substitute for those she is taking away and lets him play independently. For many of the mothers, this brings a new revelation. The baby does not accept the transfer toy; it is the end of his time with mother that upsets him, not the absence of the toys. The babies are learning, and the mothers are learning too—learning that time spent together and nurturing, affectionate behavior are not only the most important things they can give their babies but also the prerequisites for effective training.

Reprinted from "Model Programs: Mothers' Training Program," Government Printing Office, 1970 (Pamphlet of the National Center for Educational Communication, Department of Health, Education and Welfare).

Horowitz and Paden (1973), in an excellent review of the effectiveness of intervention programs, discuss the problems involved in a "deficit model" of the intellectual capabilities of lower-class children. Many investigators assume that because the language, intellectual skills, and behaviors of lower-class and minority groups differ from those of the white middle-class majority, they are in some way deficient or inferior. The issue of whether it is more useful to conceive of these groups as different rather than deficient in planning educational programs is important. Should language programs with poor black families be oriented toward eliminating their linguistic code or toward offering them an additional alternative code? The issue seems to be one of striking a constructive balance between educational enrichment and cultural annihilation.

Sex differences in cognitive development

In addition to racial and social class differences in IQ, sex differences in many aspects of cognitive development have been found. Although most standard intelligence tests have been constructed to be sex-neutral by balancing or eliminating tasks on which one sex is consistently superior to the other, sex differences in profiles of abilities still emerge. On the average girls show somewhat earlier language development and greater verbal fluency than do boys. However, on tests involving verbal comprehension or verbal reasoning this relationship is reversed. Females also excel on tests involving perception of detail, clerical skills, manual dexterity, and rote memory. In contrast, males are superior on spatial orientation and perception, arithmetical reasoning, and general information.

Girls in elementary and high school tend to receive better grades than boys, in spite of the fact that boys do as well or sometimes better on achievement tests (Carter, 1952; Coleman, 1961; Hanson, 1959). Most teachers want to maintain order in their classrooms and may respond negatively to boys because they are less conforming and cooperative and less conscientious in completing class assignments. Boys may be penalized in school because of assuming the culturally appropriate, masculine, assertive behaviors.

Even in the preschool years boys surpass girls in a variety of types of problem solving. This may be related to the finding that in the preschool years, in fact even in infants as young as thirteen months, boys are more curious and active in exploring and manipulating their environment (Goldberg & Lewis, 1969; Hutt, 1970a, 1970b, 1972).

These effects may be at least partly attributable to differences in sex-role training. Girls may be encouraged less to leave the mother and explore things around them. They may receive less reinforcement for being independent, solving problems, and doing unconventional, original things.

Torrance (1962) found that boys had more creative ideas about unusual uses for science toys than did girls. This is not surprising since in our culture scientific endeavors are encouraged more in boys than in girls. However, the investigator then discussed with teacher and parents the possibility of stereotyped sex roles interfering with intellectual potentialities. The parents and teachers were advised to encourage the girls to explore scientific toys more thoroughly. When another group of children was tested a year later, the encouragement of scientific exploration in girls was manifested by their producing just as many original ideas about the toys as boys did. However, in spite of their equivalent performance, when their peers were asked who contributed the best ideas, they said the boys did.

This study shows that girls' creative performance on scientific tasks can be improved with training and encouragement, but that stereotyped beliefs about feminine abilities may result in a lack of recognition or reward for these skills.

Females are likely to perform better on tasks they believe are sex appropriate (feminine) rather than on those that they believe are sex inappropriate (masculine) (Stein, Pohly, & Mueller, 1971). This may be why female achievement orientations are likely to be manifested in social skills.

Public achievement, particularly in competitive activities, is often threatening to females. Some girls cope with their conflict about achievement by concealing their ability, particularly from males. For example, they may tell male peers that they received lower grades than they really did (Horner, 1972). Another coping response is to decrease their efforts and intentionally perform less adequately (Weiss, 1962). Finally, a competent woman may counteract her achievement striving by being superfeminine in appearance and behavior. She may be warm, flirtatious, and submissive. She may even try to be supermother, superwife, and super-career woman by fulfilling all the demands of a conventional domestic role in addition to having a career (Stein & Bailey, 1973).

Parental influences on cognitive development Mothers who value achievement, set high achievement standards, and reward their children for satisfactory performance and punish them for substandard performance have boys and girls who have high achievement motivation and effort (Crandall, Preston, & Rabson, 1960; Rosen & D'Andrade, 1959).

There is some evidence that interactions between the sex of the parent and sex of the child must be considered in evaluating other parental influences on cognition. Some of the findings suggest that although mothers may be more important in stimulating intellectual development and achievement needs in both boys and girls, fathers may have relatively more influence on cognitive growth in daughters than in sons.

It may be that because children spend more time with their mothers than fathers in our culture, the mother is most important in determining the intellectual level of the home environment. The intelligence of mothers has been found to influence the expression of genetic predisposition for mental retardation in children. In homes in which the father is of average intelligence, but the mother is retarded, retardation is two and one-half times more frequent among the children than in homes with equally retarded fathers and normal IQ mothers (Reed & Reed, 1965).

Mothers also seem to be more important than fathers in shaping the aptitudes of their children. When university students have fathers who are less educated than their mothers, their aptitude scores are higher than those of students with more educated fathers than mothers. This occurs in spite of the fact that homes with the more educated fathers were of higher socioeconomic status. Variations in the mothers' education seemed to counteract the commonly found effect of social class factors on children's aptitudes (Willerman & Stafford, in press).

In the Fels Institute Study (Kagan & Moss, 1962; Crandall & Battle, 1970) high achievement in boys was associated with high maternal protection and little hostility during the first three years of life followed by reinforcement and encouragement for acceleration of the boys striving for achievement and independence from three to ten. In contrast mothers of high intellectually achieving girls were hostile and lacking in protectiveness in the first three years of life, which may have encouraged early independence in the girls. This was accompanied by sustained emphasis on accelerating daughters' intellectual achievement by both mother and father. Such high-achieving daughters had fathers who were affectionate and nurturant and generally satisfied with their daughters' achievement striving. However, they did not hesitate to use both appropriate praise and criticism of their daughters' achievement performance.

This suggests that factors which might lead to some alienation from the mother and a closer relationship with the father facilitate achievement in girls. It would be interesting to know how this relationship would differ if daughters with high-achieving, career-oriented mothers were compared to daughters of low-achieving mothers. It could be that with a high-achieving mother, maternal warmth would encourage the daughter to identify with the mother and emulate her achievement attitudes and performance.

SUMMARY

Intelligence tests were originally constructed to predict academic success and they remain one of our best instruments for doing so. However, test scores show considerable variability over time, and IQ cannot be considered a stable measure of intellectual capacity. Intelligence test scores should always be viewed as a measure of performance rather than ability. Under different circumstances on different measures a child who has not done well on one test may be able to demonstrate his cognitive skills. In some ways this distinction between capacity and performance is similar to that encountered in the discussion of Piagetian tasks in the previous chapter. Since under the right situation or with certain kinds of training a child who previously has been unable to solve a conservation task now can, it is suggested that these tasks are not measuring the capacity to perform these operations. In a parallel fashion, training given to young children which results in their performing more adequately on intelligence tests and in school are not changing the child's intellectual capacity. It may be changing their ability to manifest a capacity which already existed.

The IQ is best regarded as a measure reflecting the interaction of genetic and environmental factors. Heredity, environmental stimulation, and deprivation; home and cultural factors; and characteristics of the test situation influence performance on intelligence tests.

Marked differences in amount and patterns of cognitive skills are related to social class, ethnic group, and sex. Low-socioeconomic-class children score lower on almost all tests of cognitive skills; however, the patterns of skills are influenced by ethnicity. Blacks and Jews score relatively higher on tests of language skills and low on spatial skills, whereas this pattern is reversed for Chinese and Puerto Ricans.

Many hypotheses have been advanced to explain the relatively poorer performance of low-socioeconomic-class and black children. Some investigators have argued that the tests used are culturally biased toward white middle-class experience and information and thus other groups are penalized. The test situation itself is regarded as stressful and unfamiliar to lower-class children.

A controversy now rages as to whether the differences in test performance are partly based on genetic differences in social classes and ethnic groups or whether the differences can be explained entirely by experiential factors. Cultural factors associated with isolation and poverty do seem to have a marked effect on IQ.

In addition to social class and ethnic differences in cognitive development, sex differences are also found. Girls perform better on tests of verbal fluency, manual dexterity, clerical skills, and rote memory than do boys. Boys excel in spatial relations, mathematical reasoning, verbal comprehension, and reasoning and problem solving. These may in part by the consequences of social pressures for the two sexes to conform to sex role stereotypes.

Parental factors are important in shaping cognitive development. Some intervention programs which have taught and encouraged lower-class mothers to interact with their children in ways thought to facilitate cognitive growth have successfully raised the IQs of both parents and children. Parents who have high achievement standards and both reward and criticize their children's performance have intellectually achieving children. Maternal affection with boys and maternal rejection and paternal warmth for girls are also associated with achievement. There is some evidence that mothers play a more salient role than fathers in the intellectual development of their children.

In conclusion, it can be seen that cognitive development is a complex process influenced by a myriad of genetic, constitutional, environmental, and experiential factors.

REFERENCES

Bayley, N. Development of mental abilities. In P. H. Mussen (Ed.), *Carmichael's manual of child psychology.* Vol. 1. New York: Wiley, 1970. Pp. 1163-1210.

Bell, R. Q., Weller, G. M., & Waldrop, M. F. Newborn and preschooler: organization of behavior and relations between periods. *Monographs of the Society for Research in Child Development,* 1971, **36** (4, Serial No. 142), 1-145.

Bucky, S. F., & Banta, T. J. Racial factors in test performance. *Developmental Psychology,* 1972, **6,** 7-13.

Burnett, A., Beach, H. D., & Sullivan, A. M. Intelligence in a restricted environment. *Canadian Psychologist,* 1963, **4,** 126-136.

Burt, C. Intelligence and social mobility. *British Journal of Statistical Psychology,* 1961, **14,** 3-24.

Cameron, J., Livson, T. V., & Bayley, N. Infant vocalizations and their relationship to mature intelligence. *Science,* 1967, **157,** 331-333.

Carter, E. S. How invalid are marks assigned by teachers? *Journal of Educational Psychology,* 1952, **43,** 218-228.

Chilman, C. S. Programs for disadvantaged parents: Some major trends and related research. In B. Caldwell & H. Riccuiti (Eds.), *Review of child development research.* Vol. 3. Chicago: The University of Chicago Press, 1973. Pp. 403-466.

Coleman, J. S. *The adolescent society.* Glencoe, Ill.: Free Press, 1961.

Crandall, P., Preston, A., & Rabson, A. Maternal reactions and the development of independence and achievement behavior in young children. *Child Development,* 1960, **31,** 243-251.

Crandall, V. C., & Battle, E. S. The antecedents and adult correlates of academic and intellectual achievement effort. In J. Hill (Ed.), *Minnesota Symposia on Child Development.* Vol. 4. Minneapolis: The University of Minnesota Press, 1970. Pp. 60-73.

Dove, A. Taking the chitling test. *Newsweek,* July 15, 1968.

Dreger, R. M., & Miller, S. K. Comparative psychological studies of Negroes and whites in the United States. *Psychological Bulletin,* 1960, **57,** 361-402.

Dreger, R. M., & Miller, S. K. Comparative psychological studies of Negroes and whites in the United States: 1959-1965. *Psychological Bulletin Monograph Supplement,* 1968, **70**(3, Part 2), 1-58.

Gladwin, T. *East is a big bird: navigation and logic on Pulawat Atoll.* Cambridge: Harvard, 1970.

Goldberg, H., & Lewis, M. Play behavior in the year-old infant: early sex differences. *Child Development,* 1969, **40,** 21-31.

Gordon, H. Mental and scholastic tests among retarded children. Educational Pamphlet No. 44. London: Board of Education, 1923.

Haan, N. Proposed model of ego functioning: coping and defense mechanisms in relationship to IQ change. *Psychological Monographs,* 1963, **77,** 1-23.

Hanson, E. H. Do boys get a square deal in school? *Education,* 1959, **79,** 597-598.

Herrenstein, R. I. Q. *Atlantic,* 1971, **228,** 44-64.

Honzik, M. P., & Macfarlane, J. W. Personality development and intellectual functioning from 21 months to 40 years. Paper presented at meeting of American Psychological Association, Washington, D.C., September 1970.

Honzik, M. P., MacFarlane, J. W., & Allen, L. The stability of mental test performance between two and eighteen years. *Journal of Experimental Education,* 1948, **17,** 309-324.

Horner, M. S. Toward an understanding of achievement-related conflicts in women. *Journal of Social Issues,* 1972, **78,** 157-176.

Horowitz, F. D., & Paden, L. Y. The effectiveness of environmental intervention programs. In B. Caldwell & H. Riccuiti (Eds.), *Review of child development research.* Vol. 3. Chicago: The University of Chicago Press, 1973. Pp. 331-402.

Hunt, J. McV. The role of experience in the development of competence. In J. McV. Hunt (Ed.), *Human intelligence.* Brunswick, N. J.: Transaction Books, 1972.

Hutt, C. Specific and diversive exploration. In H. Reese & L. Lipsitt (Eds.), *Advances in child development behavior.* Vol. 5. London: Academic, 1970. (a)

Hutt, C. Curiosity in young children. *Science,* 1970, **6,** 68-72. (b)

Hutt, C. Neuroendocrinological, behavioral and intellectual aspects of sexual differentiation in human development. In Olmstead & Taylor (Eds.), *Gender differences—their ontogeny and significance.* London: Churchill, 1972.

Jensen, A. R. How much can we boost IQ and scholastic achievement? *Harvard Educational Review,* 1969, **39,** 1-123.

Jensen, A. R. *Genetic, educability and subpopulation differences.* London: Methuen, 1973.

Kagan, J. S. Inadequate evidence and illogical conclusions. *Harvard Educational Review,* 1969, **39,** 274-277.

Kagan, J. S., & Moss, H. A. *Birth to maturity: a study in psychological development.* New York: Wiley, 1962.

Katz, I., & Greenbaum, C. Effects of anxiety, threat and racial environment on task performance of Negro college students. *Journal of Abnormal and Social Psychology,* 1963, **66,** 562-567.

Katz, I., Roberts, S. O., & Robinson, J. M. Effects of difficulty, race of administrator and instructions on Negro digit-symbol performance. *Journal of Personality and Social Psychology,* 1965, **70,** 53-59.

Katz, I., Robinson, J. M., Epps, E. G., & Waly,

P. Effects of race of experimenter and tests vs. neutral instructions on expression of hostility in Negro boys. *Journal of Social Issues,* 1964, **20,** 54-59.

Kennedy, W. A. A follow-up normative study of Negro intelligence and achievement. *Monographs of the Society for Research in Child Development,* 1969, **34**(2), No. 126.

Kennedy, W. A., VanDeRiet, V., & White, J. C. A normative sample of intelligence and achievement of Negro elementary school children in the southeastern United States. *Monographs of the Society for Research in Child Development,* 1963, **28**(6, Serial No. 90), 13-112.

Kessen, W., Haith, M. M., & Salapatek, P. H. Human infancy: a bibliography and guide. In P. H. Mussen (Ed.), *Carmichael's manual of child psychology.* Vol. 1. New York: Wiley, 1970.

Klaus, R. A., & Gray, S. W. The early training project for disadvantaged children: a report after five years. *Monographs of the Society for Research in Child Development,* 1968, **33**(4), No. 120.

Labov, W. The logic of nonstandard English. In F. Williams (Ed.), *Language and poverty.* Chicago: Markham Publishing Company, 1970. Pp. 153-189.

Lesser, G. S., Fifer, G., & Clark, D. H. Mental abilities of children from different social class and cultural groups. *Monographs of the Society for Research in Child Development,* 1965, **30**(4, Serial No. 102), 1-115.

McCall, R. B., Appelbaum, M. I., & Hogarty, P. S. Developmental changes in mental performance. *Monographs of the Society for Research in Child Development,* 1973, **38**(3, Serial No. 150), 1-84.

McCall, R. B., Hogarty, P. S., & Hurlburt, N. Transitions in infant sensorimotor development and the prediction of childhood IQ. *American Psychologist,* 1972, **27,** 728-748.

Mercer, J. R. Sociocultural factors in labeling mental retardates. *The Peabody Journal of Education,* 1971, **48,** 188-203.

Mercer, J. R. IQ: the lethal label. *Psychology Today,* September 1972. P. 44.

Miller, J. Research, change and social responsibility: intervention research with young disadvantaged children and their parents. In *DARCEE papers and reports,* numbers 2 and 3. Nashville: George Peabody College for Teachers, 1967.

Moore, T. Language and intelligence: a longitudinal study of the first eight years. Part I: Patterns of development in boys and girls. *Human Development,* 1967, **10,** 88-106.

Osborne, R. T. Racial differences in mental growth and school achievement: a longitudinal study. *Psychological Reports,* 1970, **7,** 233–239.

Reed, E. W., & Reed, S. C. *Mental retardation: a family study.* Philadelphia: Saunders, 1965.

Rees, A. H., & Palmer, F. H. Factors related to change in mental test performance. *Developmental Psychology Monograph,* 1970, **3**(2).

Rosen, B. C., & D'Andrade, R. The psychological origins of achievement motivation. *Sociometry,* 1959, **22,** 185–218.

Scarr-Salapatek, S. Race, social class and IQ. *Science,* 1971, **174,** 1285–1292.

Scarr-Salapatek, S. Genetics and the development of intelligence. In F. Horowitz (Ed.), *Review of child development research.* Vol. 4. Chicago: The University of Chicago Press, in press.

Sherman, M., & Key, C. B. The intelligence of isolated mountain children. *Child Development,* 1932, **3,** 279–290.

Shuey, A. M. *The testing of Negro intelligence.* 2d ed. New York: Social Science Press, 1966.

Sontag, L. W., Baker, C. T., & Nelsen, V. L. Mental growth and personality: a longitudinal study. *Monographs of the Society for Research in Child Development,* 1958, **23**(68), 1–143.

Stein, A. H., & Bailey, M. M. The socialization of achievement orientation in females. *Psychological Bulletin,* 1973, **80,** 345–366.

Stein, A. H., Pohly, S. R., & Mueller, E. The influence of masculine, feminine and neutral tasks on children's achievement behavior, expectancies of success and attainment of values. *Child Development,* 1971, **42,** 195–207.

Streissguth, A. P., & Bee, H. L. Mother-child interactions and cognitive development in children. In W. W. Hartup (Ed.), *The young child: reviews of research.* Washington, D.C.: National Association for the Education of Young Children, 1972.

Torrance, E. P. *Guiding creative talent.* Englewood Cliffs, N.J.: Prentice-Hall, 1962.

Wechsler, D. *Wechsler Intelligence Scale for Children.* New York: The Psychological Corporation, 1952.

Weiss, P. Some aspects of femininity. *Dissertation Abstracts,* 1962, **23,** 1083.

Willerman, L., & Stafford, R. E. Maternal effects on intellectual functioning. *Behavior Genetics,* in press.

Williams, R. L. Black pride, academic relevance and individual achievement. *Counseling Psychologist,* 1970, **2**(1), 18–22.

Zigler, E., & Butterfield, E. C. Motivational aspects of changes in IQ test performance of culturally deprived nursery school children. *Child Development,* 1968, **39,** 1–14.

11
THE FAMILY

Socialization is the process whereby an individual's standards, skills, motives, attitudes, and behaviors are shaped to conform to those regarded as desirable and appropriate for his or her present or future role in society. Certain groups and organizations within society play key roles in socialization. Parents, siblings, peers, and teachers spend a great deal of their time communicating values and directing and modifying children's behavior. Some organizations, such as the school, the church, and legal institutions, have evolved with the specific mission of transmitting the culture's knowledge and its social and ethical standards and development, and maintaining culturally valued behaviors.

In the following chapters there will be a discussion of the role of some of the main agents and institutions involved in socialization: the family, the school, and peers. The impact of these groups on the development of morality and self-control, on the inhibition of aggression and encouragement of positive social behavior, on achievement, and on behaviors regarded as appropriate for males or females within our culture will be emphasized particularly.

Social- def.

Although many social factors and groups effect the process of socialization, the family is frequently regarded as the most influential agency in the socialization of the child. This chapter will deal with the processes and problems of socialization within the family. The formation of early emotional attachments between parent and child which serve as the basis for later parental effectiveness in teaching or modeling socially desirable standards of behavior will be presented. It will be seen that different parental characteristics, attitudes, and childrearing patterns are associated with different behaviors in children. Finally, the effects of variations in family structure, such as the number of siblings, the absence of one parent, or communal childrearing, will be discussed.

VARIATIONS IN PATTERNS OF SOCIALIZATION

The standards, goals, and methods of socialization vary among societies, within subgroups in the same society, and within a society over time. Behavior regarded as desirable and encouraged in one society would be regarded as undesirable or even pathological in another. The grandiose boasting accepted by the Kwakiutl Indians as an appropriate means of establishing status might seem more like a paranoid delusional system to other segments of the American population. The handling of poisonous snakes to demonstrate devoutness, a practice of some fundamentalist religious groups in the Appalachians and in the Southwest, might seem a trifle excessive to others. The confinement of infants in some Guatemalan villages to a small, dark, windowless, toyless hut for the first year of life because of the belief that outside fresh air, sunlight, and dirt are harmful, would be viewed as the grossest deprivation by American middle-class mothers who surround their children with educational toys, festoon cribs with spinning mobiles and busy boxes, and involve their children in a regular routine of daily sunbaths and walks in the park.

Even within the same culture, dramatic changes over time occur in the goals of socialization and the methods used to mold the values and behavior of children. In the years between 1910 and 1930, which were the heyday of American behaviorism led by John B. Watson, childrearing experts regarded the infant as an object for systematic shaping and conditioning. Little attention was paid to the needs and feelings of the child or the parent, or possible variations in genetic predispositions or temperamental characteristics of the child. Behaviorists of this era maintained an extreme environmentalist position and believed that desirable social behavior could be shaped in almost any child. Desirable social behavior could be attained if the child's antisocial behaviors were always punished and never indulged, and if positive behaviors were carefully conditioned and rewarded in a highly controlled and structured childrearing regime. The goal of the parents was to "shape in" good habits and avoid the development of, or "stamp out," bad habits. Watson advocated that the parents not indulge themselves by hugging and kissing the child, but treat children in a sensible way like young adults. He assured parents that if they behaved in an objective, unemotional way for only one week that they would be utterly ashamed of the mawkish, sentimental way they had been dealing with their child. Watson suggested:

In conclusion, won't you then remember when you are tempted to pet your child that mother love is a dangerous instrument? An instrument which may inflict a never healing wound, a wound which may make infancy unhappy, adolescence a nightmare, an instrument which may wreck your adult son or daughter's vocational future and their chances for marital happiness [Watson, 1928, p. 87].

Completely permissive attitude

Watson's vast influence was reflected in some of the popular childrearing literature of the day and even the official government booklet for parents published by the U.S. Children's Bureau entitled "Child Care." This booklet advocated never permitting the child to suck his thumb and if necessary restraining the child by tying his hands to the crib at night, and painting his fingers with foul-tasting liquids or having him wear mittens during the day. It was recommended that feeding and toilet training be carefully scheduled. Daytime feeding sessions were at fixed four-hour intervals. Children were punished for soiling themselves and were seated on the toilet at prescribed times of the day and remained there until they urinated or defecated, at which time they were praised or rewarded. Parents were advised to let infants "cry themselves out" rather than reinforce this unacceptable behavior by picking them up, and rocking and soothing them. This position seemed to emphasize all of the anxieties and drudgery and none of the joys of the parent-child relationship.

However, in the following years from the early 1930s until the mid-1960s, a more permissive attitude in which the parent was advised to be concerned with the feelings and capacities of the child emerged. This shift was due in part to the influence of Freudian psychology and its focus on the role of early deprivation and restrictions in the development of inhibitions which could serve as the foundation of many emotional problems. Another influence was the maturationally oriented child psychologists, such as Arnold Gesell, who stressed the importance of the "readiness" of the child in socialization. When the child was maturationally ready and when he was at the appropriate stage for training, weaning, toilet training, and other forms of self-control would proceed with greater ease and less stress for both mother and child. When the child was biologically ready, he would almost train himself with a little encouragement from the parent if there was a positive relationship between the parent and child.

This more relaxed attitude to childrearing was given added impetus by the continuing influence of progressive educators, such as John Dewey, and the writings of humanistic psychologists, such as A. H. Maslow and Carl Rogers, which began to appear in the 1940s. Both of these groups believed that individuals have an innate capacity to learn and develop in a constructive and creative way and to realize their potential abilities if they are free to explore and develop in an open, accepting environment.

It became fashionable during the travails of the sixties, that is, during the sit-ins, protests, and riots, to blame the obstreperous, unconventional, and anti-establishment behavior of the young on their failure to be adequately socialized due to the widespread use by their parents of Benjamin Spock's book, *Baby and Child Care*. This influential book was first published in 1946 and since then over 21 million copies have been sold in the United States alone, in addition to a wide circulation in its many translated foreign editions. Spock's book became the parents' security blanket in dealing with everything from protruding navels to discipline. The students in this course may not have read Dr. Spock, but many will have been reared according to his precepts. Dr. Spock was not purveying a radical new doctrine; he was synthesizing and communicating in a jargon-free, highly readable style the beliefs and findings of the medical and social scientists of the era. Contrary to the statements of many of his critics, Spock did not advocate a completely indulgent and permissive approach to childrearing. He emphasized the importance of a warm parent-child relationship in the child's responsiveness to discipline. A child responds to the demands of loving parents more readily than to parents that are disliked and feared. If the parents are responsive to the capacities, needs, and feelings of the child, Spock thought they should seldom have to use discipline more severe than distracting, guiding, reasoning, and explaining. Even for parents things looked better with Dr. Spock, for his frequent cry was "Enjoy your baby."

Since the mid-1960s there has been a continued emphasis on the role of parental love in the socialization of the child; however, experts now advise the parents to play a less permissive and more active role in shaping the child's behavior. The virtues of the "authoritative" versus the "authoritarian" parent are extolled. Parents should set limits and be authoritative in making decisions in areas where the child is not capable of making a reasonable judgment. However, they should listen and adapt to the child's point of view, should explain their restrictions and discipline, and should never be authoritarian; that is, they should never use their greater power to control the child in an unreasonable or hostilely punitive manner. The research findings which have led to this position will be discussed at length in the following chapters.

THE FAMILY AND THE TASKS OF SOCIALIZATION

Among the many social agencies that contribute to the socialization of the child, the family is clearly of central importance. But why is this the case? This emphasis on the great power of the family is largely attributable to the fact that family members are the first and often almost the only social contacts the child has in the early years which are critical in social development. The interaction and emotional relationship between the infant and parents will shape his expectancies and responses in subsequent social relationships.

In addition, note that the beliefs, values, and attitudes of the culture are filtered through the parents and presented to the child in a highly personalized, selective fashion. The personality, attitudes, socioeconomic class, religious affiliation, education, and sex of the parent will influence his presentation of cultural values and standards to his offspring. The desired and appropriate standards, beliefs and role behavior shaped in a daughter by a lower-class, Baptist, authoritarian father would be quite different than those presented by an educated, middle-class, atheistic, feminist mother.

Specific norms and means of attaining socialization goals vary among cultures, but there seem to be some tasks of childhood socialization which are almost universal. Children are expected to attain certain goals or master similar tasks if they are going to be successful and accepted individuals in a variety of societies. However, the specific techniques used by parents in helping their children master these apparently universal tasks and the expression of this mastery may be highly idiosyncratic.

Clausen (1968) has proposed the relationships between parental aims and activities and the socialization tasks or achievement of the child; these are presented in Table 11-

Table 11-1 TYPES OF TASKS OF EARLY CHILDHOOD SOCIALIZATION IN THE FAMILY

Parental aim or activity	Child's task or achievement
1. Provision of nurturance and physical care	Acceptance of nurturance (development of trust)
2. Training and channeling of physiological needs in toilet training, weaning, provision of solid foods, etc.	Control of the expression of biological impulses; learning acceptable channels and times of gratification
3. Teaching and skill-training in language, perceptual skills, physical skills, self-care skills in order to facilitate care, insure safety, etc.	Learning to recognize objects and cues; language learning; learning to walk, negotiate obstacles, dress, feed self, etc.
4. Orienting the child to his immediate world of kin, neighborhood, community, and society, and to his own feelings	Developing a cognitive map of one's social world; learning to fit behavior to situational demands
5. Transmitting cultural and subcultural goals and values and motivating the child to accept them for his own	Developing a sense of right and wrong; developing goals and criteria for choices, investment of effort for the common good
6. Promoting interpersonal skills, motives, and modes of feeling and behaving in relation to others	Learning to take the perspective of another person; responding selectively to the expectations of others
7. Guiding, correcting, helping the child to formulate his own goals, plan his own activities.	Achieving a measure of self-regulation and criteria for evaluating own performance

Source: J. Clausen, Perspectives on childhood socialization. In J. A. Clausen (Ed.), *Socialization and society*. Boston: Little, Brown, 1968. P. 141.

1. The timing and techniques involved in the parent's behavior and the achievement of mastery by the child for these tasks vary in different societies, but mastery of these tasks at some point in the course of socialization is essential in all cultures.

METHODOLOGICAL PROBLEMS IN THE STUDY OF PARENT-CHILD RELATIONS

Nowhere in the field of child development are greater methodological problems encountered than in the study of parent-child relations. Usually the investigator wants to determine the relationship between parental characteristics, attitudes, and childrearing practices and the personality and cognitive and social development of the child. The assumption is often made that the behavior of the parent determines the behavior of the child. However, since most childrearing studies are correlational, such cause and effect relationships cannot be inferred (Bell, 1968). The frequently reported finding of a correlation between physical punishment, rejection, and inconsistent discipline in parents and aggression or delinquency in sons does not necessarily mean that these discipline practices led to the deviant behavior in the children. It may well be that a constitutionally active, irritable, demanding son causes parents to use increasingly more severe methods of control. A parent may begin by reasoning with or lecturing the son. If this is ineffective, mild deprivation of privileges, such as no TV for a week, may be used; this measure may also be ineffective. Then the parent may begin spanking the child. Finally, if these measures are unsuccessful, the parent becomes more frustrated, punitive, and erratic in discipline and desperately tries a variety of methods to cope with the recalcitrant child's aggression; he finally rejects the child. Thus, constitutional predispositions in the child may cause the parents' childrearing practices. This is obviously an extreme example. It is more accurate to view the family in terms of an interacting unit in which the characteristics and behavior of each family member interact with and shape the responses of all other members. However, no parent who has yielded to the relentless cries of an infant at three o'clock in the morning in spite of a firm resolve to let him "cry himself out," ever doubts that the infant plays an active role in socializing the parents.

In the case of battered children, where the child is severely injured or even killed by parental mistreatment, the behavior of the child sometimes seems to contribute to the parental violence. Although the parents of battered children are frequently emotionally immature, unstable, frustrated individuals, their abused children are often reported to be difficult children (Gil, 1970). A higher than normal incidence of birth anomalies, physical and intellectual deviations, irritability, excessive crying with a peculiar and extremely irritating cry, fussiness, negativism, and other behaviors that exasperate the parents are found in many of these children. The parents feel they are being abused by the abused child. This negative perception of the battered child by his parents could be regarded as a means of their justifying their own cruelty. However, it is commonly found that other children in the families of battered children are not abused. In addition, in some cases, when abused children have been removed from their own homes and placed in foster homes, foster parents who have not previously been harsh with other children have severely mistreated and abused the "battered child."

Although it would be unfair to say the battered child always "brought it on himself," in the case of child abuse as in other parent-child interactions the child is often an active participant in shaping his parents' responses.

Questionnaires and interviews

The methods used to investigate family relations include parental questionnaires and interviews, direct observation, and laboratory analogue studies. Questionnaires and interviews often provide unreliable, inaccurate, and systematically distorted data. The task which the parent is being asked to perform during an interview or questionnaire is a difficult one. The parent is being asked to recall details which have occurred in the past, to rate him- or herself and the child in relation to dimensions of childrearing which are meaningful to psychologists but may have little to do with the way the parent thinks about parenthood, and to formulate attitudes or principles which determine his or her behavior toward the child. In the face of such a challenge, it is not surprising to find little agreement of reports over time or between different sources of information, and distortion in the direction of idealized expectations, precocity, and cultural stereotypes. Unless their child is grossly retarded, few parents report their child's development as slow. Instead the child is recalled as having walked and talked a little earlier and as having attained better grades in school than was actually the case and may be described as active and playful, a "real boy," rather than more aptly as the scourge of the neighborhood. In a 1963 study by Robbins, the retrospective reports of childrearing practices of parents of three-year-old children were compared with those that had previously been gathered over the course of the first three years as part of a longitudinal study. It was found that parental distortions in recall which occurred were in the direction of greater agreement with the opinions of experts and the writings of Dr. Spock. For example, Dr. Spock in his 1957 book, *Baby and Child Care,* approves of use of a pacifier and disapproves of thumbsucking. In this study all mothers who were inaccurate in their reports of thumbsucking and even those who at the time were recorded as having reported their concern to their physicians about their children's thumbsucking, denied that their children had ever sucked their thumbs. In contrast, most of the mothers who inaccurately recalled their use of pacifiers reported that they had used one when the actual records showed that they had not.

Parents with more than one child are also likely to have their memories of their children's past behaviors confused. On being asked to describe an individual child, often what the parent produces is a composite child. Just as parents sometimes confuse their children and call them by each others names, they confuse who did what, and to whom. Although parent attitude questionnaires and reports of early child-training practices are seldom able to predict independently assessed child behavior (Becker & Krug, 1964; Yarrow, Campbell, & Burton, 1968), some improvement in such predictions is obtained by focusing on specific current practices rather than broad retrospective attitudes (Winder & Rau, 1962; Bell, 1964; Kagan & Moss, 1962).

For example, rather than asking a mother to respond to the broad question, "Do you believe that children should not be permitted to defy or aggress against their parents?" an interviewer might begin with a general statement followed by increasingly specific probes such as:

Most parents encounter times when their child talks back to them, or gets angry at them or uses physical aggression towards them.
When _____gets angry at you, what does he (she) do?
a. Does _____ever shout at you? Answer back? How often?
b. Has _____ever struck you? Thrown things around the house? How often?
c. Stamped out of the house? Slammed doors? How often?
d. How much of this sort of thing have you allowed? What do you do?
e. (If this doesn't happen) How have you taught him (her) not to do these things?
Can you remember the most recent occasion when _____was angry or put out with you? Try and remember as many details as you can: When _____did, what was your reaction, how did _____react to any attempt on your part to discipline him (her)? In general let's try and reconstruct the actual sequence of who did what and the feelings that the two of you had.

The behavioral scientist is interested in quantifying data; therefore independent raters later would rate this section of the interview on 4-point scales specifically constructed to assess permissiveness and severity of punishment for disobedience and anger at the parent. For example:

Rating I
Permissive with respect to talking back, deliberate disobedience, shouting at parent, or other forms of showing anger at parent.
1. Not at all permissive. Would stop immediately. Would never ignore. Not permitted under any circumstances.
2. Would discourage rather firmly, but would expect some expression of anger toward parent to occur occasionally.
3. Moderately permissive. Sometime overlook, sometimes restrain, depending on circumstances.

4. Very permissive. Would not restrain child, unless he (she) likely to hurt parent.

Rating II

Punishment for talking back, or other forms of expressing anger at parent.

1. No punishment. Might talk to child, distract him (her) in some way, or explain why he (she) should not aggress toward me.
2. Mild punishment, consisting of "talking to" or mild reprimand, or withdrawing some small privilege.
3. Moderate punishment, consisting of scolding, or withdrawal of more important privileges, a mild spanking or slap, or warnings of even more severe punishment. You feel some irritation or anger as you give punishment.
4. Strong punishment. Severe scolding, perhaps shouting, or spanking or other physical punishment. Parent feels very angry with child.

This gives the psychologist a means of comparing the responses of different parents or groups of parents to similar children's behavior. It should be noted that the interview questions and the scales are structured to assess the parents' behaviors in the specific situation involving anger at the parent. There is no assumption that the parent would be similarly permissive or punitive in situations involving aggression against peers or other forms of misbehavior around the house. Different questions must be used to assess parental responses to those situations.

Another strategy is to use children's reports of parents behavior rather than parents' reports of their own attitudes and behaviors. It can be argued rather convincingly that children's perception of their parents' attitudes are more important in their development than what the parents true feelings may be. A son may feel rejected by a father who really loves him but believes that men don't show emotion and that high standards and strict discipline are necessary to develop strong moral character in the young. The child's belief that his father does not find him worthy of love rather than the father's real attitude might result in the development of feelings of inadequacy and low self-esteem in the son.

Direct observation

In order to circumvent some of the problems in interviews and questionnaires experimenters have resorted to the use of direct observation of parents and children in a variety of situations ranging from naturalistic home settings to highly structured tasks in the laboratory. Of course, that observational data is valid only to the extent that representative patterns of interaction have not been disrupted or distorted by the presence of the observer or the demands of the situation.

Studies suggest that when families are shifted from familiar to unfamiliar settings, from the home to the laboratory, or from unstructured to structured situations, there is a tendency for family members to express less negative emotion, exhibit more socially desirable responses, and assume socially prescribed behavior. Mothers are more directive and less passively attentive in the home than in the laboratory (Moustakas, Sigel, & Schalock, 1956). Similarly with a shift from the laboratory to the home there is a change from stereotyped sex-role behavior to an increase in the expression of emotion by fathers and more active participation in decision making by mothers (O'Rourke, 1963).

Attempts to minimize such distortions have been made by observing families in familiar situations, permitting a long period of adaptation through frequent sustained observations, and the use of unobtrusive measures. Some experimenters have monitored homes by television or tape recorder during the entire waking hours of the family for periods as long as a month. Other studies have had observers appear at each dinner hour over a period of several weeks. Although it seems anyone would be a little disconcerted when an observer, wearing dark glasses to conceal the direction of his gaze and making notes on a clipboard, appeared regularly with the entree, families report that they gradually almost become unaware of the observation. This is reflected in increases in less socially accepted behaviors, such as quarreling, criticizing, punishing, and using obscene language.

In making such naturalistic home observations the observer usually uses a sheet containing a list of behaviors; on this sheet the observer checks off which behaviors are occurring in a predetermined period of time. For example, if the family was going to be observed for an hour, the observer might divide the hour into 120 thirty-second units. Each time any of the behaviors on the list occurred in a single thirty-second time period, the observer would put a check beside the behavior on the list. This yields the frequency of different kinds of behaviors of family members in the hour session. In addition, by looking at the sequence of behaviors over successive thirty-second time units, a good picture of the interactions between family members emerges. If in the first thirty-second unit the baby throws his cereal, in the next mother slaps the baby, in the third baby cries, and in the fourth mother picks the baby up and cuddles and pats him, a clear stream of behavior is apparent. The analysis of such behavioral sequences allows the psychologist to answer such questions as the following: When the mother criticizes her son what is the most frequent response of the son? Does he ignore her? Argue with her? Yield and accept her criticism and show signs of remorse?

Laboratory analogue studies

Finally, there has been frequent use of laboratory analogue studies of family interaction over the past decade. In such studies a strange adult in the laboratory behaves in some manner assumed to be analogous to important parental behaviors or disciplinary practices. For example, the adult in the laboratory may be affectionate or withdraw attention and warmth, or be actively critical and punitive. The effects of these adult behaviors on the child's subsequent behaviors, such as responsiveness to rewards by the adult, attention seeking, resistance to temptation, or aggression, are then observed. Such controlled, experimental procedures permit greater inferences of cause and effect relationships within the specific laboratory setting. However, can it be assumed that these simplistic, restricted laboratory interactions of extremely short duration with strangers parallel the experience in intense, sustained, complex parent-child relations? It can be argued persuasively that an experimenter's giving children candy, praising them, and smiling differs qualitatively from the nurturance and warmth of a loving parent, or that a periodic criticism and removal of reward by a stranger is in no way similar to the overwhelming, inescapable, unpredictable threat of an erratic, punitive, rejecting parent.

Because of the limitations in all of the methods used to study family interaction, many investigators have recently begun using multiple measures of family relations, with the hope that convergence of the findings based on different assessment techniques implies greater validity of the results.

PARENT-CHILD INTERACTION

We will begin our discussion of parent-child interaction with a presentation of how emotional bonds between the parent and child develop in infancy. These affective ties are important because they will serve as the prototype for later relationships and will influence the effectiveness of parents and children in shaping each others behavior.

Attachment

At some time during the first year of life children seek to be near certain specific people, and their attempts to maintain contact frequently elicit reciprocal nurturant or attentive responses from the objects of their attention. This relationship is referred to as *attachment* or *dependency* and is characterized by strong affect. The first object of attachment is usually, but not always, the mother. Behaviors such as protest in the form of crying or pursuit at separation from the mother, approach and seeking physical contact, reduction of distress in the presence of the mother, smiling and looking at the mother, and the effectiveness of the mother as a reinforcing agent have all been used as measures of attachment. The various measures used to assess attachment are only modestly intercorrelated (Coates, Anderson, & Hartup, 1972; Maccoby & Feldman, 1972).

There is extensive interest in attachment formation not only because it is a widespread and often extremely intense and dramatic phenomenon, but also because attachment is thought to enhance the parents' effectiveness in later socialization of the child. The child who is strongly attached to his parent is more likely to be concerned about maintaining parental love and approval through adopting socialized behaviors than is the weakly attached child.

The issues in attachment which have been the focus of greatest theorizing and research have been the parental characteristics and childrearing practices associated with attachment, the sequence and timing of attachment behaviors, and the relationship of attachment to other cognitive and emotional responses, such as the development of object permanence and fear of strangers.

Theories of attachment The role of the parent in caretaking functions, which are essential for the survival of the child, especially in feeding, has been regarded by psychoanalysts and by many learning theorists as critical in attachment formation. Freudians postulate that the infant has an innate need to suck, which interacts with and is modified by actual feeding experiences. This need for oral gratification through sucking and other forms of stimulation of the mouth results in the infant becoming attached to the satisfying mother's breast and ultimately to the mother herself. Learning theorists suggest that since the caretaker is associated with the satisfaction and reduction of a variety of needs, she acquires secondary reinforcing and secondary drive properties. That is, eventually just the presence of the mother becomes satisfying and the child develops an acquired need for contact with the mother, which is referred to as attachment.

The relative importance of the specific needs involved in attachment formation has been a controversial issue. Some theorists have emphasized proximal stimulation, such as rocking, contact comfort, feeding, and cleanliness; this type of stimulation involves close contact with the child and depends largely on sensations of touch, temperature, and movement. Others have emphasized distal stimulation, in which the caretaker need not be in direct contact with the infant; this includes auditory input through the caretakers' talking or singing and visual stimulation, such as presentation of different toys and shifts in the visual field due to movement. In most parent-infant interactions it is apparent that both distal and proximal stimulation occur simultaneously. When the hungry baby cries, the mother appears, picks the infant up (thereby giving him both tactual stimulation and changing his visual field by the shift in position), and rocks, talks to, and feeds the infant. This cannot be regarded as a situation in which the child alone is gaining satisfaction. The mother is gratified by her contact with the child and her ability to terminate the unpleasant stimulation of his crying. This mutually gratifying relationship results not only in attachment of the child to the mother but in attachment of the mother to the child as well. As parent and infant gain a sense of mutual control, competence, and satisfaction in dealing with each other, the bonds of attachment develop.

Some more ethologically oriented theorists (Ainsworth, 1969; Bowlby, 1958, 1960) have generalized from observations and studies with animals and have suggested that attachment is a result of instinctive behaviors which are essential for the protection of the young and their survival in a variety of species. Infant behaviors such as crying, smiling, and babbling elicit contact with the mother, and certain characteristics of the mother, such as her voice, face, or touch, instinctively elicit attachment behavior in offspring. Thus the infant is instinctively ready to respond to specific stimuli that emanate from the caretaker with specific behaviors that will elicit and control the responses of others.

It has also been suggested that the infant will be more receptive to certain types of sensory and social input at specific stages of development. Initially proximal behaviors involving contact will be most important, but as the child matures, visual stimulation and sounds such as the mother's voice become more salient in attachment formation.

The development of attachment The development of attachment proceeds through a consistent sequence of stages. A longitudinal study of attachment, in which sixty Scottish infants were studied at four-week intervals during the first year of life with an additional follow-up session at eighteen months, investigated this sequence of attachment behaviors (Schaffer & Emerson, 1964). The amount of protest behavior manifested by the children in a variety of specific separation situations (for example, being left in a pram outside shops, being left in a crib, etc.) was reported by the mothers in monthly interviews, and monthly observations were made of the infants' fear responses to the increasing approach of the strange interviewer.

In the first six months of life the infant developed indiscriminate attachments to people: he cried for attention and contact from strangers or close acquaintances alike. However, at about seven months of age very intense attachments to specific people appeared. The child protested only when separation from certain people occurred. The mother was usually, but not always, the main person to whom the child became attached, and many children were attached to more than one person. Other studies have found the same pattern in the development of separation protest and have found that protest is highest between twelve and eighteen months (Kotelchuck, 1972). The developmental course of these attachments is presented in Figure 11-1. In looking at Figure

11-1, it is important to remember that these ages represent averages and that there is considerable variation among babies in the timing of attachments. About one month after the emergence of specific attachments, some children show fear of strangers. Infants in this study who developed specific attachments early were also found to manifest early fear of strangers.

These investigators emphasize the role of the child's level of cognitive development in the emergence of specific attachments and fear of strangers. Before such responses can occur, the infant must be able to differentiate between mother and stranger and must be aware that people still exist when they are not visible. In the Piagetian sense the child must have developed object permanence, or the knowledge that objects, including humans, have a continuous existence. The child is unlikely to protest or call for a person who is out of sight if he is not aware that they still exist when he cannot see them.

Other findings also suggest that cognitive factors play a role in the amount of protest a child shows at separation from a parent. Increased protest is likely to occur when the child is able to recognize that he is in an unfamiliar situation, when he is with strange people, or when something unexpected is occurring. In terms of Piagetian concepts, he is relating his new experiences to previously formed schemata and perceiving a discrepancy from his past experiences. Children protest less when the mother leaves them at home than in the laboratory, and they protest more in the home when the mother leaves through a door she seldom uses than when she departs through a door she uses often (Littenberg, Tulkin, & Kagan, 1971). The infant knows that he is in a strange situation or that something unusual is happening. In addition, the child is more likely to cry if the parent leaves the child in a room with a stranger rather than with the other parent (Kotelchuck, 1972; Spelke, Zelazo, Kagan, & Kotelchuck, 1973).

Although other studies show cultural influences and individual differences in the time these behaviors emerge, this general developmental pattern is frequently found. There is some evidence that the ability to discriminate mother from strangers may emerge earlier than suggested by Schaffer and Emerson. A study of infants in Ghana, Africa, showed that specific attachments emerged slightly earlier and fear of strangers later than in the Scottish sample (Ainsworth & Salter, 1963; Ainsworth, Salter, & Wittig, 1967). Similarly, a study in which three-month-old infants showed greater increases in smiling when their smiles were reinforced by the cough, smiles, and voice of their mothers than when they

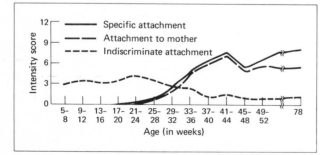

FIGURE 11-1 Developmental course of attachments. (From Schaffer, H. R., & Emerson, P. E., 1964.)

were reinforced by strangers, indicates that they must be able to discriminate between these reinforcing agents at this early age (Wahler, 1957).

Maternal behavior and attachment in infancy   Schaffer and Emerson not only described the development of attachment but examined the effects of maternal behavior on attachment. Contrary to the predictions of both psychoanalytic and learning theory, specific child-training practices associated with feeding and toilet training were *not* associated with measures of attachment, nor was the type of maternal stimulation, whether proximal or distal. Even maternal availability and amount of contact with the child was not a significant factor. Rather infants were attached to adults who responded quickly to their demands and cries and who spontaneously sought and initiated interactions with them. Hence, when a relatively unstimulating mother, that is, one who tends to avoid contact with her infant except for routine physical care, is combined with an attentive, stimulating father, the child is more likely to form a paternal attachment despite the greater amount of routine contact with the mother. As was true in the studies of the effects of early institutionalization, stimulation plus a sense of control over the environment seem to be critical factors in early infant social development. Longitudinal studies which have used direct observational measures of mother-child interactions rather than maternal reports have also found that parental stimulation, particularly in response to the infant's signals, are important in attachment formation (Ainsworth, 1964; Ainsworth & Bell, 1969; Caldwell, Wright, Honig, & Tannenbaum, 1970).

On the basis of reinforcement theory, it might be thought that rapid responding to the infant's signals such as his crying would strengthen the crying response and result in a spoiled, demanding, squalling baby. Instead there is evidence that maternal responsiveness in the first three quarters of the first year of life is associated with decreased crying in the next quarter. In contrast, early lack of maternal responsiveness is related to increased infant crying in the last three months of the first year (Ainsworth, Bell, & Stayton, in press). In addition, this type of maternal responsiveness leads to securely emotionally attached children who manifest an adaptive balance between seeking and enjoying contact with the mother and being able to use her as a "secure base" for exploration (Ainsworth, 1973; Ainsworth & Bell, 1969; Ainsworth et al., in press).

In another study Ainsworth and her colleagues observed a group of white middle-class mothers interacting with their infants for four-hour sessions every three weeks from birth until fifty-four weeks of age. At about one year of age, observations of the infants' attachment and exploratory behavior were made in a series of standard situations involving various combinations of the infant with presence or absence of the mother and a stranger.

One group of infants were clearly attached to the mother, as shown by occasional seeking to be close to and touching the mother when she was present, and intensified contact-maintaining behavior following being left alone in a strange situation. This group felt secure enough to explore and manipulate a strange environment when their mothers were present. They did not cling and whine, but were curious and manipulative in dealing with toys and other objects in the unfamiliar situation when their mother was with them. In familiar situations such as the home, with ordinary minor separations these children were minimally disturbed although they greeted the mother's return with enthusiasm. All children in this group had mothers who had permitted them to play an active role in determining the pacing, onset, and termination of feeding early in life. It should be noted again that it is not the particular child-care practice but the responsiveness and sensitivity to the infant's needs that are important in attachment.

Some of the infants showed frequent intense distress and crying when the mother was either present or absent, and either lacked interest in contact with the mother or showed ambivalence about contact by such things as intermittent proximity seeking accompanied with angry pushing away and rejection of the mother. These infants had mothers who had been insensitive in the early feeding situation.

Either extreme clinging and apprehensiveness or indifference to the mother might be regarded as undesirable. A smooth balance between exploratory and attachment behavior may serve as a positive foundation for future affectional relations and strivings for mastery. A constructive closeness to the parent should facilitate rather than stifle the type of independence necessary for later achievement and social relations.

Children's behavior and parent-child attachment   All infants do not become attached equally easily to their parents. Nor is parental attachment to children inevitable.

In Chapter 2 a distinction between cuddlers and noncuddlers was made. Cuddlers were infants who enjoyed being held and cuddled. Noncuddlers protested at being restrained and held but were soothed by visual and auditory stimulation. Attachment is slower in developing in noncuddlers. At one year of age cuddlers are more attached than noncuddlers; however by eighteen months the two types of infants seem to be equally attached.

In addition to individual differences in infants leading to variations in their pattern of attachment formation, the behavior of the infant affects the mother's attachment to the child. Many mothers report feeling distressed or deviant because they feel so little deep affection for their infants in the first few months of life. Affection in these mothers usually increases as the child begins to smile, look at, and respond more to her. In some cases the mother may be enthusiastic about the infant during pregnancy and affectionate in the early weeks after birth, but become increasingly less attached to a difficult infant. If the infant is unresponsive to holding, cries and fusses excessively, and is late in smiling and looking at the mother's eyes, the mother's feelings of attachment may never develop or may diminish (Robson & Moss, 1970).

Compatible needs between the parent and child should facilitate attachment. If the parent has a need for physical contact with her child, it may be difficult for her to adapt to a noncuddler. If she persists in holding her infant, he will become increasingly irritable and ultimately neither parent nor child may be attached to each other. In contrast, the combination of an infant who is a cuddler and a "cuddly" mother would seem to be a more auspicious foundation for attachment.

Changes in attachment with age   Although the terms attachment and dependency are frequently used interchangeably, two different types of dependency are distinguished in children beyond infancy. The first, called *emotional dependency,* involves seeking the affection, approval, and proximity of others. This is similar to the concept of attachment in infancy. The second type of dependency involves seeking help and attention and is called *instrumental dependency.*

A healthy attachment to parents should increase the child's trust in other social relationships. Some degree of emotional dependency is necessary for mature affectionate relationships. In contrast, early attachment should decrease the child's later instrumental dependency because he will have had the security necessary for exploration, curiosity, and mastery of his environment.

Changes in the objects and forms of attachment behavior occur with age. In general, children shift from parents to peers as objects of attachment; and dependency changes from clinging, touching, and proximity-seeking to attention-seeking behaviors, such as seeking reassurance, help, and approval. Dependent behavior is more stable across time for girls than for boys, perhaps because expressions of tender emotions and help-seeking are regarded as more culturally appropriate in females than males.

A marked decline in attachment behavior toward the mother in an unfamiliar situation with a stranger occurs at about age four (Marvin, 1972). In most species a decline in mother-infant attachment behaviors is accompanied by increased communication skills in the offspring. The communication may be in the form of subtle nonverbal communications. In four-year-old children a decrease in proximity seeking toward the mother is accompanied by the rather sudden emergence of a constellation of behaviors which might be labeled "coyness," which is directed toward adults (Marvin, Marvin, & Abramovitch, 1973). Coy behaviors include such things as a lowering of the head to the shoulders; a sideways glance; an open mouth with the lower lip stretched over the bottom teeth and the tongue protruding; a stance with the belly protruding; and touching gestures toward the face involving such things as scratching or picking the nose, covering the mouth or putting a finger in it, primping the hair, etc. Figure 11-2 shows

FIGURE 11-2 This girl exhibits some of the characteristics of coyness.

some of these characteristics. These behaviors are interpreted as an attempt by the child to elicit gentle, playful, nonaggressive feelings in the stranger partly by mimicking some of the characteristics of human infants which make them particularly attractive to adults, such as the rounded cheeks and belly. The child at four, rather than seeking protection from the stranger by the mother, is evolving his own methods of communicating and coping with unfamiliar people.

It might be asked whether intensity of attachment or dependency on the mother generalizes with age to attachment to others, or even whether dependency on adults is related to dependency on children. Preschool children who maintain close contact with their mothers also seek to be near their nursery school teachers (Maccoby & Feldman, 1972). In addition, the study by Rosenthal (1965, 1967a, 1967b) presented in Box 11-1 suggests that children who are highly dependent on their mothers are also dependent on adult strangers and that anxiety-producing conditions increase dependency on both the mother and the stranger in children. By nursery-school age, children who trust and gain security from their mothers also gain solace from other adults.

Although children who are dependent on one adult tend to be dependent on others, the evidence for a correlation between dependent behaviors directed toward adults and toward other children is more questionable. Although there is some suggestion that seeking attention from adults may be related to seeking attention from peers, there is no evidence that this is true of seeking proximity and physical contact. In fact, in some extreme cases under stress or disruption of the home situation, attachment to peers may be negatively related to dependency on adults, as is reported in some studies of delinquents or war orphans. Children who are unable to gain security in close relations with their parents may reject all adults and seek intimate relations elsewhere.

A famous study (Freud & Dann, 1951) of six German-Jewish orphans, separated from their parents at an early age because of World War II and placed in an institution, tells how the children formed intense, protective attachments to each other while ignoring or being actively hostile to their adult caretakers. The children had lost their parents before the age of one, most commonly in gas chambers. When they were in their fourth year of life, they arrived at Bulldog Banks, a small English country home which had been transformed into a nursery for war children. They had lived together in various concentration camps and institutions since their first year of life. Their stay at Bulldog Banks was their first experience in living in a small, intimate setting.

In their early days at Bulldog Banks they were wild and uncontrollable. They destroyed or damaged much of the furniture and all of their toys within a few days. Usually they ignored adults but when they were angry they would bite, spit, or swear at them, often called them blöder ochs (stupid fool), which seemed to be their favorite epithet for their caretakers.

The contrast between their hostile behavior toward their caretakers and their solicitous, considerate behavior toward other children in their group was surprising. In one case, when a caretaker accidentally knocked over one of the children, two of the other children threw bricks at her and called her names. The children resisted being separated from each other even for special treats such as pony rides. When one child was ill, the others wanted to remain with her. They showed little envy, jealousy, rivalry, or competition with each other. The sharing and helping behavior the children showed was remarkable in children of this age.

BOX 11-1 THE GENERALIZATION OF DEPENDENCY BEHAVIORS FROM MOTHER TO STRANGERS

This study investigated the relation between children's dependency responses to their mothers or to a stranger and the effects of stress on the frequency of dependency responses. Dependency responses of sixty-four English preschool girls toward their mother and a strange female were measured in separate sessions. Half of the girls were observed under high-anxiety-inducing conditions and half under low-anxiety-inducing conditions. The girls' dependency responses were recorded when they were in either the stressful or unstressful situation with their mother or the stranger.

The procedures to increase or minimize stress were as follows: In the low-anxiety condition the child played in an observation room with an array of various toys and pictures of smiling faces. From outside the room the sound of children's songs played at regular three-minute intervals could be heard. In contrast, in the high-anxiety condition no such benign atmosphere greeted the child. The room contained no toys, only a stainless steel tray, a slow-burning alcohol lamp, a pair of scissors, white tissue paper, and a pencil. In addition,

. . . the pictures of the smiling faces were replaced with a group of sad faces. The sound track from the adjacent room was made up of the following sounds: a loud banging on a metal object, a child crying and a high-pitched shriek. Each sound was on for about 20 seconds. The tray with the burning lamp stood on a chair next to the red door leading to the room from which the sounds came. After about 12 minutes, and following a loud continuous shriek, the red door opened very slowly and a hand in an arm-length black glove reaching in slowly, put out the lamp and withdrew, closing the door once more. Within two or three minutes, a crying sound was heard [Rosenthal, 1967, pp. 122–123].

This clearly would be an extremely stressful situation for a young child; in fact, it would be disturbing to many adults. Children who were categorized as dependent outside the testing situation showed more dependent responses toward both mother and stranger in the test situation than did low-dependent children. Children who gained solace from being close to the mother also felt more secure when they were near the stranger. Although stress increased the children's proximity-seeking responses, it did not increase their instrumental dependency responses, such as seeking help and attention. Stress increased children's desire to be near and to cling to both their mother and the stranger, but it was found that more dependency responses were directed to the mother than to the stranger under both high- and low-anxiety conditions. Although there is a generalization of dependency to the stranger, the child is more strongly attached to and more readily gains solace from the mother.

Source: Rosenthal, M. K. The generalization of dependency behaviors from mother to stranger. *Journal of Child Psychology and Psychiatry*, 1967, **8,** 117–133.

The following are typical incidents in their first seven months at Bulldog Banks:

The children were eating cake, and John began to cry when he saw there was no cake left for a second helping. Ruth and Miriam, who had not yet finished their portions, gave him the remainder of their cake and seemed happy just to pet him and comment on his eating the cake.

On another occasion when one child lost his gloves, although it was very cold another child loaned his gloves without complaining about his own discomfort.

The investigators cited the following incidents where even in fearful situations children were able to overcome their trepidation to help the others in the group:

A dog approaches the children, who are terrified. Ruth, though badly frightened herself, walks bravely to Peter who is screaming and gives him her toy rabbit to comfort him. She comforts John by lending him her necklace.

On the beach in Brighton, Ruth throws pebbles into the water. Peter is afraid of waves and does not dare to approach them. In spite of his fear, he suddenly rushes to Ruth, calling out: "Water coming, water coming," and drags her back to safety. (From A. Freud & S. Dann, 1951, pp. 150–168).

When finally positive relations with adults began to be formed, they were made on the basis of group feelings and had none of the demanding, possessive attitudes often shown by young children toward their own mothers. They began to include adults in their group and to treat them in some ways as they treated each other. This seemed to be a phase of general attachments which for some of the children was eventually followed by specific attachment toward an individual caretaker, with clinging and possessiveness appearing. During their year's stay at Bulldog Banks the intensity of the children's attachment to their surrogate mothers was never as intense as in normal mother-child relations and never as binding as those to their peers.

The parent as a teacher

Early attachment of the parent to the child and the child to the parent in infancy serve as the foundation for later family relationships. Although socialization is certainly occurring in the first year of life, it seems to become more conscious and systematic with the occurrence of greater mobility and the beginning of language in the second year. Behaviors that previously were accepted, indulged, or regarded as "cute" start to be limited. Feet are not longer permitted on the high chair tray, smearing food is frowned on, exploration is restrained by playpen bars, and serious attempts at toilet training begin. As the child is practicing his new-found motor skills and exploring the world about him, climbing out of his crib, tottering to the head of the stairs, discovering the delights of the pot and pan cupboard, or eating cigarette butts, the air may be ringing with "Nos!" "Don'ts!" and "Stops!" The child will also be cuddled, petted, and praised for his achievements, for learning to use a spoon, for naming objects, for repeating words, for dry diapers, for the many behaviors that mother and society regard as desirable. The process of socialization has begun in earnest. The parent teaches the child the rules of the society in which he must live by telling the child what the rules are and by disciplining him as he conforms to or violates acceptable standards of behavior. In addition, parents will modify their children's behavior by serving as models for the child to imitate. The effectiveness of parents as teachers depends on their emotional relationship with the child and on the number and type of controls they attempt to exert.

Dimensions of parental behavior Parents' relationships to their children have frequently been conceptualized in terms of the interaction between two sets of parental attributes which are assumed to be relatively independent: warmth-hostility and control-autonomy. In a variety of studies based on both self-report and observational measures

different kinds of families

of parent attitudes and practices these key dimensions have emerged, sometimes in conjunction with less significant factors. The first factor deals with the emotional relationship of the parent with the child, the second with controls and restrictions placed upon the child's behavior. In general the parent's love dimension is more stable over time than the control dimension. Schaffer's model of the interaction between these dimensions is presented in Figure 11-3. A useful, but oversimplified typology of parent behaviors emerges by studying the interaction of the two dimensions in each of the quadrants in Figure 11-3. The *democratic family* would be one in which the parents were loving and permissive, allowing the child considerable exploration and self-determination in an atmosphere of warmth and support. The combination of love and restrictiveness in which the child's activities are curtailed by loving, intrusive parents is frequently called the *overprotective family*. In contrast, when hostility is combined with restrictiveness, a family often labeled as *authoritarian* emerges. Finally, the combination of laxness and hostility is associated with neglect and rejection.

In addition to these dimensions, investigators have focused on the specific disciplinary techniques imposed on the child when being taught to behave in a desirable way. These disciplinary characteristics include such things as the use of reasoning and explanation versus physical forms of discipline, or the use of affection and threats of withdrawal of love versus material rewards and withdrawal of privileges, or the inconsistency or regularity with which discipline is administered. These variables are not independent. Hostile restrictiveness is related to frequent use of physical punishment and high reasoning is associated with warmth in both mothers and fathers (Becker, Peterson, Luria, Shoemaker, & Hellmer, 1962).

The critical question must now be answered: Do these variations in parental behavior relate in any systematic way to differences in social and cognitive development?

Parental attitudes, childrearing practices, and child behavior

Parental warmth or hostility. Parental warmth is regarded as important in the socialization process for two reasons. First, the child is likely to fear the disapproval and loss of

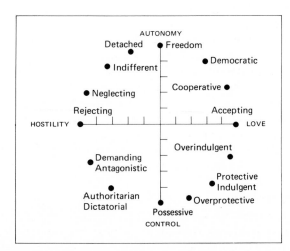

FIGURE 11-3 A circumplex model of maternal behaviors which shows the relationship of various types of maternal behavior to love-hostility and autonomy-control. (From Schaeffer, E. S., 1959.)

love of a warm parent, and therefore the need for harsh forms of discipline to gain compliance is often unnecessary. In contrast, the threat of withdrawal of love is unlikely to be an effective mechanism of socialization when used by hostile parents who have little demonstrable affection to rescind. What has the child to lose? Second, the frequent use by warm parents of reasoning and explanation permits the child to internalize social rules and identify and discriminate situations in which a given behavior is appropriate. It is easier to learn the rules of the game if someone tells you what they are and why you should play them that way. If the child reaches for a second piece of cake and his mother says, ''No, you can't have another because your brother hasn't had one yet and there's only one piece left,'' it tells the child the circumstances under which he cannot have cake. At a future time he might anticipate that if everyone in the family had had cake or if there were many pieces left he would be permitted a second. This is in marked contrast to the effects of a peremptory parental ''No!'', where the child doesn't know if eating cake is bad, eating cake with hands is not permitted, he is bad, or the parent is mad. Even on those occasions when physical punishment is utilized by warm parents, they report it is more effective in limiting their child's behavior than do hostile parents. Again, this is probably both because the child wishes to conform to the standards of warm parents and because these parents are more likely to provide information about alternative socially desirable responses available to the child. These findings are consistent with the results of the laboratory studies of punishment effectiveness that were discussed earlier in Chapter 7.

There are other reasons why hostile parents may be ineffective in inhibiting their children's behavior, particularly aggressive behavior. When physical punishment is used to control aggression, the hostile parent is also in the anomalous situation of frustrating the child, which may lead to greater arousal of anger, and of offering an aggressive model to the child. Field studies of delinquents which find the presence of a criminal parent to be associated with delinquency would seem to support this position. As might be expected under such circumstances the child usually exhibits little overt aggression in the home toward the threatening parents, but displaces it to others outside the home where he is less fearful of retaliation.

A puzzle: warmth, punitiveness, and dependency. To illustrate the complexity of the relationships between parental warmth, hostility, and type of control, let us consider the puzzling problem of dependency in children. If all we knew about a parent was that he frequently criticized and strapped his child and avoided his company, or that he enjoyed spending time with his son and often praised him and told him what a great boy he was, we would still not be able to predict dependence or independence of the child. No simple relationship exists between hostility or warmth in the parent and dependency in the child. When children have parents who are nurturant and permit or actively reinforce dependent behavior, the children are dependent; however, when parents are nurturant, but value and encourage independent behavior, their children are more socially autonomous. Loving parents who are still buttoning buttons and tying shoelaces for school-age children, doing their homework, intervening and protecting them in altercations with their peers, and solving all their problems are likely to have dependent children. In contrast, warm parents who encourage children to bathe, feed, and dress themselves early, to work through their own difficulties with their peers, and to enjoy mastering tasks in the world about them will have more independent, striving children.

The fact that warm parents are effective in shaping both the dependence and independence of their children, or the frequently reported findings that dependency is associated with warm, restrictive parents, and aggression and lack of self-control is found in the offspring of warm, indulgent parents, is not surprising. However, an unexpected finding is that dependency is frequently associated with parental hostility or rejection. Clinicians have often noted that a child who has been removed from punitive, cold parents and placed in a warm foster home will continue to yearn for his natural parents and may even run away and attempt to return to his rejecting home. How can this dependence on apparently nonnurturant parents be explained? It is difficult to explain it on the basis of the acquired reward value of the parent, since a constantly hostile parent should not be rewarding to the child and the child should seek to avoid him. However, few parents are constantly punitive; even hostile parents are intermittently rewarding as well as punishing.

A number of studies have found that withdrawal of nurturance or a combination of intermittent rewards and punishment by an adult for dependent behavior leads to more attention seeking in children than does sustained adult nurturance (Hartup, 1958; Gewirtz, 1954). Sears, Rau, and Alpert (1965) compared children's dependency responses in a laboratory situation where the mother was attentive and helpful as the child solved a puzzle, to those in a situation in which the mother was preoccupied and busy filling out a questionnaire. The child made more dependency overtures when the mother was busy, often clinging, whining, pulling at her clothing, and asking for attention.

Field studies also support the position that rejection and withdrawal of love, which may also imply intermittent reinforcement, are associated with high dependency. Some insight into this baffling situation is given in the results of a study which found that maternal rejection led to increased dependency only when the dependent response was also occasionally rewarded (Sears, Maccoby, & Levin, 1957). In most families mild punishment or nurturance withdrawal by the parent is probably only temporary and the parent will eventually yield to the child's persistent demands for attention. Even the most rejecting parent in exasperation sometimes gives in. The child, on the basis of his past experience, will expect that gratification of his dependency demands will finally be made, and he will remain focused on the parent, soliciting attention and affection until that occurs. As we have repeatedly noted, parent-child interaction is a mutually shaping process.

It will be recalled from the chapter on learning that behaviors acquired on either an intermittent reinforcement schedule or a schedule of both reward and punishment are difficult to extinguish. In real life, mixed schedules are the rule and consistent punishment is relatively rare.

Parental permissiveness or restrictiveness. The effects of parental control interact with the hostility or affection of the parent. Some degree of restriction is necessary if the child is to develop self-control. Either extreme of parental control leads to deficient development in these characteristics. Baumrind (1967) suggests that *authoritative* rather than *authoritarian* parental control is desirable; in the former, parents are not intrusive and do permit the child considerable freedom within reasonable limits, but are willing to impose restrictions in areas in which they have greater knowledge or insight. Such discipline gives the child the opportunity to explore his environment and gain interpersonal competence without the anxiety and neurotic inhibition associated with hostile, restrictive discipline practices, or the inexperience in conforming to the demands and needs of others associated with extreme permissiveness. In general, high warmth and moderate restrictiveness with the parent setting reasonable limits but being responsive and attentive to the child's needs are associated with the development of self-esteem, adaptability, competence, internalized control, and popularity with peers. This relationship is illustrated in a well-designed study by Baumrind (1967), which is presented in Box 11-2. She identified three groups of children having various characteristics and found that authoritative but not authoritarian behavior by parents led to positive emotional, social, and cognitive development in children.

BOX 11-2 PARENTAL BEHAVIORS AND THE DEVELOPMENT OF SOCIAL COMPETENCE IN CHILDREN

What parental behaviors are associated with the development of social competence or maladaptive behaviors in children? In this study, on the basis of fourteen weeks of behavioral observation of nursery school children, three groups of children exhibiting markedly different behavior were identified. Group I (energetic-friendly) children were rated higher on the following characteristics than were the other two groups: interest and curiosity in approaching novel or stressful situations, self-reliance, self-control, energy level, cheerfulness, and friendly relations with peers. Group II (conflicted-irritable) children were less cheerful and more moody, apprehensive, unhappy, easily annoyed, passively hostile and guileful, and vulnerable to stress than group I children. In interpersonal relations they alternated between aggressive, unfriendly interactions and withdrawal. Group III (impulsive-aggressive) children were even less self-reliant and controlled than group II and seemed to be almost entirely impulsive and lacking in self-control. However, they were more cheerful and recovered more readily from irritations than did group II children. Parent behavior was measured in the home, by interview in a structured observation procedure involving the mother teaching the child some simple mathematical concepts, and in a free play period. Data on parental behavior from all three procedures tended to be congruent.

The parent scores on control, maturity demands, communication, and nurturance in the structured observation and home visit observations are graphed in Figure 11-4. Parents of group I children (energetic-friendly) were more nurturant than parents in the other groups, as measured by high use of positive reinforcement and low use of punishment, and responsiveness to the child's request for support and attention. However, they were not indulgent; they were willing to direct and control the child and were less likely to yield to unpleasant, coercive demands by the child based on crying, whining, and nagging. Baumrind describes their control as *authoritative* rather than *authoritarian* since it was not necessarily extremely restrictive, punitive, rigid, or intrusive. Although these parents did not yield to the child's coercive demands, they more often explicitly altered their position on the basis of specific arguments advanced by the child. They also demanded more mature, independent behavior from their children and explained to their children the reason for their position. Group II parents (conflicted-irritable), in contrast to those in group III (impulsive-aggressive), were more persistent in enforcing their demands in the face of child opposition and coercive techniques by the child. In addition to being less effective in directing their children's behavior than parents in group II, group II parents

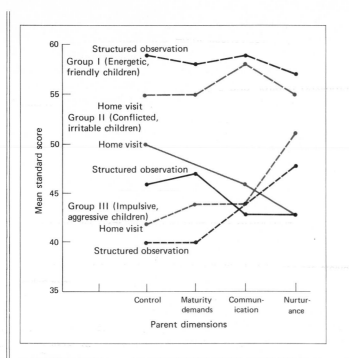

FIGURE 11-4 Profile of composited parent dimension scores from the summary ratings for the structured observation (SRSO) and the home visit sequence analysis (HVSA) for each pattern. (From Baumrind, D., 1957.)

put forth fewer maturity demands and tended to be more nurturant. Group III fathers also used less corporal punishment than did fathers of group II children.

In summary, the energetic, friendly, apparently better adjusted children had parents who provide a combination of high nurturance with high expectations and maturity demands for their children, which were clearly communicated and consistently but not inflexibly enforced. They were willing to listen and respond to reasonable demands by their children. Parents of the conflicted-irritable group seem to exhibit a combination of inflexible, frustrating, nonsupportive responses that might be aggression producing, in combination with punitive responses that may be aggression inhibiting and could well result in the neurotic-like conflict of these children. Finally, the infantilizing, lax, inconsistent discipline of parents of the impulsive-aggressive children and the parents' inability to define and maintain restrictions is associated with lack of self-control and internalization of social standards.

Source: Baumrind, D. Child care practices anteceding three patterns of preschool behavior. *Genetic Psychology Monographs,* 1967, **75,** 43–88.

In a subsequent study Baumrind (1971) used a reverse strategy and rather than initially finding the groups of children and then studying their parents, she first identified groups of parents having clusters of different attributes and then related these to the behavior of their children. The results confirmed many findings of the previous study. Sons of authoritative parents were more friendly, cooperative, and achievement-oriented than those of any other parent groups, and daughters of authoritative parents were more dominant, achievement-oriented, and independent.

Although much of the popular childrearing literature over the past two decades has extolled the virtues of permissiveness, recently concern has been expressed about the effects of lack of control on children. Bronfenbrenner (1970) has argued that children in the United States are no longer brought up by their parents, but that training of children has been relinquished to the mass media, particularly television, with its violent models, and to the anti-adult, anti-establishment, anti-social peer group. This has led to increases in rebelliousness, delinquency, aggression, indifference, and alienation. He likens this to the phenomena in William Golding's *Lord of the Flies,* where civilized values are destroyed by the "quickly rising sadism of peer power." This is contrasted to the Russian childrearing practices, which he regards as more desirable, where parents are warm and directive and use withdrawal of love as the main discipline practice. Although the children are oriented toward the influence of social groups, including peers, these groups are supervised by adults and adolescents and are trained to value respect and obedience for the social order. Many psychologists would not agree with Bronfenbrenner's position and would argue that the ideal childrearing conditions would lie somewhere between the permissiveness of American families and restrictiveness of the Russian home.

Research findings indicate that either extreme on the control scale is associated with some undesirable behavior. Warm restrictive discipline is related to politeness, neatness, and conformity; however, it is also related to immaturity, dependency, blind acceptance of authority, social withdrawal, and low creativity. At the other extreme, warm permissive parents have self-indulgent children who have little impulse control and low achievement standards. If parents do not encourage self-restraint and mastery in social and academic situations, the child is unlikely to value or to acquire such standards.

Although low achievement and impulse control are also associated with hostile permissive parents, in these families they are often accompanied by anti-social aggressive behavior in and out of the home. Finally, the combination of high hostility and restrictiveness is the most devastating to the child's development of a sense of competence. The child sees himself as controlled by powerful, malignant external forces over which he has little influence. This perception is reflected in self-doubting, fearful, rigid approaches to both achievement and interpersonal situations. The child admires but fears authority, and when he reaches adulthood he tends to express his hostility in a devious manner by holding repressive political beliefs, by discriminating against minority groups, and by advocating harsh but socially accepted forms of aggression, such as capital punishment or maximum sentences for minor legal transgressions.

The parent as a model

In addition to playing an important role in socialization by verbalizing the values of the culture and rewarding or punishing the child's behavior in relation to these cultural standards, the parent socializes the child by serving as a model for the child to imitate. Although the process is called by many names, all psychologists recognize that children emulate other persons or groups and that this process leads to increased actual or perceived similarity between the child and these persons. Psychoanalysts have called this process *identification*, learning theorists have called it *imitation* or *modeling*, and sociologists have called it the *adoption of roles.*

The question of which characteristics of a model are acquired and the specific processes involved in the acquisition of such similarities is a controversial one. If the people with whom the child comes in contact exhibit attributes valued by society, socialization is facilitated; if the child is surrounded by deviant models, culturally approved behaviors are less likely to be acquired. Children with emotionally unstable or criminal parents are more likely to develop maladaptive or delinquent patterns of behavior. The child who comes from a family with affectionate, honest, hard-working parents is more likely to demonstrate ethical behavior, a concern for others, and a need to achieve than is a child who has a viciously punitive father and an alcoholic mother and was reared in a slum populated by drug pushers, prostitutes, and pimps.

It is apparent that in most cases children identify with different attributes of a variety of models. A child may exhibit his mother's fear of dogs, his father's sense of humor, his older brother's enthusiasm for Bob Dylan, and his scout master's interest in Indian lore. The characteristics on which individuals can resemble each other seem to range from generalized attitudes, aspirations, and interests to very specific mannerisms and behaviors. Sometimes similarities are manifested as broad cognitive, personality, or social styles which will influence behavior in a variety of situations. Both child and parent may be cautious and systematic in problem solving or concerned about social approval in interpersonal relations. In some cases such shared values or styles of relating to people may cause parent and child to behave alike even in new situations where the child has had no opportunity to observe the responses of his parent. Some of the most important behaviors in which imitation is assumed to play a key role are in moral development and self-control and in the development of masculine and feminine characteristics. The development of these behaviors will be presented in the following two chapters.

Theories of identification and imitation   Since imitation begins early and since the child's major social contacts are largely limited to the family in the preschool years, the role of the parents is critical in the process of identification. Even in the first year of life the child's imitation and the parents' encouragement of imitative behaviors can be seen. The child and parent repeatedly play imitative games such as "peek-a-boo" and "waving bye-bye." The parent echoes the baby's vocalizations and encourages the infant to repeat words after her. Mothers spend hours pointing to objects, naming them, and encouraging the child to repeat the names. Although the parents are the crucial models early in life, as the child gains greater social mobility with age, the role of siblings, peers, social institutions, and mass media become increasingly important.

Various theorists have emphasized different aspects of the parent-child relationship as being most important in the process of identification. The dimensions of parental behavior that have been found to be central in identification are nurturance and warmth, parental power or dominance, and parental aggression and punishment.

Psychoanalytic theory of identification.   The earliest theory that presented a systematic view of identification, and the one from which most other theories are at least partially derived is psychoanalytic theory. In psychoanalytic theory the process of identification is regarded as critical in the formation of the *superego*. The superego comprises the *conscience* and the *ego ideal.* The ego ideal includes idealized standards of behavior, a kind of perfect image which the child uses as a comparative standard and goal for his own behavior. Freud believed that the development of standards for masculine and feminine behaviors was one of the most important aspects of the formation of the ego ideal. It is in part attributable to Freud's great influence on the conceptualization of identification that, although a wide variety of behaviors can be acquired through identification, the two which have been the focus of most research have been moral development and the development of masculinity and femininity. Freud was constantly revising his concept of identification, however, in spite of frequent modification he always described identification as involving an emotional tie with a person, usually the parent. Freud eventually evolved a separate theory of identification for males and females. The theories for the two sexes emphasized different factors during the developmental course of identification, and disparate end results in terms of characteristics of the superegos of the males and females.

Freud recognized two types of identification: the first was *anaclitic* identification, an identification based on fear of loss of love of a nurturant parent; the second was *defensive* identification, an identification with a parent perceived to be powerful and threatening, and aimed at the avoidance of punishment. Freud (1950) suggests that although both types of identification are important for all children, anaclitic identification is more influential in the development of girls and defensive identification, sometimes called *identification with the aggressor,* was more important for boys. Because of their early helplessness, both boys and girls form an initial dependency and emotional attachment on the person responsible for their care, feeding, and protection, usually the mother. Every infant suffers some separation from his mother as the mother goes through the routine of her daily life. No mother can be constantly available to the child or always respond immediately to his cries. Freud believed that when the mother leaves the child or is not attentive to the child, the child becomes apprehensive about the tensions and lack of satisfaction of physical needs which would result from extended withdrawal of the caretaker's love and attention. This infantile fear of the consequences of loss of love of the nurturant parent serves as the basis for anaclitic identification. It was believed that the child gains security and comfort by performing some of the behaviors she has observed in her mother. Imitation of the loving, nurturant parent in itself becomes anxiety reducing and rewarding.

Freud thought that later, at about ages three through five, the boy experiences the *Oedipus complex,* in which he sexually desires his mother, perceives his father as a competitor for his mother's love, and fears retaliation from the father in the form of castration for his incestuous desires. He represses his desires for his mother and resolves his Oedipus complex through identification with the threatening father. This permits the son vicariously to enjoy the mother sexually since the father with whom he now identifies has sexual relations with the mother; in this way the boy also avoids paternal aggression. Hence both anaclitic identification and identification with the aggressor can be viewed as anxiety-reducing mechanisms, the former based on fear of loss of love and the latter on fear of punishment, particularly in the form of castration.

When the child resolves his Oedipus complex by identifying with the like-sexed parent, he internalizes the rules and prohibitions of society as he perceives them in that parent. Since the child at this age regards the parent as unrealistically threatening, powerful, and demanding, the standards which the child internalizes are often more stringent than those actually exhibited by the parent.

Although some psychoanalysts acknowledged a superficial moral development before this age, sometimes called "sphincter morality" since it occurs in a period when the child and parent are concerned with toilet training, true moral behavior cannot be expected until the formation of the superego. Before age three, one may observe the child reaching for the cookie jar while dutifully repeating "No! No!", but he does take and eat the cookie. At this early age no true *internalization* of moral values can have occurred, where the child's behavior will be controlled by moral standards in the absence of external authority or the threat of punishment.

Although this internalization of parental prohibitions accompanied by anxiety for anticipated transgression and guilt following deviation is regarded as essential in normal conscience development, too rigid superego development can lead to neurosis. If the internalized standards are too threatening, too restrictive, or impossible to attain, the child may develop neurotic symptoms associated with chronic anxiety and guilt.

Many students who encounter Freud's theory of identification and the idea of every boy going through an Oedipus complex regard it as rather a wild fantasy. It does seem rather a difficult and complicated way of explaining how children develop consciences and sex-typed behaviors. In addition, the question is often raised as to how it is possible for defensive identification to play a role in the identification of girls. Since it is apparent that fear of castration would not be a threat to females, a parallel motivation to that of boys for resolution of the Oedipus complex and subsequent superego formation cannot exist in girls. Freud (1950) suggests that although females wish to replace their mothers in their fathers' affections, there is no dramatic intense resolution of the Oedipus complex based on fear of punishment. Freud maintained that the female Oedipus complex is never totally abandoned; it gradually decreases but continues to be acted out in subsequent relationships with men other than the father throughout life. Instead of fear of the aggressor leading to identification with the same-sexed parent, a prolongation and intensification of fear of loss of the mother's love based on early infantile anxieties underlies feminine identification. For Freud, this tender pre-Oedipal attachment is critical in the development of culturally appropriate feminine social and sexual responsiveness. However, Freud (1950) concludes that this less intense and complete process of identification has dire implications for the moral development of girls:

> In girls the motive for the destruction of the Oedipus complex is lacking. Castration had already had its effect, which was to force the child into the situation of the Oedipus complex. Thus the Oedipus complex escapes the fate which it meets with in boys; . . . I cannot escape the notion (though I hesitate to give it expression) that for women what is ethically normal is different from what it is in men. Their superego is never so inexorable, so impersonal, so independent of its emotional origins as we require it to be in men. Character traits which critics of every epoch have brought up against women—that they show less sense of justice than men, that they are less ready to submit to the great necessities of life, that they are more often influenced in their judgments by feelings of affection and hostility—all these would be amply accounted for by the modification in the formation of their superego which we have already inferred. We must not allow ourselves to be deflected from such conclusions by the denials of feminists, who are anxious to force us to regard the two sexes as completely equal in position and worth; but we shall, of course, willingly agree that the majority of men are also far behind the masculine ideal [Freud, 1950, pp. 196–197].

It is easy to understand why the present women's liberation movement regards Freud as a prime target!

Social learning theory of identification. Most social learning theorists would reject Freud's theory of identification (Bandura, 1969). They would argue that the behaviors attributed to identification by Freud can be more adequately explained as a result of direct teaching and modeling by parents (Gewirtz, 1969). Parents shape the child's performance by verbalizing standards of behavior, rewarding desired behaviors, and punishing unacceptable behaviors, and also by offering a model for the child to emulate. The tendency of the child to imitate will be facilitated by characteristics of the model, such as his warmth, competence, power, and success in gaining rewards. A loving, nurturant parent should be more effective in modifying children's behavior through either direct training or modeling. If a parent has been associated frequently with reduction of hunger, thirst, pain, contact comfort, temperature maintenance, and pleasant sensory input, the parent gradually comes to elicit the positive responses evoked by those physical reinforcers. The appearance, presence, or even image of the warm parent, through classical conditioning, will come to elicit pleasant emotional states which are labeled as "love" for the parent.

The motivation for the acquisition of parental behaviors may be twofold. The child maintains parental affection by behaving in a similar fashion to the parent, and also the child gains a sense of mastery over the environment by emulating the responses of a warm, competent, powerful parent (Kagan, 1964).

The traditional psychoanalytic conception of defensive identification is not accepted by most learning theorists. A competent, hostile model may be imitated because of his success and the rewards he receives; however, it is unlikely that the model's aggressiveness itself facilitates identification as a means to reduce anxiety (Bandura, 1969).

Role theory of identification. The impact of sociological theories of identification on psychological research has been mainly confined to the area of sex-role typing. Social-role theorists (Brim, 1958; Cottrell, 1942; Johnson, 1963; Parsons, 1955) have integrated into their theory of identification many of the factors regarded as critical in the previously discussed theories, such as direct teaching, imitation, nurturance, and punishment. However, they have extended their theory in several important ways: they have clearly differentiated masculine and feminine roles in our culture; they have emphasized the reciprocal learning which occurs in role relationships; and they have specified the sequence of role relationships which are important in identification.

Parsons' (1955) theory of identification is based on the delineation and differentiation of increasingly complex role relationships between the child, parents, family, and eventually the culture. These might be called "we-they" discriminations, for the child gradually identifies persons or groups with whom he shares common characteristics ("we"), and those from whom he differs ("they"). He learns that "we" boys are different than "those" girls, that "we" children are different from "those" adults. It might be expected that some "we-they" categorizations would be more important in some cultures than others. In Northern Ireland "we" Catholics versus "those" Protestants would be an early developed and influential differentiation. In this country "we" blacks versus "those" whites might be more salient.

Parsons regards the discrimination of "we males" from "those females" as one of the most important distinctions the child makes. It will be seen in the next chapter that Lawrence Kohlberg also believes this discrimination is a critical factor in sex-role typing. Parsons holds that in this culture the feminine role is basically expressive and the masculine role is instrumental. By this he means that the mother's role is oriented toward the emotional needs of the family; she is affectionate, solicitous, conciliatory, and supportive. In contrast, the father's role is one of mastering environmental problems, making decisions, and dispensing rewards and punishments. He is the provider, judge, and ultimate disciplinarian in the family. Although these roles are similar to Freud's description of the nurturing mother and threatening Oedipal father, Parsons conceives of the father as being powerful in dispensing both punishments and rewards, and as being competent rather than primarily hostile. This social power of the father is particularly important in identification.

Parsons believes that in any interpersonal interaction the child identifies with his own role and the role of the person with whom he interacts. He calls this *reciprocal role learning* since the child learns something about the performance and interaction between both roles. Hence in the most important interaction in infancy, the mother-child relationship, the child internalizes the nurturant role of the mother as a caretaker and the role of himself as one to be cared for. Through the acquisition of both roles he learns how to love and be loved. It is this primary reciprocal-love relationship with the mother and her encouragement of the boy's emulating and loving his father that initiates the boy's identification with his father. However, interaction with both parents is essential for the perception and differentiation of sex roles by both boys and girls. The discrimination and internalization of the category of "we males" or "we females" is facilitated by the opportunity to learn both sex roles in reciprocal interactions with both parents, siblings, and peers. Interactions with the father are critical in the development of femininity in girls and the opportunity to relate to the mother is important for boys. Although boys acquire masculine behaviors by imitating the powerful, decision-making father, they also learn to play an instrumental role in relation to the mother's female expressive role. Similarly girls acquire sex-appropriate behaviors not only by emulating the mother but also through learning to interact in a feminine expressive manner in relation to a masculine, instrumental father.

It is apparent that although there is considerable agreement among theories as to which variables are influential in identification, they differ in the emphasis they place on the relative importance of these variables. Psychoanalytic theorists focus on both parental nurturance and punitiveness, with perceived paternal aggressiveness and hostility being particularly important for the identification of boys. Social learning theorists emphasize the importance of parental affection and competence in making the parent an effective model and reinforcer for the child. Role theorists have stressed the importance of maternal warmth and paternal power in dispensing both rewards and punishments.

Studies of imitation

Attempts to assess the relation between various parental behaviors and identification have been focused on the three parental characteristics of greatest theoretical interest: warmth, power, and punitiveness. Evidence from imitation studies support the position that children tend to emulate nurturant or powerful models more than nonnurturant or nondominant models, whether the models are parents or strangers (Bandura & Huston, 1961; Bandura, Ross, & Ross, 1963; Hetherington, 1965; Hetherington & Frankie, 1967; Mischel & Grusec, 1966; Mussen & Parker, 1965). However there is some variation in the effects of the models' warmth and power on children's imitation according to what specific behaviors are to be modeled and whether it is a boy or girl doing the imitating. Girls tend to be more responsive to the model's warmth and boys to the model's dominance. Warmth also facilitates the imitation of task-irrelevant responses, such as gestures, mannerisms, and comments, more than task-relevant or problem-solving responses (Hetherington, Cox, Thomas, & Hunt, 1974). Children may view the parent or model who makes decisions and seems to be in control of things as more competent and more likely to succeed in problem solving. In task-relevant or problem-solving imitation it may be a matter of "Who wants to imitate a loser, even a loving loser, when you are trying to solve a problem?"

In addition, warmth of the model facilitates imitation more when the model is a parent than when the model is a strange experimenter interacting with the child in an attentive, affectionate, approving way. It may be that nurturance is difficult to communicate in short-term interactions in the laboratory with strangers, or that being with a stranger in an unfamiliar situation is more stressful than being with a parent. Stress may reduce the effects of the model's nurturance while increasing the effects of power. In a stressful situation the child may want to go along with the "boss" in order to feel more secure.

Laboratory studies give considerable support to theories of imitation and identification which emphasize the importance of the dominance and warmth or nurturance of the model or parent in the child's imitation. In contrast, laboratory studies of imitation have offered little support for the theory of defensive identification. Evidence for identification with the aggressor rests largely on clinical cases (Freud, 1923; Freud, 1946) and anecdotal reports (Bettelheim, 1969). Bettelheim reports that prisoners in Nazi concentration camps frequently adopted vocal and postural mannerisms and styles of dress resembling those of the punitive guards. They were often similarly physically and verbally abusive toward new prisoners and were brutally and irrationally cruel and authoritarian when supervising others.

Sarnoff (1951) has suggested that three conditions are essential in producing identification with the aggressor: a hostile person who directs his aggression toward another person; a victim who is dependent upon the aggressor; and a situation involving stresses and limitations that prevent escape from the aggression. Hetherington and Frankie (1967) reasoned that the home situation which would seem to most adequately fulfill these criteria and lead to identification with a hostile, dominant parent would be one in which there is a stressful, conflictual atmosphere and both parents are cold. Such a home would offer the child no escape by seeking a closer relationship with a warm, nondominant parent, and the stressful family relationship should heighten his feelings of helplessness and anxiety and his tendency toward defensive identification.

In the study presented in Box 11-3, these investigators tried to approximate this situation by studying the effects of various combinations of parents' warmth, dominance, and conflict on imitation of parents by preschool boys and girls. An attempt was made to test theories of imitation based on social power, secondary reinforcement, and identification with the aggressor. Family triads consisting of both parents and a child were brought into the laboratory, parental characteristics relative to the theoretical predictions being tested were assessed, and then the child's imitation of his parents was observed and recorded. This study is distinguished by the fact that fathers as well as mothers were included in the study and that parental behavior was directly observed rather than being obtained from retrospective reports on interviews or questionnaires.

BOX 11-3 EFFECTS OF PARENTAL DOMINANCE, WARMTH, AND CONFLICT ON IMITATION IN CHILDREN

What parental characteristics affect modeling by the child? Under what circumstances do dominance, warmth, and hostility of parents become more salient in facilitating their child's imitation? This investigation sought to answer these questions.

The subjects were eighty preschool boys and eighty girls and their parents. Each parent was visited individually in his home and presented with the Structured Family Interaction Test, an experimental task in which each parent is presented separately with a series of 12 hypothetical situations involving behavioral problems of children and asked how he or she would handle them in the absence of the other parent. Examples of the situations are:

You have friends over in the evening and your son/daughter keeps getting out of bed to see what's going on.

A neighbor comes to the door and reports that your son/daughter has been throwing rocks at passing automobiles.

You have taken your son/daughter out to dinner in a restaurant as a special treat. He/she is behaving in a generally noisy, ill-mannered way although you have warned him/her to quiet down.

After separately presenting their individual solutions, the parents are then brought together and asked to discuss the problems and to reach a compatible solution to them and indicate it by saying "agreed." Behavioral measures of dominance and conflict and ratings of warmth-hostility were obtained from this procedure for each parent. The measures of dominance include who speaks first, last, and most; who shifts his position most from his original separate solution to the joint solution; and who exhibits passive acceptance. Passive acceptance involves acceptance of the spouse's solution with no argument or discussion. An example of this measure would be a case in which the mother separately has advocated a mild punishment, such as depriving the child of television for a day, and the father severe corporal punishment, and when the parents are together the mother mildly acquiesces with no argument and says, "Yes, he's right. We'd spank her so hard she wouldn't be able to sit for a week."

It can be seen that such measures of parental dominance assess both control in terms of verbal interaction, and power in making decisions about the dispensing of rewards and punishments. The measures of parental conflict recorded during the joint interaction session included interruptions, disagreements and aggressions, simultaneous speech, inability to compromise enough to reach a mutually agreed upon decision, and total amount of time taken to reach an agreement. It is assumed that the more conflict there is, the more difficult and time-consuming it will be to attain agreement. The measure of parental warmth-hostility was based on ratings made on the basis of tape recordings of the interaction sessions. The rating scale ranged from 1 (extremely warm, nurturant and affectionate; clearly proud of the child; concerned with and enjoys the child as a person; understanding and empathic) to 6 (marked hostility, anger and punitiveness toward the child, little sympathy or attempt to understand the child's behavior, always interprets the child's behavior in the worst light).

The parents and children were then brought into the laboratory and the children were tested for imitative responses in a play situation after watching each parent alternately performing for four trials. The parents had been preinstructed and trained to go through a differing but prescribed series of verbal, postural, and motor behaviors. One parent would squat while lining up golf shots, always use blue equipment and say "Blue is my lucky color," sit sideways on a chair and throw darts with two hands, shout "good one" each time he scored, etc. The other parent would perform a different series of distinctive responses. Parents were not present during the child's play sessions in order to avoid parental intimidation or encouragement of preferential imitation of either parent.

The results yielded partial support for all theories of identification. Under certain circumstances warmth, hostility, and dominance each led to increased imitation by children. Although warmth and dominance in the parents increased imitation by both boys and girls, the effect of warmth was greatest for girls and dominance for boys. Girls tended to imitate a warm mother and boys a powerful father, as would be predicted by psychoanalytic theory. Imitation of a dominant, hostile parent was obtained only under the conditions analogous to those described by Sarnoff as those most likely to elicit defensive identification. When both parents were hostile and there was high conflict in the home, boys and girls tended to imitate the dominant parent, whether it was the mother or the father. If either the nondominant parent was warm or conflict was reduced, there was less imitation of the aggressive, powerful parent. It appears that defensive identification with a dominent, punitive model occurs only under the extremely restrictive conditions of high stress and the absence of a supportive, loving parent to whom the child may turn for protection and succor.

The results of this study suggest that no theory of identification is adequate to explain the imitation of both boys and girls under all circumstances. Under some conditions warmth, hostility, and dominance in the parents each facilitate imitation by children.

Source: Hetherington, E. M., & Frankie, G. Effects of parental dominance, warmth and conflict on imitation in children. *Journal of Personality and Social Psychology*, 1967, **6,** 119-125.

When the results of a variety of investigations are summarized, some support is found for all theories of imitation, although the effects of a model's power or dominance have been most clearly and consistently demonstrated and the effects of the models' hostility is limited to a very narrow set of circumstances. The salience of warmth, power, and aggression in a model on imitative behavior interacts with many factors in the test situation: the sex of child and sex of model; the particular behavior being imitated; and whether parents or strangers are serving as models. The role of some of these factors in moral development and the development of masculinity and femininity will be discussed in later chapters. It will then be seen even more clearly that the effects of parental characteristics differ with the specific behavior being imitated.

SOCIAL CLASS AND SOCIALIZATION

No culture is entirely homogeneous. Subgroups within a culture may have different problems to cope with and divergent values. These will be reflected in different goals and methods in socialization.

Powerlessness and poverty

Considerable concern has been focused on differences between the life situations of lower-working-class families and middle-class families in the American culture and the reflection of these differences in diverse attitudes and childrearing practices. Although the most obvious differences between these social groups is an economic one, there are other related pervasive features of their life which may be more directly relevant to the process of socialization.

The critical importance of children having the opportunity of learning to control and shape their environment has been discussed previously. Without this growing sense of power based on the responsiveness of others, the child's feelings of helplessness, incompetence, and low self-esteem are reflected in disruptions in cognitive, emotional, and adaptive processes.

In an analogous manner, powerlessness is a basic problem of the poor. They have less influence over the society in which they live and are likely to be less adequately treated by social organizations than are members of the middle class. They receive poorer health and public services, and they are more likely to have their individual rights violated by agents of the law or social workers or educators or the medical profession. Their lack of power and prestige and lack of educational and economic resources restrict the availability of options in most areas of their lives. They have little control or choice of occupations or housing and little contact with other social groups; they are tragically vulnerable to disasters such as job loss, financial stress, and illness; and they are subject to impersonal bureaucratic decisions in the legal system and in social institutions, such as welfare agencies. In addition, the low educational level, restricted experience, and lack of information of the poor make it difficult for them to understand and avail themselves of the limited resources which are open to them.

In view of the life circumstances associated with poverty, it is not surprising that many of the differences in attitudes and social relationships between lower- and middle-class families can be conceptualized in terms of a dimension of power and self-direction versus helplessness and obedience to the demands of others.

Social class and childrearing

In the 1920s and 1930s the first important studies of class differences in childrearing found that lower-class parents were more permissive but used more physical punishment than middle-class parents. Middle-class parents made greater demands and had higher expectations for their children, but they used love-oriented disciplinary techniques involving affection or withdrawal of love to control their children. Over the succeeding years, in both classes there has been an increase in permissiveness and in the use of love-oriented techniques, and more active participation by the father in childrearing. There has also been a shift away from highly differentiated, stereotyped maternal and paternal roles in the family; both the mother and father now tend to express affection toward their children and to participate actively in disciplining their children. However, parental roles continue to be more clearly delineated in lower classes.

Recent reviews suggest that current social class differences in permissiveness should be regarded as a difference in kind and timing of restrictions rather than degree of restrictiveness (Bronfenbrenner, 1961; Clausen & Williams, 1963; Hess, 1970). There is less restrictiveness among middle-class parents toward the infant and young child, but greater parental supervision and control in adolescence. Middle-class parents are more permissive in early feeding, toilet, sex, and aggression training. However, they also expect early development of responsibility and have higher achievement and academic goals for their children. The shift to greater permissiveness by the lower-class parents with older children may be attributable in part to the expectation of earlier attainment of economic independence by children in lower-class families. Most lower-class adolescents must of necessity help contribute financially to their own support, in contrast to middle-class children who usually expect to be supported through college and often graduate school, well into young adulthood.

Social class and values

Many class differences in childrearing are directly related to divergent ideas of desirable behavior, general attentiveness to the responses of the child, and variations in discipline patterns for sons and daughters.

Middle-class parents value the ability to delay gratification and work for distant goals, achievement, curiosity, honesty, consideration for others, and self-control. They are attentive to their children's opinions and feelings, are concerned with the motivations underlying their children's behavior, and use explanation and reasoning in attempting to shape these motives. They wish the child to behave appropriately because the child has internalized the parents' values and wants to do it and not because the child is acquiescing to authority. Lower-class parents are more interested in violations of proscriptions and the immediate consequences of the child's actions. They wish their child to exhibit "respectable" conduct which is in accord with social standards. Neatness, politeness, cleanliness, and especially obedience and respect for authority are regarded as prime virtues. This structuring of relationships in terms of authority and power is exhibited in a number of forms. Lower-class fathers regard love and respect from their children as equivalent to conformity with their demands (Kohn, 1959). Disobedience and aggression toward parents are not tolerated. Mothers in urban slum areas introduce their children to elementary school by focusing on how to deal with the authorities in the school system, in contrast to the middle-class mothers who orient their children toward the learning and achievement possibilities of the academic situation (Hess & Shipman, 1968).

In some ways these responses can be thought of as adaptive responses by lower-working-class parents. Vigilence toward the power structure, an awareness and sensitivity to external control, and an unwillingness to opt for long-term gratifications and achievements may be appropriate survival mechanisms in an environment where day-to-day subsistence is a problem and personal destiny in reality is often manipulated by impersonal, sometimes arbitrary, authorities. Concentration on the child's long-term inner development may be a luxury the economically deprived cannot afford.

It should be noted that in spite of these differences lower- and middle-class parents do value some of the same behaviors. For example, both groups of parents want their children to respect the rights of others and to be honest.

Social class differences in discipline of boys and girls

In addition to class differences in values and responses to children, patterns of discipline administered to sons and daughters by mothers and fathers vary with social class. Lower-class boys receive more harsh punishment than do girls, who tend to be more indulged and protected. The lower-class parent also is more likely to indulge the opposite-sex child and discipline the same-sex child. Lower-class fathers are more permissive with girls and mothers with boys. In upper-middle-class families boys and girls are treated in a more similar manner. Upper-middle-class mothers are stricter with their sons and the fathers are more likely to punish their daughters than is the case in lower-class families. Because upper-middle-class girls are treated more like boys and are less overprotected, they behave more like males and are less conforming and more independent and achievement-oriented than lower-class girls. They are less accepting of the traditional feminine role (Bronfenbrenner, 1961).

It has been proposed that there are some deleterious consequences of the greater participation by middle-class mothers in disciplining their sons and that these can lead to poor self-control and responsibility in boys. Boys are least responsible when the mother and father participate equally in disciplinary functions. Paternal involvement in discipline combined with love and attention tends to be related to responsibility and leadership in boys (Bronfenbrenner, 1961).

In spite of the reported variations in goals and socialization techniques among social classes, it should be recognized that there is considerable overlap in attitudes and practices among economic status groups and considerable variability within the social groups.

FAMILY STRUCTURE

Our discussion of the family thus far has centered on the effects of parental values, attitudes, discipline practices, and dimensions of childrearing on the behavior of the child. In addition, various aspects of the structure of the family affect its functioning. The development of the child is influenced by family size; the number and sex of siblings; the absence of one parent; and whether it is a nuclear family consisting of a mother, father, and children, or an extended family in which grandparents, aunts, uncles, or cousins may live together. Some of these factors will be discussed in this chapter. The effects of absence of a parent will be presented in the following chapter on sex-role typing.

Family size and socialization

As family size increases, opportunities for extensive contact between the parents and the individual child decrease, but opportunities for a variety of interactions with siblings expand.

A parent's attitude toward childrearing and the circumstances under which a child is reared will change as more children are added to the family. With a large number of children, particularly in families with over six children, family roles tend to become more precisely defined, chores are assigned, and discipline is more authoritarian and severe (Bossard & Boll, 1960). Parents can't afford to be indulgent with a large number of children or chaos will result. There is little time for reasoning and extended explanations. More use of hostile, restrictive control by mothers, particularly in relation to daughters, occurs in large families (Nuttall & Nuttall, 1971). In addition, as family size increases the mother exhibits not only less attention but less warmth toward individual children. Frequently older siblings are assigned the supervisory and disciplinary roles maintained by parents in smaller families. A firstborn girl of twelve in a large family may warm bottles, burp babies, change diapers, and sooth a squalling infant with the alacrity and skill of a young mother. Because the parents in large families cannot interact as closely with their children as those in smaller families, there is less opportunity for overprotection, infantalization, constant harassing, or close supervision of children. The results of this relationship are reflected in the greater independence but lower academic achievement of children from large families.

In addition to the changes in social relationships imposed by large family size, economic burdens and crowding may contribute to stresses within the family. When the large family is economically secure, many of the pressures on family members are alleviated and conflicts and authoritarianism are reduced. Since many lower-class families are large, some of the class differences in interaction patterns may be attributable to family size.

The role of siblings and birth order in socialization

In spite of the fact that the effects of birth order on the development of the child are influenced by a multitude of variables such as sex and spacing of siblings, family size, age of the mother, socioeconomic factors, and sex and age of the child studied, some interesting findings have emerged in this area.

Parent-child interactions and birth order   When differences related to birth order have been obtained, these are usually attributed to variations in interaction with parents and siblings associated with the unique life experiences found in children with that position in the family.

This is particularly true in the unusual role of the firstborn child. The eldest child is the only one who, until he is dethroned by the birth of a subsequent child, does not have to share his parents' love and attention with other siblings. There seems to be an especially intense and concerned involvement of parents and firstborn children which is maintained throughout life. Even when their children are infants, parents spend more time with, stimulate, and talk more to firstborn infants (Thoman, Liederman, & Olson, 1972). This pattern of effects differs in interactions involving the mother or father. The father talks and touches firstborn boys more than firstborn girls or later born children (Parke, in press). In contrast, mothers smile and vocalize more to firstborn girls than to other children (Thoman, Liederman, & Olson, 1972). Parents pay more attention to the firstborn not only early in life; even after the birth of other children, parents tend to direct their comments toward and pitch their conversation at the level of the eldest child (Bossard & Boll, 1956; Koch, 1955). This may be one of the reasons firstborns show accelerated verbal development. The quality as well as the quantity of parent-child interaction varies with the birth order. Parents have higher expectations, exert greater pressures toward achievement and acceptance of responsibility, and interfere more with

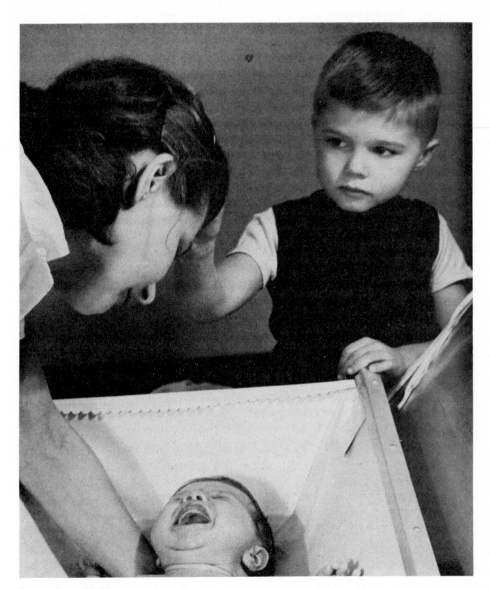

The firstborn child has to learn to share his parents' love and attention with other siblings. (Suzanne Szasz.)

the activities of first than later-born children (Lasko, 1954; Cushna, 1966; Hilton, 1967; Rothbart, 1971). Firstborn children also have greater disciplinary friction with their parents. At any age more physical punishment is likely to be administered to a firstborn than to a later born child. In contrast, parents are more consistent and relaxed in disciplinary functions with later-born children, perhaps as a result of self-confidence gained from practice in childrearing (Lasko, 1954). In a sense the firstborn is the "practice baby" on which the parent, through trial and error, learns his parenting skills.

These divergent patterns of parent-child interaction for first- and later-born children are found in studies using both parental reports and direct observation. Hilton (1967) observed that mothers of only and firstborn four-year-olds were more extreme, inconsistent, and interfering in their child's behavior on a puzzle-solving task in the laboratory than were mothers with their later-born children. Mothers of early-born children, in addition to giving their children more task-oriented instructions, were more likely to demonstrate love if the child was doing well and withdrawal of love and approval for poor performance.

There has been some suggestion that in such situations mothers are more exacting, critical, intrusive, and demanding of firstborn daughters than of sons (Cushna, 1966; Rothbart, 1971). Although there is insufficient evidence, it may be that both parents are more demanding of same-sexed eldest children.

Sibling interaction and birth order   In addition to birth order being associated with differences in parent-child relations, it is associated with variations in sibling relations. The eldest child is frequently expected to assume some responsibility and self-control toward the younger sibling who has displaced him. When the eldest child feels jealousy or hostility, he or she is likely to be restrained or punished by his parents and the younger child is likely to be protected and defended. On the other hand, the eldest child is more dominant, competent, and able to bully or, conversely, to assist and teach the younger offspring.

For eldest children the main models for social learning are the parents, whereas the younger child has both parental and sibling models. The effects of older siblings on sex-typed behavior was demonstrated by Brim (1958), who found that boys with older sisters exhibit more feminine behavior than boys with older brothers. Boys with older sisters become more dependent and withdrawn and may underachieve in school (Hodges & Balow, 1961; Koch, 1960). Girls with older brothers tend to become tomboys and show more leadership, aggressiveness, quarrelsomeness, and confidence at young ages (Koch, 1955). They also are more interested in masculine activities and occupations and less conforming and affiliative (that is, interested in being with people and making friends) (Bragg & Allen, 1967) than are girls with older sisters.

Characteristics of firstborn children   In view of the marked differences in family dynamics related to birth order it is not surprising that different characteristics are associated with firstborn and later-born children. Firstborn children remain more adult-oriented, self-controlled, conforming, anxious, and less aggressive than their siblings. The parental demands and high standards imposed on firstborns result in eldest children being more studious, conscientious, and serious. Although these children are not superior in intelligence, they excel in academic and professional achievement. This is supported by their overrepresentation in *Who's Who* and among Rhodes scholars and eminent American men of letters and science.

Emotionally and socially firstborns show less self-confidence and social poise and greater fear of failure and guilt than later borns. They are more apprehensive about pain and are more anxious than later borns in stressful situations (Schacter, 1959). This is reflected in their avoidance of dangerous or competitive sports and of occupations or activities that may result in physical harm (Nisbett, 1968). Firstborns seem less able to cope with anxiety-producing situations. In situations involving danger, such as piloting a fighter plane in combat, firstborns are less effective than later borns (Torrance, 1954). Under stressful conditions firstborns, especially firstborn girls, prefer to be with other people. In a laboratory situation where subjects expected to receive painful high-intensity shocks, firstborn females more often wished to wait in a room with another person in preference to being alone in the period preceding the experiment (Schacter, 1959).

The power failure in New York City on November 9 and 10, 1965, provided a naturalistic stress situation in which to test the generality of laboratory findings relating to anxiety and affiliation in firstborns. The blackout resulted in many people being stranded in the city and being physically uncomfortable and uncertain about what was going on. They were separated from families and friends, were often in unfamiliar situations, and were deprived of information. The experimenters collected information from people in a bus station and a hotel where there was some dim emergency lighting. Firstborns reported being more anxious than later borns in this situation, and more firstborn than later-born women had been striking up casual acquaintances and talking or interacting with someone prior to the experimental interview (Zucker, Manosevitz, & Lanyon, 1968).

The greater pressures and anxiety of the primary birth order may also be a factor in the high frequency of admission of firstborns to child guidance clinics (Phillips, 1956; Rosenoer & Whyte, 1931) and of neurotic symptoms, such as oversensitivity, sleep disorders, and timidity (MacFarlane, Allen, & Honzik, 1954), in firstborns. Later borns, on the other hand, tend to manifest conduct disorders such as aggression and hyperactivity.

The only child has frequently been regarded as a "spoiled brat" combining undesirable symptoms such as dependency, egotism, lack of self-control, and emotional disorders. However, research findings suggest that in many ways the only child has advantages over other children. Although exposed to the high parental demands and guidance of firstborns, an only child does not have to adapt to ultimate displacement and competition with siblings. As was the case with firstborns, this sustained close relationship with the parents is associated with dependency and high achievement; however, an only child is lower on anxiety, is more assertive, has higher self-esteem, and is socially more adaptable.

In social relations both outside and inside the home they seem to make more positive adjustments than children distressed by sibling rivalry. The main disadvantages suffered by only children are the problems associated with too strong an identification with the opposite-sex parent. Sutton-Smith and Rosenberg state:

> The most striking data on only children have to do with the sex role differences between male and female only children. Cushna's data (1966) show that mothers favor only boys to a much greater extent than only girls. There are other data to show that the only boy is more feminine than other males, and the only girl more masculine; moreover that the deviation in these opposite-sex directions leaves them with a greater general tendency toward sex deviation consonant with these tendencies [Sutton-Smith & Rosenberg, 1970, p. 153].

Characteristics of later-born children   The characteristics of the second or middle child in the family are less clearly defined. The middle child suffers from rivalry with a younger sibling, without the compensation of being in a power position comparable to that of the eldest. He also often experiences parental neglect since he is caught between the parents' intense relationship with the eldest sibling and nurturant, affection-ate relation with the youngest. Middle children have poor achievement, short attention spans, are readily distractible, and are often characterized as flighty. They tend to be extroverted, frequently seeking the companionship and affection of others, and are more humorous and pleasure-oriented than their siblings (Altus, 1959; Cohen, 1951). Al-though these children are externally oriented, more middle-born children are regarded as extremely unpopular by their peers than are children in any other birth order (Elkins, 1958).

The last born child is usually indulged by his parents and siblings and has a variety of sibling models available in addition to the parents. This state of security and some-times benign neglect results in a set of characteristics which have many of the positive and few of the negative attributes of firstborns. The last child has similar assets in that he is striving, persevering, achievement-oriented, and popular; however, he is more opti-mistic, self-confident, and secure than firstborns.

The effects of birth order clearly are related to the interactions and role of that position within the family. The relationships of power and dependency, of attention or relative neglect, and of differential emotional bonds and the options for action and reaction within the family system all interact in shaping the characteristics associated with sibling position.

THE COMMUNE: AN ALTERNATIVE TO THE NUCLEAR FAMILY

The nuclear family consisting of two parents and their children is the most accepted organization for rearing and socializing children in this country. However, many sociol-ogists and anthropologists have questioned both the survival of the family and whether the nuclear family is the best agency for raising children (Lasch, 1965; Linton, 1959; Zimmerman, 1972).

There are many alternatives to the nuclear family, such as the extended family, where grandparents may play an active role in childrearing, or communal childrearing, in which children "belong" to a group and are raised by the group or adults other than the parents. In addition, adoptions by single parents are now permitted in many states, and children by intent rather than misfortune may have only one parent.

The commune has had an extensive history. In this century communal living has been extensively utilized in Russia, China, and Israel. In the United States in the past two decades there has been a surge in the formation of communes. Many American com-munes can be viewed as a rejection of the constraints of the nuclear family and of the materialistic pressures of urban life in a highly industrialized society (Berger, Hackett, & Millar, 1972).

Because of the wide variations in the goals, structuring, and functioning of different communes it is difficult to make any broad generalizations about the effects of commu-nal life on the development of children. Some communes are simply clusters of nuclear families living and working together where the parents still have the main responsibility for child care. Others have arrangements where adults have free sexual relations with any member of the commune and the children belong to the group. In still others, such as the Israeli kibbutz, the children are regarded as belonging to the group and children

A commune in the United States. (Dennis Stock, Magnum Photos.)

are reared in group residences or schools apart from their parents, but the parents still play a special role in the lives of their children.

The Israeli kibbutz is perhaps the most studied form of communal living, and even among kibbutzim there are many variations.

One of the most important aspects of life in the kibbutz is the attempt to eliminate differences in sex roles. Men and women share the same types of work, working conditions, and community roles. None of the economic ties and childrearing demands that would normally bind a married couple are present in the kibbutz. The kibbutz provides for all members of its commune and assumes responsibility for child care. Marriage ties are based on mutual emotional and sexual needs.

Rabin has summarized the changes in family structure and childrearing in the kibbutz setting as follows:

> Most significant in the Kibbutz setting is the change in family structure and the important changes in the roles of parents in relation to their children. The entire process of collective education stems basically from this major social reform. Although the family continues to exist, many of its traditional characteristics have been altered or eliminated. First, the family as a physical or geographically located unit no longer exists. From birth to maturity, the child does not reside in the same residence as his parents or his other biological siblings; he resides in one of the units of the children's house or in one of the dormitories of the adolescent society. Secondly, the child's economic dependence upon the parents is eliminated. The child "belongs" to the Kibbutz. A Kibbutz member speaks of "our children," referring to all children born in the Kibbutz, not only to the ones born out of his own union. The Kibbutz often views itself as one large "family" that is responsible for and responsive to all its members. Third, it involves the parents' relinquishment of their traditional role as "socializers" of the child. In the conventional family setting the parents, and especially the mother, is the primary "teacher" of the child in the sense that she shows him how to eat, keep clean,

and control his aggression; she usually applies the appropriate sanctions provided by the culture (rewards and punishment) in an attempt to direct the child's behavior, and she often uses the giving of love or its deprivation as the means of controlling of the child. To a lesser extent, the father is a socializer in the typical nuclear family as we know it; he too applies sanctions, or sanctions are applied in his name; he also serves as a model, as does the mother, as a transmitter of the values of the larger society and culture. The parents, in psychoanalytic terms, are the sources of superego formation. Related to these facts is the child's strong emotional relation and frequent dependency upon the parents. Due to the special arrangements in the Kibbutz, these conditions do not prevail. Along with the lack of economic dependency of the child upon his parents, there is a reduced emotional dependency. The socializing of the child is distributed among the several metaplet that care for him during infancy and early childhood as well as among members of the peer group that increasingly become important figures in the life of the growing child. It has also been pointed out that parents, although they have given up their roles as controllers of behavior and as punishers, to a great extent retain the role of rewarders. The daily afternoon and evening hours, as well as the longer periods on weekends and holidays, are times when the parents are almost completely and uninterruptedly available to their children. They do not need to feed them, direct them, or punish them. They merely want to be with them, give them things, and love them. Thus, these periods are characterized by a minimum of ambivalence and by a maximum of positive interaction. This relationship has sometimes been likened to that of the relationship between grandparents and grandchildren [Rabin, 1971, pp. 7–8].

There have been contradictory reports of the effects on children of being raised in a kibbutz. Children reared in the kibbutz are described by some authors as mature, courageous, unselfish, and cooperative, with a highly developed ethical sense (Rabin, 1965; Shapira & Madsen, 1969). Delinquency and homosexuality are almost unknown in kibbutzim. Kibbutz-reared children are also reported to show more positive attitudes toward their parents than nonkibbutz children (Rabin, 1959). There is less fear, conflict, and hostility toward the parent because he has not played the role of disciplinarian.

However, other authors have described kibbutz-reared children as rigidly opinionated, having inferiority feelings, and as being overly conforming, hostile, introverted, and insecure (Spiro, 1958). In addition it has been suggested that because of the lack of an early strong attachment with his parents, the kibbutz child has a lack of a capacity for intimacy and for showing deep personal feelings (Bettelheim, 1969). Dissatisfaction of a good many children with life in the kibbutz is revealed by the large exodus of young adults from the kibbutz into the cities in spite of great communal pressure not to leave.

It seems that although great diversity in family patterns and agencies for childrearing exist, the ideal one is yet to be discovered.

SUMMARY

The family plays a critical role in the socialization of the child. The early parent-child relationships are important because they serve as the initial social relationships which will shape the child's expectancies and responses in subsequent social encounters, and because the values and attitudes of the culture are filtered through the parents in their presentation to their offspring.

The child's first attachment to specific individuals occurs at about the middle of the first year of life. Infants tend to become attached to adults who are responsive and stimulating. As children grow older, the objects and form of attachment and dependency shift from parents to peers and from clinging and proximity seeking to attention seeking.

In the course of socialization parents serve important roles as teachers and models for their children. Two basic dimensions of parental behavior in relation to their children are warmth-hostility and permissiveness-control. The interaction of these two variables is associated with different clusters of behavior in children. In general, warm parents who are moderately restrictive and use consistent love-oriented discipline practices, such as explanation, reasoning, and withdrawal of affection, have children who exhibit many behaviors regarded as socially desirable, such as adaptability, self-esteem, competence, self-control, and popularity with peers.

Children imitate a wide range of behaviors in parents. Warmth or dominance in the parents will facilitate the child's imitation. Dominance plays the most significant role in task-relevant and problem-solving imitation. Warmth of the parent is more important in the imitation of girls and dominance for boys.

Parents in different social classes have different values which may influence their socialization practices. Lower-class parents value respectability, obedience, conformity, neatness, and politeness. They are concerned more about the immediate consequences of their children's behavior rather than about the motives underlying their behavior. In shaping their children toward these goals, they tend to be more power assertive and restrictive with young children, although they are permissive with older children. In contrast, middle-class parents focus on their children's "inner development" and are concerned with the development of responsibility, internalized controls, and achievement motivation.

Structural factors such as family size, sex, and number of siblings and birth order also play an important role in child development.

Although the nuclear family is regarded as the usual unit for childrearing in the United States, organizations such as communes offer alternate systems for caring for children. Communal systems seem to have some advantages over the family in childrearing; however, some adverse effects on children have been noted.

REFERENCES

Ainsworth, M. D. Patterns of attachment behavior shown by the infant in interaction with his mother. *Merrill-Palmer Quarterly,* 1964, **10,** 51-58.

Ainsworth, M. D. Object relations, dependency and attachment: a theoretical review of the mother-infant relationship. *Child Development,* 1969, **40,** 969-1025.

Ainsworth, M. D. The development of infant-mother attachment. In B. Caldwell & H. Riccuiti (Eds.), *Review of child development research.* Vol. 3. Chicago: The University of Chicago Press, 1973.

Ainsworth, M. D., & Bell, S. M. Some contemporary patterns of mother-infant interaction in the feeding situation. In J. A. Ambrose (Ed.), *Stimulation in early infancy.* London: Academic, 1969.

Ainsworth, M. D., Bell, S. M., & Stayton, D. J. Individual differences in the development of some attachment behaviors. *Merrill-Palmer Quarterly,* in press.

Ainsworth, M., & Salter, D. The development of infant-mother interaction among the Ghanda. In B. M. Foss (Ed.), *Determinants of infant behavior.* Vol. 2. New York: Wiley, 1963.

Ainsworth, M., Salter, D., & Wittig, B. A. Attachment and exploratory behavior of one-year-olds in a strange situation. In B. M. Foss (Ed.), *Determinants of infant behavior.* Vol. 4. New York: Wiley, 1967.

Altus, W. D. Birth order, intelligence and adjustment. *Psychological Reports,* 1959, **5,** 502.

Bandura, A. Social-learning theory of identificatory processes. In D. A. Goslin (Ed.), *Handbook of socialization theory and research.* Chicago: Rand McNally, 1969. Pp. 213-269.

Bandura, A., & Huston, A. C. Identification as a process of incidental learning. *Journal of Abnormal and Social Psychology,* 1961, **63,** 311-318.

Bandura, A., Ross, D., & Ross, S. A. A comparative test of the status envy, social power and secondary reinforcement theories of identificatory learning. *Journal of Abnormal and Social Psychology,* 1963, **67,** 527-534.

Baumrind, D. Child care practices anteceding three patterns of preschool behavior. *Genetic Psychology Monographs,* 1967, **75,** 43-88.

Baumrind, D. Current patterns of parental authority. *Developmental Psychology Monograph,* 1971, **4** (No. 4, Part 2).

Becker, W. C., & Krug, R. S. A comparison of the ability of the PAS, PARI, parent self ratings and empirically keyed questionnaire scales to predict ratings of child behavior. Mimeographed report, University of Illinois, Urbana, 1964.

Becker, W. C., Peterson, D. R., Luria, Z., Shoemaker, D. J., & Hellmer, L. A. Relations of factors derived from parent-interview ratings to behavior problems of five-year-olds. *Child Development,* 1962, **33,** 509-535.

Bell, R. Q. Structuring parent-child interaction situations for direct observation. *Child Development,* 1964, **35,** 1009-1021.

Bell, R. W. A reinterpretation of the direction of effects in studies of socialization. *Psychological Review,* 1968, **75,** 81-95.

Berger, B., Hackett, B. M., & Millar, R. M. Child rearing practices in the communal family. Unpublished report to the National Institute of Mental Health, 1972.

Bettelheim, B. *The Children of the dream.* New York: Macmillan, 1969.

Bossard, J. H. S., & Boll, E. *The large family system.* Philadelphia: University of Pennsylvania Press, 1956.

Bossard, J. H. S., & Boll, E. S. *The sociology of child development.* New York: Harper & Row, 1960.

Bowlby, J. The nature of the child's tie to his mother. *International Journal of Psychoanalysis,* 1958, **39,** 35.

Bowlby, J. Symposium on ''psychoanalysis and ethology.'' II. Ethology and the development of object relations. *International Journal of Psychoanalysis,* 1960, **41,** 313.

Bragg, B., & Allen, V. L. Ordinal position and conformity. Paper presented at the American Psychological Association, Washington, D.C., September 1967.

Brim, O. G. Family structure and sex role learning by children: a further analysis of Helen Koch's data. *Sociometry,* 1958, **21,** 1-16.

Bronfenbrenner, U. Some familial antecedents of responsibility and leadership. In L. Petrullo & B. M. Bass (Eds.), *Adolescents in leadership and interpersonal behavior.* New York: Holt, 1961.

Bronfenbrenner, U. *The worlds of childhood: U.S. and U.S.S.R.* New York: Russell Sage, 1970.

Caldwell, B. M. The usefulness of the critical period hypothesis in the study of filiative behavior. *Merrill-Palmer Quarterly,* 1962, **8,** 219-242.

Caldwell, B. M., Wright, C., Honig, R., & Tannenbaum, J. Infant day care and attachment. *American Journal of Orthopsychiatry,* 1970, **40,** 397-412.

Clausen, J. A. Perspectives on childhood socialization. In J. Clausen (Ed.), *Socialization and society.* Boston: Little, Brown, 1968.

Clausen, J. A., & Williams, J. R. Sociological correlates of child behavior. In *Yearbook: National Society of Education,* Part I. Chicago: The University of Chicago Press, 1963.

Coates, B., Anderson, E. P., & Hartup, W. W. Interrelations in the attachment behavior of human infants. *Developmental Psychology,* 1972, **6,** 218-230.

Cohen, F. Psychological characteristics of the second child as compared with the first. *Indian Journal of Psychology,* 1951, **26,** 79-84.

Cottrell, L. S., Jr. The adjustment of the individual to his age and sex roles. *American Sociological Review,* 1942, **7,** 617-620.

Cushna, B. Agency and birth order differences in very early childhood. Paper presented at the meeting of the American Psychological Association, New York, September 1966.

Elkins, D. Some factors related to the choice status of ninety eighth grade children in a school society. *Genetic Psychology Monographs,* 1958, **58,** 207-272.

Freud, A. *The ego and the mechanisms of defense.* New York: International Universities Press, Inc., 1946.

Freud, A., & Dann, S. An experiment in group upbringing. In *The psychoanalytic study of the child.* Vol. 6. New York: International Universities Press, Inc., 1951.

Freud, S. *The ego and id.* London: Hogarth, 1923.

Freud, S. Some psychological consequences of the anatomical distinction between the sexes. In *Collected Papers of Sigmund Freud.* Vol. 5. London: Hogarth, 1950. Pp. 186–197.

Gewirtz, J. L. Three determinants of attention-seeking in young children. *Monographs of the Society for Research in Child Development,* 1954, **19** (2, Serial No. 59).

Gewirtz, J. L. Mechanisms of social learning: some roles of stimulation and behavior in early human development. In D. A. Goslin (Ed.), *Handbook of socialization theory and research.* Chicago: Rand McNally, 1969. Pp. 57–212.

Gil, D. G. *Violence against children.* Cambridge, Mass.: Harvard, 1970.

Hartup, W. W. Nurturance and nurturance-withdrawal in relation to the dependency behavior of young children. *Child Development,* 1958, **102,** 501–509.

Hess, R. D. Class and ethnic influences upon socialization. In P. Mussen (Ed.), *Carmichael's manual of child psychology.* Vol. 2. New York: Wiley, 1970.

Hess, R. D., & Shipman, V. C. Maternal attitudes toward the school and the role of the pupil. In A. H. Passow (Ed.), *Developing programs for the educationally disadvantaged.* New York: Columbia, 1968.

Hetherington, E. M. A developmental study of the effects of sex of the dominant parent on sex-role preference, identification and imitation in children. *Journal of Personality and Social Psychology,* 1965, **2,** 188–194.

Hetherington, E. M., Cox, M., Thomas, J., & Hunt, L. The generalizability of laboratory analogue studies of imitation. Unpublished manuscript, 1974.

Hetherington, E. M., & Frankie, G. Effects of parental dominance, warmth and conflict on imitation in children. *Journal of Personality and Social Psychology,* 1967, **6,** 119–125.

Hilton, I. Differences in the behavior of mothers toward first- and later-born children. *Journal of Personality and Social Psychology,* 1967, **7,** 282–290.

Hodges, A., & Balow, B. Learning disability in relation to family constellation. *Journal of Educational Research,* 1961, **55,** 4–42.

Johnson, M. Sex role learning in the nuclear family. *Child Development,* 1963, **34,** 319–333.

Kagan, J. Acquisition and significance of sex typing and sex role identity. In M. L. Hoffman & L. W. Hoffman (Eds.), *Review of child development research.* Vol. 2. New York: Russell Sage, 1964. Pp. 137–167.

Kagan, J., & Moss, H. A. *Birth to maturity: a study in psychological development.* New York: Wiley, 1962.

Koch, H. L. The relation of "primary mental abilities" in five and six year olds to sex of child and characteristics of his siblings. *Child Development,* 1955, **26,** 13–40.

Koch, H. L. The relation of certain formal attributes of siblings to attitudes held toward each other and toward their parents. *Monographs of the Society for Research in Child Development,* 1960, **25**(4, Whole No. 78), 1–134.

Kohlberg, L. *Stages in the development of moral thought and action.* New York: Holt, 1969.

Kohn, M. L. Social class and the exercise of parental authority. *American Sociological Review,* 1959, **24,** 352–366.

Kotelchuck, M. The nature of a child's tie to his father. Unpublished doctoral dissertation, Harvard University, 1972.

Lasch, D. *The new radicalism in America.* New York: Vantage, 1965.

Lasko, J. K. Parent behavior towards first and second children. *Genetic Psychology Monographs,* 1954, **49,** 96–137.

Levy, D. M. *Maternal overprotection.* New York: Columbia, 1943.

Linton, R. The natural history of the family. In R. Nanshen (Ed.), *The family: its function and destiny.* New York: Harper & Row, 1959. Pp. 30–52.

Littenberg, R., Tulkin, S., & Kagan, J. Cognitive components of separation anxiety. *Developmental Psychology,* 1971, **4,** 387–388.

Maccoby, E. E., & Feldman, S. S. Mother attachment and stranger reactions in the third year of life. *Monographs of the Society for Research in Child Development,* 1972, **37** (1, Serial No. 146).

MacFarlane, J. W., Allen, L., & Honzik, M. P. A developmental study of the behavior problems of normal children between twenty-one months and fourteen years. University of California Publications in Child Development, 1954, 2.

Marvin, R. S. Attachment, exploratory and communicative behavior of two-, three- and four-year-old children. Unpublished doctoral dissertation, University of Chicago, 1972.

Marvin, R. S., Marvin, C. N., & Abramovitch, L. An ethological study of the development of boy behavior in young children. Paper presented at Society for Research in Child Development, Philadelphia, 1973.

Mischel, W. A., & Grusec, J. Determinants of the rehearsal and transmission of neutral and aversive behaviors. *Journal of Person-*

ality and Social Psychology, 1966, **2,** 197-205.

Moustakas, C. E., Sigel, I. E., & Schalock, N. D. An objective method for the measurement and analysis of child-adult interaction. *Child Development,* 1956, **27,** 109-134.

Mussen, P. H., & Parker, A. L. Mother nurturance and girls' incidental imitative learning. *Journal of Personality and Social Psychology,* 1965, **2,** 94-97.

Nisbett, R. E. Birth order and participation in dangerous sports. *Journal of Personality and Social Psychology,* 1968, **8,** 351-353.

Nuttall, E., & Nuttall, R. The effects of size of family on parent-child relationships. *Proceedings of the American Psychological Association,* 1971, **6,** 267-268.

O'Rourke, J. F. Field and laboratory: the decision making behavior of family groups in two experimental conditions. *Sociometry,* 1963, **26,** 422-435.

Parke, R. Family interaction in the newborn: some findings, some observations and some unresolved issues. In K. Riegel & J. Meacham (Eds.), *Determinants of behavioral development,* in press.

Parsons, T. Family structure and the socialization of the child. In T. Parsons & R. Bales (Eds.), *Family, socialization and interaction process.* Glencoe Ill.: Free Press, 1955. Pp. 35-131.

Phillips, E. L. Cultural vs. interpsychic factors in childhood. *Journal of Clinical Psychiatry,* 1956, **12,** 400-401.

Rabin, A. I. Attitudes of kibbutz children to family and parents. *American Journal of Orthopsychiatry,* 1959, **29,** 172-179.

Rabin, A. I. *Growing up in the kibbutz.* New York: Springer, 1965.

Rabin, A. I. *Kibbutz studies.* East Lansing: The Michigan State University Press, 1971.

Robbins, L. C. The accuracy of parental record of aspects of child development and of child rearing practices. *Journal of Abnormal and Social Psychology,* 1963, **66,** 261-270.

Robson, K. S., & Moss, H. A. Patterns and determinants of maternal attachment. *Journal of Pediatrics,* 1970, **77,** 976-985.

Rosenoer, C., & Whyte, A. H. The ordinal position of problem children. *American Journal of Orthopsychiatry,* 1931, **1,** 430-434.

Rosenthal, M. K. The generalization of dependency behaviors from mother to stranger. Unpublished doctoral dissertation, Stanford University, 1965.

Rosenthal, M. K. The effect of a novel situation and anxiety on two groups of dependency behavior. *British Journal of Psychology,* 1967, **58,** 357-364. (a)

Rosenthal, M. K. The generalization of dependency behavior from mother to stranger. *Journal of Child Psychology and Psychiatry.* 1967, **8,** 117-133. (b)

Rothbart, M. K. Birth order and mother-child interaction in an achievement situation. *Journal of Personality and Social Psychology,* 1971, **17,** 113-120.

Sarnoff, I. Identification with the aggressor: some personality correlates of anti-Semitism among Jews. *Journal of Personality,* 1951, **20,** 199-218.

Schacter, S. *The Psychology of Affiliation.* Stanford, Calif.: Stanford, 1959.

Schaeffer, E. S. A circumplex model for maternal behavior. *Journal of Abnormal and Social Psychology,* 1959, **59,** 226-235.

Schaffer, H. R., & Emerson, P. E. The development of social attachments in infancy. *Monographs of the Society for Research in Child Development,* 1964, **29** (3, Serial No. 94), 5-77.

Sears, R. R., Maccoby, E. E., & Levin, H. *Patterns of Child Rearing.* New York: Harper & Row, 1957.

Sears, R. R., Rau, L., & Alpert, R. *Identification and Child Rearing.* Stanford, Calif.: Stanford, 1965.

Shapira, A., & Madsen, M. C. Cooperative and competitive behavior of Kibbutz and urban children in Israel. *Child Development,* 1969, **40,** 605-618.

Spelke, E., Zelazo, P., Kagan, J., & Kotelchuck, M. Father interaction and separation protest. *Developmental Psychology,* 1973, **9,** 83-90.

Spiro, M. E. *Children of the kibbutz.* Cambridge, Mass.: Harvard, 1958.

Sutton-Smith, B., & Rosenberg, B. G. *The sibling.* New York: Holt, 1970.

Thoman, E. B., Liederman, P. H., & Olson, J. P. Neonate-mother interaction during breast feeding. *Developmental Psychology,* 1972, **6,** 110-118.

Torrance, E. B. A psychological study of American jet aces. Paper presented at the meeting of the Western Psychological Association, Long Beach, Calif., 1954.

Wahler, R. G. Infant social attachments: a reinforcement theory interpretation and investigation. *Child Development,* 1957, **38,** 1079-1088.

Watson, J. B. *Psychological care of infant and child.* New York: Norton, 1928.

Winder, C. L., & Rau, L. Parental attitudes associated with social deviance in preadolescent boys. *Journal of Abnormal and Social Psychology,* 1962, **64,** 418-424.

Yarrow, M. R., Campbell, J. D., & Burton, R. V. *Child rearing.* San Francisco: Jossey-Bass, Inc., Publishers, 1968.

Zimmerman, C. C. The 1971 Burgess Award Address: The future of the family in America. *Journal of Marriage and the Family,* 1972, **34,** 323-349.

Zucker, R. A., Manosevitz, M., & Lanyon, R. D. Birth order, anxiety and affiliation during a crisis. *Journal of Personality and Social Psychology,* 1968, **8,** 354-359.

12
SOCIALIZATION AND THE DEVELOPMENT OF SEX ROLES

Sex-role typing is the process by which children acquire the values, motives, and behaviors appropriate to either males or females in a specific culture. Systematic attempts to communicate sex-role standards and to shape different behaviors in boys and girls begin in earliest infancy and have been described as follows:

> Sex-role differentiation usually commences immediately after birth, when the baby is named and both the infant and the nursery are given the blue or pink treatment depending upon the sex of the child. Thereafter, indoctrination into masculinity and femininity is diligently promulgated by adorning children with distinctive clothes and hair styles, selecting sex-appropriate play materials and recreational activities, promoting associations with same-sex playmates, and through non-permissive parental reactions to deviant sex-role behavior [Bandura, 1969, p. 215].

One investigator who was studying sex differences in infancy and did not want her observers to know whether they were watching boys or girls, complained that even in the first few days of life some infant girls were brought to the laboratory with pink bows tied to their wisps of hair or taped to their little bald heads. Later when another attempt at concealment of sex was made by asking mothers to dress their infants in overalls, girls appeared in pink and boys in blue overalls, and as the frustrated experimenter said, "Would you believe overalls with ruffles?"

SEX-ROLE STANDARDS

Considerable consistency in standards of appropriate sex-role behavior exists within and between cultures. These standards parallel Parsons' description of the female role as expressive and the male role as instrumental which were presented in Chapter 11. The male role is oriented toward controlling and manipulating the environment. Males are expected to be independent, assertive, dominant, and competitive in social and sexual relations. Females are expected to be more passive, loving, sensitive, and supportive in social relationships, especially in their family role as a wife and mother. Expression of warmth in personal relationships or anxiety under duress, and suppression of overt aggression and sexuality are regarded as more appropriate for women than men (Bennett & Cohen, 1959; Parsons, 1955). Although this may appear to be a rather outdated presentation of sex-role standards, studies have indicated that affection, nurturance, and passivity still are viewed as more characteristic of females and aggression, independence, competence, and dominance as characteristic of males by the majority of both elementary school children (Hartley, 1960) and adults (Hetherington, 1974; Jenkins & Vroegh, 1969; Broverman, Vogel, Broverman, Clarkson, & Rosenkrantz, 1972). Cross-cultural studies also find these stereotyped roles widespread not only in the American culture but in the majority of societies (Barry, Bacon & Child, 1957; D'Andrade, 1966).

Broverman and her colleagues (Broverman et al., 1972) report the results of a recent study in which seventy-four college men and eighty college women checked phrases which they regarded as more characteristic of males or females and evaluated the desirability of these characteristics. It can be seen in Table 12-1 that more characteristics regarded as masculine than feminine were rated as desirable. In addition, the characteristics labeled feminine and masculine fall into stereotyped sex-role clusters: a warmth-expressiveness cluster for females and a competency cluster for males.

There is, however, some variation in culturally accepted sex-role standards. In the United States female students and college-educated women between the ages of eighteen and thirty-five are more likely to perceive the feminine role as involving greater independence and achievement striving than do older or less educated females. Children with mothers who are employed in skilled occupations and professions also regard female educational and professional aspirations and the assumption of housekeeping and child-care tasks by males as more appropriate than do children whose mothers are unemployed. However, men, even young educated men, maintain more stereotyped sex-role standards than do women (Hetherington, 1974). Although adults regard sex-role standards in preschool children as less clearly delineated than those in older children, more men than women rate the behaviors of toddlers as young as eighteen months as sex-typed (Fagot, 1973). This clearer differentiation of sex roles by men is probably related to the frequently reported finding that fathers are more concerned

Table 12-1 STEREOTYPIC SEX-ROLE ITEMS
Responses from 74 college men and 80 college women

Competency cluster: masculine pole is more desirable

Feminine	Masculine
Not at all aggressive	Very aggressive
Not at all independent	Very independent
Very emotional	Not at all emotional
Does not hide emotions at all	Almost always hides emotions
Very subjective	Very objective
Very easily influenced	Not at all easily influenced
Very submissive	Very dominant
Dislikes math and science very much	Likes math and science very much
Very excitable in a minor crisis	Not at all excitable in a minor crisis
Very passive	Very active
Not at all competitive	Very competitive
Very illogical	Very logical
Very home-oriented	Very worldly
Not at all skilled in business	Very skilled in business
Very sneaky	Very direct
Does not know the way of the world	Knows the way of the world
Feelings easily hurt	Feelings not easily hurt
Not at all adventurous	Very adventurous
Has difficulty making decisions	Can make decisions easily
Cries very easily	Never cries
Almost never acts as a leader	Almost always acts as a leader
Not at all self-confident	Very self-confident
Very uncomfortable about being aggressive	Not at all uncomfortable about being aggressive
Not at all ambitious	Very ambitious
Unable to separate feelings from ideas	Easily able to separate feelings from ideas
Very dependent	Not at all dependent
Very conceited about appearance	Never conceited about appearance
Thinks women are always superior to men	Thinks men are always superior to women
Does not talk freely about sex, with men	Talks freely about sex with men

Warmth-expressiveness cluster: feminine pole is more desirable

Feminine	Masculine
Doesn't use harsh language at all	Uses very harsh language
Very talkative	Not at all talkative
Very tactful	Very blunt
Very gentle	Very rough
Very aware of feelings of others	Not at all aware of feelings of others
Very religious	Not at all religious
Very interested in own appearance	Not at all interested in own appearance
Very neat in habits	Very sloppy in habits
Very quiet	Very loud
Very strong need for security	Very little need for security
Enjoys art and literature	Does not enjoy art and literature at all
Easily expresses tender feelings	Does not express tender feelings at all easily

Source: Broverman, I. K., Vogel, S. R., Broverman, D. K., Clarkson, F. E., & Rosenkrantz, P. S. Sex-role stereotypes: a current appraisal. *Journal of Social Issues*, 1972, **28,** 63.

about their children maintaining sexually appropriate behaviors, and that the father plays a more important role in the sex-role typing of children than does the mother. It is interesting that in spite of some variations in sex-role standards among groups in the United States, almost all groups regardless of sex, social class, and education still view aggression as more characteristic of men and interpersonal sensitivity as more frequent in women, which are critical differences in Parsons' sex-role classifications (Hetherington, 1974).

One of the most frequently cited reports of divergence among cultures in sex-role standards and behavior is Margaret Mead's study of social roles in three primitive tribes: the Arapesh, the Mundugumor, and the Tchambuli (Mead, 1935). Little sex-role differentiation was prescribed by the Mundugumor and the Arapesh. However, the Arapesh exhibited behaviors which in many societies would be regarded as feminine and the Mundugumor those traditionally thought of as masculine. The Arapesh were passive, cooperative, and unassertive, whereas both men and women in the Mundugumor tribe were hostile, aggressive, cruel, and restrictive. In the Tchambuli a reversal of Parsons' traditional sex roles was found. The men were socially sensitive and concerned with the feelings of others, dependent, and interested in arts and crafts. The women were independent and aggressive and played the controlling role in decision making. Thus although the "traditional" sex roles are most common, there is enough variability within and across cultures to indicate that there is a great deal of plasticity in the development of masculine and feminine behaviors. If there are constitutionally based social and cognitive differences between males and females, they can be considerably modified by cultural forces.

SEX ROLES AND CONSTITUTIONAL FACTORS

Much to the consternation of contemporary feminists, the prevalence of stereotyped sex roles in humans and primates has led some investigators to propose that there are constitutionally determined personality and cognitive sex differences. Precisely what role genetic, biochemical, or prenatal influences play in the development of such constitutional factors remains a controversial issue. The possibility of constitutional factors in the development of sex differences has resulted in an increased interest in the role of hormonal factors in development and in the study of infants and young children when it is assumed that unlearned sex differences in behavior will have had less opportunity to be modified through experience.

Studies of young children

The description of women as "the weaker sex" appears particularly inaccurate in infancy. Male neonates are more vulnerable and less mature than females. They are miscarried more often, have a higher rate of infant mortality, and are more vulnerable to disease and many hereditary anomalies. Greater neurological maturity in females in the first few weeks of life is suggested by their greater sensitivity to touch, cold, pain, and variations in pitch and sound. It has been said that a newborn girl is similar to a four- to six-week-old boy in terms of neurological and physical maturity (Garai & Scheinfeld,

1968). The developmental acceleration in girls is apparent in later infancy in earlier walking and talking. Time of puberty as estimated by measures of skeletal maturity and the occurrence of the onset of the preadolescent growth spurt in height and weight also occurs over two years earlier in girls.

Although the male infant generally is less developmentally mature at birth, he is larger and has more mature muscular development. He also has relatively larger lungs and heart. These characteristics may prepare the male infant for a more physically active life. It seems possible that their lower sensitivity to pain and heavier muscular development may prepare the male infant for his later rough-and-tumble play, aggressiveness, and physical risk-taking behavior.

At a very early age infants are already expressing behaviors that are precursors of their later sex-typed behaviors. The greater docility and orientation toward social stimuli and interaction of girls, and the tendency of boys to be more assertive and demanding are rapidly apparent. Male neonates sleep less, are more irritable, cry more, and are more vigorously motorically active. It has been speculated that high degrees of infant activity are related to an inability to cope with and control internal tensions and impulses, and that this may be associated with later difficulty in inhibiting aggressive behavior and assertiveness found in males. In addition to such neonatal differences, greater aggressiveness and exploratory behavior in social relations and unfamiliar situations are found in boys as early as one year of age (Goldberg & Lewis, 1969; Hutt, 1970). Similarly, behaviors which are suggestive of the females' later concern with social relationships appear in infancy. Female infants talk earlier and utter more sounds (McCarthy, 1954), smile more (Moss, 1967), show a greater preference for looking at drawings of a human face rather than a geometric figure (Kagan & Lewis, 1965; Lewis, 1969), and can discriminate among upright faces earlier (Fagan, 1972) than do boys.

It might be expected that the greater social orientation and gazing at faces of females would lead to their earlier and more accurate perception of cues associated with social relations. Adults use how close people stand to each other and how much they look at each other as important cues in judging whether people like each other or not. There is some support for the greater social sensitivity of females in the finding that preschool girls learn to use proximity and eye contact in judging affiliation earlier than do boys (Post & Hetherington, 1974).

Patterns similar to those found in the first year of life are also found in older preschool children. After an extensive observational study of nursery school children it was concluded that "boys are interested in objects or things and girls in people [Hutt, 1972, p. 159]." In this study, girls spent more play time involved in social interactions, and boys in manipulation of toys and objects. In spite of the greater total time spent by girls in social interactions, boys spent over twice as much time involved in aggressive interactions and were more often both the initiators and targets of aggression. Boys also fought back against attacks and hence sustained aggressive altercations more often than did girls. Girls tended to submit and to argue rather than fight (Brindley, Clarke, Hutt, Robinson, & Wethli, 1972).

Studies of the effects of hormones on sex-typing

Some writers have suggested that hormonal differences (Beach, 1958; Young, Goy, & Phoenix, 1964) experienced prenatally or during the subsequent course of development may contribute to differences in behavior between sexes and within the same sex. Young, Goy, and Phoenix (1964) injected pregnant monkeys with testosterone (a male hormone) during the second quarter of pregnancy; this resulted in pseudohermaphroditic female offspring who exhibited not only genital alterations but also social behavior patterns which are characteristic of male monkeys. These infant female monkeys manifested masculine behaviors such as more threatening gestures, less withdrawal to approach or threat by other animals, more mounting behavior, and more rough-and-tumble play.

Subsequent studies have found that if male hormones are injected into normal female monkeys after birth but preceding puberty, the females also become much more assertive, sometimes even attaining the prime dominance status in the monkey troop. When this occurs, it is an evil day for the male monkeys in the troop. The tyrannical female restricts sexual and rough-and-tumble play between males and demands more restrained and docile behavior from her followers.

Even if such hormonal factors are present, they may be modified by the impact of social experiences. This is dramatically demonstrated in the studies of Money and his colleagues (Money, Hampson, & Hampson, 1957; Hampson & Hampson, 1961; Money, 1961; Money & Ehrhardt, 1972) of prenatal hormonal anomalies, such as high levels of androgen, which result in feminizing the male or masculinizing the female child and the subsequent mistaken sexual identity of the child. Many of the subjects in these studies were female infants who had the normal internal female reproduction system, but an enlarged clitoris which resembled a penis, and labial folds often fused and resembling a scrotum. A study of twenty-five fetally androgenized girls who were raised as girls and given corrective surgery if it was necessary, found that these girls were characterized by tomboyishness. Such girls enjoy vigorous athletic activities such as ball games. There is little rehearsal of the maternal role early in life in such things as doll play, or at adolescence in baby-sitting or caring for younger children. These girls also prefer simple utilitarian clothing, such as slacks and shorts, and show little concern with cosmetics, jewelry, or hairstyle.

In addition to play and grooming interests of these girls more closely resembling those of boys, their assertiveness and attitudes toward sexuality and achievement are similar to those more often found in males in our culture. These girls are assertive enough to be successful in establishing themselves in the dominance hierarchy of their male friends, although they do not compete for the top position in the hierarchy. They showed little concern in establishing a position in the dominance hierarchy of groups of girls, perhaps because of a lack of interest in traditional feminine games and activities.

Even in childhood the fantasies of these girls show a preference for success through achievement rather than marriage. They do show some interest in marriage and children but think in terms of a late marriage in conjunction with a career and few children. It should be noted that there is not an unusual incidence of lesbianism in these girls. Although their dating behavior tends to begin late and although their sexual fantasies tend to resemble those of males in specifically portraying the imagined sexual partner, they choose a male sexual partner in real life and in fantasy.

It has been suggested that their intense focus on achievement is based on the fact that these girls often have high IQs and perform unusually well on academic tasks. In fact, both males and females who have been exposed to high prenatal androgen levels show elevated scores on intelligence tests. It has been speculated that androgen may play a role in the development of the cerebral cortex, and that even within genitally normal females there might be a relationship between tomboyism and high IQ.

If the reassignment of the child to her correct feminine gender role occurred after the first few years of life, inadequate sex-typing and poor psychological adjustment occurred. If early reassignment occurred, normal psychosexual development in some of the subjects followed. This finding led the authors to conclude that there is a "critical period" for the establishment of gender role between eighteen months and three years.

Beach (1965), in discussing this issue, concludes:

> Without questioning the primary importance of individual experience and social learning in gender role development, the potential contribution of constitutional factors can be regarded as an unresolved issue. It is at least conceivable that there are sex differences in the functional characteristics of the male and female brain, that such differences are manifest at birth, and that they have some effect upon the acquisition of social behavior tendencies, including learning the gender role [Beach, 1965, p. 565].

Therefore, rather than innate sex differences in personality existing, such constitutional differences may only serve to mediate variations in the kinds of social and sensory input received by boys and girls. LaBarre (1954) has discussed the differences between living in a female body and a male body in terms of such things as physical strength and the necessary roles in sexual intercourse, pregnancy, and feeding of offspring. More subtle interactions between these constitutional factors and life experiences may also occur. The crying, irritable, physically active male infant may interact with a wider environment and will probably structure and contribute more to the interaction with the mother than does the more inactive, frequently sleeping, less demanding female child. Indeed, there is evidence that mothers hold, stimulate, and arouse male infants more than females, but imitate the vocalizations of females more than males (Moss, 1967). It may be the irritability and activity of the male which elicits greater physical stimulation by the mother which in turn leads to assertive behavior either through the effects of sensory input itself or through giving him a sense of greater control of his environment.

Few psychologists would accept a purely biological or purely cultural position as to the origins of sex differences in behavior and temperament. What genotypical predispositions there may be are being constantly modified by cultural forces to conform to sex-role standards. In spite of this, there is considerable overlap in the characteristics of males and females. Some males are more passive, sensitive to people, verbal, and interested in the arts than are some females. Similarly, although males seem constitutionally predisposed to be stronger, more irritable, and better adapted to successful aggressive interactions, some women are pretty hardy types, as can be witnessed at women's roller derbys or wrestling matches. In addition in the area of intellectual and occupational achievement there are outstanding female architects, mathematicians, engineers, and scientists, although males receive more encouragement in these areas.

DEVELOPMENTAL PATTERNS OF SEX-TYPING

Developmental patterns of sex-typing differ for boys and girls. Our culture is basically a male-oriented culture, with greater esteem, privileges, and status accorded to the masculine role (Brown, 1957; D'Andrade, 1966). The male role is more clearly defined and there is greater pressure for boys than girls to conform to sex-appropriate standards. Tomboys are tolerated, but sissies rejected. Parents and peers condemn boys for crying, retreating in the face of aggression, wearing feminine apparel, or playing with dolls. In contrast, an occasional temper tantrum, rough-and-tumble play, wearing jeans, or playing with trucks is at least moderately acceptable for girls. Lansky (1967) asked parents of preschool and kindergarten children to react to a series of sex-appropriate and sex-inappropriate choices of activities and objects by children. Mothers and fathers both responded more negatively to opposite sex choices by boys than by girls. Studies suggested that fathers tend to respond more negatively to feminine behaviors in boys than do mothers. Such intense concern about inappropriate sex-typed behavior as is revealed by fathers may be a manifestation of their anxieties about their own masculinity (Goodenough, 1957), and may be a pervasive masculine concern in our culture.

It has been speculated that sex-role behavior for boys is seldom defined positively as something the child should do, but more often negatively as something he should not do, and that these negative sanctions are frequently enforced by punishment (Hartley, 1959). Boys receive physical punishment more often than do girls. It even has been concluded that the basic developmental task of girls is learning how not to be a baby, and of boys is learning how not to be a girl (Emmerich, 1959). It has also been proposed that an additional difficulty in sex-role identification for boys is the necessary shift from their initial identification with the mothers to identification with the father, whereas girls need only intensify their initial maternal identification. This difficult transition plus the greater demands for conformity and harsher prohibitions utilized in sex-role training of boys may make sex-role identification more stressful for boys than for girls (Lynn, 1969). Many eight- to eleven-year-old boys express great anxiety about maintaining their sex roles, and this anxiety verges on panic at being detected in the performance of feminine activities (Hartley, 1959). Such apprehension is rarely expressed by girls.

In view of the above factors it is not surprising that boys develop appropriate behaviors earlier and more consistently than do girls. On measures of sex-role preference such as the It Scale for Children, which asks a child to select preferred masculine or feminine toys or whether the child would like to grow up to be a mommy or a daddy, girls make masculine choices until about the age of ten, when a rapid shift toward femininity occurs. There is some evidence that feminine preferences increase rapidly from age three to four (Hartup & Zook, 1960), but that girls shift toward more masculine choices from age four to ten (Brown, 1957). This might be attributed to the elementary school age girl's increasing awareness of the greater privileges and prestige of the male role, followed by her eventual capitulation to social pressures toward sexual conformity in the preadolescent period. In contrast, even in the preschool years most boys prefer and sustain a marked preference for the masculine role.

Observational studies of play patterns of boys and girls have obtained similar results in indicating that preschool and elementary school girls conform less strictly to sex-appropriate behaviors than do boys, in addition to voicing less culturally appropriate sex-role preferences. Girls are more likely to play with a truck than boys are to cuddle a doll.

Children from middle-class families conform less strictly to sex-appropriate behaviors. (Suzanne Szasz.)

The course of sex-typing varies in the lower and middle classes. Lower-class boys clearly prefer sex-appropriate toys by age four or five, middle-class boys and lower-class girls by about seven, and finally middle-class girls at age nine (Rabban, 1950). Class differences in sex-role standards for males become particularly apparent in adolescence. In a study of forty early adolescents it was found that the aggressive playground bully was the undisputed leader among low-socioeconomic-class boys, while both the sissy and the classroom conformer were likely to be rejected by their peers. In contrast, aggressive, domineering behaviors at the high socioeconomic level made a boy unpopular not only with other boys but with girls as well. Skill and daring in competitive games were highly valued instead, and even the studious adult-conformer and classroom "intellectual" was accorded much more acceptance by his peers than in lower social class groups. The sissy, however, was rejected just as he was by lower-class children. Both lower- and middle-class girls accepted the "little lady" pattern of behavior, comprising friendliness, conformity, goodness, and tidiness in girls (Pope, 1953).

These differences have been attributed to the clearer delineation of sex roles, more rigid demands for conformity to sex standards, and more conventional masculine or feminine models offered by lower-class parents. The middle-class mother is less home-oriented and feels she has more control over what happens to her and her children than the lower-class mother. She has interests and activities outside the family and may be employed in a vocation which is not regarded as suitable solely for women. The main roles of lower-class women are often focused on sexual satisfaction, housekeeping, and child care. Their employment also frequently involves traditionally feminine activities, such as cooking, housework, and child care. Lower-class men usually work in occupations regarded as uniquely masculine, such as those involving heavy labor, and their function in childrearing is often limited to that of family provider and disciplinarian. In contrast, middle-class fathers spend more time with their children and participate more actively in the tasks of routine child and household care and family recreational activities.

STABILITY OF SEX-ROLE TYPING

Masculinity or femininity appears to be a remarkably early developed and stable personality characteristic. The longitudinal Fels Institute study (Kagan & Moss, 1962), which studied the development of a group of middle-class children from birth to adulthood, found that adult heterosexual behavior could be predicted from sex-typed interests in elementary school. Figure 12-1 presents a summary of the relationship between some selected child behaviors and similar adult behaviors. Boys who were interested in competitive games, gross motor skills, and such things as mechanics, and girls who were interested in cooking, sewing, reading, and noncompetitive games were involved in sex-typed activities in adulthood. A finding of greater stability for boys than girls on this characteristic is not unexpected in the light of the ambivalence toward the feminine role experienced by many females. The earlier sex-typing of boys is again demonstrated since childhood sexuality and masculine play even in the preschool years is associated with adult sex-role interests and heterosexual activities in boys but not in girls. It was found that the stability of many of the personality characteristics investigated was related to their appropriateness to culturally accepted sex-role standards. When a characteristic conflicted with sex-role standards it led to some form of more socially acceptable substitute or derivative behavior in adulthood. When it was congruent with such standards, it tended to remain stable from childhood to maturity. Thus sex-typed interests, which are encouraged in both sexes, tend to remain stable in both males and females. In contrast, childhood sexuality and aggression are predictive of adult sexuality and anger arousal in males but not in females; and childhood passivity and dependency are predictive of these adult behaviors in females but not in males.

The sexually incongruent behaviors, which it may be assumed are eliminated through socialization practices, do emerge in derivative forms of behavior in adulthood. Anger and tantrums in girls are associated with intellectual competitiveness, masculine interests, and dependency conflict in women. Passivity in boys is related to social apprehension, noncompetitiveness, and sexual anxiety in men.

THEORIES OF SEX-ROLE TYPING

In addition to the previously discussed psychoanalytic, social learning, and role theories of identification which are assumed to explain the acquisition of a variety of behaviors

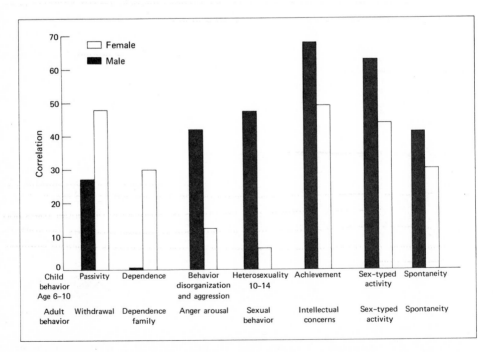

FIGURE 12-1 Summary of relations between selected child behaviors (six to ten years of age) and functionally similar adult behaviors. (From Kagan, J., & Moss, H. A. *Birth to Maturity: A Study in Psychological Development.* Copyright © 1962 by John Wiley and Sons. Reprinted by permission of publisher and author.)

including sex-typed behaviors, two theories have been proposed which deal specifically with the acquisition of sex-role typing.

Johnson's reciprocal role theory of sex-role typing

In an interesting extension of Parsons' reciprocal role theory of identification, Johnson (1963) suggests that the father may be the critical parent for sex-typing of both boys and girls since the father responds differentially to sons and daughters, but the mother does not. When the child is about five years of age, the father takes a more permissive, affectionate, and appreciative attitude toward his daughter than his son. He is the demanding, critical teacher of the son, but is warm and indulgent with the daughter. In contrast, the mother is equally loving and permissive to children of both sexes.

Johnson also emphasizes the importance of parental power, particularly the father's control in the sex-typing of boys. If children develop a sense of competence by controlling sources of love and affection and mastering the environment (Kagan, 1958), it might be expected that a child would become oriented toward the form of competence most congruent with accepted sex roles. Since the instrumental male role emphasizes problem solving and power in manipulating the environment, and the female role stresses concern and responsiveness to the needs and feelings of others, boys may learn to respond relatively more to parental control and dominance, and girls to the warmth and affective behaviors of the parents.

The role of power in the father should be particularly critical in the sex-typing of boys, in motivating the boys to emulate their father, and in offering a masculine model. If the father is perceived as powerful, the boy's striving for mastery and competence and the social sanctions reinforcing him for being masculine will lead to identification with the father. If the mother is controlling, the boy may tend to sustain his bonds with her in spite of cultural pressures for masculine behavior. Secondly, paternal dominance should be particularly important since the decisive controlling father offers a more appropriate masculine model for his son.

Kohlberg's cognitive theory of sex-role typing

Kohlberg (1966) has presented a provocative cognitive theory of the development of sex-typing. In contrast to the social learning position that sex-typing is a result of reinforcement and modeling, he argues that the child's differentiation of gender roles and his perception of himself as more similar to same-sexed models precedes, not follows, identification. His notion of the development of sex-role concepts is similar to Parsons' belief that children make "we males" and "those females" differentiations in learning social roles. When the child on the basis of physical and sex-role differences such as clothing, hair style, occupation, etc., categorizes himself as male or female, it then becomes rewarding to behave in a sex-appropriate manner and imitate same-sexed models. Thus the girl says, "I am a girl since I am more like my mother and other girls than boys; therefore I want to dress like a girl, play girl games, and feel and think like a girl."

Consistency between the child's gender, self-categorization, and appropriate behaviors and values are critical in sustaining self-esteem. That cognitive factors are important in sex-typing is clear since high IQ is related to early sex-role preferences and attitudes. Bright boys more easily and rapidly acquire and exhibit the masculine interests and play patterns expected by society.

THE FAMILY AND SEX-TYPING

Studies of effects of the family on sex-typing again find marked differences in the development of boys and girls. In accord with the predictions of Johnson, the father exerts great influence on the sex-typing of both sons and daughters. Although mothers have some effect on the development of femininity in girls, they have little influence on the masculinity of sons. Nurturance and warmth in the same-sex parent increases appropriate sex-role learning for both boys and girls (Bronson, 1959; Helper, 1955; Mussen & Distler, 1959, 1960; Mussen & Rutherford, 1963; Payne & Mussen, 1956; Sears, 1953). However, where both maternal and paternal warmth increase femininity in girls, highly masculine boys perceive their fathers but not their mothers as more nurturant and rewarding than do boys who are lower in masculinity (Hetherington, 1967).

Great consistency is found in the evidence for the effects of parental power on sex-typing. In decision making, dominant mothers and passive fathers are particularly destructive in the identification of boys although they have no effect on femininity in girls. Highly masculine boys have fathers who are decisive and dominant in setting limits and dispensing both rewards and punishments (Biller, 1968; Hetherington, 1965; Moulton, Liberty, Burnstein, & Altucher, 1966; Mussen & Distler, 1959). They play an active role in discipline of their sons. Paternal punishment seems to facilitate sex-role typing in boys only if the father is also nurturant and dominant. In contrast to the strong relationship with the development of masculinity in boys, parental power has little effect on the development of femininity in girls.

Parental characteristics other than warmth, power, and hostility might also be expected to effect sex-typing. One might speculate that the masculinity or femininity of the parents and their encouragement of sex-typed behaviors should be particularly important for the child's delineation and discrimination of gender roles. However, sex-typing of parents and encouragement of sex-typed activities by parents is not related to masculinity in boys (Angrilli, 1960; Mussen & Rutherford, 1963; Payne & Mussen, 1956). Again in girls we see the importance of the father in sex-typing; femininity in daughters is related to father's masculinity, father's approval of the mother as a model, and father's reinforcement for participation in feminine activities. It is interesting that it is not related to femininity in mothers. More feminine mothers do not have more feminine daughters (Hetherington, 1967).

FATHER ABSENCE AND SEX-ROLE TYPING

Since the father plays such a critical role in sex-role typing, it might be expected that children from homes in which the father is either permanently absent or away for long periods of time would show disruptions in sex-typing. In some ways the home in which there is no father present may resemble a mother-dominated, intact family since the mother must of necessity assume a more decisive role in rearing her children alone. The

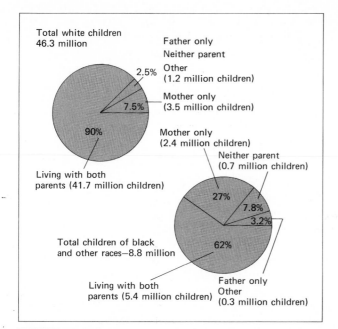

Total white children
46.3 million

Father only
Neither parent
Other
(1.2 million children)

2.5%

Mother only
(3.5 million children)

7.5%

90%

Mother only
(2.4 million children)

Neither parent
(0.7 million children)

Living with both
parents (41.7 million children)

27%

7.8%

3.2%

Total children of black
and other races—8.8 million

62%

Living with both
parents (5.4 million children)

Father only
Other
(0.3 million children)

FIGURE 12-2 Presence of parents for children under age fourteen: United States, March, 1970. (From White House Conference on Children. *Profiles of Children.* Government Printing Office, 1970, p. 22.)

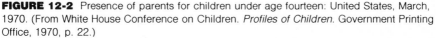

absence of a male model and lack of opportunity for interaction with a father may also contribute to difficulty in sex-typing in such homes.

Thirty to forty percent of urban children have experienced a broken home at some time before age eighteen (Langner & Michael, 1963). The 1970 Population Census shows that the American divorce rate has now increased to one in every four marriages. Figure 12-2 presents the percent of white and nonwhite families in which both parents are present, only the mother is present, or only the father is present. It can be seen that the absence of a father is more frequent in nonwhite families, and it has been found that this is particularly marked in black families.

Although there are certain disadvantages to raising children in one-parent families, such children make more satisfactory adjustments than those reared in unhappy, strife-ridden, intact families (Chombart de Laurve, 1959; Nye, 1957). There is also some evidence that the deleterious effects of a family with a single parent may be less than those of a family with a stepparent. Studies of children of remarried parents indicate that friction, competition, hostility, and ambivalence with stepparents is frequent, and is most common in adolescent children (Bowerman & Irish, 1962). Permanent separation from a father due to death or divorce, temporary separation or unavailability due to war or occupational demands, or paternal disinterest have been shown to disrupt the sex-role typing, self-control, and cognitive development of boys (Hetherington & Deur, 1971). Disruptions in sex-role typing are most apparent in preadolescent boys; however, poor intellectual performance and academic achievement and lack of self-control seem to increase through the school years. These effects are most severe if the separation has occurred before age five. In girls such effects seem to be largely limited to cognitive deficits and to deviations in relationships with males which do not emerge until adolescence.

Preschool boys who are separated from their fathers early in life are found to be less aggressive and more dependent, to have more feminine self-concepts, and to exhibit more feminine patterns of play and social interactions involving such things as the use of high verbal aggression and low physical aggression. The importance of age of separation is apparent in a study by Hetherington (1966) which involved direct observations by male recreation directors of boys in a recreation center. Boys who were six years of age or older at the time of separation from fathers did not differ from children raised in intact homes. However, if the father had left before the son was five, the son scored as less masculine on the It scale for children a measure of sex-role preference, was rated as more dependent on peers and less assertive, as engaged in fewer rough physical contact sports than father-present boys. They were demonstrating behaviors more characteristic of girls than of boys. This supports the psychoanalytic premise that there is a critical period for sex-typing in the preschool years.

Although preschool boys with absent fathers exhibit disruptions in sex-typing, the results with older boys are less consistent. Some studies have reported no differences between adolescent father-absent and father-present boys (Barclay & Cusumano, 1967), especially if the son was not deprived of his father until after age five (Biller & Bahm, 1971); others have found compensatory masculinity. Compensatory masculinity involves the exhibition of inconsistent patterns of both masculine and feminine behaviors. Such boys exhibit both excessively masculine, assertive forms of behavior, and at times feminine behaviors such as dependency. Delinquents are often found to have this combination of flamboyant, swaggering toughness and sexuality, accompanied by dependency. This has been associated with the high rates of father absence found in the homes of delinquent children. With age father-absent boys may gradually become more aware of the greater privileges and prestige of males and therefore prefer the masculine role. However, the lack of early identification with a masculine, paternal model may result in difficulty in developing a subtle, integrated repertoire of masculine behaviors.

With increasing age and wider social contacts other models, such as teachers, peers, siblings, surrogate fathers, and those in the mass media, serve to partially mitigate the effects of father absence on sex-role adoption. Models other than parents have been demonstrated to effect sex-typing. In two-child families, children who have siblings of the same sex rather than the opposite sex are rated as more appropriately sex-typed by teachers (Brim, 1958), and adolescents who report frequent childhood experiences with older members of the same sex exhibit more appropriate sex-typed interests (Steimel, 1960). In families with fathers absent, children who have older brothers are more aggressive and less dependent than children with no older male siblings (Wohlford, Santrock, Berger, & Leiberman, 1971).

The effects of paternal absence on preadolescent girls appears to be minimal. Although a study by Lynn and Sawrey (1959) of eight- and nine-year-old children of Norwegian seamen whose fathers were away for extended periods of time found the daughters to show greater dependency on the mother, a current investigation (Santrock, 1970) found no effects of father absence on the dependency, aggression, and femininity of preschool black girls.

It is only recent evidence largely based on studies of adolescents that suggests paternal absence may have a delayed effect on the sex-typing of girls. The study presented in Box 12-1 shows that father-absence is associated with disruptions in relating to other males by adolescent daughters and that the form of this disruption differs for daughters of widows and divorcees.

BOX 12-1 THE EFFECTS OF FATHER ABSENCE ON PERSONALITY
DEVELOPMENT IN ADOLESCENT DAUGHTERS

What are the effects on daughters of absence of a father? The subjects were three groups of twenty-four lower- and lower-middle-class firstborn adolescent white girls with no male siblings. The first group came from families with both parents living in the home, the second group from families in which the father was absent due to divorce, and the third in which the father had died. Both groups of girls with fathers absent had no males living in the home.

The measures included the following: observations of the girls' behavior in a recreation center; interviews, personality tests, and tests of sex-role typing of mother and daughter; and observed measures of nonverbal communication, such as posture, gestures, and eye contact, when the girls were being interviewed by a male or female interviewer.

There were few differences among the three groups of girls on traditional measures of sex-role typing. The girls in all groups had feminine interests, activities, preferences, and behaviors. However, girls with fathers absent showed different patterns of heterosexual behavior than girls from intact families. Their disturbance in relationships with males appeared either as excessive sexual anxiety, shyness, and discomfort around males or as promiscuous and inappropriately assertive behavior with male peers and adults. The former syndrome was more common when separation had occurred because of the father's death, the latter when separation was a result of divorce. These behaviors did not occur in interacting with females. In recreation center dances, males tended to congregate at one end of the hall and females at the other. The behavior of the girls was recorded during these occasions. The first, inhibited group of daughters of widows tended to remain in the cluster of other girls unless they were invited to dance. They more frequently positioned themselves in the back row than did the other group of father-absent or father-present girls. Some even spent over 90 percent of the evening hiding in the ladies' room. In contrast, the second group, the daughters of divorcees, spent more time at the boys' end of the hall, more frequently initiated encounters and asked male peers to dance, and more frequently touched the males in proximity to them. This was not related to differences in popularity since girls in all three groups were asked to dance equally often when they were in the hall.

Except for behaviors associated with proximity and attention seeking or avoidance of males there were few differences between girls with fathers absent or fathers present in sex-typed behaviors.

In interviews in the laboratory where three chairs were available to the interviewees, daughters of widows tended to seat themselves on the most distant chair, daughters of divorcees on a chair immediately adjacent to the interviewer, and girls from intact homes directly across the desk in what might be considered the most appropriate position for interactions in such situations. The daughters of widows spent the least time in mutual eye contact with the interviewer, most frequently was turned away from the interviewer, and had the most constricted body posture, often with arms tensely folded and legs crossed. The daughters of divorcees spent more time looking at the male interviewer, with their bodies oriented directly toward him. They also assumed a sprawling, open-body position with legs and arms apart, a position which some investigators of nonverbal communication would assume was a sexually receptive position. Father-present girls tended to fall between the two father-absent groups on measures of nonverbal communication. The important finding was that these differences occurred only if the interviewer was a man. With a female interviewer the differences between groups were no greater than would be expected by chance.

It seems plausible that such differences in the daughters might be the result of differences in childrearing practices and attitudes of their mothers. However, the mothers of the different groups of girls were very similar in their childrearing practices. Until the girls reached adolescence, the mothers were equally loving, consistent, and permissive. Greater conflict, inconsistency, and punitiveness and restrictiveness about sex found in divorcees after their daughters were adolescents could well be a reaction to, rather than a precursor of daughters' adolescent behavior.

The following are portions of representative interviews by mothers from each of the father-absent groups; the first is from the widowed group; and the second is from the divorced group.

_____is almost too good. She has lots of girl friends but doesn't date much. When she's with the girls she's gay and bouncy—quite a clown but she clams up when a man comes in. Even around my brother she never says much. When boys do phone she often puts them off even though she has nothing else to do. She says she has lots of time for that later, but she's sixteen now and very pretty, and all her friends have boy friends.

That kid is going to drive me over the hill. I'm at my wits end. She was so good until the last few years then Pow! At eleven she really turned on. She went boy crazy. When she was only twelve I came home early from a movie and found her in bed with a young hood and she's been bouncing from bed to bed ever since. She doesn't seem to care who it is, she can't keep her hands off men. It isn't just boys her own age; when I have men friends here she kisses them when they come in the door and sits on their knees all in a very playful fashion but it happens to them all. Her uncle is a 60-year-old priest and she even made a "ha ha" type pass at him. It almost scared him to death. I sometimes get so frantic I think I should turn her in to the cops but I remember what a good kid she used to be and I do love her. We still have a good time together when we're alone and I'm not nagging about her being a tramp. We both like to cook and get a lot of good laughs when we're puttering around in the kitchen. She's smart and good-looking—she should know she doesn't have to act like that [Hetherington, 1972, p. 322].

All of the mothers were equally feminine, reinforced their daughters for sex-appropriate behaviors, and surprisingly had equally positive attitudes toward men in general.

It was mainly in attitudes toward herself, her marriage, and her life that the divorcee differed from the widow. The divorcee is anxious and unhappy. Her attitude toward her spouse is hostile, and her memories of her marriage and life are negative. These attitudes are reflected in the critical attitude of her daughter toward the divorced father. Although she loves her daughter, she feels she had had little support from other people during her divorce and times of stress and with her difficulties in rearing a child alone. This is in marked contrast to the positive attitudes of the widows toward marriage, their lost husbands, the emotional support of friends and family at the loss of a husband, and the gratification of having children. These attitudes are reflected in the happy memories their daughters have of their fathers.

Both groups of girls with absent fathers report feeling anxious around males but have apparently developed different ways of coping with this anxiety. It may be that daughters of divorcees view their mothers' separated lives as unsatisfying and feel that for happiness it is essential to secure a man. It may also be that life with a dissatisfied, anxious mother, even if she loves the daughter, is difficult, and that these daughters are more eager to leave home than daughters of widows living with relatively happy, secure mothers with support from the extended family. In contrast, daughters of widows with their aggrandized image of their father may feel that few other males can compare favorably with him or alternately may regard all males as superior and as objects of deference and apprehension.

Source: Hetherington, E. M. Effects of father absence on personality development in adolescent daughters. *Developmental Psychology*, 1972, **7,** 303-326.

The studies of paternal absence again indicate the important role of the father in the social development of girls. Daughters learn to feel competent and to value and acquire the social skills necessary for effective heterosexual interactions by interacting with a warm, masculine, instrumental father who rewards and enjoys her femininity. However, the severity of the effects of father absence are moderated by maternal behavior. Mothers who present their husbands and their previous relationships with them in a positive manner and who are themselves stable, lessen the deleterious effects of father absence.

A follow-up study is being conducted on the girls in the study reported in Box 12-1 to see how long lasting the effects of father absence on daughters' relationships with men are, as reflected in the girls' subsequent marital relationships. Freud has suggested that girls continue to relive their relationships with their fathers through subsequent interactions with men. Do girls marry men who resemble their image of their fathers?

One difficulty in the follow-up study has been that daughters of widows are continuing to show their avoidance pattern with males and are marrying later than daughters of divorcees or girls from intact families. At this writing, only eleven daughters of widows but twenty-one daughters of divorcees and sixteen daughters from intact families out of the twenty-four in each group have married. Daughters of divorcees not only married younger, but more of them were pregnant at the time of marriage and several are already separated or divorced.

On an adjective checklist on which the girls checked adjectives which were most or least like their husband, father, or most men, both daughters of divorcees and widows report more similarity between their husbands and fathers than do girls from intact families. Freud may be right, but only for father-absent girls. Girls from father-absent families may not have the opportunity to work through their feelings about their fathers as do girls with the father present, and may seek to resolve these feelings with their mates. Girls who have had a continuous relationship with a father come to view them in a more balanced, realistic way, perceiving virtues and shortcomings. Girls with absent fathers maintain their childhood image of their fathers. Daughters of widows perceived both their husbands and fathers as having many more favorable characteristics than most men. Daughters of divorcees viewed their fathers, husbands, and most men as having predominantly undesirable characteristics. Their attitude could be characterized as "Men are no damned good, they never have been, and they'll never change." In contrast, girls from intact families view men in general and their husbands and fathers as good but not perfect, as having a substantial number of favorable attributes but also some flaws.

The appraisals of the husbands on the basis of interviews, tests, and direct observations to some extent confirm the wives' opinions. The husbands of the daughters of divorcees were less educated, had less stable employment records, and were more frequently involved in problems with the law than were the other two groups of husbands. In addition, they felt more ambivalent or hostile toward their wives and infants and were less emotionally mature and more impulsive and self-centered. In contrast, daughters of widows tended to marry husbands with more education or a higher vocational status than their parents had. These men were self-controlled almost to the point of being too inhibited. They were also nurturant, ambitious, concerned about social approval, and conventional, and they maintained stereotyped views of male and female roles. One interviewer characterized them as "repulsively straight." The results of this study indicate that the effects of fathers' absence on their daughter's interactions with males are long lasting and extend even into their marital choices. These girls seem to select mates who were similar to their images of their fathers, whereas girls from intact families were less constrained by their relationship with their father in their choice of a husband.

It should be noted that the father-absent girls in this study came from rather extreme samples in which there was not only no father but no other males in the house, including brothers, and in which the mother had not remarried. These girls could be considered as deprived of contacts with males in general, rather than just deprived of a father. Such marked differences might not be obtained with less severe conditions of male absence.

The effects of father absence on sex-typing extend beyond those of personality development into the area of cognition. Deficits in both intellectual and academic achievement have been found in father-absent children. These effects appear to be cumulative (Deutsch & Brown, 1964) and extend into adulthood. College students whose fathers have been absent for two or more years have lower American college entrance examination scores than do father-present students, although the presence of a like-sex sibling attenuates this difference (Sutton-Smith, Rosenberg, & Landy, 1968). Even less severe forms of father absence have implications for cognitive development. A study (Blanchard & Biller, 1971) of the effects of early (before age five) versus late father absence and low (less than six hours per week) versus high father availability in intact homes, found that boys with highly available fathers exceeded the other three groups on achievement tests and classroom grades. Although both boys whose fathers were seldom available and who lost their fathers after age five performed below grade level expectations, they were not as severely retarded as boys who had been separated from their fathers in the first five years of life. Separation from fathers leads to significant but less severe deficits in achievement test and IQ scores in girls (Santrock, 1972).

Studies also suggest that these deficits affect certain content areas more than others and that the pattern of deficiencies is related to sex-typed abilities. Females are usually superior to males in verbal areas, while males are superior to females in quantitative areas. Some studies have shown that boys with absent fathers tend to show higher verbal scores than mathematics scores, while boys from intact homes manifest the traditional masculine pattern of greater relative mathematical ability. This pattern is most pronounced for boys who have undergone early and long separation experiences (Carlsmith, 1964).

Two explanations have been advanced to account for this finding. It has been attributed to a more feminine cognitive style based on disrupted identification in boys lacking a father. They may be identifying with their mother and acquiring her relatively higher verbal abilities. It has also been suggested that stress interferes most with mathematical and less with verbal ability and that paternal absence is only one of a variety of stressful home situations which could result in a depression in mathematical ability in both boys and girls (Nelson & Maccoby, 1966).

Cross-cultural studies yield further evidence of the effects of early isolation from the father on masculine development. Burton and Whiting (1967) propose that in societies where the child's early social interactions are entirely confined to his mother or other females, and where the father is isolated from the infant, a process of discontinuous identification occurs. Although the child has an unusually focused and intense primary identification with his mother, boys must eventually shift to a secondary identification with the unfamiliar masculine role. Such cultures frequently utilize highly ritualized, often painful initiation rites in an effort to facilitate and formalize the abrupt transition to manhood. The high incidence of couvade in these societies suggests that the transition in sex-role identification is not entirely successful. *Couvade*, which may be a manifestation of underlying feminine identification, is a custom where the husband goes to bed as if for childbearing during the delivery of his offspring of his wife. Such a custom suggests considerable ambivalence about adoption of the masculine role.

The literature on the role of the father in intact families and the deleterious effects of father absence in the sex-role typing of sons and heterosexual relations of daughters indicates that the father may be the most important parent in the psychosexual development of offspring of either sex.

MATERNAL EMPLOYMENT AND CHILD DEVELOPMENT

An increasing number of mothers are employed. Figure 12-3 shows the percent of working white and nonwhite mothers. It can be seen that a larger percentage of non-

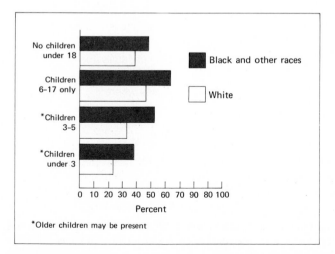

FIGURE 12-3 Percent of wives in the labor force by race and age of children: United States, 1969 (married women, husband present). (From White House Conference on Children. *Profiles of Children*. Government Printing Office, 1970, p. 62.)

white mothers work irrespective of the ages of their children. It can also be noted that mothers tend to remain in the home when their children are infants.

Maternal employment might be expected to make the mother unavailable to the child over a large portion of the day, thus altering activities and role relations in the home. Such changes in family interaction might be expected to be reflected in the adjustment to and in attitudes toward sex roles in children. In spite of dire predictions to the contrary, the results of studies of maternal employment suggest that it does not have consistent detrimental effects on children; in fact, in many studies positive consequences have been obtained. The effects of maternal employment can only be evaluated in relation to other factors, such as the reason why the mother is working, the mother's satisfaction with her role, the attitudes of and demands placed on other family members, and the adequacy of substitute care provided for the children.

When the mother works because she enjoys her occupation or in order to help out the family finances, there is less familial disruption than when maternal employment is motivated by a desire to escape from family responsibilities and from contact with her children. Nonworking mothers who have a sense of satisfaction and competence in their homemaking role, and working mothers who enjoy their employment both show more positive relations with their children than unhappy nonworking mothers who would like to be employed (Hartley, 1966; Hoffman, 1961; Yarrow, Scott, DeLeeuw, & Heineg, 1962).

When mothers work only periodically, the effect on family relationships is more detrimental than when they are regularly employed. The former situation frequently involves inadequate substitute care and lack of time for the child to adapt to his new situation. One of the factors which has been found to be particularly important in the effects of maternal employment on children has been the supervision of children whose mothers work. Eight to ten percent of American children have no supervision when their parents are absent from home (United States Department of Labor, 1965). The study presented in Box 12-2 investigated the effects of maternal employment and supervision arrangements on the health and on the cognitive, social, and personality development of lower-class black children. When inadequate care is provided, household routine breaks down: meals are irregular, there is less attention to grooming, there are fewer opportunities for family social interaction and recreation, and other family members may be forced to assume household chores. There is some evidence that preadolescent children do not assume more household duties except in cases where the mother dislikes working (Hoffman, 1961). However, adolescents and husbands are likely to increase their household duties. A few studies of maternal employment in lower-class families show that in some cases employment can lead to feelings of neglect, loneliness, and nervousness in young children; ambivalence toward the mother in adolescent daughters; and a rejection of the father as an adequate role model and resentment of adult authority in sons (Siegel, Stolz, Hitchcock, & Adamson, 1959). In contrast, a study by Hoffman (1961) reports that middle-class, employed mothers are more helpful, warm, satisfied, and relaxed in the family situation. It may be that more lower-class mothers who do not want to work are forced to do so out of financial need and that their resentment is reflected in adverse family relations.

Maternal employment may influence the child's perception of sex roles. If both parents work, their roles may be perceived as similar not only because of the maternal

BOX 12-2 THE UNSUPERVISED CHILD OF THE WORKING MOTHER

In this study the effects of lack of supervision of the children of employed mothers on the children's behavior was investigated. The subjects were 106 fifth-grade, urban ghetto dwellers with employed mothers. These children were classified into groups varying in their degree of supervision based on their reports of whether they were supervised by mature individuals (eighteen years of age and older) during breakfast, lunch hour, and after school until dinner, and during the summer vacation.

The children were administered a series of intelligence, achievement, and personality tests. In addition, they took the Parent Behavior Inventory developed by Earl Schaefer (1965) which measures children's perceptions of their parents' attitudes, discipline practices, and behavior.

Teachers described each of the children by checking adjectives which were descriptive of them on an adjective checklist. In addition, information on the children was gathered from school, hospital, and police records. Finally, an extensive interview was conducted on a subgroup of the mothers.

It was found that more girls than boys reported a lack of supervision and that the effects of lack of supervision are more detrimental for girls than for boys. Unsupervised girls exhibited difficulties in school relations as well as lowered achievement and intelligence test scores. Children who were supervised also appeared to be more self-reliant and to have a greater sense of personal freedom than those with little adult supervision.

The mother's personality and relationship with her child, as well as the conditions of her employment, modified the effects of her employment on the child.

Children who had the best relationships with their mothers had the highest verbal and language IQs, the highest achievement and reading scores, and the best personality adjustment. They showed a good balance between self-reliance involving a sense of personal freedom and stable home relationships with a sense of belonging. It is interesting that teachers also responded most positively to children from these warm, stable mother-child relationships and gave them high grades both in work habits and in citizenship.

Children who were expected to assume responsibility for household tasks and care of younger siblings showed a high degree of intellectual maturity, cognitive ability, and social adjustment. The author suggests that it is difficult to establish a cause and effect relationship in this finding. In lower-class families where there is a real need for family participation in household tasks, the assignment of responsibilities in the home may generalize to mature behavior in the classroom; on the other hand, mothers may assign more responsibility to bright, mature, competent children because they will be more reliable and able to carry out tasks. Finally, mothers who were employed full time and who enjoyed their work had children with better social and intellectual adjustment than unhappy part-time employees.

It can be seen from these results that, just as is true in families with nonworking mothers, a positive relationship with a satisfied, stable mother is one of the most important influences on child development. In addition, in families with a working mother, the consistency of the mother's employment and her pleasure in her work and the supervision provided for the child, particularly for daughters, modify the possible deleterious effects of maternal employment.

Source: Woods, M. B. The unsupervised child of the working mother. *Developmental Psychology*, 1972, **6,** 14–25.

employment, but also because the father may participate more actively in family and childbearing tasks often regarded as part of the maternal role.

In middle-class families maternal employment is related to higher educational and occupational goals in children (Banducci, 1967; Nye & Hoffman, 1963; Stein, 1973). In addition, daughters of working as compared to nonworking mothers more often perceive the woman's role as involving freedom of choice, satisfaction, and competence, and these daughters have higher self-esteem and intentions of working after marriage (Baruch, 1972; Hartley, 1966). Finally, maternal employment is associated with fewer traditional feminine interests and characteristics in daughters (Douvan & Adelson, 1966; Stein, 1973). Female college students with working mothers have fewer passive feminine characteristics and have high achievement motivation, endurance, and dominance.

An extension of the study by Broverman et al. (1972), which involved rating characteristics as masculine or feminine and as desirable or undesirable, was done with daughters and sons of employed or unemployed women. They summarize their results as follows:

> As expected, daughters of employed mothers perceived significantly smaller differences between men and women than did daughters of homemaker mothers, on both the competency cluster and the warmth-expressiveness cluster. Sons of employed mothers perceived a significantly smaller difference between women and men on the warmth-expressiveness cluster than did sons of homemaker mothers. However, the perceptions of the two groups of male Ss did not differ significantly on the competency cluster. Further analysis uncovered another significant difference: Daughters of employed mothers perceived women less negatively on the competency characteristics than did daughters of homemaker mothers. Thus, while the two groups did not differ in their perceptions of women with respect to the characteristics usually valued in women (warmth-expressiveness), daughters of employed mothers did perceive women to be more competent than did the daughters of homemaker mothers.
>
> The results of this study suggest that the stereotypic conceptions of sex roles are not immutable. Insofar as perceptions of sex roles are subject to variation as a function of the individual's experience, then societal sex-role stereotypes may also be subject to change [Broverman et al., 1972, pp. 74–75].

No general conclusions can be drawn about the constructive or detrimental results of maternal employment. The effects seem to be closely linked to characteristics and attitudes of the family members and the specific social and home situation involved. Depending on these factors some mothers should be employed, others should not.

SUMMARY

The development of sex-typed values, motives, and behaviors is influenced by both biological and cultural factors. Studies of hormonal factors and sex differences in infancy suggest that there are some constitutional differences in males and females. However, cultural differences in sex roles and the overlap in attributes of males and females show that socialization can serve as a powerful factor in modifying temperamental variations.

Although the developmental course of sex-role typing differs for boys and girls, sex-typing for children of both sexes tends to be more closely related to paternal than maternal characteristics and behavior. Masculinity in boys is facilitated by paternal power and warmth. A dominant, controlling mother and passive father is associated with disruptions in the development of masculinity in sons. Femininity in girls is facilitated by masculinity, a positive attitude toward females, and reinforcement for feminine activities and interests by the father, and by warmth in both parents.

Early separation from the father leads to deviations in sex-typing in young sons and to disruptions in later relationships with males in adolescent daughters. In addition, both boys and girls from homes in which the father is absent show deficits on IQ and achievement tests, although they are most marked for boys who have lost their fathers in the first five years of life and are more severe for boys than for girls.

Maternal employment leads to children having less stereotyped and more favorable conceptions of the feminine role. This may be partly attributable to the fact that a working mother is violating the feminine, passive, dependent stereotype. In addition, family roles alter when the mother is employed and the father participates more actively in household chores and the care of children.

REFERENCES

Angrilli, A. F. The psychosexual identification of preschool boys. *Journal of Genetic Psychology*, 1960, **97,** 329-340.

Banducci, R. The effect of mother's employment on the achievement, aspirations and expectations of the child. *Personnel and Guidance Journal*, 1967, **46,** 263-267.

Bandura, A. Social learning theory and identificatory processes. In D. A. Goslin (Ed.), *Handbook of socialization theory and research.* Chicago: Rand McNally, 1969. Pp. 213-262.

Barclay, A. G., & Cusumano, D. Father absence, cross-sex identity, and field dependent behavior in male adolescents. *Child Development*, 1967, **38,** 243-250.

Barry, H., Bacon, M., & Child, I. L. A cross cultural survey of some sex differences in socialization. *Journal of Abnormal and Social Psychology*, 1957, **55,** 327-332.

Baruch, G. K. Maternal influences upon college women's attitudes toward women and work. *Developmental Psychology*, 1972, **6,** 32-37.

Beach, F. A. Neural and chemical regulation of behavior. In H. F. Harlow & C. N. Wolsey (Eds.), *Biological and biochemical bases of behavior.* Madison, Wis.: The University of Wisconsin Press, 1958.

Beach, F. A. Retrospect and prospect. In F. Beach (Ed.), *Sex and behavior.* New York: Wiley, 1965.

Bennett, E. M., & Cohen, L. R. Men and women, personality patterns and contrasts. *Genetic Psychology Monographs*, 1959, **59,** 101-155.

Biller, H. B. A multiaspect investigation of masculine development in kindergarten age boys. *Genetic Psychology Monographs*, 1968, **76,** 89-139.

Biller, H. B., & Bahm, R. M. Father absence, perceived maternal behavior and masculinity of self-concept among junior high school boys. *Developmental Psychology*, 1971, **4,** 178-181.

Blanchard, R. W., & Biller, H. B. Father availability and academic performance among third grade boys. *Developmental Psychology* 1971, **4,** 301-305.

Bowerman, D. E., & Irish, D. P. Some relationships of stepchildren to their parents. *Marriage and Family Living*, 1962, **24,** 113-121.

Brim, O. G. Family structure and sex role learning by children: a further analysis of Helen Koch's data. *Sociometry*, 1958, **21,** 1-16.

Brindley, C., Clarke, P., Hutt, C., Robinson, I., & Wethli, E. Sex differences in the activities and social interactions of nursery school children. In R. P. Michael & J. H. Crook (Eds.), *Comparative ecology and behavior of primates.* London: Academic, 1972.

Bronson, W. C. Dimensions of ego and infantile identification. *Journal of Personality*, 1959, **27,** 532-545.

Broverman, I. K., Vogel, S. R., Broverman, D. M., Clarkson, F. E., & Rosenkrantz, P. S. Sex-role stereotypes: a current appraisal. *Journal of Social Issues*, 1972, **28,** 59-78.

Brown, D. G., Masculinity-femininity development in children. *Journal of Consulting Psychology*, 1957, **21,** 197-202.

Burton, R. V., & Whiting, J. W. M. The absent father and cross sex identity. *Merrill-Palmer Quarterly*, 1967, **7,** 85-95.

Carlsmith, L. Effect of early father absence on scholastic aptitude. *Harvard Educational Review*, 1964, **34,** 3-21.

Chombart de Laurve, Y. M. Le groupe familial et l'enfant. In *Psychopathologie sociale de l'enfant inadapte.* Paris: Centre National de la Recherche Scientifique, 1959, 175-210.

D'Andrade, R. Cross-cultural studies of sex differences in behavior. In E. Maccoby (Ed.), *The development of sex differences.* Stanford, Calif.: Stanford, 1966. Pp. 82-172.

Deutsch, M., & Brown, B. Social influences in Negro-white intelligence differences. *Journal of Social Issues,* 1964, **20,** 24-35.

Douvan, E., & Adelson, J. *The adolescent experience.* New York: Wiley, 1966.

Emmerich, W. Parental identification in young children. *Genetic Psychology Monographs,* 1959, **60,** 257-308.

Fagan, J. F. Infants' recognition memory for faces. *Journal of Experimental Child Psychology,* 1972, **14,** 453-476.

Fagot, B. I. Sex-related stereotyping of toddlers' behaviors. *Developmental Psychology,* 1973, **9,** 429.

Garai, J. E., & Scheinfeld, A. Sex differences in mental and behavioral traits. *Genetic Psychology Monographs,* 1968, **77,** 169-299.

Goldberg, S., & Lewis, M. Play behavior in the year-old infant: early sex differences. *Child Development,* 1969, **40,** 21-31.

Goodenough, E. W. Interest in persons as an aspect of sex differences in the early years. *Genetic Psychology Monographs,* 1957, **55,** 287-323.

Hampson, J. L., & Hampson, J. G. The ontogenesis of sexual behavior in men. In W. D. Young (Ed.), *Sex and internal secretions.* Vol. 2. Baltimore: Williams & Wilkins, 1961.

Hartley, R. E. Sex-role pressures and socialization of the male child. *Psychological Reports,* 1959, **5,** 457-468.

Hartley, R. E. Children's concepts of male and female roles. *Merrill Palmer Quarterly, 1960,* **6,** 83-91.

Hartley, R. E. Sex-roles from a child's viewpoint. Paper read at the Annual Meeting of the American Orthopsychiatric Association. San Francisco, April 1966.

Hartup, W. W., & Zook, E. A. Sex role preference in three- and four-year-old children. *Journal of Consulting Psychology,* 1960, **24,** 420-426.

Helper, M. M. Learning theory and the self concept. *Journal of Abnormal and Social Psychology,* 1955, **51,** 184-194.

Hetherington, E. M. A developmental study of the effects of sex of the dominant parent on sex-role preference, identification and imitation in children. *Journal of Personality and Social Psychology,* 1965, **2,** 188-194.

Hetherington, E. M. Effects of paternal absence on sex-typed behaviors in Negro and white preadolescent males. *Journal of Personality and Social Psychology,* 1966, **4,** 87-91.

Hetherington, E. M. The effects of familial variables on sex typing, on parent-child similarity and on imitation in children. In J. P. Hill (Ed.), *Minnesota symposia on child psychology.* Vol. 1. Minneapolis: The University of Minnesota Press, 1967. Pp. 82-107.

Hetherington, E. M. Effects of father absence on personality development in adolescent daughters. *Developmental Psychology,* 1972, **7,** 313-326.

Hetherington, E. M. Changing sex role stereotypes. Unpublished manuscript, 1974.

Hetherington, E. M., & Deur, J. The effects of father absence on child development. *Young Children,* 1971, **26,** 233-248.

Hoffman, L. W. Mothers' enjoyment of work and effects on the child. *Child Development,* 1961, **32,** 187-197.

Hutt, C. Specific and diverse exploration. In H. Reese & L. Lipsitt (Eds.), *Advances in child development and behavior.* Vol. 5. London: Academic, 1970. Pp. 120-181.

Hutt, C. Sex differences in human development. *Human Development,* 1972, **15,** 153-170.

Jenkins, N., & Vroegh, K. Contemporary concepts of masculinity and femininity. *Institute for Juvenile Research Reports,* 1969, 1.

Johnson, M. Sex role learning in the nuclear family. *Child Development,* 1963, **34,** 319-333.

Kagan, J. The concept of identification. *Psychological Review,* 1958, **65,** 296-305.

Kagan, J., & Lewis, M. Studies of attention in the human infant. *Behavior Development,* 1965, **11,** 95-127.

Kagan, J., & Moss, H. A. *Birth to Maturity: a study in psychological development.* New York: Wiley, 1962.

Kohlberg, L. A cognitive-developmental analysis of children's sex-role concepts and attitudes. In E. E. Maccoby (Ed.), *The development of sex differences.* Stanford, Calif.: Stanford, 1966. Pp. 82-173.

LaBarre, W. *The human animal.* Chicago: The University of Chicago Press, 1954.

Langner, T. S., & Michael, S. T. *Life stress and mental health.* New York: Free Press, 1963.

Lansky, L. M. The family structure also affects the model: sex role attitudes in parents of preschool children. *Merrill-Palmer Quarterly,* 1967, **13,** 139-150.

Lewis, M. Infants' responses to facial stimuli during the first year of life. *Developmental Psychology,* 1969, **1,** 75-86.

Lynn, D. B. *Parental and sex-role identification.* Berkeley: McCutchan Publishing Corporation, 1969.

Lynn, D. B., & Sawrey, W. L. The effects of father-absence on Norwegian boys and girls. *Journal of Abnormal and Social Psychology*, 1959, **59,** 258-262.

McCarthy, D. Language development in children. In L. Carmichael (Ed.), *Manual of child psychology.* (2d ed.) New York: Wiley, 1954. Pp. 492-630.

Mead, M. *Sex and temperament in three primitive societies.* New York: Morrow, 1935.

Money, J. Sex hormones and other variables in human eroticisms. In W. C. Young (Ed.), *Sex and internal secretions.* Vol. 2. Baltimore: Williams & Wilkins, 1961.

Money, J., & Ehrhardt, A. A. *Man and woman, boy and girl.* Baltimore: Johns Hopkins, 1972.

Money, J., Hampson, J. G., & Hampson, J. L. Imprinting and the establishment of gender role. *American Medical Association, Archives of Neurological Psychiatry*, 1957, **77,** 333-336.

Moss, H. Sex, age and state as determinants of mother-infant interaction. *Merrill-Palmer Quarterly*, 1967, **13,** 19-36.

Moulton, R. W., Liberty, P. G., Burnstein, E., & Altucher, N. Patterning of parental affection and disciplinary dominance as a determinant of guilt and sex typing. *Journal of Personality and Social Psychology*, 1966, **4,** 356-363.

Mussen, P. H., & Distler, L. Masculinity identity and father-son relationships. *Journal of Abnormal and Social Psychology*, 1959, **59,** 350-356.

Mussen, P. H., & Distler, L. Child rearing antecedents of masculine identity and kindergarten boys. *Child Development*, 1960, **31,** 89-100.

Mussen, P. H., & Rutherford, E. Parent-child relations and parental personality in relation to young children's sex role preferences. *Child Development*, 1963, **34,** 589-607.

Nelson, E. A., & Maccoby, E. E. The relationship between social development and differential abilities on the scholastic aptitude test. *Merrill-Palmer Quarterly*, 1966, **12,** 269-289.

Nye, F. I. Child adjustment in broken and unhappy unbroken homes. *Marriage and Family Living*, 1957, **19,** 356-361.

Nye, F. I. & Hoffman, L. W. *The employed mother in America.* Chicago: Rand McNally, 1963.

Parsons, T. Family structure and the socialization of the child. In T. Parsons & R. Bales (Eds.), *Family, socialization and interaction process.* Glencoe, Ill.: Free Press, 1955. Pp. 35-131.

Payne, D. E., & Mussen, P. H. Parent-child relations and father identification among adolescent boys. *Journal of Abnormal and Social Psychology*, 1956, **52,** 358-362.

Pope, B. Socio-economic contrasts in children's peer culture prestige values. *Genetic Psychology Monographs*, 1953, **48,** 157-220.

Post, B., & Hetherington, E. M. Sex differences in the use of proximity and eye contact in judgments of affiliation in preschool children. *Developmental Psychology*, 1974, **10,** 881-889.

Rabban, M. Sex role identity in young children in two diverse social groups. *Genetic Psychology Monographs*, 1950, **42,** 81-158.

Santrock, J. W. Paternal absence, sex-typing and identification. *Developmental Psychology*, 1970, **2,** 264-272.

Santrock, J. W. Relation of type and onset of father absence to cognitive development. *Child Development*, 1972, **43,** 455-469.

Sears, P. S. Child rearing factors related to playing of sex-typed roles. *American Psychologist*, 1953, **38,** 431. (Abstract)

Siegel, A. E., Stolz, L. M., Hitchcock, E. A., & Adamson, J. Dependence and independence in the children of working mothers. *Child Development*, 1959, **30,** 533-546.

Steimel, R. J. Childhood experiences and masculinity-femininity scores. *Journal of Counseling Psychology*, 1960, **7,** 212-217.

Stein, A. H. The effects of maternal employment and educational attainment on the sex-typed attributes of college females. *Social Behavior and Personality*, 1973, **1,** 111-114.

Sutton-Smith, B., Rosenberg, B. G., & Landy, F. Father-absence effect in families of different sibling compositions, *Child Development*, 1968, **38,** 1213-1221.

United States Department of Labor. Child care arrangements of the nation's working mothers, a preliminary report. Washington, D.C.: Government Printing Office, 1965.

White House Conference on Children. *Profiles on children.* Washington, D.C.: Government Printing Office, 1970.

Wohlford, P., Santrock, J. W., Berger, S. E., & Leiberman, D. Older brothers' influence on sex-typed aggressive and dependent behavior in father absent children. *Developmental Psychology*, 1971, **4,** 124-134.

Woods, M. B. The unsupervised child of the working mother. *Developmental Psychology*, 1972, **6,** 14-25.

Yarrow, M. R., Scott, P., DeLeeuw, L., & Heineg, C. Child rearing in families of working and non-working mothers. *Sociometry*, 1962, **25,** 122-140.

Young, W. C., Goy, R. W., & Phoenix, C. H. Hormones and sexual behavior. *Science*, 1964, **143,** 212-218.

13
SOCIALIZATION AND MORAL DEVELOPMENT

How do moral values and behaviors develop? How does the child change from an egocentric, self-indulgent, uncontrolled organism to an individual capable of self-control, resistance to temptation, and personal sacrifices for the welfare of others? This chapter will trace the course of moral development. Theories of the development of moral judgment will be presented. The relationship of moral judgment, moral behavior, and guilt and their consistency across situations and over time will be discussed.

A basic task of socialization in every culture is that of communicating ethical standards and shaping and enforcing the practice of "good" behaviors in the developing child. Although the specific values and behaviors regarded as desirable vary among cultures, all societies have a system of rules about the rightness and wrongness of certain behaviors. The child is expected to learn these rules and to experience emotional discomfort or guilt when violating them and satisfaction when conforming to them.

Initial control over the young child's behavior is maintained largely through immediate external social factors, such as the presence of authority figures or fear of punishment. However, with age the child's behavior seems to be increasingly maintained by internalized standards of conduct which lead to self-control in the absence of external restraints. This shift from external factors to personal feelings and ethical beliefs as the basis of moral behavior is called *internalization*; many psychologists believe internalization to be the basic process in the development of morality.

Psychological research has focused on the development of the three basic components of morality, that is, the cognitive component, the behavioral component, and the emotional component, and the relationships between these three factors and their roles in the process of internalization. The cognitive factor involves the knowledge of ethical rules and the judgments of the "goodness" or "badness" of various acts. The behavioral factor has to do with actual behavior in a variety of situations involving ethical considerations. Most studies have investigated disapproved of aspects of children's behaviors, such as cheating, lying, and the inability to delay gratification, resist temptation, or control aggression. However, recent studies of moral development have also included positive behaviors, often called *prosocial behaviors,* such as sharing, cooperation, altruism, and helping. Similarly, studies of the emotional dimension of morality have tended to be confined to negative aspects, such as feelings of guilt, often measured by confession or reparation following transgression, rather than feelings of satisfaction associated with prosocial acts. Again we find that different psychological theories have focused on different aspects of moral development. Cognitive theories have emphasized moral judgments; psychoanalytic theories have emphasized affective components of morality, particularly those of guilt and anxiety; and learning theories have emphasized ethical behavior. Both analytic and behavior theory have been greatly concerned with internalization, although they invoke different mechanisms to explain its development.

Psychoanalytic and social learning theories of moral development were presented in detail in the chapter on the family. Freud believed moral behavior and the guilt experienced when violating moral standards were the result of the formation of the superego through identification, when the child takes in the ethical standards as he perceives them in his parent. Social learning theorists use the same learning principles of conditioning, the administration of rewards and punishments, and imitation as the foundation for the acquisition of all social behaviors including moral conduct and self-control.

Thus, for psychoanalysts internalization is a result of resolution of the Oedipus complex through identification and for behavior theorists it is a result of learning.

COGNITIVE THEORIES OF MORAL DEVELOPMENT

Alternative explanations for the acceptance and development of moral standards are presented by the cognitive theorists Jean Piaget and Lawrence Kohlberg. Piaget's theory of moral development involves many of the same principles and processes of cognitive growth that were encountered in the earlier presentation of his theory of intellectual development. In fact, the key thing to remember is that for these theorists the study of moral development is just an approach to the study of intellectual development as it bears on the specific topic of ethical cognition. Since intellectual growth proceeds through a specific sequence of stages, moral judgments will also advance in stages related to the changes in the child's general cognitive development.

Jean Piaget's cognitive theory of moral development

Piaget proposes a cognitive-developmental theory of moral development in which the moral concepts of the child evolve in an unvarying sequence from an early stage, which is often called the *stage of moral realism,* to a more mature stage, referred to as *the morality of reciprocity* or *autonomous morality.* No one could reach the stage of moral reciprocity without first having passed through the stage of moral realism. According to Piaget, mature morality includes both the child's understanding and acceptance of social rules, and his concern for equality and reciprocity in human relationships which is the basis of justice. He investigated changing moral judgments in two main ways. First, he investigated shifts with age in children's attitudes toward rules in such common children's games as marbles. Second, he studied children's judgments of the seriousness of transgressions by having children listen to stories and comment on why and to what extent the behaviors of the characters in the stories were wrong.

The preschool child shows little concern or awareness of rules. In children's games such as marbles he does not try to play a systematic game with the intention of winning, but he seems to gain satisfaction from the manipulation and multiple uses of the marbles. If two three-year-olds are observed playing marbles, they may each be using different and idiosyncratic rules and thinking the point of the game is to enjoy themselves. At about age five however, the child begins to develop great concern and respect for rules. Rules are regarded as coming from external authority, usually the parents; rules are immutable, unchanging through time, and never to be questioned. What Piaget calls *moral absolutism* prevails. If a child of this age is asked if children in other countries could play marbles with different rules, he will assure the interviewer that they could not. This is reflected in the rigidity with which the child approaches social interactions, frequently falling back on a "my mommy says_____" ploy to solve disputes. In addition to rules being viewed as beyond the child's influence, any deviation from them is seen as inevitably resulting in punishment by *immanent justice.* Someone or something is going to get you one way or another! Such retribution might take the form of accidents or mishaps controlled by inanimate objects or by God. A child who has lied to his mother may later fall off his bike and skin his knees and will think, "That's what I get for lying to mother." In this stage, children also evaluate the seriousness of an act in terms of its consequences rather than according to the good or bad intentions of the actor. Behavior is assessed in terms of *objective responsibility* rather than intentionality. The two factors which contribute to the young child's moral realism are his *egocentrism,* that is, his inability to subordinate his own experience and perceive situations as others would, and his *realistic thinking,* which leads him to confuse external reality with his own thought processes and subjective experiences.

With older children at about ages nine to eleven, Piaget believes a *morality of reciprocity* begins to emerge. In contrast to the period of moral realism, moral judgments are now characterized by the recognition that social rules are arbitrary agreements which can be questioned and changed. Obedience to authority is neither necessary nor always desirable. Violations of rules are not always wrong, nor are they inevitably punished. The child considers the feelings and viewpoints of others in judging their behavior. When there is to be punishment, reciprocity in relating the punishment to the intentions of the wrongdoer and nature of the transgression should be considered; the punishment should be in the form of restitution that will make up for harm done or help teach the culprit to behave better if the situation should arise again. Finally there should be "equalitarianism" in the form of equal justice for all.

Some of these shifts in attitude from the stage of moral realism to that of moral reciprocity are vividly illustrated in the children's responses to stories reported by Piaget in his book *The Moral Judgement of the Child* (1932). Piaget would present the child with pairs of stories such as the following ones and ask the child if the children in each are equally guilty, and which child was the naughtiest and why.

> Story I. A little boy who is called John is in his room. He is called to dinner. He goes into the dining room. But behind the door there was a chair, and on the chair there was a tray with 15 cups on it. John couldn't have known that there was all this behind the door. He goes in, the door knocks against the tray, "bang" to the 15 cups and they all get broken!
> Story II. Once there was a little boy whose name was Henry. One day when his mother was out he tried to get some jam out of the cupboard. He climbed up on a chair and stretched out his arm. But the jam was too high up and he couldn't reach it and have any. But while he was trying to get it, he knocked over a cup. The cup fell down and broke. [Piaget, 1932, p. 122].

A characteristic response for a child in the stage of moral realism is given by a six-year-old:

> "Have you understood these stories?"
> "Yes."
> "What did the first boy do?"
> "He broke 15 cups."
> "And the second one?"
> "He broke a cup by moving roughly."
> "Why did the first one break the cups?"
> "Because he was clumsy. When he was getting the jam the cup fell down."
> "Is one of the boys naughtier than the other?"
> "The first one is because he knocked over 15 cups."
> "If you were the daddy, which one would you punish most?"
> "The one who broke 15 cups."
> "Why did he break them?"
> "The door shut too hard and knocked them over. He didn't do it on purpose."
> "And why did the other boy break a cup?"
> "He wanted to get the jam. He moved too far. The cup got broken."
> "Why did he want to get the jam?"
> "Because he was all alone. Because his mother wasn't there." (Piaget, 1932, p. 129)

In spite of the fact that Henry was clumsy while trying to deceive his mother, John is regarded by the child in the stage of moral realism as behaving less ethically since he destroyed more cups, although it was unintentional. In contrast, Russ, a ten-year-old, shows advances to the stage of moral reciprocity when he responds that the one who wanted to take the jam was naughtiest. He is considering intentions. When asked if it makes any difference that the other child broke more cups, he replies: "No because the one who broke 15 cups didn't do it on purpose [Piaget, 1932, p. 130]."

Moral judgments and peer interactions

It might be asked what the factors are which facilitate this essential shift in moral judgments. In contrast to psychoanalytic and social learning theories, which both emphasize the role of the parents in moral development, Piaget focuses on the contribution of peers. The movement away from moral absolutism, realism, and egocentrism can only occur in interpersonal relationships in which the child can contrast and question his point of view and those of others. Through cooperation and the making of shared decisions with peers, he becomes sensitive to the multiple roles, needs, and feelings he has in common with others. He realizes that the same act may be perceived in a variety of ways by different people and lead to different results. In a series of studies of role-taking skills (Flavell, Botkin, Fry, Wright, & Jarvis, 1968) with elementary school children, it was shown that there is a great increase in role-taking skills between the ages of eight and twelve. By age ten, children have started to understand that the other child can take their point of view while they are perceiving the role of the other. They are recognizing that both children in a social interaction can consider the feelings, emotions, and thoughts of the other. It is a kind of "I know that he knows that I know" situation. If two twelve-year-old children were playing a game where one child held a coin concealed in one hand behind his back and the other child had to guess which hand the coin is in, the child guessing might reason as follows: "Last time I guessed the coin was in his right hand. He'll think I'll figure he wouldn't keep it in the same hand twice in a row and will guess left. So to fool me he'll keep it in the right hand. So I'll guess right again." This is a very complicated procedure of reciprocal role taking which a younger child would never be able to accomplish and at which expert poker players are adept.

This increased ability to make interferences about others is based on the child's cognitive development and improved intellectual ability to solve a variety of intellectual problems. It is also related to the child's motivation to understand others and acquire social skills as he interacts more with his peers. The child realizes that it is useful to understand when someone is angry or hurt but is trying not to show it, when someone is pleased or displeased by his behavior, or when someone is tired and irritable.

As the child becomes less dependent on adults, his increased feelings of control and participation in decision making and his growing ability to take on new roles enhance the child's respect for himself and others. It frees him from the domination of external authorities and leads to a sympathy and concern with intentions in actions, which he would not be likely to attain if it weren't for the agreement and cooperation inherent in interactions with people of equal status.

Piaget suggests that this mutual solidarity and respect, which is so critical in developing a sense of social justice, can only occur when the child frees himself from relations of unilateral authority with adults, particularly with his parents. Although Piaget believes peer relations to be of the greatest importance in the development of a mature morality, he does suggest that if parents moved from their traditional position of unilateral authority and attempted to establish a more egalitarian relationship with their children, they might thereby accelerate the acquisition of reciprocal morality. If adults were willing to conform to the same rules they impose on their children and to stress their own obligations and failures in their relationships with them, they might become a more positive force in ethical development.

Lawrence Kohlberg's cognitive theory of moral development

Kohlberg (1963a, 1963b, 1969) has extended, modified, and refined Piaget's theory, based on his analysis of interviews of ten- to sixteen-year-old boys who were confronted with a series of moral dilemmas in which they must choose between acts of obedience to rules and authority or to the needs and welfare of others which conflicted with the regulations.

A representative dilemma is one in which a man needs a particular expensive drug to help his dying wife. The pharmacist who discovered and controls the supply of the drug has refused the husband's offer to give him all the money he now has, which would be about half the necessary sum, and to pay the rest later. The man must now decide whether or not to steal the drug to save his wife, that is, whether to obey the rules and laws of society or violate them to respond to the needs of his wife. What should the man do, and why?

Kohlberg formulated a series of three broad levels of moral development subdivided into six stages; each stage was based not only upon whether the boys chose an obedient or need-serving act, but also on the reasons and justification for their choices. Kohlberg believes that the order of the stages is fixed, but that stages do not occur at the same age in all people. Many people never attain the highest level of moral judgment, and some adults continue to think in immature preconventional terms of conforming only to avoid punishment and gain rewards.

Kohlberg would agree with Piaget in noting that the young child is oriented toward obedience, but for different reasons. Whereas Piaget regarded this early conformity as being based on the young child's dependency and respect for authority, in level 1, the *preconventional level,* Kohlberg regards it as based on the desire to avoid punishment and gain rewards. At level 1 there is no internalization of moral standards. At level 2, the *conventional level,* although the child identifies with his parents and conforms to what they regard as right and wrong, it is the motive to conform rather than ethical standards which have been internalized. It is only at level 3, the *postconventional level,* that moral judgment is rational and internalized and that conduct is controlled by an internalized ethical code and is relatively independent of the approval or castigation of others. At this level, moral conflict is resolved in terms of broad ethical principles and violating these principles results in guilt and self-condemnation.

The levels and stages of moral development as conceptualized by Kohlberg are as follows:

Level 1. Preconventional morality
Stage 1. Obedience and punishment orientation
  This orientation involves deference to prestigious or powerful people, usually the parents, in order to avoid punishment. The morality of an act is defined in terms of its physical consequences.
Stage 2. Naive hedonistic and instrumental orientation
  In this stage the child is conforming to gain rewards. Although there is evidence of reciprocity and sharing, it is a manipulative, self-serving reciprocity rather than one based on a true sense of justice, generosity, sympathy, or compassion. It is a kind of bartering: "I'll lend you my bike if I can play with your wagon," "I'll do my homework now if I can watch the late night movie."
Level 2. Conventional level: morality of conventional rules and conformity
Stage 3. Good boy morality
  In this stage good behavior is that which maintains approval and good relations with others. Although the child is still basing his judgments of right and wrong on the responses of others, he is concerned with their approval and disapproval rather than their physical power. He is concerned about conforming to his friends and families' standards to maintain good-

will. He is however starting to accept the social regulations of others and is judging the goodness or badness of behavior in terms of a person's intent to violate these rules.

Stage 4. Authority and social-order-maintaining morality

In this stage the individual blindly accepts social conventions and rules and believes that if society accepts the rules they should be maintained to avoid censure. It is no longer just conformity to other individuals' standards but conformity to the social order. This is the epitome of "law and order" morality involving unquestioning acceptance of social regulations. Behavior is judged as good in terms of its conformity to a rigid set of rules. It is unfortunate that most individuals in our culture do not pass beyond the conventional level of morality.

Level 3. Postconventional level: Morality of self-accepted moral principles

Stage 5. Morality of contract, individual rights, and democratically accepted law

There is a flexibility of moral beliefs in this stage that was lacking in earlier stages. Morality is based upon an agreement among individuals to conform to norms which appear necessary to maintain the social order and the rights of others. However, since it is a social contract, it can be modified when the people within society rationally discuss alternatives which might be more advantageous to a larger number of the members of the group.

Stage 6. Morality of individual principles and conscience

In this stage individuals conform both to social standards and to internalized ideals to avoid self-condemnation, rather than criticism by others. Decisions are based upon abstract principles involving justice, compassion, and equality. It is a morality based upon a respect for others. People who have attained this level of development will have highly individualistic moral beliefs which may at times conflict with the social order accepted by the majority. A greater number of nonviolent, activist students taking part in the anti-Vietnam war demonstrations had attained the postconventional level of morality than had nonactivist students.

Kohlberg, like Piaget, believes that stages of moral development are determined by the cognitive capabilities of the individuals. Like the orderly progression of Piaget's general cognitive theory of development with the attainments of one stage building on the achievements of earlier stages, moral development builds on the moral concepts in previous stages. The sequence should be invariant across cultures, although the ultimate level attained may vary among cultures and for individuals within the same society. Once an individual has attained a high level of moral cognition, especially stage 6, he will not regress and go back to earlier stages of moral judgment.

EVALUATION OF COGNITIVE THEORIES OF MORAL DEVELOPMENT

Studies of cognitive theories of moral development have focused on three main issues: first, the question of the invariance of the stages of moral development; second, its relation to other aspects of cognitive development; and third, the effects of variations in social interactions with parents and peers on moral development (Hoffman, 1970).

Invariance of stages of moral development

Figure 13-1 presents the percent of moral statements of different types or stages of development at four ages (Kohlberg, 1963b). Although Kohlberg predicts no direct relation between age and moral maturity, it can be seen that more preconventional responses are made by young children and more postconventional responses by older children.

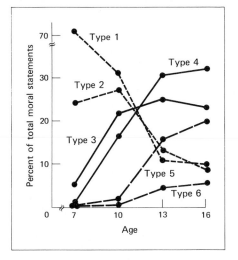

FIGURE 13-1 Use of six types of moral judgments at four ages. (From Kohlberg, L., 1963.)

Several reviews of the literature (Kohlberg, 1963b, 1964a, 1969) conclude that in industrialized Western countries such as the United States, Great Britain, France, Switzerland, etc., across a wide range of populations and social classes and for both sexes there are regular age trends of development in moral judgment. In most Western countries there is a trend from moral realism to moral reciprocity with increasing age. However, the findings in cross-cultural studies are less consistent. A study by Havinghurst and Neugarten (1955) of ten American Indian tribes found developmental increase rather than the predicted decrease in belief in immanent justice in six tribes. Also, only two of the ten groups showed the expected shift in the conception of rules toward greater flexibility with age. It seems that cultural factors can alter the sequence of Piaget's moral judgments.

In cross-cultural studies of children in Turkey, Taiwan, Yucatan, and Mexico, Kohlberg has also found that in primitive tribal or village communities the level of postconventional morality is never attained. In this country, high-socioeconomic-status children pass through the sequence of moral stages more rapidly than those in poorer economic conditions; they also ultimately are more likely to attain the postconventional levels. Cultural factors certainly seem to influence moral judgments.

It has also been argued that if moral judgments are firmly based on cognitive structures, it should be difficult to modify them by short-term laboratory manipulations. However, both progressive shifts to a more advanced level of moral judgments and regressive shifts to less mature levels have been induced by modeling. Children who observed an adult being rewarded for expressing moral judgments which were either more advanced or less advanced than their own shifted their own judgments in the direction of the model's (Bandura & MacDonald, 1963; Cowan, Langer, Heavenrich, & Nathanson, 1969; LeFurgy & Woloshin, 1969). In addition to exposure to a rewarded model influencing judgments, the kind of reasons the model gives for his decision may shift judgments. Subjects who were exposed to models' reasoning about moral dilemmas at a stage above or a stage below their own stage of moral development preferred the more advanced to the less advanced stage. In this type of study there usually are small increases in the use of the reasoning of the stage above but less often shifts to the stage below following exposure to models (Cowan et al., 1969; Keasey, 1973; Rest, Turiel, & Kohlberg, 1969; Turiel, 1966; Turiel & Rothman, 1972).

It must be concluded that although moral judgments tend to develop in a regular sequence within traditional Western culture, deviations in the ordering or speed of attainment of levels may result from variations in cultural structures and social influences.

Relation of moral judgments to other cognitive measures

It is not surprising that general cognitive maturity has been found to be related to moral maturity. Just as IQ was found to be associated with speed of development of concepts associated with sex-role typing, it is also associated with the attainment of both Piaget's and Kohlberg's stages of morality. A high level of abstract thinking is required in the development of evaluation of intent, generalized rational ethical standards, and sensitivity to the roles, perceptions, and feelings of others.

In addition to general intellectual ability, the specific ability to take the role of others is emphasized as a key cognitive skill influencing moral responses (Selman, 1974). Both Kohlberg and Piaget have stressed the shift from egocentricity to consideration of the feelings and intentions of others as an important transition in moral development. As children pass through the elementary school years, they describe others in a more differentiated, detailed, and accurate way (Scarlett, Press, & Crockett, 1971). Rather than saying all teachers are mean, they recognize some are mean and some kind. In addition, rather than describing other people's behavior in egocentric terms related to concrete instances of behavior, such as "He always hits me when no one's looking," the child by fifth grade can make nonegocentric abstractions about the other person's character: "He is a bully."

It would seem that increased differentiation and accuracy in social perception must accompany the ability to take the role of others. The child must understand the great variation and complexity in the characteristics of others before he can consider their feelings and intentions in moral situations. Measures of role-taking skills do correlate with Kohlberg's levels of moral judgments, and shifts to higher levels of moral development are preceded by increases in role-taking ability (Selman, 1971a, 1971b).

Opportunities for role taking affect moral behavior as well. Children who are given the opportunity to play the role of disciplinary agent and enforce a rule on another child are more likely to subsequently follow the rule themselves (Bosserman & Parke, 1973).

Effects of social interactions on moral development

In contrast to social learning theorists and psychoanalytic theorists, the cognitive theorists have not been as concerned with the effects of childrearing factors and parental influences on moral development. Piaget has emphasized the role of peers and Kohlberg that of social interactions involving role-taking opportunities in moral development.

There is evidence that social interactions with peers are important in moral development. Children who participate in more social activities are rated by their peers and teachers as more popular; as group leaders, these children have been found to be more mature in moral judgments (Keasey, 1971).

Some support for Kohlberg's emphasis on the importance of social role-taking experience in moral development is found in studies which show that restricted social environments, such as isolated communities, or large, impersonal, diffuse school environments where there is a lack of opportunity for intense and varied role-taking experiences are related to undifferentiated, simplistic descriptions of social roles. This might be expected to restrict the role-taking abilities basic in moral judgment.

Although Piaget argues that parents do not play a crucial role in moral development, the cognitive structuring involved in parental discipline does effect both moral judgments and moral behavior. When parents use consistent disciplinary techniques involving reasoning and explanation (Aronfreed, 1961, in press; Parke, 1973, in press) or involving discussions of the feelings of others (Hoffman & Saltzstein, 1967; Kohlberg, 1969), more mature moral judgments in addition to more self-controlled behavior occur.

Laboratory investigations of moral behavior are consistent with these field studies; children who are given a verbal rationale (for example, the object belongs to someone else) for maintaining self-control are less likely to violate a prohibition than children who are not given a rationale (Parke, 1973). Moreover, cognitively based discipline produces greater stability of self-control (Parke, 1969), and children who receive this type of training are more likely to enforce the rationale-based prohibiion on their peers as well. The giving of reasons in discipline produces not only better self-control but may transform the child into a transmitter of adult rules as well (Parke, in press).

In contrast to sex-role typing, mothers seem to play a more important role than fathers in the moral development of children (Hoffman & Saltzstein, 1967; LaVoie, 1973). This may be because mothers seek information about their children's feelings and their interpretation of their transgressions before punishing the child, whereas fathers favor immediate punishment without discussion. There is more communication between mother and child about discipline (LaVoie, 1973). In addition to offering more verbal cognitive structuring of the moral contingencies in the situation, the mother may offer a more positive social model of sensitivities and concern with the perceptions and feelings of others.

The child as moral philosopher

The view of the child as a moral philosopher has been criticized [by Justin Aronfreed (in press)] as an extremely narrow and incomplete theory of the development of morality. Moral conduct does not seem rational. Aronfreed points out that a restricted focus on cognition leads to a neglect of the emotional processes which are so integral in the control of behavior.

Knowing what is right frequently does not seem to be the critical factor in self-controlled behavior. Moral judgments seem to be more closely related to the complex reasoning processes necessary in offering mature verbal solutions to moral dilemmas, than to morality. Discrepancies between moral knowledge and actual conduct indicate that the emotions elicited when a child considers the array of possible responses he can make in a situation are often not adequate to direct his behavior toward the most mature response of which he is capable. He may not feel anxious enough at the prospect of transgressing to control his behavior. A child may have reached stage 3, the level of "good boy morality." In spite of the fact that he thinks it is critical to maintain parental approval, when his younger brother breaks his favorite toy he may kick him even if the parent is present and will disapprove of his action. The child may later even be able to offer mature reasoning that it was wrong to hit young children because they don't really know what they are doing. Aronfreed proposes that cognitive factors in morality only become important in moral conduct when emotions become attached to the moral ideas because of past experiences and discipline.

In addition to the deficits in cognitive theories as a means of explaining moral conduct, Aronfreed points out that children seem to have a repertoire of levels of moral judgments available. Although a child may have attained a stage 4 level of morality in one situation, in other situations his responses may be less mature. Similarly under stress conditions, such as in prisoner of war camps, people who previously have demonstrated mature moral principles and behavior manifest unethical conduct.

In summary, Aronfreed feels that cognitive theories of moral development may have more to do with general intellectual competence than morality, and that these theories are inadequate to deal with many of the important issues in the development of morality. If one is concerned with moral actions rather than moral thoughts these cognitive theories of morality are inadequate.

WHICH CHILDREN CHEAT AND WHEN?

Situational factors play an important role in the performance of honest or dishonest behavior. The characteristics of the situation interact with the motives, values, past experiences, and attributes of the child to produce transgressions or resistance to temptation. Different children cheat in different situations for different reasons.

Sex differences and cheating

There are no consistent sex differences in honesty. Although teachers rate girls as being more self-controlled, trustworthy, and obedient than boys and although girls are less likely to admit cheating than are boys, the frequency of their cheating behavior tends to be similar (Krebs, 1969). Unfortunately, the frequency of cheating on examinations is high for both sexes, ranging from 50 to 80 percent in studies of elementary school, high school, and college students. Academic cheating does not seem to moderate with age. Girls are more likely to manifest antisocial behavior if they think there is little risk of being caught. Boys are more willing to take chances.

Intelligence and cheating

A frequently reported finding is that bright students cheat less (Hartshorne & May, 1928; Hetherington & Feldman, 1964; Johnson & Gormley, 1972; Kanfer & Duerfeldt, 1968; Nelsen, Grinder, & Biaggio, 1969). This is often explained by saying bright students have less need to cheat since on the basis of their past academic success they know they are likely to do well on tests. Some support is given this position by the finding that the correlation between IQ and cheating disappears when the task is a nonacademic game-type task, when risk of detection is minimized, or when an exam is particularly difficult (Hartshorne & May, 1928; Howells, 1938). When the situation is unfamiliar or the going gets tough, bright children cheat too.

Another possible explanation for the correlation between IQ and honesty is suggested by the results of studies which show that bright students are better able to judge the chances of being caught cheating or to figure out what an experimenter is up to, and that a deception procedure must be very subtle to trap them.

Motivation and cheating

Motivational factors play an important role in honest or dishonest behavior. There is a complex interaction between the need to achieve, the extent of possible gains, fear of failure, and the possibility of detection. Children who have a high need to achieve and fear of failure are likely to cheat when they think they are not performing as well as their peers on a test (Gilligan, 1963; Shelton & Hill, 1969). It has been proposed that under these circumstances cheating is an attempt to avoid self-criticism and devaluation by peers (Hill & Kochendorfer, 1969; Shelton & Hill, 1969). When children think there is a high probability of being caught, they are less likely to cheat even when they are not doing well because this would result in such a loss of self-esteem and public regard.

When the gains involved in cheating are high, there is an increase in the frequency of cheating and a willingness to take greater risks. Students who are working their way through college cheat more than nonworking students (Parr, 1936). They have more to lose by failure. Similarly as the pressure for academic and vocational success on males increases, there is an acceleration of cheating in the late high school and college years (Hetherington & Feldman, 1964; Feldman & Feldman, 1967). Students attribute much of the cheating in a university to the highly competitive atmosphere and the impact failure would have on future vocational opportunities and admissions to graduate schools (Smith, Ryan, & Diggins, 1972). The interaction between motivation and fear of failure is vividly illustrated in a study by Pearlin and his associates (Pearlin, 1971; Pearlin, Yarrow & Scarr, 1967). These investigators found that although parental pressure toward achievement is related to greater academic success in children, these pressures may also result in a greater motivation to cheat. If parents had high aspirations for their children and pressured them toward success, but were of a low income level, this resulted in the greatest cheating. The motivation to succeed was great but because of financial restrictions the possibility of realizing the parents' goals was limited. It has also been found that if parents put great pressures on a child of limited intellectual ability to succeed, it will result in more dishonest behavior.

Group membership and cheating

Finally, the standards of the group with which the individual is involved and the behavior of those about him influence his moral behavior. There is a high correlation between the honesty of children and that of their siblings and parents (Hartshorne & May, 1928). Dishonesty and criminality in parents is also associated with delinquency in children (McCord, McCord, & Zola, 1959). This might be attributed to shared ethical standards within the family, to modeling of each other's behavior, or to exposure to the same childrearing and disciplinary factors.

Groups other than the family influence honesty. When students come together in a classroom or academic institution, they become more similar in their patterns of honesty. They modify their behavior according to the norms of the group, the behavior they see around them, and the verbalized standards of other members of the group. There is less cheating in schools which are on the honor system and where internalized control is expected than in schools where exams are closely monitored (Canning, 1956; Bonjean & McGee, 1965). In addition, within an academic institution there is less cheating within certain majors and living groups. There is greater cheating among fraternity and sorority members than nonaffiliated members (Bonjean & McGee, 1965; Bowers, 1964; Hetherington & Feldman, 1964). Even within a classroom the student who happens to be assigned a seat among students who cheat is more likely to increase his dishonest behavior.

Moreover, the impact of the peer group on moral behavior is evident very early (Parke, in press). Observations of nursery school age children revealed that three- to five-year-olds cheated less in a resistance to temptation situation; that is, in a room with toys, if they were told that the peer group had decided that no one should play with the toys. However, the child's relationship with the peer group is important: peer endorsement of rules produces the highest degree of self-control in children who are observed to be well-integrated into the peer group.

REINFORCEMENT, PUNISHMENT, AND MODELING AS DETERMINANTS OF SELF-CONTROL

Consistent with a social learning analysis of self-control, rewards and punishments for resistance to temptation are important situational determinants of dishonesty in children. As we saw earlier in Chapter 7, a variety of factors, including timing, intensity, consistency, and the nature of the agent-child relationship, will determine the effectiveness of punishment for producing resistance to deviation (Parke, 1972, 1973). A particularly effective technique for producing self-control is to encourage an alternative, socially acceptable behavior that is incompatible with the prohibited behavior (Perry & Parke, 1975).

However, it is not only externally administered rewards and punishments that are important in self-control. Research has focused on the active role that the child himself can play in the self-control process. Children who are taught to self-verbalize a prohibitory rule during the adult's absence show better resistance to temptation than those who receive only an adult prohibition (Hartig & Kanfer, 1973). Exposure to a self-verbalizing model achieves a similar effect not only in the short run, but over a lengthy delay as well (Toner, Parke, & Yussen, 1974). Children who see a model instruct himself not to cheat show more resistance to cheating both immediately and after a week's delay.

Finally, the consequences to the deviant model can alter degrees of cheating in observers. Children who observe a model rewarded for deviant activity are more likely to violate a rule than are observers who see a punished model (Walters & Parke, 1964; Slaby & Parke, 1971). Clearly reinforcement, punishment, and modeling can have an important impact on the child's moral behavior.

WHICH CHILDREN HELP AND SHARE AND WHEN?

Although there has been a voluminous amount of research done on antisocial behavior, it has only been within the past decade that psychologists have become involved in the study of more positive, altruistic aspects of social behavior, such as cooperation, helping, and sharing. Therefore, much less is known about why and when prosocial behavior occurs.

Cultural factors, cooperation, and sharing

As was found in studies of honesty and resistance to temptation, cultural factors and group norms play an important role in positive social behavior. The Anglo-American culture, particularly the middle-class urban groups, is a highly competitive culture, and cross-cultural research has consistently demonstrated that the attitudes of Anglo-American children interfere with their ability to cooperate with others in problem solving, even when such cooperation would be to their advantage. Children raised in cultures which place less value on self-sufficiency and competition, such as Mexican or black American families, are more able to work cooperatively together for common goals (Kagan & Madsen, 1971, 1972; Madsen & Shapira, 1970). Societies in which the norm of cooperation and orientation to the group goals is systematically inculcated in the educational system, such as in Russia or in the Israeli kibbutz, also show more cooperative behavior than do Anglo-Americans.

The self-concern generated by a competitive orientation, and a focus on status needs and self-sufficiency, interfere with behaviors such as giving and sharing with others. In one study it was found that nursery school age boys who were highly competitive in games and were viewed as competitive in the classroom by their teachers were less likely to share candy with their two best friends than were less competitive children (Rutherford & Mussen, 1968). It has been proposed that any kind of self-concern will interfere with the individual's inclination to consider the needs and feelings of others (Berkowitz, 1972).

Preaching and practicing sharing

What kind of social values, family situation, and parental behaviors might lead to a lessening of self-concern and an interest in the feelings and welfare of others, which seems so basic in cooperative, helping, or sharing behaviors? Most parents advocate good conduct for their children. Only a deviant minority advocate selfishness or dishonesty. However, many parents oozing virtuous platitudes seem to have self-centered children. Laboratory studies and naturalistic studies indicate that although both what adults say about altruism and their demonstrated altruistic behavior influence altruism in children, there is a tendency for the model's verbalizations to have more effect on what the child says, and the model's behavior more effect on what the child does. An interesting series of laboratory analogue studies was performed to investigate the "Don't do as I do, do as I say" conflict which confronts most children in listening to their parents' moralistic preachings while viewing their sometimes questionable ethical practices (Bryan & Walbek, 1970a, 1970b; Bryan & Schwartz, 1971). The effects of moral exhortation and the behavioral examples of filmed models on children's reactions in helping

Altruistic behavior is infrequent in children and must be learned. (Suzanne Szasz.)

situations were investigated. Third- and fourth-grade children were exposed to an altruistic model (one who donated to the March of Dimes) or a greedy model (one who
hoarded all of his winnings in an experimental game). One-third of the children within
each group heard the model exhort charitable actions (for example, "It's good to donate
to poor children. Children should help other children."), one-third heard the model
preach selfishness (for example, "No sir, why should we give any of our money to other
people? It is not good to donate to the poor people."), and one-third heard neutral
preachings (for example, "I hope I win some money today."). The hypocrisy conditions
were those where the model's behavior and preaching were discrepant. Following the
viewing of the model, the child was left alone to play a game and had the option of
anonymously donating his or her winnings to poor children. After the game, the children
were asked to evaluate the attractiveness of the model. Children were more likely to
make self-sacrificing responses if the model had donated to the March of Dimes. Exhortations concerning charity failed to alter the altruistic behavior of the child. As is usually
found, the filmed model's actions were a greater source of influence upon the observ-

er's behavior than his words were. However, what the model said was an important influence on the child's judgment of the model's attraction. While the model's verbalizations of the virtues of giving did not change the child's behavior, such exhortations did play a significant role, as did the model's acts, in determining the model's attractiveness. With young children the child regards either a generously talking or acting person positively; the discrepancy or hypocrisy involved in the selfish person mouthing altruistic platitudes does not mean he is a bad fellow. "The preacher of charity and practitioner of greed is not disparaged, his character is vindicated simply by his verbal allegiance to the norm of giving [Bryan & Schwartz, 1971, p. 56]."

However, with older children, particularly children above the age of nine, such hypocrisy is perceived negatively and approval from "hypocrites" is aversive to children. When a selfish-acting, generous-sounding model praises a child for a charitable act, the child is likely to give less than he would with no social approval. He avoids doing what the hypocrite says (Midlarsky, Bryan, & Brickman, 1973). With age and increasing cognitive and interpersonal skills, children may be more able to perceive discrepancies and disapprove of the deviousness in hypocrisy.

The study presented in Box 13-1 of adults who were actively involved in the civil rights movement in the early 1960s suggests that parents' hypocrisy in preaching and practicing may have marked effects on the helping behavior of their children.

Nurturance and altruism

Although the effects of nurturance on altruistic behavior in the laboratory situation are not consistent, its effects on prosocial behavior in naturalistic settings involving parents or other adults with whom the child has had long-term contact, such as teachers, seems clear.

It might be expected that nurturance would play a particularly important role in the development of altruism, since while nurturant parents are exhibiting concern and care and responsiveness to the needs of the child, they are offering a model of altruism to the child. In addition, since nurturance makes the child feel valued and secure, he may more readily be able to orient to the needs and feelings of those about him since his own needs are satisfied. Children who are self-confident, happy, and successful are more likely to be altruistic (Isen, 1970; Isen, Horn, & Rosenhan, 1973; Isen & Levin, 1972; Kazdin & Bryan, 1971; Moore, Underwood, & Rosenhan, 1973; Mussen, Rutherford, Harris, & Keasey, 1970).

The study by Yarrow, Scott, and Waxler (1973) presented in Box 13-2 is noteworthy for several reasons. It uses a procedure of interaction with nurturant or nonnurturant caretakers which is sustained enough to approximate real-life encounters with adults such as teachers. In addition it evaluates the effectiveness of training in helping behavior in the original training situation and in realistic encounters with distress in a natural setting. It is also one of the few studies which has attempted to assess the long-term effects of such training procedures and of the nurturance of the caretaker. The findings are very clear. In the real-life situation only the nurturant model who had taught and exemplified altruistic behavior in her actions caused an increase in helping behavior in children.

BOX 13-1 HELPING IN THE CIVIL RIGHTS MOVEMENT

What kind of people were active in the civil rights movement of the late 1950s and early 1960s? Who marched, protested, and picketed? What kinds of parents produced these activists?

Rosenhan distinguished between two groups of activists: the fully committed and the partially committed. The *fully committed* had left their homes, jobs, and schools and had been immersed in the civil rights movement for over a year. In contrast, the *partially committed* had sacrificed little. They had participated in one or two marches but had not given up their other activities. The fully committed were guided by internalized moral standards involving a deep commitment to equality, what Rosenhan calls *autonomous altruism.* The partially committed were motivated by social conformity, or *normative altruism;* that is, they were concerned with approval from their group, the camaraderie of being involved in a common movement, and short-term personal rewards rather than altruistic motives.

What kind of parental characteristics might have led to these two different types of activism in their children? The fully committed had parents who had themselves been activists and had been concerned with the welfare of others; parents who had been involved in protesting Nazi atrocities, the Spanish Civil War, religious restrictions, etc. Their children spoke of the emotion they shared with their parents on these occasions. One subject described being carried on his father's shoulders during the Sacco-Vanzetti parades. In addition, these fully committed activists had always had a warm relationship with their parents despite the fact that they sometimes had disagreements. Thus these young people had parents who they loved, who served as warm, altruistic models.

In contrast, the partially committed had negative or ambivalent feelings toward their parents. They reported their relations while they had been in the home as hostile, and they were still rejecting and avoiding their parents. Rosenhan summarizes some of the feelings toward their parents of the partially committed as follows:

By contrast, the Partially Committed had parents who were at best mere verbal supporters of prosocial moralities and, at worst, hypocritical about those moralities. It was common for our Partially Committed to report that their parents preached one thing and practiced another. Moreover, the Partially Committed were so angered by the discrepancy between parental posture and action that we had reason to believe that our respondents had undergone a "crisis of hypocrisy" during their childhood which resulted in an inability to make enduring commitments to prosocial (as to other) matters later on [Rosenhan, 1972, pp. 342-343].

These findings are in agreement with the laboratory studies. As children grow older, hypocrisy in adults leads to negative and adverse responses. Parents should practice what they preach.

Source: From Rosenhan, D. L. Prosocial behavior of children. In W. W. Hartup (Ed.), *The young child.* Vol. 2. Washington: National Association for the Education of Young Children, 1972. Pp. 340-359.

BOX 13-2 LEARNING CONCERN FOR OTHERS

How do children learn to help others?

The study was designed to test the relative effectiveness of two types of moral training and nurturance of models on three and one-half- to five and one-half-year-old nursery school children. In the first training condition, adults modeled *principles* of altruism (what one should do and is expected to do) rather than altruistic *practices*. Helping was learned as an abstract impersonal lesson, unrelated to personal experience. In the second type of training, adults *taught* principles and also *exemplified* them in living. The child observed and experienced the adult's concern and involvement in the feelings and welfare of others.

Half of the children in each training condition were exposed to a nurturant, attentive caretaker who was sympathetic and offered help and support and praise freely. The other children were exposed to a nonnurturant adult caretaker who ignored or critically evaluated the children.

The study comprised six phases. In phase I, pretraining measures of helping others in distress were obtained from the children's responses to a series of pictures depicting the misfortunes of others and from four behavioral incidents of distress. The pictorial incidents involved such things as a child skating and falling down, a child falling off a bike with his knee bleeding, and a lady dropping packages. The behavioral incidents were interwoven naturally into play activities and involved such things as a kitten tangled in yarn struggling toward its mother, the experimenter accidentally knocking over a flower vase, an adult with a bandaged finger having difficulty buttoning her sweater, etc.

The child's response in terms of recognition of the misfortune, expressions of sympathy, attempts to alleviate the situation, and self-centered expressions of concern about themselves were recorded. The effectiveness of training later involved a comparion of these pretraining measures with similar post-training measures.

In phase 2, the children interacted with a nurturant or nonnurturant adult in half-hour play sessions, five days a week for two weeks. The adults playing the nurturant roles were sympathetic, protective, and friendly; they expressed praise and confidence in the child freely; and they responded to the child's demands for attention. The nonnurturant adult disregarded or criticized the child and played an uninvolved, aloof, supervisory role. This amount of interaction is much longer than is customarily used in experimental studies, where often experimenters assume a brief, fiteen-minute interaction will be sufficient for the child to perceive the experimenter as nurturant or rejective.

Phase 3 involved again measuring altruistic responses on a battery of tests parallel to that used in phase 1. These measures were taken before the moral training procedures began in order to establish whether the nurturance interactions alone might lead to increased altruism.

In phase 4, half of the children with the nurturant or nonnurturant caretaker were exposed to one of two training conditions. The adults continued in their established nurturance roles while carrying out the training.

In both training conditions helpfulness was portrayed through play materials (dioramas). Three-dimensional models and toy actors were used to portray situations of misfortune. The adult model expressed altruism in the form of sympathy, help, and relief by remedying the situation through the toy actors. This modeling was regarded as being midway between modeling percept and behavior. The child was allowed to take a turn with the toys in a similar diorama following the adult's performance. The type A training group received only the diorama procedure; however, the extended type B training condition involved the adult modeling altruism on a series of pictures and behavioral incidents as well as the dioramas. For example, in one behavioral incident the adult confederate accidentally bumps her head on a table and the experimenter responds with concern and help.

In phase 5, the children were tested on a new series of pictures and behavioral incidents two days after the termination of training. In addition, in order to measure durability and generalization of the helping response, two weeks later children were measured outside the training situation of the nursery school. They were taken to a house adjacent to the school to see a mother and a year-old baby. While they were there, the child had the opportunity to pick up a spilled basket of spools and buttons to retrieve toys the baby had dropped out of the crib, and so on.

Finally, phase 6 involved a long-term test of retention of the experimental influences six months after training had terminated. The diorama was used as a prop in questioning the child about the principles underlying his offers of help.

It was found that the type A training, where altruism was modeled only in the form of diorama lessons, was less effective in increasing altruistic responses than that involving dioramas and pictures plus altruism in actual behavioral interaction. On the tests two days after training terminated, type A training was found to increase altruism only in the specific type of situation (that is, the dioramas) on which training had been done. It generalized to new diorama situations, but it did not generalize to pictures and behavioral incidents. The extended type B training led to increases of altruism on both dioramas and pictures but not in the behavioral incidents. This was disappointing since responses in the behavioral incidents depend on the child's unprodded awareness of the distress and his inclination to enter into the event, and are more related to the kinds of real-life helping situations with which parents are concerned.

However, on the follow-up condition two weeks later in the naturalistic home situation, it was found that helping and expressions of sympathy were more common from children who had received the extended type B training from a nurturant adult, than children in any other group. Eighty-four percent of these children spontaneously gave help as compared to less than 25 percent in the pretraining behavioral incidents. "Thus the optimal condition for the development of sympathetic helpful behavior was one in which children observed an adult manifesting altruism at every level—in principle and in practice both toward the child and toward others in distress [Yarrow, Scott, & Waxler, 1973, p. 251]."

Modeling in symbolic form using characters in the diorama was effective in developing symbolic altruism. The child rapidly learned to respond in the diorama situation. He really learned the adult's verbal and play-acting principle of helping regardless of the nurturance or nonnurturance of the model. However, altruistic responses in real situations involving people in need were learned only with extended training within an established nurturant relationship.

Source: From Yarrow, M. R., Scott, P. M., & Waxler, C. Z. Learning concern for others. *Developmental Psychology,* 1973, **8,** 240–260.

The facilitating effects of nurturance of parents and caretakers on altruism in children is more marked than it is in resistance to temptation and honesty where factors such as moderate levels of restrictiveness, consistency of discipline, and honesty of the parents

Helping behavior in children. (Suzanne Szasz.)

are more important. A nurturant parent who is concerned about the child's needs and feelings and is responsive to them develops a child who is concerned and helpful with others (Hetherington, Hunt, Cox, & Thomas, 1974).

CONSISTENCY OF MORAL DEVELOPMENT

Three types of consistency of moral development can be distinguished. The first is consistency between moral judgment, affect, and behavior. The second involves the generality of morality from one situation to another. The third is the consistency of moral development over time. Does the aggressive, egocentric, dishonest preschool or early-elementary school child evolve into the antisocial adolescent or adult?

Consistency between moral judgments and moral behavior

The available evidence suggests considerable discrepancies between moral judgment, self-control, and indications of guilt following transgressions. Some studies, particularly of young children, have found no relationship between cognitive indexes of internalization, such as responses to Piaget's or Kohlberg's moral dilemmas, and resistance to temptation in laboratory situations in which the child believed he could cheat without risk of detection (Grinder, 1964; Medinnus, 1966; Nelson, Grinder, & Challas, 1968); others have found only modest relationships (Hoffman, 1963a, 1963b; Kohlberg, 1964a, 1969). Experimental studies of cheating behavior of older subjects show that subjects who are in the two most advanced stages of Kohlberg's classifications of moral development (stage 5 of the morality of contract and stage 6 of the morality of individual principles and conscience) are less likely to cheat than those at earlier levels (Grim, Kohlberg, & White, 1968; Krebs, 1967; Lehrer, 1967). In a procedure used by Milgrim (1963) in which adult subjects were asked to give increasingly painful electric shocks to another person who they believed had agreed to submit to the procedure, Kohlberg (1965) reports that most of the subjects at stage 6 in moral judgments refused to shock the other subject when he showed signs of pain. In contrast, the majority of subjects at lower levels complied.

Some relationship of cognitive level of moral development and behavior is also demonstrated in a study of college students' participation in the 1964 Berkeley free speech movement during disruptions at the University of California. Eighty percent of students at stage 6 participated in civil disobedience, whereas about 50 percent at stage 5 and only 10 percent at stages 3 and 4 were involved in activist protest (Haan, Smith, & Block, 1968). The authors assume that the orientation to their conscience as a directing agent of stage 6 students led them to protest the violation of ethical principles by this country's war activities.

In contrast, with children rather than adults as subjects, few relationships between moral judgments and behavior have been obtained. In one study no relationship was found between the intensity of the shock administered to a peer in a situation using a procedure similar to that of Milgrim and Kohlberg's levels of moral maturity with elementary school children (Podd, 1972). Still other investigators have found no relation between moral judgment and cheating in children (Nelsen, Grinder & Biaggio, 1969; Nakasato & Aoyamo, 1972).

Consistency between moral behavior and guilt

In a similar manner, with young subjects few consistent relationships between moral behavior and guilt have been obtained. Resistance to temptation and remorse after transgression tend to be uncorrelated and are sometimes found to be related to different sets of childrearing variables in young children (Sears, Rau, & Alpert, 1965). It has even been found that self-condemnation following transgression is unrelated to the tendency to correct the damage done (Aronfreed, 1963). However, with older children and adults several studies have found some relationship between self-blaming responses and self-control in the form of resistance to temptation (Grinder & McMichael, 1963; MacKinnon, 1938) or a low incidence of delinquent behavior (Bandura & Walters, 1959; McCord and McCord, 1958). With increasing age there seems to be some convergence of the three aspects of morality. The relations between cognition, emotions, and conduct are more integrated in adults than in children.

Consistency across situations

Although this lack of generality across the three dimensions of morality in children constitutes a theoretical challenge to psychologists who support a unitary theory of internalization of moral development, there appears to be more consistency within than between factors. In what is probably the classic and most extensive investigation of moral behavior ever attempted, Hartshorne and May (1928) studied the responses of 11,000 school-age children who were given the opportunity to cheat, steal, and lie in a wide variety of situations: in athletics, social events, the school, the home, alone, or with peers. Burton (1963) took only the measures which were reliable from the original studies in deceit and found strong evidence for a general factor of moral behavior. Burton concludes that each child does have a different general predisposition to behave morally or immorally in a variety of situations. The more similar the situations, the greater the consistency in self-control; the less the situations resemble each other, the less generality of moral behavior is obtained. Measures of cheating on different achievement tests in the classroom are going to correlate more highly with each other than with measures of cheating on games in the home. Other studies have found positive correlations between a variety of tests of resistance to temptation in nursery school children (Sears et al., 1965) and between measures of dishonesty in classroom tests with adolescents (Barbu, 1951) and college students (Hetherington & Feldman, 1964). Such findings do not minimize the importance of situational variables such as fear of detection, peer support for deviant behavior, and the instigation of other powerful motivational factors, such as achievement needs in moral conduct. However, they do suggest that some children are more likely to yield to such demands than are others.

Parallel findings are obtained in the consistency of moral judgments across a variety of dimensions and situations. Although there is some modest consistency in level of moral maturity across the situations and dilemmas used to measure level of moral judgment, it varies according to the degree of shared factors in stories. Is the main issue in both stories the intentions of the person performing an act, or does one story involve intentionality and the other immanent justice? If both involve the same moral dimension, the correlation in level of moral maturity in judgments will be higher than if the dimensions differ (Johnson, 1962).

Stability of morality over time

The longitudinal findings on the stability of self-control over lengthier developmental periods are sparse. They tend to be related to measures of control of aggressive responses rather than resistance to temptation. Since aggression is a strongly sex-typed behavior in our own society, it might be expected that the stability of such behavior would differ for boys and girls. Although childhood temper tantrums and antisocial aggression are related to aggressive retaliation, ease of anger arousal, and competitiveness in adult males, childhood aggression is more likely to be associated with achievement striving (Kagan, & Moss, 1962) or aggression anxiety and prosocial aggression in females. Since overt aggression is unacceptable in females in our culture, it tends to be modified or appear in derivative forms with increasing age, whereas the stability over time and direct expression of aggression is greater for males.

Studies of early behavior of adolescent delinquents suggest that in the early school years these children were already manifesting poor self-control and antisocial behavior (Conger & Miller, 1966; Havinghurst, Bowman, Leddle, Matthews, & Pierce, 1962; Mulligan, Douglas, Hammond, & Tizzard, 1963). Predelinquents are often underachievers who challenge the teacher's authority, cheat, quarrel, and fight; this behavior leads to unpopularity with peers. Such findings suggest some stability over time of lack of self-control and internalization.

SUMMARY

The socialization of moral beliefs and behavior is one of the main tasks in all cultures. Different theorists have focused on different aspects of moral development. Psychoanalytic theorists have focused relatively more on affective components of morality, such as guilt and remorse; social learning theorists on moral conduct; and cognitive theorists on moral judgments.

Jean Piaget and Lawrence Kohlberg have both proposed theories involving invariant sequences of stages of moral development related to the increasing cognitive complexity of the child and the ability to perceive and respond to the intentions and feelings of others.

Piaget has emphasized the role of peers and Kohlberg the importance of varied opportunities for role taking in the development of moral judgments. Both have tended to minimize the influence of parents in the development of moral judgments. However, there is considerable evidence that consistent discipline involving reasoning and explanation and concern with the feelings of others leads to both more mature moral judgments and more self-control. In addition, nurturance and altruistic behavior in parents is related to the development of altruism in children.

Cheating is related to motivational factors, such as the need to achieve, the extent of possible gains, and fear of failure and detection. In addition, group norms and the behavior of others around the child are related to honest or dishonest behavior.

Altruistic behavior is influenced by cultural values. An emphasis on competition interferes with the development of altruistic behavior.

In studies involving the modeling of adults' behavior, children's altruistic behavior is most effected by the conduct of the adult and his imitative verbalizations by what the adult says.

It would be inaccurate to speak of honest or dishonest or moral and immoral people. The moral judgments, behaviors, and expressions of remorse which are all aspects of moral development are strongly influenced by situational factors. Some people are honest in certain situations. However, the evidence suggests that as the elements of situations and type of behavior assessed become more similar, more consistency of moral judgments and conduct occurs. More consistency among various dimensions of moral development also occurs with increasing age.

REFERENCES

Aronfreed, J. The nature, variety and social patterning of moral responses to transgression. *Journal of Abnormal and Social Psychology,* 1961, **63,** 223-240.

Aronfreed, J. The effects of experimental socialization paradigms upon two moral responses to transgression. *Journal of Abnormal and Social Psychology,* 1963, **66,** 437-448.

Aronfreed, J. Moral development from the standpoint of a general psychological theory. In T. Lickona (Ed.), *Man and morality.* New York: Holt, in press.

Bandura, A., & MacDonald, F. J. Influence of social reinforcement and the behavior of models in shaping children's moral judgments. *Journal of Abnormal and Social Psychology,* 1963, **67,** 274-281.

Bandura, A., & Walters, R. H. *Adolescent aggression.* New York: Ronald, 1959.

Barbu, Z. Studies in children's honesty. *Quarterly Bulletin, British Psychological Society,* 1951, **2,** 53-57.

Berkowitz, L. Social norms, feelings and other factors affecting helping and altruism. In L. Berkowitz (Ed.), *Advances in experimental social psychology.* New York: Academic, 1972. Pp. 63-108.

Bonjean, C. M., & McGee, R. Scholastic dishonesty among undergraduates in differing systems of social control. *Sociology of Education,* 1965, **38,** 127-137.

Bosserman, R., & Parke, R. D. The effect of assuming the role of rule enforcer on subsequent self-control. Paper presented at the meeting of the Society for Research in Child Development, Philadelphia, 1973.

Bowers, W. J. *Student dishonesty and its control in college.* New York: Columbia University Bureau of Applied Social Research, 1964.

Bryan, J. H., & Schwartz, T. H. The effects of film material upon children's behavior. *Psychological Bulletin,* 1971, **75,** 50-59.

Bryan, J. H., & Walbek, N. H. Preaching and practicing generosity: children's action and reactions. *Child Development,* 1970, **41,** 329-353. (a)

Bryan, J. H., & Walbek, N. H. The impact of words and deeds concerning altruism upon children. *Child Development,* 1970, **41,** 747-757. (b)

Burton, R. V. The generality of honesty reconsidered. *Psychological Review,* 1963, **70,** 481-499.

Canning, R. Does an honor system reduce classroom cheating? An experimental answer. *Journal of Experimental Education,* 1956, **24,** 291-296.

Conger, J. J., & Miller, W. C. *Personality, social class and delinquency.* New York: Wiley, 1966.

Cowan, P. A., Langer, J., Heavenrich, J., & Nathanson, M. Social learning and Piaget's cognitive theory of moral development. *Journal of Personality and Social Psychology,* 1969, **11,** 261-274.

Feldman, S. E., & Feldman, M. T. Transition of sex differences in cheating. *Psychological Reports,* 1967, **20,** 957-958.

Flavell, J., Botkin, P., Fry, C., Wright, J., & Jarvis, P. E. *The development of role-taking and communication skills in children.* New York: Wiley, 1968.

Gilligan, C. F. Responses to temptation: an analysis of motives. Unpublished doctoral dissertation. Harvard University, 1963.

Grim, P., Kohlberg, L., & White S. Some relationships between conscience and attentional processes. *Journal of Personality and Social Psychology,* 1968, **8,** 239-253.

Grinder, R. Relations between behavioral and cognitive dimensions of conscience on middle childhood. *Child Development,* 1964, **35,** 881-893.

Grinder, R. E., & McMichael, R. Cultural influences on conscience development: resistance to temptation and guilt among Samoans and American Caucasians. *Journal of Abnormal and Social Psychology,* 1963, **66,** 503-507.

Haan, N., Smith, M. B., & Block, J. The moral reasoning of young adults: political-social behavior, family background and personality correlation. *Journal of Personality and Social Psychology,* 1968, **10,** 183-201.

Hartig, M., & Kanfer, F. H. The role of verbal self-instructions in children's resistance to temptation. *Journal of Personality and Social Psychology,* 1973, **25,** 259-267.

Hartshorne, H., & May, M. S. *Moral studies in the nature of character:* Vol. 1, Studies in deceit; Vol. 2, Studies in self-control; Vol. 3, Studies in the organization of character. New York: Macmillan, 1928-1930.

Havinghurst, R. J., Bowman, P. H., Leddle, G. P., Matthews, C. V., & Pierce, J. V. *Growing up in River City.* New York: Wiley, 1962.

Havinghurst, R. J., & Neugarten, B. L. *American Indian and white children.* Chicago: The University of Chicago Press, 1955.

Hetherington, E. M., & Feldman, S. E. College cheating as a function of subject and situational variables. *Journal of Educational Psychology,* 1964, **55,** 212-218.

Hetherington, E. M., Hunt, L., Cox, M., & Thomas, J. The effects of characteristics of parents and strangers on altruism in children. Unpublished manuscript, 1974.

Hill, J. P., & Kochendorfer, P. A. Knowledge of achievement anxiety and knowledge of peer performance. *Developmental Psychology,* 1969, **1,** 449-455.

Hoffman, M. L. Child rearing practices and moral development: generalizations from empirical research. *Child Development,* 1963, **34,** 295-318. (a)

Hoffman, M. L. Parent discipline and the child's consideration of others. *Child Development,* 1963, **34,** 573-588. (b)

Hoffman, M. L. Moral development. In P. H. Mussen (Ed.), *Carmichael's manual of child psychology.* Vol. 2. New York: Wiley, 1970. Pp. 261-330.

Hoffman, M. L., & Saltzstein, H. D. Parent discipline and the child's moral development. *Journal of Personality and Social Psychology,* 1967, **5,** 45-57.

Howells, T. H. Factors influencing honesty. *Journal of Social Psychology,* 1938, **9,** 97-102.

Isen, A. M. Success, failure, attention, and reaction to others: the warm glow of success. *Journal of Personality and Social Psychology,* 1970, **15,** 294-301.

Isen, A. M., & Levin, P. F. The effect of feeling good on helping: Cookies and kindness. *Journal of Personality and Social Psychology,* 1972, **21,** 384-388.

Isen, A. M., Horn, N., & Rosenhan, D. L. Effects of success and failure on children's generosity. *Journal of Personality and Social Psychology,* 1973, **27,** 239-247.

Johnson, R. C. A study of children's moral judgments. *Child Development,* 1962, **33,** 327-354.

Johnson, C. D., & Gormley, J. Academic cheating: the contribution of sex, personality and situational variables. *Developmental Psychology,* 1972, **6,** 320-325.

Kagan, J., & Moss, H. A. *Birth to maturity: a study in psychological development.* New York: Wiley, 1962.

Kagan, S., & Madsen, M. C. Cooperation and competition of Mexican, Mexican-American, and Anglo-American children of two ages under four instructional sets. *Developmental Psychology,* 1971, **5,** 32-39.

Kagan, S., & Madsen, M. C. Experimental analyses of cooperation and competition of Anglo-American and Mexican children. *Developmental Psychology,* 1972, **6,** 49-59.

Kanfer, F. H., & Duerfeldt, P. H. Age, class standing, and commitment as determinants of cheating in children. *Child Development,* 1968, **39,** 545-557.

Kazdin, A. E., & Bryan, J. H. Competence and volunteering. *Journal of Experimental Social Psychology,* 1971, **7,** 87-97.

Keasey, C. B. Social participation as a factor in the moral development of preadolescents. *Developmental Psychology,* 1971, **5,** 216-220.

Keasey, C. B. Experimentally induced changes in moral opinions and reasoning. *Journal of Personality and Social Psychology,* 1973, **26,** 30-38.

Kohlberg, L. Moral development and identification. In H. W. Stevenson (Ed.), *Child psychology. 62nd Yearbook of the National Society for the Study of Education.* Chicago: The University of Chicago Press, 1963. (a)

Kohlberg, L. The development of children's orientations towards a moral order. 1. Sequence in the development of moral thought. *Vita Humana,* 1963, **6,** 11-33. (b)

Kohlberg, L. Development of moral character and ideology. In M. L. Hoffman & L. W. Hoffman (Eds.), *Review of child development research.* Vol. 1. New York: Russell Sage Foundation, 1964. (a)

Kohlberg, L. Sex differences in morality. In E. E. Maccoby (Ed.), *Sex role development.* New York: Social Science Research Council, 1964. (b)

Kohlberg, L. Relationships between the development of moral judgment and moral conduct. Paper presented at the meeting of the Society for Research In Child Development, Minneapolis, March 26, 1965.

Kohlberg, L. *Stages in the development of moral thought and action.* New York: Holt, 1969.

Krebs, R. L. Some relationships between moral judgment, attention and resistance to temptation. Unpublished doctoral dissertation, The University of Chicago, 1967.

Krebs, R. L. Teacher perceptions of children's moral behavior. *Psychology in the Schools,* 1969, **6,** 394-395.

LaVoie, J. C. Punishment and adolescent self control. *Developmental Psychology,* 1973, **8,** 16-24.

LeFurgy, W. G., & Woloshin, G. W. Immediate and long term effects of experimentally induced social influences in the modification of adolescents' moral judgments. *Journal of Abnormal and Social Psychology,* 1969, **12,** 104-110.

Lehrer, L. Sex differences in moral behavior and attitudes. Unpublished doctoral dissertation, The University of Chicago, 1967.

MacKinnon, D. W. Violation of prohibitions. In H. A. Murray, *Explorations in personality.* New York: Oxford University Press, 1938. Pp. 491-501.

McCord, J., & McCord, W. The effect of parental role model on criminality. *Journal of Social Issues,* 1958, **14,** 66-75.

McCord, W., McCord, J., & Zola, K. *Origins of crime.* New York: Columbia University Press, 1959.

Madsen, M. C., & Shapira, A. Cooperative and competitive behavior of urban Afro-American, Anglo-American, Mexican-American and Mexican village children. *Developmental Psychology,* 1970, **3,** 16-20.

Medinnus, G. R. Behavioral and cognitive measures of conscience development. *Journal of Genetic Psychology,* 1966, **109,** 147-150.

Midlarsky, E., Bryan, J. H., & Brickman, P. Aversive approval: interactive effects of modeling and reinforcement on altruistic behavior. *Child Development,* 1973, **44,** 321-328.

Milgrim, S. Behavioral study of obedience. *Journal of Abnormal and Social Psychology,* 1963, **67,** 371-378.

Moore, B. S., Underwood, B., & Rosenhan, D. Affect and altruism. *Developmental Psychology,* 1973, **8,** 99-104.

Mulligan, G., Douglas, J. W. B., Hammond, W. A., & Tizard, J. Delinquency and symptoms of maladjustment: the findings of a longitudinal study. *Proceedings of the Royal Society of Medicine,* 1963, **56,** 1083-1086.

Mussen, P., Rutherford, E., Harris, S., & Keasey, C. Honesty and altruism among preadolescents. *Developmental Psychology,* 1970, **3,** 169-194.

Nakasato, Y., & Aoyama, Y. Some relations between children's resistance to temptation and their moral judgment. *Reports of the National Research Institute of Police Science: research on prevention of crime and delinquency,* 1972, **13,** 62-70.

Nelsen, E. A., Grinder, R. E., & Biaggio, A. M. Relationships among behavioral cognitive-developmental and self report measures of morality and personality. *Multivariate Behavioral Research,* 1969, **4,** 483-500.

Nelsen, E. A., Grinder, R. E., & Challas, J. H. Resistance to temptation and moral judgment: behavioral correlates of Kohlberg's measure of moral development. Mimeographed paper, University of Wisconsin, 1968.

Parr, F. W. The problem of student honesty. *Journal of Higher Education,* 1936, **7,** 318-326.

Parke, R. D. Effectiveness of punishment as an interaction of intensity, timing, agent nurturance and cognitive-structuring. *Child Development,* 1969, **40,** 213-235.

Parke, R. D. The role of punishment in the socialization process. In R. A. Hoppe, G. A. Milton, & E. C. Simmel, (Eds.), *Early experiences and the processes of socialization.* New York: Academic, 1970. Pp. 81-108.

Parke, R. D. Some effects of punishment on children's behavior. In W. W. Hartup (Ed.), *The young child.* Vol. 2. Washington: National Association for the Education of Young Children, 1972. Pp. 264-283.

Parke, R. D. Explorations in punishment, discipline and self-control. In P. J. Elich, (Ed.), *Social learning.* Bellingham: Western Washington State Press, 1973.

Parke, R. D. Rules, roles and resistance to deviation in children. In A. Pick (Ed.), *Minnesota symposium on child psychology.* Vol. 8. Minneapolis: The University of Minnesota Press, in press.

Pearlin, L. I. *Class context and family relations: a cross national study.* Boston: Little, Brown, 1971.

Pearlin, L. I., Yarrow, M. R., & Scarr, H. A. Unintended effects of parental aspirations: the case of children's cheating. *American Journal of Sociology,* 1967, **73,** 73-83.

Perry, D. G., & Parke, R. D. Punishment and alternative response training as determinants of response inhibition in children. *Genetic Psychology Monographs,* in press.

Piaget, J. *The Moral judgment of the child.* New York: Harcourt, Brace, 1932.

Podd, M. H. Ego identity status and morality: the relationship between two developmental constructs. *Developmental Psychology,* 1972, **6,** 497-507.

Rest, J., Turiel, E., & Kohlberg, L. Level of moral development as a determinant of preference and comprehension of moral judgments made by others. *Journal of Personality,* 1969, **37,** 225-252.

Rosenhan, D. L. Prosocial behavior of children. In W. W. Hartup (Ed.), *The young child.* Vol. 2. Washington: National Association for the Education of Young Children, 1972. Pp. 340-359.

Rutherford, E., & Mussen, P. H. Generosity in nursery school boys. *Child Development,* 1968, **39,** 755-765.

Scarlett, H., Press, A., & Crockett, W. Children's descriptions of peers: a Wernerian developmental analysis. *Child Development,* 1971, **42,** 439-453.

Sears, R. R., Rau, L., & Alpert, R. *Identification and child rearing.* Stanford, Calif.: Stanford, 1965.

Selman, R. L. Taking another's perspective: role taking development in early childhood. *Child Development,* 1971, **42,** 1721-1734. (a)

Selman, R. L. The relation of role-taking ability to the development of moral judgment in children. *Child Development,* 1971, **42,** 79-91. (b)

Selman, R. L. Stages of role taking and moral judgment as guides to social intervention.

In T. Lickona (Ed.), *Man and morality.* New York: Holt, in press.

Shelton, J., & Hill, J. P. Effects on cheating of achievement anxiety and knowledge of peer performance. *Developmental Psychology,* 1969, **1,** 449-455.

Slaby, R. G., & Parke, R. D. The effect on resistance to deviation of observing a model's affective reaction to response consequences. *Developmental Psychology,* 1972, **5,** 40-47.

Smith, C. P., Ryan, E. R., & Diggins, D. R. Moral decision making: cheating on examinations. *Journal of Personality,* 1972, **40,** 640-660.

Toner, I. J., Parke, R. D., & Yussen, S. R. The effects of model self-verbalization on self-control. Unpublished manuscript, 1973.

Turiel, E. An experimental test of the sequentiality of developmental stages in the child's moral judgments. *Journal of Personality and Social Psychology,* 1966, **3,** 611-618.

Turiel, E., & Rothman, G. R. The influence of reasoning on behavioral choices at different stages of moral development. *Child Development,* 1972, **43,** 741-756.

Walters, R. H., & Parke, R. D. Influence of response consequences to a social model on resistance to deviation. *Journal of Experimental Child Psychology,* 1964, **1,** 269-280.

Yarrow, M. R., Scott, P. M., & Waxler, C. Z. Learning concern for others. *Developmental Psychology,* 1973, **8,** 240-260.

14

THE PEER GROUP AS A SOCIALIZATION AGENCY

In recent years there has been increasing recognition of the importance of extrafamilial agents in the socialization process. With the rise in maternal employment and the increase in the availability of pre-elementary school education, the role of peers and teachers has been brought into sharp focus. The purpose of the next two chapters will be to examine the contribution of the peer group and the school to childhood socialization.

In this chapter a number of issues concerning the role of the peer group in socialization are examined. First, how early are peers influential and what are the developmental trends in peer interaction? What factors influence the developmental changes in the role of peers in social development? Next, the factors that influence the formation of peer groups, as well as the determinants of conflict between groups, will be examined. Why do children conform to peer standards, and does conformity shift with age? Next, what are the determinants of peer acceptance? How important are personality factors, physical appearance, and children's names in determining popularity? Finally, a cross-cultural examination of the peer group will be presented.

DEVELOPMENTAL TRENDS IN PEER INTERACTION

Even in the first year of life infants are responsive to their peers. However, the early forms of social interaction between infants are limited to responding to the crying of another infant or looking at another baby. In the latter half of the first year, the patterns of interaction become more complex. Recent research by Durfee and Lee (1973) described the changes that take place in infant-infant interaction in a free play situation between six and twelve months of age. The ways of initiating contact changed with increasing age, from visual scrutiny of a peer, to approach and exploration of another infant and his toys, to more clearly social overtures, such as a smile or the offering of a toy. This type of sharing behavior, however, only occurred very often toward the end of the first year. Some of these shifts in approach and interaction are, of course, due to the maturation of the infant's motor capacities. As Figure 14-1 illustrates, the occurrence of the different types of activity while in contact follow the same pattern as initiating behavior. The typical periods of contact were brief (five to ten seconds) to moderately long (thirty to sixty seconds); longer contacts occurred only about 10 percent of the time. As the child develops, one of the most interesting shifts is from asocial to social contacts. At six months of age, 50 percent of the contacts were one-way, with the other baby never getting involved. From eight months on, contact is more interactive, with both infants in a dyad participating. These data suggest that peer interaction has its origins as early as the first year of life.

Although infants are responsive to peers as well as to adults, the importance of peers increases markedly in the preschool years. This increase is not merely quantitative since changes in the form of the interchange occur as well. The classic description of the

Toward the end of the first year, infants sometimes engage in sharing behavior. (Suzanne Szasz.)

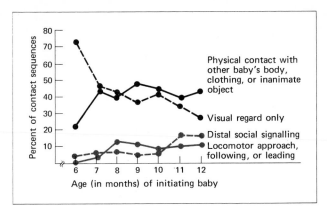

FIGURE 14-1 Predominant type of activity during interaction between infants. (From Durfee, J. T., & Lee, L. C., 1973.)

developmental course of peer interaction was provided many years ago by Parten and Newhall (1943). Basing their study on observations of children from two to five years of age, these investigators offered a three-phase sequence of peer play patterns: a solitary phase in which the child plays by himself; a period of parallel play in which children play beside but do not interact directly with other children; and finally, the advent of cooperative play, by the time the child is ready to enter elementary school. However, as the observational study of infants that we discussed earlier indicates, this classic description probably underestimates the complexity of early peer interaction.

Other research has not only confirmed this observation that peers become more important as the child matures but has provided information concerning the impact of this increased peer orientation on adult-child relations. Does the child simply become more responsive to all social agents—peers as well as adults—with increasing age, or does peer influence increase at the expense of adults? Between two and five years of age, children interact increasingly more frequently with their peers and less often with their teachers; even teacher-initiated bids for attention are ignored more frequently (Heathers, 1955).

Parent-child relations follow a similar pattern: as they grow older, children tend to interact less with all adults, including parents (Barker & Wright, 1955; Wright, 1967). In one of their investigations, a group of children ranging from two to eleven years of age were "tracked" by an observer for a full day with the aim of providing as complete a record as possible of the child's activities. This record of the child's "stream of behavior" was divided into discrete "episodes" (behavioral units with clear-cut beginning and termination points, such as eating dinner and combing hair), and the frequency with which parents, teachers, and peers were involved in each behavioral episode was plotted. As Figure 14-2 shows, parent-child interaction decreases markedly as the child grows older; the importance of peers, as expected, shows an upward trend with increasing age.

Factors affecting age changes in peer interaction

There is a variety of possible reasons for these shifts in interaction patterns during childhood. First, there are structural changes, such as school attendance, which drasti-

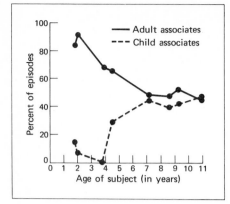

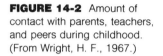

FIGURE 14-2 Amount of contact with parents, teachers, and peers during childhood. (From Wright, H. F., 1967.)

cally increase opportunities for peer interaction. However, as the Heathers study (1955) has already indicated, two-year-olds simply take less advantage of their opportunities for peer exchanges than older children; obviously, while proximity is necessary, it is by no means the sole factor accounting for these developmental changes. In addition, children's social skills, such as role taking and communication abilities, improve with age, making peer-peer interactions more likely and more successful. Moreover, as children mature they become more and more adequate sources of positive reinforcement for one another and serve increasingly as social models for each other. Paralleling these changes are shifts in cultural norms concerning the appropriateness of peer group participation for the older child: adults not only permit, but actively encourage, increased peer interaction.

Communication skills and peer interaction

As children grow older their communication skills increase, and this increased skill is an important contributor to the increased influence of the peer group on the older child. Once you have listened to a two-year-old attempt to converse with a peer, it will no longer be surprising that very young children's peer interactions are brief and limited. The speech patterns of the two-year-old have an egocentric quality; in other words, the child's speech is often characterized by idiosyncratic terms and references, which gives one the impression that the child is talking to himself rather than to his audience. Only as children grow older do they appreciate that the viewpoint of the listener must be considered if communication is to be effective. The implication of this observation for peer interaction is obvious: As children sharpen their communication skills, sustained and rewarding peer-peer exchanges are likely to increase.

Evidence documenting this shift in communication competence over age comes from a recent study by Krauss and Glucksberg (1969) presented in Box 14-1. Further evidence that the emergence of communication skills follows a developmental course was provided in another study (Glucksberg, Krauss, & Westburg, 1966) in which nursery-school children were completely unable to communicate effectively about novel graphic forms to a peer. Data directly linking communication competence and peer interaction come from a recent study by Rubin (1972). This investigator argued that the emerging ability to communicate clearly and effectively does, in fact, make peer exchanges more rewarding for both and in turn may affect popularity among peers. Children from kindergarten and second, fourth, and sixth grades both selected their three favorite classmates and then participated in the type of communication task described in Box 14-1. Kindergarten and second-grade children who were skillful communicators were more popular than those who performed poorly on the communication task. The effect was not present at the later grades, where most children are relatively effective communicators. These results suggest that the ability to take another person's point of view may play a role in determining the child's popularity during the early school years.

This research nicely illustrates the relationship between cognitive and social development in children. In earlier chapters we observed that a decline in egocentric thinking was important for the understanding of such basic cognitive concepts as conservation of volume and weight. These same shifts in egocentrism affect social communication and result in more rewarding peer relations.

BOX 14-1 THE DEVELOPMENT OF COMMUNICATION EFFECTIVENESS

Does communication effectiveness improve across age? To find out, Krauss and Glucksberg gave children at four age levels, kindergarten and grades one, three, and five, the task of communicating a description of a set of novel graphic designs to a partner of the same age. Figure 14-3 illustrates the novel figures which are printed on wooden blocks. In the experimental situation there are two subjects, designated the speaker and listener, each of whom has a duplicate set of the design blocks. The speaker is required to stack his blocks on a peg and at the same time to instruct his partner, the listener, which block to stack on her peg. No restrictions are placed on verbal communication, and the object of the game is to tell the partner the correct block so that listener and speaker have identical stacks of blocks at the end of the trial. Success is rewarded by a small plastic trinket. Before using the novel forms, the children were given practice trials with animal-

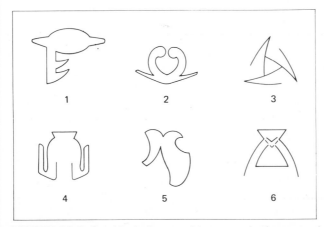

FIGURE 14-3 Graphic designs used in communication research. (From Krauss, R., & Glucksberg, S., 1969.)

shaped blocks in full view of one another. After they learned the game, they were separated by an opaque screen and provided eight trials with the novel figures. The developmental trends were clear-cut, as evidenced by Figure 14-4, which shows the mean
number of errors that the children made over the series of trials. While the kindergarten
age subjects failed to show any improvement, the older subjects in grades three and five
steadily reduced their error rate so that by the last few trials they were performing the
game without a mistake. Clearly, communication effectiveness does improve as the child
develops.

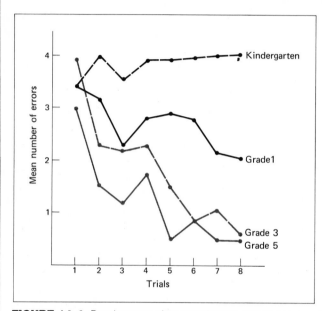

FIGURE 14-4 Development of communication skill across age. (From Krauss, R., &
Glucksberg, S., 1969.)

Source: Krauss, R. H., & Glucksberg, S. The development of communication: competence as a
function of age. *Child Development,* 1969, **42,** 255-266.

Peers as reinforcing agents

As children grow older the salience of peers as reinforcing agents and as models
increases. Many parents, particularly of adolescents, bemoan the fact that their children
ignore their wise advice while listening to and emulating their peers. Even throughout
the preschool years, the frequency with which peers reinforce each other increases.

A recent study by Charlesworth and Hartup (1967) has documented the shift in the
reinforcing capacity of peers that occurs in three- and four-year-olds. These investigators gathered normative information on the amount and kinds of positive social reinforcement dispensed by three- and four-year-old children to each other in a nursery
school setting. The following kinds of social categories were scored:

1. *Giving positive attention and approval:* attending, offering praise and approval, offering help, smiling, informing someone of another child's needs, general conversation.
2. *Giving affection and personal acceptance:* physical and verbal.
3. *Submission:* passive acceptance, imitation, sharing, accepting another's idea or help, allowing another child to play, compromise, following an order or request with pleasure and cooperation.

Four-year-olds socially reinforced their peers at a higher rate than did three-year-old children. Moreover, older children tended to distribute their reinforcements over a larger number of recipients than did younger children. Regardless of age, however, there was a marked tendency for boys to direct their reinforcement to boys, while girls gave more reinforcements to other girls than to opposite-sexed peers. This is consistent with numerous findings (Moore, 1967) that young children tend to prefer to interact with peers of the same sex. Another issue concerns the development of reciprocity: Do young children tend to reinforce the same individuals that reinforce them? The relationship between giving and receiving of positive reinforcement was large ($r = .79$). Similarly the child who tended to reinforce a large number of different peers received reinforcement from many children. Even by three and four years of age, therefore, giving and receiving have developed into reciprocal activities.

Home and background factors may also contribute to the patterns of reinforcement used by preschool children in peer interactions. Recall from the chapter on the assessment of intelligence that middle-class parents use more praise and less punishment in interaction with their children than do lower-class parents.

On the basis of these findings, Feshbach and Devor (1969) argued that "if a child duplicates in his social transactions with peers, modal patterns of reinforcement observed at home, then peer interaction and influences may vary with social class [Feshbach & Devor, 1969, p. 1]." Specifically, these investigators predicted that middle-class Caucasian children would make greater use of positive reinforcement, while children from more deprived backgrounds would manifest greater instances of negative reinforcement. Rather than assess spontaneous occurrences of positive and negative social reinforcement, Feshbach and Devor experimentally arranged the four-year-olds in the study to teach a younger child how to solve a simple wooden puzzle. The extent to which the child-teacher used positive and negative reinforcements in carrying out his instructional task was recorded by observers. The positive category included statements of praise, encouragement, and affirmation, such as "that's a girl" or "she did it," while the negative category included criticism, negations, and derogatory comments, such as "wrong way" or "you skipped." Although all "teachers" were equally effective, the children differed in their relative use of positive and negative reinforcers. Middle-class Caucasian children used a greater number of positive reinforcers than the lower-class group. There was a slight tendency for the lower-class subjects to use more negative reinforcements in instructing a younger child than the middle-class children; however, the effect was less marked than in the case of positive reinforcement. More recently, Feshbach (1973) has reported similar results for middle- and lower-class children in England and Israel. Differences previously reported in relation to parental reinforcement patterns across social class appear to be reflected, at least in part, in peer behavior. The differential encouragement and positive support that the middle-class Caucasian child

The reactions of other children are often reinforcers of aggressive behavior. (Suzanne Szasz.)

receives from his peer group may contribute to his greater school achievement and intellectual accomplishment. Moreover, it is clear that no typical reinforcement pattern can be described; the social class of the child required consideration.

There is no doubt that peer reinforcement in the form of attention and approval does affect the behavior patterns of the peer recipient. A study by Wahler (1967) will illustrate this effect. Instead of merely observing peer interactions, Wahler directly intervened and trained a group of youngsters to serve as experimenter confederates. Wahler instructed the peers of five children to attend to only certain behaviors and to ignore other social responses. Eddie, a five-year-old boy, will illustrate the procedures used. First, the aspects of Eddie's behavior that were consistent and stable parts of his response repertoires were noted, namely, cooperative behavior (playing a game initiated by peers), solitary play (playing alone), and shouting. Two other five-year-old boys were selected to "shape" Eddie's behavior. They were taught to ignore the boy whenever he made a cooperative overture; as expected, ignoring this class of responses produced a marked reduction of cooperative behaviors. At the same time, solitary play and shouting increased in rate during this period. To demonstrate that Eddie's behavior was under peer reinforcement control, Wahler next instructed his young assistants to resume their attention to Eddie's cooperative behavior. The result was more cooperative responses from

Eddie. Using other five-year-olds, Wahler was able to demonstrate similar effects for a variety of other social responses, including speech, aggression, and play behavior. As Box 14-2 illustrates, the reactions of other children during social exchanges, such as an aggressive encounter, are another important form of control in peer-peer interaction.

BOX 14-2 PEER REACTIONS AS REINFORCERS OF AGGRESSIVE
BEHAVIOR

The aim of the Patterson, Littman, and Bricker (1967) research was to demonstrate the important role that peer group reactions play in reinforcing aggressive behavior in nursery school children. To investigate the problem of how the peer group contributes to aggression development, these investigators trained a group of students to make observations of the aggressive exchanges between children in a nursery school setting. The eighteen boys and eighteen girls participating in the study were observed for thirty-three 2½ -hour sessions. By gathering detailed information they were able to assess how the reaction of the target or victim of an aggressive attack affected the subsequent behavior of the aggressor. When the target child responded by withdrawing, by acquiescing, or by crying, the attacker in subsequent interactions was likely to perform the same aggressive act (punch, kick, etc.) toward the same victim. In other words, these reactions functioned as positive reinforcers for the aggressor. [As the child matures, the effects of these feedback cues changes, as illustrated by Buss's (1966) finding that distress responses in the victim of an aggressive attack will lessen, not increase, aggression in adults.] In contrast, if the aggressive behavior was followed by negative reinforcement, such as teacher intervention, attempts at recovery of property (for example, a toy), or retaliation (for example, hitting the aggressor), then the aggressive agent had a high probability of either choosing a new victim or altering the form of his aggression. Not only is aggression controlled by peer feedback, but nonaggressive children may learn to behave aggressively, particularly if they are frequently the victims of an aggressive attack. The best way to understand how this type of learning occurs is to examine closely what happens to a typical victim. First, children who are victimized by peers are provided with many opportunities to counterattack their aggressors. After frequent attacks, even a passive victim will finally strike back, and by counterattacking, the number of future attacks are often decreased—a highly reinforcing outcome for the victim. Over repeated occasions, the victim's aggressive responses are therefore strengthened, thus making it more probable that he will *initiate* aggressive attacks in future situations. In fact, this is precisely the pattern that these investigators discovered. Over the period of the study they found a striking association between the frequency with which children were victimized by aggressive acts of peers, the frequency of their successful counterattacks, and increases in their aggressive behavior. Even passive, nonassertive children may learn to be aggressive—in self-defense! The study suggests that peers as well as adults are important reinforcing agents and that the reactions or feedback provided by the victim constitute an important class of reinforcing events for both controlling *and* developing aggressive and assertive behaviors.

Source: From Patterson, G. R., Littman, R. A., and Bricker, W. Assertive behavior in children: a step toward a theory of aggression. *Monographs of the Society for Research in Child Development,* 1967, **32** (Serial No. 113).

Peers as models

Peers influence each other by serving not only as reinforcing agents but also as *social models*. Much research in the past few years has shown that children acquire a variety of social responses by observing the behavior of their peers. Moreover, as Piaget (1951) has suggested, the capacity for imitating others increases with age. It is likely, therefore, that this expanding capacity for modeling peer behavior increases peer influence and so contributes to the increased influence of peers as the child develops. Although there is little direct evidence of the extent to which children imitate peer versus adult models at different age levels, a study by O'Connor (1969) leaves little doubt that observing peer models can increase the amount of peer group participation. For his study, O'Connor selected a group of severely withdrawn children from a nursery school class. These social isolates share many of the characteristics of younger, immature children in that they, too, have not acquired the social skills necessary for successful peer interaction. Half of the children in this investigation saw a twenty-minute sound film portraying scenes of peer interaction in a nursery school setting. In a typical scene a child watches his peers play, then joins the group and is rewarded for his participation. The other children, for example, talk to him, smile, and generally respond in a positive fashion to his involvement in the play group. In the early stages of the film, very calm activities (for example, sharing a toy with another child) were displayed, while in later scenes both the vigor of the social exchanges and the size of the peer group increased. To ensure that the viewers attended to the critical aspects of the film, the film's sound track described the social behaviors and their consequences as shown in the visual display. A control group of isolates saw a film of the acrobatic antics of dolphins. After the film, children returned to their classrooms and the amount of social interaction was assessed. The impressive changes produced by the brief twenty-minute exposure to peer models are shown in Figure 14-5. The developmental implication of these data is clear: young children may learn, in part, how to interact with each other by observing the successful interchanges of older peer models.

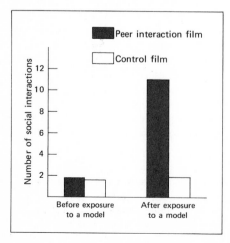

FIGURE 14-5 Impact of modeling on social interaction patterns. (Adapted from O'Connor, Robert D., 1969.)

As in the case of reinforcement patterns, a variety of factors determines the extent to which a child imitates his peers. The nature of the child's typical interactions with his peer group is one important determinant of peer imitation. Hartup and Coates (1967) recorded the frequency of reinforcements dispensed and received by each child in his nursery school class (see discussion of the study by Charlesworth & Hartup given earlier in this chapter). On the basis of these observations, children were classified as either high or low in terms of their amount of previous peer interaction. Some children, then, saw a model who had a similar history of peer reinforcements as themselves; children who received frequent peer reinforcements in their daily interactions saw a model who also had a history of high levels of peer reward. On the other hand, children who received few peer reinforcements were exposed to a child model who had a similar history of low peer group involvement. Other children saw a model who had a different history of interaction than themselves. For example, low-interaction children saw a model who was typically associated with high levels of peer reinforcement. The impact of the model was measured by the amount of imitation; the model in all cases acted in an altruistic fashion by sharing his winnings from a maze game with another child. As Figure 14-6 shows, both the child's past history of reinforcement and his prior relationship with the model are important determinants of peer imitation. As other studies have shown, similarity between observer and model is likely to increase imitation (Rosenkrans, 1967).

While the above studies illustrate the important role that peer models can play in the child's social development, a variety of other behaviors can be acquired and modified by exposure to peers, including aggression (Hicks, 1965), moral judgements (Bandura & McDonald, 1963), and resistance to deviation (Walters & Parke, 1964). Some of these studies are discussed in detail in other chapters.

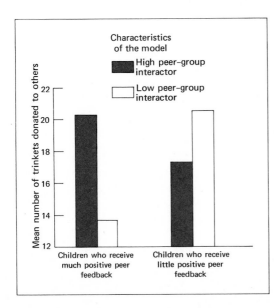

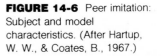

FIGURE 14-6 Peer imitation: Subject and model characteristics. (After Hartup, W. W., & Coates, B., 1967.)

Adult influences on peer interaction

Adults as well as peers play an influential role in accounting for the increases in peer group participation as the child develops. In fact, this increase in social interaction of children as they mature is not only an empirical fact but also a *cultural expectation* of adult socialization agents, such as parents and teachers. For example, a teacher is likely to permit and even encourage a three-year-old to make social overtures to her. But she is likely to expect—and reward—more *peer*-directed and less teacher-directed behavior in a five-year-old. Too many social overtures and too much attention seeking by older children may even be aversive to the teacher. In addition to rewarding children for interaction with peers, teachers probably provide more opportunities for peer interaction as the child matures.

The potential role that adults can play in shaping peer interaction is illustrated in the following study (Allen, Hart, Buell, Harris, & Wolf, 1964). The aim was to increase systematically the amount of social participation of an "isolate" in a nursery school class by adult social reinforcement. Typically, the target child played alone and restricted his interaction to the teachers; rarely, if ever, did he interact with the other children. Systematic observation indicated that isolate play usually attracted and maintained the attention of the teacher and that the teacher seldom attended to the child when he was interacting with his peers. To reverse this, Allen and his coworkers instructed the teacher to attend regularly if the child approached other children and interacted with them. Solitary play was ignored. When teacher attention was contingent on peer interaction, isolate play declined markedly in strength while social play increased two- or threefold. Nearly a month later, the amount of peer participation was still high. This experiment illustrates that once the child becomes an active peer group participant, the social reinforcers received from his peers in the course of a typical play sequence often will be sufficient to maintain peer interaction, even when adult attention is removed.

Adults can influence peer interaction patterns through their choice of play materials as well. To demonstrate this effect, Quilitch and Risely (1973) chose two sets of toys: "isolate" toys (for example, gyroscope, play dough) were primarily played with by one child at a time, and "social" toys (for example, pick-up sticks and checkers) were more often played with by two or more children. Then they provided groups of seven-year-old children with the two types of toys and observed the play patterns. Social play occurred only 16 percent of the time with the isolate toys, while peer interaction occurred 70 percent of the time when the children were provided with social toys. In short, adults can influence the amount of peer social interaction not only by direct encouragement but also by the types of toys that they make available to children.

In conclusion, the age shifts that we have been discussing in this section probably represent a complex interaction of changes in teacher and parent expectations and behaviors, along with changes in the social competence of the child. Together these two sets of factors make successful peer interaction more likely as the child grows older.

GROUP FORMATION AND INTERGROUP CONFLICT

Children not only interact more as they develop, but they form groups that possess common goals and aims. In addition, groups usually develop a hierarchical organization or structure that designates each member's relationship to other members of the group and that facilitates the interaction among its members. A study in Box 14-3 illustrates the developmental trends in children's understanding of group hierarchies based on toughness. The bases for social hierarchies shift across age, situation, and sex. In younger children, toughness may be the most important dimension on which to order members of a group. Later such things as appearance, athletic prowess, or academic performance may play a more important role in determining group status.

BOX 14-3 THE DEVELOPMENT OF GROUP HIERARCHIES

How early do children recognize their status in relation to other members of their peer group? To answer this question, Edelman and Omark (1973) asked children to compare themselves to their classmates by answering the question "Who is toughest?" Nursery-school-age children had only limited awareness of dominance relationships; when asked the question "Who is toughest?", they often responded "Me." By kindergarten there was some awareness of a dominance hierarchy, and by the first grade there was 60 percent agreement among classmates on who, in fact, was tougher. In the second and third grades the agreement reached 70 percent. However, there were clear sex differences, with boys being nominated for the top 40 percent of the positions in the classroom hierarchy of toughness while girls were generally in the bottom 40 percent of the class. However, girls were just as accurate as boys in their judgments of the toughness of their classmates. Since the girls have a low rate of interaction with boys, the girls' accurate perception of toughness probably is learned through watching the boys.

Social development is usually closely related to changes in cognitive development. These investigators tested this assumption by comparing children's ability to order a series of sticks of various lengths with their ability to order their classmates on a toughness dimension. They argued that a similar ability is involved in both tasks; namely, the logical operation of seriation, whereby a set of objects is ordered along a dimension such that $a > b > c$, etc. In addition they were asked to justify or explain the reasons for their decisions. Interestingly, the children's ability to understand the stick problem and the people problem showed a parallel developmental course; both increased markedly between kindergarten and first grade. Whether children first acquire the operation of seriation or whether "the developing dominance hierarchy may form a part of the necessary social experience for this aspect of the child's cognitive development [Edelman & Omark, 1973, p. 6]," these data do illustrate the close relationship between the child's cognitive and social development.

Source: Edelman, M. S., & Omark, D. R. Dominance hierarchies in young children. *Social Science Information*, 1973, **12,** 1.

Group formation

What are the conditions that promote the formation of a group? A study by Sherif (1956) illustrates the process of group formation in a summer camp setting in Oklahoma. When the twenty-two eleven-year-old boys who participated in the project arrived at the camp they were divided into two sets. Proximity is important in group formation, but the opportunity for sharing a variety of activities which have common appeal value to the individuals also is an important determinant. In addition, if the activities require coopera-tion among the members of the group for their attainment, a group structure will emerge more readily. So, Sherif arranged for each set of boys to engage in a series of different camping activities which they all valued, such as hiking and crafts. Tasks that required coordinated activity and which would be conducive to division of labor and to the specification of clear status and role positions were also arranged. For example, the boys were provided the ingredients for a meal in unprepared form (for example, meat, watermelon, Kool-Aid) at a time when they were hungry. To turn these ingredients into a meal required cooperation of all group members in preparation and serving. Moreover, each group developed its own rules of conduct and its own special interests. To further distinguish themselves from the other group, the boys adopted group names, The Rat-tlers and The Eagles. As a result of their shared experience, these two sets of strangers changed into groups with norms, names, and a clear hierarchial structure of leadership and status positions.

Intergroup conflict

While participating together may promote group formation, other factors, such as com-petition with other groups, are extremely influential in increasing group solidarity and group pride. However, intergroup competition may have other effects, namely increas-ing hostility and friction between competing groups. Here is a description of the out-come of a tournament of competitive games: baseball, tug of war, and a treasure hunt that Sherif arranged as part of the Robber's Cave experiment.

> The tournament started in a spirit of good sportsmanship. But as it progressed good feeling soon evaporated. The members of each group began to call their rivals "stinkers," and "cheaters." They refused to have anything more to do with individuals in the opposing group. The boys . . . turned against buddies whom they had chosen as "best friends," when they first arrived at the camp. A large proportion of the boys in each group gave negative ratings to all the boys in the other group. The rival groups made threatening posters and planned raids, collecting secret hoards of green apples for ammunition. To the Robber's Cave came the Eagles, after a defeat in a tournament game, and burned a banner left behind by the Rattlers; the next morning the Rattlers seized the Eagles's flag when they arrived on the athletic field. From that time on, name-calling, scuffles, and raids were the rule of the day [Sherif, 1956, p.5].

Competition was clearly effective in increasing hostility, rivalry, and conflict although it enhanced in-group identification and strengthened group solidarity. These findings offer little support to advocates of competitive sports as a safe outlet for reducing aggression (Lorenz, 1966). Rather, competition either between groups or between individuals (Nel-son, Gelfand, & Hartmann, 1969) is likely to increase, not decrease, aggression.

Reduction in intergroup hostility

Sherif, in a further phase of the project, set out to reduce the conflict that he so cleverly engineered. First, he gave the members of the conflicting groups opportunities for non-competitive, highly pleasant social contacts, such as going to the movies or sharing the same dining room. The results were disastrous: the boys simply took advantage of these occasions to vent their hostilities against one another; if anything, the conflict was heightened rather than reduced by this approach. Next, Sherif provided the groups with a series of tasks that required their cooperative effort to solve. This tactic was much more successful. Sherif cites the following examples of the kinds of experimentally produced crises that forced the rivals to "pull together":

> One was a breakdown in the water supply. Water came to our camp in pipes from a tank about a mile away. We arranged to interrupt it and then called the boys together to inform them of the crisis. Both groups promptly volunteered to search the water line for trouble. They worked together harmoniously, and before the end of the afternoon they had located and corrected the difficulty. . . . On another occasion, just when everyone was hungry and the camp truck was about to go to town for food, it developed that the engine wouldn't start, and the boys had to pull together to get the vehicle going. [Sherif, 1956, p. 5].

Figure 14-7 illustrates how the provision of these "superordinate" goals restored positive intergroup attitudes and feelings.

Sherif has eloquently summarized the implications of his research program:

> Efforts to reduce friction and prejudice between groups in our society have usually followed rather different methods. Much attention has been given to bringing members of hostile groups together socially, to communicating accurate and favorable information about one group to the other, and to bringing the leaders of groups together to enlist their influence. But as everyone knows, such measures sometimes reduce inter-group tensions and sometimes not. Social contacts, as our experiments demonstrated, may only serve as occasions for intensifying conflict. Favorable information about a disliked group may be ignored or reinterpreted to fit stereotyped notions about the group. Leaders cannot act without regard for the prevailing temper in their own groups.
>
> What our limited experiments have shown is that the possibilities for achieving harmony are greatly enhanced when groups are brought together to work toward common ends. Then favorable information about a disliked group is seen in a new light, and leaders are in a position to take bolder steps toward cooperation. In short, hostility gives way when groups pull together to achieve overriding goals which are real and compelling to all concerned [Sherif, 1956, p. 6].

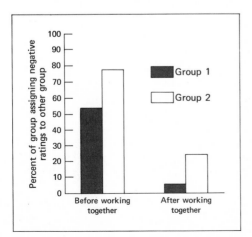

FIGURE 14-7 Ratings of opposing groups before and after working together on a common task. (Adapted from Sherif, M., 1956.)

CONFORMITY TO THE PEER GROUP

Another way in which peer social influence is reflected is in conformity to peer group norms and standards of conduct. Probably the classic study of peer conformity was conducted over twenty years ago by Berenda (1950). It was an ingenious investigation and has served as a model for numerous other conformity experiments. It merits a detailed exposition, and to capture the flavor of the situation it will be described from the standpoint of a typical subject in this study. Two age groups were included: seven-to ten- and ten-to-thirteen-year-old boys and girls. When the unsuspecting child arrived at the experimental room for a day of "special work," eight of his most intelligent class-mates were already waiting in line outside of the room. The task that the experimenter posed appeared straightforward: simply to judge which of the series of lines matched the length of a standard stimulus line. Figure 14-8 illustrates a typical card used in the study. However, the situation soon became a rather perplexing one for the naïve child. Although he was certain that he had picked the correct matching line, his classmates always picked a longer or shorter line and never the correct one. Of course, the situation was rigged; his classmates were in league with the experimenter, and they had been coached to give erroneous responses. How, then, do children respond when their own perceptual judgment of reality seriously conflicts with the ostensible judgments of their peer group? Another group of children made the judgments alone so that the effects of peer pressure could be properly assessed. Individuals differ, of course, but a large percentage give in to peer pressure. In Berenda's experiment, 93 percent of the seven-to ten-year-olds responded correctly under control conditions, while only 43 percent of the same children gave the correct answer in the experimental condition (for example, under group pressure). Similarly, 94 percent of the ten- to thirteen-year-olds' judgments were correct when alone, but only 54 percent of these subjects picked the right line in the group situation. In other words, when the children made their judgments in the presence of the false peer feedback, there were significantly greater numbers of errone-ous judgments than when they judged the lines alone.

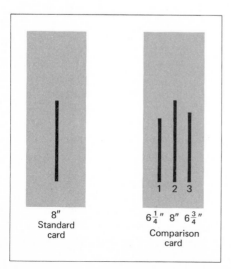

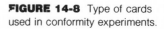

FIGURE 14-8 Type of cards used in conformity experiments.

Are children of all ages equally susceptible to peer pressures? Or do children conform more to their peer groups as they mature? Recently Allen and Newston (1972) examined conformity to peers at four age points: grades one, four, seven, and ten. In one phase children were required to match a line in length with one of a variety of comparison lines, while in another phase opinion items consisting of such statements as "Kittens make good pets" or "On weekends, students my age should be allowed to stay up later than on school days" were used. In each case the subject thought four peers disagreed with his answer. The results showed that overall conformity *decreased* as the child developed. It is important to note that there was not a significantly high degree of conformity during adolescence; conformity was more likely at younger ages. Probably the increases in the certainty of one's judgment and the self-confidence and independence to withstand group pressure that occur with age account for these findings.

As in the case of a number of age-related changes, the type of situation is important. For example, Hoving, Hamm, and Galvin (1969) have found increases in conformity from the second to the eighth grades in situations where the correct answer is ambiguous. It is clear that no simple conclusion about developmental trends can be drawn.

Different agents may be more influential at different age levels, with peers assuming increased importance as the child grows older. Allen and Newston (1972) compared the conformity of students from four grade levels (kindergarten, fourth, seventh, and tenth) when under pressure from four classmates or when under adult influence. Of particular interest was their finding that the adult influence was effective *only* for first-grade children. As we have already seen, peer influence was evident across all grade levels; however, the effectiveness of the adult agent dropped off sharply and remained at a low level in the other grades.

Age, of course, is only one of a host of individual difference factors that determine children's conformity. Sex of the child frequently has been found to be important, with girls typically conforming more than boys (for example, Iscoe, Williams & Harvey, 1963). While this finding is consistent with cultural sex-role expectations of the passive, dependent female and the assertive, independent male, one cannot legitimately conclude that girls are *always* more conforming than boys. Situational variables require consideration as well. If the conformity task is presented as an "achievement" task, boys, who are more achievement-oriented than girls, are likely to show greater peer compliance (Sampson & Hancock, 1967). On the other hand, if the conformity context makes salient feminine sex-typed motivations, such as affiliative and social acceptance tendencies, girls show greater susceptibility to social influence than boys (Patel & Gordon, 1960). The extent to which conformity is viewed as congruent with sex-role standards, then, must be considered before sex differences in peer conformity can be predicted.

What about the peer group status of the child being pressured to conform? One might think that the lower the child is in the group hierarchy the more compliant he would be. However, Harvey and Consalvi (1960) suggest otherwise. In fact, in their studies of cliques of delinquent adolescent boys, they found the least conformity among the very high and the very low status members. Most conforming were the middle-ranking adolescents, who may have been upward-oriented and therefore may have been using conformity to group norms as a technique to improve their group position.

The social influence of peers is reflected in conformity to peer group dress. (Omikron.)

In addition, the characteristics of the influence source, the nature of the group, and characteristics of the task also influence conformity. Children are more likely to yield to the opinions of a prestigious competent peer (Gelfand, 1962) and to conform when faced with a difficult, rather than an easy, problem-solving situation (Berenda, 1950). This seems to parallel the findings in imitation studies that power and competence of the model and task difficulty affect modeling. In addition, group size, the relationship among the members, the degree of agreement, and the importance of the issue to the group also affect conformity responses (Hartup, 1970).

It is clear, therefore, that no simple statement concerning peer conformity is legitimate. Peer conformity occurs, but to varying degrees at different ages, in different situations, and with different kinds of peers.

Ways of reducing conformity

The other side of the conformity issue is of interest as well. How can conformity be reduced? Under what conditions will an individual resist group pressures to conform? Obviously the learning of this kind of independence is an important developmental task if the child is to be more than a mere "follower." Many studies indicate that a partner who will provide a subject with social support in his attempts to resist majority pressure significantly reduces conformity in situations similar to that of the Berenda study (Asch, 1956; Allen & Levine, 1968). Recently Allen and Newston (1972) studied the effects of social support in order to determine whether independence in children could be increased by the technique. Subjects participated in five-person groups and were given feedback concerning the answers of the four other group members. Some children were exposed to a group giving unanimously incorrect or unpopular answers on about half the trials. In contrast, a second group heard three of the four members give erroneous answers, while the fourth person acted as a partner who gave the *correct* answer just prior to the student's turn. Even though the critical child was in the minority, the presence of the "partner" markedly reduced group conformity.

A more dramatic illustration of the power of peer support in *reducing* conformity derives from Milgram's (1974) study of obedience to authority in which subjects were encouraged by the experimenter to give what they believed were increasingly painful and dangerous shocks to another subject. If a peer urged the subject to continue, he was more likely to go to the most severe shock levels. However, if peers themselves refused to go on, the subject also was more likely to defy the experimenter. Without peer support twenty-six subjects out of thirty went onto the highest level of shock; with the support of defiant peers only four obeyed the instructions. In fact, peer rebellion was the most effective way of undercutting the experimenter's authority in this kind of situation. Clearly, peer influence can be constructive.

DETERMINANTS OF PEER ACCEPTANCE

We have seen the importance of peer groups in determining conformity in children, and we have seen that children's modeling behavior will be determined in part by the characteristics of the model, for example, his popularity, his prestige, and his resemblance to the imitator. It is of interest, therefore, to examine the characteristics of peers which may make them acceptable, and in so doing, to determine those individuals in the environment who will most influence the development of the child. The traditional approach to this issue has been simply to list the twenty behaviors and personality traits that distinguished popular children from their unpopular age-mates. However, the usefulness of this approach is questionable. As noted in the chapter on sex-role typing, the characteristics which are associated with popularity among social class groups vary and most studies of popularity have not controlled for the socioeconomic and ethnic compositions of their groups. Consequently, it is difficult to make generalizations about personality characteristics and popularity. The main conclusion from this literature is that popular children are those who have attributes valued in any given subgroup. In short, children who are perceived as competent within the norms of their group are popular. Good adjustment, friendliness, low anxiety, a reasonable level of self-esteem, and some responsiveness and sensitivity to the needs and feelings of other members of the peer group seem to be associated with popularity in most groups. If the group values toughness in males, a boy who is competently aggressive will be popular. If it values athletic prowess or intellectual achievement, competence in those areas will be associated with popularity. In short, the nature of the group and the situation must be considered before any statements can be made about personality factors in popularity.

Moreover, there are other important factors affecting peer popularity. Two kinds of determinants will be considered: physical appearance and children's names.

Physical characteristics and peer acceptance

Body build   Are children with various types of body builds treated differently by their peers? Is it true that fat, chubby children have a tougher time gaining peer acceptance than more muscular children? To answer these questions Staffieri (1967) asked children to rate different body types and then related these evaluations to peer popularity scores. Three common body types, distinguished earlier by Sheldon, Stevens, and Tucker (1940), were used. One type, the *endomorph,* is characterized by a softness and spherical appearance and an underdevelopment of muscle and bone. The *mesomorph* individual has an athletic build, muscular, broad-shouldered, and large-boned. The third type, the *ectomorph,* is thin and has poor muscular development. Six- to ten-year-old boys exposed to full body silhouettes of either child or adult endomorphs, mesomorphs, or ectomorphs were asked to assign a list of descriptive adjectives to the types as well as to designate their preferred body type. The results were clear: all the adjectives assigned to the mesomorph image were favorable. For example, the children expected a person with this muscular, athletic build to be brave, happy, good-looking, strong, helpful, and intelligent—a clearly positive set of traits; the adjectives assigned to the endomorph, primarily a socially aggressive type, were unfavorable, such as argumentative, dishonest, and stupid; finally, the ectomorph, a generally socially submissive type, was described as weak, quiet, and worried. Similar results have been found for older boys (ten to twenty years of age) (Lerner, 1969) and for adults (Brodsky, 1954). As would be expected, by age seven the boys showed a clear preference for looking like the mesomorph.

But is there a link between these stereotypes of body builds and peer acceptance? Fortunately, Staffieri (1967) collected data concerning this relationship and found that mesomorphs were selected by classmates as one of "five best friends" more often than endo- or ectomorphic children. In fact, the endomorphic boys were the least popular of the three body types. These data are consistent with a social learning view of the physique-temperament relation and suggest that this link may be mediated by commonly accepted stereotypes existing within the culture concerning the behavior expected of individuals with varying kinds of body build. There are data which indicate that individuals behave to some extent in a manner consistent with others' expectations (for example, Rosenthal, 1966). As Staffieri notes, "once the individual accepts the expectation as being true of himself the literature suggests that he will act in a manner to fulfill the belief, thus providing added continuity to behavior which was originally emitted because of expectation [Staffieri, 1967, p. 101]." Moreover, it is likely that these stereotyped responses will find support through differential peer and adult reinforcement of behaviors that are consistent with their expectations. The issue is still open, but these data leave little doubt that physical characteristics are important predictors of peer acceptance. To what extent a genetic, constitutional argument rather than a social learning approach is valid remains to be determined.

Rate of maturation and peer acceptance   Another way of approaching the issue of physical characteristics and peer acceptance is by examining the effects of the *rate* of physical growth. Although norms can be described for the rate at which individuals reach physical maturity, there are sufficiently wide individual differences to warrant a distinction between early and late maturing individuals. Physical maturity has been indexed in a variety of ways. Among the common measures are appearance of pubic hair for boys and the onset of menarche for girls. The rate of skeletal growth is another popular and reliable index of physical maturity. Studies carried out at the University of California indicate clearly that the rate of physical maturation can affect the child's social and emotional adjustment. However, boys and girls not only differ in the speed of reaching physical maturity, with girls ahead of boys, but the sex of the child determines the advantages and disadvantages of being an early or late maturer as well. For boys, it appears to be advantageous to peer acceptance to reach the developmental milestone of pubescence early, but for girls late maturity may be advantageous. Let us examine the evidence in more detail.

Jones and Bayley (1950), in their pioneering study in this area, selected sixteen early-maturing and sixteen late-maturing boys from the extremes of a normal public school population and tracked their development over the six-year period of adolescence. Observations made in a number of free-play settings indicated that the boys who were slower in their physical development were rated lower in physical attractiveness, masculinity, and grooming than were their faster-developing peers. Behavioral ratings indicated that the late maturers were more childish, more eager, less relaxed, and generally higher in attention-seeking behaviors. Peer evaluations generally confirmed this profile; the late maturer is regarded as restless, bossy, talkative, attention-seeking, and less likely to have older friends.

Moreover, the early maturers were overrepresented in terms of both athletic honors and election to important student offices, which suggests that the early maturer is accorded greater peer acceptance. Other investigators (Ames, 1956) found that both sociability and popularity are positively correlated with the rate of maturity.

The differences in appearance between early and late maturers tend to diminish as the child grows older, and by young adulthood height, weight, and body build distinctions have disappeared. However, reaching maturity at different rates seems to have long lasting effects on social behavior. Jones (1957), for example, found that the early and late maturers in their early thirties possess many of the same characteristics that distinguished them during adolescence. In adulthood, the male early maturer still has a clear social advantage; he is more sociable and more likely to be accorded prestige, popularity, and recognition by his peers.

For girls, a very different and less consistent picture emerges. The California research (Everett, 1943) suggests that the late-maturing girl, unlike her male counterpart, is likely to have the social advantage. Adult ratings indicated that the late maturer was more sociable and more likely to be allotted a prominent position in her peer group. Similarly, Ames (1956) found a negative correlation between rate of maturing and peer popularity. However, later research by Faust (1960) suggested that peer prestige may not be accorded consistently to the late-maturing girl. It depends on the age level of the peers and their resulting value system. Studying girls in the sixth through ninth grades, this investigator classified her subjects as prepuberal, puberal, or postpuberal and then had peers rate one another on a number of prestige dimensions. While the late maturers were the most prestigeful in the sixth grade, they lost their advantage in the later grades. In the seventh- and ninth-grade levels, the early maturers were accorded more peer prestige. Probably the shift is due to the awakening interest in heterosexual relationships; the greater popularity of the faster-maturing girls among members of the opposite sex undoubtedly enhanced their standing among their female peers. Clearly, the values of the age group are important such that "for girls neither physical acceleration nor physical retardation is consistently advantageous [Faust, 1960, p. 181]." Finally, rate of maturation is a poor long-term predictor in the case of girls, with few relationships existing between adult status and adolescent growth rate.

Names and peer acceptance

It is clear, then, that physical characteristics have important implications for peer group interaction and peer acceptance. In Box 14-4 we will examine another determinant of peer popularity, children's names.

THE PEER GROUP IN CROSS-CULTURAL PERSPECTIVE

So far we have cited only American research on the role of peers in socialization. A question can legitimately be raised, therefore, concerning the generality of this review. Are peers equally important in all cultures or in all parts of one culture? Is America a uniquely peer-oriented culture? Even within cultures, patterns of peer interaction may differ; for example, comparison of urban and rural peers indicate that Israeli children reared in rural kibbutzim are more cooperative than city-reared children (Shapira & Madsen, 1969). Therefore, it is not surprising that there are cross-cultural variations that deviate in both directions from the American pattern; in some countries, peers play an even more influential role, while in others the family and adult agents are more important. For example, Maslow and Diaz-Guerrero (1960) suggest that Mexican, in contrast to American, children are more family-oriented and less under the influence of peers. Often this family orientation is maintained by the parents' direct discouragement of peer interaction. Some informal observations by Martha Wolfenstein (1955) of French parents and their children in various parks in Paris nicely illustrate this phenomenon.

> For the French, each family circle is peculiarly self-inclosed, with the family members closely bound to one another and a feeling of extreme wariness about intrusion from outside. This feeling is carried over when parents take their children to play in the park. The children do not leave their parents to join other children in a communal play area. In fact, there are few communal play facilities—an occasional sand pile, some swings and carrousels, to which one must pay admission and to which the children are escorted by the parents. The usual procedure is for the mother (or other adult who brings the children to the park) to establish herself on a bench while the children squat directly at her feet and play there in the sand of the path. Where there is a sand pile, children frequently fill their buckets there and then carry the sand to where mother is sitting and deposit it at her feet. What one sees in the park, therefore, is not so much groups of children playing together while the adults who have brought them for this purpose sit on the side lines, but rather a series of little family enclaves. . . . The adults do not seem interested in friendly overtures between children of different families, showing little of the usual eagerness of American parents that their children should make friends and be a success with their age mates [Wolfenstein, 1955, p. 99–100].

This attitude is reflected in the educational level as well. In Europe "the 'bebe' is ex-

BOX 14-4 WHAT'S IN A NAME?

> "What's in a name? That which we call a rose
> By any other name would smell as sweet."
> *Romeo and Juliet,* Act II, Scene ii

Although Shakespeare's famous line may be good poetry and good horticulture, it doesn't apply to children's names. At least this is the implication of the study of McDavid and Harari (1966) of the relation between the social desirability of children's names and peer popularity. Ten- to twelve-year-old boys and girls who were members of four different youth groups at an urban community center were asked to rate the attractiveness of a list of first names. In making their ratings, the children were told to concentrate on the names and not on people bearing these names. Two sets of scores were derived: first, the desirability of names occurring in their own group; and second, a rating of the attractiveness of names that were not associated with anyone in their own group. This latter index provided a rating that was relatively free of contamination from direct familiarity with a particular person. Is there any relationship between peer popularity and children's names? To find out, a month later the investigators asked the children in each of the four groups to pick the three most popular and three least popular members of their own group. When the attractiveness rankings of the names were correlated with the popularity scores, those that had the more attractive names were rated as more popular ($r = +.63$). However, this may simply mean that children rated the names of people that they already liked as more attractive. A better test involved relating the child's popularity score with the rating of his name by another group of children who didn't know him. If names per se are really important determinants of popularity, children who are well liked by their peers should have names that even strangers find attractive. This approach involves relating the peer popularity scores of one class with the attractiveness scores that these names received from children in a different class who didn't know children with those names. Again, the popular children were found to have the most attractive names ($r = +.49$). The implication is clear: "The child who bears a generally unpopular or unattractive name may be handicapped in his social interactions with peers [McDavid & Harari, 1966, p. 458]." Naming a child a relatively rare and unusual name, such as Thelonius or Tondeleyo, may provide a child increased distinctiveness and individuality, but the price may be peer rejection. We have to be careful in generalizing, however, since different subcultures in our society value different kinds of names. Many blacks, for example, have chosen unusual Moslem names, such as "Ali" and "Kahil," as a way of emphasizing their cultural distinctiveness. Depending on the reference group, names may be popular or unpopular and, hence, so may the bearers of these names. However, the basis for this link between names and popularity still remains a mystery. For example, is the actual behavior of children with odd names clearly distinguished from the behavior of children with names like Bob and Susan? If so, how early do these patterns develop? Moreover, is the unpopularity of these children a result of early rejection by peers who discriminate against them because of their names, or are parents who choose peculiar names for their children likely to encourage atypical behaviors in their offspring, thus contributing directly to their subsequent unpopularity? In any case (with apologies to Gertrude Stein), "a name is not a name is not a name."

Source: McDavid, J. W., & Harari, H. Stereotyping of names and popularity in grade school children. *Child Development,* 1966, **37,** 453-459.

pected to look to his mother for guidance [Boehm, 1957, p. 87]." Similarly the family is expected to assume much more responsibility for "character education" or social skill development in Europe; the school is directly concerned with traditional academic learning and knowledge. Consequently one would expect more opportunities for and encouragement of peer-peer interactions in American schools. In fact, this is the case. In Europe the child works alone, while in the United States children are encouraged to work together and to help each other. Cooperative class projects tend to be more common in American than in European schools where individual products are more highly valued. In fact, as Reisman (1950) suggests in *The Lonely Crowd,* the American teacher has become a "peer group facilitator and mediator [p. 91]."

As a result of this combination of family and school influences, one would expect European children to be less susceptible to peer influence than their American counterparts. Boehm (1957) tested this hypothesis in a comparative study of twenty-nine Swiss children and forty American elementary-school-age children. To assess the relative impact of peer versus adult influence, subjects first heard a story involving children of their own age. For example: "A group of children want to give a surprise birthday party for their scout leader. One boy has accepted the responsibility of decorating the room. He wonders whom he could ask for advice [Boehm, 1957, p. 89]." A uniform questionnaire was not used; rather Piaget's "method clinique" was employed, by which the investigator probes, formulating each question on the basis of the answer the subject has given to the preceding one. Here are some typical questions:

1. Whom do you think he might ask?
2. He had thought of asking his home-room teacher, a whiz in English, history, and arithmetic, who knows nothing of art, or to ask another student who is so artistic that he has won a scholarship to the museum's art classes. Whom do you think he decided to ask?
3. He did ask both, and their advice differed. Whose advice do you think he followed?
4. He thought both ideas were equally good. Which one do you think he followed?
5. If he chooses the student's idea, will he be very embarrassed toward the teacher whose advice he did not follow [Boehm, 1957, p. 90]?

The results clear supported the hypothesis: 69.5 percent of the twenty-three Swiss subjects insisted that teachers and parents always give the best advice, even in matters requiring special talent. The American children's greater reliance on the peer group was obvious: only three out of forty children, or 7.5 percent, preferred the teacher's advice to that of the gifted child. Moreover, all three of these children were quite young, six years of age. The Swiss children (91 percent) expected that the teacher would express anger if his advice was ignored, while only six percent of the American sample expressed this view. These data suggest that emancipation from adults comes earlier for American than Swiss children; on the other hand, American children appear to have greater confidence in their peers and are more dependent on their age-mates than Swiss children.

Other cross-cultural research suggests that this difference in peer and adult orientations observed in the American-Swiss comparison is not unique. Children in the Soviet Union are particularly resistant to peer pressures which conflict with adult societal values. This finding comes from the Cornell University cross-cultural programs (Devereux,

1965, 1966, 1970; Bronfenbrenner, Devereux, Suci, & Rodgers, 1965; Bronfenbrenner, 1967) in which sixth-grade children in England, Germany, the Soviet Union, and the United States participated. In order to assess the responsiveness of these children to conflicting peer and adult pressures, a "dilemmas test" was devised which consisted of thirty hypothetical conflict situations; each situation pitted an adult-endorsed norm against peer pressure to violate the adult standard. Here is one item:

The "Lost" test

> You and your friends accidentally find a sheet of paper which the teacher must have lost. On this sheet are the questions and answers for a quiz that you are going to have tomorrow. Some of the kids suggest that you not say anything to the teacher about it, so that all of you can get better marks. What would you really do? Suppose your friends decide to go ahead. Would you go along with them or refuse?

Refuse to go along with my friends	Go along with my friends
Absolutely certain Fairly certain I guess so	Absolutely certain Fairly certain I guess so

[Bronfenbrenner, 1967, p. 201]

Other items dealt with such situations as going to a movie recommended by friends but disapproved of by parents, neglecting homework to join friends, standing guard while friends put a rubber snake in the teacher's desk, leaving a sick friend to go to a movie with the gang, joining friends in pilfering fruit from an orchard with a "no trespassing" sign, wearing styles approved by peers but not by parents, running away after breaking a window accidentally while playing ball, etc.

The Russian children were most resistant to peer influence, with significantly less resistance being demonstrated by both the American and German children. The English children showed the greatest responsiveness to peer group pressure. As in the case of the Boehm data, opportunity for peer contact and interaction is probably important. Both cross-cultural and within-cultural comparisons point in this direction. For example, the English children spent more time with their peers and less time with their parents than did Russian children. Similarly the American children yielded more readily to peer pressure, while level of association with parents, particularly with the mother, was positively related to the ability to resist deviant peer pressure. The kind of peer group, however, must be considered as well. Children who were members of groups with a high record of actual misconduct were less able to remain adult-oriented than children who were in less deviant groups. Apparently "most any gang corrupts, and a bad gang corrupts absolutely [Devereux, 1970, p. 24]."

Let us examine the Russian-American differences more closely, for the contrasts are shown even more clearly in a recent study by Bronfenbrenner (1967). Groups of Russian children and groups of American children were asked to respond to the dilemmas test under three different conditions: a neutral condition in which they were told that their answers would be kept strictly confidential; an adult-exposure condition in which they were informed that their answers would be posted on a chart for parents and teachers; and a peer-exposure condition in which the answers would later be shown to the class. The results revealed a number of cross-cultural differences. First, the Russian children showed less inclination to engage in antisocial activity, which attests to their greater acceptance of adult social values. Although the exposure-to-adult condition tended to increase the adherence to socially acceptable behavior in both cultures, the peer condition had opposite effects on the Soviet and American children. In the case of the Russian children, anticipation that classmates will eventually see their answers had the same effect as the adult-exposure manipulation: adherence to the social norms increased. American children, on the other hand, were more likely to violate the socially appropriate norms in the peer condition. Clearly, in the Russian culture the peer group operates to enforce and uphold social norms, while in the United States the evidence suggests greater norm conflict under peer influence.

The reason for this cross-national difference in the role played by the peer group becomes clear upon examination of Soviet socialization practices. Bronfenbrenner (1962) has provided a detailed account of the role played by peers in the Soviet education system. According to this review, from the earliest years in school the peer group is employed to assist adult authorities teach and enforce the dominant social values of the society. The social group or collective, rather than the individual, is the main unit of concern; evaluation of the individual's behavior is mainly in terms of its relevance to the goals and aims of the collective. The allegiance to the group is further strengthened by awarding group rewards or administering group punishment; the group, in short, is held responsible for the actions of its individual members. To promote group identification and pride, interclass and interschool competitions are frequently held. In the school the social unit may be the row of pupils in a classroom and later the "cell" of the Communist youth organization. Bronfenbrenner suggests that this peer collective rivals and, at an early age, surpasses the family as the principal agent of socialization. From the earliest grades, peer monitors are selected to keep records of their group's progress and to evaluate and criticize deviant behaviors. In fact, one of the principal methods of social control is public recognition and criticism. Children are taught that it is their civic responsibility to observe and report on the behavior of their peers. The following excerpts of conversation from a third-grade class (or link) illustrate some of these processes:

> "What are you fooling around for? You're holding up the whole link" whispers Kolya to his neighbor during the preparation period for the lesson. And during the break he teaches her how to better organize her books and pads in her knapsack.
> "Count more carefully" says Olga to her girlfriend. "See, on account of you our link got behind today. You come to me and we'll count together at home [Bronfenbrenner, 1970, p. 70]."

These examples illuminate some of the techniques typically employed by the peer group to enforce the social norms. In light of this description, with the emphasis on congruence between peer and adult norms, Bronfenbrenner's cross-cultural finding of the contrasting roles played by Soviet and American peers is understandable. In the Soviet Union the peer group is a mechanism for maintaining the adult system; in America, at least in adolescence, the peer group is often in the vanguard of efforts to alter the existing system.

SUMMARY

In this chapter the peer group, one important extrafamilial socialization agent, is examined.

Although even infants are responsive to their age-mates, the importance of peers increases rapidly and markedly in the preschool years. A number of factors affecting age changes in peer-peer interaction was discussed. First, as children mature they develop more sophisticated communication skills which make possible more complex and sustained exchanges between children. Second, peers learn to reinforce one another as they grow older; much of this reinforcement is reciprocal, with the child who rewards his peers frequently receiving many payoffs from other children. Peers influence each other by serving as social models, and many young children probably learn how to interact with their peers by observing the successful interchanges of older peer models. Individual differences are important; both the child's past history of reinforcement from the peer group and the subjects' prior experiences with the model determine the amount of peer imitation. Children who usually received frequent attention from their peers tended to imitate models who were associated with this kind of reinforcement pattern. Similarly children who typically received few reinforcers from peers tended to imitate a nonrewarding child most often.

Adults play an important part in the developmental increase in peer interaction. Not only do adults expect more peer-group participation as the child matures, but they often provide more opportunities for peer interaction and are more likely to reward this type of social behavior when it occurs.

In the next section, conditio s that promote group formation, such as the cooperative participation in achieving sha ɔd goals, were discussed. Intergroup competition is a factor that heightens group solidarity although it increases hostility and conflict between groups. When conflicting groups work together to achieve a common aim, hostility is often reduced.

In the next section a number of factors that affect the degree to which children conform to their peer group were examined. For example, the age of the child must be considered since children of all ages are not equally susceptible to peer pressure. In uncertain situations, peers tend to conform more as they mature, while peer influence tends to decline with age in situations where the correct response is clear. Also, the sex of the child as well as his group status is important. The prestige and competence of the influence source must be considered, with children being more influenced by a high-prestige peer than by a low-status individual. Situational factors, such as the nature of the pressure group and the task, are other determinants of peer group conformity. Clearly, children do conform but to different degrees at different ages, in different situations, and with different kinds of peers. Peers can offer support to one another and help resist group pressure. Even in situations where children are under a great deal of pressure to conform to a demand—sometimes an unreasonable or illegitimate one—the presence of a supporting partner often aids in resisting conformity pressures.

What determines peer popularity? No simple answer is possible. First, children of different social strata value different characteristics in their age-mates. Aggressive behavior, for example, may lead to popularity and prestige among lower-class males, while this same behavior may lead to rejection in middle-class boys. Two neglected determinants of peer acceptance, namely, physical characteristics and children's names, were considered in this chapter. Data were presented indicating that boys with muscular body builds were more likely to be popular than their thin or chubby peers. Similarly the rate of maturation is an important factor in peer acceptance. Boys who mature early tend to have a social advantage over late-maturing males. For girls, on the other hand, rate of maturation tends not to be reliable as a predictor of popularity and prestige.

Are children's names important? Apparently they are. Children with peculiar names tend to be less socially accepted than children with more common names. Whether or not names per se are important or whether oddly named children really are odd remains a mystery.

In the final section of the chapter, the role of peers in other cultures was examined. In some societies, peers play an even more influential role than in our culture, while in others the family and adult socializing agencies are more important. Particular attention was paid to a comparison of American and Russian children. Unlike our culture, where peer and adult values often clash, in Russia the peer and adult norms are more usually congruent, with peers serving to enforce rather than change adult social values.

REFERENCES

Allen, K., Hart, B. M., Buell, J. S., Harris, F. R., & Wolf, M. M. Effects of social reinforcement on isolate behavior of a nursery school child. *Child Development*, 1964, **35,** 511-518.

Allen, V. L., & Levine, J. M. Social support, dissent, and conformity. *Sociometry*, 1968, **31,** 138-149.

Allen, V. L., & Newtson, D. The development of conformity and independence. *Journal of Personality and Social Psychology*, 1972, **22,** 18-30.

Ames, R. A longitudinal study of social participation. Unpublished doctoral dissertation, University of California, 1956.

Asch, S. Studies of independence and conformity: a minority of one against a unanimous majority. *Psychological Monographs*, 1956, **70** (9, Whole No. 416).

Bandura, A., & McDonald, F. J. The influence of social reinforcement and the behavior of models in shaping children's moral judgments. *Journal of Abnormal and Social Psychology*, 1963, **67,** 274-281.

Barker, R. G., & Wright, H. F. *Midwest and its children*. New York: Harper & Row, 1955.

Berenda, R. W. *The influence of the group on the judgments of children*. New York: Columbia University, King's Crown Press, 1950.

Boehm, L. The development of independence: a comparative study. *Child Development*, 1957, **28,** 85-92.

Brodsky, C. M. *A study of norms for body form-behavior relationships*. Washington: Catholic, 1954.

Bronfenbrenner, U. Soviet methods of character education. *American Psychologist*, 1962, **17,** 550-564.

Bronfenbrenner, U. Response to pressure from peers versus adults among Soviet and American school children. *International Journal of Psychology*, 1967, **2,** 199-207.

Bronfenbrenner, U. *Two worlds of childhood: U.S. and U.S.S.R.* New York: Russell Sage Foundation, 1970.

Bronfrenbrenner, U. Devereux, E. C., Suci, G., & Rogers, R. R. Adults and peers as sources of conformity and autonomy. Paper presented at the Conference for Socialization for Competence, Social Science Research Council, Puerto Rico, 1965.

Buss, A. H. The effect of harm on subsequent aggression. *Journal of Experimental Research in Personality*, 1966, **1,** 249-255.

Charlesworth, R., & Hartup, W. W. Positive social reinforcement in the nursery school peer group. *Child Development*, 1967, **38,** 993-1002.

Devereux, E. C. Socialization in cross-cultural perspective: a comparative study of England, Germany, and the United States. Unpublished manuscript, Cornell University, 1965.

Devereux, E. C. Authority, guilt, and conformity to adult standards among German school children: a pilot experimental study. Unpublished manuscript, Cornell University, 1966.

Devereux, E. C. The role of peer-group experience in moral development. In J. P. Hill (Ed.), *Minnesota symposium on child psychology*. Vol. 4. Minneapolis: The University of Minnesota Press, 1970. Pp. 94-140.

Durfee, J. T., & Lee, L. C. Infant-infant interaction in a daycare setting. Paper presented at the meeting of the American Psychological Association, Montreal, Canada, August 1973.

Edelman, M. S., & Omark, D. R. Dominance hierarchies in young children. *Social Science Information*, 1973, **12**, 1.

Everett, E. G. Behavioral characteristics of early and late maturing girls. Unpublished Masters thesis, University of California, 1943.

Faust, M. S. Developmental maturity as a determinant of prestige in adolescent girls. *Child Development*, 1960, **31**, 173-184.

Feshbach, N. D. Reinforcement patterns of children. In A. Pick (Ed.), *Minnesota symposium on child psychology.* Vol. 7. Minneapolis: The University of Minnesota Press, 1973. Pp. 87-116.

Feshbach, N. D., & Devor, G. Teaching styles in four-year-olds. *Child Development*, 1969, **40**, 183-190.

Gelfand, D. The influence of self-esteem on rate of verbal conditioning and social matching behavior. *Journal of Abnormal Social Psychology*, 1962, **65**, 259-265.

Glucksberg, S., Krauss, R. M., & Weisberg, R. Referential communication in nursery school children: method and preliminary findings. *Journal of Experimental Child Psychology*, 1966, **3**, 333-342.

Hartup, W. W. Peer interaction and social organization. In P. H. Mussen (Ed.), *Manual of child psychology.* New York: Wiley, 1970. Pp. 361-456.

Hartup, W. W., & Coates, B. Imitation of a peer as a function of reinforcement from the peer group and rewardingness of the model. *Child Development*, 1967, **38**, 1003-1016.

Harvey, O. J., & Consalvi, C. Status and conformity to pressures in informal groups. *Journal of Abnormal Social Psychology*, 1960, **60**, 182-187.

Heathers, G. Emotional dependence and independence in nursery school play. *Journal of Genetic Psychology*, 1955, **77**, 37-58.

Hicks, D. Imitation and retention of film mediated aggressive peer and adult models. *Journal of Personality and Social Psychology*, 1965, **2**, 97-100.

Hoving, K. L., Hamm, M., & Galvin, P. Social influence as a function of stimulus ambiguity at three age levels. *Developmental Psychology*, 1969, **1**, 631-636.

Iscoe, I., Williams, M., & Harvey, J. Modification of children's judgments by a simulated group technique: A normative developmental study. *Child Development*, 1963, **34**, 963-978.

Jones, M. C. The later careers of boys who were early or late maturing. *Child Development*, 1957, **28**, 113-128.

Jones, M. C., & Bayley, N. Physical maturing among boys as related to behavior. *Journal of Educational Psychology*, 1950, **41**, 129-148.

Krauss, R. M., & Glucksberg, S. The development of communication competence as a function of age. *Child Development*, 1969, **40**, 255-266.

Kuhlen, R. G., & Lee, B. J. Personality characteristics and social acceptability in adolescence. *Journal of Educational Psychology*, 1943, **34**, 321-340.

Lerner, R. M. The development of stereotyped expectancies of body build relations. *Child Development*, 1969, **40**, 137-141.

Longstreth, L. E. *Psychological development of the child.* New York: Ronald, 1968.

Lorenz, K. *On aggression.* London: Methuen, 1966.

Maslow, A. H., & Diaz-Guerrero, R. Delinquency as a value disturbance. In J. G. Peatman and E. L. Hartley (Eds.), *Fertschrift for Gardner Murphy.* New York: Harper & Row, 1960. Pp. 228-240.

McDavid, J. W., & Harari, H. Stereotyping of names and popularity in grade school children. *Child Development*, 1966, **37**, 453-459.

Milgram, S. *Obedience to authority.* New York: Harper & Row, 1974.

Moore, S. G. *Correlates of peer acceptance in nursery school children.* In W. W. Hartup & N. L. Smothergill (Eds.), *The young child.* Washington, D.C.: National Association for the Education of Young Children, 1967. Pp. 229-247.

Nelson, J. D., Gelfand, D. M., & Hartmann, D. P. Children's aggression following competition and exposure to an aggressive model. *Child Development*, 1969, **40**, 1085-1097.

O'Connor, R. D. Modification of social withdrawal through symbolic modeling. *Journal of Applied Behavior Analysis*, 1969, **2**, 15-22.

Parten, M., & Newhall, S. W. Social behavior of preschool children. In R. G. Barker, J. S. Kounin, & H. F. Wright (Eds.), *Child behavior and development.* New York: McGraw-Hill, 1943. Pp. 509-525.

Patel, H. S., & Gordon, J. E. Some personal and situational determinants of yielding to influence. *Journal of Abnormal Social Psychology*, 1960, **61**, 411-418.

Patterson, G. R., Littman, R. A., & Bricker, W. Assertive behavior in children: a step toward a theory of aggression. *Monographs of the Society for Research in Child Development*, 1967, **32** (Serial No. 113).

Piaget, J. *Play, dreams and imitation.* New York: Norton, 1951.

Quilitch, H. R., & Risley, T. R. The effects of play materials on social play. *Journal of Applied Behavior Analysis,* 1973, **6,** 573-578.

Reisman, D. *The lonely crowd.* New York: Anchor Books, 1950.

Rosenkrans, M. A. Imitation in children as a function of perceived similarity to a social model and vicarious reinforcement. *Journal of Personality and Social Psychology,* 1967, **7,** 307-315.

Rosenthal, R. *Experimenter effects in behavioral research.* New York: Appleton-Century-Crofts, 1966.

Rubin, K. H. Relationship between egocentric communication and popularity among peers. *Developmental Psychology,* 1972, **7,** 364.

Sampson, E. E., & Hancock, T. An examination of the relationship between ordinal position, personality, and conformity: an extension, replication, and partial verification. *Journal of Personality and Social Psychology,* 1967, **5,** 398-407.

Shapira, A., & Madsen, M. C. Cooperative and competitive behavior of kibbutz and urban children in Israel. *Child Development,* 1969, **40,** 609-617.

Sheldon, W. H., Stevens, S. S., & Tucker, W. B. *The varieties of human physique.* New York: Harper, 1940.

Sherif, M. Experiments in group conflict. *Scientific American,* 1956, 54-58.

Staffieri, J. R. A study of social stereotype of body image in children. *Journal of Personality and Social Psychology,* 1967, **7,** 101-104.

Wahler, R. G. Child-child interactions in free field settings: Some experimental analyses. *Journal of Experimental Child Psychology,* 1967, **5,** 278-293.

Walters, R. H., & Parke, R. D. Influence of response consequences to a social model on resistance to deviation. *Journal of Experimental Child Psychology,* 1964, **1,** 269-280.

Wolfenstein, M. French parents take their children to the park. In M. Mead & M. Wolfenstein (Eds.), *Childhood in contemporary cultures.* Chicago: The University of Chicago Press, 1955. Pp. 99-117.

Wright, H. F. *Recording and analyzing child behavior.* New York: Harper & Row, 1967.

15
THE SCHOOL AS A SOCIALIZATION AGENCY

Most psychological theories of child development under the influence of Freud stress the early experiences of the child in the family as the main determinants of his future social, emotional, and even his intellectual development. As we have seen, a second major force in the socialization process is the peer group. A third and often neglected agent is the school. Probably no other institution has as much opportunity as the school to shape the developing child. After a child enters the first grade, an increasingly large proportion of his life will be dominated by the school. Even if he is not there, the demands of the school through home assignments and the social obligations and ties of school clubs and activities make the school a salient force in the child's daily existence. In this chapter we will focus on the ways in which the school exerts its socializing influence and on the consequences of this influence. First, some of the structural features of schools will be considered, such as school size, classroom size, and seating arrangements. Second, the effects of the central character in the school drama, the teacher, will be examined. How important is the fact that most teachers in elementary school are female? Do variations in teaching styles affect the child's attitudes toward school and his academic progress? Third, the role of the textbook will be discussed: does it mislead and misinform young children as some experts claim, or has its influence been exaggerated? Finally, the relationship of the school system to the lower-class child will be considered.

THE IMPORTANCE OF SCHOOL

Although impressive, merely underlining the increasingly large amount of time that children spend in the classroom is hardly convincing evidence that the school has an impact on the child's development. More substantial documentation is necessary. One of the most influential kinds of evidence concerning the importance of the school as a socializing force has come from studies in which the relative impacts of the family and of the school are directly assessed. Bronfenbrenner and his colleagues (Bronfenbrenner, Devereux, Suci, & Rodgers, 1965) found that the child's report of his teacher's behavior toward him was a more important predictor of his moral value orientation than reports of parental behavior. A child who had a positive relationship with his teacher was particularly likely to endorse adult moral values. Others (Schmuck & Van Egmond, 1965) have reported parallel effects: the pupil-teacher relationship is not only linked with academic performance but, in the case of boys, is more important than parental attitudes in determining values. These reports present a clear challenge to traditional family-oriented theories of socialization. While neither study denies the impact of parental influence, both dramatically illustrate the need for a greater recognition of the importance of the school as a socialization agency.

Variations within the school setting have an important impact on the child's emotional and social adjustment as well as on his academic progress. In order to explore this impact, the effects of the physical structure of the school environment need to be examined.

THE EFFECTS OF THE PHYSICAL STRUCTURE OF THE SCHOOL ENVIRONMENT

Although most discussions of the school concentrate on teachers, tactics, and texts, the structural features of the school environment merit consideration. Does the size of the school that a child attends make any difference? Similarly, do such factors as seating arrangements, class size, wall color, and ventilation affect the child's scholastic achievement, his attitudes toward school, or the degree to which he actively participates in class and extracurricular functions? Although it is impossible to answer all of these questions, recent research has given us answers to at least some of them.

Big school, small school: the effect of school size

> The large school has authority: its grand exterior dimensions, its long halls and myriad rooms and its tides of students all carry an implication of power and rightness. The small

school lacks such certainty: its modest building, its short halls and few rooms and its students, who move more in trickles than in tides, give an impression of a casual or not quite decisive educational environment [Barker & Gump, 1964, p. 195].

But that is only an outside view. And appearances are often deceiving. To find out how schools of different sizes look from the inside was the aim of a research project conducted by Roger Barker and Paul Gump of the University of Kansas. These investigators

This academy, built in 1763, was one of the earliest schools. Consider the psychological limitations of such a school environment. (Omikron.)

were concerned with the extent of student participation in extracurricular functions in small and large schools. They wanted to learn whether or not large schools offer more, and more varied, activities for their students than smaller schools and whether this meant that the student in the large school has a richer experience. High schools ranging in size from 35 to 2,287 students participated in the study; all were located in an economically, culturally, and politically homogeneous region of eastern Kansas and all were controlled by the same state authority. The results were surprising. Although the largest school had twenty times as many students as a small school in a nearby county, there were only five times as many extracurricular activities. More importantly, the large and small school do not differ greatly in terms of the variety of activities that they offer. The small school is small in enrollment but not necessarily limited in opportunities for activity and participation. Barker and Gump compare it to a small engine in that "it possesses the essential parts of a large entity but has fewer replications and differentiations of some of the parts [Barker & Gump, 1964, p. 195]." With fewer students but nearly as many participation opportunities, one would expect that more students would be more involved in more activities in more important ways in the smaller setting. This is precisely what the researchers found. The proportion of students who participated in district music festivals and dramatic, journalistic, and student government competitions was three to twenty times as great in the small, as contrasted with the large, institution. Figure 15-1 presents a graphic picture of this relationship. A student at a small school would participate in twice as many activities over his high school career. Moreover, there would be greater variety in his activities if he attended a small school. The kinds of positions occupied by students at large and small schools differed as well. The small school adolescent was more likely to hold a position of importance and responsibility than his peer at a larger school. In light of these findings, it was not surprising to learn that the rewards and satisfactions derived from participation differed for students in these two types of environments. Students from the small schools reported

> More satisfaction relating to the development of competence, to being challenged, to engaging in important actions, to being involved in group activites and to achieving moral and cultural values [while large school students reported] more satisfaction dealing with vicarious enjoyment, with large entity affiliation, with learning about their school's persons and affairs and with gaining "points" via participation [Barker & Gump, 1964, p. 197].

Further analysis revealed that these differences were largely due to the fact that a greater number of pupils held responsible positions in small schools.

There is one other way in which the two types of institutions differed. In the small school setting there were many more pressures to participate; students, themselves felt more obligation and responsibility to play an active role in their school functions and they felt that their peers expected them to participate more. One outcome is that there were fewer "outsiders," that is, students who were left out of most extracurricular activities, in the smaller schools. Comparisons of marginal students, or potential dropouts, with regular students indicated that the marginal students felt few pressures to participate in large schools. On the other hand, in small settings the two types of students felt similar pressures to participate in extracurricular affairs. This greater sense of identification and involvement of the marginal students in the smaller school may be part of the reason that dropout rates are lower in small schools.

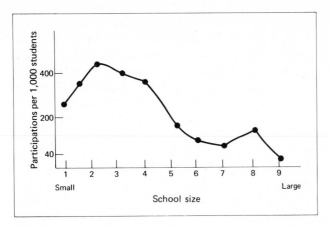

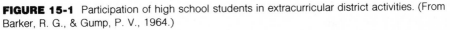

FIGURE 15-1 Participation of high school students in extracurricular district activities. (From Barker, R. G., & Gump, P. V., 1964.)

The question of whether or not school size affects academic progress is, unfortunately, left unanswered. Class size rather than institution size probably would be a better predictor in this realm. However, if we view the school as a socialization agency, it is clear that much of the school's influence in transmitting social and cultural values comes through these extracurricular functions. Not only does the research of Barker and Gump provide important information about the impact of school size on student behaviors, but it also serves as a reminder that much of the learning taking place in school is not in the classroom. The main implication of this study lies in the answer to the question that guided their research: "What size should a school be? . . . sufficiently small that all of its students are needed for its enterprises. A school should be small enough that students are not redundant [Barker & Gump, 1964, p. 202]."

The spatial arrangement of the classroom

One of the most obvious features of the learning environment is the *rectangular* classroom. Why not a round class or a square one? Or does it matter anyway? According to one design expert:

> The present rectangular room with its straight row of chairs and wide windows was intended to provide for ventilation, light, quick departure, ease of surveillance and a host of other legitimate needs as they existed in the early 1900's. . . . The typical long narrow shape resulted from a desire to get light across the room. The front of each room was determined by window location, since pupils had to be seated so that window light came over the left shoulder. Despite new developments in lighting, acoustics and structures, most schools are still boxes filled with cubes each containing a specified number of chairs in straight rows. There have been attempts to break away from this rigid pattern, but experimental schools are the exception rather than the rule [Sommer, 1969, p. 98–99].

Maria Montessori once described the children who have to exist in these traditional classrooms as "butterflies mounted on pins, fastened each to a desk, spreading the useless wings of barren and meaningless knowledge they have acquired [Montessori, 1964, p. 81]."

Does a pupil's location within the classroom make a difference? Are individuals in front more active than those in the rear? Were those in the center more active than those at the aisles, regardless of the type of room? Consider the seminar room first. Sommer (1969) compared the participation of college students at the side tables with those sitting directly opposite the instructor. Students sitting opposite the teacher participated most, while those at the side tables talked very little. Finally, while students tended to avoid chairs adjacent to the teacher, when they were ''stuck'' in these positions they pretended that they weren't there by being silent.

Participation in straight row arrangements seems to be determined by location as well. Sommer found that first-row students participate more than students near the rear and centrally located students participate more than the fringe dwellers. This location-participation relationship is a very common one and by no means restricted to college students. In a study of elementary and high school classes, it was reported that the center-front pattern emerged regardless of grade level (first, sixth, and eleventh), sex or age of teacher, or subject matter (mathematics or social studies) (Adams & Biddle, 1970). This effect was so consistent that this spatial location was termed the *action zone* of the classroom. Figure 15-2 illustrates the relationship. The reasons for the effect are unclear. Do interested students sit closer to the teacher, or do students take a greater interest if they do sit closer to the teacher?

Seat choices may have psychological implications. Levinger and Gunner (1967) found that students who typically sat at the rear of a classroom placed greater psychological distance between themselves and the teacher; these investigators had used a projective test in which students arranged geometric forms and silhouettes on a felt background to index psychological distance in their study. How such ''distance'' develops is not clear. Children may sit near the back of the class because of some fear of or alienation from the teacher; on the other hand, the psychological barrier may develop out of the spatial arrangements themselves.

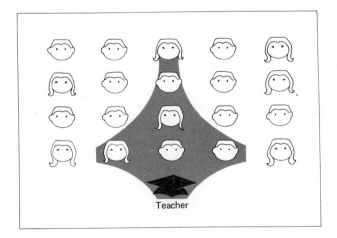

FIGURE 15-2 Area of maximum amount of teacher-pupil interaction (shaded area) in classroom. (From Adams, R. S., & Biddle, B. T., 1970.)

Finally, what about class size? In spite of the frequency of discussion and debate concerning the "optimal" class size, there is a surprising paucity of relevant investigations. An exception is an early study by Dawe (1934), in which she examined the effects of kindergarten size on pupil participation. In classes ranging in size from fifteen to forty-six children, the number of comments made by each child during a controlled discussion period was recorded. As class size increased, not only did the total amount of discussion decrease but a smaller percent of the children participated; when they did talk, their average amount of participation was likely to be less as well. Nearly forty years later, Tuana (1969) found a similar inverse relationship between participation and class size at the college level. It will come as no surprise to college students to learn that a mere 2.3 questions per class was typical in the large lecture class. As in the earlier classroom studies, those students in the two front rows of the center section of a lecture hall asked almost half of the questions. Another third of the questions came from students sitting along the side aisles. The "faceless mass" in the middle, to use Sommer's description, participated very little. This suggests that the location-participation link may be even stronger as class size increases. The result, of course, is an increasingly large proportion of children being excluded systematically from an active role in their education. If children do learn more by participating more, then the data are clear: smaller classes are preferable.

The findings concerning participation, size, and seating are consistent with a more general proposition governing social interaction, namely, that verbal communication is more likely when the potential conversationalists have eye-to-eye contact. In general, if you sit closer, you will participate more.

In light of these findings, it is encouraging to see trends toward greater flexibility in arranging classroom space. Moveable furniture is becoming increasingly popular, as in the "school without walls," an open-plan architecture designed for team teaching in which several grades share a large open space. However, merely providing flexible space and movable furniture does not guarantee that innovative teaching will necessarily follow. In one Texas experiment involving fully portable furniture, Sanders (1958) found that the equipment rarely moved in actual practice. This failure to take advantage of the flexible facilities is even more surprising in light of the fact that only 1.4 minutes were required to make a major rearrangement of the furniture. Other investigators have found similar results. For example, in one comparison of traditional and modern classrooms the teachers were "quick to emphasize that the large classroom had not changed their teaching methods [Rolfe, 1961, p. 192, cited by Sommer, 1969]." Clearly, teachers must learn to use space and facilities; without direct instruction concerning the possibilities offered by new classroom arrangements, it is unlikely that few substantial changes in individual class activities or teaching techniques will actually take place. As Sommer wryly commented, "if the school traditions make straight row arrangements immutable, even though the chairs are portable, portable chairs serve only to increase the workload of the janitors who have to straighten the rows every evening [Sommer, 1969, p. 104]."

THE TEACHER

By far the most important figures in the school are the teachers. In this section we will examine who they are, what they do, and what effects they have on their pupils' academic progress and social and emotional adjustment. First, the status of the teacher will be examined. Is it important that the teacher is usually female and middle-class? Second, the effect of variations in teacher expectations, attitudes, and beliefs will be discussed. For example, do teachers' expectations concerning the success of their charges affect academic performance? The teacher plays a variety of roles in the classroom as organizer, disciplinarian, and social model. In the final section, the manner in which she manages each of these roles comes under scrutiny.

Teacher-pupil interaction: the effects of sex of child

Children come in all shapes, sizes, and dispositions, and teachers respond to these individual differences in their daily interactions with students. Children differ in their sex as well, and teachers do treat boys and girls differently. In many ways schools are feminine: they value quiet, obedience, and passivity, and these are many of the qualities, unfortunately, that the culture dictates as sex-role appropriate for girls. The boisterous, assertive, competitive, and independent qualities which are encouraged in boys are often frowned upon in school. It is not surprising that in the early grades, at least, girls tend to like school more than boys and do better than boys in their academic work.

Male teachers help to counteract the female-oriented atmosphere of most schools. (Suzanne Szasz.)

For boys, on the other hand, school is not a happy place: they have more difficulty in adjusting to school routines, create more problems for their teachers, and generally perform not only at a lower level than their female classmates but often well below their abilities. Boys, then, appear uninterested and unmotivated under the feminine regime of the early elementary school years. But why? Part of the reason stems from the fact that boys are in conflict. On the one hand, they are encouraged by parents and peers to be active and assertive. On the other hand, at school these same behaviors are less likely to meet with approval. Supporting evidence comes from a recent observational study of nursery-school-age children by Fagot and Patterson (1969). These investigators found that the female teachers reinforced feminine behaviors more frequently than they did male-appropriate behaviors—in both girls and boys. Of the occasions on which teachers reinforced the boys' sex-typed play, 87 percent of the reinforced behaviors were classified as feminine. Boys were being selectively encouraged to engage in feminine activities (for example, quiet games), while male-appropriate behaviors (for example, aggression and rough play) were largely ignored. As Fagot and Patterson were able to show, peers were largely responsible for encouraging appropriate sex-typed responses, and in spite of the teachers' reinforcement pattern, masculine behaviors were maintained. Under a male teacher the preschool boy fares better. In nursery schools with both male and female teachers, Lee and Wolinsky (1973) found that in spite of the fact that:

> Male and female teachers are more disapproving of boys than of girls, male teachers are generally more approving of boys than female teachers are. There was also a strong tendency for teachers to favor children of the same sex in leadership assignments and for male teachers to relate to male-typed activities. The boys strongly perceived themselves as affiliated with the male teacher; the girls perceptions cut across sex-role lines, in that they expressed more or less equal affiliation with male and female teachers [Lee & Wolinsky, 1973, p. 351].

In summary, the introduction of a male teacher into the classroom made school a more congenial place for young boys.

But male teachers are still a rarity in preschool and elementary schools. To find out whether boys receive more disapproval than girls in the primary grades, we turn to a study by Meyer and Thompson (1956). Their data show that school teachers do not simply ignore masculine behaviors but may explicitly attempt to suppress these behaviors. These investigators plotted the frequency with which teachers approved and disapproved of the typical classroom behaviors of sixth-grade boys and girls. Although there were few sex differences in the frequency with which teachers approved their male and female charges, disapproval rate varied markedly with the sex of the child. As Figure 15-3 shows, teachers in all three classrooms were much more likely to disapprove of the boys' rather than of the girls' behavior. These data lend indirect support to the notion that "masculine behavior is not tolerated by the typical teacher [Meyer & Thompson, 1956, p. 393]." Moreover, the children themselves were aware of the teachers' typical reinforcement schedule. When asked to select which classmate would probably receive teacher disapproval or approval in a variety of different hypothetical situations, children of both sexes overwhelmingly nominated boys as the typical recipients of the teacher's scorn. Not only do teachers approve feminine behaviors more, but in older children at

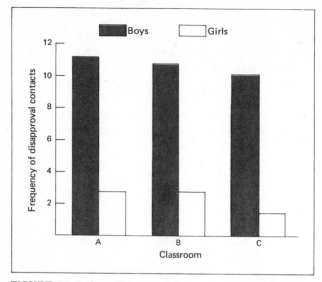

FIGURE 15-3 Sex differences in frequency of teacher's disapproval contacts. (Adapted from Meyer, W. T., & Thompson, G. G., 1956.)

least, they tend to punish the typical masculine behaviors displayed by boys in classroom settings. Combined with the teacher herself, a feminine sex-role model, it is not surprising that children tend to perceive school and school-related objects and activities as feminine (Kagan, 1964).

More recent research (Stein, 1971, 1973) has established a clear set of relationships between children's perception of the sex-role appropriateness of different activities (for example, mechanical, artistic, reading, math) and their motivation to achieve in these tasks. Sixth and ninth graders rated how "boyish" or "girlish" a variety of activities were and then indicated the importance of accomplishment in each of these areas. In addition, the children indicated how well they thought they would perform and what minimum standard of performance they would be satisfied with. For activities that were viewed as sex-appropriate, the children attached more importance to achievement, set higher minimum standards, and expected to do better than on sex-role-inappropriate activities.

What are the implications of the young boy's perception of school as a sex-inappropriate institution? One of the obvious effects is that he is less likely to be as motivated and interested in school-related activities as girls, who, of course, view school as consistent with their own sex-role identity. It is not surprising, therefore, to find that girls outperform their opposite-sexed peers in the early grades. Sex ratios in reading problems range from 3:1 to as high as six boys to one girl in some surveys (Tyler, 1947; Bentzen, 1963). Although this difference in reading achievement may in part be due to the fact that boys' cognitive development is slower than girls, it is possible that boys simply fail to excel in the feminine environment of the early elementary school years.

Recent evidence from a Japanese study suggests that boys' reading difficulties could be lessened if the school were de-feminized by the introduction of more male teachers in the early grades. On the island of Hokkaido in northern Japan, approximately 60 percent of the teachers in the first and second grades are male. In this community boys do not have more frequent difficulties in reading; rather boys and girls are equally represented with about 9 percent of each sex experiencing reading problems (cited by Janis, Mahl, Kagan, & Holt, 1969). It is worth noting that the presence of the male teacher does not appear to disrupt the learning progress of young girls, while it simultaneously increases the academic achievement of the boys.

Although not all investigations in North America have supported this finding, there is some American evidence to support the Japanese investigation; boys taught by male teachers did better in reading than boys taught by female teachers (Shinedling & Pederson, 1970). In combination with the study of male teachers in nursery school that we discussed earlier, it suggests that the introduction of more male teachers into schools may be beneficial, but it is unlikely that this change alone will solve the problem of boys' reading.

Moreover, there is an apparent paradox which must be resolved. Up to this point, the argument has centered almost exclusively on the detrimental effects of the school environment on boys. What are the effects on girls? Girls may have an advantage in the early grades but the advantage is short-lived. Girls' achievement levels decrease as they grow older, and by college the proportion of female underachievers exceeds the proportion of male underachievers (Ralph, Goldberg, & Passow, 1966). The kinds of passive and dependent behaviors that teachers accept and encourage in girls may, in the long run, be detrimental for later academic success. Intellectual achievement is negatively related to dependency. Independence, assertiveness, and nonconformity are more likely to lead to creative problem solving and high levels of achievement. A recent study (Box 15-1) offers some direct evidence concerning the ways that teachers may be contributing to these sex differences in later achievement. As early as the preschool level, teachers were encouraging dependency in girls, while teachers punished aggression in boys. They also provided males more opportunities to learn independent problem-solving skills. Boys may be in conflict early, but they do have more opportunities to acquire the skills necessary for later achievement. On the other hand, girls may have a less stressful time in the early school years but in the long run may be under a serious handicap in competitive achievement-oriented situations.

Perhaps the problem lies more with our sex-role stereotypes for boys and girls than with teachers alone. As it stands, the female sex role is consistent with the student role, while the male role does not mesh as well with the demands of being a student. As Brophy and Good (1970) note:

> The historical pattern of sex differences typically found in American schools is likely to persist until and unless changes are made in the role of student (less emphasis on passivity and inactive modes of learning) and/or the sex roles assigned to young boys and girls (less differentiation between the sexes; more stress on independent problem solving in girls and on achievement behavior and verbal skills in boys) [Brophy & Good, 1973, p. 373].

Schools will probably be a better place for children, regardless of their sex, if we change our narrow sex-typed notions of appropriate behavior.

BOX 15-1 TEACHER TREATMENT OF BOYS AND GIRLS

Do preschool teachers respond differently to boys and girls? To find out, Serbin, O'Leary, Kent, and Tonick (1973) observed teacher reactions to dependent and disruptive behaviors. Teachers were more likely to respond when boys were aggressive than when girls were behaving in this way. Loud reprimands were more likely to be used to control boys than girls; however, it should be noted that loud reprimands maintain disruptive behavior at a high level (O'Leary, Kaufman, Kass, & Drabman, 1970). Alternatively, teachers encouraged dependent behavior in girls; when girls were physically close to the teacher, they received greater attention than did boys. Perhaps most striking was the rate of teacher attention to children who were participating in class activities. Teachers praised and hugged boys more and provided more instruction to boys. Specifically, boys received more brief directions (telling child to do something) as well as detailed instruction in how to do things for "oneself." This skill training may be particularly crucial for later achievement in problem solving and other cognitive tasks. It appears that dependent behavior is encouraged in girls and independent skills are trained in boys. The pattern of teacher reinforcement is, of course, consistent with parental patterns of reaction to boys and girls (cf. Stein, 1973).

Source: Serbin, L. A., O'Leary, D. K., Kent, R. N., & Tonick, J. J. A comparison of teacher response to the preacademic and problem behavior of boys and girls. *Child Development*, 1973, **44,** 796–804.

The teacher and classroom behavior

Although the typical teacher can be described as white, middle-class, and female, it would be hazardous to attempt a description of "typical" teacher behavior. Each teacher has a great deal of freedom and flexibility in the classroom; individual differences in beliefs, attitudes, and styles of interacting with children are evident. For a number of years researchers have been attempting to assess the effects of these variations in teacher-pupil interaction. A variety of questions have been posed. Do teacher expectations of success or failure affect actual student performance? Are variations in classroom organization which allow different degrees of pupil participation in classroom decision making important? Emphasis has been placed on the effects that these different types of teacher styles and control tactics have on the child's academic progress as well as on the students' social and emotional development.

Teacher expectation and academic success

Although many teachers would probably deny it, most of them form impressions early in the school year concerning the probable performance of the incoming group of students. These expectations come from a variety of sources, such as the pupil's past academic record, his achievement test scores, his family background, his appearance, and his classroom conduct history. Do these prejudgments of the child's performance have an impact on his actual scholastic success or failure? It is possible to investigate the impact of these naturally developed expectations on the child's performance by soliciting predictions from teachers early in the year and then determining how closely the child's output conforms to the teacher's prediction. A more powerful technique

involves experimentally planting an expectation concerning certain children in a classroom and then assessing to what degree the expectations will be fulfilled. Rosenthal and
Jacobsen of Harvard University (1966, 1968) have recently carried out such an experiment. In a number of elementary school classes, teachers were informed that 20 percent
of their students were "intellectual bloomers who would show unusual intellectual gains
during the academic year [Rosenthal & Jacobsen, 1968, p. 66]." The critical 20 percent
was, of course, randomly chosen. In order to assess the impact of teacher expectations,
the children were administered an IQ test before the experiment commenced and again
after eight months of additional classroom experience with the "expectant" teacher.
Would the children labeled as academic bloomers show a larger improvement than
nonlabeled control children in the same classroom? For the school as a whole, those
children for whom the teachers had been led to expect greater intellectual gain showed
a significantly greater increase in IQ scores than did the remaining students. However,
as Figure 15-4 indicates, the effect was most marked in the lower grade levels. In fact,
the lower the grade level, the greater was the effect.

But is the gain reflected in academic performance as well? To find out, the children's
report cards were examined and in one area, reading, there were marked effects. Children who were expected to do well were judged by their teachers to show greater
advances in their reading ability. Again, the gains were most marked at the lower levels.
Finally, classroom behavior was affected, as indicated by the fact that the "experimental" pupils were rated as higher in "intellectual curiosity" than the control children.

To determine whether these advantages would persist when contact with the expectant teacher was terminated, Rosenthal and Jacobsen retested the children after two full
academic years. Before this final retest the children had spent a year with a teacher who
had not been given favorable expectations. Although the younger children had been
easier to influence initially, they had lost their advantage by the final follow-up evaluation. However, after the delay the older children, that is, those in the third to sixth
grades, who had shown smaller gains in the early stages still showed the effect of the

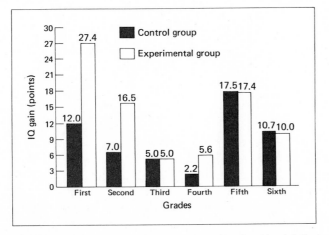

FIGURE 15-4 Teacher expectancy of students' making intellectual gains and actual gains
made by students in total IQ in six grades. (From Rosenthal, R., & Jacobson, L., 1966.)

original expectancy manipulation. As the authors suggest, continued contact with the expectant teacher seems to be necessary for maintaining the effect in younger children, while older pupils are better able to maintain their advantage autonomously.

However, Rosenthal and his self-fulfilling prophecy in the classroom has met with severe methodological criticism (Elashoff & Snow, 1971; Jensen, 1969; Thorndike, 1968). In spite of some failures to find a pygmalion effect, there has been corroboration of the central finding by other investigators in several different school systems with different populations, such as preschoolers in a Head Start program, retardates, and institutionalized adolescent female offenders. Nor is the expectancy effect restricted to academic learning situations; Burham and Hartsough (1968) have demonstrated the expectancy effect with swimming ability in a group of children at a summer camp.

How can we explain the pygmalion effect? Rosenthal (1973b) has proposed four factors that may account for the effect. First, people who are led to expect good performance from a pupil may create a warmer social-emotional *climate* for their special students; research has indicated that when teachers think they are dealing with a bright student, they are more friendly and supportive than when they view their students as less capable.

Another factor is *feedback* for the student's performance; how often does the teacher respond to the child by rewarding his right answer or correcting his errors. A study by Brophy and Good (1970) illustrates that this may be a factor in the expectancy effect. After teachers named their high and low achievers, these investigators recorded the amount of feedback provided these two types of pupils. The teachers ignored only 3 percent of the high achiever's answers, but they ignored 15 percent of the low achiever's responses. Students that teachers view as high achievers may do better, in part, because they get more feedback from their teachers.

A third factor is *input*, or the amount of teaching that children may receive. Beez (1968) led some teachers in a Head Start program to expect poor performance from their "below average" children while other teachers expected good performance from their "bright" children. Teachers taught the bright children more. For example, 87 percent of the teachers of the bright children taught eight or more words, while only 13 percent of the teachers of the below average children tried to teach that number of words. Table 15-1 summarizes these teacher differences for the two groups of children. As a result, the teacher expectations were confirmed: over 75 percent of the bright children learned five or more words, while only thirteen percent of the dull children learned five words.

Table 15-1 TEACHING DIFFERENCES FOR ABOVE- AND BELOW-AVERAGE STUDENTS

Number of words taught	Teachers expectation	
	Below average	Above average
11 or more	0%	47%
9 or 10	3.0%	33%
7 or 8	22.5%	10%
5 or 6	50.0%	3%
4 or less	22.5%	7%

(Adapted from Beez, 1968.)

Expectancies of good performance may not only translate into more teacher input but may also lead teachers to demand more *output* from students as well. As Rosenthal (1973b) notes, teachers ''call on such students more often, ask them harder questions, give them more time to answer and prompt them toward the correct answer [Rosenthal, 1973b, p. 62].'' In summary, at least four factors may aid in explaining the pygmalion effect: the climate of the classroom; differences in teacher feedback; teacher input; and opportunities for student output. The case is not closed, but these studies do raise an important question: ''How much of the improvement in intellectual performance attributed to the contemporary educational programs is due to the content and methods of the programs and how much is due to the favorable expectancies of the teachers and administrators involved? [Rosenthal & Jacobsen, 1966, p. 118].''

The teacher as a classroom organizer

The teacher can organize her classroom in a multitude of ways. For example, she can arrange to have students participate in the decision making; she can organize her class into small groups; she can arrange for students to help each other; or she can organize classroom activities in the traditional manner. In this section we will focus on the consequences of different types of classroom organization.

One of the most influential studies in this area is the classic investigation of Kurt Lewin and his colleagues (Lewin, Lippitt, & White, 1939) on the impact of experimentally established ''group climates'' on children's social behavior. The ten-year-old boys in this study worked in five-person groups under three different types of leaders: authoritarian, in which all decisions were made by the leader; democratic, in which teacher and children shared in the decision making; or laissez-faire, in which the leader offered minimal direction and participated only upon student request. The democratic leadership style was superior to the other two leadership approaches in a variety of ways. The boys in the democratic groups were more productive (even in the leader's absence), happier with both their leader and their group, and less hostile toward each other. The laissez-faire leadership produced disorganization, boredom, inefficiency, and quarrels, while the boys in the authoritarian groups were either passive or rebellious, were aggressive in their peer interaction, and showed little capacity to work efficiently in the leader's absence.

Group participation in classroom organization   Other evidence that classroom organization is important came from a later study by Bovard (1951) in which he compared the effects of group-versus teacher-centered teaching procedures. In the group-centered situation, student-student interaction was encouraged, group decisions were permitted on minor procedural matters, and the teacher's role was structured more as a member of the group. In the leader-centered group, student-to-student conversation was more limited and verbal interaction was channeled through the teacher. Students under the two regimes differed in a variety of ways. First, group-centered members showed a greater tolerance for divergent opinions than their peers in leader-centered groups. However, they showed a greater flexibility as well, as reflected in their greater conformity to a group norm in later phases of decision making; also the individuals in the group-centered program liked each other and their group more than did the leader-

A group-centered classroom.
(Suzanne Szasz.)

centered students. Finally, there was suggestive evidence that there was a stronger feeling of group solidarity fostered by the group-centered procedure. A wide variety of studies since the Bovard investigation (McKeachie, 1963) has confirmed the finding that students generally favor group-centered classroom climates. It is far less clear that the pupil's academic progress is affected by the type of classroom organization. However, some recent research by Harvey, Prather, White, and Hoffmeister (1968) indicates that there may be academic advantages associated with student participation in classroom organization and decision making.

In their research, Harvey and his associates contrasted two groups of teachers. One group encouraged free expression of feelings, allowed peer determination of classroom rules, and permitted a wide diversity of simultaneous classroom activity. The teachers in the comparison group were less flexible, more dictatorial, and more punitive; little opportunity for pupil involvement in classroom organization was permitted. As expected, student behaviors varied significantly under these two types of classroom regimes. Student involvement was higher in the classroom of the first group of teachers, as indicated by freer expression of feelings, more voluntary participation, higher independence, and a larger voice in classroom activities. Activity level, as reflected in both the amount and diversity of goal-relevant activity, was higher in these classes. Third, these pupils were higher in achievement; the accuracy of the information that they acquired was higher and the appropriateness of their solutions were all superior under the regime of this type of teacher. In contrast, the pupils under the more authoritarian classroom regime were more oriented toward specific facts; they also placed a greater emphasis on rote answers and solutions. Novelty of their answers, in turn, tended to be lower. Finally, the pupils of the authoritarian teachers tended to be less helpful, less cooperative, and more aggressive. In short, classroom organization clearly does affect the way in which pupils behave. These data point to a need for more flexible teachers who are willing to permit greater student involvement in classroom organization.

Individual differences and classroom organization In our discussion so far we have ignored individual differences; rather, we have assumed that all students, regardless of background or personality, will respond in the same way to different types of classroom organization. But this may be an erroneous assumption. One needs to consider personality factors in evaluating the effects of different organizational arrangements. As Stern (1963) has noted, "student centered instruction was preferred by students who reject traditional sources of authority, have strong needs for demonstrating their personal independence and are characterized by a high drive for academic achievement [Stern, 1963, p. 428]." It is not simply preference; some children even perform better under certain types of regimes. A study which clearly demonstrates this interdependence between the type of child and the kind of classroom organization is presented in Box 15-2.

The teacher as a reinforcing agent

The teacher is a powerful figure in the classroom hierarchy and, through grades and glances and smiles and frowns, can have an enormous impact on her charges. Teachers vary in their typical reinforcing style. Some rely on positive reinforcement to encourage, stimulate, and control their pupils; others prefer punishment, reproof, and disapproval. Do children learn best when the teacher is warm and positive, or do they learn just as well from a punitive instructor? What are the most effective disciplinary techniques for classroom control? How successful have been the recent attempts to apply

---

BOX 15-2 READING ACHIEVEMENT AND CLASSROOM ORGANIZATION

Grimes and Allinsmith (1961) compared the reading achievement of highly anxious and highly compulsive children under two types of classroom regimes. Anxious children were characterized as restless, distractable, and fidgety, while compulsive children were defined as those who were upset by disorder and lack of organization. Under one regime, children learned to read under the phonics method, which is a highly structured, rule-bound approach; in addition, the classroom using this structured approach tended to be more authoritarian than the comparison classrooms, which employed the whole-word approach to reading, a less structured system of teaching. In this approach, the child is exposed to whole words from the outset and learns to read by experience in the reading process itself. The rule-bound, step-by-step character of the phonic approach is absent.

As Figures 15-5 and 15-6 indicate, children low in anxiety and compulsivity were relatively unaffected by the type of atmosphere. However, highly anxious children performed very poorly in the unstructured school and slightly better than their less anxious peers in the structured learning situation. On the other hand, the lack of structure did not affect the low-compulsive children; however, highly compulsive children performed markedly better under a structured classroom teaching regime. "The choice of instructional methods makes a big difference for certain kinds of people, and a search for the 'best' way to teach can succeed only when the learner's personality is taken into account [Grimes & Allinsmith, 1961, p. 271]."

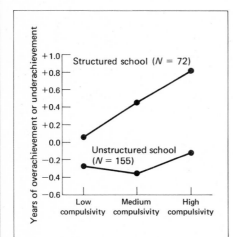

FIGURE 15-5 School achievement of compulsive children in two types of schools. (From Grimes, J. W., & Allinsmith, W., 1961.)

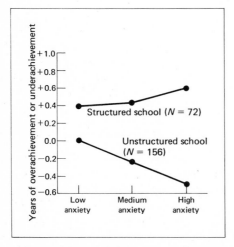

FIGURE 15-6 School achievement of anxious children in two types of schools. (From Grimes, J. W., & Allinsmith, W., 1961.)

Source: Grimes, J. W., & Allinsmith, W. Compulsivity, anxiety, and school achievement. *Merrill-Palmer Quarterly*, 1961, **7,** 247-269.

positive reinforcement control programs to classrooms? These are some of the questions that are discussed in this section.

First, no definitive answer can be given concerning the effects of positive and negative reinforcement on student academic progress. While some studies suggest that positive approaches produce better performance (for example, Anderson, White, & Wash, 1966), other studies indicate that individual differences must be considered before any conclusions can be drawn. For example, a number of years ago, Thompson and Hunnicutt (1944) reported that positive and negative feedback had quite different effects on extroverts and introverts. Praise produced high achievement in introverted students, while negative feedback was more effective with extroverted pupils. More recently Van de Reit (1964) found that criticism was more effective than praise in improving performance among underachievers; positive reinforcement, on the other hand, produced faster learning among students who were already achieving at a normal level.

Teacher reinforcement style has effects on other aspects of the child's development as well. Both the child's self-esteem and his peer group status are affected: both are higher under a positive classroom regime. Davidson and Lang (1960) found that children who perceive their teachers as having positive feelings about them have better scholastic performance and a more positive self-concept. A closely related study tapped another aspect of this issue: the effect of teacher approval-disapproval schedules on the child's peer group status. Tenth-grade children who were randomly chosen to receive increased teacher attention were more popular with their peers than their classmates who were systematically ignored by their teachers (Flanders & Havumaki, 1960).

In summary, teacher reinforcement style has important effects not only on academic achievement but on self-esteem and peer relations as well. Both pupil personality and school performance should be considered in evaluating the effects of positive and negative teacher feedback.

Classroom discipline: some new approaches

A question that our discussion so far has touched on only tangentially concerns the effectiveness of different teacher-control techniques for achieving and maintaining classroom order and discipline. Although it might be predicted intuitively that praise is more effective than disapproval, a systematic analysis of the use of praise is necessary before any conclusions concerning its effectiveness can be drawn legitimately. Other questions require consideration as well. How important are classmates in achieving classroom control? Can the power of the peer group be effectively harnessed by the teacher to achieve more effective discipline?

Modeling effects in classroom discipline First, rebukes, threats, and other forms of social disapproval are often ineffective; in fact one study showed that the frequency of inappropriate "standing up" behavior was increased, not decreased, by an accelerated use of "sit down" commands by the teacher (Madsen, Becher, Thomas, Koser, & Plager, 1968). Moreover, as our earlier teacher discussion of imitation would predict, disciplinary tactics are by no means restricted to the child toward whom the disapproval is directed. Often the use of disapproval and criticism has indirect effects, or "ripple effects," on the disciplined child's classmates. However, Kounin and Gump (1958, 1961) have found that disciplining one pupil does not necessarily deter other pupils from misbehaving. Rather, the ripple effect varied with the status of the target pupil with the effect being greatest when the teacher disciplined a child who was highly respected by his peers; if the child was low in status, there was little effect. Other studies (for example, Bandura, 1971) confirm that observers will imitate high status and prestigious models more readily than low-status models. The particular kind of control technique employed made a difference: clarity and firmness increased conformity in other misbehaving children, while rough intervention tactics (for example, threats and physical punishment) only disrupted the classroom learning process. Finally, the effect varied as a function of the child's familiarity with the school or classroom environment. The most marked observer reaction occurred on the first day; later the observers probably could anticipate the teacher's response to their own misbehavior and this knowledge may alter or in some cases weaken the ripple effect.

Operant reinforcement in the classroom Recent attempts to apply positive operant reinforcement principles to classroom control have been more successful. In some cases, social reinforcement in the form of verbal approval has been employed as a means of establishing classroom control, whereby teachers are taught to dispense praise immediately upon the occurrence of appropriate behaviors and to ignore undesirable responses. A striking example of the application of social reinforcement to classroom situations can be found in Box 15-3.

BOX 15-3 REINFORCEMENT OF INCOMPATIBLE BEHAVIOR

The encouragement of alternative responses that are inconsistent with the expression of disruptive classroom behavior, such as cooperative behaviors, is a particularly important technique for controlling undesirable behavior.

Brown and Elliot (1965) applied this technique to a practical problem: controlling aggression in a nursery school class of twenty-seven boys. Instead of disrupting the routine by introducing experimenters who would interact with the children, these investigators trained the teachers to carry out their research program. The following instructions to the teachers nicely illustrate the aim:

We will try to ignore aggression and reward cooperative and peaceful behavior. Of course, if someone is using a hammer on another's head, we would step in, but just to separate the two and leave. It will be difficult at first, because we tend to watch and be quiet when nothing is happening, and now our attention will, as much as possible, be directed toward cooperative, or nonaggressive behavior. It would be good to let the most aggressive boys see that the others are getting the attention if it is possible. A pat on the head, "That's good Mike," "Hello Chris and Mark, how are you today?," "Look what Eric made," etc., may have more rewarding power than we think. On the other hand, it is just as important during this week to have no reprimands, no "Say you're sorry," "Aren't you sorry?" Not that these aren't useful ways of teaching proper behavior, but they will only cloud the effects of our other manner of treatment. It would be best not even to look at a shove or small fight if we are sure no harm is being done; as I mentioned before, if it is necessary we should just separate the children and leave."

Prior to the treatment phase, observations of the boys' aggressive responses were gathered for a week. Two weeks later the first treatment period was initiated and it lasted for two weeks. Ratings were taken during the second week of this period. Teachers were then told that the experiment was over and that they were no longer constrained in their behavior toward aggressive acts. In order to assess the durability of the treatment, a set of ratings was taken three weeks later. Finally, the treatment was reinstituted for two weeks. The results summarized in Table 15-2 showed dramatic reduction in the frequency of aggressive responses following treatment.

This study illustrates not only the importance of reinforcement of prosocial behavior for controlling aggression, but also demonstrates the often paradoxical role played by teacher "attention." Note that when the teachers were allowed to attend to the aggressive behaviors that they were previously ignoring as part of the treatment, the frequency of physical aggression increased. Naturally, the teacher in "paying attention" to the aggressive child hopes to decrease the frequency of this kind of behavior. However, as this study and a variety of other systematic observational studies (for example, Harris, Wolf, & Baer, 1964) have clearly shown, attending to deviant responses with a mild rebuke or reprimand may often serve to maintain or even increase aggressive and troublesome behaviors. Possibly, behaving aggressively is used by children as an attention-seeking tactic. However, as the Brown and Elliot study suggests, this is less likely to occur in situations where the child is provided alternative means of gaining adult attention. There is another important feature of this technique. It avoids some of the undesirable consequences usually associated with the use of punishment for suppressing aggression. For instance, it is unlikely that this approach would lead to increase in aggressive behavior in situations different from the disciplinary context.

Table 15-2 AVERAGE NUMBER OF RESPONSES IN THE VARIOUS CATEGORIES OF AGGRESSION

Time of observation	Categories of aggression		
	Physical	Verbal	Total
Pretreatment	41.2	22.8	64.0
First treatment	26.0	17.4	43.4
Follow-up	37.8	13.8	51.6
Second treatment	21.0	4.6	25.6

(From: Brown & Elliot, 1965, p. 8.)

Source: Brown, P., & Elliott, R. Control of aggression in a nursery school class. *Journal of Experimental Child Psychology*, 1965, **2,** 103–107.

However, in some cases ignoring disruptive behavior and praising appropriate responses is not powerful enough to establish control. This may be particularly likely in a classroom where a few individual children continue to be disruptive under a praise-and-ignore regime. When other children observe their peers behaving disruptively without any negative consequence, they may become disruptive themselves.

A technique that has proven effective in establishing classroom control is the combination of material or token rewards and social reinforcements. A study by O'Leary, Becker, Evans, and Saudargas (1969) illustrates the operation of a token reinforcement program in a classroom setting. Under this program, children accumulated points or tokens for good behavior. They could then exchange the tokens for material rewards, for example, candy, peanuts, comics, dolls, and other toys. The experimenters assessed the effectiveness of the token scheme by first measuring the amount of disruptive behavior under ordinary classroom conditions. These observations provided them with a standard comparison against which the success of the program could be contrasted. Before introducing the tokens, these investigators attempted to achieve classroom control by other methods including the introduction of a set of classroom rules (for example, we sit in our seats, we do not talk in the hall, etc.) and a reorganization of the academic program into thirty-minute sessions. In addition, they tried a social reinforcement program, whereby the teachers smiled, nodded, and verbally encouraged *only* appropriate behaviors. As Figure 15-7 shows, none of these changes significantly altered the frequency of disruptive classroom behavior. However, by adding the token program to these procedures, the investigators achieved a marked drop in disruptive behavior. There is little doubt that the token program was critical in producing classroom control: when the tokens were withdrawn for a five-week period, disruptive behavior increased. Reinstatement of the tokens led to a drop in undesirable behaviors. In a follow-up period tokens were again withdrawn, but replaced with a modified reward system in order to see whether appropriate behavior could be maintained under more normal classroom conditions. While retaining the praise, rules, and educational structure, a systematic "star system" was introduced. Under this system, children were awarded gold paper stars for good behavior. The child with the largest number of stars

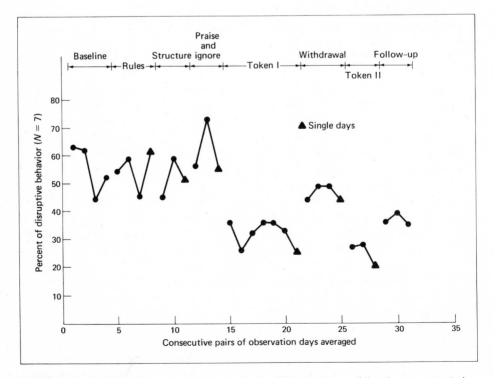

FIGURE 15-7 Amount of disruptive behavior during different phases of the classroom control project. (From O'Leary, K. D., Becker, W. C., Evans, M. B., & Saudargas, R. A., 1969.)

at the end of the week received a piece of candy. This particular procedure represented an important shift from the earlier token program since this new system relied much more heavily on reinforcers existing within the natural education setting, such as stars, peer pressure, and prestige. This system was just as effective as the token procedure in maintaining misbehaviors at a relatively low level.

This study is a variant of the "token economy" that has been used on a much broader scale to modify the behavior of delinquents, retardates, and even schizophrenics (Allyon & Azrin, 1968).

O'Leary and his colleagues noted that such a program may exert indirect influence on other kinds of pupil behavior as well. The class showed a greater than average gain in academic performance as assessed by pre- and post-measures on the California Achievement Test. Moreover, attendance jumped from 86 percent in the pretoken phases to a near perfect 99 percent in the token and follow-up periods of the study. The investigators stressed the tentative nature of both findings; more systematic analysis is necessary to assess the effects of a token system on academic performance and school attendance. Hopefully, future research will confirm these trends. Such confirmation appears likely since the main outcome of the token program was to provide the teacher with more time to devote to her central task, teaching, than to disciplining her pupils.

The importance of the peer group in achieving classroom control has been investigated as well. Two recent experimental studies will illustrate. In one study (Barrish, Sanders, & Wolf, 1969) a fourth-grade class was divided into two teams and any misbehavior (for example, talking in class or leaving your seat without permission) by *any* team member resulted in a loss of privileges for the whole team. The privileges were events which are available in almost every classroom, such as extra recess, first to line up for lunch, time for special projects, stars, and of course the fun of winning the contest. These investigators found that individual contingencies resulting in group consequences were very effective in reducing disruptive classrooms. However, the effect was present only in the class period (math) where the peer game was in effect; there was little generalization to other periods (for example, reading). Only when the game was introduced in the reading class did a drop in disruptive behavior occur. This suggests that " 'generalization' is no magical process, but rather a behavioral change which must be engineered like any other change [O'Leary et al., 1969, p. 13]."

A related study by Schmidt and Ulrich (1969) indicated that team competition may not be necessary. These investigators were able to lower the level of classroom noise by making any individual violation of a previously specified noise ceiling result in loss of privileges (extra time in gym period) not just for the individual but for the whole class. This procedure seemed to work just as well as the competition procedure used by Barrish and his colleagues and avoided some of the undesirable consequences that between-group competition may produce, such as increased intergroup hostility (Sherif & Sherif, 1953; see Chapter 14). As Bronfenbrenner notes in his recent *Two Worlds of Childhood: U.S. & U.S.S.R.* (1970), the technique of peer control is used regularly in Russian school classrooms.

The peer-teacher approach   Peers can not only aid in controlling their classmates, but they can function as peer-teachers as well. Older children are cast in the role of assistant teachers and given responsibility for teaching younger children. Although the details of different programs vary, most involve some kind of instruction session for the "helpers" in which they learn the techniques of relating to and teaching younger children. In addition, to coordinate the tutoring program with the younger child's regular classroom experience, assistants often meet with the teacher of the child that they are aiding. The results are encouraging and indicate that both tutor and pupil benefit in a variety of ways.

First, both participants show greater academic progress in the tutorial subject. Cloward (1967) found significant changes in reading achievement over a five-month period: not only did the tutored pupils show a gain of 6.2 months in reading level in contrast to a gain of only 3.5 months for nontutored control children, but the tutors gained as well. In fact, over a seven-month period the tutors improved an average of nineteen months in reading level.

More recently, Allen and Feldman (1973) found that the experience of being a tutor can benefit low-achieving children. Children who are low achievers often have a record of failure and tend to be passive participants in any learning exchange. Motivation and involvement will increase in the tutoring situation and so these investigators argued that low achievers would learn better when placed in the role of peer-teacher than when studying alone. Ten low-achieving fifth graders whose reading scores were at least one year below average grade level served as tutors; ten third graders were the tutees or learners. Subjects participated for ten consecutive weekdays for a two-week period; for every alternate day the fifth-grade tutor either taught a third grader for twenty minutes or studied the material alone. By the end of the two-week period, tutoring resulted in significantly better performance than studying alone for the low-achieving fifth-grade children. These gains were made in spite of the fact that the third graders learned equally with the tutor or studying alone. The tutoring effect in this case had more impact on the tutors than the tutees. While follow-up studies are necessary to determine the stability of these gains, these results point clearly to the effectiveness of the peer-teacher program.

Moreover, other benefits have been reported. Lippitt and Lippitt (1968), for example, recently summarized some of these additional effects:

> Teachers of younger children who receive help say that their youngsters show increased self-respect, self-confidence, and pride in their progress. They are less tense, can express themselves more clearly, are better groomed, and have improved atttendance records.
>
> As for the older students, working with their juniors provides valuable learning experiences in addition to giving them a chance to be appreciated by teachers and younger students. They learn how to help someone else learn. They learn to relate to a younger child. They get a chance to work through, at a safe emotional distance, some of the problems they have in relation to their own peers or younger siblings. Ordinarily, older children might not be interested in the social skills involved in getting along with people, but they are highly motivated to learn them when learning those skills enables them to do a better job of helping the younger children.
>
> Academically, too, older students benefit from being crossage helpers. Children who might have had no interest in reviewing subject matter which they did not understand when they were in the lower grades make a tremendous effort to fill the gaps when they are responsible for helping someone else understand [Lippitt & Lippitt, 1968, p. 4].

Although other investigators have reported similar effects (for example, Myers, 1968; Deering, 1968; Kuppel, 1964), systematic research is required to determine the critical factors that account for the effectiveness of these programs.

The teacher as a social model

Just as parents and peers serve as models for the developing child, recent evidence suggests that young children imitate their teachers as well. However, not all teachers are likely to be imitated, nor are all children equally likely to copy their teacher's actions. In a recent study Portuges and Feshbach (1971) have isolated some of the teacher and observer characteristics that affect the degree of teacher imitation. Groups of eight- to ten-year-old boys and girls were shown movies of a female teacher presenting a geography lesson, using either a rewarding or critical teaching style. The "positive" teacher responded approvingly to correct answers, while the negative model rebuked the pupils in the film for their errors. In addition, the models exhibited different distinctive incidental movements, such as cupping the ear or clasping the hands. To assess the extent to which the children would imitate the teacher-model's distinctive mannerisms, the children were required to "teach a geography lesson" to two life-sized dolls. The rewarding teacher was imitated more than the negative instructor. The use of a positive approach, then, apparently enhances teacher influence by making it more likely that the pupils will imitate the teacher's behavior. However, the strength of the effect varied with the sex and social class of the observing child. Girls imitated the female teacher-model more than the boys did; in light of our earlier discussion, girls probably view the role of teacher as more sex-appropriate than do boys. Moreover, middle-class children imitated more of the teacher's gestures than did lower-class observers. It was the middle-class girls who imitated the model to the greatest degree, while lower-class boys were the least influenced by the teacher-model. The implications of this social class difference will be explored in detail in a later section. Other studies suggest that the children may imitate their teacher's typical problem-solving style. As we saw earlier in our discussion of cognitive style (see Chapter 8), impulsive children exposed to reflective teachers become more reflective in their problem-solving strategies (Yando & Kagan, 1968). Teachers as well as parents and peers serve as influential models for children.

We have examined teachers and tactics; now we turn to an evaluation of texts.

TEXTBOOKS

What's wrong with primary readers?

In the past decade there has been a reawakening of interest and concern with children's readers. Educators have recognized that children are influenced not only by their teachers and peers but also by the reading material to which they are exposed. Primers serve an important socializing function. Many of the attitudes and cultural values that are slowly emerging during the early school years are directly shaped by the content and themes of these textbooks. In addition, these readers play an important role in determining the child's attitudes toward the task of reading itself. Particularly for children who have had little encouragement to read before entering school and, therefore, have little appreciation of the value of books and the rewards of reading, primers with lively, interesting, and relevant content would seem to be necessary to interest them in books and reading.

However, most evaluations of available readers give these texts a failing grade. Here is one such evaluation of the current status of the American reader:

> The reading textbooks used in the first grade were inappropriate in terms of interest value. They concealed the results of life in America, hiding not only its difficulties and problems, but also much of its excitement and joy. They featured Dick and Jane in the clean, Caucasian, correct suburbs, in houses surrounded by white fences, playing happily with happy peers and happy parents. They contained a dearth of moral content which could have high interest values. They presented a monstrous repetition of pollyanish family activities. They offered no new knowledge. They contradicted the everyday experiences of children in general since most American children seldom, if ever, experience the affect-less situations depicted in the books. . . . the stories were so predictable in outcomes that little, if any, of a child's incentive to continue reading was derived from the story content [Blom, Waite, & Zimet, 1970, p. 433].

Other surveys have unearthed further deficiencies. For example, Klineberg (1963) has pointed out that in addition to distorting the picture of current American society, these texts pay little attention to foreign nationalities. Maybe it is just as well, for when other national groups are depicted it is often in stereotyped terms or in an unfavorable light. It is not surprising that American children are markedly ethnocentric.

Moreover, textbooks carry hidden agendas to the young about sex-role mythologies in our society (Saario, Jacklin, & Tittle, 1973). A recent analysis of first-, second-, and third-grade readers revealed evidence of a stereotypic portrayal of male and female roles. Boys were portrayed as demonstrating significantly higher amounts of aggression, physical exertion, and problem solving, while girls were often cast as characters engaged in fantasy, carrying out directions, and making statements about themselves. Nor were these rigid sex-role pictures restricted to child story characters. Adult males were portrayed more often as engaging in constructive and productive behaviors, physical activity, and in more problem-solving behavior. On the other hand, adult females were presented as conforming and were usually found in home or school settings. Males were found more frequently outdoors or in business. Finally, young male characters significantly more often receive positive outcomes as a result of their *own* actions; girl characters receive positive outcomes, but they are more often because of circumstance. This kind of sex-role stereotyping, in fact, starts very early in children's literature: other studies of picture books for preschoolers reveal a very similar pattern (Weitzman, Eifler, Hokada, & Ross, 1972).

Direct evidence that the children themselves are dissatisfied with their classroom readers comes from a recent comparison of the content of first-grade primers and the library selections made by first graders when they had a free choice (Wiberg & Trost, 1970). The marked discrepancies between the two sets of books underlined the differences between children's reading interests and primer content. Unlike the play and Pollyannaish themes of the primers, the children's library choices emphasized folk tales, lessons from life, nature, and real-life events that had both sad and happy endings. Activities involving boys and older children were more frequent in the library books, as were stories about foreign countries. Moreover, although boys and girls read the same books in the classroom, clear sex differences in book preferences were evident when the children were given a choice. Boys preferred books with boy activity stories and prank and information themes. Girls, on the other hand, showed no preference in terms of the sex appropriateness of the activity, but did choose pet books frequently. These data suggest that if children's interest in reading is to be stimulated, some radical redesigning of primers is necessary. The children themselves can, in fact, point the way to more realistic and relevant texts. Not only do young children know what they want; what they want is probably better for them!

Some implications of traditional readers

What are the implications of these elementary school readers for the child's academic progress and for his emotional, social, and cultural development? One would expect that children would be much more involved and motivated if the content of the reading material were relevant to their own background, interests, and experience. It is likely that many children simply "tune out" at a very early age due to the perceived irrelevance of school as reflected in these primers. If this is the case, one would expect differences between reading ability of children exposed to the "Dick and Jane" stories and those taught to read with more sophisticated, realistic, and relevant materials.

Recently, Asher and Markell (1974) have demonstrated that the interest value of stories can affect reading scores, especially for boys. Fifth graders were given passages to read that were of either high or low interest. When boys had the chance to read stories about astronauts and airplanes, they read much better than when they read low-interest stories. Moreover, the typical difference in reading level between boys and girls was not present when the material was interesting. Girls, on the other hand, tended to be less affected by the interest level of the stories (see Figure 15-8). Although there is no simple solution to the problem of lower reading achievement of boys in elementary school, this study suggests that more attention should be paid to motivational factors. Boys can read better if the material turns them on!

Typical texts may have a detrimental impact on girls in the long run by reinforcing sex-role feminine stereotypes of passivity or dependency. Texts merely reinforce the lesson provided by teachers and parents concerning female roles. As noted earlier in this chapter, changing these stereotypes may help to increase the achievement level of girls in high school and college.

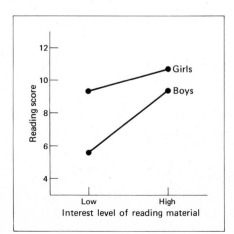

FIGURE 15-8 Reading level of boys and girls with low and high interest material. (From Asher, S., & Markell, R. A., in press.)

Nontraditional readers

Similarly Whipple (1963) found differences in measures of word recognition and oral reading accuracy between children taught with traditional primers and those introduced to reading through a multiethnic reading text. The children using the new text, one which more realistically emphasized the different ethnic and racial groups in American society, had higher scores on both measures. Probably these effects would be particularly marked for non-Caucasian, non-middle-class children. Is it at all surprising that these children feel alienated from the school system when the system presents such a uniformly consistent but irrelevant and foreign set of values? Even for white middle-class children the misrepresentation of our society promoted in the typical primer has detrimental effects. Readers provide an excellent device for exposing these socially naïve children to some of the other racial and ethnic groups that compose American society— a needed lesson in cultural learning. Possibly many of the stereotypes that often underlie current white middle-class prejudices would be eliminated by a more realistic presentation of the current American scene.

Fortunately readers are changing, and a number of publishing firms have produced primers that include children of more than one ethnic background as story characters. But have they been successful in avoiding the white middle-class bias of the traditional textbook? In an attempt to find out whether the changes were more than skin-deep, that is, whether the basic primer remained, with the occasional addition of a black story character, Blom, Waite, and Zimet (1970) examined a sample of these multiethnic readers. The results to date have been mixed. A majority of these "new" readers fail to recognize that suburbia is not the only American environment; suburban settings still predominate to the exclusion of urban locales. "What is being depicted is a Negro family living in a happy, stable, white suburban neighborhood [Blom et al., 1967, p. 179]." Moreover, many of the ostensibly multiethnic books contain few significant characters of ethnic background other than white Anglo-Saxons. And when other races and nationalities are represented, some books, at least, tend to emphasize their lack of success to a greater degree than they do in the traditional "white" stories. Possibly more serious is the fact that in at least one series investigated by Waite (1968), the characteristics of the nonwhite story characters (blacks) reflected the stereotypes and prejudices current in American society. The black youngster was depicted as athletic, less intelligent, impulsive, and distractible, while his white counterpart in the story was presented much more sympathetically, for example, reflective, more intelligent, and socially secure. The portrayal of the fathers in these stories reflected a similar prejudicial bias. The white male was economically more successful and more consistently masculine than the black father. "While the conscious intent of the authors was socially responsive, prejudicial values and attitudes clearly emerged in spite of conscious attempts to avoid them [Blom et al., 1970, p. 449]."

A recent study by Graebner (1972) came to similar conclusions concerning the presentation of the sexes in contemporary readers. The same sex-role stereotypes that characterized the 1961–63 texts were still there in 1971. Almost no change had occurred in the portrayal of the sexes; the study concluded that texts "have not kept pace with a changing society [Graebner, 1972, p. 52]."

A closing comment on texts

Perhaps the most appropriate way to close this section is to offer the following plea that texts not only need to recognize differences in sex and race, but should be generally more aware that:

> The real world is more varied than the one depicted in elementary readers. Boys and girls, and men and women, are fat and skinny, short and tall. Boys and men are sometimes gentle, sometimes dreamers. Artists, doctors, lawyers, and college professors are sometimes mothers as well. Rather than limiting possibilities, elementary texts should seek to maximize individual development and self-esteem by displaying a wide range of models and activities. If the average is the only model presented to a child and therefore assumed to be the child's goal, most children—and most adults—would probably be unable to match the model [Saario, Jacklin, & Tittle, 1973, p. 399].

THE LOWER-CLASS CHILD AND THE SCHOOL

It has been estimated that the school has a cumulative effect on the lower-class child such that "by the third grade he is approximately one year behind academically, by the sixth grade two years behind, by grade eight two and one half to three years retarded academically and by the ninth grade a top candidate for dropping out [Rioux, 1968, p. 92]." For the middle-class child the picture is very different; rather than dropping out, he is much more likely to go to college than his lower-class peer.

Why the social class difference? Many answers have been offered. Recall our earlier discussions of the cognitive and linguistic differences between lower- and middle-class children. At that time, it was noted that those differences are present and detectable before the child ever reaches the schoolroom. So it may not be entirely the school's fault; children of lower-class backgrounds are simply not as well prepared to fit into the middle-class culture. But it is the aim of education presumably to teach the child regardless of his background.

The middle-class bias of the school

First of all, the fact that the school is a middle-class institution, espousing middle-class values and staffed by middle-class teachers, puts the child from a lower-class background at a disadvantage from the outset.

> The lower class child experiences the middle class oriented school as discontinuous with his home environment and further, comes to it unprepared in the basic skills on which the curriculum is founded. The school becomes a place which makes puzzling demands and where failure is frequent and feelings of competence are subsequently not generated. Motivation decreases and the school loses its effectiveness . . . [Deutsch, 1964, p. 255].

In contrast, for the middle-class child,

> The school is very central and is contiguous with the totality of his life experiences. As a result there are few incongruities between his school experiences and any others he is likely to have had and there are intrinsic motivating and molding properties in the school situation

to which he has been sensitized. . . . faculty orientation with his family orientation [Deutsch, 1964, p. 255].

Simply by virtue of his class membership, the middle-class child has an advantage over his lower-class peers.

Parent attitudes toward the school

Part of the reason for this feeling of discontinuity stems from the different orientation to the school system that middle- and lower-class parents provide their children. There are clear social class differences in the manner that children are introduced to the school. Hess and Shipman (1967) studied this problem by asking black middle- and lower-class mothers to indicate "what she would tell her child on the first day of school before he left the house [p. 69]." It was assumed that the answer to this inquiry would tap the parental attitude toward the school. The lower-class mothers tended to give their children un-qualified commands concerning how to behave in school. Little or no rationale for their directives were provided: "sit down," "don't holler," and "mind the teacher" were typical of the answers. On the other hand, the middle-class mothers tended to use a more cognitive, rational orientation which provided the child with some explanation for the rules that the school would impose on his behavior. For example, a middle-class mother might instruct her child: "You shouldn't talk in school because the teacher can't teach so well and you won't learn your lessons properly." Consider the implications of these different orientations for the child in the classroom. The child who is given the imperative orientation is likely to view the school as a rigid authoritarian institution gov-erned by inflexible and unexplained rules and regulations. This attitude may lead to overzealous acceptance of absolute answers and less likelihood of inquiry, curiosity, and debate. His interest and involvement would probably be low. In contrast, the child given the rational, cognitive orientation will be more likely to expect that answers should have reasons underlying them. A spirit of inquiry is kindled in the middle-class child which probably delights his teacher and, in turn, aids his progress. In fact, if these motivational and attitudinal consequences are true, one would expect performance dif-ferences between the two groups. Hess and Shipman found a clear relationship be-tween the mother's orientation and the child's mental performance; the use of an im-perative approach was associated with low performance in several areas, including lower IQ scores among children of imperative mothers.

Moreover, the differences are not simply in the initial orientations but also in the amount and quality of home support for academic achievement. A number of studies has indicated that the child's perception of parental support and interest in his aca-demic progress is significantly related to the child's actual school performance and the child's attitude toward school. Class differences are clear: there is more likely to be support from middle-class parents than from lower-class parents for scholastic achieve-ment and success.

Lower-class parents are not only less likely to provide encouragement, but they are often less able to help the child in his school tasks. Often their own education is limited and, as the child moves to higher grades, the parents are increasingly unable to assist their children or even appreciate the usefulness and relevance of the school's demands. Incidentally, the frustration experienced by many middle-class parents in trying to com-prehend the "new math," for example, suggests that this problem is not restricted to lower-class parents. With increasing specialization and curriculum innovation it may be necessary to teach the parents as well.

The problem of appropriate models

There are other problems encountered by lower-class children which tend to lessen their chances for scholastic success. While the middle-class children can adopt their parents as models of scholastic achievement, the lower-class children must look elsewhere. Their parents are simply inappropriate models from which to learn the attitudes and values necessary for school success. The teacher, of course, provides an alternative model, and if the child could identify with and emulate the actions and attitudes of his middle-class teacher, chances of succeeding in the school system would increase. However, as Portuges and Feshbach (1972) found in their recent study of social class differences in teacher imitation, middle-class white children imitated the teacher more than did the lower-class black children. This is consistent with other evidence that middle-class children are more likely to aspire to the teaching profession than are lower-class children. Whether or not these black students were rejecting the teaching role or merely the *white* teacher is left unanswered. One might expect that more black teachers with whom the disadvantaged black pupils could more readily identify would result in a more positive attitude toward school among black students. If he does adopt the teacher as his primary model, this may emphasize further the discontinuity between his home life and the school.

Social class differences in peer group influences

Perhaps peers could provide appropriate models for academic achievement. This is not likely. In contrast to the middle-class peer group where a child is often held in esteem for outstanding academic work, the lower-class child is likely to be rejected by his peers for this kind of success. Only "sissies" and "teacher's pets" do well in school, according to lower-class peer group codes; prestige and status is allotted more frequently to the disruptive, underachieving child who delights his classmates by disrupting the teacher. For the lower-class child, peers generally provide poor models for academic success.

Social class differences in teacher attitudes

How much of the blame should the teacher assume for the failures of the lower-class child? The teacher, of course, has been a favorite target; a number of investigators have blamed the white middle-class teacher's lack of appreciation of the problems of the disadvantaged as a primary cause of the lower-class child's scholastic plight. An angry and outspoken advocate of this view is Clark (1965). In his words:

> The clash of cultures in the classroom is essentially a class war, a socioeconomic and racial warefare being waged on the battleground of our schools with middle-class and middle-class aspiring teachers provided with a powerful arsenal of half-truths, prejudices and rationalizations arrayed against hopelessly outclassed working class youngsters [Clark, 1965, p. 129].

Support for the claim that teachers fail to understand and appreciate the differences in background, experience, and values of lower-class children comes from a study by

Groff (1963). In his search for the reasons for dissatisfactions in teaching the culturally disadvantaged child, he found that 40 percent of the 294 teachers interviewed cited the "peculiarities" in the personalities of the children as the major cause of dissatisfaction.

There is little doubt that this is due to the middle-class outlook of the teachers. In an investigation by Gottlieb (1964), the attitudes of white middle-class teachers and black teachers with lower-class origins were compared. When asked to indicate the factors that contributed to job dissatisfaction, the white teachers cited "clientele" factors, such as lack of parental interest and student behavior or discipline problems. In contrast, the black teachers tended to see such factors as lack of proper equipment and over-crowded conditions—rather than the students—as their major sources of discontent. Teacher race and background were related to their perceptions of their students as well. When asked to check those adjectives which came closest to describing the outstanding characteristics of their children, white teachers most frequently selected "talkative," "lazy," "fun-loving," "high-strung," and "rebellious" to describe their lower-class pupils. Black teachers, however, saw their pupils in a much more positive light and checked such adjectives as "happy," "cooperative," "fun-loving," "energetic," and "ambitious."

> It would appear that the Negro teachers are less critical and less pessimistic in their evaluations of these students than the white teachers, probably because many of them have themselves come from backgrounds similar to that of their students and yet have managed to overcome social barriers and status [Gottlieb, 1964, p. 353].

However, it is not just the failure to appreciate differences in customs, values, and background that leads to the lower-class child's lack of success; it is the commonly shared expectation that lower-class children will fail. Their failure, in a sense, becomes a self-fulfilling prophecy. However, as noted earlier in the chapter, by providing teachers with more positive expectations, pupil performance can be improved. And this effect is not restricted to middle-class children.

Teacher expectancy and student performance

Rosenthal and Jacobsen (1968) included a sample of Mexican-American children in their extensive study of this problem in order to evaluate the effects of teacher expectancies on minority group children. Their results indicated clearly that the lower-class Mexican-American children as well as the middle-class children benefited from the planted expectations. Moreover, there was a tendency for these pupils to gain more than their non-Mexican peers. In fact, the more "Mexican-looking" the pupil appeared as rated by their teachers, the greater was the IQ gain. Probably the teachers' preexperimental expectancies for these individuals were lowest of all, and their surprise may have led the teachers to take a special interest in these children. The main point is clear: disadvantaged children can benefit from changes in teacher expectancies even though there were no special programs to aid and assist them. Simply altering the teachers' attitudes may be sufficient to bring about at least some improvement.

Implications for the lower-class child

What are the implications of this failure to understand the lower-class child? Often resentment, dissatisfaction, and a sense of bewilderment characterizes the middle-class teacher in ghetto schools. Attempts to teach are often abandoned in favor of primitive control tactics. In fact, Deutsch (1960) has estimated that lower-class children receive one-third less actual teaching than their middle-class peers. The teacher spends almost 80 percent of the school day disciplining her charges or engaging in noneducational duties, such as collecting milk money. The teacher then becomes redefined as a disciplinarian and, since she spends less time in educating her students, they learn less, become increasingly bored, and become even more disruptive. The result is a vicious circle: a tougher control policy and even less teaching. To the teacher in this situation:

> School is not an enthusiastic learning center where everybody is academically alert, where people desire to learn something now because it is worth knowing. Instead it is a place where a major part of the teachers' time must be devoted to maintaining discipline among children who never before have known it. Thus, it is often felt that years of excellent preparation go for naught [Cheyney, 1966, p. 79].

The upshot is that many teachers tend to regard being assigned to teach in lower-class schools not as a challenge but simply as a less desirable, less prestigious placement. For many it is merely a necessary first step to a "better" job; the aim is not to learn to adjust to the situation but to apply for transfers as soon as the system's regulations permit.

Clearly any program aimed at improving the academic progress of lower-class children should not be restricted to content and curriculum innovations. Drastic alterations in teacher preparation and teacher attitudes are necessary. This education should include an extensive exposure to lower-class life and lower-class values. The implication of Rosenthal's research is clear: once teachers decide that lower-class pupils can learn, maybe they will learn. One lesson that Head Start has taught us is that children of all backgrounds can learn.

SUMMARY

The school is an extremely influential, although often neglected, socializing force. In this chapter several factors that affect the kind and extent of the school's influence were examined. First, the physical structure of the school environment came under scrutiny. School size, for example, determines the extent of involvement in extracurricular activities; children at small high schools are not only more likely to participate but are also more likely to occupy positions of prestige and importance. One result is that there are few potential dropouts in small schools. Next, the impact of the size, shape, and seating arrangements of the classroom were examined. Both class size and the pupil's location in the class determines the extent to which he participates in classroom activities. While participation is higher in smaller classrooms, the child located in the front and center of the class, the action zone, participates more than children seated in other parts of the room.

The most important individual in the academic drama is, of course, the teacher. First, the interaction patterns between teachers and children of different sexes were examined. Teacher disapproval of male sex-typed behavior may result in a clash between female teachers and young boys; this in turn may account for the poor adjustment and lower achievement of boys in the early elementary grades. Teacher encouragement of dependency in young girls, however, may account for the lower levels of achievement in older female students. Teachers have a great deal of flexibility and freedom in the classroom; individual differences in beliefs, attitudes, and styles of interacting with children are evident. The effects of variations in teacher behavior were explored in the next section of this chapter. Often teachers form early impressions and expectations concerning a pupil's probable success. Evidence shows that these expectations, even when they are experimentally induced, have a powerful impact on the child's academic progress. A self-fulfilling prophecy is evident: children succeed when teachers believe they will do well, while pupils are likely to perform poorly when instructors expect them to fail. Next, the effects of different classroom organizations were discussed. Students generally prefer a group-centered classroom in which they are allowed some opportunity to participate in the decision making. Recent evidence suggests that this type of arrangement even may be correlated with better academic performance. However, this is still an unresolved issue and, in the final analysis, any conclusion about the advantages of a traditional, authoritarian regime over more pupil-oriented arrangements must take into account the kind of pupils involved. Different personalities apparently function better under different types of classroom organizational arrangements.

One promising technique in classroom organizations is the peer-teacher approach, where older children are cast in the role of assistant teachers and given responsibility for teaching younger peers. Early evaluations indicate that both the helper and the child who is assisted benefit from this arrangement.

Is the teacher's preferred reinforcement style important? Do children learn just as well under a teacher who is positive and encouraging as under a punitive teacher? While there is no clear-cut answer to this question, there is some indication that self-esteem and peer group status are correlated with a positive classroom teacher. Recent applications of behavior modification techniques for controlling children's classroom behavior were examined and found to be successful. This is particularly true when these programs have used material or token reinforcers for shaping appropriate behavior. Generally speaking, positive approaches to classroom discipline work better than punitive approaches.

Finally, the teacher may influence her charges by serving as a social model. Evidence was presented indicating that a rewarding teacher tends to be imitated more than a negative instructor tends to be. Again, the sex and social class of the child observers must be considered. Middle-class girls, for example, tend to imitate a teacher model to the greatest extent, while lower-class boys are influenced relatively little by a teacher model. The impact of the teacher as model is not restricted to reinforcing style; the typical problem-solving style of the teacher is often imitated by her students as well.

After this discussion of teachers and their tactics, primary-school textbooks were examined. Texts are important vehicles for learning and reinforcing attitudes and social values. Unfortunately, most current primers are grossly inadequate; rather than presenting a realistic picture of American culture, the typical text offers a Pollyannaish substitute. This is not merely an adult evaluation: children's library choices indicate that children themselves prefer very different kinds of books than those usually available as primary readers. Tentative evidence indicated that children provided with more reality-oriented interesting readers scored higher on a variety of reading and language measures. Although texts are changing, many of the white, middle-class, suburban biases still persist in more recent "new look" primers.

In the final section, the impact of the schools on the academic progress of the lower-class child was examined. A number of factors militate against the success of the lower-class child. In this chapter, some of the reasons underlying the school's inability to effectively educate lower-class children were presented. The incongruity between the attitudes and motivations of the lower-class child and the middle-class school was seen as an important factor. The school is a strange and often hostile environment for the lower-class child. Even if he does succeed, he is unlikely to receive either parental support or peer acceptance for his accomplishments. Some have blamed the teachers for their failure to appreciate the differences in background, experience, and values of the disadvantaged pupil. In fact, comparisons of middle-class white and lower-class black instructors suggests that this charge has validity; teachers from lower-class origins were more accepting and less pessimistic in their evaluations of their lower-class charges than were middle-class teachers. Clearly, any program aimed at solving the problems of the lower-class child's chronic academic failure must include alterations in teacher preparation. Curriculum and content changes are not enough; teacher attitudes toward children must change as well.

REFERENCES

Adams, R. S., & Biddle, B. J. *Realities of teaching.* New York: Holt, 1970.

Allen, V. L., & Feldman, R. S. Learning through tutoring: low achieving children as tutors. *Journal of Educational Psychology,* 1973, **42,** 1-5.

Allyon, T., & Azrin, N. H. *A motivating environment for therapy and rehabilitation.* New York: Appleton-Century-Crofts, 1968.

Anderson, D. F., & Rosenthal, R. Some effects of interpersonal expectancy and social interaction on institutionalized retarded children. *Proceedings of the 76th Annual Convention of the American Psychological Association,* 1968, **4,** 479-480.

Anderson, H. E., White, W. F., & Wash, J. A. Generalized effects of praise and reproof. *Journal of Educational Psychology,* 1966, **17,** 169-173.

Asher, S., & Markell, R. A. Sex differnces in comprehension of high and low interest reading material. *Journal of Educational Psychology,* in press.

Bandura, A. (Ed.). *Psychological modeling.* Chicago: Aldine, 1971.

Barker, R. G., & Gump, P. V. *Big school, small school,* Stanford, Calif.: Stanford, 1964.

Barrish, H. H., Saunders, M., & Wolf, M. M. Good behavior game: effects of individual contingencies for group consequences on disruptive behavior in a classroom. *Journal of Applied Behavior Analysis,* 1969, **2,** 119-124.

Beez, W. V. Influence of biased psychological reports on teacher behavior and pupil performance. *Proceedings of the 76th Annual Convention of the American Psychological Association,* 1968, **4,** 605-606.

Bentzen, F. Sex ratios in learning and behavior disorders. *American Journal of Orthopsychiatry,* 1963, **33,** 92-98.

Blom, G. E., Waite, R. R., & Zimet, S. G. A motivational content analysis of children's primers. In P. H. Mussen, J. J. Conger, & J. Kagan (Eds.), *Readings in child development and personality.* New York: Harper & Row, 1970.

Bovard, E. W., Jr. The psychology of classroom interaction. *Journal of Educational Research,* 1951, **45,** 215-224.

Bronfenbrenner, U. *Two worlds of childhood: U.S. & U.S.S.R.* New York: Russell Sage Foundation, 1970.

Bronfenbrenner, U., Devereux, E. C., Jr., Suci, G. J., & Rodgers, R. R. Adults and peers as sources of conformity and autonomy. Unpublished study. Ithaca, N.Y.: Cornell University, Dept. of Child Development and Family Relations, 1965.

Brophy, J. E., & Good, T. L. Teachers' communication of differential expectations for children's classroom performance: some behavioral data. *Journal of Educational Psychology*, 1970, **61,** 365-374.

Brown, P., & Elliott, R. Control of aggression in a nursery school class. *Journal of Experimental Child Psychology*, 1965, **2,** 103-107.

Burham, J. R., & Hartsough, D. M. Effects of experimenter's expectancies on children's ability to learn to swim. Paper presented at the Meeting of the Midwestern Psychological Association, Chicago, May 1968.

Busch, F. *Interest, relevance, and learning to read.* Teachers College Record, 1970.

Cheyney, A. B. Teachers of the culturally disadvantaged. *Exceptional Children*, 1966, **33,** 83-88.

Clark, K. B. *Dark ghetto: dilemmas of social power.* New York: Harper & Row, 1965.

Cloward, R. D. Studies in tutoring. *Journal of Experimental Education*, 1967, **36,** 14-25.

Davidson, H. H., & Lang, G. Children's perceptions of their teachers' feelings toward them related to self-perception, school achievement, and behavior. *Journal of Experimental Education*, 1960, **29,** 107-118.

Dawe, H. C. The influence of size of kindergarten group upon performance. *Child Development*, 1934, **5,** 295-303.

Deering, M. Youth tutoring youth. Supervisor's Manual. National Commission on Resources for Youth, Inc. New York, 1968.

Deutsch, M. Minority group and class status as related to social and personality factors in scholastic achievement. *Monographs of the Society for Applied Anthropology*, 1960, **2**.

Deutsch, M. Facilitating development in the preschool child: Social and psychological Perspectives. *Merrill-Palmer Quarterly*, 1964, **10,** 249-263.

Elashoff, J. D., & Snow, R. E. *Pygmalion reconsidered.* Worthington, Ohio: Charles A. Jones Publishing Co., 1971.

Fagot, B. I., & Patterson, C. R. An *in vivo* analysis of reinforcing contingencies for sex role behaviors in the preschool child. *Developmental Psychology*, 1969, **1,** 563-568.

Flanders, N. H., & Havumaki, S. The effect of teacher-pupil contacts involving praise on the sociometric choices of students. *Journal of Educational Psychology*, 1960, **51,** 65-68.

Gottlieb, D. Teaching and students: the views of Negro and white teachers. *Sociology of Education*, 1966, **37,** 345-353.

Gottman, J. J. Unpublished data. University of Wisconsin, 1969.

Graebner, D. B. A decade of sexism in readers. *The Reading Teacher*, 1972 (October), **26**.

Grimes, J. W., & Allinsmith, W. Compulsivity, anxiety, and school achievement. *Merrill-Palmer Quarterly*, 1961, **7,** 247-269.

Groff, P. J. The social status of teachers. *Journal of Educational Sociology*, 1962, **36,** 20-25.

Groff, P. J. Dissatisfactions in teaching the culturally deprived child. *Phi Delta Kappan*, 1963, **45,** 76.

Harris, F. R., Wolf, M. M., & Baer, D. M. Effects of adult social reinforcement on child behavior. *Young Children*, 1964, **20,** 8-17.

Hartley, R. E. Sex role primers and the socialization of the male child. *Psychological Reports*, 1959, **5,** 457-468.

Harvey, O. J., Prather, M., White, B. J., & Hoffmeister, J. K. Teachers' beliefs, classroom atmosphere and student behavior. *American Educational Research Journal*, 1968, **5,** 151-166.

Harvey, O. J., White, B. J., Prather, M., & Alter, R. D., & Hoffmeister, J. K. Teachers' belief systems and preschool atmospheres. *Journal of Educational Psychology*, 1966, **57,** 373-381.

Hess, R., & Shipman, V. Cognitive elements in maternal behavior. In J. Hill (Ed.), *Minnesota Symposium on Child Psychology.* Minneapolis: The University of Minnesota Press, 1967. Pp. 57-81.

Himmelweit, H. T., & Swift, B. A model for the understanding of school as a socializing agent. In P. H. Mussen, J. Langer, & M. Covington (Eds.), *Trends and issues in developmental psychology.* New York: Holt, 1969. Pp. 154-181.

Janis, I. L., Mahl, G. F., Kagan, J., & Holt, R. R. *Personality: dynamics, development and assessment.* New York: Harcourt, Brace & World, 1969.

Jensen, A. R. Review of Pygmalion in the classroom. *American Scientist* 1969, **51,** 44A-45A.

Kagan, J. The child's sex role classification of school objects. *Child Development*, 1964, **35,** 1051-1056.

Kagan, J., & Moss, H. *Birth to maturity.* New York: Wiley, 1962.

Klineberg, O. Life is fun in a smiling, fair skinned world. *Saturday Review*, 1963, **87,** 75-77.

Kounin, J. S., & Gump, P. V. The ripple effect in discipline. *The Elementary School Journal*, 1958, **59,** 158-162.

Kounin, J. S., & Gump, P. V. The comparative influence of punitive and non-punitive teachers upon children's concepts of school misconduct. *Journal of Educational Psychology*, 1961, **52,** 44–49.

Kuppel, H. Student tutors for floundering classmates. *School Activites*, 1964, **35,** 255–256.

Lee, P. C., & Wolinsky, A. L. Male teachers of young children: a preliminary empirical study. *Young Children*, 1973, **28,** 342–353.

Levinger, G., & Gunner, J. The interpersonal grid: felt and tape techniques for the measurements of social relationships. *Psychonomic Science*, 1967, **8,** 113–174.

Lewin, K., Lippitt, R., & White, R. K. Patterns of aggressive behavior in experimentally created "social climates." *Journal of Social Psychology*, 1939, **10,** 271–299.

Lippitt, P., & Lippitt, R. Cross-age helpers. *National Education Association*, March 1968, 1–6.

Longstreth, L. *The Psychological Development of the Child.* New York: Ronald, 1968.

Madsen, C. H., Becher, W. C., Thomas, D. R., Koser, L., & Plager, E. An analysis of the reinforcing function of "sit down" comments. In R. K. Parker (Ed.), *Readings in Educational Psychology.* Boston: Allyn and Bacon, 1968.

McKeachie, W. J. Research on teaching at the college and university level. In N. L. Gage (Ed.), *Handbook of research on teaching.* Chicago: Rand McNally, 1963. Pp. 1118–1172.

Meichenbaum, D. H., Bowers, K. S., & Ross, R. R. A behavioral analysis of teacher expectancy effect. *Journal of Personality and Social Psychology*, 1969, **13,** 306–316.

Meyer, W. T., & Thompson, G. G. Sex differences in the distribution of teacher approval and disapproval among ninth grade children. *Journal of Educational Psychology*, 1956, **47,** 385–396.

Michenbaum, D. H., Bowers, K. S., & Ross, R. R. A behavioral analysis of teacher expectancy effect. *Journal of Personality and Social Psychology*, 1969, **13,** 306–316.

Montessori, M. *Spontaneous activity in education.* Cambridge, Mass.: Robert Bentley, Inc., 1964.

O'Leary, K. D., Becker, W. C. Evans, M. B., & Saudargas, R. A. A token reinforcement program in a public school: a replication and systematic analysis. *Journal of Applied Behavior Analysis*, 1969, **2,** 3–13.

O'Leary, K. D., Kaufman, K., Kass, R. & Drabman, R. The effects of loud and soft reprimands on behavior of disruptive students. *Exceptional Children*, 1970, **37,** 145–155.

Portuges, S. H., & Feshbach, N. D. The influence of sex and social class upon imitation of teachers by elementary school children. *Child Development*, 1972, **43,** 981–989.

Ralph, J. B., Goldberg, M. L., & Passow, A. H. *Bright underachievers.* New York: Teachers College, 1966.

Rioux, J. W. The disadvantaged child in school. In J. Helmuth (Ed.), *The disadvantaged child.* New York: Brunner/Mazel, 1968.

Rosenthal, R. On the social psychology of the self-fulfilling prophecy: further evidence for pygmalion effects and their mediating mechanisms. In M. King (Ed.), *Reading and school achievement: cognitive and affective influences.* New Brunswick, N.J.: Rutgers, 1973. (a)

Rosenthal, R. The pygmalion effect lives. *Psychology Today*, September 1973, 46–63. (b)

Rosenthal, R., & Jacobsen, L. Teachers' expectancies: determinants of pupils' IQ gains. *Psychological Reports*, 1966, **19,** 115–118.

Rosenthal, R., & Jacobsen, L. *Pygmalion in the classroom.* New York: Holt, 1968.

Ryans, D. G. Some relationships between pupil behavior and certain teacher characteristics. *Journal of Educational Psychology*, 1961, **52,** 82–90.

Saario, T. N., Jacklin, C. N., & Tittle, C. K. Sex role stereotyping in the public schools. *Harvard Educational Review*, 1973, **43,** 386–416.

Sanders, D. C. Innovations in elementary school classroom seating. *Bureau of Laboratory Schools Publication No. 10.* Austin: University of Texas, 1958.

Schmidt, G. W., & Ulrich, R. E. Effects of group contingent events upon classroom noise. *Journal of Applied Behavior Analysis*, 1969, **2,** 171–179.

Schmuck, R. A., & Van Egmond, E. Sex differences in the relationship of interpersonal perceptions to academic performance. *Psychology in the Schools*, 1965, **2,** 32–40.

Serbin, L. A., O'Leary, D. K., Kent, R. N., & Tonick, I. J. A comparison of teacher response to the preacademic and problem behavior of boys and girls. *Child Development*, 1973, **44,** 796–804.

Sherif, M., & Sherif, C. W. *Groups in harmony and tension. An integration of studies on intergroup relations.* New York: Harper & Row, 1953.

Shinedling, M. M., & Pederson, D. M. Effects of sex of teacher and student on children's gains in quantitative and verbal performance. *Journal of Psychology*, 1970, **76,** 79–84.

Sommer, R. *Personal space.* Englewood Cliffs, N.J.: Prentice-Hall, 1969.

Stein, A. H. The effects sex-role standards for achievement and sex-role preference on three determinants of achievement motivation. *Developmental Psychology,* 1971, **4,** 219-231.

Stein, A. H., & Bailey, M. M. The socialization of achievement orientation in females. *Psychological Bulletin,* 1973, **80,** 345-366.

Stern, G. G. Measuring noncognitive variables in research on teaching. In N. L. Gage (Ed.), *Handbook of research on teaching.* Chicago: Rand McNally, 1963. Pp. 398-447.

Thompson, G. G., & Hunnicutt, C. W. The effect of repeated praise or blame on the work achievement of "introverts" and "extroverts." *Journal of Educational Psychology,* 1944, **35,** 157-166.

Thorndike, R. L. Review of R. Rosenthal and L. Jocobson, "Pygmalion in the classroom." *American Educational Research Journal,* 1968, **5,** 708-711.

Tuana, S. Unpublished research. In Sommer, R.: *Personal space.* Englewood Cliffs, N.J.: Prentice-Hall, 1969. P. 118.

Tyler, L. E. *The Psychology of human differences.* New York: Appleton-Century-Crofts, 1947.

Van de Reit, H. Effects of praise and reproof on paired associate learning in educationally retarded children. *Journal of Educational Psychology,* 1964, **55,** 139-143.

Waite, R. R. Further attempts to integrate and urbanize first grade reading textbooks: a research study. *The Journal of Negro Education,* Winter 1968, 62-69.

Weitzman, L., Eifler, D., Hokada, E., & Ross, C. Sex-role socialization. *American Journal of Sociology,* 1972, **77,** 1125-1150.

Whipple, G. *Appraisal of the city schools reading program.* Detroit: Detroit Public Schools Division for Improvement of Instruction, Language Education Department, 1963.

White, W. F., & Dekle, O. T. Effect of teachers motivational cues on achievement level in elementary grades. *Psychological Reports,* 1966, **18,** 351-356.

Wiberg, J. L., & Trost, M. A comparison between the content of first grade primers and free choice library selections made by first grade students. *Elementary English,* 1970, **47,** 792-798.

Yando, R. M., & Kagan, J. The effect of teacher tempo on the child. *Child Development,* 1968, **39,** 27-34.

Zimet, S. G. Children's interest and story preferences: a critical review of the literature. *The Elementary School Journal,* 1966, **67,** 123-130.

INDEX